THE ROUGH GUIDE TO
COSTA RICA

ROUGH
GUIDES

This eighth edition updated by
Stephen Keeling and Shafik Meghji

Contents

Introduction to
Costa Rica

Democratic and prosperous, Costa Rica is Central America's biggest tourist destination. The draw is not ancient Mesoamerican ruins or Spanish colonial history, but nature; the country is one of the most biodiverse areas on the planet, an ecological treasure-trove whose wide range of habitats – lush rainforests and untouched beaches, steaming volcanoes and dense mangrove swamps – supports an incredible variety of wildlife, from those loveable sloths and tiny, fluorescent green frogs to brightly plumed macaws and toucans. And it's also peaceful; with its long democratic tradition Costa Rica is an oasis of political stability.

Though this idyllic image might not do justice to the full complexities of contemporary Costa Rican society, it's true that the country's complete absence of military forces (the army was abolished in 1948) stands in sharp contrast to the brutal internal conflicts that have ravaged its neighbours. This reputation for peacefulness has been an important factor in the spectacular growth of Costa Rica's tourist industry – almost three million people visit the country annually, mainly from North America. Most of all, though, it is Costa Rica's outstanding natural beauty, and the wildlife that accompanies it, that has made it one of the world's prime **ecotourism** destinations, with visitors flocking here to hike trails through ancient rainforest, peer into active volcanoes or explore the Americas' last vestiges of high-altitude cloudforest, home to jaguars, spider monkeys and resplendent quetzals.

Admittedly, tourism has made Costa Rica less of an "authentic" experience than many travellers would like: some towns seemingly exist purely to provide visitors with a place to sleep and a tour to take, while previously remote spots are being bought up by foreign entrepreneurs. And as more hotels open, malls go up and potholed tracks get tarmacked over, there's no doubt that Costa Rica is experiencing a significant social change, with the darker side of outside involvement in the country – sex tourism, conflicts between foreign property-owners and poorer locals and, in particular, drug trafficking – all on the increase.

ABOVE PLAYA CARRILLO **OPPOSITE** VOLCÁN IRAZÚ

Costa Rica's **economy** is the most diversified in Central America, and has become even more so since the country finally entered into the then-controversial Central American Free Trade Agreement (CAFTA) in 2009, enhancing its economic ties with the US in the process. Computer processors and medical supplies now sit alongside coffee and bananas as key exports, although the country's revenue from tourism still outstrips everything else. It is thanks to this money, in particular, that Costa Ricans – or Ticos, as they are generally known – now enjoy the highest rates of literacy, health care, education and life expectancy on the isthmus. That said, Costa Rica is certainly not the wealthy, globalized country that it's often portrayed to be – a significant percentage of people still live below the poverty line. While it is modernizing fast, its character continues to be rooted in **distinct local cultures**, from the Afro-Caribbean province of Limón, with its Creole cuisine, games and patois, to the traditional *ladino* values embodied by the

BIODIVERSITY UNDER PROTECTION

Despite its small size, Costa Rica possesses over five percent of the world's total **biodiversity**, around 165 times the amount of life forms it might otherwise be expected to support. This is in part due to its position as a transition zone between temperate North and tropical South America, and also thanks to its complex system of interlocking **microclimates**, created by differences in topography and altitude. This biological abundance is now safeguarded by one of the world's most enlightened and dedicated conservation programmes – about 25 percent of Costa Rica's land is protected, most of it through the country's extensive network of national parks and wildlife refuges.

Costa Rica's **national parks** range from the tropical jungle lowlands of Corcovado on the Osa Peninsula to the grassy volcanic uplands of Rincón de la Vieja in Guanacaste, an impressive and varied range of terrain that has enhanced the country's popularity with ecotourists. Outside the park system, however, land is assailed by **deforestation** – ironically, there are now no more significant patches of forest left anywhere in the country outside of protected areas.

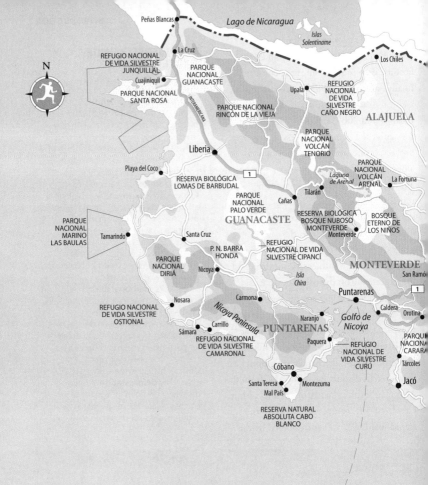

Peñas Blancas

Lago de Nicaragua

Islas Solentiname

La Cruz

Los Chiles

REFUGIO NACIONAL
DE VIDA SILVESTRE
JUNQUILLAL

PARQUE
NACIONAL
GUANACASTE

Cuajiniquil

Upala

REFUGIO
NACIONAL
DE VIDA
SILVESTRE
CAÑO NEGRO

ALAJUELA

PARQUE NACIONAL
SANTA ROSA

PARQUE NACIONAL
RINCÓN DE LA VIEJA

PARQUE
NACIONAL
VOLCÁN
TENORIO

PARQUE
NACIONAL
VOLCÁN
ARENAL

Liberia

La Fortuna

Playa del Coco

*Laguna
de Arenal*

RESERVA BIOLÓGICA
LOMAS DE BARBUDAL

Tilarán

PARQUE
NACIONAL
PALO VERDE

Cañas

RESERVA BIOLÓGICA
BOSQUE NUBOSO
MONTEVERDE

BOSQUE
ETERNO DE
LOS NIÑOS

GUANACASTE

Monteverde

PARQUE
NACIONAL
MARINO
LAS BAULAS

Tamarindo

Santa Cruz

P. N. BARRA
HONDA

REFUGIO
NACIONAL DE VIDA
SILVESTRE CIPANCÍ

MONTEVERDE

San Ramón

PARQUE
NACIONAL
DIRIÁ

Nicoya

*Isla
Chira*

Puntarenas

Nosara

Carmona

Caldera

Orotina

REFUGIO NACIONAL
DE VIDA SILVESTRE
OSTIONAL

Nicoya Peninsula

PUNTARENAS

Naranjo

*Golfo de
Nicoya*

PARQUE
NACIONAL
CARARA

Sámara

Carrillo

REFUGIO
NACIONAL DE
VIDA SILVESTRE
CAMARONAL

Paquera

REFUGIO DE
VIDA SILVESTRE
CURÚ

Tárcoles

Cóbano

Jacó

Santa Teresa

Montezuma

Mal País

RESERVA NATURAL
ABSOLUTA CABO
BLANCO

PACIFIC OCEAN

Isla del Coco

Bahía Chatham

Bahía Wafer

PARQUE NACIONAL
ISLA DEL COCO

Bahía Yglesias

0   3
kilometres

Isla del Coco is 535 kilometres southwest of Costa Rica

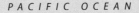 *Isla del Coco (see inset)*

sabanero, or cowboys, of Guanacaste. Above all, the country still has the highest rural population density in Latin America, and society continues to revolve around the twin axes of countryside and family: wherever you go, you're sure to be left with mental snapshots of rural life, whether it be horsemen trotting by on dirt roads, coffee-plantation day-labourers setting off to work in the mists of the highlands or avocado-pickers cycling home at sunset.

Where to go

Although almost everyone passes through it, hardly anyone falls in love with **San José**, Costa Rica's capital. Though often dismissed as an ugly urban sprawl, "Chepe" enjoys a dramatic setting amid jagged mountain peaks and is home to the country's finest museums, as well as some excellent cafés and restaurants, a lively university district and a burgeoning arts scene. The surrounding **Valle Central**, Costa Rica's agricultural heartland and coffee-growing region, supports the vast majority of the country's population and features several of its most impressive volcanoes, including steaming Volcán Poás and Volcán Irazú, its deep-green crater lake set in a strange lunar landscape high above the regional capital of Cartago.

While nowhere in the country is further than nine hours' drive from San José, the far north and the far south are less visited than other regions. The broad alluvial plains of the **Zona Norte** are dominated by the now-dormant cone of Volcán Arenal, which looms large over the friendly tourist hangout of La Fortuna, while the dense rainforest of the Sarapiquí region harbours monkeys, poison-dart frogs and countless species of bird, including the endangered great green macaw. Up by the border with Nicaragua, the seasonal wetlands of the Refugio Nacional de Vida Silvestre Caño Negro provide a haven for water birds, along with gangs of basking caimans.

Author picks

Our authors have tramped around towns and trekked through jungles, rafted down rivers and paddled up canals, and consumed more coffee than is probably good for them. Here are a few of their favourite things…

Basílica de Nuestra Señora de Los Ángeles In a country not necessarily known for its architectural heritage, Cartago's showpiece church (p.143) is a stunner, with a gilded interior to match.

Time with the OTS Spend a few days with the Organization of Tropical Studies at their biological stations in La Selva (p.72) or Palo Verde (p.245) and you'll see why their guides are rated some of the best in the country.

Little-known beaches Escape the crowds at the gorgeous beaches of Playa Junquillal in Guanacaste (p.281) and Ojochal's Playa Tortuga on the southern Pacific coast (p.377).

Sodas Basic, cheap and unfailingly friendly, Costa Rica's ubiquitous *sodas* are a great place to tuck into a plate of *gallo pinto* or a traditional *casado*. Try *La Casona Típica* in San José (p.108), *Soda Luz* in Orosí (p.148) or *Johanna* in Golfito (p.389).

Off-the-beaten-track reserves The most famous national parks can get crowded in peak season, so try Parque Nacional Juan Castro Blanco (p.129), take a multiday hike in the Bosque Eterno de los Niños (p.312) or visit Parque Nacional Los Quetzales, home of the iconic resplendent quetzal (p.364).

Kayaking around Curú There are few more enjoyable ways of watching wildlife than paddling a kayak through the limpid waters of the southern Nicoya Peninsula (p.321), camping on beaches and spotting monkeys, sloths and seabirds along the way.

Traditional cafés San José's traditional cafés are wonderfully atmospheric places for people-watching and sampling Costa Rican coffee. Try the elegant *Alma de Café* inside the Teatro Nacional, rustic *Café Rojo* or colonial-style *Café Hacienda Real* in Escazú (p.108).

> Our author recommendations don't end here. We've flagged up our favourite places – a perfectly sited hotel, an atmospheric café, a special restaurant – throughout the Guide, highlighted with the ★ symbol.

FROM TOP SEA-KAYAKING, REFUGIO DE VIDA SILVESTRE CURÚ; EATING AT A *SODA*; BIRDWATCHING, PARQUE NACIONAL PALO VERDE

In the northwest, cowboy culture dominates the cattle-ranching province of **Guanacaste**, with exuberant ragtag rodeos and large cattle haciendas occupying the hot, baked landscape that surrounds the attractive regional capital of Liberia. The province's beaches are some of the best – and, in parts, most developed – in the country, with Sámara and Nosara, on the Nicoya Peninsula, providing picture-postcard scenery and superb sunsets.

Further down the **Pacific coast**, the surf-oriented sands of Montezuma and Santa Teresa/Mal País, on the southern Nicoya Peninsula, draw travellers looking to kick back for a few days (or weeks), while popular Parque Nacional Manuel Antonio, Costa Rica's smallest national park, also enjoys a sublime ocean setting and has equally tempting beaches. Further inland, nestled in the cool highlands of the Tilarán Cordillera, Monteverde has become the country's number-one tourist attraction, pulling in the visitors who flock here to walk through some of the most enchanting cloudforest in the Americas.

Limón Province, on the Caribbean coast, is markedly different to the rest of the country. It's home to the descendants of the Afro-Caribbeans who came to Costa Rica at the end of the nineteenth century to work on the San José–Limón railroad – their language (Creole English), religion (Protestantism) and West Indian traditions remain relatively intact to this day. The reason most visitors venture here, however, is for Parque Nacional Tortuguero, and the three species of marine turtle that lay their eggs on its beaches each year.

RUMBLE IN THE JUNGLE

Costa Rica is set in one of the most **geologically active** areas on Earth. Ringed by the convergence of five major tectonic plates, it sits on the western edge of the Caribbean Plate, at the point where it slides beneath the Cocos Plate; this subduction (where one plate sinks into the Earth's mantle) formed a chain of volcanoes that stretches 1500km from Guatemala to northern Panama. Costa Rica itself is home to some 112 **volcanoes**, though only five (including the major visitor attractions of Volcán Poás and Volcán Irazú) are considered active – Volcán Arenal, for so long the most active volcano in the country, has been in a resting phase since July 2010.

The ongoing friction between the Caribbean and Cocos plates causes around 1500 **earthquakes** in Costa Rica each year, although only a small proportion of these are actually felt and fewer still are strong enough to cause significant damage – the worst incident in recent times was the earthquake that struck near Cinchona, 50km north of San José, in January 2009, when forty people were killed.

Travellers looking to venture off the beaten track will be happiest in the rugged **Zona Sur**, home to Cerro Chirripó, the highest point in the country, and, further south on the outstretched feeler of the Osa Peninsula, **Parque Nacional Corcovado**, which protects the last significant area of tropical wet forest on the Pacific coast of the isthmus. Corcovado is probably the best destination in the country for walkers – and also one of the few places where you have a fighting chance of seeing some of the more exotic wildlife for which Costa Rica is famed, such as the scarlet macaw.

When to go

Although Costa Rica lies between eight and eleven degrees north of the equator, temperatures (see box, p.80), governed by the vastly varying altitudes, are by no means universally high, and can plummet to below freezing at higher altitudes. Local microclimates predominate and make weather unpredictable, though to an extent you can depend upon the **two-season rule**. In the dry season (roughly mid-Nov to April), most areas are just that: dry all day, with occasional northern winds blowing in during January or February and cooling things off; otherwise, you can depend on sunshine and warm temperatures. In the wet season (roughly May to mid-Nov), you'll have sunny mornings and afternoon rains. The rains are heaviest in September and October and, although they can be fierce, will impede you from travelling only in the more remote areas of the country – the Nicoya Peninsula and Zona Sur especially – where dirt roads become impassable to all but the sturdiest 4WDs.

Costa Rica is generally booked solid during the peak season, the North American winter months, when bargains are few and far between. The crowds peter out after Easter, but return again to an extent in July and August. Travellers who prefer to play it by ear are much better off coming during the low or rainy season (euphemistically called the "green season"), when many hotels offer discounts. The months of November, April (after Easter) and May are the **best times to visit**, when the rains have either just started or just died off, and the country is refreshed, green and relatively untouristy.

OPPOSITE RAINFOREST IN PARQUE NACIONAL VOLCÁN ARENAL

things not to miss

It's not possible to see everything that Costa Rica has to offer in one trip – and we don't suggest you try. What follows is a selective and subjective taste of the country's highlights: stunning national parks, brooding volcanoes, gorgeous beaches and exhilarating outdoor activities. All highlights are colour-coded by chapter and have a page reference to take you straight into the Guide, where you can find out more.

1 TREKKING IN PARQUE NACIONAL CORCOVADO

Page 390

Straddling the Osa Peninsula in the far south of the country, this biologically rich, coastal rainforest is one of Costa Rica's finest destinations for walking and wildlife-spotting.

2 TEATRO NACIONAL, SAN JOSÉ

Page 93

Central America's grandest theatre, extravagantly done out in gold and marble and built in imitation of the Palais Garnier in Paris.

3 TURTLE-WATCHING

Pages 173, 274 & 295

View some of the thousands of turtles – leatherback, hawksbill, olive ridley and green – that come ashore to lay their eggs each year, and, if you're lucky, watch their hatchlings' perilous journeys back to sea.

4 VOLCÁN ARENAL
Page 214

The lava may have stopped spewing, but Arenal is still a magnificent sight, and the surrounding area is one giant adventure playground – soak in volcanic hot springs, zipwire through the forest canopy or sign up for any number of other outdoor activities.

5 PARQUE NACIONAL SANTA ROSA
Page 260

This magnificent park protects a rare stretch of dry tropical rainforest – and the wildlife that calls it home.

6 INDIGENOUS COSTA RICA
Pages 193, 220 & 379

Learn how the Maleku use medicinal plants, shop for crafts at a women's co-operative in the Gulf of Nicoya or take a walking tour with the Bribrí – just some of the ways of gaining a better insight into Costa Rica's remaining indigenous communities.

7 MUSEO DE ORO PRECOLOMBINO
Page 92

One of the country's best museums, with a dazzling display that features more than 1500 pre-Columbian gold pieces.

8

9

8 PARQUE NACIONAL MANUEL ANTONIO

Page 349

This perennially popular park boasts white-sand beaches, tropical forests full of sloths and monkeys, and stunning coastal scenery peppered with striking rock formations.

9 REFUGIO NACIONAL DE VIDA SILVESTRE CAÑO NEGRO

Page 224

Crammed with caimans and home to hundreds of species of bird, this isolated reserve near the Nicaraguan border is one of the most important wetlands in the world.

10 ISLAS TORTUGA

Page 323

Pristine white sands, palm trees and lush jungle await on these tropical islands off the Nicoya Peninsula.

11 RESERVA RARA AVIS

Page 232

Costa Rica's premier ecotourism destination flourishes with primitive ferns and has more kinds of plants, birds and butterflies than the whole of Europe.

14

12 STAYING AT AN ECOLODGE
Pages 56 & 389

From rustic simplicity to luxury in the jungle, Costa Rica has some of the Americas' best ecolodges, all offering a variety of ways to immerse yourself in the natural world. Try *Lapa Ríos* in the Osa Peninsula (pictured).

13 NAUYACA WATERFALLS
Page 375

Costa Rica is laced with jungle cascades, and these are some of the country's most captivating.

14 PLAYA COCLES
Page 192

One of the most appealing beaches on the entire Caribbean coast, a long stretch of fine sand backed by swaying palms and sprayed by barrelling waves, just a couple of kilometres from the laidback backpackers' haunt of Puerto Viejo de Talamanca.

15 JAGUAR RESCUE CENTER
Page 193

This wildlife rehab centre provides close encounters with howler monkeys, sloths, snakes and other injured animals before they're released back into the wild.

15

20

16 WHITEWATER RAFTING
Page 66

Whitewater rafting is one of Costa Rica's most exciting outdoor activities, whether you're floating down the Peñas Blancas or riding Class-V rapids on the Pacuare.

17 EL DÍA DE LA RAZA, PUERTO LIMÓN
Page 165

Young bloods and grandparents alike take to the streets during Costa Rica's most exuberant carnival.

18 MONTEVERDE
Page 302

Experience the bird's-eye view – and a touch of vertigo – from a suspended bridge in the lush Monteverde cloudforest.

19 VOLCÁN POÁS
Page 132

Poás is one of the world's more easily accessible active volcanoes, with a history of eruptions that goes back eleven million years.

18

19

20 SURFING
Page 69

Boasting nearly 1300km of palm-fringed coastline, and a variety of beach breaks, reef breaks, long lefts and river mouths, Costa Rica has a wave for just about every surfer out there.

21 COFFEE
Page 58

Sample an aromatic cup of Costa Rica's most famous export, and the foundation of the country's prosperity.

22 PARQUE NACIONAL RINCÓN DE LA VIEJA
Page 251

Clouds of sulphurous smoke and steaming mud pots dot the desiccated slopes of Volcán Rincón de la Vieja, one of the country's most thermally active areas.

23 EXPLORING THE TORTUGUERO CANAL
Page 171

Take a slow boat north from Puerto Limón along the Tortuguero Canal, past luxuriant vegetation and colourful wooden houses on stilts.

20

21

Itineraries

The following itineraries will give you a taste of everything that's addictive about Costa Rica, from the wildlife-rich wetlands of the north and the remote rainforests of the south, to surf-lashed Pacific beaches and nesting turtles on the Atlantic coast. You may not be able to cover everything, but even picking a few highlights will give you a deeper insight into the country's natural wonders.

CLASSIC COSTA RICA

All the big hitters, from volcanoes to beaches via wildlife-rich national parks, can be ticked off on a simple, fairly central two-week circuit.

❶ **San José** The oft-overlooked capital has Costa Rica's best museums and its widest range of restaurants, and is worth at least a night at the beginning or end of your trip. See p.84

❷ **Poás or Irazú** Two active volcanoes lie a short hop from San José: choose Volcán Poás for its boiling acid pools, Volcán Irazú for its milky-green crater lake and views of both oceans. See p.132 & p.144

❸ **Parque Nacional Tortuguero** Even if you're not here for the turtle-nesting seasons, you'll see plenty of other jungle wildlife as you paddle through the network of forest-fringed canals. See p.171

❹ **The Arenal region** Volcán Arenal itself may be quiet, but the bustling town of La Fortuna is still an essential stop for walks in the national park and all manner of other outdoor activities. See p.214

❺ **Monteverde** Arguably the most famous reserve in Costa Rica, where you can hike through the cloudforest in search of resplendent quetzals. See p.302

❻ **Parque Nacional Manuel Antonio** Further south along the coast, Manuel Antonio is Costa Rica's smallest national park – and also its most popular. Finish your trip spotting sloths and squirrel monkeys, or relaxing on a white-sand beach. See p.349

WILDLIFE-WATCHING

Diverse and abundant, Costa Rica's wildlife is the country's single biggest attraction. Allow a minimum of three weeks for the below, longer if you want to go deeper into Corcovado.

❶ **Parque Nacional Tortuguero** Green, hawksbill and giant leatherback turtles, plus howler monkeys, sloths and caimans – not a bad way to start any trip. See p.169

❷ **Reserva Rara Avis** Remote jungle lodge in the heart of the Sarapiquí region, with an impressive bird list and a bounty of unusual reptiles and amphibians. See p.232

❸ **Refugío Nacional de Vida Silvestre Mixto Maquenque** This important wedge of protected rainforest on the border with Nicaragua represents the country's last refuge of the stunning great green macaw. See p.237

❹ **Refugío Nacional de Vida Silvestre Caño Negro** Wily caimans bask on the riverbanks during the dry season; migratory birds swell the resident populations during the wet. See p.224

❺ **Refugío Nacional de Vida Silvestre Ostional** At certain times of the year, thousands of olive ridley turtles storm the beaches at

ABOVE HUMMINGBIRDS

Ostional, in one of nature's most spectacular sights. **See p.295**

❻ **Parque Nacional Carara** The hot northern lowlands meet the humid southern Pacific at Carara, meaning even greater varieties of wildlife, from armadillos and agoutis to both types of toucan. **See p.337**

❼ **Parque Nacional Corcovado** The one place in the country where you have a realistic chance of seeing a tapir, an ocelot or even the famously elusive jaguar. **See p.390**

OUTDOOR ACTIVITIES

Costa Rica is one giant natural playground. You could spend months just surfing the waves at Santa Teresa and Mal País, but three weeks should be enough to cover the below.

❶ **The Río Pacuare** Start your trip by tackling one of the wildest rivers in Central America and some-time host of the World Whitewater Rafting Championships. **See p.152**

❷ **Arenal** Hike the old lava-flow trails of Parque Nacional Volcán Arenal and take a dip in volcano-fed hot springs: the pricey Balneario

Tabacón is the most popular, the smaller Ecotermales Fortuna the most relaxed. **See p.206**

❸ **Monteverde** Birdwatching tours and guided night walks, of course, but also hanging bridges and ziplines – the canopy-tour craze that has swept the country (and the world) started in Monteverde. **See p.302**

❹ **Santa Teresa and Mal País** Popular surfer hangouts on the southern tip of the Nicoya Peninsula, offering a variety of beginner-friendly and much more challenging beach and reef breaks. **See p.334**

❺ **Isla del Coco** It's a long way to go and expensive to get there, but Isla del Coco, 535km off mainland Costa Rica (and some 36hr in a boat from Puntarenas), is simply the best scuba-diving destination in the country. **See p.320**

❻ **Parque Nacional Chirripó** Climb up through cloudforest and alpine paramo, and past crestones and glacial lakes as you tackle Cerro Chirripó, Costa Rica's highest point. **See p.368**

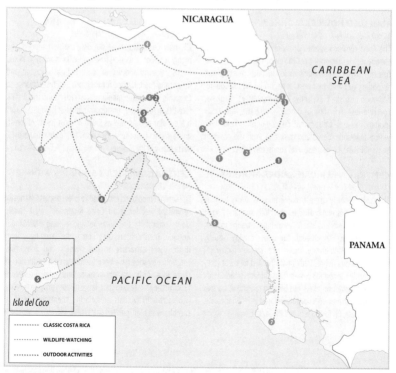

NICARAGUA

CARIBBEAN SEA

PACIFIC OCEAN

PANAMA

Isla del Coco

.... CLASSIC COSTA RICA

.... WILDLIFE-WATCHING

.... OUTDOOR ACTIVITIES

Wildlife

Thanks to Costa Rica's celebrated position as a land bridge between the temperate zone to the north and the Neotropics to the south, the country's varied animal life features tropical forms like the jaguar, temperate-zone animals such as deer and some unusual, seemingly hybrid combinations like the coati. Many of the country's more exotic mammals (*mamíferos*) are nocturnal or endangered, or have been made shy by years of hunting and human encroachment; as such, you are far more likely to come into contact with some of the smaller and more abundant species. Amphibians and reptiles (*anfibios y reptiles*) are much more evident, though, and birdlife is particularly numerous, with 850 species of bird (*ave*), more than the US and Canada combined.

This field guide helps you identify some z the more common and distinctive animals that you might spot in Costa Rica, together with their Spanish names. The abbreviations used below are:

EB Estación Biológica
PN Parque Nacional
RB Reserva Biológica

RBBN Reserva Biológica Bosque Nuboso
RNA Reserva Natural Absoluta
RNdVS Refugio Nacional de Vida Silvestre

MONKEYS

Costa Rica is home to four species of monkey. As their diets consist of slightly different foods, it is not unusual to see mixed-species groups foraging together, with spider monkeys on the lookout mainly for fruit, howler monkeys favouring leaves, and white capuchin and squirrel monkeys feeding mostly on insects. Although comparatively prevalent, Costa Rican monkeys are threatened by habitat loss, which limits their movement and exposes them to disease.

MANTLED HOWLER MONKEY (*MONO CONGO* or *MONO AULLADOR*) *ALOUATTA PALLIATA*

The most common species of monkey in Costa Rica, the shaggy howler monkey lives in troupes of around ten to fifteen, led by a dominant male, in both primary and secondary wet and dry forest, in particular PN Tortuguero. Although also the least active of the country's monkeys, covering less than 1km of ground a day, they are easily located: the male's distinctive, rasping gorilla-like bellow, which announces dawn and dusk and even the onset of heavy rain, can be heard several kilometres away.

CENTRAL AMERICAN SPIDER MONKEY (*MONO COLORADO* or *MONO ARAÑA*) *ATELES GEOFFROYI*

The spider monkey takes its name from its ability to glide through the trees, gibbon-like, using its long arms and fingers and its strong prehensile tail – watching a troupe making their gymnastic way through the upper canopy (usually following a well-worn trail known as a "monkey highway") is a magical experience. Traditionally hunted for meat (they are allegedly the region's best-tasting primate) so now wary of humans, spider monkeys can be seen ranging in troupes of up to forty in mature, undisturbed forest in PN Guanacaste, PN Santa Rosa, PN Tortuguero and PN Santa Elena.

WHITE-FACED CAPUCHIN MONKEY (*MONO CARABLANCO*) *CEBUS CAPUCINUS*

The only Costa Rican ape not listed as endangered, the highly intelligent white-faced capuchin monkey is noted for its dexterity and use of tools, both as weapons and for getting food. Named for their physical resemblance to Capuchin friars, the monkeys' distinctly humanoid pink face (it's actually the surrounding fur that is white) makes it a popular pet. As well as living in most forms of forest, white-faced capuchins are also found in mangroves, particularly in PN Manuel Antonio and RNA Cabo Blanco.

CENTRAL AMERICAN SQUIRREL MONKEY (*MONO TITÍ*) *SAIMIRI OERSTEDII*

The squirrel monkey is restricted to a few pockets of mostly secondary wet forest on Costa Rica's southwest Pacific slope, principally the areas in and around PN Manuel Antonio. Their delicate grey and white faces have long made them attractive to pet owners and zoos, and consequently they have been hunted to near extinction in Costa Rica. Although uncommon, and small in stature (30cm), they are easy to spot, large troupes of up to seventy hyperactive individuals announcing themselves with a cacophony of high-pitched chattering.

SLOTHS

True to their name, Costa Rica's two species of sloth (*perezoso*, which means "lazy" in Spanish) are inherently adverse to movement, with an extremely slow metabolism that allows them to sleep for up to twenty hours a day. Their sharp, taloned claws are best suited to the arboreal world, and yet once a week, risking life and limb, they descend to the forest floor to defecate – though experts still debate why they do this, one theory is that it marks the tree as being "occupied" to other sloths and animals.

HOFFMANN'S TWO-TOED SLOTH
(PEREZOSO DE DOS DEDOS) CHOLOEPUS HOFFMANNI

Mostly nocturnal, the two-toed sloth is common in both primary and secondary wet forest, and more mobile than its three-toed cousin, but is still difficult to spot – the greasy green algae that often covers their brown hair camouflages them from their main predators, eagles, and means that, from a distance, they can easily be mistaken for a hornet's nest. They prefer disturbed growth, particularly in PN Tortuguero, RBBN Monteverde and EB La Selva – look for them hanging out in the mid- and upper branches of cecropia and guarumo trees.

BROWN-THROATED THREE-TOED SLOTH
(PEREZOSO DE TRES DEDOS) BRADYPUS VARIEGATUS

Diurnal and nocturnal, the three-toed sloth is the one you're more likely to see on the move, but even then they can spend more than eighty percent of the time asleep. They also prefer disturbed growth, and can often be seen curled around the V-shaped intersections between branches in PN Manuel Antonio, PN Corcovado, PN Cahuita and PN Tortuguero. Apart from the difference in digits on their hands (both species have three toes on their feet), they have greyer, wirier hair than two-toed sloths, with a brown stripe on their back, black eye masks and a stubby tail (two-toed sloths are tail-less).

CATS

Costa Rica has half of the New World's dozen wild cat species, which in descending size order are the jaguar, puma (*puma*), jaguarundi (*león breñero*), ocelot, margay (*caucel*) and oncilla (*tigrillo*); the very rare black panther is in fact a melanistic (dark) form of jaguar. Nocturnal and shy at the best of times, they are incredibly difficult to spot – indeed, all six are listed as endangered – and require areas of (rapidly disappearing) pristine wilderness to thrive.

JAGUAR *(TIGRE) FELIS ONCA*

The largest of Costa Rica's cats, the semi-sacred jaguar was once common throughout Central America, especially in the lowland forests and mangroves of coastal areas, but is now an endangered species, hunted by man – incredibly, right up until the 1980s – for its valuable pelt and because of its reputation as a predator of calves and pigs. A solitary nocturnal hunter, the jaguar stalks its prey – whatever's most abundant, from turtles to tapirs – often killing it by biting straight through the skull. You may spot tracks (four rounded toe prints, about 10cm wide) in the morning mud, though deep-forest hiking in PN Corcovado offers the only real (and very rare) chance of seeing one in the wild.

OCELOT *(MANIGORDO) FELIS PARDALIS*

The sleek and elegant-looking ocelot, with its beautiful roseate patterning, is similar in appearance to the jaguar, though considerably smaller, and is another animal you are very unlikely to see – it is threatened due to habitat loss and a slow reproductive cycle. Mostly nocturnal, ocelots spend up to twelve hours roaming through primary and secondary forest (occasional sightings include PN Tortuguero and RB Tirimbina) and across open country for a variety of prey, particularly rodents. Its tracks are fairly easy to distinguish, with the forepaw print wider than the hind paw – hence its Spanish name ("Fat Hand").

1 TWO-TOED SLOTH 2 THREE-TOED SLOTH 3 JAGUAR 4 OCELOT >

RACCOON FAMILY

There are seven members of the raccoon (or Procyonidae) family in Costa Rica, an omnivorous group of New World species that have long tails to aid their arboreal antics and are united by their strong hearing and night vision and their excellent sense of smell. The most unusual-looking species is the brilliantly named kinkajou, though the one you're most likely to see is the ubiquitous coati.

KINKAJOU (MARTILLA) POTOS FLAVUS

Ranging in colour from russet orange to grey brown, the kinkajou uses its long, narrow tongue to eat fruit, nectar and insects, and is most often seen hanging from branches by its prehensile tail. Common in primary and secondary forests, including RBBN Monteverde and EB La Selva, it is one of the most frequently seen of Costa Rica's nocturnal mammals; look out for the orange reflection of its eyes in torchlight. The kinkajou is slightly bigger than the similar-looking olingo, which is absent from the Pacific slope, and uses its tail like a fifth limb as it moves about the forest canopy (olingos favour jumping).

WHITE-NOSED COATI (PIZOTE) NASUA NARICA

With its long muzzle and ringed tail, held aloft to aid its balance, the coati (often mistakenly called coatimundi) looks like a confused combination of a raccoon, domestic cat and an anteater. The coati is very common, and its habituation to humans and comparative abundance makes it easy to spot: coatis are regularly seen in roadside bands of a dozen or more, on the scrounge for food, or scavenging in national-park car parks. Groups are made up of females and their young only, save for mating season, when a solitary male joins them temporarily – he is banished soon after, as he will harm the pups.

RODENTS

There are 47 species of rodent in Costa Rica, ranging from pocket gophers and spiny rats to the Mexican hairy porcupine. The majority are common across the country, with most of them contributing to their surrounding environment by dispersing seeds and providing an important link on the food chain for larger carnivores; the important exceptions are the black rat, brown rat and house mouse, introduced species that are responsible for contaminating food, spreading disease and often adversely affecting native ecosystems.

CENTRAL AMERICAN AGOUTI (GAUTUSA)
DASYPROCTA PUNCTATA

Often seen on trails or foraging along the forest floor, the rabbit-like agouti is common in both primary and secondary forest, and – thanks to their comparative abundance and diurnal activities – is the Costa Rican rodent you are most likely to come across, particularly if you're spending much time in PN Manuel Antonio or PN Carara. Agoutis spend most of their time alone (though monogamous pairs will share territory), and will follow troupes of white-faced capuchin and spider monkeys, feeding on fallen titbits. They make their dens in hollow trees or log piles.

PACA (TEPEZCUINTLE) AGOUTI PACA

Roughly fifty percent larger than the agouti, the solitary paca is nocturnal and uncommon, and so less readily seen. They make their dens near forest rivers; their burrows contain one or more secret exits (known as *uzús*), through which a paca will burst if cornered, often jumping into the water to escape danger. Pacas are easily distinguishable thanks to their rows of white spots, but can sometimes be mistaken for baby tapirs (see p.32), though the latter has a longer snout, a more defined streak patterning and white-tipped ears.

BATS

With 109 species in Costa Rica, bats make up over half of the country's mammal species; most of them are spotted whizzing about at dusk, though you can also see them hanging out by day, sleeping on the underside of branches, where they look like rows of small grey triangles. For the best bat-viewing opportunities, head to PN Barra Honda caves on the Nicoya Peninsula, where they roost in huge numbers.

GREATER FISHING BAT (MURCIÉLAGO PESCADOR) NOCTILIO LEPORINUS

Costa Rica is home to both species of fishing bat (also known as bulldog bats, due to their stout heads, folded faces and large canines), although it is easy enough to tell the two apart – as the name suggests, the greater fishing bat is much larger than the lesser variety (about 12cm in length, compared to 6cm), and its clawlike feet are proportionately much bigger. It is only found below elevations of around 200m; you may see one skimming the water in PN Tortuguero, casting its aural net in front in search of food – being blind, it fishes by sonar.

WHITE TENT BAT (MURCIÉLAGO BLANCO) ECTOPHYLLA ALBA

One of only two whitish bats in Costa Rica (the other is the larger northern ghost bat), the furry, ball-like white tent bat roosts in small groups underneath the leaves of heliconia plants, rattlesnake plants and banana plants. Look for folded-down midsections in horizontal leaves that are close to the ground; the bats create their protective "tents" by gnawing through the leaf veins. White tent bats only inhabit forests on the Atlantic slope, and, although generally uncommon, are relatively abundant in EB La Selva.

OTHER MAMMALS

NORTHERN TAMANDUA (COLLARED ANTEATER) (OSA HORMIGUERO) TAMANDUA MEXICANA

Of the two species of anteater that inhabit Costa Rica (the giant anteater, a third, was once found on both the Caribbean and Pacific slopes but is now thought to be extinct in Costa Rica), you're more likely to see the northern tamandua or collared anteater, which is more prevalent than the silky anteater, though largely nocturnal. It hunts ants, termites and occasionally bees, digging into nests using its sharp claws and vacuuming them up with its proboscis-like sticky tongue. Good places to spy one include PN Rincón de la Vieja and Reserva Rara Avis – look for large gashes in termite mounds (smaller scuffs are usually the work of other animals), and its distinctive interlocking paw tracks.

COLLARED PECCARY (SAÍNO) TAYASSU TAJACU

Of the two barely distinguishable species of peccary, a kind of wild boar, that forage through the rainforest undergrowth in Costa Rica, the collared peccary is the much more frequently seen, particularly in PN Corcovado, PN Santa Rosa and PN Braulio Carrillo. While they may clack their teeth when aggravated, collared peccaries are much less aggressive than the more elusive white-lipped variety (chancho de monte), which are essentially restricted to PN Corcovado. Longer-haired than their cousins, they can travel in battalions of several hundred and are dangerous when threatened; the best route of escape is to climb a tree.

BAIRD'S TAPIR (DANTA) TAPIRUS BAIRDII

One of the largest, most extraordinary-looking mammals in the Neotropics, the Baird's tapir resembles an overgrown pig with a sawn-off elephant's trunk stuck on its face. Their antediluvian look comes from their prehensile snout, small ears and delicate cloven feet; adults have a stout reddish-brown body, young have additional white streaks. Weighing as much as 300kg (and vegetarian), they are extremely shy in the wild, largely nocturnal, and stick to densely forested or rugged land. Consequently, they are very rarely seen by casual rainforest walkers, though you may spot one in the inner reaches of PN Corcovado, and there have been occasional sightings at Rara Avis – look in muddy areas around water.

WEST INDIAN MANATEE (MANATÍ or VACA MARINA) TRICHECHUS MANATUS

Among Costa Rica's marine mammals, the sea cow or manatee is arguably the most beguiling, an amiable herbivore that is elephantine in size and well intentioned, not to mention endangered. Manatees all over the Caribbean are declining in number, due to the disappearance and pollution of the fresh- and saltwater riverways in which they live. Your only reasonable chance of seeing one is in the Tortuguero canals in Limón Province, where they sometimes break the surface (main sightings are early morning), though there are a few in the more recently protected lagoons of the RNdVS Mixto Maquenque, near the border with Nicaragua – at first, you might mistake it for a tarpon, but the manatee's overlapping snout and long whiskers are quite distinctive.

TURTLES

Five species of marine turtle visit Costa Rica's shores: greens, hawksbills, leatherbacks and olive ridleys, and the strange blunt-nosed loggerhead, which seems not to nest in Costa Rica, but can sometimes be seen in Caribbean coastal waters. Nesting takes place mostly at night, when hundreds of turtles come ashore at a certain time of year, visiting the same beach each time (the same beach, in fact, on which they themselves hatched) and laying hundreds of thousands of eggs. They are found in shallow and (in the case of the leatherback and olive ridley) deep ocean, and shallow bays, estuaries and lagoons.

LEATHERBACK TURTLE (TORTUGA BAULA)
DERMOCHELYS CORIACEA

The leatherback turtle (see box, p.276) is the largest of Costa Rica's sea turtles, growing to a length of around 2m and weighing around 300kg. Leatherbacks have a soft, dark-grey ridged carapace – not a shell like other sea turtles, but actually a network of bones overlaid with a very tough leathery skin (hence the name). Although they nest in most numbers at PN Marino Las Baulas on the western Nicoya Peninsula (Oct–Feb), leatherbacks also come ashore elsewhere, including PN Tortuguero and RNdVS Gandoca-Manzanillo (both March–May). Their numbers have dwindled considerably due to loss of beachfront habitat and manmade hazards such as rubbish dumping (they can choke on plastic bags, which they mistake for jellyfish), and they are now listed as endangered.

GREEN TURTLE (TORTUGA VERDE) CHELONIA MYDAS

The green turtle, long prized for the delicacy of its flesh, has become nearly synonymous with its favoured nesting grounds in PN Tortuguero (Pacific greens, as opposed to Atlantic greens, nest at PN Santa Rosa and PN Manuel Antonio), with some turtles travelling 2000km to reach their breeding beaches (they nest July–Oct). Green turtles have a heart-shaped shell and are similar in appearance to the hawksbill, which have closer mosaic patterns on their flippers. Green turtles were classified as endangered as long ago as the 1950s, but are making a bit of a comeback thanks in part to the protection offered by areas like Tortuguero.

HAWKSBILL TURTLE (TORTUGA CAREY)
ERETMOCHELYS IMBRICATA

The hawksbill turtle, so-named for its distinctive hooked "beak", is found all over the tropics, often preferring rocky shores and coral reefs. It used to be hunted extensively on the Caribbean coast for its meat and shell, but this is now banned; poaching does still occur, however, despite their being listed as endangered, and you should avoid buying any tortoiseshell that you see for sale. Hawksbills have heart-shaped shells, like green turtles, but with mottled tortoise-shell patterns. Unlike greens and olive ridleys, hawksbills prefer to nest alone, coming ashore on beaches in PN Tortuguero, PN Santa Rosa and PN Marino Ballena (July–Oct).

OLIVE RIDLEY TURTLE (TORTUGA LORA)
LEPIDOCHELYS OLIVACEA

Growing to around 70cm, the olive ridley is the smallest of Costa Rica's sea turtles. Like greens and hawksbills, they also have a heart-shaped shell, although their distinctive colouring tells them apart. They nest (July–Nov) on just a few beaches along the Pacific coast, principally Playa Nancite in PN Santa Rosa and RNdVS Ostional, coming ashore in their thousands (an event known as an *arribada*; see box below) – unusually, often during the day. Despite these seemingly huge *arribadas*, olive ridleys are also unfortunately listed as endangered.

ARRIBA THE ARRIBADA!

Olive ridley turtles are one of only two species of marine turtle that nest in vast numbers (kemp's ridleys being the other), a mass gathering of up to eight thousand turtles known as an **arribada** (Spanish for "arrival"). *Arribadas* can last over twelve hours, with a steady stream of females crawling slowly out of the water to a free patch of sand beyond the high tide line where they will begin to lay their eggs. Each individual will lay around one hundred eggs over the course of a few days; according to estimates, more than **eleven million eggs** may be deposited during a single *arribada*. It is the sheer number of eggs that is the evolutionary reason behind the unusual behaviour of the olive ridleys: with so many eggs and hatchlings for predators to prey on, the likelihood of a hatchling making it out to sea increases dramatically. Despite the mass layings, however, the odds are still stacked overwhelmingly against the young turtles – only one out of every three hundred hatchlings from the protected beaches of the Refugio Nacional de Vida Silvestre Ostional, for example, will reach adulthood.

1 LEATHERBACK TURTLE 2 GREEN TURTLE 3 HAWKSBILL TURTLE 4 OLIVE RIDLEY TURTLE >

CROCODILIANS AND LIZARDS

AMERICAN CROCODILE (*COCODRILO*) *CROCODYLUS ACUTUS*

Travelling along Costa Rica's waterways, you may well see crocodiles hanging out on the riverbanks, basking in the sun, or lounging in the muddy shallows – you have a decent chance of spotting one in PN Tortuguero, RNdVS Mixto Maquenque and RNdVS Gandoca-Manzanillo, and are virtually guaranteed to see them under the so-called Crocodile Bridge near Tárcoles on the Pacific coast (see p.338). Crocodiles live in both freshwater and brackish water, mostly in lowland rivers, lagoons and estuaries but also occasionally in the sea, near the mouth of rivers. They are aggressive and dangerous, and have been known to kill humans in Costa Rica. Crocodiles have a longer, more pointed snout than caimans, with two projecting teeth, one on either side of the lower jaw, which caimans lack.

SPECTACLED CAIMAN (*CAIMÁN* or *GUAJIPAL*) *CAIMAN CROCODILUS*

Smaller and lighter in colour (tan or brown) than "flatter"-looking crocodiles, and with a shorter snout, caimans inhabit lowland rivers, swamps and wetlands, particularly PN Tortuguero, PN Palo Verde and RNdVS Caño Negro, where they will sometimes perch on submerged tree branches, scuttling away at your approach; in the dry season, large numbers gather in diminishing pools of water with only their eyes and snout visible. Caimans feed on various aquatic wildlife and carrion, and will even eat other young caimans. Although common locally, caimans (like crocodiles) are under constant threat from hunters, who sell their skin to make shoes and handbags.

GREEN IGUANA (*IGUANA VERDE* or *GALLINA DE PALO*) *IGUANA IGUANA*

Pot-bellied iguanas are the most ubiquitous of Costa Rica's lizards, as common here as chickens are in Europe or the US (indeed, their Spanish name means "tree chicken", though this is a reference more to the taste of their meat). Masters of camouflage, they like basking on high branches over water, or on riverbank rocks. Their colours vary from lime green to orangey brown (a yellow or orange head indicates a breeding male). Green iguanas are distinguished from their spiny-tailed cousins by the comb-like yellow crest along their spine; a large, circular scale below their ear; and a hanging throat sac (dewlap), which is used to regulate body temperature and for courtship and territorial displays. Despite their size (they can grow up to 2m), they are very shy, and when you do spot them, it's likely that they'll be scurrying away in an ungainly fashion.

SPINY-TAILED IGUANA (BLACK IGUANA) (*IGUANA NEGRA*) *CTENOSAURAS IMILIS*

More terrestrial than the green iguana, the tetchier spiny-tailed or black iguana can often be seen on or by the side of roads, or at the back of Pacific-coast beaches, basking on logs on the forest floor. Apart from the difference in colour, they can be told apart from the green iguana by the bands of spiny scales that encircle their tail and the black stripes that extend to their dorsal crest. They are the world's fastest lizard, escaping predators by hitting speeds of up to 35km/h.

EMERALD BASILISK LIZARD (*BASILISCA VERDE*) *BASILISCUS PLUMIFRONS*

One of the more incredible reptilian sights in and around the rivers and wetlands of Costa Rica is the tiny form of a basilisk lizard skittering across the water: its partially webbed hind feet, and the speed at which it can move them, enable the basilisk to "walk" on water (for up to 4.5m), earning it the nickname "Jesus Christ" lizard. When not in flight, basilisks are regularly seen in damp leaf litter and on low-hanging branches. Emerald basilisk lizards – which are easy to spot in PN Palo Verde and RNdVS Caño Negro – are more colourful than brown (Pacific slope) and striped (Caribbean slope) basilisks. It's also easy enough to differentiate between the sexes: males have three crests along their back, females have two.

SNAKES

Of the 162 species of snake (*serpientes* or *culebras*) that call Costa Rica home, only 22 are venomous. These are usually well camouflaged, but some, such as the highly venomous coral snake (*corallilo*), advertise their danger with a flamboyance of colour: although retiring, they are easily spotted (and avoided) thanks to their bright rings of carmine red, yellow and black (though note that the many-banded coral snake has only red and black rings). Snakes are largely nocturnal, and for the most part far more wary of you than you are of them, so the chances of actually spotting one – let alone getting bitten (see p.61) – are very slim.

FER-DE-LANCE (*TERCIOPELO*) *BOTHROPS ASPER*

The fer-de-lance pit viper has adapted quite well to cleared areas and grassy uplands, although you are far more likely to see them in places that have heavy rainfall (such as the Limón coast) and near streams or rivers at night (they are absent from Guanacaste's dry forest and the Nicoya Peninsula). Though it can reach more than 2m in length, the *terciopelo* ("velvet") is very difficult to spot – its brown body, marked with cream chevrons and dark triangles resembling "X"s (sometimes an hourglass), resembles a big pile of leaves. Along with the bushmaster, the fer-de-lance is one of the few snakes that may attack without provocation, and is extremely dangerous (its venom can kill within 2hr).

CENTRAL AMERICAN BUSHMASTER

(*MATABUEY*) *LACHESIS STENOPHRYS*

The largest venomous snake in the Americas (reaching 3m), the bushmaster is extremely aggressive and packs a highly potent bite (its Spanish name translates as "bull killer").

Fortunately, it is rarely spotted, as it is restricted to remote primary wet forests on the Caribbean slope (the black-headed bushmaster is endemic to the Osa Peninsula), prefers dense and mountainous territory and is nocturnal. Bushmasters are recognized by their thick, triangular head, with a broad, dark stripe running behind the eye, and the dark triangles that run down from the ridge along their back.

EYELASH VIPER (*BOCARACÁ*) *BOTHRIECHIS SCHLEGELII*

The very pretty eyelash viper is usually tan or bright green or decked out in a lichen-like pattern of browns, greys and mottled green, but is sometimes brilliant yellow when inhabiting golden palm-fruit groves. Largely arboreal and generally well camouflaged, it takes its name from the raised scales around its eyes – other notable features are its large triangular head, which is clearly distinguishable from its neck, and vertical pupils. Eyelash vipers are quite venomous to humans and should be given a wide berth if seen hanging from a branch or negotiating a path through the groves.

FROGS

There are many, many frogs (*ranas*) in Costa Rica, the most famous of which are the brilliantly coloured miniature poison-dart frogs. With markings as varied as wallpaper, they are relatively easy to see, but you should never touch one – these frogs secrete some of the most powerful natural toxins known to man through their skin, directly targeting the heart muscle, paralyzing it and causing immediate death. You will most likely see Costa Rica's frogs around dusk or at night; some of them make a regular and dignified procession down paths and trails, sitting motionless for long periods before hopping off again.

RED-EYED TREE FROG (*RANA CALZONUDA*)
AGALYCHNIS CALLIDRYAS

The nocturnal red-eyed tree frog is physically striking: relatively large, it is an alarming bright green, with orange hands and feet and dark blue thighs; its eyes are pure red, to scare off potential predators. Very common and abundant in wet forest, swamps and small pools, red-eyed tree frogs are particularly active during the wet season, and on humid nights you can often hear breeding males calling (a short "chuck" or "chuck-chuck") for the larger female.

FLEISCHMANN'S GLASS FROG (*RANA DE CRISTAL*) *HYALINO BATRACHIUM FLEISCHMANNI*

The extraordinary Fleischmann's glass frog is a living biological lesson – their inexplicably transparent belly affords you the dubious pleasure of observing its viscera and digestive processes through its skin. Glass frogs are fairly common and widespread in moist and wet forest,

where they are usually found on leaves overhanging fast-flowing water, so you have a good chance of spotting one; they are most active on rainy nights, when the male calls (a whistle-like "wheet") from the underside of a leaf.

STRAWBERRY POISON-DART FROG
(*RANA VENENOSA ROJA Y AZUL*) *OOPHAGA PUMILIO*

If you're spending any time on the Caribbean side of the country, you are almost guaranteed to see the diminutive but extravagantly coloured strawberry poison-dart frog, also known as the "Blue Jeans" thanks to its dark-blue hind legs. They are very common and abundant in wet forest, particularly the Sarapiquí – look in the leaf litter round the base of trees for them feeding on ants (if their colouring doesn't give them away, their loud "buzz-buzz-buzz" croak will). If you're lucky, you may even spot a female carrying her tadpoles, piggy-back style, one at a time, to take refuge in small water pools that form in treetop plants.

BIRDS

Birds, both migratory and indigenous, are abundant in Costa Rica – indeed, with nearly 900 different species, the country is home to more varieties than in the US and Canada – and most visitors take a birdwatching trip (see p.71) of one sort or another while they're here. Costa Rica's national bird is the rather dour-looking clay-coloured robin (*el yigüirro*), a somewhat surprising choice given that the competition includes some of the most colourful species in the Americas. Many birds are best observed while feeding – quetzals, for instance, are most often sighted when they are foraging from their favoured aguacatillo tree, and you might catch a glimpse of a hummingbird hovering over a flower as it sups on its nectar.

MAGNIFICENT FRIGATEBIRD *(RABIHORCADO MAGNO) FREGATA MAGNIFICENS*

The magnificent frigatebird is a very common sight along the Pacific coast (less so on the Caribbean side of the country), where they are often spotted just offshore or in mangrove keys, or circling over fishing boats at harbours and docks – they are easily recognized by their sleek forked tail and large wingspan (up to 2m). Due to its absorbent plumage, the frigatebird rarely dives underwater, instead feeding by snatching food from the sea or other birds. The male is the more "magnificent" of the two, inflating its enormous scarlet pouch (gular sac) to attract females.

BOAT-BILLED HERON *(PICO CUCHARA) COCHLEARIUS COCHLEARIUS*

The chunky, funny-looking boat-billed heron is fairly common in Costa Rica's wetlands, mangroves and coastal lowlands. Its large eyes and sensitive bill enable the heron to hunt at night, but it is easier to see during the day, resting in trees near the water's edge. Its call is a throaty croak, which helps locate it amid the branches, though there's little chance of missing this species; its eponymous beak snaps shut loudly when disturbed.

ROSEATE SPOONBILL *(ESPATULA ROSADA) PLATALEA AJAJA*

As the only pink bird in Costa Rica, there is no mistaking the roseate spoonbill. Common in coastal waters and open wetland in the Pacific lowlands, particularly around the Río Tempisque and in the Gulf of Nicoya, it is restricted to RNdVS Caño Negro on the Caribbean side of the country – birds are usually seen feeding in groups in shallow fresh- and saltwater, trawling for food with their flattened, spatula-shaped bill. The spoonbill's unique pink plumage is attained through its diet of crustaceans.

NORTHERN JACANA *(JACANA CENTROAMERICANA) JACANA SPINOSA*

Anyone spending much time in the wetlands of PN Palo Verde and RNdVS Caño Negro and the waterways of PN Tortuguero will come to know the northern jacana rather well – it is common in wetlands, ponds and rivers across the country but is particularly prevalent in these three protected areas. A rather ungainly looking bird, the northern jacana's giant spindly feet and elongated toes enable it to walk on floating vegetation in search of insects and seeds. It is easily agitated, displaying its recognizable lemon-yellow underwings when taking flight. Northern jacanas are usually seen in pairs, though the female mates with several males, who care for separate clutches of eggs.

LAUGHING FALCON *(GUACO) HERPETOTHERES CACHINNANS*

Of Costa Rica's raptors, the laughing falcon, found all over the country, probably has the most distinct call, which sounds exactly like its Spanish name – the "laughing" bit comes from a much lower-pitched variation, which resembles muted human laughter. The falcon preys on reptiles, including venomous snakes, biting off the head before bringing the body back to its eyrie, where it drapes it over a branch, sings a duet with its mate and proceeds to dine.

RED-CAPPED MANAKIN *(SALTARIN CABECIRROJO) PIPRA MENTALIS*

The diminutive star of many a wildlife documentary, the red-capped manakin is famous for its flamboyant leks, where males gather to woo females with elaborate courtship displays that range from short swoops to a variety of nifty tree-branch moves. Aside from the eponymous "helmet", males are also easily identified by their bright yellow thighs; like most manakins, the female is a dull green colour. They are common in primary rainforest on the Caribbean and central and southern Pacific slopes, and are regularly filmed at EB La Selva.

MONTEZUMA OROPENDOLA *(OROPÉNDOLA DE MOCTEZUMA) PSAROCOLIUS MONTEZUMA*

You are unlikely to visit Costa Rica without seeing a Montezuma oropendola. These large, russet-coloured birds are very common in gardens, wet forests and forest fringes of the Caribbean lowlands (less so higher up, and rarer on the northwest Pacific slope) and are easily distinguished thanks to their outsized beaks, pretty facial markings and golden tails. Courting males are even more noticeable, tipping off their perch and flicking their wings while uttering a long, warbling call that ends with a loud gurgle. Oropendolas live in noisy colonies of skilfully woven hanging nests (*oropéndola* means "gold pendulum"), which dangle from tall trees like Christmas decorations.

SCARLET MACAW (LAPA ROJA) ARA MACAO

The endangered scarlet macaw, with its liberal splashes of red, yellow and blue, was once common on the Pacific coast of southern Mexico and Central America. The birds, which are easily distinguished from the rest of Costa Rica's predominantly green parrot species, live in lowland forested areas, but these days your best chance of spotting them is in the dense cover of PN Corcovado and the Osa Peninsula, although their numbers are on the increase in PN Carara and the RNdVS Curú, and to a lesser extent PN Palo Verde and RB Lomas Barbudal. They are usually spotted in or near their tree-trunk nesting holes, wrestling seeds, fruit and nuts from the upper branches, or while flying high in pairs (they are monogamous) and calling to one another with their distinctive raucous squawk.

VIOLET SABREWING (ALA DE SABLE VOLÁCEO) CAMPYLOPTERUS HEMILEUCURS

Of the fifty-plus species of hummingbird (colibrí) in Costa Rica, the violet sabrewing is the largest, and one of the most beautiful, its deep, iridescent purple plumage shimmering like sequins. Its wings are big enough for you to hear them beating, but despite its size, the sabrewing is timid and easily scared off feeding sites by smaller birds. Sabrewings prefer the forest understorey but are often seen hovering around heliconia and banana plants and are a regular at nectar-feeders – RBBN Monteverde is a good place to spot them.

RESPLENDENT QUETZAL (QUETZAL) PHAROMACHRUS MOCINNO

With a range historically extending from southern Mexico to northern Panama, the dazzling resplendent quetzal was highly prized by the Aztecs and the Maya. In the language of the Aztecs, quetzali means, roughly, "beautiful", and along with jade, the jewel-coloured feathers were used as currency in Maya cities. Top of most visitors' birdwatching wish-list, the quetzal is unfortunately endangered due to the destruction of its favoured cloudforest habitat, and the male in particular – who possesses the distinctive streamer-like feather train, up to 1.5m long – is still pursued by poachers. These days the remaining cloudforests, particularly RBBN Monteverde, PN Los Quetzales and the area around San Gerardo de Dota in the Zona Sur, are among the best places to see them (March–May is most favourable).

BLUE-CROWNED MOTMOT (BARRANQUERO) MOMOTUS MOMOTA

The blue-crowned motmot is readily seen in gardens and forest fringes of the Valle Central, and also in the Pacific lowlands. As its name suggests, this particular member of the motmot family sports a turquoise-blue cap, though it is more noticeable for its distinctive pendulous tail, which ends in twin racket-shaped tips. The blue-crowned motmot nests in burrows in earthbanks and is able to sit motionless for a long time, perched on a branch in the lower canopy, before darting out for prey such as insects and small lizards.

CHESTNUT-MANDIBLED TOUCAN (DIOS TEDÉ) RAMPHASTOS SWAINSONII

Costa Rica is home to six members of the toucan family, which include toucanets and aracaris, the largest of which is the chestnut-mandibled toucan. Named for the two-tone brown colour in their bill, which differentiates them from the flamboyantly adorned keel-billed toucan (tucán pico iris), chestnut-mandibled toucans are fairly common in coastal lowlands, wet forests and clearings across the country, although they're generally easier to see on the Pacific slope (you are most likely to see keel-billed toucans, however, in the Caribbean lowlands, particularly the Sarapiquí area); both varieties are often spotted at dawn and dusk – though sometimes as early as in the afternoon as 4 or 4.30pm – sitting in the open upper branches of secondary forest. The chestnut-mandibled toucan's Spanish name is derived from its onomatopoeic call; the keel-billed toucan's is more of a monotonous croak.

THREE-WATTLED BELLBIRD (CAMPENERO TRICARUNCULADO) PROCNIASTRICA RUNCULATUS

Spend a few days in the cloudforests of PN Santa Elena and RBBN Monteverde and you're likely to hear the distinctly un-bell-like metallic "eenk" of the three-wattled bellbird, a strange-looking bird whose appearance is defined by the black, wormlike strands that dangle from its beak; audible from almost a kilometre away, its call is considered one of the loudest bird songs on earth. Despite a variety of ongoing conservation efforts, the bellbird is becoming increasingly less common in wet and humid forests; between March and June, you may also spot them in the Tilarán and Talamanca cordilleras, to which they migrate during the breeding season.

BARE-NECKED UMBRELLABIRD (PÁJARO-SOMBRILLA CUELLINUDO) CEPHALOPTERUS GLABRICOLLIS

Endemic to Costa Rica and western Panama, the bare-necked umbrellabird is a difficult species to spot – confined to a strip along the Caribbean slope from Volcán Miravalles south, it is uncommon, and generally silent. But there's no mistaking this bizarre-looking bird if you are lucky enough to see one: it has a cropped, overhanging crest, which makes it look like it's sporting a bad basin-style hairpiece. During the breeding season (March–June), the male is even more distinctive, inflating his impressive scarlet throat sac during courting displays. Usually found in wet-forest lowlands, but migrates to higher altitudes to breed.

HOTEL BED AND BREAKFAST SIGN

Basics

Getting there

Costa Rica has two international airports. Juan Santamaría (SJO), just outside San José, receives the majority of flights, though Daniel Oduber Quiros (LIR), near the northern city of Liberia, handles an increasing range from the US, Canada and the UK. In recent years, direct flights from Europe have grown in number, though the majority of routes pass through the US – this means passengers have to comply with US entry requirements, even if merely transiting the country.

Airfares always depend on the **season**, with the highest being around July, August and December to mid-January; you'll get the best prices during the wet summer (May–Nov). Flying at weekends is usually more expensive than during the week; the price ranges quoted below assume midweek travel.

Fares on all routes fluctuate significantly: compare prices at ⓦ roughguides.com/flights before booking.

From the UK and Ireland

There are now direct flights **from the UK** to Costa Rica: British Airways flies **to San José** and Thomson flies **to Liberia**. Fares can be as low as £430 for either route, though generally hover around £500–650. You can sometimes find cheaper fares by flying via Madrid (with Iberia), Paris (with Air France), the US (with American Airlines, Delta, United and US Airways) or Canada (with Air Canada), though this will obviously extend your journey time.

There are no direct flights **from Ireland** to Costa Rica, so you have to travel via the UK, the US or mainland Europe; expect to pay €600–750.

A BETTER KIND OF TRAVEL

At Rough Guides we are passionately committed to travel. We believe it helps us understand the world we live in and the people we share it with – and of course tourism is vital to many developing economies. But the scale of modern tourism has also damaged some places irreparably, and climate change is accelerated by most forms of transport, especially flying. All Rough Guides' flights are carbon-offset, and every year we donate money to a variety of environmental charities.

DEPARTURE TAX

Most airlines now include Costa Rica's US$29 **departure tax** in their ticket prices. If your airline does not include it, you'll have to pay it at the airport in US dollars or colones, by cash or credit card. Note that credit-card payments are treated as a cash advance and incur a charge of around US$10.

From the US and Canada

Daily direct flights depart **for San José** from numerous cities in **the US**, including Miami (around 2hr 45min), Orlando (around 3hr), Houston (around 3hr 40min), Dallas (around 4hr), Denver (around 5hr 15min), New York (around 5hr 30min) and Los Angeles (around 6hr). American Airlines usually offers the cheapest fares **from Miami** and **Dallas** (starting at US$400 in high season), while United's flights **from Houston** start at around US$450; American Airlines and United both fly from many US cities to Dallas, Miami or Houston to connect with flights to Costa Rica. JetBlue and Spirit Airlines run services from **Florida** (both Orlando and Fort Lauderdale), with fares around US$375 for a flight from Orlando but as low as US$200 on one of Spirit's early morning departures from Fort Lauderdale. JetBlue also flies from New York **to Liberia** (5hr 15min), from around US$380, while Avianca offers good-value fares **from New York** to San José (via San Salvador; around US$450). Spirit Airlines also has low-cost flights (around US$350), though these involve a long wait in Fort Lauderdale. **From LA**, the best deals are generally with Avianca (again via San Salvador); flights start at around US$600.

Air Canada has a few direct flights between San José and **Canada**, with fares from Toronto, Vancouver and Montreal starting at around Can$650. The airline also has a number of flights via the US, as do American Airlines and Delta, among others.

From Australia, New Zealand and South Africa

There are no direct flights from Australia, New Zealand or South Africa to Costa Rica – the quickest and easiest option is to fly via the US or Canada. Note that it's best to book several weeks (or months) ahead.

From Australia, the cheapest fares **to San José** from Sydney tend to be via Los Angeles with Delta (from Aus$2000 in high season); American Airlines' fares to San José via LA are usually slightly higher. Fares from all eastern Australian cities are typically the same – those from Perth and Darwin are a little more.

From New Zealand, the best through-tickets **to San José** are with Delta, departing from either Auckland or Christchurch and travelling via Sydney/ Brisbane and Los Angeles (from around NZ$2500 in high season).

From South Africa, the least convoluted route to San José is with Delta from Johannesburg via Atlanta (around ZAR15,000).

From neighbouring countries

Costa Rican airlines Sansa (Ⓦflysansa.com) and Nature Air (Ⓦnatureair.com) have regular flights from San José to **Nicaragua** (Managua) and **Panama** (Bocas del Toro). Expect to pay from around US$120 one way.

Overland to Costa Rica

Costa Rica's main international bus company, Tica Bus (☎2221 0006, Ⓦticabus.com), runs a good **overland bus** service between Mexico (Tapachula), Guatemala, El Salvador, Honduras, Nicaragua and Costa Rica, continuing on south to Panama. It's a very popular route, and you'll need to reserve your tickets up to a month in advance in the high season (and up to three months in Dec).

Tica Bus has daily (except Good Friday) buses between San José and destinations including **Managua** (from US$28.75; 11hr), **Guatemala City** (from US$86.50; 60hr, with overnights in Managua and El Salvador at your own expense) and **Panama City** (from US$42; 16hr).

Alternatively, TransNica (☎2223 4242, Ⓦtransnica .com) runs buses (5 daily; 11hr; from US$28) between San José and **Managua**, while Central Line (☎2221 9115, Ⓦtransportescentralline.com) runs services via **Granada** (2 daily; 11hr; US$29). Expreso Panamá (☎507 314 6837, Ⓦexpreso panama.com) has a daily service to **Panama City**, departing at 11pm (US$40).

The main northern **border crossing** with Nicaragua is at Peñas Blancas (see p.268) on the Interamericana. Further east, you'll find another crossing at Los Chiles (see p.223) to/from San Carlos on the shores of Lago Nicaragua. The main route south, to and from Panama, is again along the Interamericana, at Paso Canoas (see p.405). On the Caribbean coast, Sixaola is a smaller crossing, across one of the most decrepit bridges in the world (a new one is in the pipeline), while in the southern

highlands a little-used route links San Vito with the border town of Río Sereno.

Agents and operators

TRAVEL AGENTS

eBookers UK ☎0203 320 3320, Ⓦebookers.com. Low fares on an extensive range of scheduled flights.

Flightcentre UK ☎0870 499 0040, US ☎1 877 992 4732, Canada ☎1 877 967 5302, Australia ☎13 31 33, New Zealand ☎0800 243544, South Africa ☎0877 405000; Ⓦflightcentre.com. Rock-bottom fares worldwide.

Journey Latin America UK ☎0203 603 8765, Ⓦjourneylatin america.co.uk. Latin American specialists, adept at arranging unusual itineraries at competitive fares. They also offer tours (see opposite).

North South Travel UK ☎01245 608 291, Ⓦnorthsouthtravel .co.uk. Friendly, competitive travel agency, offering discounted fares worldwide. Profits are used to support projects in the developing world, especially the promotion of sustainable tourism.

STA Travel UK ☎0333 321 0099, US ☎1 800 781 4040, Australia ☎13 47 82, New Zealand ☎0800 474 400, South Africa ☎0861 781781; Ⓦstatravel.co.uk. Worldwide specialists in independent travel; also student IDs, travel insurance, car rental, rail passes, and more. Good discounts for students and under-26s.

Trailfinders UK ☎0207 368 1200, Ireland ☎021 464 8800; Ⓦtrailfinders.com. One of the best-informed and most efficient agents for independent travellers.

Travel CUTS Canada ☎1 800 667 2887, Ⓦtravelcuts.com. Canadian youth and student travel firm.

USIT Ireland ☎01 602 1906, Ⓦusit.ie. Ireland's main student and youth travel specialists.

TOUR OPERATORS

In addition to the below, there are some excellent tour operators in Costa Rica itself (see p.53).

Adventures Abroad UK ☎01142 473400, US & Canada ☎1 800 665 3998, Australia ☎2 9680 2828; Ⓦadventures-abroad.com. Adventure specialists, with one- to three-week trips throughout Costa Rica and other Central American countries (from £1635).

Backroads US ☎1 800 462 2848, Ⓦbackroads.com. Cycling, hiking and multisport tours designed for the young at heart, with the emphasis on going at your own pace. Accommodation ranges from "casual inns" to "premier" hotels. Also family-friendly options and singles trips.

★ **Chill Expeditions** US ☎1 800 5517887, Ⓦchillexpeditions .com. Small-group and private trips, with a company dedicated to creating a healthier and more sustainable Costa Rica through eco-centred travel.

Contours Australia ☎1 300 135391, Ⓦcontourstravel.com.au. Specialists in Latin America, with a decent range of trips across Costa Rica – their eight-day Best of Costa Rica tour takes in Parque Nacional Tortuguero, Volcán Arenal and Monteverde (Aus$1523).

★ **Costa Rica Undiscovered** UK ☎020 7370 6646, Ⓦcostarica undiscovered.com. Tour operator specializing in Costa Rican sustainable tourism, and following the code of ethics outlined by Sustainable Travel

International and the Rainforest Alliance. Offers everything from day-tours in Parque Nacional Tortuguero to week-long yoga breaks.

Exodus UK ☎ 0845 287 7562, ⓦ exodus.co.uk. Experienced adventure-tour operators offering a range of Central American itineraries, with a popular sixteen-day Discover Costa Rica tour including visits to Parque Nacional Tortuguero, Reserva Santa Elena and Parque Nacional Piedras Blancas (£2519).

GeoEx US ☎ 1 888 570 7108, ⓦ geoex.com. Luxury adventure travel and cultural tours, including rainforest and river trips, plus customized itineraries; the nine-day Costa Rica Family Discovery tour costs from US$6375.

Global Exchange US ☎ 415 255 7296, ⓦ globalexchange.org. Human rights organization offering "Reality Tours" to meet local activists and participate in educational workshops. They run annual trips to Costa Rica (one to the Caribbean coast, two to the Pacific) concentrating on ecotourism and sustainability (US$1539).

Journey Latin America UK ☎ 0203 432 3949, ⓦ journeylatin america.co.uk. Specialist in flights, packages and adventurous, tailor-made trips to Latin America, including numerous tours of Costa Rica – for example, a fifteen-day wildlife-focused trip (from £3639) and the fifteen-day "Value Central America" trip, which also takes in Guatemala and Belize (from £3228).

Journeys International US ☎ 1 800 255 8735, ⓦ journeys 0international.com. Award-winning operator focusing on ecotourism and small-group trips, with ones specializing in photography and writing (from US$2000).

Nature Expeditions International US ☎ 1 800 869 0639, ⓦ naturexp.com. Small-group expeditions led by specialists in anthropology, biology and natural history; Costa Rican trips offer optional lectures on the environment, ecotourism and local cultures (from US$4150).

Peregrine UK ☎ 0808 274 5438, ⓦ peregrineadventures.com. Experienced small-group adventure specialists offering a number of good-value tours, from 10 to 43 days (from £2420).

Rainbow Tours UK ☎ 020 7666 1260, ⓦ rainbowtours.co.uk. Highly respected and experienced tour operator with a strong focus on wildlife-watching; their dozen itineraries include family-friendly options (from £2310).

Rickshaw Travel UK ☎ 01273 322399, ⓦ rickshawtravel.co.uk. This well-run outfit specializes in two- to four-day "bite-size" tours and activities that you can combine to create your own, personalized itinerary. Trips include visiting an indigenous Bribrí village (from £188), treetop walks and ziplining in Monteverde (from £145) and a tour of Rincon de la Vieja (from £188).

Road Scholar US ☎ 1 800 454 5768, ⓦ roadscholar.org. Extensive selection of educational and activity programmes, including photography trips, birdwatching tours and "study cruises". Participants must be over 55, though companions may be younger.

Sunvil Holidays UK ☎ 0208 568 4499, ⓦ sunvil.co.uk. Flexible fly/drive itineraries and tailor-made tours, specializing in luxury and wildlife-watching trips, with accommodation in a number of areas including Caño Negro, Santa Teresa and the Osa Peninsula.

TravelLocal UK ☎ 01865 242 709, ⓦ travellocal.com. An innovative agency that enables you to create tailor-made holidays through Tico travel experts based in Costa Rica (and around the world).

Wildlife Worldwide UK ☎ 0845 130 6982, ⓦ wildlifeworldwide .com. Tailor-made trips for wildlife and wilderness enthusiasts, visiting more off-the-beaten-track places such as Parque Nacional Braulio Carrillo and Refugio Nacional de Vida Silvestre Gandoca-Manzanillo (from £2995).

Getting around

Costa Rica's public bus system is excellent, inexpensive and relatively frequent, even in remote areas. Privately run shuttle buses offer quicker but more expensive transfers, while taxis also regularly do long- as well as short-distance trips, and are decent value if you're travelling in a group. Car rental is more common here than in the rest of Central America, but is quite expensive, especially if you're hiring a 4WD. Driving can also be quite a hair-raising experience, with precipitous drops in the highlands and potholed roads just about everywhere else.

Domestic airlines are reasonably economical and can be quite a time-saver, especially since Costa Rica's difficult terrain makes driving distances longer than they appear on the map. **Tour operators** in San José organize individual itineraries and packages with transport included, well worth checking out before making any decisions about heading out on your own.

By bus

Travelling by public **bus** is by far the cheapest way to get around Costa Rica – the most expensive journey in the country (from San José to Paso Canoas on the Panamanian border) costs just US$14. **San José** is the hub for virtually all bus services in the country (see p.103); indeed, it's often impossible to travel from

---

SOME USEFUL ROAD-SIGN MEANINGS

No Hay Paso No Entry
Ceda El Paso Give Way
Una Via One Way
Despacio Slow
Peligroso Danger
Carretera En Mal Estado Road In Bad Condition
Hombres Trabajando En La Via Men Working In The Road
Salida De Camiones Truck Exit

FINDING YOUR WAY AROUND COSTA RICAN TOWNS

As in most Central American countries, Costa Rica's major urban areas are laid out on a **grid system**, with the main plaza in the middle of town. Calles run north–south, avenidas east–west. Generally, calles east of the plaza are odd-numbered, while those to the west are even-numbered; avenidas are even-numbered south of the park and odd-numbered to the north. However, there are a number of peculiarities that are essential to get to grips with if you want to find your way around with ease. The following rules apply to all cities except Limón.

Exact street numbers tend not to exist, and you'll typically see **addresses** written as follows: *Bar Esmeralda, Av 2, C 5/7*, which means that *Bar Esmeralda* is on Avenida 2, between Calle 5 and Calle 7. *Bar Lotto*, C 5, at Av 2, on the other hand, is on or near the corner of Calle 5 and Avenida 2. Apartado (Aptdo) means "post code", and bis means, technically, "encore": if you see "Av 6 bis" in an address, for example, it refers to another Avenida 6, right next to the original one.

Many **directions**, in both written and verbal form, are given in terms of metres rather than blocks (in general, one block is equivalent to 100m). Thus "de la Escuela Presidente Vargas, 125 metros al sur, cincuenta metros al oeste", translates as "from the Presidente Vargas School, 125 metres south [one block and a quarter] and 50 metres west [half a block]". More confusingly, verbal directions are commonly given in relation to landmarks that everyone – except the visitor – knows and recognizes. Even more frustratingly, some of these landmarks may not even exist any longer. This is something to get the hang of fast: taxi drivers will often look completely bewildered if given street directions, but as soon you come up with a landmark (the town church, the *parque central*, a *Pops Heladería*), the proverbial light bulb goes on.

one place to another without backtracking to the capital. Tickets for some of the popular routes ought to be **booked in advance**, though you may be lucky enough to get on without a reservation. **Tickets** on most mid- to long-distance and popular routes are issued with a date and a seat number; make sure the date is correct, as you cannot normally change your ticket or get a refund. Neither can you buy **return** bus tickets on Costa Rican buses, which can be quite inconvenient if you're heading to very popular destinations like Monteverde or Manuel Antonio at busy times – you'll need to buy your return ticket as soon as you arrive to guarantee yourself a seat.

Bus **schedules** change with impressive frequency, so be sure to check in advance; you can download a comprehensive timetable from the ICT website (Ⓦ visitcostarica.com); alternatively, check Ⓦ thebusschedule.com/EN/cr.

The majority of the country's buses are in good shape, although most lack air conditioning and there's very little room for luggage, or long legs. Most comfortable (generally) are the **Tica Buses** – modern, air-conditioned vehicles with good seats, adequate baggage space and very courteous drivers – that run from San José to Panama City and Managua, and on to Tegucigalpa, San Salvador, Guatemala City, and Tapachula in Mexico (see p.105). Most buses in Costa Rica have buzzers or bells to signal to the driver that you want to get off, though you may still find a few people using the old system of whistling, or shouting "*¡Parada!*" ("Stop!") – despite signs requesting otherwise. The

atmosphere on board is generally friendly, and while there are no **toilets** on the buses, drivers make (admittedly infrequent) stops on longer runs. Often, there'll be a lunch or dinner stop at a roadside restaurant or service station; failing that, there is always a bevy of hardy food and drinks sellers who leap onto the bus proffering their wares.

The **local buses** that make short hops between towns and nearby villages and attractions, such as the services that run from Heredia to Santa Bárbara, are less comfortable and more crowded, though they can be convenient to use, and the journeys are short. Finding the bus stop you need, however, can be difficult, as they tend to move about town with alarming frequency – you'll probably need to ask around to find the current departure point.

By shuttle bus

In recent years, travellers have begun to make much more use of the network of a/c **shuttle buses** that connect most of Costa Rica's main tourist destinations. While these often cost over five times as much as the public buses, they are significantly faster and more comfortable, and will pick up and drop off at hotels. The main operator is **Interbus** (Ⓣ 4100 0888, Ⓦ www.interbusonline .com), which has comprehensive routes across the country; their fares range from US$42 to US$92. The similar but slightly more expensive **Gray Line** (Ⓣ 2220 2126, Ⓦ graylinecostarica.com) runs direct services between many tourist spots, as well as a variety of passes that offer unlimited use of their routes, starting from US$240 for a week.

By car

Although there's little traffic outside San José and the Valle Central, the common perception of **driving** in Costa Rica is of endless dodging around cows and potholes, while big trucks nudge your rear bumper in an effort to get you to go faster around the next blind bend. The reality is somewhat different. While many minor roads are indeed badly potholed and unsurfaced, driving is relatively easy, and with your own vehicle you can see the country at your own pace without having to adhere to bus or plane schedules – road signage, however, is poor, particularly in the Valle Central, so a good map (see p.78) is essential.

You only need a **valid driver's licence** issued in your home country to drive a car in Costa Rica (for up to three months). The general **speed limit** on highways is 80kph, reducing to 40kph elsewhere and 25kph in built-up areas; the speed limit is marked on the road surface or on signs. Fines (*multas*) for motoring offences are steep: talking on a mobile phone or driving without a seatbelt can incur fines of US$187–196; running a red light could cost you US$374–391; while if you're caught speeding (speed traps are fairly common), you may have to pay up to US$553–578 (the same, oddly, that you can be fined

if caught making a "U" turn). If a motorist – especially a trucker – in the oncoming direction flashes his headlights at you, you can be almost certain that traffic cops with speed-trapping radar are up ahead. Although traffic cops routinely accept bribes to tear up tickets, it's a very serious offence and should not be attempted under any circumstances.

Petrol is comparatively expensive (by North American standards, at least) at about US$3.83 per gallon (fuel prices are regulated by the government, so you'll pay the same at all petrol stations). Most cars take regular; all petrol stations (*bomboneras* or *gasolineras*) are serviced.

If you're unlucky enough to have an **accident** in Costa Rica, don't attempt to move the car until the traffic police (☎2222 9330 or ☎2222 9245) arrive: call the National Insurance Institute (☎2287 6000, Ⓦins-cr.com), who will send an inspector to check the vehicles involved to assess who caused the accident – vital if you're using a rental car.

Car rental

Expect to pay from about US$40 per day for a regular vehicle, and up to US$80 for an intermediate 4WD (both including full insurance); extras such as additional driver, child seats, mobile phone and cool box will push the price up further – though note that the excellent Vamos Rent-A-Car (see p.52) include these as standard. Rental days are

---

CAR SAFETY IN COSTA RICA

Although the majority of the country's roads are fairly light on traffic, the **road accident** rate is phenomenal – while most Ticos blame bad road conditions, the real cause is more often poor driving. Sections of washed out, unmarked or unlit road add to the hazards, as do big trans-isthmus trucks. Another hazard is **car crime** (break-ins are an unfortunately regular occurrence) and **scams**, such as thieves puncturing your tyres and then robbing you after stopping to "help". Most people have a memorable, and uneventful, time driving around Costa Rica, but it will help if you consider the following:

- Drive defensively.
- Keep your doors locked and windows shut, especially in San José.
- Keep valuables in the boot or out of sight.
- Avoid driving at night, when wild animals are more active.
- If someone suspicious approaches your vehicle at a red light or stop sign, sound your horn.
- Do not pull over for flashing headlights – note that an emergency or police vehicle has red or blue flashing lights.
- If you get lost, find a public place, like a service station, to consult your map or ask for directions.
- If someone tells you something is wrong with your vehicle, do not stop immediately. Drive to the nearest service station or other well-lit public area.
- Do not park at remote trailheads – leave your car at the nearest manned ranger station.
- Be aware of steep roadside gullies, used to channel rainwater runoff, when turning or reversing.
- Do not pick up hitchhikers.
- In case of emergency, call ☎911.

DISTANCE CHART (IN KM)

	Alajuela	Cahuita	Cartago	Dominical	Golfito	Guápiles	Heredia	Jacó	Liberia	Limón
Alajuela		192	40	179	331	64	12	100	200	148
Cahuita	192	-	195	334	486	128	175	287	392	44
Cartago	40	195	-	139	291	70	35	131	240	151
Dominical	179	334	139	-	152	219	174	118	309	290
Golfito	331	486	291	152	-	371	326	270	461	442
Guápiles	64	128	70	219	371	-	47	159	264	84
Heredia	12	175	35	174	326	47	-	112	205	131
Jacó	100	287	131	118	270	159	112	-	191	243
Liberia	200	392	240	309	461	264	205	191	-	348
Limón	148	44	151	290	442	84	131	243	348	-
Nicoya	185	377	225	295	442	249	197	161	83	333
Paso Canoas	337	492	291	162	54	379	332	284	471	448
Peñas Blancas	277	469	317	377	524	341	289	259	77	425
Puerto Jiménez	354	509	314	175	127	394	349	293	454	465
Puerto Viejo de Sarapiquí	79	168	119	241	393	57	67	179	272	124
Puerto Viejo de Talamanca	209	17	212	351	503	145	192	304	409	61
Puntarenas	98	290	138	187	339	162	103	75	132	246
Quepos	175	377	182	43	195	239	187	75	263	333
San Carlos	56	225	96	235	387	97	68	144	185	181
San Isidro de El General	153	308	111	28	180	180	146	251	351	264
San José	17	175	23	162	309	47	12	117	217	131
Tamarindo	257	449	297	357	524	321	269	239	69	405
Tilarán	174	366	214	274	421	236	186	156	70	322
Turrialba	85	150	45	187	336	70	80	176	285	106

Nicoya	Paso Canoas	Peñas Blancas	Puerto Jiménez	Puerto Viejo de Sarapiquí	Puerto Viejo de Talamanca	Puntarenas	Quepos	San Carlos	San Isidro de El General	San José	Tamarindo	Tilarán	Turrialba
185	337	277	354	79	209	98	175	56	153	17	257	174	85
377	492	469	509	168	17	290	377	225	308	175	449	366	150
225	291	317	314	119	212	138	182	96	111	23	297	214	45
295	162	377	175	241	351	187	43	235	28	162	357	274	187
442	54	524	127	393	503	339	195	387	180	309	524	421	336
249	379	341	394	57	145	162	239	97	180	47	321	236	70
197	332	289	349	67	192	103	187	68	146	12	269	186	80
161	284	259	293	179	304	75	75	144	251	117	239	156	176
83	471	77	454	272	409	132	263	185	351	217	69	70	285
333	448	425	465	124	61	246	333	181	264	131	405	322	106
-	452	160	465	264	394	118	242	210	336	202	72	95	272
452	-	534	159	399	509	355	209	393	186	320	534	431	342
160	534	-	547	383	486	210	334	223	428	304	146	173	355
465	159	547	-	416	526	362	218	410	203	332	527	444	359
264	399	383	416	-	185	170	254	57	201	67	336	253	164
394	509	486	526	185	-	307	394	242	325	192	466	383	167
118	355	210	362	170	307	-	150	108	249	115	190	107	183
242	209	334	218	254	394	150	-	119	326	192	314	231	227
210	393	223	410	57	242	108	119	-	209	73	272	115	141
336	186	428	203	201	325	249	326	209	-	134	408	325	156
202	320	304	332	67	192	115	192	73	134	-	274	191	68
72	534	146	527	336	466	190	314	272	408	274	-	139	335
95	431	173	444	253	383	107	231	115	325	191	139	-	252
272	342	355	359	164	167	183	227	141	156	68	335	252	-

CAR RENTAL ESSENTIALS

You have to exercise caution when **renting a car** in Costa Rica. While the agencies listed above are all recommended for their service, it is not uncommon for rental companies to claim for "damage" they insist you inflicted on the vehicle, and you may wish to rent a car through a Costa Rican ICT-accredited **travel agent** (see opposite), which could work out cheaper than renting on your own and will help guard against false claims of damage and other accusations.

Make sure to **check the car** carefully before you sign off the damage sheet. Scan the bodywork for dents and scuffs, and check the oil, brake fluid and fuel gauge (to make sure it's full) and that there is a spare tyre with good air pressure and a jack. Look up the Spanish for relevant terminology first, so you can at least scrutinize the rental company's assessment: "rayas", for example, means scratches. Keep a copy of this document on you.

Take the full **insurance**, not just the basic CDW (Collision Damage Waiver); because of the country's high accident rate, you need to be covered for damage to the vehicle, yourself and any third party, and public property.

---

calculated on a 24-hour basis: thus, if you pick up your car on a Tuesday at 3pm for a week, you have to return it before 3pm the following Tuesday. It's well worth hiring a Sat Nav, as road signs in Costa Rica are few and far between.

The **minimum age** for rental is usually 21, though sometimes it's as low as 18, and you'll need a credit card (either Visa or MasterCard) which has sufficient credit for the entire cost of the rental. Most **car-rental companies** are located in San José and at or around the international airports near Alajuela and Liberia (note that airport rentals incur an additional twelve percent charge), though you can also rent cars in various towns around the country. Local agencies invariably provide a much better deal than the major overseas operators (Vamos and Adobe are particularly recommended), and while prices vary considerably from agency to agency, renting outside San José is usually a bit more expensive. During peak season (especially Christmas, but any time from December to March), it's wise to reserve a car before you arrive. Picking up your car in another part of Costa Rica and dropping it off at the airport when you leave normally entails a charge of US$30 or more, though it may be waived if you're taking the vehicle for more than a few days.

Buying basic **insurance** is mandatory, even if you have your own. "Basic" insurance in Costa Rica tends to only cover damage by you to other people's vehicles, not your own, and given the rudimentary state of some of the roads and the aggressive driving of some of the people on them, it is worth paying extra for full insurance, although this will add to your car-rental costs considerably (full insurance starts at around US$30 per day).

If you're planning to visit the Nicoya Peninsula, Santa Elena and Monteverde or remote parts of the Zona Sur, it's definitely worth paying the extra

money for a **4WD**; indeed, in some areas of the country during the rainy season (May–Nov), it's a necessity. While a 4WD doesn't grant you immunity to the laws of physics, it does provide greater traction in the wet and higher clearance for rough roads and river crossings. Furthermore, in smaller vehicles, punctures are a depressingly regular experience, and although getting them repaired is a matter of a couple of minutes' hammering at the rim at the local garage, you've got better things to be doing on your holiday.

CAR RENTALS AROUND SAN JOSÉ

Adobe 10 Plaza Aventura ☎ 2542 4848, ⓦ adobecar.com
Alamo Juan Santamaría International Airport ☎ 2242 7733, ⓦ alamocostarica.com
Budget Paseo Colón, at C 30 ☎ 2255 4240, ⓦ budget.co.cr
Hertz Paseo Colón, at C 38 ☎ 2221 1818, ⓦ hertz.com
National Juan Santamaría International Airport ☎ 2242 7878, ⓦ natcar.com
Payless Juan Santamaría International Airport ☎ 2432 4747, ⓦ paylesscr.com
Vamos Rent-A-Car C 4, at Plaza Aeropuerto ☎ 2432 5258, ⓦ vamosrentacar.com

By motorcycle

For riders with a decent amount of experience, a **motorcycle** is one of the best ways to discover the diversity of Costa Rica. You will need a valid motorcycle licence or endorsement in order to rent a bike; smaller motorcycles for day-trips (125–155cc) can be rented in some beach towns (ie Jacó and Tamarindo), with daily rates from around US$40.

Those who want to tour the country can rent larger motorcycles (250cc and above) or book **guided tours** out of San José. Once outside the metropolitan area, an endless number of curvy back-roads and scenic gravel trails awaits – while the notorious road conditions of Costa Rica can be tiring in a car, they are usually great fun on a dual-sport motorcycle (Enduro motorcycle), with its good suspension.

MOTORBIKE RENTALS IN SAN JOSÉ

Costa Rica Motorcycle Tours ☎ 2225 6000, ⓦ costarica motorcycletours.com. Rental (from US$150/day) and tours on new BMWs (650–1200cc).

Wild Rider Motorcycles Paseo Colón, C 30/32 ☎ 2258 4604 or ☎ 8844 6568, ⓦ wild-rider.com. Very helpful German-run motorcycle rental (from US$70/day for 3 days) and tours, using Honda and 250–650cc Suzuki bikes.

By bicycle

Costa Rica's terrain makes for easy **cycling** compared with neighbouring countries, and as there's a good range of places to stay and eat, you don't need to carry the extra weight of a tent, sleeping bag and stove. Always bring warm clothes and a hi-vis jacket, however, wherever you are. As for **equipment**, rear panniers and a small handlebar bag (for maps and camera) should be enough. Bring a puncture repair kit, even if your tyres are supposedly unbustable. You'll need a bike with a triple front gear – this gives you 15 to 21 gears, and you will really need the low ones, especially if cycling in the highlands. Make sure, too, that you carry and drink lots of water – five to eight litres a day in the coastal lowlands.

There is very little **traffic** outside the Valle Central, and despite their tactics with other cars (and pedestrians), Costa Rican drivers are some of the most courteous in Central America to cyclists. That said, however, bus and truck drivers do tend to forget about you as soon as they pass, sometimes forcing you off the road. **Roads** are generally good for cyclists, who can dodge the potholes and wandering cattle more easily than drivers. Bear in mind that if you cycle up to Monteverde, one of the most popular routes in the country, you're in for a slow trip: besides being steep, there's not much traction on the loose gravel roads. Although road signs will tell you that cycling on the Interamericana (Panamerican Highway, or Hwy-1) is not permitted, you will quickly see that people do so anyway.

San José's best **cycle shop** is Ciclo Los Ases, 100m east of the Gimnasio Nacional, on Av 10 (☎ 2255 0535, ⓦ facebook.com/ciclo.losases). They have all the parts you might need, can fix your bike and may even be able to give you a bicycle carton for the plane.

By plane

Costa Rica's two **domestic carriers**, Sansa and NatureAir, offer reasonably economical flights between San José and many beach destinations and provincial towns. They can be particularly handy for accessing the more remote corners of the country – the flight from San José to Puerto Jiménez on the Osa Peninsula, for example, takes just fifty minutes compared to four and a half hours on the bus. Both carriers fly small twin-propeller aircraft (so bad weather can have an impact on schedules) and service more or less the same destinations.

NatureAir (☎ 2299 6000, ⓦ natureair.com), which flies from Tobías Bolaños Airport in Pavas, 7km west of San José, generally has bigger planes and more frequent services. **Sansa** (☎ 2290 4100, ⓦ flysansa .com) flies from Juan Santamaría airport, 17km northwest of San José. Rates start around US$60 for the shortest hops on both airlines, and last-minute deals are sometimes available on flights that aren't fully booked. On both reserve as far in advance as possible (at least two weeks in high season), and even then be advised that a booking means almost nothing until the seat is actually paid for. Reconfirm your flight in advance of the day of departure and again on the day, if possible, as their **schedules** (see p.103) can change at short notice. Note that some airports have **departure/arrival taxes**: Arenal (US$7), Tambor (US$2.50) and Quepos (US$3).

If you're travelling in a large group, **air-charter taxis** can prove a reasonably cheap way to get to the country's more remote areas. NatureAir and Alfa Romeo Air (☎ 8632 8150, ⓦ alfaromeoair.com) both run charters, on five- to eighteen-seater planes; Alfa Romeo's flight from San José to Tortuguero, for example, costs US$550.

Tour operators

There are scores of **tour operators** in Costa Rica, some very good, some not so – bear in mind that although you may save a few dollars by going with the cheapest agency, you could end up on a badly organized tour with poor accommodation and underqualified guides. Go with a reputable tour operator – such as those listed below, which are all licensed (and regulated) by the ICT, and in the relevant sections of each chapter – and not with one of the freelance "guides" who may approach you at the bus station or on the street. The following is not a comprehensive list, but all those that we've listed are experienced and recommended, offering a good range of services and tours.

TOUR OPERATORS IN AND AROUND SAN JOSÉ

★ **ACTUAR** 250m north of Parque La Amistad, Pavas ☎ 2290 7514, ⓦ actuarcostarica.com. The Costa Rican Association of Community-based Rural Tourism, whose highly rewarding trips give a real insight into co-operatives, locally owned coffee farms and indigenous reserves, among other grassroots organizations.

Camino Travel C 1, Av Central/1 ☎ 2234 2530, ⓦ caminotravel .com. Young, enthusiastic staff with high standards (and a mainly European clientele) offering upmarket and independent travel, including individual tours with quality accommodation. They can also help with transport information and car rental. From US$30 for a day-tour of Santa Cruz and the pottery village of Guaitíl.

Cooprena Simbiosis Tours 200m west and 75m south of CNFL, Sabana Sur ☎ 2290 8646, ⓦ turismoruralcr.com. Tour company offering community-based rural tourism and volunteer programmes alongside various day-trips; some of their excellent hiking trips are held in conjunction with local co-operatives, and involve staying in community lodges.

★ **Costa Rica Expeditions** C Central, at Av 3 ☎ 2257 0766, ⓦ costaricaexpeditions.com. The longest-established and most experienced of the major tour operators, with superior accommodation in Tortuguero, Monteverde and Corcovado, a superlative staff of guides and tremendous resources. You can drop into the busy downtown office and talk to a consultant about individual tours.

Ecole Travel C 7, Av 0/1 ☎ 2234 1669, ⓦ ecoletravel.com. Long-established, rightly popular agency offering well-priced tours to Tortuguero (2/3 days; from US$219), the Celeste river (2/3 days; from US$185) and the Osa Peninsula (3/4 days; from US$375), among many others. They work with ACTUAR on their community-based tourism trips and boast a maximum Certificate of Sustainable Tourism rating (see p.173).

Expediciones Tropicales C 3 bis, Av 11/13 ☎ 2257 4171, ⓦ costarica info.com. Highly regarded agency with knowledgeable guides who run popular combination day-tours of Volcán Poás and nearby sights (from US$64), as well as a host of other trips from San José at competitive prices. They can also organize short-term minivan or bus rental (including driver).

Horizontes Nature Tours C 28, Av 1/3 ☎ 2222 2022, ⓦ horizontes .com. Popular agency concentrating on rainforest walking and hiking, volcanoes and birdwatching, all with an emphasis on natural and cultural history; their eight-day tour of Carara and Palo Verde national parks costs about US$1600.

Serendipity Adventures Apdo 90 7150, Turrialba ☎ 2556 5852, ⓦ serendipityadventures.com. This superior travel agency offers individual custom-made tours for self-formed groups with a sense of adventure, mostly to little-visited parts of Costa Rica. They're experts in canyoning and abseiling, and are the only operators in Costa Rica to offer hot-air balloon trips (from US$385).

Accommodation

Most towns in Costa Rica have a wide range of places to stay, and even the smallest settlements usually have simple lodgings. Prices are higher than you'd pay in other Central American countries, but they're by no means exorbitant – certainly not when compared to the US or Western Europe. Budget accommodation ranges from the extremely basic, where US$25 will get you little more than a room and a bed, to reasonably well-equipped accommodation with a clean, comfortable en-suite room, a fan and possibly a TV for around US$40 a night. In the middle and upper price ranges, facilities and services are generally of a very good standard throughout the country.

The larger places to stay in Costa Rica are usually called **hotels**. **Posadas**, **hostals**, **hospedajes** and **pensiones** are smaller, though *posadas* can sometimes be quite swanky, especially in rural areas. **Casas** tend to be private guesthouses or B&Bs, while **albergues** are the equivalent of lodges. **Cabinas** are common in Costa Rica, particularly in coastal areas: they're usually either a string of motel-style rooms in an annexe away from the main building or, more often, separate self-contained units. Usually – although not always – they tend towards the basic, and are most often frequented by budget travellers. Smarter versions may be called "villas" or "chalets". Anything called a **motel** – as in most of Latin America – is unlikely to be used for sleeping.

Almost every hotel, guesthouse and hostel in Costa Rica provides free wi-fi access.

Few hotels at the lower end of the price range have double beds, and it's more common to find two or three single beds in a room. **Single travellers** will generally be charged the single rate even if they're occupying a double room, though this is sometimes not the case in popular beach towns and at peak seasons.

Bear in mind that in Costa Rican hotels, the term "**hot water**" can be misleading. Showers are often equipped with squat plastic nozzles (water heaters), inside which is an electric element that heats the water to a warm, rather than hot, temperature.

> ### ACCOMMODATION PRICES
>
> All the prices quoted for accommodation in this book are for the least expensive double room or dorm bed in high season for one night, and include the thirteen percent national tax that is automatically added onto hotel bills. Breakfast is included in the price; exceptions are noted. Camping prices are per person, pitching your own tent, unless stated otherwise.

STAYING WITH A COSTA RICAN FAMILY

There's no better way to experience life off the tourist trail and to practise your Spanish than by **staying with a Tico family**. Usually enjoyable, sometimes transformative, this can be a fantastic experience, and at the very least is sure to provide genuine contact with Costa Ricans.

Most **homestay programmes** are organized by the country's various **language schools** and cater mainly to students. However, some schools may be willing to put you in contact with a family even if you are not a student at the school in question. The **Ilisa Language School** (☏ 2280 0700, ⊛ ilisa.com), one of San José's largest, is particularly helpful in this regard. Stays can last from one week to several months, and many travellers use the family home as a base while touring the country. You'll have your own key, but in most cases it would be frowned upon if you brought someone home for the night. The one rule that always applies is that guests and hosts communicate in Spanish.

For a **non-study-based** option, try **Bells' Home Hospitality** (☏ 2225 4752, ⊛ homestay -thebells.com), run by long-time resident Vernon Bell and his wife Marcela, who arrange for individuals, couples and families to stay in private rooms in a family home, with private or shared bathroom; singles cost US\$35, doubles US\$60, and there are reduced rates for stays of two weeks or longer (breakfast is included in the price). Another recommended organization is the **Monteverde Institute** (☏ 2645 5053, ⊛ monteverde-institute.org), which offers accommodation in a range of rural family homes near the Santa Elena and Monteverde reserves for US\$23 per night including meals and laundry.

Another way to find homestays is to visit ⊛ **homestay.com**, which has a range of options across the country (and, indeed, throughout Central America). For longer-term **apartment rentals and houseshares** try ⊛ airbnb.com or adverts in the *Tico Times* (although homestays and flats listed here tend to be expensive), the (Spanish) classifieds in *La Nación* and the notice boards of hostels and guesthouses.

Some of the nozzles have a button that actually turns on the element. Under no circumstances should you touch this button or get anywhere near the nozzle when wet – these contraptions may not be quite as bad as their tongue-in-cheek name of "suicide showers" suggests, but there's still a distinct possibility you could get a nasty shock. The trick to getting fairly hot water is not to turn on the pressure too high. Keep a little coming through to heat the water more efficiently.

Reservations

Costa Rica's hotels tend to be chock-full in high season (Nov–April), especially at Christmas, New Year and Easter, so **reserve well ahead**, particularly for hostels and hotels in popular spots; book online or with a credit card by email. Once on the ground, it's a good idea to phone or email again to reconfirm your reservation.

If you prefer to be a little more spontaneous, travelling in the low season, from roughly after Easter to mid-November, can be easier; during this period, you can safely wait until you arrive in the country to make reservations. During these months, it's even possible to show up at hotels on spec – there will probably be space, and possibly even a low-season discount of as much as thirty to fifty percent.

Pensiones and hotels

When travelling, most Costa Ricans and nationals of other Central American countries stick to the lower end of the market and patronize traditional **pensiones** (a fast-dying breed in Costa Rica, especially in San José) or established Costa Rican-owned hotels. If you do likewise, you may well get a better price than at the tourist or foreign-owned hotels, although this is not a hard-and-fast rule. Though standards are generally high, you should expect to get what you pay for: usually clean but dim, spartan rooms with cold-water showers. If you've got the option of looking at several places, it's perfectly acceptable to ask to see the room first.

The majority of accommodation catering to foreigners is in the **mid range**, and as such is reasonably priced – although still more expensive than similar accommodation in other Central American countries. Hotels at the lower end of this price category will often offer very good value, giving you a/c (which, it has to be said, is not really necessary in most places; a ceiling fan generally does fine) and a private bathroom with hot water and towels. At the upper end of this price range, a few extras, like TV, may be thrown in.

TOP 5 ECOLODGES

As the original ecotourist destination (see p.428), Costa Rica has some of the best **ecolodges** in the Americas, and there can be few more gratifying ways to spend your holiday than by lushing it up in a luxury lodge in the middle of the rainforest, safe in the knowledge that you're having no negative impact on your surroundings and that your money is going to a good cause.

Finca Rosa Blanca Coffee Plantation & Inn Gorgeous, idiosyncratically designed rooms and suites on an organic coffee plantation in the Valle Central. Solar heating and recycling (including a vermiculture compost) are just some of their sustainable practices. See p.122.

Lapa Ríos High-end lodge built using renewable resources on the diversity-rich Osa Peninsula. Protects its own thousand-acre conservancy, invests heavily in the local community and regional wildlife projects and is completely locally staffed. See p.389.

Rancho Margot Self-sufficient organic farm and holistic retreat with a range of accommodation to suit all budgets – join in with milking the cows or help in the herb garden. See p.216.

Rara Avis Waterfall Lodge Remote rainforest lodge that doubles as a research station, set in thick primary forest that's home to a variety of unique flora and thrilling fauna. See p.233.

El Silencio Lodge & Spa Inviting hillside cabins overlooking swathes of cloudforest (much of it the lodge's private reserve). There are carbon-offsetting initiatives and waste-management programmes, most of the staff are local, and profits go towards primary school projects. See p.130.

Resorts, lodges and B&Bs

Costa Rica's many "resorts" range from swanky hotels in popular places like Manuel Antonio to lush **rainforest ecolodges** in areas of outstanding natural beauty – the sort of hideaways that have their own jacuzzis, swimming pools, spas, gourmet restaurants and even private stretches of jungle. These rank among the finest – and most expensive – places to stay in the country, though prices can fall dramatically out of season, when you might be able to get yourself a night of luxury for as little as US$150.

A new breed of **B&Bs** (often owned by expats) has sprung up in recent years, similar to their North American or UK counterparts, offering rooms in homes or converted homes with a "family atmosphere", insightful local advice and a full breakfast. As well as those listed in the Guide, you can search online for Costa Rican B&Bs at ⓦbedandbreakfast.com.

Camping

Though **camping** is fairly widespread in Costa Rica, gone are the days when you could pitch your tent on just about any beach or field. With the influx of visitors, local residents (especially in small beachside communities) have grown tired of campers leaving rubbish on the beach – you'll have a far better relationship with them if you politely ask locals whether it's OK to camp first.

In beach towns, you'll usually find at least one well-equipped **private campsite**, with good facilities including toilets, drinking water and cooking grills; staff may also offer to guard your clothes and tent while you're at the beach. You may also find hotels, usually at the lower end of the price scale, where you can pitch your tent on the grounds and use the showers and bathrooms for a fee. Though not all **national parks** have campsites, the ones that do usually offer high standards and at least basic facilities, with toilets, water and cooking grills

A CAMPING CHECKLIST

- Tent
- Backpack (with waterproof cover)
- Lightweight (summer) sleeping bag, except for climbing Chirripó, where you may need a three-season bag
- Sleeping-bag liner (optional)
- Rain gear
- Mosquito net
- Maps
- Torch
- Knife
- Camping stove (bought once in Costa Rica)
- Matches, in a waterproof box
- Firelighter
- Compass
- Insect repellent
- Water bottles
- Toilet paper
- Hat
- Hiking boots
- Sunglasses
- Sunblock
- Plastic bags (for wet clothes/rubbish)

– all for US$5–10 per person per day. In some national parks, you can bunk down at the **ranger station** if you call well in advance.

There are three general **rules of camping** in Costa Rica: never leave your tent (or anything of value inside it) unattended, or it may not be there when you get back; never leave your tent open except to get in and out, unless you fancy sharing your sleeping quarters with snakes, frogs, insects or curious coati; and always take your rubbish with you when you leave.

Youth hostels

Costa Rica has over two hundred **hostels**, offering dorm beds for as little as US$10 a night; most have a range of double (from around US$30), triple and family rooms, and many offer additional services including free wi-fi, laundry and luggage storage. Bed linen, towels and soap are generally included in the price. There are only three **official youth hostels** affiliated with Hostelling International – *Jardines Arenal* in La Fortuna, *Vista Serena Hostel* in Manuel Antonio (see p.352) and *Hostel Casa Yoses* in San José – which cost from US$12 per night. As with all accommodation in Costa Rica, bookings should ideally be made several months in advance if you're visiting in high season.

YOUTH HOSTEL ASSOCIATIONS
UK AND IRELAND
Youth Hostels Association (YHA) UK ☎ 0800 019 1700, ⓦ yha.org.uk
Scottish Youth Hostels Association UK ☎ 0845 293 7373, ⓦ syha.org.uk
Irish Youth Hostel Association Ireland ☎ 01 830 4555, ⓦ anoige.ie
Hostelling International Northern Ireland Northern Ireland ☎ 028 9032 4733, ⓦ hini.org.uk

US AND CANADA
Hostelling International USA (American Youth Hostels) US ☎ 240 650 2100, ⓦ hiusa.org
Hostelling International Canada Canada ☎ 1800 663 5777, ⓦ hihostels.ca

AUSTRALIA AND NEW ZEALAND
Youth Hostel Association Australia Australia ⓦ yha.com.au
Youth Hostel Association New Zealand New Zealand ☎ 0800 278 299, International ☎ 0643 379 9970; ⓦ yha.co.nz

Food and drink

Costa Rican food – called comida típica ("native" or "local" food) by Ticos – is best described as unpretentious. Simple it **may be, but it's tasty nonetheless, especially when it comes to the interesting regional variations found along the Caribbean coast, with its Creole-influenced cooking, and in Guanacaste, where there are vestiges of the ancient indigenous peoples' use of maize. For more on the cuisine of these areas, see the relevant chapters in the Guide.**

Típico dishes you'll find all over Costa Rica include rice and some kind of meat or fish, often served as part of a special plate with coleslaw salad and plantain, in which case it's called a **casado** (literally, "married person"). The ubiquitous **gallo pinto** ("painted rooster"), often described as the national dish of Costa Rica, is a filling breakfast combination of red and white beans with rice, sometimes served with *huevos revueltos* (scrambled eggs). The heavy concentration on starch and protein reveals the rural origins of Costa Rican food: *gallo pinto* is food for people who are going out to work it off.

Of the dishes found on menus all over the country, particularly recommended are *chicarrones* (fried pork rind), **ceviche** (raw fish "cooked" in lime juice with coriander and peppers), **pargo** (red snapper), **corvina** (sea bass) and any of the ice creams and **desserts**, though these can be too sickly for many tastes. The fresh **fruit** is especially good, either eaten by itself or drunk in *refrescos* (see p.58). Papayas, pineapple and bananas are all cheap and plentiful, along with some less familiar fruits like *mamones chinos* (a kind of lychee), *anona* (custard fruit), *pejibaye* (peach palm fruit) and *marañón*, whose seed is the cashew nut. Look out, too, for fresh strawberries around Volcán Poás and sweet, fleshy guanábana (soursop) along the Caribbean coast.

Eating out

Eating out in Costa Rica will cost more than you might think, and has become even more expensive over the past few years. Main dishes start at around US$10 in San José, and can be more than double that in some of the more popular coastal towns. Then there are those sneaky **extra charges**: the service charge (10 percent) and the sales tax (13 percent), which bring the meal to a total of 23 percent more than the menu price. Add this all up, and dinner for two can easily come to US$30 or more for a single course and a couple of beers. **Tipping** (see p.81) is not necessary, however. Costa Rica's best restaurants are on the outskirts of San José, and in popular tourist destinations such as Tamarindo, Manuel Antonio and around La Fortuna.

The most economical places to dine in Costa Rica – and where most workers eat lunch, their main meal – are the ubiquitous **sodas**, halfway between the North American diner and the British greasy spoon. *Sodas* offer filling set *platos del día* (daily specials) for about US$6.50, as well as *casados* and other hearty *típico* classics; most do not add sales tax. You usually have to go to the cash register to get your bill. *Sodas* also often have takeaway windows where you can pick up snacks such as churros, delicious little fingers of fried dough and sugar. Many *sodas* are vegetarian, and in general **vegetarians** do quite well in Costa Rica – most menus will have a vegetable option, and asking for dishes to be served without meat is perfectly acceptable.

Because Costa Ricans start the day early, they are less likely to hang about late in restaurants in the evening, and establishments are usually empty or **closed** by 10pm. Smoking has been banned in restaurants (among many other places) since 2012.

Drinking

Costa Rica is famous for its **coffee**, and it's usual to end a meal with a small cup, traditionally served in a pitcher with heated milk on the side. Most of the best blends are exported, so premium coffee is generally only served in high-end restaurants and sold in shops.

Always popular are **refrescos**, cool drinks made with fresh fruit, ice and either milk (*leche*) or water (*agua*), all whipped up in a blender; you can buy them at stalls or in cartons, though the latter tend to be sugary. **Batidos** (smoothies) are a thicker, tastier variation. You'll find **herb teas** throughout the country; those served in the Caribbean province of Limón are especially good. In Guanacaste, you can sample the distinctive **corn-based drinks** *horchata* and *pinolillo*, made with milk and sugar, and with a grainy consistency.

Costa Rica has several local brands of **lager**, a godsend in the steamy tropics. Most popular is Imperial, with its characteristic eagle logo, but Bavaria Gold is the best of the bunch, with a cleaner taste and more complex flavour; they also produce a decent dark beer, while Pilsen and the lemon-flavoured Rock Ice are also worth a try. Craft breweries, meanwhile, are springing up all the time.

Wine, once a rare commodity, has become far more common in mid- and top-range restaurants, where you'll often find good Chilean and Argentine varieties on offer, as well as (for a premium) Spanish brands. **Spirits** tend to be associated with serious drinking, usually by men in bars, and are rarely consumed by local women in public; the indigenous sugarcane-based drink, **guaro**, of which Cacique is the most popular brand, is a bit rough but good with lime sodas or in a cocktail. For an after-dinner tipple, try Café Rica, a creamy **liqueur** made with the local coffee.

Bars

Costa Rica has a variety of **places to drink**, from shady macho domains to pretty beachside bars, with some particularly cosmopolitan nightspots in San José. The capital is also the place to find the country's last remaining **boca bars**, atmospheric places that serve *bocas* (tasty little tapas-like snacks) with drinks (see box, p.112); though historically these were free, nowadays even in the most traditional places you'll probably have to pay for them. In even the smallest town with any foreign population

---

COFFEE

There are two types of coffee available in Costa Rica: **export quality** (*grano d'oro*, literally the "golden bean"), typically packaged by either Café Britt or Café Rey and served in good hotels and restaurants; and the **lower-grade blend**, usually sold for the home market. Costa Rica's export-grade coffee is renowned the world over for its mellowness and smoothness. The stuff produced for the domestic market, however, is another matter entirely; some of it is even pre-sweetened, so if you ask for it with sugar (*con azúcar*), you'll get a saccharine shock.

All coffee in Costa Rica is Arabica; it's illegal to grow anything else. Among the best brews you'll find are **La Carpintera**, a smooth, rich, hard bean grown on Cerro de la Carpintera in the Valle Central, and **Zurqui**, the oldest cultivated bean in the country, grown for over 150 years on the flanks of Volcán Barva. Strong, but with a silky, gentle taste, **Café el Gran Vito**, grown by Italian immigrants near San Vito in the extreme south of the country, is an unusual grade of export bean, harder to find than those grown in the Valle Central.

Several small coffee producers run **tours** of their plantations, allowing you to see the coffee-cultivating process up close and to try their home-grown roasts on site. The Valle Central, home to five of the country's eight regional varieties, offers the greatest range (see box, p.122), though there are also a couple of tours worth trying near Monteverde (see box, p.307).

– either resident or tourist – you'll notice a sharp split between the places frequented by locals and those that cater to foreigners. Gringo grottoes abound, especially in beach towns, and tend to have a wide bar stock, at least compared to the limited *guaro*-and-beer menu of the local joints. In many places, especially port cities like Limón, Puntarenas and Golfito, there is the usual contingent of rough-and-ready bars where testosterone-fuelled men go to drink gallons and fight. It's usually pretty obvious which ones they are – they advertise their seediness with a giant Imperial placard parked right in front of the door so you can't see what's going on inside.

Most bars **open** between 8.30 and 11am, and **close** at around 11pm or midnight. Sunday night is usually dead: many bars don't open at all and others close early. Though Friday and Saturday nights are the busiest, the **best nights** to go out are often weeknights (particularly Thursdays), when you can enjoy live music, happy hours and other specials. **Karaoke** is incredibly popular, and if you spend much time in bars, you'll soon pick out the well-loved Tico classics. The **drinking age** is 18, and many bars only admit those with ID (*cédula*); a photocopy of your passport is acceptable.

Health

Health-wise, travelling in Costa Rica is generally very safe. Food tends to be hygienically prepared, so bugs and upsets are normally limited to the usual "traveller's tummy". Water supplies in most places are clean and bacteria-free, and outbreaks of serious infectious diseases such as cholera are rare.

In general, as in the rest of Latin America, it tends to be local people, often poor or without proper sanitation or access to healthcare, who contract infectious diseases. Costa Rica's **healthcare** is of a high standard, but facilities at major public hospitals vary widely, so use private hospitals and clinics where possible – and get extensive health insurance before you travel (see p.77). The capital's two excellent **private hospitals**, CIMA San José and Clínica Biblica (see p.115), are equipped to handle medical, surgical and maternity cases, and have 24-hour emergency rooms; the latter also has a good paediatric unit.

Inoculations

No **inoculations** are required before you enter Costa Rica unless you're travelling from a country that has yellow fever, such as Colombia, in which case you must be able to produce an up-to-date inoculation certificate. You may, however, want to make sure that your polio, tetanus, typhoid, diphtheria and hepatitis A jabs are up to date, though none of the diseases is a major risk. Rabies, a potentially fatal illness, should be taken very seriously if you're going to be spending a significant amount of time in the countryside. There is a vaccine comprising a course of three injections that has to be started at least a month before departure. If you're not vaccinated, stay away from dogs, monkeys and any other potentially biting or scratching animals. If you do get scratched or bitten, wash the wound at once, with alcohol or iodine if possible, and seek medical help immediately.

The sun

Costa Rica is just eight to eleven degrees north of the Equator, which means a blazing-hot sun directly overhead. To guard against **sunburn** take at least factor 15 sunscreen (start on factor 30) and a good hat, and wear both even on slightly overcast days, especially in coastal areas. Even in places at higher altitudes where it doesn't feel excessively hot, such as San José and the surrounding Valle Central, you should protect yourself. **Dehydration** is another possible problem, so keep your fluid levels up, and take rehydration salts (Gastrolyte is readily available) if necessary. **Diarrhoea** can be brought on by too much sun and heat sickness, and it's a good idea to bring an over-the-counter remedy such as Imodium from home – it should only be taken for short periods, however, and only when really necessary (such as travelling for long periods on a bus) as extensive use leads to constipation and only serves to keep whatever is making you ill inside you.

Drinking water

The only areas of Costa Rica where it's best not to drink the tap water (or ice cubes, or drinks made with tap water) are the port cities of **Limón** and **Puntarenas**. Bottled water is available in these towns; drink from these and stick with known brands, even if they are more expensive. Though you'll be safe drinking tap water elsewhere in the country, it is possible to pick up **giardia**, a bacterium that causes stomach upset and diarrhoea, by drinking out of streams and rivers – campers should stock up on water from the national parks' water-spouts, where it's been treated for drinking.

The time-honoured method of **boiling** will effectively sterilize water, although it will not remove

---

A TRAVELLER'S FIRST-AID KIT

Among the items you might want to carry with you, especially if you're planning to go hiking, are:

- Prescription medicines
- Antiseptic cream
- Plasters/Band-Aids
- Imodium for emergency diarrhoea treatment, plus rehydration salts
- Paracetamol/Aspirin
- Rehydration sachets
- Calamine lotion
- Hypodermic needles (see p.62) and sterilized skin wipes
- Iodine soap for washing cuts (guards against humidity-encouraged infections)
- Insect repellent
- Sulphur powder (fights the sand fleas/chiggers that are ubiquitous in some of Costa Rica's beach areas)

Note that most of Costa Rica's major towns have well-stocked **pharmacies** (*farmacias* or *boticas*) where trained pharmacists are licensed to dispense a wide range of drugs (essentially anything other than antibiotics or psychotropic drugs, for which you'll need a prescription).

---

unpleasant tastes. A minimum boiling time of five minutes (longer at higher altitudes) is sufficient to kill microorganisms. Boiling water is not always convenient, however, as it is time-consuming and requires supplies of fuel or a travel kettle and power source – **chemical sterilization** can be carried out using either chlorine or iodine tablets or (better) a tincture of iodine liquid; add five drops to one litre of water and leave to stand for thirty minutes. **Pregnant women** or people with **thyroid problems** should consult their doctor before using iodine sterilizing tablets or iodine-based purifiers. Inexpensive iodine-removal filters are recommended if treated water is being used continuously for more than a month or if it is being given to babies.

Malaria, dengue fever, Zika and Chikungunya

Although some sources of information – including perhaps your GP – will tell you that you don't need to worry about **malaria** in Costa Rica, there is a small risk if you're travelling to the **southern Caribbean coast**, especially Puerto Limón and south towards Cahuita and Puerto Viejo de Talamanca. Fewer than one hundred cases of malaria are reported annually, and the World Health Organization is optimistically predicting Costa Rica could eradicate the disease by 2018, but if you want to make absolutely sure of not contracting the illness, and intend to travel extensively anywhere along the southern Caribbean, you should take a course of prophylactics (usually chloroquine rather

than mefloquine), available from your doctor or a clinic.

Dengue fever is more of a concern: in 2013 there were a record 50,000 cases reported in the country, more than double the amount of the previous year; the Nicoya Peninsula was the worst-affected area. Numbers have since declined, but may well rise again in the future. Most cases occur during the rainy season when the mosquito population is at its height, and usually in urban or semi-urban areas; note that, unlike malaria, the dengue-carrying mosquito often bites during the day. The symptoms are similar to malaria, but with extreme aches and pains in the bones and joints, along with fever and dizziness. On rare occasions, the illness may develop potentially fatal complications, although this usually only affects people who have caught the disease more than once. The only cure for dengue fever is rest and painkillers.

There were well over a hundred **Zika virus** cases in Costa Rica in 2016, mostly in the Puntarenas and Guanacaste provinces. For most people it results in a mild infection and is not harmful; it can, however, be dangerous for pregnant women, as there is evidence that it causes birth defects. Symptoms include a rash, itching all over the body, fever, headache, joint and muscle pain, conjunctivitis, lower back pain, and pain behind the eyes.

Another mosquito-borne virus to be aware of is **Chikungunya fever**, of which there were over 1400 cases in Costa Rica in 2016. Symptoms include fever, headache, fatigue, nausea, muscle and joint pain, and a rash. It usually resolves itself within a few days, and serious complications are not common.

For malaria, dengue fever, the Zika virus and Chikungunya fever, the best course of action is **prevention**: to avoid getting bitten by mosquitoes (*zancudos*), cover up with long sleeves and long trousers, use insect repellents (containing DEET) on exposed skin and, where necessary, sleep under a mosquito net. If you do get ill, seek medical attention as early as possible.

Snakes

Snakes abound, but the risk of being bitten is incredibly small – there has been no instance of a tourist receiving a fatal bite in recent years. Most of the victims of Costa Rica's more venomous snakes – such as the fer-de-lance and the dreaded bushmaster (see p.38) – are field labourers who do not have the time or resources to get to a hospital (there are around five such deaths each year). Just in case, however, travellers hiking off the beaten track may want to take specific **antivenins** plus sterile hypodermic needles; if you're worried, you can buy antivenin at the Instituto Clodomiro Picado, the University of Costa Rica's snake farm in Coronado, outside San José (☎2511 7888, 🌐icp.ucr.ac.cr), where herpetologists (people who study snakes) are glad to talk to visitors about precautions.

If you have no antivenin and are unlucky enough to get bitten, do not try to catch or kill the specimen for identification, as you only risk getting bitten again. Clean the wound with soap and water (do not try to suck out the venom), bandage it firmly, apply a splint to keep the limb immobile (do not apply a tourniquet) and get to the nearest hospital as soon as possible.

In general, **prevention** is better than cure. As a rule of thumb, you should approach rainforest cover and grassy uplands – the kind of terrain you find in Guanacaste and the Nicoya Peninsula – with caution. Always watch where you put your feet and, if you need to hold something to keep your balance, make sure the "vine" you're grabbing isn't, in fact, a surprised snake. Be particularly wary at dawn or dusk – before 5.30am or after 6pm – though note that many snakes start moving as early as 4.30pm, particularly in dense cloudforest cover. In addition, be careful in "sunspots", places in thick rainforest where the sun penetrates through to the ground or onto a tree; snakes like to hang out here, absorbing the warmth. Above all, though, don't be too alarmed: thousands of tourists troop through Costa Rica's rainforests and grasslands each year without encountering a single snake.

Spiders

Most spiders in Costa Rica are harmless, but one species that's definitely worth avoiding is the Brazilian wandering spider or **banana spider**, a large, aggressive arachnid covered in dark brown hair, and often with some bright red patches. It hides under logs and dried banana leaves and in other dark places during the daytime, coming out at night to stalk the forest floor in search of prey. It is recognized as the most venomous spider in the world, carrying a cocktail of toxins that can cause priapism, convulsions and paralysis; bites are rare in Costa Rica (banana plantation workers, rather than tourists, are most at risk), but if you are bitten, you should seek medical attention immediately.

Purrujas, chiggers, ants and bees

Costa Rica is home to a quarter of a million different species of **insect** (*bicho*), and while most are perfectly harmless there are a few that can give you a nasty bite or sting. In hot, slightly swampy lowland areas, such as the coastal Osa and southern Nicoya peninsulas, you may come across **purrujas**, similar to blackflies or midges. They can inflict itchy bites, as can the **chiggers** (*colorados*) that inhabit scrub and secondary-growth areas, attaching themselves to the skin, leech-like, in order to feed.

Of the country's numerous species of ant, the ones to watch out for are the enormous **bullet ants**, which resemble moving blackberries. Prevalent in low-lying forests, they hold the distinction of causing the world's most painful insect sting – their colloquial name of *veinticuatro* ("24") refers to the fact that if you get bitten by one it will hurt for 24 hours.

Among Costa Rica's many bee species (*abejas*) are aggressive **Africanized bees**, which migrated from Africa to Brazil and then north to Costa Rica, where they have colonized certain localities. Although you have to disturb their nests before they'll bother you, people sensitive or allergic to bee-stings should avoid Parque Nacional Palo Verde.

Sharks

Sharks (*tiburón*) are generally found on beaches where turtles nest, especially along the northern Caribbean coast, on Playa Ostional in the Nicoya Peninsula (although not – so far – as far south as Playa Nosara) and in the waters surrounding Parque Nacional Corcovado. **Bull sharks**, an aggressive species and one of the few sharks that can live in both fresh water and sea water, have been known to enter the rivers in the areas mentioned above, as well as the Río San Juan on their way between Lago Nicaragua and the sea.

HIV and AIDS

HIV and **AIDS** (in Spanish, SIDA) are present in the country – an estimated 10,000 adults in Costa Rica are living with HIV – but aren't prevalent. That said, the same common-sense rules apply here as all over the world: sex without a condom, especially in some of the popular beach towns, is a serious health risk. **Condoms** sold in Costa Rica are not of the quality you'll find at home; it's best to bring them with you. Though hospitals and clinics use sterilized equipment, you may want to bring sealed hypodermic syringes anyway.

MEDICAL RESOURCES

Canadian Society for International Health Canada ☎ 613 241 5785, ⓦ csih.org. Extensive list of travel health centres.

CDC US ☎ 1800 232 6348, ⓦ cdc.gov/travel. Official US government travel health site.

Hospital for Tropical Diseases Travel Clinic UK ⓦ www.thehtd .org/travelclinic.aspx. Pre- and post-trip advice and help with the prevention, diagnosis and treatment of tropical diseases and travel-related infections.

International Society for Travel Medicine US ☎ 1404 373 8282, ⓦ istm.org. Has a full list of clinics specializing in international travel health. Publishes outbreak warnings, suggested inoculations, precautions and other background information for travellers.

MASTA (Medical Advisory Service for Travellers Abroad) UK ⓦ masta-travel-health.com. Has a range of travel clinics across the UK.

NHS UK ⓦ www.fitfortravel.nhs.uk. Information and advice on recommended inoculations, malaria risk and the general health situation in listed countries.

The Travel Doctor ⓦ traveldoctor.com.au. Lists travel clinics in Australia, New Zealand and South Africa.

Tropical Medical Bureau Ireland ☎ 1850 487 674, ⓦ tmb.ie. Travel clinics in Dublin and 21 other locations across the Republic of Ireland.

The media

Though the Costa Rican media generally pumps out relatively anodyne and conservative coverage of local and regional issues (shadowing the antics of the president and the political elite with dogged tenacity), it's possible to find good investigative journalism. There are also a number of interesting local radio stations, though TV coverage leaves a lot to be desired.

Newspapers

In San José, all **domestic newspapers** are sold on the street by vendors. Elsewhere, you can find them in newsagents and *pulperías* (general stores). All are tabloid format, with colourful, eye-catching layouts and presentation.

Though the Costa Rican press is free, it does indulge in a certain follow-the-leader journalism. Said leader is the daily **La Nación** (ⓦ nacion.com), voice of the (right-of-centre) establishment and owned by the country's biggest media consortium; other highbrow dailies and television channels more or less parrot its line. Historically, *La Nación* has been known for its exposure of scandals and corruption, as in the Banco Anglo corruption scandal and in highlighting Costa Rica's continuing drug-trafficking problems. It also comes with a useful daily pull-out arts section with listings of what's on in San José, and the classifieds are handy for long-term accommodation.

Also quite serious is **La República** (ⓦ larepublica .net), even if they have a tendency to slap a football photo on the front page no matter what's happening in the world. Alternative voices include **El Heraldo** (ⓦ elheraldo.net), a small but high-quality daily, and **La Prensa Libre** (ⓦ prensalibre.cr), the very good left-leaning paper. **Al Día** (ⓦ aldia.cr) is a popular daily sports paper.

The weekly **Semanario Universidad** (ⓦ semanario universidad.ucr.cr), the voice of the University of Costa Rica, certainly goes out on more of a limb than the big dailies, with particularly good coverage of the arts and the current political scene; you can find it on or around campus in San José's university district of San Pedro, and in libraries.

The well-regarded, online-only English-language paper **Tico Times** (ⓦ ticotimes.net) is a good source of information. As for the **foreign press**, you can pick up recent copies of *The New York Times*, *International Herald Tribune*, *USA Today*, *Miami Herald*, *Newsweek*, *Time* and sometimes the *Financial Times* in the souvenir shop beside the *Gran Hotel Costa Rica* in downtown San José. Of the capital's bookshops, Librerías Lehmann and Librería Internacional keep good stocks of mainstream and non-mainstream foreign magazines (see p.114); the Mark Twain Library at the Centro Cultural Costarricense Norteamericano (see p.115) also receives English-language publications.

Radio

There are lots of **commercial radio stations** in Costa Rica, all pumping out techno and house, along with a bit of salsa, annoying commercials and the odd bout of government-sponsored pseudo-propaganda promoting the general wonder that is Costa Rica. Some of the more interesting **local radio stations** have only limited airtime, such as Radio Costa Rica (930AM), while others, such as Radio Alajuela (1120AM), stop broadcasting early on Sundays. A fascinating programme is *El Club del Taxista Costarricense* – the "Costa Rican Taxi Driver's Club" – broadcast by Radio Actual FM (107.1FM) on Mondays to Fridays from 6 to 7pm. This social and political talk show, which started broadcasting in 1973, was initially directed only at taxi drivers, but its populist appeal has led to it being adopted by the general population. Radio Dos (99.5FM) has a weekday English-language morning show, *Good Morning*, which runs from 6 to 9am.

Television

Costa Rican **televisions** beam out a range of wonderfully awful Mexican or Venezuelan *telenovelas* (soap operas) and some not-so-bad domestic news programmes. Costa Rica is also the graveyard for 1970s American TV.

Canal 7, owned by Teletica, is the main national station, particularly strong in local and regional news. Other than its news show, **Telenoticias**, Costa Rica has few home-grown products, and Canal 7's programming comprises a mix of bought-in shows from Spanish-speaking countries plus a few from the US. Repretel's **Canal 6** is the main competitor, very similar in content, while **Canal 19** mostly shows US programmes and movies dubbed into Spanish. The **Mexican cable channels** are good for news, and even have reports from Europe. Many places also subscribe to CNN and other cable channels, such as HBO, Fox and ESPN.

Holidays and festivals

Though you shouldn't expect the kind of colour and verve that you'll find in fiestas in Mexico or Guatemala, Costa Rica has its fair share of lively holidays and festivals, or feriados, when all banks, post offices, museums and government offices close. In particular, don't try to travel anywhere during Semana Santa, Holy (Easter) Week: the whole country shuts down from Holy Thursday until after Easter Monday, and buses don't run. Likewise, the week from Christmas to New Year is invariably a time of traffic nightmares, overcrowded beach towns and suspended transport services.

Provincial holidays, such as Independence Day in Guanacaste (July 25) and the Limón Carnival (the week preceding Oct 12), affect local services only, but have a serious impact, with municipal shutdowns similar to those experienced at festival time.

January 1 New Year's Day. Celebrated with a big dance in San José's Parque Central.

January Fiesta de Palmares. Two weeks of dancing, music and horse parades in the small town of Palmares.

February Puntarenas Carnival. Ten days of parades, music and fireworks around the middle of the month.

February/March Monteverde Music Fest. National and international musicians gather in the cloudforest town for a month of song and dance.

March Festival Imperial. Alajuela's annual rock festival is the biggest of its kind in Costa Rica, attracting a crowd of over thirty thousand.

March El Día de los Boyeros. The Escazú barrio of San José celebrates the historical importance of oxcart drivers on the second Sunday in March with colourful parades of painted oxcarts and driving competitions, plus plenty of traditional food and dancing.

March 19 El Día de San José (St Joseph's Day). The patron saint of San José Province is celebrated with fairs, parades and church services.

Ash Wednesday Countrywide processions; in Guanacaste, they're marked by horse, cow and bull parades, with bullfights (in which the bull is not harmed) in Liberia.

Holy Week (Semana Santa) Dates vary annually, but businesses will often close for the entire week preceding Easter weekend.

April International Arts Festival. Every two years (even numbers), San José plays host to ten days of theatre shows, concerts, dance performances and art exhibitions.

April 11 El Día de Juan Santamaría. Public holiday (and longer festivities) to commemorate the national hero who fought at the Battle of Rivas against the American adventurer William Walker in 1856.

May 1 El Día del Trabajo (Labour Day). The president delivers his annual "state of the nation" address while everyone else heads to the beach.

May 29 Corpus Christi Day. Countrywide national holiday, typically focused around a traditional feast.

June 29 St Peter's and St Paul's Day. Street festivities in towns named after these saints (Pedro and Pablo).

July Virgen del Mar (Virgin of the Sea). Elaborately decorated boats fill the Gulf of Nicoya on the Saturday nearest to the 16th, celebrating the patron saint of Puntarenas.

July 25 El Día de Guanacaste (Guanacaste Province only). Celebrations mark the annexation of Guanacaste from Nicaragua in 1824.

August 2 El Día de La Negrita (Virgin of Los Ángeles Day). Worshippers make a pilgrimage to the basilica in Cartago to venerate the miraculous Black Virgin of Los Ángeles (La Negrita), the patron saint of Costa Rica.

August 15 Assumption Day and Mother's Day. Family get-togethers and occasional street parades and community events mark what is traditionally a big deal in Costa Rica.

September 15 Independence Day. Big patriotic parades celebrating Costa Rica's independence from Spain in 1821.The highlight is a student relay race across the entire Central American isthmus, carrying a "freedom torch" from Guatemala to Cartago (the original capital of Costa Rica).

October 12 El Día de la Raza (Columbus Day; Limón Province only). Celebrations to mark Christopher Columbus's landing at Isla Uvita are centred on the Limón Carnival, which takes place in the week prior to October 12, and on the day itself.

November 2 El Día de los Muertos (All Souls' Day). Families visit cemeteries to pay their respects to their ancestors.

Christmas Week The week before Christmas is celebrated in San José with fireworks, bullfights and funfairs.

December 25 Christmas Day. Family-oriented celebrations with trips to the beach.

December 27 San José Carnival. Huge parade with colourful floats and plenty of music.

National parks and reserves

Costa Rica protects just over a quarter of its total territory under the aegis of a carefully structured system of national parks, wildlife refuges and biological reserves – in all, there are nearly two hundred designated protected areas. Gradually established over the last 45 years or so (see p.424), the role of these parks in conserving the country's rich fauna and flora is generally lauded.

The parks and reserves harbour approximately five percent of the world's total **wildlife species** and **life zones**, among them rainforests, cloudforests, paramo (high-altitude moorlands), swamps, lagoons, marshes and mangroves, and the last remaining patches of tropical dry forest in the isthmus. Also protected are areas of historical significance, including a very few pre-Columbian settlements, a number of active volcanoes and places considered to be of immense scenic beauty – valleys, waterfalls, dry lowlands and beaches. Costa Rica has also taken measures to safeguard beaches where marine turtles lay their eggs.

Definitions

A **national park** (*parque nacional*) is typically a large chunk of relatively untouched wilderness – usually more than 2500 acres – dedicated to preserving features of outstanding ecological, environmental or scenic interest. These are generally the most established of the protected areas, typically offering walking, hiking or snorkelling opportunities. Though habitation, construction of hotels and hunting of animals is prohibited in all national parks (indeed, since 2012, trophy hunting has been prohibited full stop), "**buffer zones**" are increasingly being designated around them, where people are permitted to engage in a limited amount of agriculture. In most cases, park boundaries are surveyed but not demarcated – rangers and locals know what land is within the park and what is not – so don't expect fences or signs to tell you where you are.

Although it also protects valuable ecosystems and conserves areas for scientific research, a **biological reserve** (*reserva biológica*) generally has less of scenic or recreational interest than a national park, though fishing is usually still prohibited. A **national wildlife refuge** (*refugio nacional de vida silvestre* or *refugio nacional de fauna silvestre*) is designated to protect the habitat of wildlife species. It will not be at all obviously demarcated, with few, if any, services, rangers or trails, and, the Refugio Nacional de Vida Silvestre Caño Negro notwithstanding, is generally little visited by tourists. An "**absolute**" **reserve** (*reserva absoluta*) is purely dedicated to scientific research, with no public entry permitted – the one exception being the Reserva Natural Absoluta Cabo Blanco, on the tip of the southern Nicoya Peninsula, which was Costa Rica's first piece of nationally protected land and grants visitors similar access to a national wildlife refuge or national park.

There are also a number of **privately owned reserves**, chief among them community-initiated projects such as the now famous reserves at Monteverde and nearby Santa Elena. While the money you pay to enter these does not go directly to the government, they are almost always not-for-profit places; the vast majority are conscientiously managed and have links with national and international conservation organizations.

Visiting the parks

Despite their role in attracting tourists to the country, national parks – and the national park system in general – are underfunded, and facilities at some of the more remote and less visited parks (such as Juan Castro Blanco el Agua, Volcán Turrialba and La Cangreja) can be surprisingly threadbare or even nonexistent. Most parks,

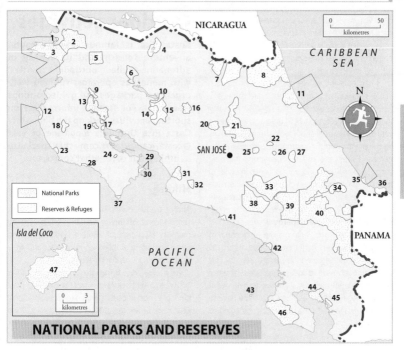

NATIONAL PARKS AND RESERVES

NATIONAL PARKS AND PRINCIPAL BIOLOGICAL RESERVES, WILDLIFE REFUGES AND PRIVATE RESERVES

1 Refugio Nacional de Vida Silvestre Bahía Junquillal

2 Parque Nacional Guanacaste

3 Parque Nacional Santa Rosa

4 Refugio Nacional de Vida Silvestre Caño Negro

5 Parque Nacional Rincón de la Vieja

6 Parque Nacional Volcán Tenorio

7 Refugio Nacional de Vida Silvestre Mixto Maquenque

8 Refugio Nacional de Vida Silvestre Barra del Colorado

9 Reserva Biológica Lomas Barbudal

10 Parque Nacional Volcán Arenal

11 Parque Nacional Tortuguero

12 Parque Nacional Marino Las Baulas

13 Parque Nacional Palo Verde

14 Reserva Biológica Bosque Nuboso Monteverde & Reserva Santa Elena

15 Bosque Eterno de los Niños

16 Parque Nacional Juan Castro Blanco

17 Refugio Nacional de Vida Silvestre Cipancí

18 Parque Nacional Diriá

19 Parque Nacional Barra Honda

20 Parque Nacional Volcán Poás

21 Parque Nacional Braulio Carrillo

22 Parque Nacional Volcán Turrialba

23 Refugio Nacional de Vida Silvestre Ostional

24 Refugio Nacional de Vida Silvestre Reserva Karen Mogensen

25 Parque Nacional Volcán Irazú

26 Monumento Nacional Guayabo

27 Parque Nacional Barbilla

28 Refugio Nacional de Vida Silvestre Camaronal

29 Reserva Biológica de Guayabo y Negritos

30 Refugio Nacional de Vida Silvestre Curú

31 Parque Nacional Carara

32 Parque Nacional La Cangreja

33 Parque Nacional Tapantí–Macizo Cerro de la Muerte

34 Reserva Biológica Hitoy-Cerere

35 Parque Nacional Cahuita

36 Refugio Nacional de Vida Silvestre Gandoca-Manzanillo

37 Reserva Natural Absoluta Cabo Blanco

38 Parque Nacional Los Quetzales

39 Parque Nacional Chirripó

40 Parque Internacional La Amistad (Costa Rica & Panama)

41 Parque Nacional Manuel Antonio

42 Parque Nacional Marino Ballena

43 Reserva Biológica Isla del Caño

44 Parque Nacional Piedras Blancas

45 Refugio Nacional de Vida Silvestre Golfito

46 Parque Nacional Corcovado

47 Parque Nacional Isla del Coco

however, have an entrance **puesto**, or ranger station, often little more than a small hut where you pay your fee (usually around US$10) and pick up a general map. Typically, the main ranger stations – from where the internal administration of the park is carried out, and where the rangers (or *guardaparques*) sleep, eat and hang out – are some way from the entrance *puesto*; it's a good idea to pay these a visit, as you can talk to the *guardaparques* (if your Spanish is good) about local terrain, conditions and recent wildlife spottings, enquire about drinking water and use the bathroom. In some parks, such as Corcovado, you can sleep in or camp near the main stations, which usually provide basic but adequate accommodation, be it on a campsite or a bunk, in a friendly atmosphere.

In general, the **guardaparques** are extremely knowledgeable and informative. Independent travellers and hikers might want to ask about the possibility of joining them on patrol during the day (you'll probably have to speak some Spanish), while the more adventurous can volunteer to help out at remote ranger stations (see box, p.74); you have to be pretty brave to do this, as you are expected to do everything that a ranger does, which includes patrolling the park (often at night) against poachers.

Outside the most visited parks – Volcán Poás, Volcán Irazú, Santa Rosa and Manuel Antonio – **opening hours** are erratic. Most are open daily, from around 8am to 3.30 or 4pm, though there are exceptions. In all cases, especially the volcanoes, arrive as early in the morning as possible to make the most of the day and, in particular, the weather (especially in the wet season); early morning is also the best time to spot the wildlife that the parks protect. You'll usually find a *guardaparque* somewhere, even if he or she is not at the ranger station – if you hang around for a while and call "¡*Upe!*" (what people say when entering houses and farms in the countryside), someone will usually appear.

Costa Rica's protected areas are overseen by the Sistema Nacional de Areas de Conservación (National System of Conservation Areas), or **SINAC** (☎ 2522 6500, ⓦ www.sinac.go.cr), which operates within MINAE and can provide information on individual parks, transport and camping facilities. The only central office where you can make reservations and buy **permits**, where required, is the **Fundación de Parques Nacionales** (Av 15, at C 25, Barrio Escalante, San José ☎ 2257 2239, ⓦ fpn-cr .org), who will contact those parks for which you sometimes need reservations, chiefly Santa Rosa (see p.260), Corcovado (see p.390) and Chirripó (see p.366); other parks can be visited on spec.

Outdoor activities

Costa Rica is famous for year-round adventure tourism and its variety of adrenaline-fuelled outdoor activities, with numerous operators running well-organized packages and guided outings (see p.53). For further information on sporting activities, pick up the bimonthly Costa Rica Outdoors magazine or visit ⓦ costaricaoutdoors.com – they specialize in fishing, but cover other sports, too.

Hiking

Almost everyone who comes to Costa Rica does some sort of **hiking** or **walking**, whether it be multiday hikes through remote rainforest, scaling Cerro Chirripó or ambling along beaches and well-maintained national park trails.

Make sure you **bring** sturdy shoes or hiking boots, and lightweight rain gear. It helps to have binoculars, too. In certain areas, like Parque Nacional Corcovado – where you'll be doing more walking than you've probably ever done before, unless you're in the Marines – most people also bring a tent. In the high paramo of Chirripó, you'll need to bring at least a sleeping bag.

There are a number of things you have to be careful of when hiking. The chief danger is **dehydration**: always carry lots of water with you, preferably bottled, or a canteen, and bring a hat and sunscreen to protect yourself against sunstroke (and use both, even if it's cloudy).

Each year many hikers **get lost**, although they're nearly almost always found before it's too late. If you're venturing into a remote and unfamiliar area, bring a map and compass and make sure you know how to use both. To lessen anxiety if you do get lost, make sure you have matches, a torch and, if you are at a fairly high altitude, warm clothing. It gets cold at night above 1500m, and it would be ironic (and put quite a damper on your holiday) to end up with hypothermia in the tropics.

Whitewater rafting

After hiking, **whitewater rafting** is probably the most popular activity in Costa Rica. Some of the best rapids south of the Colorado are here, and there's a growing mini-industry of rafting outfitters, most of them in San José, Turrialba and La Virgen.

Whitewater rafting entails getting in a rubber dinghy with about eight other people (including

TOP 5 HIKES

Costa Rica's national parks and wildlife refuges are home to some truly spectacular **trails**, enabling you to hike deep into verdant rainforest, past bubbling mud pools or along surf-lashed beaches. Below are a few of our favourites.

Cerro Chirripó A long, cold and sometimes wet slog up and across alpine-esque moorland rewards you (on a clear day) with superb views from Costa Rica's highest point. See p.368.

Estación Biológica Pocosol Arguably the most adventurous trek in the country, the two-day hike from Monteverde to this research station on the eastern edge of the Bosque Eterno de los Niños traverses unmarked trails and is accompanied by armed rangers. See p.312.

Sendero Laguna Meándrica Perhaps the finest birding trail of any national park in the country (and that's saying something), this 4.3km round-trip in the western half of Parque Nacional Carara leads through transitionary terrain to a croc-filled lake that's home to myriad species of bird. See p.338.

Sendero Las Pailas Terrific 6km circuit, taking in the best of Parque Nacional Rincón de la Vieja: sulphur pools, geothermal "stoves" and thermal mud pots, all within the shadow of a smoking volcano. See p.253.

Sendero Los Patos–Sirena Tough 20km trek through the dense rainforest cover of Parque Nacional Corcovado, offering experienced hikers the chance to spot some of Costa Rica's more elusive large mammals, including tapir and collared peccary. See p.393.

a guide) and negotiating exhilarating rapids of varying difficulty. Overall it's very safe, and the ample life jackets and helmets help. Most trips last a day, though some companies run overnight or multiday excursions; **costs** range between US$60 and US$150 for a day, including transport, equipment and lunch. Dress to get wet, with a bathing suit, shorts and surfer sandals or gym shoes.

Rafters rate their rivers from Class I (easiest) to Class V (pretty hard – don't venture onto one of these unless you know what you're doing). The **most difficult** rivers in Costa Rica are the Class III–IV+ Pacuare and Reventazón, both reached from Turrialba (see box, p.152); the Class IV Río Naranjo, near Quepos (see p.347); and the Class V Upper Balsa, accessed from La Fortuna (see p.207). The **moderately easy** Río Sarapiquí (see box, p.228) is a Class II river with some Class III rapids and a fearsome Class IV upper section; the Río Savegre, near Quepos (see p.347) runs Class II–III rapids. The **gentlest** of all is the Río Corobicí (see box, p.244), a lazy ride along Class I flat water.

OUTFITTERS

Aguas Bravas ☎ 2292 2072, ⓦ aguasbravascr.com. One of the largest rafting specialists in the country, operating on the Balsa, the Sarapiquí, the Pacuare and the Chirripó, close to San José.

Aventuras Naturales ☎ 2225 3939, ⓦ tourcostarica.com. Focuses on running the Sarapiquí and the Pacuare rivers – its two- to seven-day trips on the latter include overnight stays at their sumptuous *Pacuare Jungle Lodge*.

Exploradores Outdoors ☎ 2222 6262, ⓦ exploradoresoutdoors .com. A focused selection of one- and two-day trips on the Pacuare and the Reventazón (El Carmen section).

Ríos Tropicales ☎ 2233 6455, ⓦ riostropicales.com. One of the larger outfitters, with challenging one- to four-day trips on the Pacuare, plus day-rides on half a dozen other rivers, including the Reventazón, the Tenorio and the Cucaracho in Guanacaste – a good choice for experienced rafters.

Kayaking

More than twenty rivers in Costa Rica offer good **kayaking** opportunities, especially the Sarapiquí, Reventazón, Pacuare and Corobicí, while several tour operators run paddling trips among the wildlife-rich mangroves of Isla Damas and Bahía Drake. La Virgen in the Zona Norte is a good base for customized kayaking tours, with a number of specialist operators or lodges renting boats, equipment and guides (see box, p.335). The "Week of Rivers" trip run by Costa Rica Rios (US & Canada ☎ 1 888 434 0776, UK ☎ 0800 612 8718; ⓦ costaricarios.com) takes in four of the country's best kayaking rivers and includes three days (US$1699).

Sea-kayaking has become increasingly popular. This is for experienced kayakers only, and should never be attempted without a guide – the number of rivers, rapids and streams pouring from the mountains into the oceans on both coasts can make currents treacherous, and kayaking dangerous without proper supervision. One of the best operators is Seascape Kayak Tours (☎ 8314 8605, ⓦ seascapekayaktours.com), who run recommended trips around the Refugio Nacional de Vida Silvestre Curú on the southern Nicoya Peninsula (see p.237).

RIPTIDES

Riptides are always found on beaches with relatively heavy surf, and can also form near river estuaries; some are permanent, while others "migrate" up and down a beach. If caught in a riptide – and you'll know when you're in one as they can move at an alarming rate of up to 10kph – you should follow the advice below:

Don't panic While riptides may drag you out to sea a bit, they won't take you far beyond the breakers, where they lose their energy and dissipate. They also won't drag you under (that's an undertow), and there are far fewer of those on Costa Rica's beaches. Relax as much as possible – panicking will exhaust you fast and cause you to take in water.

Don't swim against the current This is a pointless exercise. Instead, float, call for help and wait until the current dies down. Then swim back towards the beach at a 45-degree angle, not straight in; by swimming at an angle, you'll avoid getting caught in the current again.

BEACHES WITH RIPTIDES

Some of the most popular and frequented **beaches** in Costa Rica are, ironically, also the worst for riptides. Take extra care when swimming at the following destinations:

Playa Avellana (Guanacaste)
Playa Bonita (Limón)
Playa Cahuita (the first 400m of beach; Limón)
Playa Doña Ana (Central Pacific)
Playa Espadilla (Manuel Antonio, Central Pacific)
Playa Jacó (Central Pacific)
Playa Junquillal (Guanacaste)
Playa Tamarindo (Guanacaste)
Punta Uva (Limón)

Canopy tours, hanging bridges and aerial trams

The **canopy tour** craze that started in Monteverde in the early 1990s has taken the country by storm, and now pretty much any tourist town worth its salt has a **zipline** or two. The standard tour consists of whizzing from lofty platform to platform via traverse cables, and while you're moving too fast to see much wildlife, it's definitely a thrill. In recent years, Tarzan swings and Superman cables (which you ride horizontally, arms stretched out) have upped the ante, and several places now let you zipline at night. Monteverde (see box, p.305) and the area around Volcán Arenal (see box, p.207) have some of the best canopy tours in Costa Rica.

More sedate, and more worthwhile for wildlife-watching, are the **hanging bridges** complexes, where you can experience spectacular views as you walk across the wobbly structures over serious heights. Several bridges take you right alongside the canopy of tall trees; most places offer tours with a naturalist guide, which can be a great way of gaining a better insight into life in the treetops. Again, Monteverde and Volcán Arenal are recommended places to take a "sky walk".

For an even more relaxing meander through the canopy, try riding on an **aerial tram**, a gondola-like cable car that slowly circuits the upper reaches of the rainforest. Several places that operate canopy tours and hanging bridges also have aerial trams, though the most famous is the Rainforest Aerial Tram (now known as the Rainforest Adventures Costa Rica Atlantic), just outside Parque Nacional Braulio Carrillo (see p.141); there's also a Pacific branch, just north of Jacó (see p.340).

Swimming

Costa Rica has lovely **beaches**, most of them on the Pacific coast. You do have to be careful swimming at many of them, however, as around 250 **drownings** occur each year – about five a week. Most are the result of **riptides**, strong, swift-moving currents that go from the beach out to sea in a kind of funnel (see box above). It's also important to be aware of fairly heavy **swells**. These waves might not look that big from the beach but can have a mighty pull when you get near their break point. Many people are hurt coming out of the sea, backs to the waves, which then clobber them from behind – it's best to come out of the sea sideways, so that there is minimum body-resistance to the water.

In addition to the above **precautions**, never swim alone, don't swim at beaches where turtles nest (this means, more often than not, sharks), never swim near river estuaries (pollution and riptides) and always ask locals about the general character of the beach before you swim.

Surfing

Surfing is one of Costa Rica's biggest draws and is very good on both coasts, although there are certain beaches that are suitable during only certain months. You can surf all year round on the **Pacific**: running north to south the most popular beaches are Naranjo, Tamarindo, Boca de Barranca, Jacó, Hermosa, Quepos, Dominical and, in the extreme south near the Panama border, Pavones. On the **Caribbean**, the best year-round beaches are at Puerto Viejo de Talamanca and Punta Uva, further down the coast.

There are numerous camps and schools where you can **learn to surf** in Tamarindo (see box, p.378), Santa Teresa/Mal País (see box, p.334) and Jacó (see box, p.341). Costa Rica is small enough that if things are quiet on one coast, it's fairly easy to pack up your kit and hit the other (buses will take your board for an additional US$2 or so, more on shuttle buses). Serious surfers spending some time in the country will find *The Surfer's Guide to Costa Rica and SW Nicaragua* by Mike Parise an invaluable guide.

You can check **tide times** online at ⦿ crsurf.com.

The Pacific

The **north Pacific coast** and **Nicoya Peninsula** are the country's prime surfing areas, with a wide variety of reef and beach breaks, and lefts and rights of varying power and velocity. **Playa Potrero Grande** (also known as Ollie's Point and made famous in the surf flick *Endless Summer II*) is only accessible by boat from Playas del Coco and offers a very fast, right point break. Within Parque Nacional Santa Rosa, **Playa Naranjo** (or Witch's Rock) gives one of the best breaks in the country and has the added attraction of good camping facilities, though you'll need your own 4WD to reach them.

Moving down to the long western back of the Nicoya Peninsula, **Playa Tamarindo** has three (very popular) sites for surfing, though they don't offer a really demanding or wild ride and parts of the beach are plagued by rocks. **Playa Langosta**, just south of Tamarindo, offers more demanding right and left beach breaks. **Playa Avellana** has a good beach break, with very hollow rights and lefts, while the faster **Playa Negra** nearby has a right point

break that is one of the best in the country. **Playa Sámara and Playa Nosara** offer fairly gentle beach breaks (Sámara is particularly good for beginners), though things hot up a bit as you work your way towards the tip of the peninsula, where *playas* **Manzanillo**, **Santa Teresa**, **Carmen** (best for beginners), **Mal País** and, on the east coast, **Montezuma**, have consistent breaks.

Near Puntarenas on the **central Pacific coast**, **Boca Barranca** is a river-mouth break with a very long left, while **Puerto Caldera** also has a good left. **Playa Tivives** (beach break) and **Valor** (a rocky point break) have good lefts and rights, as does the point break at **Playa Escondida**. **Playa Jacó** is not always dependable for good beach breaks, and the surf is not too big, though it's within easy reach of **Roca Loca**, a rocky point break to the north, and, to the south, **Playa Hermosa**, a good spot for more experienced surfers, with a very strong beach break. The adjacent *playas* **Esterillos Oeste**, **Esterillos Este**, **Bejuco** and **Bocas Damas** offer similarly good beach breaks.

On the **south Pacific coast**, the river mouth at **Quepos** has a small left point break, while **Playa Espadilla** at Manuel Antonio is good when the wind is up, with beach breaks and left and right waves. Southwards from here, **Playa El Rey** offers left and right beach breaks, but you're best off continuing to **Dominical** and some really great surfing, with strong lefts and rights and beautiful surroundings. Down at the very south of the country, **Bahía Drake** gets going on a big swell. A much more reliable wave hits the shore at **Playa Pavones**, allegedly the longest left point in the world, very fast and with a good formation; it's offset by the nearby right point break at **Matapalo**. Only hardcore surfers tend to tackle the remote reef break at **Punta Burica**.

The Caribbean

The best surfing beaches on the **Caribbean coast** lie in the south, from Cahuita to Manzanillo villages. **Playa Negra** at Cahuita has an excellent beach break, with the added bonus of year-round waves. **Puerto Viejo de Talamanca** is home to **La Salsa Brava**, one of the few legitimate "big waves" in Costa Rica, a very thick, tubular wave formed by deep water rocketing towards a shallow reef. Further south, **Manzanillo** has a very fast beach break in lovely surroundings.

Up towards Puerto Limón, there are a couple of beaches that, while not in the class of Puerto Viejo, can offer experienced surfers a few good waves. **Westfalia**'s left and right beach breaks only really work on a small swell, while **Playa Bonita**, a few kilometres north of Limón, is known for its powerful

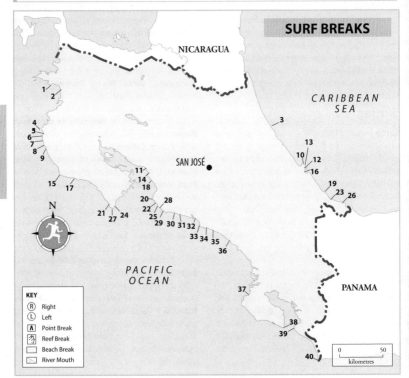

SURF BREAKS

MAJOR SURF BREAKS

1 Petrero Grande (Ollie's Point) (R) (A)

2 Playa Naranjo (Witch's Rock) (R) (L) □

3 North Caribbean Coast (R) (L) □

4 Playa Grande (R) (L) □

5 Playa Tamarindo (R) (L) (A) ▷

6 Playa Langosta (R) (L) (A)

7 Playa Avellanas (R) (L) □

8 Playa Negra (R) (A)

9 Playa Junquillal (R) (L) (A)

10 Portete (R) ⌇

11 Boca Barranca (L) ▷

12 Isla Uvita (L) ⌇

13 Playa Bonita (L) (A) ⌇

14 Puerto Caldera (L) (A)

15 Playa Nosara (R) (L) □

16 Westfalia (R) (L) □

17 Playa Sámara (R) (L) □

18 Playa Tivives/Valor (R) (L) □ ⌇

19 Playa Negra (R) (L) □

20 Playa Escondida (L) (A)

21 Santa Teresa, Playa Carmen & Mal País (R) (L) □ ⌇

22 Playa Jacó (R) (L) □

23 Puerto Viejo de Talamanca (La Salsa Brava) (R) (L) ⌇

24 Montezuma (R) (L) (A) □

25 Roca Loca (R) ⌇

26 Manzanillo (R) (L) □

27 Cabuya (L) (A) ⌇

28 Playa Hermosa (R) (L) □

29 Playa Esterillos Oeste (R) (L) □

30 Playa Esterillos Este (R) (L) □

31 Playa Bejuco (R) (L) □

32 Boca Damas (R) (L) □

33 Quepos (L) ▷

34 Playa Espadilla (R) (L) □

35 Playa El Rey (R) (L) □

36 Playa Dominical (R) (L) □

37 Bahía Drake (R) (L) ⌇

38 Matapalo (R)

39 Playa Pavones (L) (A)

40 Punta Burica (R) (L) ⌇

and dangerous left; only people who really know what they are doing should try this. The right point break at **Portete** is easier to handle, though the left-breaking waves at **Isla Uvita**, just off the coast from Puerto Limón, are also considered tricky. The **north Caribbean coast** has a number of decent beach breaks, which you can reach along the canals north of Moín.

Diving and snorkelling

Though **diving** is less of a big deal in Costa Rica than in Belize or Honduras' Bay Islands, there are a few worthwhile dive sites around the country; the best, however, lie some 535km off Costa Rica's Pacific coast in the waters around **Parque Nacional Isla del Coco** (see box, p.320).

You can also theoretically **snorkel** all along the Pacific coast – Playa Flamingo in northern Guanacaste has clear waters though not a lot to see, while Playa Panama and Bahía Ballena also have good snorkelling. For people who want to see an abundance of underwater life, the small **reef** near Manzanillo on the Caribbean coast is the best; the nearby reef at Cahuita has suffered in recent years from erosion and is now dying.

DIVING OPERATORS

Aquamor Talamanca Adventures ✆ 2759 9012, Ⓦ greencoast .com/aquamor.htm. Excellent dive operation situated within the Refugio Nacional de Vida Silvestre Gandoca-Manzanillo. Employs local captains and works in alliance with the Talamanca Dolphin Foundation.

Bill Beard's Costa Rica ✆ 1 877 853 0538, Ⓦ billbeardcostarica .com. Experienced operator running trips in the northern Guanacaste region, including around Isla Murciélago in Parque Nacional Santa Rosa, as well as trips to Isla del Caño off the Osa Peninsula. PADI certification courses available.

Costa Rica Adventure Divers ✆ 2231 5806, Ⓦ costaricadiving .com. Boat dives, dive courses and snorkelling around Bahía Drake and the pristine reef of nearby Isla del Caño.

Rich Coast Diving ✆ 2670 0176, Ⓦ richcoastdiving.com. Snorkelling and scuba-diving trips in northern Guanacaste, plus PADI certification courses.

Fishing and sportfishing

Both coasts are blessed with the kind of big fish serious anglers love, marlin (*aguja*), sailfish (*pez vela*), tarpon (*sábalo*) and snook (*robalo*) among them. Sportfishing is just that: sport, with the vast majority of fish returned to the sea alive. Its most obvious characteristic, though, is its tremendous **expense** – day-trips start at around US$400, while multiday packages can cost upwards of US$3500. **Quepos** (see p.347) and **Golfito** (see p.396) have long been

good places to do some fishing, while **Barra del Colorado** (see p.176) in the northeast and **Playa Flamingo** (see p.273) in Guanacaste have turned into monothematic costly sportfishing destinations. Although good fishing is possible all year round, the catch is seasonal (Pacific marlin, for example, can only be caught Nov–April); January and February are the most popular months.

Casual anglers can find cheaper and more low-key fishing opportunities in the country's many trout-rich **freshwater rivers**, or in **Laguna de Arenal** and the **Refugio Nacional de Vida Silvestre Caño Negro**, where fishing for rainbow bass (*guapote*) is especially good.

Birdwatching

One oft-repeated statistic you'll hear about Costa Rica is that the country boasts more than 885 species of bird (including migratory ones), a higher number than all of North America. Consequently, the **birding** is hugely impressive, and it's likely that you'll spot hummingbirds, toucans, kingfishers and a variety of trogons (the best time to see migratory birds is the dry season). The iconic resplendent quetzal, found in the higher elevations of Monteverde and the Cordillera de Talamanca, is elusive, but can still be spotted – the tiny hamlet of San Gerardo de Dota (see p.362), close to Cerro de la Muerte, and the nearby Parque Nacional Los Quetzales are by far the best places to see them.

A good **guide** is worth its weight in gold and will be able to pick out all sorts of species that you might otherwise miss; the wildlife guide at the start of this book (see p.40) will help you identify some of the more common and unusual birds, but anyone with more than a casual interest will probably also want to carry a more comprehensive birdwatching **field guide** with them (see p.433).

Most **lodges** include some sort of birdwatching trip among their excursions, and several cater specifically for birders, including *Rancho Naturalista* (see p.152) and *Bosque de Paz* (see p.130), which organize day-trips and multiday tours.

SPECIALIST BIRDWATCHING OPERATORS

Costa Rica Gateway ✆ 2433 8278, Ⓦ costaricagateway.com. Well-run operator offering over a dozen one- and two-week tours using birder-friendly lodges; can also help put together tailor-made trips including transport, accommodation and local guides.

Costa Rican Bird Route ✆ 1 608 3448, Ⓦ costaricanbirdroute .com. Network of eighteen private reserves and lodges in the Zona Norte, including *Selva Verde Lodge*, *Laguna del Lagarto* and the Estación Biológica La Selva, which harbours over five hundred of the country's bird species. Their four-day Great Green Macaw tour is the only multiday trip in the country that focuses on observing, photographing and learning about this endangered species. See box, p.234.

★ **Organization of Tropical Studies** ☎ 2524 0607, ⓦ ots .ac.cr. Custom-made itineraries taking in the research stations operated by the OTS (such as La Selva and Palo Verde), and their varying habitats and species, with some of the best naturalist guides in the country. Also offers day-long birdwatching workshops at La Selva and Las Cruces – an excellent introduction to birdwatching in the tropics.

Mountain biking

Only certain places in Costa Rica lend themselves well to **mountain biking**. In general, the best areas for extensive biking are Parque Nacional Corcovado, the road from Montezuma to the Reserva Natural Absoluta Cabo Blanco on the southern Nicoya Peninsula, and Parque Nacional Santa Rosa. The La Fortuna and Volcán Arenal area is also increasingly popular: you can bike to see the volcano (although not up it) and around the pretty Laguna de Arenal. Some tour operators, such as Desafío (ⓦ desafío costarica.com), also offer mountain biking as part of the transfer from La Fortuna to Monteverde.

There are plenty of bike **rental shops** throughout the country, and you may also be able to rent one from local tour agencies; bike rental costs around US$5 an hour or US$10–20 for the day.

BIKE TOUR OPERATORS

Bike Arenal ☎ 2479 7150, ⓦ bikearenal.com. Runs exhilarating week-long rides through the Zona Norte and along the Pacific coast, with a paved-road option for the less adventurous. Their scenic one-day tour around Laguna de Arenal is the closest you can get to Volcán Arenal on two wheels.

Coast to Coast Adventures ☎ 2280 8054, ⓦ coasttocoast adventures.com. Multi-activity operator with mountain-bike sections in the Valle Orosí and across the southern Nicoya Peninsula.

Serendipity Adventures ☎ 2556 5852, ⓦ serendipityadventures .com. Adventure specialists offering all-inclusive customized biking tours along the Caribbean coast, around the Valle Central and in the Zona Norte.

Horseriding

Almost everywhere you go in Costa Rica, with the exception of waterlogged northern Limón Province, you should be able to hook up with a **horseriding tour**. Guanacaste is probably the best area in the country for riding, with a cluster of excellent haciendas (working cattle ranches) that also cater to tourists, offering bed and breakfast and horse hire.

Riding **on the beach** on the Nicoya Peninsula, especially in Montezuma in the south and Sámara

on the west coast, is also very popular; however, there has been a history of mistreatment of horses in these places (if you see any cases of mistreatment, complain to the local tourist information centre or local residents). The horseriding operators we recommend in the Guide have a good reputation for animal welfare.

TOUR OPERATORS

★ **Horsetrek Monteverde** ☎ 1 866 811 0522 or ☎ 8359 3485, ⓦ horsetrekmonteverde.com. Trips on well-cared-for horses around Monteverde and horseriding as part of a multiday transfer between the cloudforest and La Fortuna; their eight-day Trails of the Campesinos takes in Monteverde, Guanacaste and Arenal (from US$1595). They can also arrange bespoke horse tours across the country.

Travelling with children

Costa Rica is the most child-friendly destination in Central America: historically peaceful, easy to get around and with a good healthcare system, it boasts a bounty of exotic wildlife and enough outdoor activities to keep even the most adrenaline-fuelled teenager quiet for a week or two.

Like most other Latin countries, children are a fundamental part of society in Costa Rica, and you'll be made to feel more than welcome in **hotels and restaurants** and on guided tours and trips. Very few hotels do not accept children (we've noted in the Guide those that don't), and you'll find that the comparatively early opening hours in restaurants actually favour the routines of younger families.

Costa Rica is also a very **safe** destination to travel around, with a long history of political stability and far less crime than in neighbouring countries. You don't need specific inoculations to visit (and malaria is only present in the southern Caribbean) and most tourist places have a high standard of food hygiene, so **health** problems (see p.59) are rarely an issue – though Costa Rica's position near the equator means that you should take the necessary precautions with the sun. In the unlikely scenario that you do require medical help, note that the (private) healthcare system in Costa Rica is excellent, with a couple of top-notch clinics in San José (see p.115), while the capital's Hospital Nacional de Niños (C 14, at Av Central; ☎ 2222 0122, ⓦ hnn.sa.cr) has the best paediatric specialists in Central America.

Activities

Costa Rica's incredible **wildlife** will undoubtedly provide your children with the most abiding memories of their trip, and you'd struggle to spend a couple of weeks in the country and not see a Blue Morpho butterfly, a colourful keel-billed toucan or a sloth or howler monkey working their way through the rainforest canopy – these last two are particularly prevalent in Tortuguero and Manuel Antonio national parks. Most parks have well-maintained **trails**, many of which are short circuits; travellers with very young children will find pushchair-friendly paths at Poás (see p.132) and Carara (see p.337) national parks and the Reserva Santa Elena (see p.309), while the main-crater viewpoint at Parque Nacional Volcán Irazú (see p.144) is also reachable with a buggy.

Butterfly farms are a big hit for younger children. It can sometimes seem that every small rural village has its own *finca de la mariposa*, but one of the best – and most interesting for the adults – is the Butterfly Conservatory at El Castillo, near La Fortuna (see p.216), the biggest in the country. Similarly, **frog gardens**, or ranariums, should also appeal thanks to the variety of croaking, whirring, garishly coloured species that are easily spotted hopping about; most major tourist centres, such as Monteverde, have a frog garden, while several private wildlife reserves run evening frog walks.

Costa Rica's two long coastlines are backed by some beautiful beaches, though **swimming** should be supervised at all times – the same waves that make the country so popular with surfers can be dangerous for children, while some of the best beaches are plagued by riptides (see box, p.68). Older children can rent **bodyboards and surfboards** in major surfing resorts such as Tamarindo and Santa Teresa/Mal País.

Taking a dip in an outdoor **hot spring** is a novel experience likely to be enjoyed by young children and teenagers alike. Most complexes have a variety of pools (of varying temperatures), many "fed" by waterfalls that you can perch under, and some have water slides as well; the springs around Volcán Arenal (see p.207) make great spots for a thermally heated soak.

The variety of outdoor activities available to teenagers is seemingly endless, and few will be able to resist hurtling through the treetops attached to cables on a **zipline** (see p.68); **hanging bridges** (see p.68) offer a more relaxing alternative for exploring the upper canopy **caving** in Parque Nacional Barra Honda (see p.285) and Venado, near La Fortuna (see p.220). Older teenagers can try their hand at **whitewater rafting** (see p.66) by tackling the raging rapids of the Pacuare and Reventazón rivers, among others, though there are also "safari floats" on much calmer waters that will appeal to all the family.

Studying and volunteering

Costa Rica is a great place to broaden your mind, and an increasing number of visitors kick off their travels through the country with an immersive language course, or break up their vacation with a few days of volunteering, which can range from helping maintain trails in a cloudforest reserve to measuring turtles on the Pacific coast. There are also a great number of opportunities for travellers with more time and a scientific interest in the country's flora and fauna to enrol in a research project.

Study programmes and learning Spanish

There are scores of language schools in Costa Rica, with San José and the Valle Central offering a wealth of **Spanish courses**. Though you can arrange a place through organizations based in your home country (see p.55), the best way to choose (at least in the low season, May–Nov) is to visit a few, perhaps sit in on a class or two, and judge the school according to your own needs; in the high season, many classes will have been booked in advance. Note that courses in Costa Rica generally cost more than in Mexico or Guatemala.

Some of the **language schools** listed here are Tico-run; some are branches of international (usually North American) education networks. Instructors are almost invariably Costa Ricans who speak some English. School notice boards are an excellent source of information and contact for travel opportunities, apartment shares and social activities. Most schools have a number of Costa Rican families on their books with whom they regularly place students for **homestays**. If you want **private tuition**, any of the places listed below can recommend a tutor – rates run from US$20 to US$30 per hour.

LANGUAGE SCHOOLS

Academia Latinoamericana de Español ☎ 2224 9917, 🌐 alespanish.com. Friendly school running small-group courses (20hr weekly; US$190), with morning or afternoon schedules; homestay programmes (which include breakfast, dinner and laundry) cost a further US$180/week; all materials included.

Conversa ☎ 2203 2071, 🌐 conversa.com. Well-established institute whose classes have a maximum of four students (5hr 30min daily for a "super-intensive" course) with thorough teaching that puts the emphasis on grammar; stay either with a Tico family or at the centre's five-acre former dairy farm, 10km outside San José. Not cheap (US$815–920/week), though the price also includes Latin dance and cooking classes and community activities.

Costa Rican Language Academy (CRLA) ☎ 2280 1685, 🌐 spanishandmore.com. Small, friendly and Costa Rican-owned school, with a conversational approach to learning, based on current affairs, and with a variety of options (3–6hr/day, 4–5 days/week). One-week (4hr/day) programmes, including Latin dance and cooking classes, cost just US$488 including homestay accommodation.

Costa Rica Spanish Institute (COSI) ☎ 2234 1001, 🌐 cosi.co.cr. Small classes in San José, as well as a "Beach and Rainforest Programme" in Parque Nacional Manuel Antonio (around US$40 extra/week). Homestays are arranged (or you can stay in an apartment or hotel), as are tours and cultural activities. One-week (4hr/day) programmes cost from US$780 including homestay accommodation.

Instituto Para Estudiantes Extranjeros ☎ 2030 7855, 🌐 ipee .com. Small school that prides itself on a cosy atmosphere, total-immersion methodology and small groups (max six people), with year-round courses, from one week to six months or more. Facilities include free internet, and they can also arrange field trips and excursions and homestays. One-week (4hr/day) programmes cost around US$450 including homestay accommodation.

Montaña Linda Spanish School ☎ 2533 3640, 🌐 montanalinda .com. Popular school in the gorgeous Valle Orosí run by a friendly and knowledgeable team. Tuition is either one-to-one (nine months of the year) or in tiny classes up to a maximum of three people (3hr/day), with the choice of grammar or conversation. Accommodation is provided in a nearby hostel, homestay or guesthouse (starting from US$195/week in the hostel, including classes), and a wide range of tours and sightseeing activities are available.

Universal de Idiomas ☎ 2257 0441, 🌐 universal-edu.com. Well-established school with programmes offering three to six hours of tuition daily. Tours can also be arranged. Four-day (4hr/day) programmes cost from US$200 (excluding accommodation).

Volunteer work and research projects

There's a considerable range of **volunteer work** and **research projects** in Costa Rica – some include food and lodging, and many can be organized from overseas. You'll be required to spend at least a week working on a project (such as monitoring sea turtles, helping conserve

endangered parrots or working with rural communities), sometimes up to three months, though the extra insight you'll gain – and, of course, the enormous sense of achievement – are ample rewards.

A good resource **in the US** for volunteer work programmes is *Transitions Abroad* (☎ 1 802 442 4827, 🌐 transitionsabroad.com), a bimonthly magazine and website focusing on living and working overseas. Prospective **British** volunteers should contact the Costa Rican Embassy in London (see p.76). In **Australia**, details of current student exchanges and study programmes are available either from the Costa Rican consul (see p.76), or from the American Field Service (AFS) in Sydney (☎ 02 9215 0077, 🌐 afs.org .au); in **New Zealand** and **South Africa**, you should contact the AFS, in Wellington (☎ 04 494 6020, 🌐 afsnzl.org.nz) and Johannesburg (☎ 011 447 2673, 🌐 afs.org.za), respectively.

Volunteer South America (🌐 volunteersouth america.net) is also useful, with a list of free and low-cost volunteer placements across Latin America, including Costa Rica.

VOLUNTEER PROGRAMMES

In addition to the programmes recommended below, many private reserves take volunteers directly, including the Reserva Biológica Bosque Nuboso Monteverde and the Reserva Santa Elena (see box, p.313).

ASVO ☎ 2258 4430, 🌐 asvocr.org. NGO enabling volunteers to work in national parks and wildlife refuges, local schools and communities, from monitoring turtle nests in the Refugio Nacional de Vida Silvestre Gandoca-Manzanillo to helping in a cheese factory in Zapotal.

Earthwatch US ☎ 1 800 776 0188, UK ☎ 01865 318838, Australia ☎ 03 9016 7590; 🌐 earthwatch.org. Projects range from studying leatherback turtles in Guanacaste to monitoring the effects of climate change on Costa Rica's caterpillars.

Friends of the Osa ☎ 2735 5756, 🌐 osaconservation.org. Hands-on help at a sea-turtle project on the southern tip of the Osa Peninsula, measuring turtles, monitoring nesting sites and hatchlings, and patrolling the beach at night. Placements are a minimum of one week.

Monteverde Institute ☎ 2645 5053, 🌐 monteverde-institute .org. Regular volunteer opportunities on a variety of wildlife and community initiatives in and around Monteverde.

Proyecto Campanario ☎ 2289 8694, 🌐 campanario.org. Research station and ecotourist project on the Osa Peninsula, which sometimes offers free or discounted lodging and meals in exchange for a minimum of three months' work on and around the reserve.

Reserva Rara Avis ☎ 2764 1111, 🌐 rara-avis.com. This off-the-beaten-track rainforest lodge and research station in the Zona Norte (see p.233) regularly requires volunteers to help with guiding, research or conservation projects. Placements are a minimum of three months.

Sea Turtle Conservancy ☎ 1 352 373 6441, 🌐 conserveturtles .org. Volunteer research work on leatherback and green turtles or Neotropical birds at Parque Nacional Tortuguero.

Travel essentials

Costs

Costa Rica is the most **expensive** country in Central America. Just about everything – from ice cream and groceries to hotel rooms and car rental – costs more than you might expect. Some prices, especially for high-end accommodation, are comparable to those in the US, which never fails to astonish American travellers and those coming from the cheaper neighbouring countries. That said, you can, with a little foresight, travel fairly economically throughout the country.

The high cost of living is due in part to the **taxes**, which are levied in hotels (13 percent) and restaurants (23 percent, including a service charge/tip) and also to the International Monetary Fund, whose restructuring policies of balancing the country's payments deficit have raised prices. Even on a rock-bottom **budget**, you're looking at spending at least US$50 a day for a hostel or basic lodge, three meals and bus tickets. Staying in mid-range accommodation, eating in smarter restaurants and taking part in the odd activity will usually cost you over US$120 a day, while the sky's the limit at the upper end, where one night in a swanky hotel can set you back over US$500 in some places. And that's not including any tipping you might do (see p.81).

The good news is that **bus travel**, geared towards locals, is always cheap – often less than US$1.50 for local buses, and US$5–7.50 for long-distance buses (3hr or more).

Crime and safety

Costa Rica is one of the safest countries in Latin America, and crime tends to be opportunistic rather than violent. **Pickpockets** and **luggage theft** are the greatest problems, particularly in San José and other larger cities (be extra vigilant in bus terminals and markets). If you do have anything stolen, report it immediately at the nearest police station (*estación de policía*, or *guardia rural* in the countryside).

Car-related crime, especially involving rental vehicles, is on the rise, so make sure you park securely, particularly at night (see box, p.49). A common scam is for people to pre-puncture rental-car tyres, follow the vehicle and then pull over to "offer assistance"; beware of seemingly good Samaritans on the roadside.

Drug-trafficking is a growing problem in Costa Rica (see p.419), and dealers in tourist hangouts such as Jacó and Tamarindo occasionally approach travellers. Drug possession carries stiff penalties in Costa Rica.

Electricity

The **electrical current** in Costa Rica is 110 volts – the same as Canada and the US – although plugs are two-pronged, without the round grounding prong.

Emergencies

The national **emergency number** is ☎911.

INTO NICARAGUA AND PANAMA

To cross the border from Costa Rica **into Panama** (at Paso Canoas, Sixaola or Río Sereno), most nationalities need a tourist card (US$5), valid for thirty days; nationals of the UK, Ireland, the US, Canada, Australia and New Zealand do not need a visa. You may also need a return ticket back to Costa Rica (or an onward ticket out of Panama to another country), but bear in mind that immigration requirements frequently change, seemingly on a whim, so always check with the Panamanian consulate before setting off. Panama has no paper currency of its own, and US dollars – called *balboas* – are used; it does have its own coins, however, which are equivalent to US coins and in wide circulation. Also beware that you cannot take any **fruit or vegetables** across the border (they will be confiscated if you try). Note that Panama is one hour ahead of Costa Rica.

Few nationalities require a visa to cross **into Nicaragua** (at Peñas Blancas or Los Chiles), but if needed, this must be done at the Nicaraguan consulate in San José (see p.115). Everyone, however, has to pay the US$10 entry fee (it costs US$2 going the other way). Note that if you needed a visa to enter Costa Rica, you should make sure you've got a double-entry stamp or you won't be allowed back into Costa Rica.

The local currency is the córdoba, for which you can exchange colones or dollars in Peñas Blancas and Los Chiles before arriving in Sapoa or San Carlos de Nicaragua, respectively.

Entry requirements

Citizens of the UK, Ireland, the US, Canada, Australia, New Zealand, South Africa and most Western European countries can obtain a ninety-day entry stamp for Costa Rica without needing a **visa**. Whatever your nationality, you must in theory show your passport (with more than six months remaining), a valid onward (or return) air or bus ticket, a visa for your next country (if applicable) and proof of "sufficient funds" (around US$500), though if you arrive by air the last is rarely asked for. Most other nationalities need a visa (a thirty-day visa costs US$32); always check first with a Costa Rican consulate concerning current regulations. The websites of the ICT (Ⓦ visitcostarica.com) and Costa Rica's US embassy (Ⓦ costarica-embassy.org) give up-to-date requirements.

Your **entrance stamp** is very important: no matter where you arrive, make sure you get it. You have to carry your passport (or a photocopy) with you at all times in Costa Rica; if you are asked for it and cannot produce it, you may well be detained and fined.

The easiest way to **extend your entry permit** is to leave Costa Rica for 72 hours – for Panama or Nicaragua, say – and then re-enter, fulfilling the same requirements as on your original trip. You should then be given another ninety-day (or thirty-day) stamp, although it is at the discretion of the immigration officer. If you prefer not to leave the country, you can apply for a permit or visa extension at the *migración* near San José (see p.115), a time-consuming and often costly business. You'll need to bring all relevant documents – passport and three passport photographs, onward air or bus ticket – as well as proof of sufficient funds (US$100 for every month's stay); note that requirements change, so check in advance. If you do not have a ticket out of Costa Rica, you may have to buy one in order to get your extension. Bus tickets are more easily refunded than air tickets; some airlines refuse to cash in onward tickets unless you can produce or buy another one out of the country. If you **overstay your limit**, you'll need to go to the Departamento de Migración in San José with your passport and onward ticket and will be charged an overstayers' fee of US$100 per month.

COSTA RICAN EMBASSIES AND CONSULATES ABROAD

Australia Consulate-General, Suite 301 B, Level 3, 50 Margaret St, Sydney, NSW 2000 ☎ 02 9262 3883
Canada 350 Spark St, Suite 701 (Office Tower), Ottawa, Ontario, K1R 7S8 ☎ 613 562 2855, Ⓦ costaricaembassy.com

Ireland No representation; contact the UK embassy.
New Zealand No representation; contact the Australian consulate-general.
South Africa 14 Talton Road, Forest Town, Johannesburg ☎ 11 486 4716, ✉ bish@mega.co.za
UK Flat 1, 14 Lancaster Gate, London, W2 3LH ☎ 0207 706 8844, Ⓦ costaricanembassy.co.uk
US 2112 S St NW, Washington, DC 20008 ☎ 202 499 2991, Ⓦ costarica-embassy.org

Information

The best source of information about Costa Rica is the **Instituto Costarricense de Turismo (ICT)** in La Urucain San José (☎ 22915764, Ⓦ visitcostarica.com). Their office is near the Plaza de la Cultura in central San José (see p.106), where the friendly, bilingual staff will do their best to answer your queries; they can also give you a free city map and a useful bus timetable – which is also available online (see below). Outside the capital, there are seven regional ICT offices offering limited information and advice, as well as small ICT booths at the four main entry points to the country: the Juan Santamaría and Daniel Oduber airports and at Peñas Blancas on the Nicaraguan border and Paso Canoas on the Panamanian border; otherwise, you'll have to rely on locally run initiatives, often set up by a small business association or the chamber of commerce, or hotels and tourist agencies.

A number of Costa Rican **tour operators**, based in San José (see p.54), can offer information and guidance when planning a trip around the country, though bear in mind that they may not be as objective as they could be.

USEFUL WEBSITES

In addition to the below, most of Costa Rica's newspapers, such as *La Nación*, have online editions, which are good resources for current affairs, cultural events and the like (see p.62).
Ⓦ **anywhere.com/costa-rica** Useful online guide, with practical advice, destination guides, thematic maps and transport information.
Ⓦ **canatur.org** Website of the Costa Rican National Tourism Chamber.
Ⓦ **lab.org.uk** The website of the London-based charity/publisher Latin America Bureau (or LAB) is a useful source of news, information and analysis on countries throughout the region, including Costa Rica.
Ⓦ **ticotimes.net** The website of the English-language *Tico Times* newspaper.
Ⓦ **visitcostarica.com** Comprehensive website of the tourist board, including a very handy countrywide bus schedule.

GOVERNMENT WEBSITES

Australian Department of Foreign Affairs Ⓦ dfat.gov.au
British Foreign & Commonwealth Office Ⓦ fco.gov.uk

Canadian Department of Foreign Affairs Ⓦ international.gc.ca
Irish Department of Foreign Affairs Ⓦ dfa.ie
New Zealand Ministry of Foreign Affairs Ⓦ mfat.govt.nz
South African Department of Foreign Affairs Ⓦ dirco.gov.za
US State Department Ⓦ state.gov

Insurance

It's always a good idea to take out **insurance** before travelling. A typical policy usually provides cover for the loss of baggage, tickets and – up to a certain limit – cash or cheques, as well as cancellation or curtailment of your journey. It's particularly important to have one that includes **health cover**, too, since while private medical treatment in Costa Rica is likely to be cheaper than in your home country, it can still be expensive.

You can buy a policy from a specialist travel insurance company – such as World Nomads, who work with Rough Guides (see box, below). When choosing a policy, always check whether **medical benefits** will be paid as treatment proceeds or only after you return home, and if there is a **24-hour medical emergency number**. When securing baggage cover, make sure that the per-article limit – typically under £500 and sometimes as little as £100 – will cover your most valuable possession. Most policies exclude so-called **dangerous sports** unless an extra premium is paid: in Costa Rica, this can mean scuba diving, whitewater rafting, surfing and windsurfing.

If you need **to make a claim**, you should keep receipts for medicines and medical treatment, and in the event you have anything stolen, you must obtain an official statement from the police: tell them *"He sidorobado"* ("I've been robbed") and they'll provide you with the necessary paperwork.

Internet

Virtually all hostels and hotels, and many restaurants and bars, provide free wi-fi access. The majority of Costa Rican towns have at least one **internet café** (around US$1/hr in major towns, more in remote areas where they rely on slower satellite link-up), though these are becoming increasingly rare with the proliferation of free wi-fi hotspots.

Laundry

There are very few **launderettes** in Costa Rica, and they're practically all in San José (see p.115); in the main tourist towns, though, you'll usually be able to find someone running a small **laundry service**, charging by the kilo (around US$1.50). Most hotels can do your laundry, although charges are often outrageously high.

LGBT Costa Rica

Costa Rica has a good reputation among LGBT travellers and continues to be generally hassle-free for gay and lesbian visitors. The country has a large gay community by Central American standards, and to a smaller extent a sizeable lesbian one, too; it's pretty much confined to San José (which holds a **Gay Pride Festival** every June), though there is also a burgeoning scene in Manuel Antonio.

Outside of these two places, macho attitudes still exist, and gay and lesbian travellers should be discreet – there have been some incidents of police harassing gay men in bars. That said, there's no need to assume, as some do, that everyone is a raving hetero-Catholic poised to discriminate against homosexuals. Part of this general **tolerance** is due to the subtle tradition in Costa Rican life and politics summed up in the Spanish expression *"quedarbien"*, which translates roughly as "don't rock the boat" or "leave well alone". People don't ask you about your sexual orientation or make assumptions, but they don't necessarily expect you to talk about it unprompted, either.

Where once it was difficult to find an entrée into gay life (especially for women) without knowing local gays and lesbians, there are now several **points of contact** in Costa Rica for gay and lesbian travellers. Online, try Costa Rica Gay Map (Ⓦcostaricagaymap .com), which provides information about gay-friendly accommodation and nightlife, or Costa Rica Gay Vacation (Ⓦcostaricagayvacation.com), a travel agent that specializes in gay and lesbian holidays to Costa Rica. For a more informal introduction to the scene in the country itself, head to *La Avispa*, an LGBT-friendly disco in San José (see p.113).

Mail

Even the smallest town has a **post office** (*correo*), with fairly uniform opening hours (see opposite), but the most reliable place to mail letters overseas is from San José's Correo Central (see p.115). Airmail letters to the US and Canada take around a week to arrive; letters to Europe take ten days or so; letters to Australasia and South Africa take three or four weeks.

Most post offices have a **poste restante** (*lista de correos*) – an efficient and safe way to receive letter mail, especially at the main office in San José. They will hold letters for up to four weeks for a small fee (though in smaller post offices you may not be charged at all). Bring a photocopy of your passport when picking up mail, and make sure that correspondents address letters to you under your name exactly as it appears on your passport.

One thing you can't fail to notice is the paucity of **postboxes** in Costa Rica. In the capital, unless your hotel has regular mail pick-up, your only resort is to hike down to the Correo Central. In outlying or isolated areas of the country, you will have to rely on hotels' or local businesses' private mailboxes. In most cases, especially in Limón Province, where mail is very slow, it's probably quicker to wait until you return to San José and send your correspondence from there.

Although letters are handled fairly efficiently, **packages** are another thing altogether – the parcel service, both coming and going, gets snarled in paperwork and labyrinthine customs regulations, besides being very expensive and very slow. If you must send parcels, take them unsealed to the post office for inspection.

Maps

The **maps** dished out by Costa Rican embassies and the ICT are basic and somewhat out of date, so arm yourself with some general maps before you go. The best **road maps**, clearly showing all the major routes and national parks, are the *Costa Rica Road Map* (1:650,000; Berndtson & Berndtson;

Ⓦberndtson.com) and the annually updated *Costa Rica Waterproof Travel Map* (1:470,000; Toucan Maps; Ⓦmapcr.com), which also has a very useful, highly detailed section of the Valle Central and San José, plus area maps of Monteverde, Volcán Arenal, Tamarindo and Manuel Antonio, among others.

In Costa Rica, it's a good idea to go to one of San José's big downtown bookshops, such as Librería Internacional (see p.114), and look through their stock of **maps**, which are contoured and show major topographical features such as river crossings and high-tide marks; you can buy them in individual sections. You can also go to the government maps bureau, the **Instituto Geográfico Nacional** (C 9, Av 20/22, San José), which sells more lavishly detailed colour maps of specific areas of the country; while out of date, the smaller-scale series is useful for serious hiking trips.

Considering it's such a popular hiking destination, there are surprisingly few good maps of Costa Rica's **national parks**. Those given out at ranger stations are very general; your best bet is to get hold of the Fundación Neotrópica (Ⓦneotropica.org) 1:500,000 map (available from the major San José bookshops), which shows national parks and protected areas; alternatively, while the maps in the book *National Parks of Costa Rica* (also usually available in San José) suffer from being rather cramped, not too detailed and of little practical use for walking the trails, they do at least show contours and give a general idea of the terrain, the animals you might see and the annual rainfall.

Money

The official currency of Costa Rica is the **colón** (plural colones; ₡); you'll often hear them colloquially referred to as "pesos". There are two types of **coins** in circulation: the old silver ones, which come in denominations of 5, 10 and 20, and newer gold coins, which come in denominations of 5, 10, 25, 50, 100 and 500. The silver and gold coins are completely interchangeable, with the exception of public payphones, which don't accept gold coins. **Notes** are available in 1000, 2000, 5000, 10,000 (sometimes called the "rojo"), 20,000 and 50,000 colones. The colón floats freely against the US dollar, which in practice has meant that it devalues by some ten percent per year; at the time of writing, the **exchange rate** was around 540 colones to the dollar, 666 colones to the pound and 567 colones to the euro. Obtaining colones outside Costa Rica is virtually impossible: wait until you arrive and get some at the airport or border posts. While the

US dollar has long been the second currency of Costa Rica and is widely accepted; many hostels, hotels and travel agencies quote their services in dollars, though you can pay in either currency (as a rule of thumb, it is generally cheaper to pay for something in the currency the price is quoted in).

Outside San José and Juan Santamaría International Airport, there are effectively no official **bureaux de change**. In general, legitimate money-changing entails going to a bank, a hotel (usually upper-end) or, in outlying areas of the country, to whoever will do it – a tour agency, the friend of the owner of your hotel who has a Chinese restaurant… That said, it's unlikely that you'll need to change US dollars into colones, but if you do, or if you are changing other currencies such as sterling or euros, you'll find that the efficient private banks (such as Banco Popular and the Banco de San José) are much faster but charge scandalous commissions; the state banks such as Banco Nacional don't charge such high commissions but are slow and bureaucratic. Whichever bank you use, make sure you take your passport with you as identification. All in all, it's far easier to withdraw cash from **ATMs** (*cajeros automático*) as and when you need it; international Visa and MasterCard debit cards are accepted at any ATM, and some dispense dollars as well as colones.

When heading for the more remote areas, try to carry sufficient colones with you, especially in small denominations – banking facilities can be scarcer here, and you may have trouble changing a 5000 note in the middle of the Nicoya Peninsula, for example. Going around with stacks of mouldy-smelling colones may not seem safe, but you should be all right if you keep them in a money belt, and it will save hours of time waiting in line. Some banks may not accept bent, smudged or torn dollars. It's also worth noting that, due to an influx of counterfeit **US$100 notes** a few years ago, some shops, and even banks, are unwilling to accept them; if you bring any into the country, make sure that they are in mint condition.

Opening hours

Banks are generally open Monday to Friday 8.30 or 9am to 3 or 4pm, with some in the bigger towns also open 9am to noon on Saturday. **Post offices** are open Monday to Friday 8am to 4.30 or 5.30pm (sometimes with an hour's break between noon and 1pm), and Saturdays 8am to noon; government offices, Monday to Friday 8am to 5pm; and **shops** Monday to Saturday 9am to 6 or 7pm. In rural areas, shops generally close for lunch. Practically the only places open on Sundays are shopping malls and **supermarkets**, which are generally open daily from 7 or 8am to 8pm, though sometimes they don't close until 9 or 10pm.

Phones

The **country code** for all of Costa Rica is ☎ **506**. There are no area codes, and all phone numbers have eight digits: in 2008, a "2" was added to the beginning of landline numbers, and an "8" to mobile numbers, though not all signs, brochures and business cards have been updated. Calls **within Costa Rica** are inexpensive and **calling long-distance** can work out very reasonably if you ring directly through a public telephone network, and avoid calling from your hotel or another private business.

With the proliferation of free wi-fi, Skype is the best way to make **international calls**. Alternatively, purchase a phonecard (*tarjeta telefónica*), available from most grocery stores, street kiosks and pharmacies; you'll need card number 199 (card number 197 is for domestic calls only), which comes in varying denominations. You can also **call collect** to virtually any foreign country from any phone or payphone in Costa Rica; dial ☎ 09 (or ☎ 116 to get an English-speaking operator, a more expensive option), then tell them the country code, area code and number; note that this method costs twice as much as dialling direct.

Another way of making calls is by purchasing a prepaid SIM card for your **mobile phone** from the booths in the arrivals area at Juan Santamaría and Daniel Obuder Quiros airports, or from telecommunications offices around the country; cards start at

---

USEFUL PHONE NUMBERS

International information ☎ 124
International operator (for collect calls) ☎ 116

CALLING HOME FROM ABROAD

Note that the initial zero is omitted from the area code when dialling the UK, Ireland, Australia and New Zealand from abroad.
Australia international access code + 61
Ireland international access code + 353
New Zealand international access code + 64
South Africa international access code + 27
UK international access code + 44
US and Canada international access code + 1

2000 colones and can (for a fee) be topped up online; a thirty-day data package costs US$15–20. Your phone will need to work on the 1800mhz range (any quad band and most tri-band phones; there's an approved list on the ICE website ⓦgrupoice.com) and must be unlocked (check with your provider).

Photography

Film is extremely expensive in Costa Rica, so if you've got a conventional camera bring lots from home. Although the incredibly bright equatorial light means that 100 ISO will do for most situations, remember that rainforest cover can be very dark, and if you want to take photographs at dusk you'll need 400 ISO or even higher.

Sex work

Sex work is legal in Costa Rica, and is particularly prevalent in San José and Jacó. While there is street-walking (largely confined to the streets of the capital, especially those in the red-light district immediately west and south of the Parque Central), many sex workers work out of bars.

In recent years, Costa Rica has gained a reputation as a destination for sex tourism (see p.430) and, even more disturbingly, foreign paedophiles. The government is trying to combat this with a public information campaign and strict prison sentences for anyone caught having sex with a minor.

Shopping

Costa Rica does not have a particularly impressive crafts or artisan tradition. There are some interesting souvenirs, such as carved wooden salad bowls, plates and trays, however, and wherever you go, you'll see hand-painted wooden **replica ox-carts**, originating from Sarchí in the Valle Central (see p.128) – perennial favourites, especially when made into miniature drinks trolleys.

Reproductions of the **pre-Columbian pendants and earrings** displayed in San José's Museo Nacional, the Museo de Oro and the Museo del Jade are sold both on the street and in shops. Much of it isn't real gold, however, but gold-plated, which chips and peels.

Costa Rican **coffee** (see box, p.122) is one of the best gifts to take home. Make sure you buy export brands Café Britt or Café Rey – or better yet, home-grown roasts straight from the coffee plantations themselves (see boxes, p.122 & p.148) – and not the lower-grade sweetened coffee sold locally. It's often cheaper to buy bags in the supermarket rather than in souvenir shops, and cheaper still to buy beans at San José's Mercado Central.

Indigenous crafts are available at places such as the Reserva Indígena Maleku (see p.220) and the Reserva Indígena KéköLdi (see box, p.193), but in the general absence of a real home-grown crafts or textile tradition, generic **Indonesian** dresses and clothing – batiked and colourful printed cloth – are widely sold in the beach communities of Montezuma, Cahuita, Tamarindo and Quepos. In some cases, this craze for all things Indonesian extends to slippers, silver and bamboo jewellery – and prices are reasonable.

If you have qualms about buying goods made from **tropical hardwoods**, ask the salesperson what kind of wood the object is made from, and avoid mahogany, laurel, purple heart and almond (which is illegal anyway). Other goods to steer clear

AVERAGE TEMPERATURE AND RAINFALL

	Jan	Feb	Mar	Apr	May	Jun	Jul	Aug	Sep	Oct	Nov	Dec
SAN JOSÉ												
min/max (°C)	14/24	14/24	15/26	17/26	17/27	17/26	17/25	16/26	16/26	16/25	16/25	14/24
min/max (°F)	57/75	57/75	59/79	63/79	63/81	63/79	63/77	61/79	61/79	61/77	61/77	57/75
rainfall (mm)	15	5	20	46	229	241	211	241	305	300	145	41
TORTUGUERO												
min/max (°C)	22/30	22/30	24/31	24/33	25/33	25/33	24/32	25/33	25/33	24/33	23/31	22/30
min/max (°F)	72/86	72/86	75/88	75/91	77/91	77/91	75/90	77/91	77/91	74/91	73/88	72/86
rainfall (mm)	233	445	181	142	236	341	499	317	323	360	442	349
MANUEL ANTONIO												
min/max (°C)	21/31	21/31	22/32	22/32	22/32	22/31	21/31	21/30	22/30	22/30	22/30	21/30
min/max (°F)	70/88	70/88	72/90	72/90	72/90	72/88	70/88	70/86	72/86	72/86	72/86	70/86
rainfall (mm)	72	36	60	167	392	433	461	478	528	644	388	169

of are coral, anything made from tortoise shells, and furs, such as ocelot or jaguar.

Time

Costa Rica is in North America's **Central Standard time zone** (the same as Winnipeg, New Orleans and Mexico City) and six hours behind **GMT**; daylight saving time is not observed.

Tipping

Unless **service** has been exceptional, you do not need to leave a tip in restaurants, where a ten percent service charge is automatically levied. **Taxi drivers** are not usually tipped, either. When it comes to **nature guides**, however, the rules become blurred. Many people – especially North Americans, who are more accustomed to tipping – routinely tip guides up to US$10 per day. If you are utterly delighted with a guide, it seems fair to offer a tip, although be warned that some guides may be made uncomfortable by your offer.

Toilets

The only place you'll find so-called public conveniences – they're really reserved for customers – is in fast-food outlets in San José, petrol stations and roadside restaurants. When travelling in the outlying areas of the country, you may want to take a roll of **toilet paper** with you. Note that except in the poshest hotels, which have their own sewage system/septic tank, you should not put toilet paper down the toilet. Sewage systems are not built to deal with paper, and you'll only cause a blockage. There's always a receptacle provided for toilet paper.

Travellers with disabilities

While public transport isn't **wheelchair-accessible**, an increasing number of hotels are, particularly those in the mid- and top-end brackets. Travellers with disabilities will also find short but **accessible trails** at an increasing number of national parks, including Poás (see p.132), Rincon de la Vieja (see p.251) and Carara (see p.337) national parks, as well as the Reserva Santa Elena (see p.309). The main-crater viewpoint at Parque Nacional Volcán Irazú (see p.144) is also accessible to wheelchair users. A good starting point is to contact Serendipity Adventures (see p.54), who can organize dedicated adventure trips for travellers with disabilities that include whitewater rafting and abseiling.

Women travellers

Educated urban women play an active role in Costa Rica's public life and workforce – indeed, in 2010, the country voted in its **first female president** (see p.419) – while women in more traditional positions are generally accorded the respect due to their roles as mothers and heads of families. Despite this, however, women may be subjected to a certain amount of machismo.

In general, people are friendly and helpful to solo **women travellers**, who get the *pobrecita* (poor little thing) vote, because they're *solita* (all alone), without family or man. Nonetheless, Costa Rican men may throw out unsolicited comments at women in the street: "*mi amor*", "*guapa*", "*machita*" ("blondie") and so on. If they don't feel like articulating a whole word, they may stare or hiss – there's a saying used by local women: "Costa Rica is full of snakes, and they're all men".

Blonde, fair-skinned women are in for quite a bit of this, whereas if you look even remotely Latin you'll get less attention. This is not to say you'll be exempt from these so-called compliments, and even in groups, women are targets. Walk with a man, however, and the whole street theatre disappears as if by magic.

None of this is necessarily an expression of sexual interest: it has more to do with a man displaying his masculinity to his buddies than any desire to get to know you. The best way to deal with these incidents is to ignore them; retorts or put-downs are often seen as encouragement, and may make the situation worse.

Sexual assault figures in Costa Rica are low by international standards, you don't get groped and you rarely hear *piropos* outside of towns. But for some women, the machismo attitude can be endlessly tiring, and may even mar their stay in the country.

In recent years, there has been a spate of incidents allegedly involving Rohypnol, the so-called **date-rape drug** (legal and available over the counter in Costa Rica), whereby women have been invited for a drink by a man, or sent a drink from a man in a bar, which turns out to be spiked with the drug (often by the bartender, who's in on the game). In the worst cases, the women have woken up hours later having no recollection of the missing time, and believe they were raped. This is not to encourage paranoia, but the obvious thing to do is not accept opened drinks from men and be careful about accepting invitations to go to bars with unknown men. If you do, order a beer and ask to open the bottle yourself.

San José

TEATRO NACIONAL

1

San José

Sprawling smack in the middle of the fertile Valle Central, San José, capital of Costa Rica and the only city of any size, has a spectacular setting, ringed by the jagged silhouettes of soaring mountains – some of them volcanoes – on all sides. On a sunny morning, the sight of the blue-black peaks piercing the sky is undeniably beautiful. At night, from high up on one of these mountains, the valley floor twinkles like a million Chinese lanterns.

That's where the compliments largely end, however. Costa Ricans can be notoriously hard on the place, calling it, with a mixture of familiarity and contempt, "Chepe"– the diminutive of the name José – and writing it off as a maelstrom of stress junkies, rampant crime and other urban horrors. Travellers, meanwhile, tend to view it as an unavoidable stopover jarringly at odds with expectations and impressions of the rest of the country.

Going by first impressions it's easy to see why this is the case. San José certainly doesn't exude immediate appeal, with its nondescript buildings and aggressive street life full of umbrella-wielding pedestrians, narrow streets, noisy food stalls and homicidal drivers. Scratch the surface, though, and you'll find a civilized city, with museums and galleries and plenty of places to walk, meet people, enjoy a meal, and go dancing. It's also relatively manageable, with less of the chaos and crowds that plague most other Latin American cities. San José is a surprisingly green and open city: small, carefully landscaped parks and paved-over plazas punctuate the **centre** of town. Cafés and art galleries line the streets, and some colonial-era wooden houses have survived in the leafy barrios of Amón and Otoya.

On the west side of the centre, the **Mercado Central** is an intriguing warren of stalls and canteens, while the main drag of Paseo Colón (Avenida Central) ends at the tranquil green expanse of **Parque La Sabana**. Further afield, the comfortable districts of **Escazú** and hip **San Pedro** (home to the Universidad de Costa Rica), merit a visit in their own right. Of the city's museums, the major draws are the exemplary **Museo de Oro Precolombino**, featuring over two thousand pieces of pre-Columbian gold, and the **Museo del Jade**, the Americas' largest collection of the precious stone. Less visited, the Museo Nacional offers an overview of the nation's history and some interesting archeological finds, while the Museo de Arte y Diseño Contemporáneo displays some of the most striking contemporary works in the region. All the attractions lie near each other, and you can cover everything of interest in a couple of days.

Brief history

San José traces its roots to the establishment of a parish around 1736 in an area known as Boca del Monte – the Catholic Church was aiming to give a focal point to the scattered populace already living in the area. The first simple chapel dedicated to **San José** (St Joseph) was completed two years later, but the area was initially known as **Villa Nueva de la Boca del Monte**. For the next sixty years it remained a muddy village of a few squalid adobe houses, until coffee was first planted in the Valle Central in 1808 (see p.122), triggering the settlement's expansion.

MERCADO CENTRAL

Highlights

❶ Museo de Oro Precolombino Striking underground collection featuring intricate gold pieces by Diquís masters. **See p.92**

❷ Museo del Jade The largest and most spectacular collection of jade in the Americas is displayed in this stylish museum, the country's most impressive. **See p.96**

❸ Café Hacienda Real Head out to Escazú to enjoy gourmet coffee and the historic ambience at this 1920s colonial-style café. **See p.108**

❹ Grano de Oro San José's finest hotel and restaurant has a lovely, leafy patio and is justly celebrated for its sensational piña colada cheesecake. **See p.111**

❺ Bar Jazz Café A consistently stellar slate of live acts and top-notch acoustics makes San Pedro an essential stop for jazz aficionados. **See p.112**

❻ Mercado Central Enormous, labyrinthine food market where cri mson sides of beef and crispy *chicharrones* (deep-fried pork skins) share the aisles with teetering mounds of papaya and sacks of pungent coffee beans. **See p.114**

HIGHLIGHTS ARE MARKED ON MAPS ON P.86 & PP.90–91

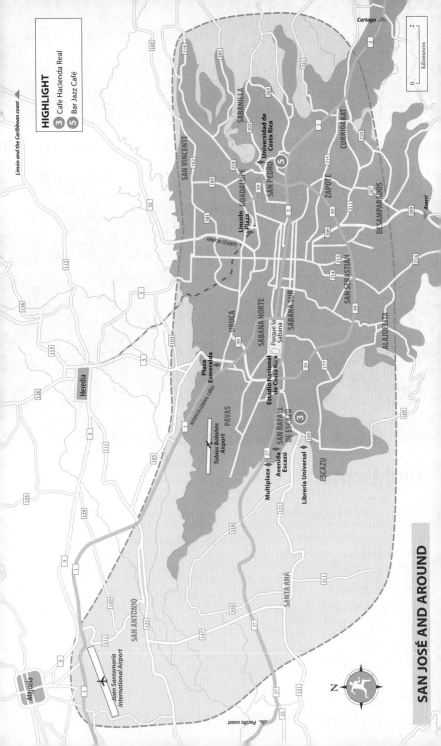

SAN JOSÉ AND AROUND

ORIENTATION IN SAN JOSÉ

The centre is subdivided into little neighbourhoods (*barrios*) that flow seamlessly in and out of one another. Barrios **Amón** and **Otoya**, in the north, are the prettiest, lined with the genteel mansions of former coffee barons. To the east and southeast are **La California** and **Los Yoses**, home to most of the embassies and the Centro Cultural Costarricense Norteamericano. The esteemed Universidad de Costa Rica rises amid the lively student bars and cafés of the **San Pedro** *barrio*, further east of the city centre.

San José, along with most Costa Rican towns of any size, is planned on a grid system. It's intersected east–west by **Avenida Central** (called Paseo Colón west of Mercado de la Coca-Cola) and north–south by **Calle Central** ("Central" is sometimes shortened to "0" on signs). From Avenida Central, parallel avenidas run to the north (odd numbers) and to the south (even numbers). From Calle Central, even-numbered calles run to the west and odd numbers to the east. Avenidas 8 and 9, therefore, are actually quite far apart. Similarly, calles 23 and 24 are at opposite ends of the city. When you see **bis** ("again") in an address it denotes a separate street, usually a dead end (*calle sin salida*), next to the avenida or calle to which it refers. Av 8 bis, for example, is between Av 8 and 10.

Most times, locals – and especially taxi drivers – won't have a clue what you're talking about if you try to use street numbers to find an address. When possible, give directions in relation to local **landmarks**, buildings, businesses, parks or institutions. In addition, people use **metres** to signify distance: in local parlance 100 metres equals one city block. There are precious few street signs, so it's helpful to count streets as you go along so as not to miss your turn. Note that most roads are one-way, usually (but not always) the opposite direction to the previous road.

The single most crucial event in determining the city's future importance, however, was the Province of Nicaragua and Costa Rica's **declaration of independence** from the Spanish Crown in 1821. Following the declaration, Mexico's self-proclaimed "emperor", General Agustín de Iturbide, ordered Costa Rica's immediate annexation, a demand which caused a rift between the citizens of Heredia and Cartago, who supported the move, and those of Alajuela and San José, who saw it for what it was: a panicky imperialist attempt to stifle Latin America's burgeoning independence movements. A short **civil war** broke out, won in 1823 by the *independentistas*, who moved the capital from Cartago to San José in the same year. However, it wasn't until 1838 (after the conclusion of another civil war, the "Guerra de la Liga", in 1835), that San José's status was irrevocably confirmed.

Into the nineteenth century

Despite its capital status, San José remained a one-horse town until well into the nineteenth century. The framed sepia photographs in the venerable *Balcón de Europa* restaurant show wide dirt roads traversed by horse-drawn carts, with simple adobe buildings and a few spindly telegraph wires. Like the fictional town of Macondo in García Márquez's *One Hundred Years of Solitude*, this provincial backwater attracted piano-teaching European flotsam – usually young men looking to make their careers in the hinterland – who would wash up in the drawing rooms of the country's nascent bourgeoisie. Accounts written by early foreign tourists to San José give the impression of a tiny, stultifying backwater society: "The president of the republic has to sit with his followers on a wooden bench", they wrote, aghast, after attending a church service. In the city's houses they found dark-skinned young women, bound tight in white crinoline dresses, patiently conjugating French verbs, reflecting the degree to which Costa Rica's earliest cultural affiliations and aspirations lay with France. Even the mansions of former *finqueros* (coffee barons) in San José's Barrio Amón – especially the Alianza Francesa – resemble mansions in New Orleans or Port-au-Prince, with their delicate French ironwork, Moorish-influenced lattices, long, cool corridors of deep-blooded wood and brightly painted exteriors.

SAFETY IN SAN JOSÉ

San José is much safer than most Central American cities, but petty crime is a problem – be particularly wary in the streets around Mercado de la Coca-Cola and Parque Central. A few places have a bad reputation day and night, including seedy Barrio México in the northwest of the centre (where most of the bus stations are located) and the red-light districts of C 12, Av 8/10 and Av 4/6, C 4/12, just southwest of the centre. The **dangers** are mainly mugging, purse-snatching or jewellery-snatching rather than serious assault, and many people walk around without encountering any problems at all, especially during the day. However, taxis are cheap enough that it's not worth taking the risk in those areas.

CROSSING STREETS

You have to be careful when crossing the street in San José, as drivers are very aggressive, and pedestrian fatalities are distressingly common (you'll see lots of stories about "*atropellados*" – literally "the run-overed" – in the national newspaper). There are a few ground rules, however, that can help minimize your chances of ending up in hospital.
- If possible, always try to cross the road at an official crossing point alongside other pedestrians. Note that there are only a handful of pedestrian lights in the entire city.
- Don't expect anyone to stop for you under any circumstances. You have to get out of their way – not vice versa.
- Run if it looks like the light is changing.
- Take particular care negotiating the city's very wide roadside storm-drains.

By the 1850s, fuelled largely by the tobacco boom, the city's prosperity had become demonstrable, with a profusion of leafy parks, a few paved avenues and some fine examples of European-style architecture. Grand urban houses were built to accommodate the burgeoning middle class of coffee middlemen and industrialists; these Europhile aspirations culminated in 1894 with the construction of the splendid **Teatro Nacional** – for which every molecule of material, as well as the finest craftsmen, were transported from Europe.

The twentieth century and beyond

During the twentieth century, San José came to dominate nearly all aspects of Costa Rican life. The **Universidad de Costa Rica** was founded here in 1941, and since the 1970s the city has become the Central American headquarters for many foreign nongovernmental organizations, which has considerably raised its international profile – **Pope John Paul II**'s 1983 visit to the city is still regarded as one of the nation's most important events. Multinationals, industry and agribusiness have based their national and regional offices here, creating what at times seems to be a largely middle-class city, inhabited by an army of neatly suited, briefcase-toting office and embassy workers. Though San José is indeed one of the safest and least violent cities in Central America, economic inequality remains a serious issue, and homelessness (some two thousand people live on the streets), drug addiction, alcoholism and prostitution are major and clearly visible problems in poorer neighbourhoods.

Central San José

Compact **central San José** contains the lion's share of the city's major attractions, all of which are a short walk from each other on or just off Avenida Central. Despite holding the bustling **Mercado Central**, the regal **Teatro Nacional** and San José's more renowned **museums**, the area has a low-key charm that is punctuated only by the shouts of street hawkers selling their wares.

Parque Central

Av 2, C Central/2

At the heart of the city centre, **Parque Central** is punctuated by tall royal palms and a weird, Gaudí-esque bandstand dating from the 1940s (the Art Deco *kiosco* was actually a gift from Nicaraguan dictator Anastasio Somoza). It's the oldest public space in the city, landscaped in the 1880s on the spot where Central American independence was declared in 1821 (and where Central American president Francisco Morazán was executed in 1842). Green parrots roost nightly in the palms; come twilight, their noisy chatter drowns out the constant rumble of traffic. Less frantic than many of the city's squares, it's a pleasant place to snack on the lychee-like *mamones chinos* (rambutans) or papayas sold by the nearby fruit vendors. The barely contained hubbub of pedestrianized Calle 2 and its assorted electronics and shoe shops overtakes the park's western side.

Catedral Metropolitana and Teatro Melico Salazar

Parque Central • **Catedral Metropolitana** Mon–Sat 6am–noon & 3–6pm, Sun 6am–9pm • Free • ☎ 2221 3820, ⓦ arquisanjose.org • **Teatro Melico Salazar** Free guided visits can be arranged by appointment • ☎ 2221 5172, ⓦ teatromelico.go.cr

At the eastern edge of the Parque Central looms the huge, Baroque-style **Catedral Metropolitana**, the current building dating from the 1870s but renovated several times after earthquakes. It's well worth a peek inside for its colourful frescoes and stained glass. On the square's northeastern corner, the Neoclassical **Teatro Melico Salazar** (see p.113) is one of Costa Rica's premier theatres, completed in 1928 and second only to the Teatro Nacional a few blocks further east.

Avenida Central and around

One block north of Parque Central, the pedestrianized **Avenida Central** bisects the city from east to west. Despite the constant ebb and flow of people and preponderance of modern, concrete architecture, it's a lively stretch of street that makes for a good introduction to contemporary city life. Department stores dot the avenue, including Universal, which has a small book department (see p.114), the cavernous book–stationery shop Librería Lehmann (see p.114) and, further east, a clutch of *sodas* and fast-food outlets.

Plaza Juan Rafael Mora

C 2, at Av 1/3

One block north of Avenida Central, **Plaza Juan Rafael Mora** maintains a refined European air, hemmed in by two stately buildings. On the east side is swanky **Club Unión** and its fashionable café (see p.108), while opposite stands the monumental confection of the central post office, one of the most beautiful structures in the city. A statue of **Juan Rafael Mora Porras** (president of Costa Rica 1849–59) stands in the centre of the plaza – the national hero's birthplace is marked with a stone memorial just to the south on Calle 2.

Edificio de Correos y Telégrafos

C 2, at Av 1/3 (Plaza Juan Rafael Mora) • Museo Filatélico Mon–Fri 8am–5pm • Free admission if stamps purchased on the ground floor • ☎ 2223 6918

Completed in 1917 in a French Neo-Renaissance style, the ornate, light green facade of the **Edificio de Correos y Telégrafos** (central post office) isn't matched by the rather down-at-heel interior, though aficionados should check out the **Museo Filatélico** (postal museum) and its historic stamp collection on the second floor.

Mercado Central

Av Central/1, C 6/8 • Mon–Sat 6.30am–6.30pm • Free

The squat **Mercado Central** dates back to 1880, and though it's more orderly than the usual chickens-and-*campesinos* Latin American city markets, it's still quite an

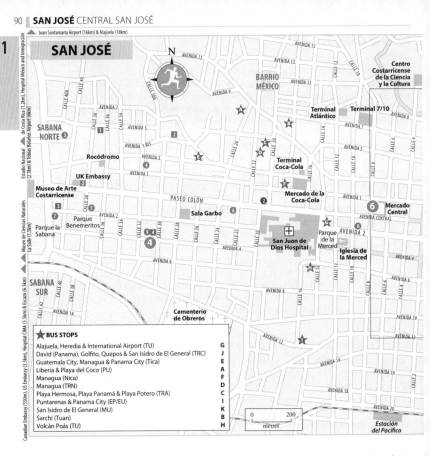

▲ Juan Santamaría Airport (16km) & Alajuela (18km)

SAN JOSÉ

N

AVENIDA 13

AVENIDA 15

AVENIDA 13

BARRIO
MÉXICO

AVENIDA 11

Centro
Costarricense
de la Ciencia
y la Cultura

AVENIDA 9

AVENIDA 7

Terminal
Atlántico

Terminal 7/10

AVENIDA 7

SABANA
NORTE ❸

Terminal
Coca-Cola

AVENIDA 5

Rocódromo

Mercado de la
Coca-Cola ❷

AVENIDA 1

UK Embassy

PASEO COLÓN

Mercado
Central ❻

AVENIDA CENTRAL

Museo de Arte
Costarricense

Sala Garbo ❻

San Juan de
Dios Hospital

Parque
de la
Merced

Iglesia de
la Merced

AVENIDA 2

Parque la
Sabana

Parque
Benemeritos

AVENIDA 2

AVENIDA 4

AVENIDA 4

AVENIDA 6

SABANA
SUR

AVENIDA 8

AVENIDA 6

Cementerio
de Obreros

AVENIDA 10

AVENIDA 14

AVENIDA 12

AVENIDA 12

AVENIDA 14

🚌 BUS STOPS

Alajuela, Heredia & International Airport (TU)	G
David (Panama), Golfito, Quepos & San Isidro de El General (TRC)	J
Guatemala City, Managua & Panama City (Tica)	E
Liberia & Playa del Coco (PU)	A
Managua (Nica)	F
Managua (TRN)	D
Playa Hermosa, Playa Panamá & Playa Potero (TRA)	C
Puntarenas & Panama City (EP/EU)	I
San Isidro de El General (MU)	K
Sarchí (Tuan)	B
Volcán Poás (TU)	H

AVENIDA 16

AVENIDA 18

AVENIDA 20

Estación
del Pacífico

0   200
metres

Left margin (top to bottom): ▲ de Costa Rica (1.2km), Hospital México and Immigración; Estadio Nacional (2.3km) & Tobías Bolaños Airport (6km); Museo de Ciencias Naturales La Salle (1.5km); Canadian Embassy (550m), US Embassy (3.5km), Hospital CIMA (5.5km) & Escazú (6.5km)

experience. Entering the labyrinthine building, your senses are assaulted by colourful arrangements of strange fruits and vegetables, dangling sides of beef and elaborate, silvery rows of fish. At certain times of the day (lunch and late afternoon, for example), the Mercado Central can be overwhelmed by an almighty crush of people – while at other times you'll be able to enjoy a relaxed wander through wide uncrowded alleys of rural commerce. The market's cooked-food stalls are certainly the best place in town to get a cheap bite to eat – especially *Lola Mora* – and the view from a counter stool is fascinating, as traders and their customers jostle for regional produce from *chayotes* (a pear-shaped vegetable) to *piñas* (pineapples) and *cas* (a sweet-sour pale fruit). With a little Spanish, and a pinch of confidence, shopping for fruit and vegetables here can be miles cheaper than in the supermarket. Note that the area north of the market, Barrio México, is a seedy, generally rough area and best avoided.

Iglesia de la Merced

C 12, Av 2/4 • Mon–Sat 6am–noon & 3–6pm, Sun 6am–9pm • Free

In a city not really known for its historic churches, the **Iglesia de la Merced** stands out, built in stages one block south of Avenida Central on the Parque de la Merced between 1894 and 1907. The French Neogothic-style edifice features a gorgeous interior of narrow, frescoed pillars, a delicate mahogany arched roof, painted tiled floor and stained glass. There's also a rare image by Costa Rican master sculptor Manuel María Zúñiga (1890–1979), dubbed *Cristo Agonizante* ("Christ in Agony").

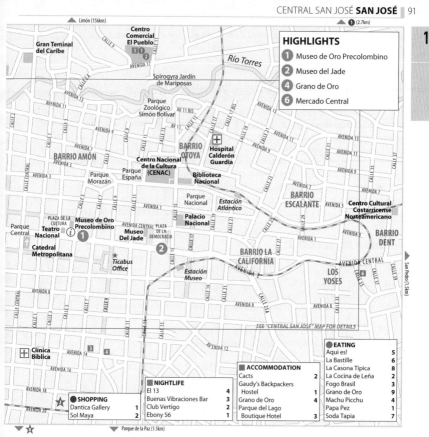

The map shows the following labels:

Limón (156km)

Centro Comercial El Pueblo

Gran Teminal del Caribe

CALLE 9

AVENIDA 17

Río Torres

(2.7km)

HIGHLIGHTS

1 Museo de Oro Precolombino

2 Museo del Jade

4 Grano de Oro

6 Mercado Central

Spirogyra Jardín de Mariposas

AVENIDA 13

Parque Zoológico Simón Bolívar

AV 11 BIS

AV 11

CALLE 17 BIS

AVENIDA 13

AVENIDA 11

CALLE 21

CALLE 1

AVENIDA 9

AVENIDA 13

AVENIDA 7

BARRIO OTOYA

Hospital Calderón Guardia

AVENIDA 11

BARRIO AMÓN

AVENIDA 5

Centro Nacional de la Cultura (CENAC)

AVENIDA 9

AVENIDA 3

Parque Morazán

Parque España

Biblioteca Nacional

AVENIDA 7

BARRIO ESCALANTE

AVENIDA 5

Centro Cultural Costarricense Norteamericano

CALLE CENTRAL

AVENIDA 3

Parque Nacional

Estación Atlántico

AVENIDA 3

BARRIO DENT

PLAZA DE LA CULTURA

Teatro Nacional

Museo de Oro Precolombino

AVENIDA CENTRAL

Palacio Nacional

AVENIDA 1

Parque Central

PLAZA DE LA DEMOCRACIA

Museo Del Jade

BARRIO LA CALIFORNIA

AVENIDA CENTRAL

Catedral Metropolitana

Ticabus Office

LOS YOSES

San Pedro (1.5km)

Estación Museo

AVENIDA 8

AVENIDA 8

CALLE 19

CALLE 21

CALLE 25

CALLE 33

CALLE 35

AVENIDA 8

SEE "CENTRAL SAN JOSÉ" MAP FOR DETAILS

Clínica Bíblica

AVENIDA 14

AVENIDA 12

AVENIDA 16

AVENIDA 18

AVENIDA 20

Parque de la Paz (1.5km)

SHOPPING
Dantica Gallery ... 1
Sol Maya ... 2

NIGHTLIFE
El 13 ... 4
Buenas Vibraciones Bar ... 3
Club Vertigo ... 2
Ebony 56 ... 1

ACCOMMODATION
Cacts ... 2
Gaudy's Backpackers Hostel ... 1
Grano de Oro ... 4
Parque del Lago Boutique Hotel ... 3

EATING
Aqui es! ... 5
La Bastille ... 6
La Casona Típica ... 8
La Cocina de Leña ... 2
Fogo Brasil ... 3
Grano de Oro ... 9
Machu Picchu ... 4
Papa Pez ... 1
Soda Tapia ... 7

Plaza de la Cultura

Av Central, C 3/5

Two blocks east of the Parque Central, the **Plaza de la Cultura** (and the adjacent Plaza Juan Mora Fernández) was created in the late 1970s thanks to funding from the Banco Central de Costa Rica, which now houses its priceless historic collections in a complex beneath the square. The plaza itself is dominated by the Teatro Nacional, rising elegantly over the square's southern side. Note that the plaza's famed outdoor *Café Parisienne* will be closed for renovation along with *Gran Hotel Costa Rica* until at least early 2018.

Museos del Banco Central

Plaza de la Cultura • Daily 9.15am–5pm • ₡5500/US$11 • ☎ 2243 4202, ⏎ museosdelbancocentral.org

The Plaza de la Cultura cleverly conceals one of San José's treasures, the **Museos del Banco Central**. The bunker-like underground museum complex is unprepossessing but the gold exhibits on display are truly impressive – all the more extraordinary if you take into account the relative paucity of pre-Columbian artefacts in Costa Rica (compared with Mexico, say, or Guatemala). Most of the exquisitely delicate goldwork is by the **Diquís**, ancient inhabitants of southwestern Costa Rica.

Museo de Numismática

The top (entrance) floor of the complex features a couple of temporary galleries and the marginally interesting **Museo de Numismática**, with a collection of Costa Rican coins

1

and notes from 1502 to the present day. Look out for the old five-colón note, decorated with a delicate, brightly coloured panorama of Costa Rican society.

Museo de Oro Precolombino

The main highlight of the complex is the **Museo de Oro Precolombino**, housed on the lower second and third floors (along with the rotating Visual Arts Gallery) – as the name suggests, gold displays are the highlight here, interspersed with exhibits arranged chronologically to chart the history of indigenous Costa Rican society from the Neolithic to Spanish periods. Skilfully crafted (and painted) ceramics, tools and jade carvings also help to tell the story of daily life in the region, with sections on burial rituals, the role of women, shamans and other themes. Though larger torques (or "discs" of hammered gold) are displayed, most of the gold pieces are small and unbelievably detailed, with a preponderance of disturbing, evil-looking animals. Information panels (in English and Spanish) suggest that one of the chief functions of these portents of evil – frogs, snakes and insects – was to

COSTA RICAN GOLD

Little, if anything, is known of the prehistory of the **Diquís**, who were responsible for most of the goldwork at the Museo de Oro Precolombino. However, the history of gold-working in the New World is fairly well documented. It was first recorded (around 2000 BC) in Peru, from where it spread northwards, reaching Mexico and the Central American isthmus by 700–900 AD. All the ancient American peoples favoured more or less the same methods and styles, using a gold-copper alloy (called *tumbaga*) and designs featuring extremely intricate shapes, with carefully rendered facial expressions and a preference for ingenious but rather diabolical-looking zoomorphic representations – growling peccaries, threatening birds of prey, and a two-headed figure, each mouth playing its own flute. The precise function of these intricately crafted creations is still the subject of some debate since many of the objects show no sign of having been worn (there are no grooves in the pendant links to indicate they were worn on chains). Archeologists believe they may have been intended for ceremonial burial and, indeed, some were even "killed" or ritually mutilated before being entombed. Alternatively, some may have been worn as charms protecting the bearer against illness and evil spirits.

THE PRESTIGE OF GOLD

The Diquís would have obtained the gold by panning in rivers, and it is speculated that in Osa, at least, the rivers routinely washed up gold at their feet. Diquís *caciques* (chiefs) and other social elites used their gold in the same way it is used today – to advertise wealth and social prestige. Ornaments and insignias were often reserved for the use of a particular *cacique* and his family, and these special pieces were traded as truce offerings and political gifts between various rulers, maintaining contacts between the *caciques* of distant regions. Indeed, it was the removal of native distinctions of social rank following the Spanish Conquest of the country in the seventeenth century that heralded the almost immediate collapse of the Costa Rican gold-making industry.

THE RICH COAST

Although the Diquís were the undisputed masters of design, archeological digs in the Reventazón Valley suggest that gold-working could also be found among the peoples of the Atlantic watershed zone. When Columbus first came ashore in 1502, he saw the local (Talamancan) peoples wearing gold mirror-pendants and headbands and rashly assumed he had struck it rich – hence the country's name. An early document of a subsequent expedition to the Caribbean coastal region of Costa Rica, now housed in archives in Cartago, contains the impressions of native wealth recorded by one gold-crazed Spaniard in Diego de Sojo's 1587 expedition: "The rivers abound with gold… and the Indians extract gold with calabashes in very large grains… from these same hills Captain Muñoz… took from the tombs of the dead… such a great quantity of gold as to swell two large chests of the kind in which shoes and nails for the cavalry are brought over from Castile."

protect the bearer against illness. The Diquís believed that sickness was transmitted to people through spirits in animal form. Watch out, too, for angry-looking arachnids, ready to bite or sting; jaguars and alligators carrying the pathetic dangling legs of human victims in their jaws; grinning bats with wings spread; turtles, crabs, frogs, iguanas and armadillos; and even a few spiny lobsters. A nine-minute video on loop (with English subtitles) adds context.

Teatro Nacional

C 5, at Av 2 • Tours hourly Tues–Sun 9am–4pm (1hr; English guides available) • Tours ₡5000/US$10 • ☎ 2010 1143, ⓦ teatronacional.go.cr

Reputedly modelled on the Palais Garnier in Paris, San José's heavily colonnaded, grey-brown **Teatro Nacional** is tucked in behind the Plaza de la Cultura and oozes an unmistakeable Old World air in the heart of the tropics. Indeed, the theatre's marbled stairways, gilt cherubs and red velvet carpets would look more at home in Europe than in Central America.

Teatro Nacional's story is an intriguing one, illuminating the industrious, no-nonsense attitude of the city's elite, who demonstrated the national pride and yearning for cultural achievement that came to characterize Costa Rican society in the twentieth century. In 1890, the world-famous Italian prima donna Adelina Patti was making a tour through the Americas, but could not perform in Costa Rica as there was no appropriate theatre. Mortified, and determined to raise funds for the construction of a national theatre, the president of Costa Rica (José Joaquín Rodríguez Zeledón) responded by levying a tax on every bag of coffee exported. Within a couple of years the coffers were full to bursting; European craftsmen and architects were employed, and by 1897 the building was ready for its inauguration, a stylish affair with singers from the Opéra de Paris performing *Faust*.

The interior

The theatre itself is lavishly done in red plush, gold and marble, with richly detailed frescoes and marble statues personifying "Dance", "Music" and "Fame". The upstairs "salons" are decorated in mint- and jade-green, trimmed with gold, and lined with heavy portraits of *finqueros* (rich farmers). Look for the mural depicting the coffee harvest, the *Alegoría al Café y al Banano* (once featured on the five-colón note), a gentle reminder of the agricultural source of wealth that made this urban luxury possible. All in all, the building remains in remarkably good condition, despite the dual onslaught of the climate and a succession of earthquakes (the devastating earthquake of 1991 closed the place for two years). Above all it is the details that leave a lasting impression: plump cherubim, elegantly numbered boxes fanning out in a wheel-spoke circle, heavy hardwood doors and intricate glasswork in the bathrooms.

Even if you're not coming to see a performance (see p.113) you can take a **tour** of the post-Baroque splendour – and just off the foyer is an elegant café (see p.108), which serves good coffee, juices and European-style cakes.

Barrio Chino and Plaza de las Artes

San José's modest Chinatown, **Barrio Chino**, is marked by a traditional Chinese gate across Calle 9 at Avenida 2. The district was created in 2012 as a joint project between China and Costa Rica, and though it's nothing like the Chinatowns in Europe and North America (as yet), there are a smattering of cheap and cheerful Chinese restaurants in the streets south of here (see p.110). Pedestrian-only Calle 9 (aka **Paseo de los Estudiantes**) leads through tranquil **Plaza de las Artes** all the way to Avenida 14, where it ends with a statue of Confucius. The plaza itself is dominated by the **Iglesia Nuestra Señora de la Soledad**, an elegant neo-Baroque church completed in 1910.

1

CENTRAL SAN JOSÉ

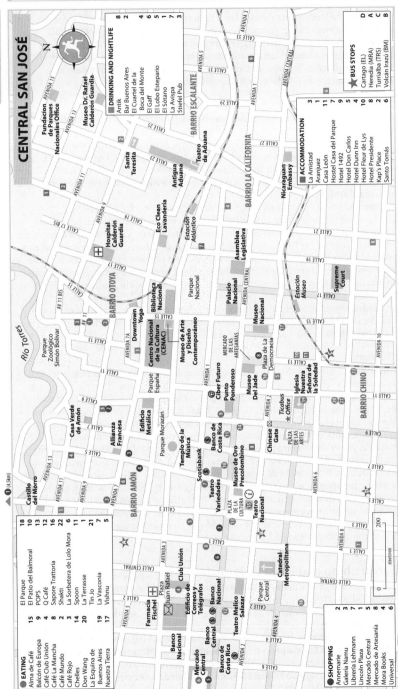

● EATING

Alma de Café	15
Balcón de Europa	9
Café Club Unión	8
Café La Mancha	2
Café Mundo	3
Café Rojo	14
Chelles	20
Don Wang	
La Esquina de	
Buenos Aires	19
Nuestra Tierra	17

El Parque	18
El Patio del Balmoral	10
POPS	13
Q Café	12
Sapore Trattoria	16
Shakti	22
La Sorbetera de Lolo Mora	6
Spoon	11
La Terrasse	1
Tin Jo	21
La Vasconia	7
Vishnu	5

■ SHOPPING

Annemarie	2
Galería Namu	3
Librería Lehmann	7
Lincoln Plaza	1
Mercado Central	5
Mercado de Artesanía	8
Mora Books	4
Universal	6

● DRINKING AND NIGHTLIFE

Antik	8
Bar Buenos Aires	2
El Cuartel de la	
Boca del Monte	4
El Gaff	6
El Lobo Estepario	5
El Sótano	1
La Avispa	7
Stiefel Pub	3

■ ACCOMMODATION

La Amistad	3
Aranjuez	1
Casa León	11
Hostel Casa del Parque	9
Hotel 1492	5
Hotel Don Carlos	4
Hotel Dunn Inn	10
Hotel Fleur de Lys	8
Hotel Presidente	7
Kap's Place	
Santo Tomás	6

★ BUS STOPS

Cartago (EL)	D
Heredia (MRA)	A
Turrialba (TRS)	C
Volcán Irazú (BM)	B

Parque España and around

C 11, Av 3/7 • Daily 24hr

1

Lined with tropical trees, the verdant **Parque España** is surrounded by several grand buildings. On the western corner, facing Avenida 5, stands the **Edificio Metálico** (Metal Building, also known as the "Escuela Metálica"), so-called because its exterior is made entirely out of metal plates shipped from Belgium in 1896. Though the prospect sounds dour, the effect is very pretty, if slightly military. Today it's one of the nation's foremost primary schools. Just west of Parque España lies **Parque Morazan**, centred on the landmark grey-domed bandstand floridly known as the Templo de la Música, completed in 1920.

CENAC

C 15, Av 3/7 • Free • ☎ 2255 3188

Sprawling across the entire eastern border of the Parque España, the former National Liquor Factory (Fábrica Nacional de Licores) was built in the 1850s and remained in use until 1981. Today it houses the **Centro Nacional de la Cultura** (**CENAC**), an arts complex that includes the Museo de Arte y Diseño Contemporáneo, Teatro 1887, the Teatro de la Danza (wander around during the day for glimpses of dancers and musicians rehearsing) and Galería 1887, a contemporary art gallery (daily 8am–4pm; free). Many *josefinos* still refer to the buildings as the old *liquoría*; indeed you can still see a massive old distilling machine in the grounds, complete with the nameplate of its Birmingham (UK) manufacturers.

Museo de Arte y Diseño Contemporáneo

C 15, at Av 3 • Tues–Sat 9.30am–5pm • ₡1500/US$3 • ☎ 2257 9370, ⓦ madc.cr

The main attraction in CENAC is the cutting-edge **Museo de Arte y Diseño Contemporáneo** (Museum of Contemporary Art and Design). Opened in 1994 under the direction of dynamic local artist Virginia Pérez-Ratton, it's a highly modern space, with a cosmopolitan, multimedia approach – there's an area specially designed for outdoor installations by up-and-coming Central American artists.

Parque Nacional and around

Av 1/3, C 15/19

San José's **Parque Nacional**, one of the city's finest open spaces, marks the civic heart of the capital. Overlooked by rows of mop-headed palms and thick deciduous trees, it's popular with courting couples and older men discussing the state of the nation. After gaining notoriety as a hangout for muggers and prostitutes, it was equipped with tall lamps to add extra light and is today much safer. Even so, it's still probably not a good idea to wander around here after dark.

Asamblea Legislativa

Av Central, C15/17 • Free • ☎ 2243 2000, ⓦ asamblea.go.cr

You can hear government debates Costa Rican-style at the nation's unicameral legislature (**Asamblea Legislativa**), just south of the Parque Nacional. The fun usually starts at 4pm, but check first if the legislature is in session. The complex comprises two buildings. The most photogenic (on the eastern side of the block) is known as the **Castillo Azul** ("The Blue Castle"), a magnificent Neoclassical residence built in 1908 for the politician and coffee baron Máximo Fernández Alvarado – it was used as the presidential residence from 1914 to 1920, and after a variety of functions has served as offices for the legislature since 1989. Construction on the main **legislative building** – also intended to be the presidential residence – began in 1937, but was halted during World War II. By the time it was completed in 1958, the legislature had moved in. The current Casa Presidencial is now an ugly concrete bunker in the district of Zapote.

1 Plaza de la Democracía

C 13/17, Av Central/2

A block southwest of the Parque Nacional sit the terraces of **Plaza de la Democracía**, constructed in 1989 (and substantially remodelled in 2009) to mark President Oscar Arias's key involvement in the Central American Peace Plan. Though it primarily acts as a gateway to the Museo Nacional (see below), at its western end is the **Mercado de las Artesanías** (daily 8am–8pm), a row of **craft stalls** selling hammocks, thick Ecuadorian sweaters, leather bracelets and jewellery. You can also buy Guatemalan textiles and decorative *molas* (patchwork textiles in vibrant colours) made by the Guna people of Panama, though at steeper prices than elsewhere in Central America. Other stalls sell T-shirts and wooden crafts and trinkets. The traders are friendly and won't pressure you; a bit of gentle bargaining is a must.

Museo del Jade

Av Central, C 13/15 • Daily 10am–5pm • US$15 • ☎ 2521 6610, ⓦ www.museodeljadeins.com

On the west side of the Plaza de la Democracía lies one of the city's finest museums, the **Museo del Jade** (Jade Museum), home to the world's largest collection of American jade.

As in China and the East, jade was much prized in ancient Costa Rica as a stone with religious or mystical significance, and for Neolithic civilizations it was an object of great power. Only slightly less hard than quartz, it's well known for its durability, and is a good material for weapons and cutting tools like axes and blades. As no quarries of the stone have been found in Costa Rica, the big mystery is how the pre-Columbian societies here got hold of so much of it. The reigning theories are that it came from Guatemala, where the Motagua Valley is home to one of the world's six known jade quarries, or that it was traded or sold down the isthmus by the Olmecs of Mexico. This would also explain the Maya insignia on some of the pieces – symbols that had no meaning for Costa Rica's pre-Columbian inhabitants. Jade exhibits an extraordinary range of nuanced colour, from a milky-white green and soft grey to a deep green; the latter was associated with agricultural fertility and particularly prized by the inhabitants of the Americas around 600 BC. No two pieces in the collection are alike in hue and opacity, though, as in the Museo de Oro, you'll see a lot of **axe-gods**: anthropomorphic bird-cum-human forms shaped like an axe and worn as a pendant, as well as a variety of ornate necklaces and fertility symbols.

Museo Nacional

C 17, Av Central/2 • Tues–Sat 8.30am–4.30pm, Sun 9am–4.30pm • US$9 • ☎ 2257 1433, ⓦ museocostarica.go.cr

The east side of Plaza de la Democracía is crowned by the impressive **Museo Nacional**, occupying the former Bellavista Barracks, a fort-like edifice constructed 1917–32. Bullet holes from the 1948 insurrection (see p.414) can still be seen on the north side of the building's thick walls. The museum's collection, though rather haphazard, gives a fascinating introduction to the history of Costa Rica. You enter via the **Jardín de Mariposas**, a tranquil butterfly garden thick with giant Blue Morphos, before climbing into the complex proper. The lower **Calabozos** (dungeons) level houses temporary art exhibits, though the cells retain some of their historic graffiti. The main exhibits begin in the **Sala Precolombina**, where the nation's indigenous history is chronicled starting with a display of Neolithic tools and early pottery. This remains the single most important archeological exhibition in the country; the jade carvings, bone ornaments, sculpted tomb slabs and funerary offerings, in particular, show precise geometric patterns and incredible attention to detail, but the really astounding pieces are the ornate "flying panel" **metates**, corn-grinding tables used by the Chorotega peoples of present-day Guanacaste, each with three legs and meticulously sculpted from a single piece of volcanic stone.

The artfully restored **Casas de los Comandantes** (officers' quarters) contain period rooms and temporary historical exhibits, while the **Casa Colonial** section is dominated by the massive but spartan furniture and cheesy Spanish religious iconography of the

1

colonial era. Exhibits make clear how slowly culture and education advanced in Costa Rica, giving a sense of a country struggling to extricate itself from terrible cultural and social backwardness – in European terms – until well into the twenty-first century. In the same room are examples of **colonial art**, which replaced indigenous art forms with scores of lamentable gilt-and-pink Virgin Marys.

The **Sala de Oro Indígena** explains the function of gold in the indigenous social hierarchy, with descriptions on which objects were used to identify warriors, chiefs and shamans – the highlight here are wonderful anthropomorphic gold figures. Finally, the newly renovated **Sala Historia de Patria** covers the history of the country from the arrival of the Spanish to the present day, with an eclectic spread of exhibits that cover everything from the development of coffee to the advent of the railways.

Barrios Amón and Otoya

Weaving its way north up the hill from the Parque España then down to the Río Torres, the historic **Barrio Amón** leads into another old district, **Otoya**. Lined with stately buildings and the former homes of the Costa Rican coffee gentry, these two neighbourhoods are among the most attractive in San José. After decades of neglect they are currently undergoing something of a rediscovery by hoteliers and café and restaurant owners, though the area remains seedy in parts – take care at night. Established in the late 1890s, Amón is home to fine examples of "neo-Victorian" tropical architecture, with low-slung wooden houses ringed by wide verandas and iron railings. Striking examples include the turreted **Castillo del Moro** (C 3, at Av 13), a whimsical Mudéjar structure built in 1930 (it's privately owned), and the mint-green former **Casa Verde de Amón** hotel (at C 7, at Av 9), built around 1910 and recently restored by Tecnológico de Costa Rica (the Costa Rica Institute of Technology).

Alianza Francesa
C 5, at Av 7 • Mon–Sat 8am–6pm • Free • ☎ 2257 1438

The headquarters of the **Alianza Francesa** (Alliance Française) in San José since 1965, this artfully restored Neoclassical building is a prefabricated metal structure dating from 1890. Inside you'll find *Le Café* (serving coffee and snacks) and temporary art exhibitions.

Museo Dr. Rafael Calderón Guardia
Av 11, C 25/27, Barrio Escalante • Mon–Sat 9am–5pm • Free • ☎ 2222 6392

Though it's a little out of the way (900m northwest of Parque Nacional), anyone interested in Costa Rican history should make time for the **Museo Dr. Rafael Calderón Guardia**, a rare memorial to one of the nation's most controversial political figures. The museum occupies an elegant mansion completed around 1912 and purchased in the 1940s by **Dr. Rafael Ángel Calderón Guardia**, Costa Rica's president from 1940 to 1944 (see p.414). Galleries inside (Spanish labels only) focus on his family, his presidency and some of his major achievements, which include the establishment of social security, healthcare, the national university and the Labour Code.

Spirogyra Jardín de Mariposas
Opposite El Pueblo, off Av 17 • Mon–Fri 9am–2pm, Sat & Sun 9am–3pm • US$7 • ☎ 2222 9237, ⓦ butterflygardencr.com

The compact **Spirogyra Jardín de Mariposas**, just over 1km northeast of Parque Morazán (across the Río Torres), has a wide variety of **butterflies** fluttering about, with daily guided tours pointing out particularly unusual and pretty ones. It exudes a tranquility far removed from the rest of the city, and the sight of brilliant Blue Morphos and dense foliage is a good primer for what you'll see once you explore further afield.

Centro Costarricense de la Ciencia y la Cultura

C 4, at Av 15 • Tues–Fri 8am–4.30pm, Sat & Sun 9.30am–5pm • Museo de los Niños ₡2300 (under-15s ₡2000), Galería Nacional free • ☎ 2258 4929, ⓦ museocr.org

At the northern end of Calle 4, 1km north of Parque Central, is the **Centro Costarricense de la Ciencia y la Cultura**. Located in a former prison (the Cárcel Pública de San José, a yellow fort-like structure in use from 1910 to 1979), this complex houses a small theatre (the Teatro Auditorio Nacional), as well as the **Galería Nacional**. Making good use of original prison cells, the gallery showcases contemporary Costa Rican art, with an emphasis on photography and sculpture. Most of the complex, however, is devoted to the mildly interesting **Museo de los Niños** (or Children's Museum), where Costa Rican kids learn about their country's history, culture and science through interactive displays.

San Pedro

Some 2.5km east of Plaza de la Democracía, the suburb of **San Pedro** is dominated by the main campus of the Universidad de Costa Rica. Once you leave traffic-choked Avenida Central you'll find a lively student quarter, plus a few elegant old residential houses. There's not much else to see beyond the slightly scrappy **Parque Kennedy** (Av Central, at C 57) and its modest **Iglesia de San Pedro**, and the area is best known for some of the city's best restaurants and nightlife (see p.111) – though hordes of raucous college students means that it's often not the most relaxing spot to be on a Friday or Saturday night, at least during term time.

Universidad de Costa Rica

C Central, at C de Amarguras • ☎ 2511 0000, ⓦ ucr.ac.cr • Buses from Av Central, at C 9 (daily 6am–10pm; every 15min)

The lush, jungle campus of the **Universidad de Costa Rica** is one of the greenest in Central America, an attractive backdrop to the most prestigious educational institution in the country. Inaugurated in 1941, the overall campus atmosphere is busy, egalitarian and stimulating, though the architecture is a decidedly uninspiring blend of prefab concrete and Modernist design.

The only real sight here is the quirky Museo de Insectos (see below), though there are several cheap cafeterias dotted around the campus and the Facultad de Bellas Artes has a wonderful open-air **theatre** used for frequent concerts (Teatro de Bellas Artes; ⓦbellasartes .ucr.ac.cr). The three or four blocks surrounding the university (especially **Calle de la Amargura**, aka Calle 3) are lined with lively bars and restaurants, though in most of them you'll feel more comfortable if you're under 30. For Spanish-speakers this is a great place to meet people, watch movies and browse in the several well-stocked bookshops.

Museo de Insectos

Universidad de Costa Rica • Mon–Fri 8am–noon & 1–4.45pm (ring the bell) • ₡1400 • ☎ 2511 5318, ⓦ miucr.ucr.ac.cr

Oddly located in the basement of the Facultad de Artes Musicales (School of Music), the excellent **Museo de Insectos** hosts as extensive an insect collection as you're ever likely to see. Pride of place is given to butterflies, which come in a bewildering variety of shapes, sizes and colours. If you're worried you might miss out on spying a harlequin beetle out in the wild – or perhaps you'd rather see one securely mounted on a wall – this is *the* place to go.

Parque La Sabana

Av Central, C 42/68 • Open daily 24hr • Free

At the very western end of Paseo Colón (Avenida Central), the solid expanse of green today known as **Parque La Sabana** served as San José's international airport from 1940 until 1958 (and welcomed small aircraft until the early 1970s). It is now home to the country's most prominent museum devoted to national art, as well as the Estadio Nacional de Costa Rica (see p.115). Most people, though, come to the park simply to enjoy an afternoon stroll amid leafy trees shading a central lake and modern sculptures. On Sunday afternoons, hordes of local families feed the resident geese and eat ice cream. Just outside the park's southern boundary is the futuristic air-traffic-control-tower shape of the **Contraloría de la República**: this is the government's administrative headquarters.

Museo de Arte Costarricense

Av Central, at C 42 • Tues–Sun 9am–4pm • Free • ☎ 2256 1281, ⓦ musarco.go.cr

The white Neocolonial edifice of the old air terminal at the eastern end of Parque La Sabana has been converted into the attractive **Museo de Arte Costarricense**, with a small but fine collection of mainly twentieth-century Costa Rican paintings displayed in a handsome setting. Most of the galleries here rotate, but highlights of the permanent collection include numerous sculptures and paintings by the celebrated **Juan Manuel Sánchez**, the outstanding landscapes of **Teodorico Quirós**, with their Cézanne-inspired palettes of russets and burnt siennas, along with Enrique Echandi, Margarita Berthau, abstract painter Lola Fernández and a scattershot selection of foreign artists including Diego Rivera and Alexander Calder.

Salon Dorado

The remarkable **Salon Dorado** upstairs is always on view – four full walls of bas-relief stucco carvings overlaid with sumptuous gold, portraying somewhat idealized scenes of Costa Rica's history since the Spanish arrived. Created by French sculptor Louis Féron between 1939 and 1940, the western wall features imagined scenes from the lives of the indigenous peoples, followed on the north wall by Columbus's arrival ("Discovery and Conquest"), to which the indigenous peoples improbably respond by falling to their knees and praying solemnly. The two remaining walls represent the Colonial and Independence periods respectively, including images of Costa Rican agrarian gods of horses, oxen and chickens, and an image of this very building when it was San José's airport, little biplanes buzzing around it like mosquitoes.

Museo de Ciencias Naturales La Salle

Av 12, at C 68 • Mon–Sat 8am–4pm, Sun 9am–5pm • US$3 • ☎ 2232 1306, ⓦ museolasalle.ed.cr

On the southwest corner of Parque La Sabana, across the road in the Ministerio de Agricultura y Ganadería complex, is the quirky natural-science museum **Museo de Ciencias Naturales La Salle**. Walk in to the Ministerio complex, and after about 400m you'll see the painted wall proclaiming the museum; the entrance is at the back. It's an offbeat collection, with displays ranging from pickled fish and snakes coiled in formaldehyde to some rather forlorn taxidermy exhibits – age and humidity have taken their toll. Highlights include the model of the huge **baula**, or leatherback turtle, the biggest reptile on earth, and the **dusky grouper** fish, a serious contender for first prize in the Ugliest Animal in the World contest. Tonnes of crumbly fossils and an enormous selection of pinned butterflies (twelve cases alone of titanium-bright Blue Morphos) finish off the collection. Live tortoises, virtually motionless, doze in the courtyard garden.

Escazú

If you have half a day to spare consider a short bus ride out to **Escazú**, one of San José's more affluent suburbs, some 9km west of the centre (buses run every few minutes from central San José, Av 6, at C 14). There's little in the way of sights, but the views from the upper town are spectacular and plenty of cafés and restaurants line the streets. As a popular home for Europeans and Americans and city commuters, Escazú has a reputation for being a bit posh in Costa Rica, but it's a fairly typical Valle Central community for the most part (the newest development clings to the highway at the far north end of the area) and locals far outnumber foreign residents. Spreading up along its namesake mountain from a valley floor, the town comprises three separate neighbourhoods; take the bus to the top (San Antonio) if you want to see all three.

San Rafael

From the main San José highway (Carr Próspero Fernández, or Hwy-27), Via 105 runs straight into modern **San Rafael**, the commercial hub of Escazú, where most of the upscale shops and galleries are located (though giant **Multiplaza** and the fancy **Avenida Escazú** complex are further along the highway). Via 105 is essentially the main drag these days, lined with strip malls and dreary international fast-food chains; *Café Hacienda Real* (see p.108) is a notable exception. A block west of Via 105 lies the former main square (now turned into a football pitch), **Plaza San Rafael**. The elegant, all-white **Iglesia San Rafael Arcángel** on the south side was completed in 1950 in a Spanish neo-Baroque style. The hacienda-themed **Plaza Colonial** mall on the west side of Plaza San Rafael contains a few boutiques and decent open-air cafés.

ESCAZÚ

0 – 200 metres

121

Plaza Colonial   Plaza San Rafael

SAN RAFAEL

Iglesia San Rafael Arcángel

Costa Rica Country Club

Plaza Atlantis

AVENIDA 20

AVENIDA 22

AVENIDA 24

AVENIDA26

AVENIDA 28   Palacio Municipal

SAN MIGUEL (ESCAZÚ CENTRO)

AVENIDA CENTRAL

AVENIDA 32   Parque Central   Iglesia San Miguel Arcángel

AVENIDA 34

AVENIDA 36

TOMÁS FERNAL 124

VIA 105

CALLE 124

CALLE 40   CALLE 42

CALLE 134

CALLE 40

CALLE 132   CALLE 28

VIA 110

AVENIDA 30

(800m & Central San José (4km)

(550m & Central San José (6km)

(550m & Central San José (6km)

Multiplaza shopping centre (2.5km) & Krama Yoga Center (3.5km)

(500m)

San Antonio (2km)

● EATING	
Café Hacienda Real	2
La Cascada	1

■ ACCOMMODATION	
Casa de las Tías	1
Costa Verde Inn	3
Posada El Quijote	2

1

San Miguel

Just over 1km south from San Rafael on Via 105 lies **San Miguel** (also known as Escazú Centro), the site of the original town and far more laidback, its rural character reflecting its ranching origins. Fronting the central, leafy square – the Parque Central de Escazú – the **Iglesia San Miguel Arcángel** (irregular hours) dates back to 1799, though it was completely rebuilt in a rather unusual Romanesque style in the late nineteenth century, at odds with the rest of the square's more understated buildings. The square is also the site of Escazú's excellent **farmers' market** (Sat 7am–noon), which draws *josefinos* from across the city for the impressive selection of fresh produce and artisanal foods.

San Antonio

From the east side of Parque Central de Escazú, Via 105 (aka Calle 132) runs up the mountain for another 2km to the centre of **San Antonio**, the most residential and rustic of the three neighbourhoods. Plaza San Antonio is mostly used for football practice these days, but the red-roofed church, **Iglesia de San Antonio de Padua** (daily 6am–7pm), is the prettiest in Escazú, with stellar views back down the mountain and across the San José valley. The church was only completed in 1929, with the twin towers added in 1937.

ARRIVAL AND DEPARTURE   SAN JOSÉ

Arrival in San José, whether by **plane** or **bus**, is straightforward. Though Liberia is gaining tracking as an arrival point for international flights, José is undisputedly the transport hub of Costa Rica. Most bus services, flights and car rental agencies are located here. Chances are, wherever you plan to go – and however you plan to get there – you'll have to first go through San José.

BY PLANE

Most international flights arrive at Juan Santamaría International Airport (☎ 2443 2622), 17km northwest of San José and 3km southeast of Alajuela (see p.124). There's a small tourist office in baggage claim (manned Mon–Fri 9am–5pm, but open daily 24hr; ☎ 2443 1535), which can supply maps and give advice on accommodation. There's a post office (Mon–Fri 8am–5pm), an ATM machine (handily situated next to the departure tax desk), and a bank, downstairs on the departure level (Mon–Fri 6.30am–6pm, Sat & Sun 7am–1pm).

AIRPORT TAXIS

The fastest way to get into central San José from the airport is by taxi, which takes about 20–30min in light traffic and costs US$30–35. Official airport taxis are orange and line up outside the terminal; it's currently a little chaotic (but generally safe), as there is no organized system and drivers stampede for your business while you're practically still in customs. Take a deep breath and make sure to agree on the fare before you get in the cab. Some taxi drivers take travellers who haven't made accommodation bookings to hotels where they get commission – these are often more expensive than you were bargaining for, so be firm about where you want to go. Taxi drivers accept US dollars as well as colones, although they tend not to accept notes larger than US$20; some now accept credit cards as well (check before you get in).

SHUTTLE BUSES

The cheaper alternatives to taxis are shuttle buses, which can be arranged in advance and drop off at hotels – try EasyRide (☎ 4033 6847, ⓦ easyridecr.com), which charges US$49 (one way) for up to four people (if you're a single traveller, you should be able to join a shared minibus for around US$13–15). If you haven't arranged a ride in advance, Interbus (interbuscostarica.com) and Gray Line (☎ 2291 2222, ⓦ graylinecostarica.com) have desks in baggage claim and offer similar rates.

PUBLIC BUSES

The Alajuela–San José public bus (4am–11pm every 10min; every 30min 11pm–4am) stops right outside the airport's undercover car park. Though it's much cheaper than a taxi, there are no proper luggage racks inside and the buses are nearly always full – you can just about get away with it if you're carrying only a light backpack or small bag. Drivers will indicate which buses are on their way to San José (a 30min journey) and which to Alajuela (5–10min). The fare to San José is ₡540 (local currency only); pay the driver. The bus drops passengers in town at Av 2, at C 12/14 near the Hospital de San Juan de Dios, where there are plenty of taxis.

DEPARTURE TAX

The departure tax for international flights is US$29; it is best to pay in cash as credit card transactions are treated as a cash advance. Note that airlines are gradually adding this tax to their ticket prices – make sure you don't pay twice.

DOMESTIC FLIGHTS

Domestic flights from San José are run by Sansa (part of the TACA/Avianca regional airline system), and NatureAir, a private company. Sansa (☎ 2257 9444, ⓦ flysansa.com) flies from a tiny dedicated terminal just next door to Juan Santamaría International Airport main terminal (you have to leave the main terminal, left as you exit arrivals, but it's just a few minutes' walk). They change their schedules frequently, so it's best to phone ahead or double-confirm when booking. NatureAir (☎ 2220 3054 or ☎ 2296 1102, ⓦ natureair.com) also runs most of its flights from Juan Santamaría (main terminal). The one exception is the daily service between Liberia and Tamarindo (one in each direction), which operates from Tobías Bolaños airport in Pavas, 7km west of San José. Although the information below gives as accurate a rundown of the routes as possible, flight durations are subject to change at the last minute. Both NatureAir and Sansa fly small propeller planes that are often grounded by inclement weather. Keep in mind that, in the event of a cancellation, both airlines offer credit (for one year) rather than money back. Some of the routings, particularly those to the Nicoya Peninsula, tend to be roundabout, often with one or two stops (only nonstop flights are listed below). Fares for both airlines generally range from US$65 one way to US$120–150 return for most destinations.

Destinations via Sansa Bahía Drake (3 daily; 50min); Golfito (4 daily; 1hr); Liberia (4 daily; 45min); Limón (3 daily; 40min); Nosara (1 daily; 45min); Palmar Sur (1 daily; 50min); Puerto Jiménez (7 daily; 50min); Quepos (6 daily; 30min); Tamarindo (2 daily; 50min); Tambor (8 daily; 30min); Tortuguero (Mon, Wed & Fri 3 daily; 30min).

Destinations via NatureAir Bahía Drake (1 daily; 35min); Golfito (1 daily; 40min); Liberia (2 daily; 35min); Nosara (1 daily; 50min); Puerto Jiménez (1 daily; 40min); Quepos (3 daily; 20min); Tamarindo (1 daily; 40min); Tambor (3 daily; 25min); Tortuguero (1 daily; 25min).

BY SHUTTLE BUS

Most of the nation's shuttle bus operators (see p.48) run routes from San José to all the major tourist destinations. They offer smaller, usually more comfortable minibuses

that will pick up from your hotel; they are much more expensive than public buses however, and can even take longer, depending on the pick-up schedule. Sample one-way prices include: Arenal/La Fortuna (US$60); Cahuita (US$60); David, Panama (US$70); Dominical (US$55); Jacó (US$40); Liberia (US$60); Monteverde (US$50); Playas del Coco (US$60); and Tamarindo (US$60).

BY BUS

From San José there are few places in Costa Rica that can't be reached by bus; get a complete timetable at the tourism office (see p.106) when you arrive or check routes online at ⓦ thebusschedule.com. As schedules are prone to change, exact departure times are not given here, though some details are given under individual destinations elsewhere in the book.

BUS TERMINALS

San José's main domestic bus station is Terminal 7/10 (entrance on C 8, at Av 7). It's a relatively new facility with tickets (look for *Boletería*) sold on the upper floors – which is more like a shopping mall, with food court and even free wi-fi – and buses departing from bays on street level. Terminal 7/10 (like most of the other bus terminals) is located in Barrio México, one of the roughest parts of the city, though it's safe enough during the day. Few buses now depart from the extra-seedy area around Mercado de la Coca-Cola, five blocks west of the Mercado Central; the small terminal at the back of the market (entrance C 16, Av 1/3) now only serves Atenas, Naranjo and Orotina. Most buses for the Caribbean coast depart from Gran Terminal del Caribe (C Central, at Av 15), while the Terminal Atlántico (C 12, at Av 9) serves several other tourist destinations. Taxis line up at all of these terminals.

DOMESTIC BUS ROUTES

The buses listed below are express services from San José. Regional bus information is covered in the relevant accounts in the Guide. For destinations, these initials are used: PN = Parque Nacional; RNdVS = Refugio Nacional de Vida Silvestre; MN = Monumento National. The initials following each destination correspond to the bus companies that serve the route, or the terminal from which they depart – addresses are listed in the bus companies box (see p.104).

LUGGAGE ON LONG-DISTANCE BUSES

Thefts from the luggage racks of long-distance bus services are not uncommon, especially on the Monteverde and Manuel Antonio routes. The accepted wisdom is, if possible, to **take your luggage onto the bus** with you. Even then, make sure all compartments are locked and that you have nothing valuable inside easily unzipped pockets. If you have to put your bags in the luggage hold, make sure only the driver or his helper handles them, and get a seat from where you can keep an eye on luggage during stops.

1

BUS COMPANIES IN SAN JOSÉ

A bewildering number of **bus companies** use San José as their hub. The following is a rundown of their head-office addresses and/or phone numbers, and the abbreviations that we use in our listings.

ME	Autotransportes MEPE, Terminal Atlántico (☎2257 8129, ⊛mepecr.com)
BM	Buses Metrópoli, Av 2, C 1/3 (☎2536 6052)
EA	Empresa Alfaro, Terminal 7/10 (☎2222 2666, ⊛empresaalfaro.com)
EG	Empresarios Guápileños, Gran Terminal del Caribe (☎2222 0610, ⊛grupo caribenos.com)
EL	Empresa Lumaca, C 5, at Av 10 (☎2537 2320)
EP	Expreso Panamá C 16, Av 10/12 (☎2256 8721, ⊛expresopanama.com)
EU	Empresarios Unidos, C 16, Av 10/12 (☎2221 6600, ⊛eupsacr.com)
MRA	Microbuses Rápidos Heredianos, C 1, Av 7/9 (☎2223 8392)
MU	MUSOC, C Central, Av 22/24 (☎2222 2422)
Nica	Nicabus, Av 1, C 18/20 (near Mercado de la Coca-Cola; ☎2221 2679, ⊛nicabus.com.ni)
PU	Pulmitan de Liberia, C 24, Av 5/7 (☎2222 0610, ⊛grupocaribenos.com)
TB	Transportes Blanco, Terminal Atlántico (☎2257 4121)
TC	Transportes Caribeños, Gran Terminal del Caribe (☎2222 0610, ⊛grupocaribenos.com)
TCO	Transportes Cóbano, Terminal 7/10 (☎2642 1112)
Tica	Ticabus, Av 3, C 26/28 (☎2296 9788, ⊛ticabus.com)
TIL	Transportes Tilarán, Terminal 7/10 (☎2222 3854)
TJ	Transportes Jacó, Terminal 7/10 (☎2223 1109)
TRA	Tralapa, Av 5, C 20/22 (☎2680 0392)
TRC	Tracopa, C 5, Av 18/20 (☎2221 4214, ⊛tracopacr.com)
TRN	Transnica, C 22, Av 3/5 (☎2223 4242, ⊛transnica.com)
TRS	Transtusa, C 13, Av 6/8 (☎4036 1800, ⊛transtusacr.com)
TSC	Transportes San José-Venecia (San Carlos), Terminal 7/10 (☎2255 4318)
TU	Tuasa, Av 2, C 12/14 (☎2442 6900)
Tuan	Tuan, C 18, Av 5/7 (☎2441 3781)

TO/FROM VALLE CENTRAL AND THE HIGHLANDS

Alajuela and the airport (daily every 10min, 4am–10pm; 35min). **TU**.

Cartago (daily every 5min; 45min). **EL**.

Heredia (daily every 10min; 30min). **MRA**; **TU**.

Sarchí (4 daily Mon–Fri, 1–2 Sat; 1hr 30min). **Tuan**.

Turrialba (for MN Guayabo; 17 daily; 2hr 30min). **TRS**.

Volcán Irazú (daily 8am; 2hr). **BM**.

Volcán Poás (1 daily 9.15am; 1hr 30min). **TU** (buses depart Av 6, at C 14, 100m south of the main Tuasa terminal).

TO/FROM LIMÓN PROVINCE AND THE CARIBBEAN COAST

Cahuita (4 daily; 4hr). **ME**.

Guápiles (for PN Braulio Carrillo; daily every 45min; 1hr 30min). **EG**.

Limón (25 daily; 2hr 30min). **TC**.

Puerto Viejo de Talamanca (5 daily; 4hr 30min). **ME**.

TO/FROM THE ZONA NORTE

La Fortuna (for Volcán Arenal; 3 daily; 4hr). **TSC**.

Los Chiles (for RNdVS Caño Negro; 2 daily; 5hr). **TSC**.

Puerto Viejo de Sarapiquí (10 daily; 2hr). **TC**.

TO/FROM GUANACASTE

Liberia (17 daily; 4hr 30min). **PU**.

Nosara (1 daily; 6hr). **EA**.

Playa del Coco (3 daily; 5hr). **PU**.

Playa Hermosa (2 daily; 6hr). **TRA**.

Playa Panamá (2 daily; 6hr). **TRA**.

Playa Potrero (2 daily; 6hr). **TRA**.

Sámara (1 daily; 5hr). **EA**.

Santa Cruz (9 daily; 5hr). **EA**.

Tamarindo (2 daily; 5hr 30min). **EA**.

TO/FROM CENTRAL PACIFIC AND SOUTHERN NICOYA

Mal País (1–2 daily; 5hr 15min). **TCO**.

Monteverde (2 daily; 5hr). **TIL**.

Montezuma (2 daily; 5hr). **TCO**.

Nicoya (6 daily; 5hr). **EA**.

Playa Jacó (8 daily; 2hr 30min). **TJ**.

Puntarenas (hourly; 2hr 20min). **EU**.

Quepos (for PN Manuel Antonio; 6 daily; 3hr 45min). **TRC**.

TO/FROM THE ZONA SUR
Golfito (3 daily; 8hr). **TRC**.
Puerto Jiménez (for PN Corcovado; 2 daily; 8hr). **TB**.
San Isidro de El General (for PN Chirripó; 14 daily; 3hr). **MU**; **TRC**.

INTERNATIONAL BUS ROUTES
Most international buses from Nicaragua, Honduras, Guatemala and Panama pull into the Ticabus station, C 3, Av 26/28 (☎ 2296 9788, ⊛ ticabus.com), several blocks

west of the city centre; you can also buy tickets at the Tica office (Av 4, C 9/11, near Plaza de las Artes). Advance purchase – at least a week in advance, particularly for Managua and Panama City – is necessary for all routes. Services to San Salvador (El Salvador), Tegucigalpa (Honduras), Guatemala City and Tapachula (Mexico) require an overnight in Managua (Nicaragua).
David, Panama (2 daily; 9hr). **TRC**.
Guatemala City (3–4 daily; 60hr with overnight in Managua & El Salvador). **Tica**.
Managua (11hr). **Nica** (2 daily); **TRN** (5 daily); **Tica** (4 daily).
Panama City (16hr). **EP** (1 daily); **Tica** (2 daily).

GETTING AROUND

San José is easily negotiated **on foot**. Several blocks in the city centre around the Plaza de la Cultura have been completely pedestrianized. There is little need to take **buses** within the city centre, though the suburban buses are useful, particularly if you are heading out to Parque La Sabana, a 30min walk west along Paseo Colón. Escazú is a 20min ride to the west, and San Pedro and the Universidad de Costa Rica are a 10min ride to the east. After the buses stop running, taxis become the best way to get around. **Street crime** is an issue, and most *josefinos* advise against walking alone after dark.

BY TRAIN

San José has been trying to develop an urban rail system for years, but the current service is infrequent and is targeted primarily at commuters (just 5–6 daily trains, early mornings and evenings) on lines that snake around the centre. The current Tren Urbano (15km) links Estación de Tren Freses in Curridabat with UCR (for Universidad Costa Rica and San Pedro), Estación al Atlántico (near Parque Nacional) and Contraloria (Parque La Sabana). In addition, there are extensions to Alajuela (50min), Heredia (30min) and Cartago (45min), from Estación del Atlántico. Fares are cheap, around ₡240–550. The system may be extended further – see ⊛ incofer.go.cr.

BY BUS

Fast, cheap and frequent buses connect the centre of the city with virtually all San José's neighbourhoods and suburbs, and generally run from 5am until 10/11pm every day. Most buses to San Pedro, Tres Ríos and other points east leave

from the stretch of Avenida Central between C 9 and C 15. You can pick up buses for Paseo Colón and Parque La Sabana (labelled "Sabana-Cementerio") at the bus shelters on Av 2, C 5/7. All buses have their routes clearly marked on their windshields, and usually the fare too. This is payable either to the driver or his helper when you board and is usually ₡245–290 (in the city), though the faster, more comfortable *busetas de lujo* (luxury buses) to the suburbs cost upwards of ₡450; push the bell when you'd like to stop.

BY TAXI

Taxis are plentiful, even at odd hours of the night and early morning. Licensed vehicles are red with a yellow triangle on the side, and have "SJP" ("San José Público") licence plates. The starter fare – ₡625 at the time of research – is shown on the red digital read-out, and you should always make sure that the meter is on before you start (ask the driver to *toca la maría, por favor*, "turn on the meter please"). Some drivers may claim that the meter doesn't

---

USEFUL BUS ROUTES

The following is a rundown of the main inner-city routes, all of which stop along Avenida Central or Avenida 2. If in doubt, ask "*¿dónde está la parada para…?*" ("Where is the stop for…?").
Sabana–Cementerio buses travel west along Paseo Colón to Parque La Sabana, and are ideal for going to any of the shops, theatres and restaurants clustered around Paseo Colón, the Museo de Arte Costarricense or Parque La Sabana.
Sabana–Estadio services run basically the same route, with a tour around Parque La Sabana. Good for the neighbourhoods of Sabana norte and Sabana sur.
Sabanilla–Bethania buses run east through Los Yoses and beyond to the quiet residential suburb of Sabanilla.
San Pedro (also **La U**) or **Tres Ríos** buses will also take you east through Los Yoses and on to the Universidad de Costa Rica and the hip neighbourhood of San Pedro. Other buses serving San Pedro are: Vargas Araya, Santa Marta, Granadilla, Curridabat and Cedros.

1

work – if this is the case, agree on a fare before you start out, or find another taxi whose meter is working. Most drivers are honest – don't immediately assume everyone's trying to cheat you. Fares (officially ₡600/km) within the centre will rarely top ₡2500 or double that to get out to the suburbs. US dollars are not always accepted in taxis – check in advance. If they are, US dollars will invariably be exchanged at US$1 for ₡500 (much poorer than the bank exchange rate), and your change will be given in colones. Tipping is not expected. There are several taxi companies in the city; two of the more reliable are Coopeirazu (☏ 2254 0533) and Coopetaxi (☏ 2235 9966).

BY CAR

Renting a car specifically for getting around San José is a bad idea. Most of the city's streets are one-way, though sometimes unmarked as such. Cars left on the street anywhere near the city centre are almost certain to be broken into or stolen. If you do rent a car (see p.49), always use the secure *parqueos* (guarded car parks) that dot the city: most close at 8 or 8.30pm, although there are some 24hr parks, including one on Av Central, at C 19. Some hotels have on-site parking. If you have to leave your car on the street, look for a man whose job it is to guard cars, and expect to pay at least ₡1000/day. If driving in the centre of the city, keep your windows rolled up and your doors locked so no one can reach in.

BY BICYCLE

It's unfortunately not a good idea to cycle in San José. Diesel fumes, potholes and aggressive drivers don't make for pleasant cycling, although riding in the suburbs or Parque La Sabana is easier and much less hazardous to your health.

INFORMATION

Tourist office At the time of research San José's Instituto Costarricense de Turismo (ICT; Mon–Fri 9am–5pm; ☏ 2299 5800, ⓦ visitcostarica.com) tourist office was in the Antiguo Banco Anglo building, Av Central, C 1/3, though it may (eventually) move back to beneath the eastern edge of the Plaza de la Cultura. It gives out free maps, hotel brochures and – most crucially – comprehensive booklets detailing the national bus schedule.

ACCOMMODATION

San José has plenty of quality **hotel** rooms, with reasonable prices in all categories. Unless otherwise indicated, wi-fi is included, but breakfast is not. Many of San José's rock-bottom hotels have cold-water showers only. Unless you're particularly hardy, you'll want some form of heated water, as San José can get chilly, especially from December to March. Though staying in one of the hotels in the **city centre** is convenient, the downside is noise and, in many places, a lack of atmosphere. At night it can be a touch unsavoury, and many city-centre hotels host prostitutes. Note that downtown's venerable *Gran Hotel Costa Rica* should reopen by early 2018 as a newly refurbished five-star hotel. Not too far from downtown, in quieter areas such as Paseo Colón, Los Yoses and **barrios Amón and Otoya**, are more expensive hotels, many of them in old colonial homes. To the west of the city is **Escazú**. The vast majority of B&Bs here are owned by foreign nationals, and charge higher prices than elsewhere in town. East of the city but closer to the centre than Escazú is studenty **San Pedro**, with better connections to downtown and a more cosmopolitan atmosphere.

CENTRAL SAN JOSÉ

Casa León Av 6, C 13/15 ☏ 2221 1651, ⓦ hotelcasaleon .com; map p.94. This Swiss-run small guesthouse has dorms and basic private rooms with a spotlessly clean shared bathroom and kitchen (free coffee). There is laundry service and luggage storage. The house is a little hard to find; look for it next to the train tracks and tell your taxi driver it's in a *calle sin salida* (cul-de-sac). Dorms US$25, doubles US$35

★ **Hostel Casa del Parque** C 19, Av 1/3 ☏ 2233 3437, ⓦ hostelcasadelparque.com; map p.94. With a serene location adjacent to Parque Nacional, this small, family-run hostel is easily one of the city's better budget choices. The dorm has ten full-size beds and there are six private rooms (some with private bathrooms) – all are clean and comfortable. The friendly staff can book tours and the common areas are smarter than you'd expect for this price bracket. Dorm US$14, doubles US$40

Hotel 1492 Av 1, C 31/33 ☏ 2280 6265, ⓦ hotel1492 .com; map p.94. On a quiet stretch of Av 1, this comfortable hotel has ten well-appointed rooms, some surrounding an elegant antique- and art-filled atrium and others adjoining a small tropical garden. All have private shower and cable TV. The friendly staff can arrange tours. US$40

★ **Hotel Fleur de Lys** C 13, Av 2/6 ☏ 2223 1206, ⓦ hotel fleurdelys.com; map p.94. Wonderfully restored Swiss-run hotel set in a brilliant pink Victorian mansion. Rooms are individually furnished with local artwork, and feature cable TV, en suites and fans. Breakfast included. US$88

Hotel Presidente Av Central, at C 7 ☏ 2010 0000, ⓦ hotel-presidente.com; map p.94. Plush, immaculate hotel smack in the middle of downtown. Over ninety rooms, each tastefully designed and well-appointed with cable TV, a/c and safe – some have a jacuzzi. There's a spa on-site, as well as a gym. Breakfast included. US$95

BARRIOS AMÓN, OTOYA AND ARANJUEZ

La Amistad Av 11, at C 13 ☏ 2258 0021, ⓦ hotel amistad.com; map p.94. Set in a large 1920s mansion in historic Barrio Otoya, this American-owned hotel has over thirty rooms all with cable TV, in-room safe, private bathroom and queen-sized beds; there are also six penthouse suites with a/c. Serious breakfast buffet included. Doubles US$85, penthouse suite US$115

★**Aranjuez** C 19, Av 11/13 ☎ 2256 1825, ⓦ hotel aranjuez.com; map p.94. In quiet Barrio Aranjuez yet still close to the centre, with 35 stylish rooms set in five interconnected houses dating from the 1930s. Relax in the pretty garden around the back, where organic waste from the hotel is used as fertilizer. They serve a good buffet breakfast (included in the rate) and can arrange package tours to *Laguna Lodge* in Tortuguero (see p.175). The 36 rooms either have shared or private bathroom; all have cable TV. Be sure to reserve ahead. Private bath US$62, shared bath US$42

Hotel Don Carlos C 9, Av 7/9 ☎ 2221 6707, ⓦ doncarloshotel.com; map p.94. An elegant landmark hotel, once the home of Tomás Guardia Gutiérrez (Costa Rican president in the 1870s), now filled with replicas of pre-Columbian art and a lovely kitsch breakfast terrace/cocktail lounge with a fountain and a pretty tiled mural of the city – hand-painted by Costa Rican artist Mario Aroyabe. All rooms have cable TV and safe (some also have private patios) and there's a small pool, plus an excellent gift shop, Boutique Annemarie (see p.114). Breakfast included. US$85

Hotel Dunn Inn Av 11, at C 5 ☎ 2222 3232, ⓦ hotel dunninn.com; map p.94. Attractive and inviting hotel in Barrio Amón with 28 sunny rooms of various sizes. All are adorned with custom furnishings and have cable TV. There's a pretty restaurant and bar on-site and the staff have a wealth of local information. US$60

Kap's Place C 19, Av 11/13 ☎ 2221 1169, ⓦ kapsplace .com; map p.94. One of the city's best mid-range choices, this family-friendly hotel is run by the unstintingly helpful Karla Arias, who is an endless source of information on all things San José. There are several different types of accommodation available; all have private bathrooms, cable TV and colourful decoration. There's a fully equipped communal kitchen. Tours arranged on request. US$55

★**Santo Tomás** Av 7, C 3/5 ☎ 2255 0448, ⓦ hotelsanto tomas.com; map p.94. In quiet, elegant Barrio Amón, near downtown, this American-owned hotel is one of San José's best boutique options. It occupies an old mansion awash in soft lighting and decorated with burnished wood and Persian rugs. The twenty rooms vary widely in size, character and price, though all have cable TV. There's a small swimming pool, a hot tub, an excellent open-air restaurant and a travel service. Breakfast included. US$60

WEST OF THE CENTRE

Cacts C 28/30, at Av 3 bis ☎ 2221 6546 or 2928, ⓦ hotelcacts.com; map pp.90–91. *Cacts* has 25 rooms, all with ceiling fans (deluxe rooms also have TV); all but four have private bathrooms. There's a tropical garden,

swimming pool, jacuzzi and sunny roof terrace, where you can enjoy the complimentary breakfast buffet of fresh fruits and baked goods. The friendly owners run a travel agency and can book tours and make reservations. US$7

Gaudy's Backpackers Hostel Av 5, C 36/38 ☎ 2248 0086, ⓦ backpacker.co.cr; map pp.90–91. Popular hostel with clean and very comfy dorms, decent hot showers and kitchen, laundry and shuttle to/from the airport (US$24). Breakfast included, and well-priced tours offered. Dorms US$13, doubles US$35

★**Grano de Oro** C 30, Av 2/4 ☎ 2255 3322 ⓦ hotel granodeoro.com; map pp.90–91. In a quiet location, housed in an elegant turn-of-the-twentieth-century mansion. Its tasteful en suites have been decorated in a faux-Victorian style, with wrought-iron beds and wood-beamed ceilings, plus all mod cons. Several of the deluxe rooms even come with their own private gardens. There's a rooftop sun-terrace featuring a pair of jacuzzis, lush, fountain-filled gardens, and one of the city's top restaurants (see p.111). Service is on point, too. US$186

Parque del Lago Boutique Hotel Paseo Colón, C 40/42 ☎ 2547 2000, ⓦ parquedellago.com; map pp.90–91. Modern hotel near Parque La Sabana with elegant, contemporary-style rooms, cable TV and free bikes. Breakfast included. US$82

SAN PEDRO

★**Hostel Bekuo** Av 8, C 39/41 ☎ 2234 1091, ⓦ hostelbekuo.com; map p.99. A great place to meet fellow travellers, this is one of the city's best hostels, with clean dorms plus a few private doubles (some with private bathroom). Facilities include a fully equipped kitchen, pool table, darts, cable TV in the common lounge, unlimited free calls to the US and Canada and shared computers. Rates include breakfast of pancakes, fresh fruit and toast. Airport transfers US$30. Dorms US$13, doubles US$32

Hostel Urbano C 57, Montes de Oca (in front of Parque Kennedy) ☎ 2281 0707, ⓦ hostelurbano.com; map p.99. An excellent hostel, featuring clean, modern dorms with pinewood bunks, shared kitchen and plenty of tour advice – and you can leave luggage here for free for up to a week. Dorms US$13, doubles US$33

Hotel Milvia Av 1, at C 75 (50m east of the Muñoz y Nanne supermarket) ☎ 2225 4543, ⓦ novanet.co.cr /milvia; map p.99. Mid-range hotel in a lovely old Caribbean-style plantation house beautifully decorated with antiques and modern Costa Rican art. Located in a residential area, with a soothing fountain, garden, sun terrace and mountain views. Simple breakfast included – lunch and dinner available on request (costs extra). US$70

TripOn Open House C 39, at Av 15 (Barrio Escalante) ☎ 2280 5244, ⓦ triponopenhouse.com; map p.99. Justly popular hostel in a quiet residential area, with attractively decorated dorms with hardwood bunks, spotless kitchen and

1

pool table. Wholesome breakfast of cereal, toast and fresh fruits included. Dorms US$13, doubles US$38

ESCAZÚ

Casa de las Tías San Rafael de Escazú, southeast of El Cruce Shopping Centre; take the east turn by the Restaurante Cerutti ☎2289 5517, ⓦcasadelastias .com; map p.101. Set on a garden estate (home of a former Costa Rican Labour Minister), this quiet, friendly B&B has just five en-suite rooms (with hot water), each individually decorated. Breakfast included. US$100

Costa Verde Inn On an unmarked side street off Av 32 ☎2228 4080, ⓦcostaverdeinn.com; map p.101. Exceedingly friendly and airy B&B with large, nicely appointed rooms, small pool, jacuzzi, garden and open dining area. The helpful staff can arrange numerous tours. US$65

Posada El Quijote 800m south of El Cruce Shopping Centre, just east of Chango's restaurant ☎2289 8401, ⓦquijote.cr; map p.101. Renovated, tranquil inn with eight spacious rooms adorned in Spanish colonial style and comfortably furnished, with bathroom, hot water and cable TV. Breakfast (included) is served in the lovely garden. US$85

EATING

For a Central American city of its size, San José has a reasonable variety of restaurants – Italian, Thai and even macrobiotic – along with simple Costa Rican places, such as **sodas**, that offer dishes beginning and ending with rice (rice-and-shrimp, rice-and-chicken, rice-and-meat). Sadly, **fast-food outlets** in San José are proliferating so rapidly that at times it can look like a veritable jungle of *Pizza Hut*s, *Taco Bell*s and *KFC*s, not to mention *McDonald's*. Happily, local **café** chains also abound; some, like *Giacomín*, have old-world European aspirations; others, such as *Spoon*, are resolutely Costa Rican. Working *josefinos* eat their **main meal** between noon and 2pm, and at this time *sodas* especially get very busy. Many of the more upmarket restaurants close at 3pm and open again in the evening.

CAFÉS AND BAKERIES

★**Alma de Café** Av 2, C 3/5 (Teatro Nacional) ☎2010 1119, ⓦalmadecafe.net; map p.94. Good coffee (₡995) and espresso, fruit drinks, sandwiches (₡4000–6000) and fantastic cakes (from ₡2500) served amid Neoclassical decor – marble, crystal and ceiling murals. Settle in at a window table and check out the goings-on in Plaza de la Cultura. Mon–Sat 9am–7pm, Sun 9am–4pm.

Café Club Unión C 2, Av 1/3 ☎2257 1555, ⓦclubunion .com; map p.94. Fashionable glassed-in café, serving quality espresso and pastries, allowing a perfect view of the historic post office across the street. Mon–Fri 8am–7pm, Sat 8am–5pm.

★**Café Hacienda Real** Via 105, San Rafael ☎4035 6561, ⓦgoldenbean.net; map p.101. Amazing find just off traffic-choked Via 105, a boutique coffee roaster in a 1920s colonial-style house with a garden, genuinely friendly staff, top-quality coffee, comfy chairs and delicious snacks. One of the city's highlights. Mon 9am–7pm, Sun 10am–6pm.

Café La Mancha C 1, Av Central/1 ☎2221 5591; map p.94. Housed in the courtyard of the stately Edificio Steinvorth, this small café is a great place to absorb the city's all too rarely appreciated historical roots. Serves pastries, sandwiches, cappuccino and espresso made with beans sourced from La Cabaña farm in the Tarrazú region – you can also purchase bags of the café's own La Mancha brand of coffee. Mon–Sat 10am–7pm.

★**Café Rojo** Av 7, C 3/5 ☎2221 2425; map p.94. Café housed in a gorgeous old property in Barrio Amón, with simple wood tables, friendly staff, mint-flavoured water, seasonal menus and light meals (from *pupusas* to muffins) for under ₡5000. Mon–Thurs & Sun noon–7pm, Sat noon–8pm.

Q Café Av Central, at C 2 ☎2221 0707; map p.94. Sleek, upmarket café on Avenida Central (it's on the second floor above *Café Tostados*) that's a great spot to idle away a couple of hours, especially while sipping their signature espresso accented with slivers of chocolate ("Café Q"; ₡2650) or one of their several other house-blend coffee drinks (from ₡1100). They also serve hamburgers and various pastries (₡1450–3650). Mon–Sat 9am–9pm, Sun 10am–8pm.

Spoon Av Central, C 5/7 ☎2222 5172, ⓦspooncr.com; map p.94. Popular chain packed with *josefinos* ordering birthday cakes to try or takeaway. The coffee, served with hot milk on the side, can be a little too bitter, but the choice of cookies and cakes is endless. They serve full breakfasts and lunches at a good price. Mon–Fri 8am–8pm, Sat 9am–8pm, Sun 10am–6pm.

SODAS, SNACKS AND ICE CREAM

Sodas generally open early, close late and are cheap – a *plato del día* lunch will rarely set you back more than ₡3500. They also have *empanadas* and sandwiches to take away – combine these with a stop at one of the fruit stalls on any street corner and you've got a quick, cheap lunch. The pieces of papaya and pineapple sold in neatly packaged plastic bags have been washed and peeled by the vendors and should be safe, but if in doubt, wash again. Snacks sold at the Mercado Central (see p.114) are as tasty as anywhere.

La Casona Típica Av 2, at C 10 ☎2248 0701; map pp.90–91. An incongruous white, blue and red clapboard shack that serves up, as the name implies, *comida típica* at rock-bottom prices. The rice and beans and various *casados* are all a great deal at around ₡2000–2400. Daily 7am–10pm.

Chelles Av Central, at C 9 ☎ 2221 1369; map p.94. This spartan bar, with bare fluorescent lighting and a TV blaring away in the corner, has been a San José institution for over hundred years, opening around 1909. It remains a great place to sit and watch your fellow customers or the street action outside. Aproned waitresses serve up cold, cheap beer, snacks and *casados*. Daily 24hr.

El Parque C 2, Av 4/6 ☎ 2258 3681; map p.94. This *soda* caters to everyone from businessmen grabbing a cup of coffee on their way to the office and retail workers popping out for a quick lunchtime snack to late-night bar hoppers looking to eat themselves sober. Try *plato de días* (daily 11.30am–4.30pm) such as *pinto con huevo* (rice, beans and eggs), a bargain at just ₡2850. Breakfast plates from ₡1700. Daily 24hr.

★**POPS** Av Central, C 1/3 ⓦ pops.co.cr; map p.94. This beloved local ice-cream chain occupies prime real estate on the corner of Plaza de la Cultura, with cones for ₡1100, and all sorts of sundaes and flavours available, from chocolate and banana to guanábana and *dulce de leche*. Daily 9am–9.45pm.

Soda Tapia C 42, at Av 2 ☎ 4033 2390; map pp.90–91. Huge, old-fashioned Costa Rican diner running since 1965, open to the street with views (across the busy ring road) of Parque La Sabana and the art museum. Especially handy for late-night snacks, with sandwiches and burgers (₡3500) for those weary of *casados*. Mon–Thurs 6am–2am, Fri & Sat 24hr (from 6am), Sun 6am–1am.

★**La Sorbetera de Lolo Mora** Mercado Central ☎ 2256 5000; map p.94. Home-made ice cream stall in the heart of the central market that dates back to 1901. They serve one delicious flavour, a blend of vanilla and cinnamon, and also sell delicious milkshakes and fruit ices (from ₡1500). Mon–Sat 7am–6pm.

La Vasconia Av 1, at C 5 ☎ 2223 4857; map p.94. Get off the tourist trail and dig into cheap breakfasts, *arroz con pollo* and *empanadas* alongside Costa Rican workers at this casual *soda*. Adorning the walls are thousands of photos of the national football team (some dating back to 1905) and there's karaoke nightly, for better or worse. Most mains cost ₡2500–4000. Mon–Fri 9am–1.30am, Sat 11am–2am.

Vishnu Av 1, C 1/3 ☎ 2223 4434; map p.94. This cheery vegetarian *soda* is an obligatory pit stop for healthy dishes in San José. Enjoy delicious, reasonably priced *platos del día* with brown rice and also generous vegetable dishes and soups. The vegetarian club sandwich with chips will set you back a mere ₡3000; fruit plates with yoghurt are around ₡2500; and the set breakfast is ₡1500. Daily 8am–8pm.

RESTAURANTS

Many of the city's best restaurants are in the relatively wealthy and cosmopolitan neighbourhoods of San Pedro, along Paseo Colón, and in Escazú. Wherever you choose, eating out in San José can set your budget back considerably. Prices are generally steep, and the 23 percent tax added to your bill (which includes a ten percent "service charge") make it even more expensive. In central San José, you'll find plenty of cheaper snack bars and *sodas*, where the restaurant tax doesn't apply.

CENTRAL SAN JOSÉ

Balcón de Europa C 9, Av Central/1 ☎ 2221 4841; map p.94. The pasta and other Italian staples (most

---

EL PUEBLO

Once one of San Jose's most enduring tourist attractions, the **El Pueblo** complex (off Av 17, C 9/11, north of the Río Torres; ☎ 2221 9434) has definitely lost its appeal in recent years, though it remains on the surface a thoroughly attractive, faux-Spanish colonial mall. It's virtually empty during the day (despite several antique shops remaining open) and it's essentially a late-night bar and club zone, with a reputation, sadly, for violence. The restaurants are still pretty good, though – and because so many bars and clubs are located here, plenty of folks have a great time on Friday and Saturday nights crawling from place to place. Note, however, that fights are common (though they rarely involve shootings or serious injury). The following listings may still be worth checking out – ask your host/hotel before setting out.

La Cocina de Leña ☎ 2222 1003; map pp.90–91. Some see this as an example of Tico food at its best, superb meals cooked in a wooden oven and served in faux-rustic surroundings. Others see it as a glorified *soda* selling overpriced staples to gullible tourists. The truth lies somewhere in between. The succulent chicken dishes are recommended and it's certainly handy if you're making a night of it in the bars and discos of El Pueblo. *Menús* for ₡2800–3500. Mon–Thurs 11.30am–2pm & 5–11pm, Fri & Sat 11am–midnight, Sun 11am–11pm.

Ebony 56 ☎ 2223 2195; map pp.90–91. One of the most popular among El Pueblo's glut of discos. Several large dancefloors play salsa and US and European dance music with the odd 1980s/1990s pop hit thrown in. Thurs–Sun 8pm–4am.

Papa Pez ☎ 2233 8145, ⓦ lukascr.com; map pp.90–91. With excellent seafood and friendly service, this restaurant is especially known for fresh ceviche, seafood soup and sea bass dishes. Mains ₡2500–5000. Mon–Sat 11.30am–11pm, Sun 11.30am–5pm.

1

₡8000–10,000) are nothing special, but the atmosphere at this city landmark is great. Sepia photos of San José's early days line the wood-panelled walls, along with treacly snippets of "wisdom". Monster cheeses dominate the dining room, as does the strummer who serenades each table. Tues–Sun 11am–11pm.

★**Café Mundo** Av 9, at C 15, Barrio Otoya ☎ 2222 6190; map p.94. One of the finest restaurants in San José, the Italian-influenced cuisine is a delight, served in a beautiful dark-wood dining room or, if the weather is nice, on a leafy terrace. The Caesar (₡3000) and Niçoise (from ₡5500) salads are large but still a bit overpriced. If you're on a budget, just come for a cappuccino (₡1500). At night the bar attracts a largely gay clientele. Mon–Thurs 11am–10.30pm, Fri 11am–midnight, Sat 5pm–midnight.

Don Wang C 11, Av 6/8 ☎ 2233 6484, 🌐donwang restaurant.com; map p.94. If you have a craving for East Asian food, this Chinese restaurant is the place to go, serving reasonably authentic Hong Kong-style dim sum, Chinese classics, curries, Thai food and Japanese dishes, with tables set around a tranquil koi pond. Hotpots are a speciality and there are several vegetarian and seafood dishes on offer (most mains are around ₡6000). Mon–Thurs 11am–3.30pm & 5.30–10pm, Fri 11am–3.30pm & 5.30–11pm, Sat 11am–11pm, Sun 11am–10pm.

★**La Esquina de Buenos Aires** C 11, at Av 4 ☎ 2223 1909; map p.94. A block and a half from Plaza de la Democracía and adjacent to the Iglesia Nuestra Señora de La Soledad, this is a gem of a steakhouse and easily the best in San José. Well-executed Argentine *parrillas* feature heavily, including *lomito* (tenderloin) and *ojo de bife* (ribeye). Prices are very reasonable, with steaks starting at around ₡8000, and the tango music and decor evoking a bygone Buenos Aires (with old prints and pictures from Argentina) can't be beaten. Mon–Sun 11am–3pm & 6pm–midnight.

Nuestra Tierra Av 2, at C 15 ☎ 2258 6500; map p.94. Hugely popular in spite of its gimmicky feel, *Nuestra Tierra* offers reliable Tico standards and a dining experience that is anything but dull. Expect to be regaled by dancing singers, a persistent din, hefty portions and a bill that is more than you might expect (specials from ₡3000, but mains as high as ₡13,000). Daily 24hr.

El Patio del Balmoral Av Central, C 7/9 ☎ 2222 5022; map p.94. Smack in the middle of the pedestrianized portion of Av Central, this pleasant restaurant with an interior courtyard (and separate café section for espresso and cake, plus *El Bar* upstairs, open Mon–Thurs 4–10pm, Fri & Sat 4–11pm) has a wide range of international salads and entrees, such as fish and chips and fettuccine Alfredo *(menu de día ₡4500–6000)*. The portions are enormous; a breakfast here could easily carry you through to dinner. Restaurant & café Mon–Thurs 6am–10pm, Fri & Sat 6am–11pm, Sun 6am–9pm; bar Mon–Thurs 4–10pm, Fri & Sat 4–11pm.

Sapore Trattoria Av 2, at C 13 ☎ 2222 8901, 🌐sapore trattoria.com; map p.94. Restaurant close to the southern end of the craft market, offering superbly crafted and very authentic Italian food, including a range of pastas (₡6450–9950), pizzas (from ₡5500) and fish and meat dishes such as tilapia with shellfish (₡9450). Mon–Thurs 11.30am–10.30pm, Fri & Sat 11.30am–11.30pm, Sun noon–9pm.

Shakti C 13, at Av 8 ☎ 2222 4475, 🌐restauranteshakti .com; map p.94. The self-proclaimed "home of healthy food" offers filling *platos del día* of *sopa negra* or salad, a hearty vegetarian *casado*, a *refresco* plus tea or coffee, all for around ₡3500. Tasty breakfast specials include granola, fruit juice and coffee or tea for just ₡2000. It's popular for lunch, so go early or late for a seat. Mon–Sat 7.30am–7pm.

★**La Terrasse** Av 9, at C 15, Barrio Otoya ☎ 2221 5742; map p.94. Just a bit north of *Café Mundo*, this handsome, intimate spot in a historic house dating from 1927 serves rich French-style dishes from lauded chef Patricia Richer, such as a creamy veal stew (₡9800) and duck with blackberries and red wine (₡16,000). Reservations essential. Mon–Fri noon–2pm & 7–10pm, Sat 7–10pm.

Tin Jo C 11, Av 6/8 ☎ 2221 7605, 🌐tinjo.com; map p.94. Quiet, popular and fairly formal Asian restaurant with a choice of Chinese, Indian, Indonesian, Thai, Burmese or Japanese cuisine. The lemongrass soup (₡3100), bean-thread noodle salad in lime juice (₡5000) and coconut milk curries (₡7000) are particularly recommended. Dinner with wine is around ₡25,000 for two; skip the alcohol, or go for lunch, and you'll get away with half that. Mon–Thurs 11.30am–2.30pm & 6–10pm, Fri 11.30am–2.30pm & 6–11pm, Sat noon–3.30pm & 6–10pm, Sun noon–9pm.

WEST OF THE CENTRE

Aqui es! Av 2, at C 38 ☎ 2221 5727, 🌐restaurante aquies.com; map pp.90–91. Atmospheric Argentine steakhouse in a historic building overlooking Parque Auxiliadora. The steaks can be hit-and-miss, but it also knocks out decent pastas, pizzas, fresh salads and desserts, plus jugs of sangria, Argentine wine and *empanadas*. Mains ₡6000–10,000. Mon–Thurs 11am–6.30pm, Fri 11am–10.30pm, Sat noon–10.30pm.

La Bastille Av Central, at C 22 ☎ 2255 4994; map pp.90–91. Swanky restaurant/gallery with a dining room bedecked in garishly coloured modern art, including some strange Gaudí-esque chairs. Though the decor is strictly "love it or hate it", the French–Italian cuisine is some of the finest in the city – the ravioli is particularly recommended. Around ₡25,000 for two with wine. Mon–Fri noon–2pm & 6–10pm.

Fogo Brasil Av de las Américas, at C 40 (100m east of the Nissan dealership, La Sabana) ☎ 2248 1111, 🌐fogobrasilcr.com; map pp.90–91. A true carnivore's delight, this Brazilian steakhouse is a popular stop-off on the way to or from the airport. The skewered red meat is adroitly cooked and doled out until you practically have to plead for mercy. Against all odds, there's a massive salad bar, too. It's pricey, though, and dinner for two could cost upwards of ₡50,000. Daily 11.30am–11.30pm.

★**Grano de Oro** C 30, Av 2/4 ☎ 2253 3322, ⊛ hotelgranodeoro.com; map pp.90–91. Top-end restaurant, in the hotel of the same name (see p.107), with hacienda-style decor, romantic courtyard setting and a regularly changing menu. Breakfast is particularly good: try the pancakes with roasted banana and caramelized macadamia nuts or the poached eggs in a truffle cream. The lunch and dinner menus (mains ₡9000–17,500) are similarly appealing – the amazing desserts include a piña colada cheesecake and the signature "Grano de Oro Pie", a creamy blend of coffee and chocolate – and there's also a well-stocked wine cellar featuring over 2000 bottles. Daily 6am–10pm.

★**Machu Picchu** C 32, Av 1/3 ☎ 2222 7384; map pp.90–91. Velvet llamas hang on the walls at this San José favourite, one of the top South American restaurants in town. The appetizers, including ceviche and Peruvian *bocas*, tend to be more interesting than the main dishes. Around ₡18,000 for two with beer or wine; the Pisco sour should not be missed. Mon–Sat noon–10pm, Sun noon–6pm.

SAN PEDRO

★**La Cascada** C 108, just off Via 167, San Rafael ☎ 2228 0906, ⊛ lacascadasteak.com; map p.99. This difficult-to-find restaurant (there's no sign) with ho-hum decor is

actually one of the best steakhouses in San José. Hugely popular, it's often full of Tico families, especially on Sunday afternoons. The hunks of beef, such as the house tenderloin (*lomito en salsa pimienta*, ₡16,500), are fantastic, and the filling plates all come with rice and veggies. Mon–Fri 11.30am–3pm & 6–10pm, Sat & Sun noon–10pm.

Le Chandelier Av 12a (100m west and 100m south of the Instituto Costarricense de Electricidad building in Los Yoses) ☎ 2225 3980, ⊛ lechandeliercr.com; map p.99. Exquisite French food prepared by the restaurant's Swiss owner. Try the lobster in pastry or the delicious trout with almonds (set *menú* from ₡7450). The decor is homely, with exposed ceiling beams and a crackling fireplace. Mon–Fri 11.30am–midnight, Sat 6.30pm–midnight.

★**Mantras Veggie Café and Teahouse** C 35, Av 11/13, Barrio Escalante ☎ 2253 6715; map p.99. While *Mantras* definitely draws its share of vegetarians and vegans, it pulls in just as many meat lovers with its colourful and exceedingly tasty dishes. The menu isn't extensive, but there isn't any filler and the entrees, such as raw courgette pasta (₡5000), pop with flavour. Be sure to save room for the inventive raw and organic desserts. Mon–Fri 8.30am–5pm, Sat 8.30am–3pm.

NaPraia Seafood & Raw Bar Blvd Dent (just off Via 39) ☎ 2234 0133; map p.99. Spot that attracts a fashionable crowd, especially at the weekends, with high-quality seafood, friendly service, excellent ceviche, wines and craft beers. Mon–Thurs 11.30am–10pm, Fri & Sat 11.30am–11pm, Sun 11.30am–4pm.

DRINKING

When it comes to going out at night, young *josefinos*, students and foreigners in the know stay away from downtown (where prostitution is particularly prevalent, especially at the bars in the notorious *Del Rey Hotel*) and head instead to Los Yoses or San Pedro. Avenida Central in **Los Yoses** is a well-known "yuppie trail" of bars, packed with middle- and upper-middle-class Ticos imbibing and conversing. **San Pedro's** Calle de la Amargura nightlife is geared more towards the university population, with a strip of studenty bars to the east of the UCR entrance. Those looking to kick back with locals should head to a *boca* bar (see box, p.112).

Bar Buenos Aires Av 9, at C 23 ☎ 2221 6738; map p.94. Open since around 1910, this classic old-school *boca* bar is adorned with a fabulous array of historic photos of San José and frequented by a host of local characters. Mon–Sat 11am–2.30am.

Bar Río Av 2, C 43/45 ☎ 2225 8371; map p.99. Wildly popular and long-running Los Yoses sports bar with a large terrace – it's the local for *Hostel Bekuo* (see p.107). Inside, several large TVs usually show football matches, and in the back is a large dance area. Live music on Tues and the occasional weekend. The starchy fast-food menu, such as quesadillas and nachos for around ₡4000, is a good way to soak up the alcohol. Mon & Tues 3pm–midnight, Wed & Thurs 3pm–1am, Fri & Sat noon–4am, Sun 4pm–midnight.

Caccio's Calle de la Amargura, 200m east and 25m

north of San Pedro Church ☎ 2224 3261; map p.99. This insanely popular student hangout, where guys wearing baseball caps sing along loudly to pop songs and drink jugs of booze dyed in garish colours, is a great spot to meet Ticos. Knock back cheap, cold beer while munching on pizza. Daily 11am–1am.

El Cuartel de la Boca del Monte Av 1, C 21/23 ☎ 2221 0327; map p.94. Lively, long-established bar – with great lunch, dinner and *bocas* (₡3500–10,000) – that still packs in *josefinos*. Particularly full on Mon and Wed, when there's live music (Latin, rock and reggae) by up-and-coming bands. Mon–Thurs 11.30am–2pm & 6pm–midnight, Fri 11.30am–2pm & 6pm–2am, Sat 6pm–2am.

El Gaff C 29, at Av 8, Los Yoses ☎ 2234 1596; map p.94. Friendly local pub serving tasty house and craft beer plus decent bar food (think huge, juicy burgers

1

BOCA BARS

In Costa Rica, *bocas* (appetizers) are the tasty little snacks traditionally served free in bars. **Boca bars** are a largely urban tradition, and although you find them in other parts of the country, the really famous ones are all in San José. Because of mounting costs, however, and the erosion of local traditions, few places serve *bocas* gratis any more. Several bars have a *boca* menu, among them *El Cuartel de la Boca del Monte* (see p.111) near Los Yoses, but the authentic *boca* bars are concentrated in suburban working- or lower-middle-class residential neighbourhoods. They have a distinctive, welcoming feel – friends and family spending the evening together – and are very busy most nights. Saturday is the hardest night to get a table; get there before 7.30pm. You'll be handed a menu of free *bocas* (one beer gets you one *boca*, so keep drinking and you can keep eating). The catch is that the beer costs more than elsewhere, but even so, the little plates of food are generous enough to make this a bargain way to eat out. Typical *bocas* include deep-fried plantains with black-bean paste, small plates of rice and meat, shish kebabs, tacos and *empanadas*.

One of the most authentic and well-known *boca* bars is the working-class, long-established *Bar México* in Barrio México (C 16, Av 11/13; ☎ 2221 8025). It's a pretty rough neighbourhood, so go by taxi. Alternatively, you'll find a varied clientele – but conspicuously few foreigners – at *Los Perales* and *El Sesteo* (both Mon–Sat 7pm–midnight) in the eastern suburb of Curridabat. They're about 100m from each other on the same street, but hard to find on your own; taxi drivers will know them.

and pizza). Tues–Thurs 6pm–1am, Fri noon–1am, Sat 4pm–1am.

★**Lupulus Beer Shop** Centro Comercial Calle Real, Hwy-2 (Interamericana), C 65a/65b, San Pedro ☎ 2234 6392; map p.99. Small but lively craft beer pub (serving pints from Costa Rica's Craft Brewing Co, among others), that also serves exquisite burgers – including an excellent lamb burger (₡4000). Mon–Fri 6pm–midnight, Sat 3pm–midnight.

★**Stiefel Pub** Av 7, at C 11, Barrio Otoya ☎ 8854 4824; map p.94. Superb selection of craft beers from Costa Rica (and elsewhere in the region), which you can get in that cheesy glass known as "Das Boot" (*stiefel* means "boots" in German, slang for "let's go for a beer"). Tables, lamps and the bar are made from recycled materials, and punters are encouraged to add to the chalk scrawling on the walls. Mon–Fri 11.30am–2pm & 6pm–2am, Sat 6pm–2am.

NIGHTLIFE

San José pulsates with the country's most diverse nightlife, and is home to scores of lounge bars, clubs and live music venues. For full details of what's on, check the *Cartelera* in the *Tiempo Libre* section of *La Nación*, which lists live music along with all sorts of other activities, or the *San José Volando* (🌐 sanjosevolando.com). One way to make the most out of the scene is to make use of the safe and secure bus operated by Carpe Chepe (🌐 carpechepe.com/la-carreta-app), which runs daily 8.30pm–2.30am, making a loop of major venues every 1hr 30min (one ticket ₡1000, all-night pass ₡4000).

Antik Av 10, at C 21 ☎ 4033 3324, 🌐 antik.cr; map p.94. This elegant, historic mansion (Casa Matute Gómez) has been turned into a fashionable club and lounge with three levels: restaurant and cocktail bar on the first (ground) floor; the basement dancefloor (mostly electronic music, Fri & Sat only); and the second-floor balcony featuring more ambient beats from local DJs. Thurs–Sat 8pm–4am.

★**Bar Jazz Café** Hwy-2 (Interamericana), at C 65, San Pedro ☎ 2253 8933, 🌐 jazzcafecostarica .com; map p.99. The best venue in San José for live jazz, with an air of intimacy and consistently good bands. The cover charge varies from ₡3000 to ₡5000 (sometimes including a glass of wine) and is well worth it. Mon–Fri 5pm–midnight, Sat & Sun noon–midnight.

Club Vertigo Paseo Colón, C 36/38 ☎ 2257 8424, 🌐 vertigocr.com; map pp.90–91. When a big-name international DJ tours Central America, a date at *Club Vertigo* is pretty much a certainty. The lines are inevitably long – particularly on Sat – and the dress code is somewhat strict for San José, but they're small prices to pay for a vibe that can't be matched elsewhere in town. The action is split between two rooms, and the music you'll hear in each differs nightly, though it's usually trance and house amping up the joint. Daily 10pm–6am.

Dope Club Paseo de la Segunda República (opposite Taco Bell), San Pedro ☎ 8838 8589; map p.99. One of the city's hottest live music and DJ venues – local students especially love Ladies Night on Tues. Tues & Thurs–Sat 9pm–4am.

El Lobo Esteparío Av 2, at C 13 ☎ 2256 3934; map p.94. Bar and club named after Hermann Hesse's *Steppenwolf*, featuring everything from live poetry readings to rock concerts. Mon–Thurs & Sun 4pm–12.45am, Fri & Sat 4pm–2am.

El Sótano C3, at Av 11, Barrio Amón ☎ 2221 2302, ⓦ amonsolar.com; map p.94. Jazz, live music, and club-night venue set in a beautiful house built in 1920, with several quieter spaces for drinks and food, a stage on the main floor, an art gallery on the second floor and a basement favoured for jazz concerts. Cover around ₡3000 for live performances. Mon–Sat 3pm–2am.

Terra U C de la Amargura, one block east of Iglesia de San Pedro ☎ 2283 7728; map p.99. With three open-air levels and a heaving dancefloor, this is one of San José's weekend hotspots. Latin and Jamaican dance hits predominate. Music videos (and occasional football match highlights) play on the big-screen TVs. Mon–Sat 10.30am–2.30am, Sun 3pm–2.30am.

LGBT NIGHTLIFE
San José is one of the best places in Central America for gay nightlife. The spots we've included are the most established, and it helps if you have a local LGBT contact to help you hunt down small local clubs.

El 13 Av 14, at C 9 ☎ 2221 3947; map pp.90–91. Gay-friendly place famed for its *charanga* nights (a Cuban dance music popularized in the 1940s). Wed–Sun 6pm–2am.

La Avispa C 1, Av 8/10 ☎ 2223 5343, ⓦ laavispa.com; map pp.90–91. Friendly, landmark LGBT disco-bar, "The Wasp" has three dancefloors and several pool tables housed in a distinct black-and-yellow building. The big nights are Tues and Sun, while Thurs is karaoke. There's a varying cover charge at weekends, usually ₡3000 or less. Thurs–Sat 8pm–6am, Sun 5pm–6am.

Buenas Vibraciones Bar Av 14, C 7/9 ☎ 2223 4573; map pp.90–91. Lesbian-owned bar popular with both lesbians and gay men, and a great place to check out the local scene. Fri & Sat 9pm–3am.

ENTERTAINMENT

The quality of the performing arts in San José is very high. *Josefinos* especially like **theatre**, and there's a healthy range of venues for a city this size, staging a variety of inventive productions at affordable prices. If you speak even a little Spanish it's worth checking to see what's on.

THEATRES
The city's premier venues are the Teatro Nacional and the Teatro Melico Salazar; here you can see performances by the National Symphonic Orchestra and National Lyric Company (June–Aug), as well as visiting orchestras and singers, usually from Spain or other Spanish-speaking countries.

Teatro de Bellas Artes Universidad de Costa Rica, San Pedro ☎ 2511 8931, ⓦ bellasartes.ucr.ac.cr. Generally excellent and innovative student productions with new spins on classical and contemporary works (usually Spanish only).

Teatro Eugene O'Neill Centro Cultural, Los Yoses, San Pedro ☎ 2207 7562. Works by modern playwrights and innovative independent productions in one of the larger theatres in the country.

Teatro Laurence Olivier Av 2, C 26/28, in the Sala Garbo building ☎ 2222 1034. Modern theatre specializing in contemporary productions, plus occasional jazz concerts and film festivals.

Teatro Melico Salazar C Central, at Av 2 ☎ 2295 6032, ⓦ teatromelico.go.cr. San José's "workhorse" theatre dates from 1928 and stages occasional performances of traditional Costa Rican song and dance, including classic and modern productions by Costa Rica's Compañía Nacional de Danza (National Dance Company); ticket costs are low.

Teatro Nacional C 5, at Av 2 ☎ 2010 1111, ⓦ teatro nacional.go.cr. The city's premier theatre opened in 1897 and hosts opera, ballet and concerts (National Symphonic Orchestra), as well as drama.

CINEMAS
Going to the movies in San José is a bargain at around ₡3000, and most cinemas show the latest films, which are almost always subtitled; Lincoln Plaza is a good place to see a current Hollywood movie (see p.94). The few that are dubbed will have the phrase "*hablado en Español*" in the newspaper listings or on the posters. For Spanish-language art movies, head to Sala Garbo.

SALSA LIKE A JOSEFINO
One of the best ways to meet people and prepare yourself for San José nightlife is to take a few **salsa lessons** at one of the city's many *academias de baile*. You don't necessarily need a partner, and you can go with a friend or in a group. The tuition is serious, but the atmosphere is usually relaxed. The best classes in San José are at Ritmofit in San Pedro (Av 3, at C 65; ☎ 2234 5490); at Malecón (C 17/19, Av 2; ☎ 2222 3214); and at Merecumbé, which has various branches, the most central of which is in San Pedro (Av 8, at C 65;' ☎ 2224 3531).

Alianza Francesa Av 7, at C 5, Barrio Amón ☎ 2257 1438. Occasional French-language films, usually dubbed or subtitled in Spanish.

CCM Cinemas San Pedro San Pedro Mall ☎ 2280 9585. American-style multiplex with ten screens, full surround sound and popcorn on tap.

Sala Garbo Av 2, at C 28 ☎ 2223 1960. Popular arthouse cinema showing independent films from around the world, usually in the original language with Spanish subtitles.

Teatro Variedades C 5, Av Central/1 ☎ 2222 6104. Oldest theatre in the city (opened in 1892), now a downtown movie house with Rococo-style decor showing good foreign and occasionally Spanish-language films.

SHOPPING

San José's **souvenir and crafts shops** are pricey compared to the rest of Central America; it's best to buy from the larger shops run by government-regulated crafts co-operatives, from which more of the money filters down to the artisans. You'll see an abundance of pre-Columbian gold jewellery copies, Costa Rican liqueurs (Café Rica is the best known), coffee (the supermarkets have just about any variety you could hope to take home), T-shirts with jungle and animal scenes, weirdly realistic wooden snakes, leather rockers from the village of Sarchí (see p.128), walking sticks, simple leather bracelets, hammocks and a vast array of woodcarvings, from miniature everyday rural scenes to giant, colourfully hand-painted Sarchí ox-carts. It's worth bargaining, although goods in the city's **markets** tend to already be a little cheaper than in the shops.

SOUVENIRS AND CRAFTS

Boutique Annemarie Hotel Don Carlos, C 9, at Av 9 ☎ 2221 6707; map p.94. A good selection of pre-Columbian artefacts and jewellery reproductions are on sale in the gift shop of this hotel (see p.107).

★**Dantica Gallery** Lincoln Plaza shopping mall, 3/F, Moravia ☎ 2519 9036; map pp.90–91. Excellent gallery operated by the owners of *Dantica Lodge* in San Gerardo de Dota (see p.363), featuring a range of brightly-coloured masks, jewellery and woodwork. To the northeast of downtown and a bit out of the way, but well worth seeking out. Mon–Sat 10am–9pm, Sun 10am–8pm.

Galería Namu Av 7, C 5/7 ☎ 2256 3412, ⓦ galerianamu .com; map p.94. Top-notch fairtrade gallery specializing in indigenous artwork, such as Wounaan baskets and Boruca masks. Mon–Sat 9am–6.30pm, Jan–April also Sun 1–5pm.

Mercado Central Av Central/1, C 6/8; map p.94. *The* place to buy coffee beans, but make sure they're export quality – ask for Grano d'Oro ("Golden Bean"). It's not just coffee; a veritable warren (see p.89), there are a lot of tacky tourist offerings as well as some decent handmade items, though it's a real hunt to find them. Mon–Sat 8am–5pm.

Mercado de las Artesanías Av 2, at C 15 bis; map p.94. A block from Parque Nacional, this orderly market sells souvenirs and crafts, featuring Sarchí ox-carts, and Sarchí jewellery. Though you can find it cheaper elsewhere in the country, the quality is usually fairly good. Daily 8.30am–5pm.

Sol Maya Paseo Colón, C 18/20 ☎ 2221 0864; map pp.90–91. Rather pricey indigenous and Guatemalan arts and crafts in La Sabana; the clothes on sale are a better deal. Mon–Fri 8am–6pm.

BOOKSHOPS

★**Librería Internacional** San Pedro Mall ☎ 2234 1096, ⓦ libreriainternacional.com; map p.99. San José's best bookshop, with a well-stocked Latin American literature section, including Costa Rican authors, and a good selection of both fiction and nonfiction in English as well as maps and tourist guides. Mon–Sat 10am–8pm, Sun 10am–7pm.

Librería Lehmann Av Central, C 1/3 ☎ 2223 1212, ⓦ librerialehmann.com; map p.94. A good selection of mass-market Spanish-language fiction and nonfiction, as well as maps, children's books and a small collection of English-language books. Mon–Fri 8am–6.30pm, Sat 9am–5pm, Sun 11am–4pm.

Mora Books C 5, Av 5/7 (west side of the Aurola Holiday Inn, Parque Morazán) ☎ 8383 8385, ⓦ morabooks .com; map p.94. A pleasant shop with a good selection of secondhand English-language books, guidebooks, magazines and comics. Daily 11am–7pm.

Universal Av Central, at C 1 ☎ 2222 2222, ⓦ universal cr.com; map p.94. Major department store with a small, Spanish-only book section on the third floor. Mon–Fri 8.30am–7.30pm, Sat 9am–7pm, Sun 9am–6pm.

SHOPPING MALLS

Lincoln Plaza C 55, Av 61/65, Moravia ☎ 2519 9043, ⓦ lincolnplaza.cr; map p.94. Opened in 2012, this is José's slickest mall, with a massive food court, a huge range of national and international shops on its gleaming three floors, and one of the best cinemas in the city. Mon–Sat 10am–9pm, Sun 10am–8pm.

San Pedro Mall Av Central, at C 49 ☎ 2283 7540, ⓦ tumallsanpedro.com; map p.99. At the very end of Barrio Dent is the truly ugly but wildly popular San Pedro Mall. A terracotta-coloured multistorey building festooned with plants and simulated waterfalls, inside it's a jumble of US chain stores and fast-food outlets. Mon–Sat 10am–9pm, Sun 10am–8pm.

SPORTS AND OUTDOOR ACTIVITIES

FOOTBALL

Estadio Nacional de Costa Rica The western edge of Parque La Sabana ☎ 2284 8700. Opened in 2011, this 35,000-seat venue hosts games by the Costa Rican national football team. A somewhat controversial project – it was funded by the Chinese government and built exclusively by Chinese workers – it is nonetheless a far more inviting place to see a match (it's much easier to get to and is a lot more comfortable and modern) than the Estadio Ricardo Saprissa.

ROCK CLIMBING

Rocódromo Av 3, C 36/38 ☎ 2221 6934, ⊛ maventura .com. An impressive rock-climbing facility at the back of the Mundo Aventura store, with daily passes only ₡3000. Mon–Fri 1–8.30pm, Sat 9am–3pm.

YOGA

Downtown Yoga C 15, Av 7/7B, Barrio Otoya ☎ 6280 6169, ⊛ downtownyogacostarica.com. Central, friendly yoga studio with at least two mixed-style classes (one class ₡5000) in English most days.

Krama Yoga Center C Mango (1km north of the Multiplaza shopping centre roundabout), Escazú ☎ 2215 3535, ⊛ kramayoga.com. It's not easy to reach without a car, but this studio delivers the most complete yoga experience in San José. Single vinyasa and hot yoga classes, among others, are US$19. Mon–Fri 7.30am–8pm, Sat 9am–2pm, Sun 10.30am–1pm.

DIRECTORY

Embassies and consulates Canada, C 54, Oficentro Ejecutivo La Sabana Building 5, 3/F, south of Parque La Sabana (☎ 2242 4400); UK, 11/F, Edificio Centro Colón, Paseo Colón, C 38/40 (☎ 2258 2025); US, opposite the Centro Comercial del Oeste Pavas, C 98 – take the bus to Pavas from Av 1, at C18 (☎ 2519 2000, ⊛ costarica.usembassy.gov); Australia, Honorary Consul (main embassy in Mexico City), Centro Corporativo Plaza Roble, Edificio El Pórtico, San Rafael de Escazú (☎ 2201 0000); nearest Irish (☎ +52 55 5520 5803), New Zealand (☎ +52 55 528 39460) and South African (☎ +521 55 1100 4970) embassies are in Mexico City. Few nationalities require a visa (see box, p.76) to cross into Nicaragua or Panama but both countries have embassies here: Nicaragua, Av Central, C 25/27 (Mon–Fri 8am–4pm; ☎ 2222 2373 or ☎ 2233 8747); Panama, Av 10, at C 69, San Pedro (Mon–Fri 9am–2pm; ☎ 2281 2442).

Hospitals The city's public (social security) hospital is San Juan de Dios, Paseo Colón, C 14/16 (☎ 2257 6282). Of the private hospitals, foreigners are most often referred to Clínica Biblica, Av 14, C Central/1 (☎ 2522 1000, ⊛ clinicabiblica.com). CIMA San José, 500m west of the tollbooths on the Prospero Fernández Freeway (☎ 2208 1000, ⊛ hospitalcima.com), is also a good private hospital.

Immigration Costa Rican *Inmigración* (Mon–Fri 8am–4pm; ☎ 2299 8100) is on the airport highway in Uruca, opposite the Hospital México and next to the Dirección General de Aviación Civil; take an Alajuela bus and get off at the stop underneath the overhead walkway. Get there early, if you want visa extensions or exit visas. Larger travel agencies can take care of the paperwork for you for a fee (roughly US$10–25).

Internet access Most of the hotels and guesthouses in San José offer wi-fi (and computer terminals), usually for free, and internet cafés (at least the centre) are dwindling. Try Ciber Futuro, C 11, Av Central/1 (₡200/30min, ₡350/1hr).

Laundry Offered by most accommodation. Otherwise, try Laundry Room, C 57, at Av 1, San Pedro (Mon–Fri 9am–4.30pm, Sat 8am–noon), or Eco Clean Lavandería, Av 7, at C 19 (Mon–Sat 6am–10pm).

Libraries and cultural centres Biblioteca Nacional, C 15, Av 3/3bis (Mon–Fri 8am–6pm), and Centro Cultural Costarricense Norteamericano, 100m north of the Los Yoses supermarket in Barrio Dent, San Pedro (Mon–Fri 8am–6pm, Sat 8am–2pm; ☎ 2207 7500, ⊛ centrocultural.cr).

Money and exchange Some hotels will change currency, but you will get a much better rate at banks in San José (you must bring your passport); try Banco de Costa Rica, Av 2, C 4/6 (Mon–Fri 9am–3pm); Banco Nacional, Av Central, C 2/4 (Mon–Fri 9am–3pm); Scotiabank, C 5, Av Central/2 (Mon–Fri 8.30am–6.30pm, Sat 9am–1pm). Most international debit and credit cards should work at these banks' ATMs. Banco de Costa Rica and Banco Nacional limit foreign account holders to US$100 (or equivalent) per transaction, or US$200 (or equivalent) per day.

Pharmacies Farmacia Fischel, Av 3, at C 2, underneath Club Unión (Mon–Sat 7am–7pm, Sun 8am–5pm; ☎ 2248 1692), is one of the oldest pharmacies in the city and has a good stock of both conventional and herbal remedies. There are other locations throughout the city. Other options include Clínica Biblica, Av 14, C Central/1 (open daily 24hr; ☎ 2257 5252), and the many pharmacies in the blocks surrounding the Hospital Calderon Guardia, 100m northeast of the Biblioteca Nacional, in Barrio Otoya.

Post office The Correo Central, C 2, Av 1/3 (Mon–Fri 7.30am–6pm, Sat 7.30am–noon; ☎ 2258 8762), is two blocks east and one block north of the Mercado Central. They'll hold letters for up to four weeks (you'll need a passport to collect your post).

The Valle Central and the highlands

VOLCÁN POÁS

2

The Valle Central and the highlands

Costa Rica's Valle Central ("Central Valley") and the surrounding highlands form the cultural and geographical fulcrum of the country. Rising between 3000 and 4000m, this wide-hipped inter-mountain plateau is often referred to as the Meseta Central or "Central Tableland". It has a patchwork-quilt beauty, especially when lit up by the early morning sun, with staggered green coffee terraces set in sharp contrast to the blue-black summits of the nearby mountains. Many of these are volcanoes – the Valle Central is edged by a chain of volcanic peaks, running from Poás in the north to Turrialba in the east – and their volatile nature can sometimes give the region an air of unease.

The sight of **Poás**, **Irazú** and **Turrialba** spewing and snorting, raining a light covering of fertile volcanic ash on the surrounding farmland, is a fairly common one, though seismic activity in recent years has been a lot more significant: in January 2009, an earthquake devastated the area around Poás, and a year later Turrialba erupted for the first time in nearly 150 years, causing nearby villages to be evacuated.

Although occupying a relatively small area, the fertile Valle Central supports roughly two-thirds of Costa Rica's population, the majority of whom live in San José (covered in Chapter 1) or one of the provincial capitals of **Alajuela**, **Heredia** and **Cartago**. The tremendous pressure on land is noticeable even on short forays from San José: urban areas, suburbs and highway communities blend into each other, and in some places, every spare patch of soil sprouts coffee bushes, fruit trees or vegetables.

Away from the big cities, the countryside is blanketed by coffee plantations – several of which can be explored on tours (see box, p.122) – though sizeable tracts of land have been protected around the valley's fringes, most noticeably at **Parque Nacional Braulio Carrillo** and **Parque Nacional Tapantí–Macizo Cerro de la Muerte**. In addition to the volcanoes and their surrounding national parks, the region boasts whitewater rafting on the Río Pacuare near the town of **Turrialba**; craft shopping at **Sarchí**; the bucolic **Orosí** valley; the popular **La Paz Waterfall Gardens** nature park; and ancient ruins at **Monumento Nacional Guayabo**, one of Costa Rica's most significant archeological sites.

INFORMATION AND GETTING AROUND   THE VALLE CENTRAL

Accommodation While the provincial capitals each have their own strong identity, there is little in them to entice you to linger – with the exception of Alajuela – and most people use San José as a base for forays into the Valle

Central or stay at one of the (often very appealing) lodges scattered throughout the countryside.
Getting around Many Ticos commute from the Valle Central and the surrounding highlands to work in San

WHITEWATER RAFTING ON THE RÍO PACUARE

Highlights

❶ Coffee tours Learn about the finer points of coffee tasting – and, indeed, the whole coffee-making process – on a tour of the region's many plantations. **See p.122**

❷ Villa Blanca Cloudforest Hotel and Nature Reserve Relax by the fireplace in your luxury *casita* on the edge of a misty cloudforest alive with butterflies and echoing with birdsong. See p.131

❸ Volcán Poás Take in smoke-shrouded craters at the otherworldly Volcán Poás, which is easily accessible from Alajuela. **See p.132**

❹ Volcán Irazú Stark lunar landscapes and fantastic views (if you get a clear day) make Irazú

the Valle Central's second must-visit volcano. **See p.144**

❺ Orosí Soak in riverside hot springs or brush up on your Spanish in this beguiling village, home to Costa Rica's oldest working church and set amid the cool, coffee-studded hills of the Valle Orosí. **See p.146**

❻ CATIE Hands-on tours of the excellent botanical gardens are just one of the draws at this unique research station. **See p.150**

❼ Whitewater rafting Tackle the churning whitewaters of the Reventazón and Pacuare rivers, near Turrialba. **See p.152**

HIGHLIGHTS ARE MARKED ON THE MAP ON P.120

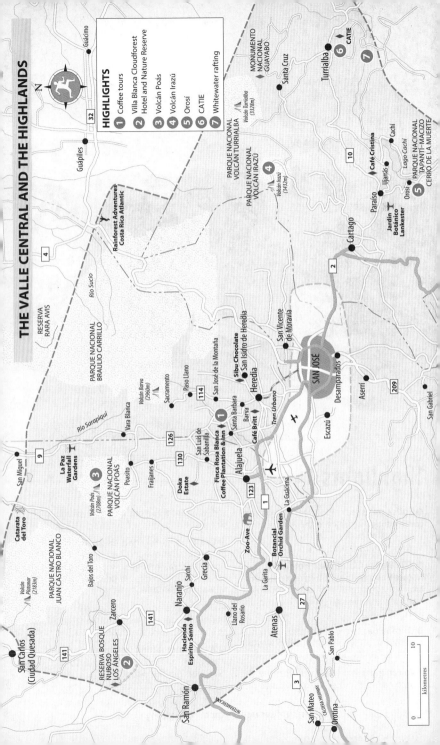

THE VALLE CENTRAL AND THE HIGHLANDS

N

32

HIGHLIGHTS

1. Coffee tours
2. Villa Blanca Cloudforest Hotel and Nature Reserve
3. Volcán Poás
4. Volcán Irazú
5. Orosi
6. CATIE
7. Whitewater rafting

Guácimo

Guápiles

4

RESERVA RARA AVIS

Río Sucio

PARQUE NACIONAL BRAULIO CARRILLO

Rainforest Adventures Costa Rica Atlantic

MONUMENTO NACIONAL GUAYABO

CATIE

6 7

Turrialba

Santa Cruz

Volcán Turrialba (3328m)

PARQUE NACIONAL VOLCÁN TURRIALBA

PARQUE NACIONAL VOLCÁN IRAZÚ

Volcán Irazú (3432m)

4

Café Cristina

10

Cachí

Ujarrás

Lago Cachí

Orosí

PARQUE NACIONAL TAPANTÍ-MACIZO CERRO DE LA MUERTE

5

Paraíso

Jardín Botánico Lankester

Cartago

2

San Vicente de Moravia

San Isidro de Heredia

Sibu Chocolate

Volcán Barva (2906m)

Sacramento

Paso Llano

114

San José de la Montaña

Heredia

Barva

Santa Bárbara

Tren Urbano

SAN JOSÉ

Desamparados

Aserrí

209

San Gabriel

Río Sarapiquí

Vara Blanca

9

San Miguel

126

San Luis de Sabanilla

130

Café Britt

Coffee Plantation & Inn

Finca Rosa Blanca

Alajuela

123

La Garita

La Guácima

Escazú

San Pablo

Catarata del Toro

Volcán Platanar (2183m)

PARQUE NACIONAL JUAN CASTRO BLANCO

La Paz Waterfall Gardens

PARQUE NACIONAL VOLCÁN POÁS

Volcán Poás (2708m)

3

Poasito

Fraijanes

Doka Estate

Zoo-Ave

Botanical Orchid Garden

27

Atenas

1

Bajos del Toro

Zarcero

141

Sarchí

Grecia

Llano del Rosario

San Carlos (Ciudad Quesada)

141

RESERVA BOSQUE NUBOSO LOS ÁNGELES

2

Hacienda Espíritu Santo

Naranjo

San Ramón

INTERAMERICANA

CALDERA HIGHWAY

3

San Mateo

Orotina

San Pablo

0   10
kilometres

THE VALLE CENTRAL IN A NUTSHELL

One easy, albeit fairly whistle-stop, way of visiting the Valle Central's major sights is on a **tour** from San José (see p.54). All kinds of packages exist, but some of the most popular are organized by Expediciones Tropicales (☎ 2233 5151, ⓦ expedicionestropicales.com). Their full-day tour of the northern Valle Central (US$129) visits Volcán Poás, the Doka coffee estate and the La Paz Waterfall Gardens, while their jaunt around the southern highlights (US$102) takes in Volcán Irazú, the botanical gardens at Lankester and the beautiful Valle Orosí; prices include breakfast, lunch and a guide.

2

José via an efficient bus and train network. However, some interesting areas – notably Irazú and Tapantí – remain frustratingly out of reach of public transport. In many cases the only recourse is to rent a car, though this is expensive and the mountainous terrain and narrow, winding, unlit roads can make driving difficult, if not dangerous. A better option perhaps is to take a taxi from the nearest town, or join an organized tour from San José (see box above) or one of the provincial capitals. Note that congestion around the capital is increasingly bad, particularly during the morning and late afternoon rush hours.

Brief history

Relatively little is known about the Valle Central's **indigenous** inhabitants, except that they lived in the valley for at least twelve thousand years, cultivating corn and grouping themselves in small settlements like the one excavated at **Guayabo**, a short drive from the town of Turrialba.

Spanish colonization

In 1560, the Spanish started to **colonize** the area, founding **Garcimuñoz**, in the west of the region, in 1561, and a further settlement at modern-day Cartago three years later. Though the first settlers found fertile land, the rich pickings they had expected didn't materialize: the region had few settlements and no roads (until 1824 there was only the Camino Real, a mule path to Nicaragua, and a thin ox-cart track to Puntarenas) and, crucially, far less **free labour** than they had hoped – the indigenous population proved largely unwilling to submit to Spanish rule, either to the system of slave labour known as *encomienda* (see p.410), or to the taxation forced upon them. Some tribes and leaders collaborated with the settlers, but in general they did what they could to resist the servitude the Spanish tried to impose, often fleeing to the jungles of Talamanca. Forced to till their own fields, many of the first settler families ended up living in as "primitive" a state as the peoples they had hoped to exploit. Indeed, money was so scarce that in 1709 the settlers adopted the cacao bean – the currency of the indigenous peoples – as a kind of barter currency, and it was used as such until the 1850s, when it was finally replaced by officially minted coins.

Coffee to cattle

In 1808, Costa Rica's governor, Tomás de Acosta, brought **coffee** here from Jamaica; a highland plant, it flourished in the mineral-rich soil of the Valle Central. Legislators, keen to develop a cash crop, offered incentives to farmers – San José's town council gave free land and coffee seedlings to settlers, while families in Cartago were ordered to plant coffee bushes in their backyards. In 1832, there were enough beans available for export, and real wealth – at least for the exporters and coffee brokers – came in 1844, when the London market for Costa Rican coffee opened up. It was the country's main source of income until war and declining prices devastated the domestic market in the 1930s.

Heredia and Cartago provinces still earn much of their money from coffee, and today the Valle Central remains the country's most economically productive region. **Fruit**, including mangoes and strawberries, is cultivated in Alajuela; **vegetables** thrive in the volcanic soil near Poás and Irazú; and on the slopes of Irazú and Barva, Holstein **cattle** provide much of the country's milk. Venture anywhere outside the urban areas and you will see evidence of the continued presence of the yeoman farmer, as small plots and family holdings survive despite the population pressure that continues to erode available farmland.

Alajuela and around

At first sight, it can be hard to distinguish **ALAJUELA** from San José, but slowly the pleasant realization dawns that you can smell bougainvillea rather than petrol fumes as you walk down the street. The city was founded in 1657 and remains a largely agricultural centre. Its most cherished historical figure is the drummer-boy-cum-martyr **Juan Santamaría**, hero of the 1856 Battle of Rivas (see box, p.265) and subject of his own **museum**, about the only formal attraction in the centre; he also has his own festival, the **Día de Juan Santamaría** (April 11, the anniversary of the great battle), when the townsfolk kick up their heels with bands, parades and fireworks.

Alajuela can be seen in half a day or so, but it makes a convenient base for visiting the surrounding sights (most of the Valle Central's main attractions lie within a 30km radius, and the city is considerably warmer than San José) or a useful place to stay if you've an early-morning flight to catch – the **airport** is just a five-minute bus ride away, compared to forty minutes or more from the capital.

Museo Juan Santamaría

Parque Central • Tues–Sat 10am–6pm • Free • ☎ 2441 4775, ⓦ museojuansantamaria.go.cr

Most impressive of the old colonial buildings that fringe the Parque Central is the sturdy whitewashed former jail that now houses the **Museo Juan Santamaría**, entered

---

ANYONE FOR COFFEE?

Some of the world's finest coffee grows on the cultivated slopes of the Valle Central, and a number of the region's *fincas* and estates run **tours** of their plantations (generally US$15–35; 1hr–2hr 30min), which take you through the process from planting and picking to drying and roasting. The area is home to five of the country's eight regional **coffee regions**: from west to east, they are the Valle Occidental, the Valle Central, Tres Ríos, Orosí and Turrialba. Differences in altitude, soil composition and production methods mean that the beans harvested from each estate have their own individual characteristics, which a good barista can help you detect. Coffee tasting, or **cupping** (*catación*), is an art in itself, and at the end of most tours you'll learn how to measure a cup's uniformity, its complexity, dry fragrance, wet aroma, brightness (actually its acidity) and body, as well as the finish it leaves on the palate.

The following *fincas* and estates are open year-round but are best visited during the **picking season** (Oct–Feb), when you can often get involved in harvesting the bright red berries and roasting them yourself:

Café Britt Barva; Valle Central. Slick group tours from the country's largest coffee exporter, including a musical rendition of the history of Costa Rican coffee, plus more insightful tasting tours for aficionados. See p.136.

Café Cristina Paraíso; Orosí. Owner-led tours (by appointment only) of this environmentally sound family set-up on the edge of the beautiful Valle Orosí. See p.148.

Doka Estate San Luis de Sabanilla; Valle Central. Doka, which produces Café Tres Generaciones, boasts the oldest *beneficio* (water mill) in Costa Rica and offers ox-cart rides around its estate. See p.126.

Finca Rosa Blanca Coffee Plantation & Inn Santa Bárbara; Valle Central. Highly personal insight into the workings of a small-scale organic coffee farm – and its sustainable practices – with an experienced and informative barista. See p.137.

Hacienda Espíritu Santo Naranjo; Valle Occidental. Part of a co-operative of producers in the Naranjo area, whose friendly guides lead you on a historical tour through their compact plantation. See p.129.

ALAJUELA

1 (3km), 2 (5.5km), 3 (6.5km), 4 (7km), 5 (7km), Doka Estate (10km) & Volcán Poás (38km)

Zoo-Ave (7km), La Garita (14km) & Atenas (23km)

Estadio Alejandro Morera Soto (300m)

Iglesia de Santo Cristo de la Agonía (200m)

Heredia (12km) & San José (18km)

AVENIDA 9
AVENIDA 7
AVENIDA 5
AVENIDA 3
AVENIDA 1
AVENIDA CENTRAL
AVENIDA 2
AVENIDA 4
AVENIDA 6
AVENIDA 8
AVENIDA 8
AVENIDA 10
AVENIDA 10
AVENIDA 12
AVENIDA 16
AVENIDA 20

CALLE 10
CALLE 8
CALLE 6
CALLE 4
CALLE 2
CALLE CENTRAL
CALLE 1
CALLE 3

Police
Museo Juan Santamaría
Banco de San José
Banco Nacional
Catedral de Alajuela
Parque Central
Scotiabank
★ Taxis
Mercado Central
Tienda Llobet
Tuasa terminal
Estación al Pacífico
Banco de Costa Rica
Teatro Municipal de Alajuela
Parque Juan Santamaría
Local Buses
Parque Los Niños
★ Station Wagon Alajuela buses

La Radial bus station

Hospital San Rafael

Interamericana (2km) & Juan Santamaría International Airport (2.2km)

● SHOPPING
Goodlight Books   1

■ ACCOMMODATION
Cortez Azul   7
Hostel Trotamundos   8
Hotel 1915   6
Hotel Buena Vista   3
Maleku Hostel   10
Pura Vida Retreat & Spa   4
Tacacori EcoLodge   5
Villa Pacande   1
Los Volcanes   9
Xandari Resort & Spa   2

● EATING
Café Delicias   3
Café Don Mayo   4
El Chante Vegano   1
Jalapeños Central   2
Restaurante Chiwake   5

0   100
metres

2

through a pretty tiled courtyard garden lined with long wooden benches. The curiously monastic atmosphere of the rooms is almost more interesting than the small collection, which runs the gamut from mid-nineteenth-century maps of Costa Rica to crumbly portraits of figures involved in the battle of 1856. Temporary exhibitions showcase local crafts or modern art, while the auditorium hosts cultural lectures (in Spanish) on regional topics.

2 Catedral de Alajuela

Parque Central • No fixed opening hours • Free

Flanking the eastern end of the square, the white-domed **Catedral de Alajuela** possesses no great architectural merit – not helped by the damage it received in an earthquake in 1990 – though it does have pretty floor tiles, round stained-glass windows and a large cupola bizarrely decorated with *trompe l'oeil* balconies.

Iglesia de Santo Cristo de la Agonía

5 blocks east of the Parque Central • No fixed opening hours • Free

The **Iglesia de Santo Cristo de la Agonía** was constructed in 1935, but looks much older, with a Baroque exterior painted in two-tone cream. Head inside for a look at the lovely wooden, gilt-edged altar, with naive Latin American motifs and gilt-painted columns edging the bright tiled floor. Realist murals, apparently painted from life, show various stages in the development of Christianity in Costa Rica, depicting monsignors and indigenous people gathering with middle-class citizens to receive the Word.

ARRIVAL AND DEPARTURE	ALAJUELA AND AROUND

By plane Most international flights arrive at Juan Santamaría International Airport, under 3km from Alajuela; most hotels and hostels include airport pick-up, or you can take a taxi (around ₡3000) or catch a bus (signed, unsurprisingly, "Alajuela") into town.

By local bus The Tuasa buses that run frequently to and from San José and Heredia use the station on C 8, four blocks west of the Parque Central. Station Wagon Alajuela buses from San José drop you off on Av 4, 50m southwest of Parque Juan Santamaría, a few minutes' walk from the centre. The daily bus to Volcán Poás uses the Tuasa terminal. Other local services leave from the Estacíon al Pacífico on Av 2, C 8/10, or from one of the surrounding jumble of bus stops.

Destinations Atenas (every 30min; 1hr); Grecia (every 30min; 1hr); La Garita, for Zoo-Ave (every 30min; 15min); Heredia (every 15min; 45min); Naranjo (every 30min; 1hr 35min); Sabanilla, for Doka Estate (every 30min; 40min); San José (every 10min; 20min); Sarchí (every 30min; 1hr 15min); Volcán Poás (departs 9.15am, returns 2.30pm; around 1hr 30min).

IN A LIGA THEIR OWN

Football (*fútbol*) is big in Costa Rica, even more so since the country's stirring performances in the 2014 World Cup, when the Ticos beat Uruguay and Italy, drew with England and knocked out Greece on penalties, before losing (also on penalties) to the Netherlands in the quarter-finals. Alajuela is home to one of the most historic teams in the country: **Liga Deportivo Alajuelense** (☎ 2443 1617, ⓦ lda.cr), who ply their trade at the impressive 18,000-seat Estadio Alejandro Morera Soto, northeast of the centre on C 9, at Av 9. One of the original founders of the national league in 1921, LDA have won the Primera División 29 times, most recently in 2013. Their great rivals are Deportivo Saprissa from San José – derbies between the two teams, known as the **Clásico de Costa Rica**, can be fiery affairs, and are certainly worth catching if you can.

Matches are played on Sundays during the winter (late July to late Dec) and summer (mid-Jan to mid-May) championships; **tickets** start around US$20 and can be bought at the stadium, or in advance on ☎ 2206 7770 or at ⓦ specialticket.net.

By long-distance bus Buses for destinations further afield depart from La Radial station (officially known as Multicentro La Estacíon), 75m south of the Shell station, on C 4. Many other buses travelling from northern Costa Rica to San José stop at the airport, from where you can quickly and easily reach Alajuela.

Destinations La Fortuna (3 daily; 3hr 30min); Liberia (10 daily; 4hr); Puntarenas (every 30min–1hr; 2hr 10min); San Carlos (14 daily; 2hr).

By car If you're driving from San José, head in the direction of the airport on Hwy-1 (the Interamericana, or Autopista General Cañas). The turn-off to Alajuela is 17km northwest of San José – don't use the underpass or you'll end up at the airport.

By train The much-delayed railway link between Alajuela and San José was still not up and running at the time of research, but may well be by the time you read this. Check ⓦ trenurbano.co.cr for updates.

GETTING AROUND AND INFORMATION

By car Most car rental agencies in and around the airport will bring your car to your hotel in Alajuela; otherwise, try the in-house travel agency at *Hotel 1915* (see p.125).

Goodlight Books The best source of information in town – alongside some of the better hotels and hostels – is Goodlight Books on Av 3, C 1/3 (daily 9am–6pm; ☎ 2430 4083), where staff can usually help with public transport questions and the like.

ACCOMMODATION

Due to its proximity to the airport, **accommodation** fills up quickly, and it's important to reserve ahead even in the rainy season. Hotels in Alajuela itself are generally underwhelming; the finest options are actually just **outside town**, including the *Xandari Resort & Spa*, one of Costa Rica's loveliest hotels. Most places can organize **tours** of the surrounding attractions.

IN TOWN

Cortez Azul Av 5, C 2/4 ☎ 2443 6145, ⓦ hotel cortezazul.com. This hostel is run by a welcoming local artist (whose works hang on the walls) and has a dorm and a selection of rooms, most with shared bathrooms. The cheapest rooms are pretty claustrophobic, so it's well worth going for one of the larger US$30–35 options. There's also a communal kitchen looking onto a small garden, and staff can arrange car hire and tours. Dorm US$12, doubles US$20

Hostel Trotamundos Av 5, C 2/4 ☎ 2430 5832, ⓦ hosteltrotamundos.com. Inexpensive and cheerful, this busy hostel is no palace, but the dorms and rooms (with shared bathrooms) are comfortable enough for a night or two. Make sure you pack your earplugs though – it can get very noisy. Rates include a free airport drop-off. Dorms US$12, doubles US$35

Hotel 1915 C 2, Av 5/7 ☎ 2440 7163, ⓦ 1915hotel .com. Alajuela's oldest hotel is also its finest, with elegantly subtle rooms dotted around a large living area split by an imposing staircase. All the rooms are en suite and come with fridge and TV; those with a/c cost an extra US$20, while family-sized apartments cost US$110. The in-house tour agency can also arrange car rental and flights. US$65

★**Maleku Hostel** Just off Av 20, opposite Hospital San Rafael ☎ 2430 4304, ⓦ malekuhostel.com. This great-value, family-run hostel is the best budget option in Alajuela, offering large, clean rooms (with shared bathrooms) and comfortable beds. The friendly staff – on hand for travel advice – set the sociable scene. Free airport transfers, too. Dorms US$15, doubles US$38

★**Los Volcanes** Av 3, C Central/2 ☎ 2441 0525, ⓦ hotellosvolcanes.com. Dating back to the 1920s, and once home to the Red Cross, this townhouse is now a charming low-cost hotel. Standard rooms (with shared bathrooms) are comfortable enough, but it's worth paying extra to enjoy the a/c and flat-screen TV that comes with the superior ones (US$70–81). The friendly owner runs a travel agency and offers a free shuttle service to/from the airport. US$52

OUT OF TOWN

Hotel Buena Vista 6.5km northeast of Alajuela ☎ 2442 8595, ⓦ hotelbuenavistacr.com. This peaceful hotel's prime hilltop location offers superlative views of the Poás, Barva and Irazú volcanoes. The en suites are spacious and elegantly decorated, there's a good restaurant on-site, and rates include airport transfers. US$180

Pura Vida Retreat & Spa 6.2km north of Alajuela ☎ 2483 0033, ⓦ rrresorts.com. Accommodation at this lifestyle retreat for yoga enthusiasts ranges from swish pagodas (US$510) with jacuzzis to luxury "tentalows" with shared bathrooms. Most people come here on a package: three-night "mind + body + spirit" retreats start at US$1390 for two and include yoga classes, guided tours, a massage at the on-site spa and oodles of nutritious nosh. Rates include full board. US$260

Tacacori EcoLodge 7km north of Alajuela on the road to Carizal ☎ 2430 5846, ⓦ tacacori.com. Charming, French-run lodge with a strong environmental ethos and bright *casitas* (each sleeping up to two) featuring queen-sized beds set amid orchid-filled gardens. Rates include a good breakfast, but there's no restaurant. US$128

Villa Pacande Opposite Escuela de Hiquis, 3km north of Alajuela on the road to Poás ☎ 2431 0783, ⓦ villapacande.com. Great budget option if you want to stay in the countryside just outside town. Rooms (triples

2

and quads also available) in this airy villa have comfy beds and smart tiled flooring, and there's a lovely suntrap garden. The bus into Alajuela passes every 20min, or a taxi costs around ₡3000. US$45

★**Xandari Resort & Spa** 5.5km north of Alajuela, clearly signposted from the main road to Poás ☎ 2443 2020, ⌨ xandari.com/costarica. Designed and decorated by its creative owners (he's an architect, she's an artist), this blissfully tranquil luxury hotel sits high above the city, with splendid views over the Valle Central. The spacious villas

(sleeping up to two), each with their own terrace, feel very private, hidden throughout the tropical gardens, and the Star Suite (sleeping up to six; US$701) is aptly named to say the least. Pamper yourself at the spa, splash about in the three swimming pools or wander through the attractive grounds, complete with waterfalls and a verdant coffee plantation. The top-notch restaurant's constantly changing menu features organic vegetables grown in their own greenhouse. One of the villas, an Ultra Plus (US$452), can accommodate travellers with disabilities. US$322

EATING

Alajuela has several decent **restaurants**, and you can dig into particularly tasty ceviche and *casados* at the friendly **Mercado Central** (daily 11am–10pm), around which there are also several inexpensive Chinese joints. Alajuela's **nightlife**, though, is fairly limited, and most bars close around 11pm.

Café Delicias Av 1, at C 1 ☎ 2440 3681, ⌨ cafedelicias .com. Breezy, open-sided café serving good coffee (₡1100–3000), breakfasts, sandwiches, pastries and cakes. It's a relaxing spot, despite the colour-clash of the lime-green ceiling and red and yellow walls. Mon–Sat 8am–9pm.

Café Don Mayo Av 2, at C 2 ☎ 2430 6920, ⌨ cafedon mayocr.com. Run by a local producer, this "Brew and Espresso Bar" serves up excellent coffee (₡990–3300) – made by machine, AeroPress, Chemex filter or French press, depending on your preference – as well as cakes, pastries, sandwiches and simple breakfasts. Daily 9am–6pm.

El Chante Vegano Av 5, C 3/5 ☎ 8911 4787, ⌨ el chantevegano.com. If you've overindulged, this vegan (and organic) restaurant is the place to come. The menu features wholesome soups, salads, sandwiches, pizzas, and juices: the quinoa burger and the falafel-filled pitas are both worth a look. Mains ₡3800–6000. Tues–Sun 11am–8pm.

★**Jalapeños Central** C 1, Av 1/3 ☎ 2430 4027,

⌨ facebook.com/JalapenosCentralCR. Run by a Colombian-American, this cheerful Tex-Mex joint offers fajitas, quesadillas, tacos, burritos, enchiladas and more, plus good-value set lunches (₡3685) and dinners (₡4510), and potent margaritas. The colourful dining room is decked out with US licence plates, sombreros and cuddly chilli toys. The owner also runs *Sr Patacon & Dona Arepa*, a few doors down, which serves up tasty fried plantains and *arepas* (cornmeal tortillas; around ₡2300); both menus are available at both restaurants. Mon–Sat 11.30am–9pm, Sun 11.30am–8pm.

Restaurante Chiwake Av 8, at C 3 ☎ 2430 7887, ⌨ chiwakecr.com. Excellent Peruvian restaurant, authentic down to its Pisco sours. There's a wide range of fish, prawn and octopus ceviches (₡4100–8500), plus classics like *aji de gallina* (shredded chicken in a smooth, spicy sauce) and *lomito saltado* (steak strips, onions, tomatoes, chips and rice in a spicy sauce). Mon & Sun noon–9pm, Tues–Thurs noon–10pm, Fri & Sat noon–11pm.

SHOPPING

Goodlight Books Av 3, C 1/3 ☎ 2430 4083. Offers an extensive selection of secondhand English-language novels, travel guides, maps and phrasebooks, as well as a

range of Spanish-, French- and German-language books. You can also get good coffee, *empanadas* and cakes. Daily 9am–6pm.

DIRECTORY

Banks and exchange Banco Nacional, opposite the Parque Central; Banco de Costa Rica, C 2, Av Central/2; Scotiabank, Av Central, at C1. All have 24hr ATMs.
Hospital San Rafael, Av 12 (☎ 2436 1000).

Police Public ☎ 2440 8889 or ☎ 2440 8890, emergencies ☎ 911. There's a police station on C2, Av 3/5.
Post office C 1, at Av 5 (Mon–Fri 8am–5.30pm, Sat 8am–noon).

Doka Estate

10km north of Alajuela • Tours daily 9am, 10am, 11am, 1.30pm & 2.30pm, Mon–Fri also 3.30pm; 1hr • US$20 • ☎ 2449 5152, ⌨ dokaestate.com • Buses run from Alajuela to the nearby town of Sabanilla, from where a taxi costs around ₡3000 (a taxi direct from Alajuela costs about ₡14,000); the estate can also arrange transportation (phone for details)

Set amid rolling coffee fields, the **Doka Estate** is one of the most historic coffee farms in the country. The Vargas family have been growing beans here for over seventy years – their *beneficio* (water mill) is the oldest in Costa Rica – and today produce a variety of roasts for Café Tres Generaciones. You can only visit on a **tour**, on which enthusiastic guides cover the entire coffee-making process and you finish with a free tasting – look out for their Peaberry Estate, a smooth medium roast containing the *caracolillo* bean, a mutation that gives the cup a sweeter flavour. The tour also takes in Doka's small butterfly farm (included in the price), and you can grab breakfast or lunch at the on-site restaurant (daily 7–9am & 11.30am–2pm).

Zoo-Ave

7km west of Alajuela • Daily 9am–5pm • US$20 • ☎ 2433 8989, ⓦ rescateanimalzooave.org • La Garita buses from Alajuela pass right by Zoo-Ave (daily every 30min–1hr; 15min)

Central America's largest aviary, **Zoo-Ave** is just about the best place in the country – besides the wild – to see Costa Rica's fabulous **birds**. The exceptionally well run rescue and rehabilitation centre has large, clean cages and carefully tended grounds. Many of the birds fly free, fluttering around in a flurry of raucous colours: look out for the kaleidoscopic scarlet macaws and wonderful blue parrots. Other birds include chestnut-mandibled toucans and resplendent quetzals – Zoo-Ave is one of the few places in the world where you can get up close to these mythical creatures – and you'll also see **primates**, from monkeys to marmosets, plus a variety of the country's resident **reptiles**, including crocodiles and iguanas.

La Garita and Atenas

Famed for their wonderful weather, **LA GARITA**, 14km west of Alajuela, and **ATENAS**, a further 9km along Hwy-3, were deemed by *National Geographic* to have the best climate in the world; fruits, ornamental plants and flowers flourish here, as does maize, a fact most evident in the corn restaurants that line the road between the two. The area has a noted botanical garden, but sees less tourist traffic since the opening of the Caldera Highway in 2010, which links San José to the Pacific and has superseded Hwy-3 as the quickest route to the coast.

At the time of writing, the **bungee jump** operations just north of La Garita were suspended; if you're interested, check locally to see if they've reopened when you visit.

Botanical Orchid Garden

Off Hwy-3, just beyond La Garita • Tues–Sun 8.30am–5pm, last entry 4.30pm • US$12, under-13s US$6 • ☎ 2487 8095, ⓦ orchidgardencr.com • Buses from Alajuela to Atenas (daily every 30min; 1hr) can drop you off on Hwy-3, from where it's an 800m walk up to the gardens

A welcome recipient of the area's clement climate, the **Botanical Orchid Garden** is home to some 150 orchid species, half of them native. Walking trails (accessible to wheelchairs and buggies) lead through extensive gardens awash with colour (the blooms are at their peak from Jan–March); keep an eye out for the *Guaria morada*, a delicate purple orchid that is Costa Rica's national flower.

ACCOMMODATION   **LA GARITA AND ATENAS**

B&B Vista Atenas Sabana Larga, 3km west of Atenas ☎ 2446 4272, ⓦ vistaatenas.com. Perched on a steep hill in Sabana Larga, this peaceful B&B offers lovely views across the Valle Central, particularly from the pool terrace. The welcoming Belgian owner fosters a homely ambience – many of the guests in the *cabinas* (sleeping up to two) are long-term, repeat visitors – and has made her property ecofriendly, with a solar-powered hot-water system and

freshwater well to the replanted grounds. Doubles <u>US$75</u>, *cabinas* <u>US$80</u>

Orchid Tree Río Grande, 4km southeast of Atenas ☎ 2446 0852, ⓦ orchidtreecostarica.net. The airy *Orchid Tree* has four tastefully furnished, spacious en suites, with a vague Balinese influence – for example, the open-sided living areas. There's also an inviting swimming pool (with a wet bar), set in lush tropical gardens. <u>US$90</u>

2

Sarchí and around

Touted as Costa Rica's centre for arts and crafts, **SARCHÍ**, 30km northwest of Alajuela, is famous for producing the brightly painted ox-carts (*carretas*) that have become the country's national symbol. Its setting is pretty enough, between precipitous verdant hills, but don't expect to see picturesque scenes of craftsmen sitting in small historic shops, sculpting marble or carving wood – Sarchí is an overly commercialized, touristy village, and most of the factories are rather soulless showrooms. In a few, however, you can watch carts and furniture being painted and assembled, and at the very least, the ox-carts and rocking chairs are less expensive here than elsewhere in the country.

Straggling along the road for several kilometres, the village is split by the Río Trojas into **Sarchí Sur**, essentially a collection of roadside workshops (*fábricas*) and furniture stores (*mueblerías*), and **Sarchí Norte**, a residential area further up the hill. Besides the shops and factories, the town's only site of interest is Sarchí Norte's pretty pink-and-white **church**; inside, its tiles are delicate pastel shades of pink and green. The **giant ox-cart** in the little park fronting the church is a record-breaking 14m long and weighs in at two tonnes; it was built in 2006 by Taller Eloy Alfaro, the only workshop in the country still making ox-carts the traditional way (see box below).

Iglesia de la Nuestra Señora de las Mercedes, Grecia

Grecia is 12km southwest of Sarchí; the church faces the town square • Frequent buses run to Grecia from Alajuela (every 30min; around 1hr) and San José (from La Coca-Cola; every 30min; around 1hr)

The small town of **GRECIA** is noticeable for its remarkable *fin-de-siècle* church, the **Iglesia de la Nuestra Señora de las Mercedes**. After their first church burned down, the

---

THE CARRETA DE SARCHÍ

The **Carreta de Sarchí** or Sarchí ox-cart was first produced by enterprising local families for the immigrant settlers who arrived at the beginning of the twentieth century to run the coffee plantations. The original designs featured simple geometric shapes, though the ox-carts sold today are kaleidoscopically painted, square creations built to be hauled by a single ox or team of two oxen. Moorish in origin, the designs can be traced back to immigrants from the Spanish provinces of Andalucía and Granada. Full-scale carts (US$1000-plus) are rarely sold, but many smaller-scale coffee-table-sized replicas are made for tourists (US$250–500), while dinky desktop versions can be picked up for around US$5.

FÁBRICAS DE CARRETAS

Cooperativa de Artesanías y Mueblerías de Sarchí Sarchí Norte, on the right-hand side of the main road just after the petrol station (look for the large spinning ox-cart wheel out front) ☏ 2454 4050, ⊛ coopearsarl.com/coopearsa_rl/index.html. While their prices are generally lower than the rest, they haven't skimped on quality: this is as good a place as any to browse for ox-carts, made by water-wheel-powered machines. They also stock traditional wooden handicrafts and furniture. Daily 8am–6pm.

Fábrica de Carretas Joaquín Chaverri Sarchí Sur, on the left-hand side of the main road as you enter the village ☏ 2454 4411, ⊛ facebook.com /FabricaDeCarretasJoaquinChaverri. Wander around the painting workshop and see dozens of ox-carts in progress at Sarchí's largest ox-cart factory, which has been in business since 1903. They'll arrange shipping and transport for souvenirs, and accept credit cards. Daily 8am–5pm.

Taller Eloy Alfaro Sarchí Norte, 125m up Calle 1 de Eva, one block east of the football field ☏ 2454 4131. Alfaro and his sons have been crafting *carretas* since 1923, and you can watch the younger generation still using age-old methods in their rickety wooden workshop, the last of its kind in Sarchí. Mon–Sat 5.30am–9pm, Sun 6am–9pm.

prudent residents decided to take no chances and built the second out of pounded sheets of metal, imported from Belgium. The white-trimmed rust-coloured result is surprisingly beautiful, with an altar that's a testament to Latin American Baroque froth, made entirely from intricate marble and rising up into the eaves of the church like a wedding cake.

Hacienda Espíritu Santo

5km northwest of Sarchí, just outside the town of Naranjo • Tours daily 9am, 11am, 1pm & 3pm; 1hr 30min • US$25 • ☎ 2450 3838, Ⓦ espiritusantocoffeetour.com • Local buses run from Sarchí to Naranjo (daily every 30min; 20min); Espíritu Santo is a signposted 800m walk west from the Banco Nacional, opposite the Parque Central in the middle of town

The red berries lining the fields at **Hacienda Espíritu Santo**, a co-operative coffee plantation, end up in the bags of Café Bandola that you'll see in all the stores around here. Thanks to the local climate, the beans are of the Valle Occidental variety – something that is explored in greater depth on one of the hacienda's **tours** (the only way to visit), which also cover the nursery, mill and roasting room, as well as a walk around the plantation itself. Tours end with that all-important tasting.

ARRIVAL AND DEPARTURE

By bus Buses from Alajuela leave daily for Sarchí every 30min (1hr 15min); buses back can be hailed on the main road from Sarchí Norte to Sarchí Sur. From San José, a daily express service (Mon–Fri 12.15pm, 5.30pm & 5.55pm, Sat

SARCHÍ AND AROUND

noon; 1hr 30min) runs from La Coca-Cola; buses return via Alajuela. Alternatively, take the bus to Naranjo from La Coca-Cola (daily every 30min), and switch there for a local service to Sarchí.

ACCOMMODATION

Hotel Daniel Zamora C 2 ☎ 2454 4596. The best of Sarchí's handful of hotels is *Hotel Daniel Zamora*, located opposite the eastern end of the football field. It resembles

a motel, with simple but clean rooms with a/c and private bathrooms. <u>US$40</u>

DIRECTORY

Banks and exchange Banco Nacional, on the main road opposite the football field, changes dollars, as does a smaller branch in the Plaza de la Artesanía.

Post office The post office is 50m east of the football field (Mon–Fri 8am–5pm).

Parque Nacional Juan Castro Blanco and around

7km north of the village of Bajos del Toro • Daily 8am–4pm. There's theoretically a US$10 entry fee, but rarely anyone to collect it

Harbouring the headwaters for five rivers, the 143-square-kilometre **PARQUE NACIONAL JUAN CASTRO BLANCO** is one of Costa Rica's least-explored national parks, partly due to its isolated location but mostly because of its seemingly permanent status as a national-park-in-waiting – scant marked trails and minimal tourist infrastructure in the surrounding villages has made it something of an off-the-beaten-path destination for **hikers** and **wildlife** enthusiasts. Created in 1992 to protect the Platanar and Porvenir volcanoes from logging, more than half the park consists of lush primary forest. Rare species of bird, such as resplendent quetzal and black guan, can be spotted here, while armadillo, tapir, red brocket deer and white-faced capuchin monkeys also roam the park. The five rivers in Juan Castro Blanco are also filled with trout, which has made the park a popular destination for anglers. If you need a guide, try the hotels and restaurants in **Bajos del Toro** – which is not much more than a cluster of corrugated houses – as most can hook you up with a knowledgeable local.

Catarata del Toro

6km north of Bajos del Toro • Mon–Sat 7am–5pm • US$14, under-13s US$7 • ☎ 2761 0681, ⓦ www.catarata-del-toro.com

Beyond Bajos del Toro the road climbs for another 6km before coming to the **Catarata del Toro**, a private reserve with a hugely impressive waterfall that plunges 100m into the caldera of an extinct volcano. Trails lead through primary forest to the base of the falls or around the crater rim; the more adventurous can abseil right alongside the thundering cascade (US$50). You can also stay here (see below).

2

ARRIVAL AND TOURS

By car If you want to visit independently, you'll need your own car. The smoother road from Sarchí is the easiest approach, the rough roads from San Carlos or Zarcero the more spectacular, providing tremendous

PN JUAN CASTRO BLANCO AND AROUND

views as you zigzag down into Bajos del Toro, 7km from the park entrance.

Tours Mapache Tours (☎ 2479 8333, ⓦ mapachetours.com) in La Fortuna can arrange full-day tours (around US$100).

ACCOMMODATION

★ **Bosque de Paz** 1.5km west of Bajos del Toro, on the road to Zarcero ☎ 2234 6676, ⓦ bosquedepaz.com. Top birdwatching lodge, set in its own cloudforest reserve that features 22km of walking trails and is home to over 330 species of bird, including quetzal and three-wattled bellbird. The dozen attractively rustic rooms have wrought-iron beds and look out onto the surrounding forest. US$246

Catarata del Toro 6km north of Bajos del Toro ☎ 2761 0681, ⓦ www.catarata-del-toro.com. The three wooden cabins located within the Catarata del Toro reserve are simple and (for the area) good value, though they have little in the way of mod cons. They sleep up to four people each, but the rates here are based on double occupancy. There's also an open-sided restaurant. US$80

★ **El Silencio Lodge & Spa** Just south of Bajos del Toro, on the road to Sarchí ☎ 2761 0301, ⓦ elsilenciolodge.com. Nestled at the foot of a thick wall of cloudforest, the eye-wateringly-expensive, ultra-stylish suites and villas (sleep up to six; two wheelchair-accessible) at this tranquil eco-retreat have bamboo-shrouded outdoor jacuzzis and wooden terraces that enjoy glorious jungle views. There's a bevy of treatments available at the therapeutically sited spa, and various guided hikes head off into the lodge's private reserve. Profits help fund a local social programme. Two-night minimum stay (rates here are per night and include a guided hike with an "eco-concierge"). Suites US$407, villas US$777

San Ramón

At the far western edge of the Valle Central, the colonial town and agricultural centre of **SAN RAMÓN** sits amid verdant rolling hills surrounded by coffee plantations and sugar cane fields. As a crossroads town between San José and La Fortuna, Liberia and the Pacific coast, it receives plenty of tourist traffic, and its leafy Parque Central, home to the imposing Gothic-style **Iglesia de San Ramón** and a couple of museums, makes a decent destination while waiting for onward connections.

Centro Cultural e Histórico José Figueres Ferrer

Opposite the northern side of the church • Tues–Sat 10am–6pm • Free • ☎ 2447 2178, ⓦ centrojosefigueres.org

Known as the "City of Poets and Presidents", San Ramón has given birth to no fewer than five of Costa Rica's former leaders, most notably the visionary and social reformer **José "Don Pepe" Figueres Ferrer** (see p.414), who famously abolished the military in 1948. His childhood home has been converted into the **Centro Cultural e Histórico José Figueres Ferrer**, a museum dedicated to his life and politics, which also hosts rolling art and photographic exhibitions.

ARRIVAL AND INFORMATION

By bus Buses arrive at and depart from C 16, Av 1/3, 150m west of the Mercado Central.

SAN RAMÓN

Destinations Alajuela (hourly; 45min); San Carlos (3 daily; 1hr 30min); San José (hourly; 1hr); Zarcero (7–8 daily; 1hr).

ACCOMMODATION AND EATING

Aromas Café 150m southwest of the Parque Central · ☎ 2447 1414, ⓦ aromascafecr.com. Clean, airy café with a garden courtyard out back; fill up on empanadas, sandwiches or a small selection of mains, or indulge in some coconut flan or lemon pie (₡900–1500). Daily 8am–7pm.

La Posada Hotel Four blocks north of the church ☎ 2445 7359, ⓦ posadahotel.net. The best accommodation option in San Ramón, La Posada Hotel has rooms with wide-screen TV, super-clean bathrooms and regal decorative flourishes such as ornate wooden bedheads. Breakfast, though, costs extra. US$60

2

Reserva Bosque Nuboso Los Ángeles

Around 20km northwest of San Ramón · Daily 8am–4pm · US$20, paid at the office, some 500m from the reserve itself · Guides cost US$30–40 and are available from the reserve office · ☎ 2461 0643

The **RESERVA BOSQUE NUBOSO LOS ÁNGELES** is a less crowded alternative to the larger and far more famous cloudforest at Monteverde. Climbing from 700m to nearly 1400m, Los Ángeles' twenty square kilometres contain a number of habitats and microclimates, including dark, impenetrable cloudforest, often shrouded in light misty cloud and resounding with the calls of monkeys.

Both of the easy dirt-track **trails** – Sendero Anastacio Alfaro (2km; 50min) and Sendero Alberto Brenes (4km; 2hr 30min) – give a great introduction to the reserve's flora and fauna, and you'll stand a good chance of spotting coatis and raccoons. Additional activities include **horseriding** (US$20/hr) and a **zipline canopy tour** (US$50); book at the reserve office.

ARRIVAL AND DEPARTURE — RESERVA BOSQUE NUBOSO LOS ÁNGELES

By car To reach the reserve from San Ramón, head north and take the right fork opposite the hospital towards La Fortuna and follow the road until you reach the hamlet of Los Ángeles Norte, from where Villa Blanca (see below) and the reserve are well signed (note that the last 9km is down a bumpy potholed track).

By taxi A taxi from San Ramón costs US$25–30.

ACCOMMODATION

★Villa Blanca Cloud Forest Hotel and Nature Reserve Reserva Bosque Nubosoe Los Ángeles ☎ 2461 0300, ⓦ villablanca-costarica.com. The traditional en-suite casitas (sleeping up to four) at Villa Blanca come complete with wood-burning stoves and are set within the Reserva Bosque Nuboso Los Ángeles. The hotel was the first in Costa Rica to host an INBio Research Station, here to investigate the reserve's staggering variety of moths (some 3000 species). You'll spot a fair few of them on the short trail that runs around the forest fringes, while the hotel runs various guided day and night tours deeper into the reserve (US$26/2hr). There's also an on-site spa (treatments from US$75), and a fine-dining restaurant, though its prices reflect the captive audience. US$237

Zarcero

ZARCERO, 52km northwest of Alajuela on Hwy-141, sits at more than 1700m, almost at the highest point of this stretch of the Cordillera Central in an astounding landscape where precipitous inclines plunge into deep gorges, and contented Holstein cattle munch grass in the valleys. A pleasant mountain town, Zarcero's focal point is its Parque Central, dotted with a motley collection of fabulous, Doctor Seuss-like **topiary sculptures**: an elephant, a helicopter, a dinosaur, along with Gaudí-esque archways of scented hedges, all the work of Costa Rican landscape gardener Evangelisto Blanco.

Zarcero is also known for its organic produce as well as a fresh, white, relatively bland **cheese**, called palmito (heart-of-palm, which is what it looks like); you can buy it from any of the shops near the bus stop on the south side of the main square.

ARRIVAL AND DEPARTURE ZARCERO

By bus Daily buses leave from C 12, Av 7/9 in San José every 45min and from La Coca-Cola at 9.15am, 12.20pm, 4.20pm and 5.20pm (both 1hr 30min), arriving in Zarcero on the northern side of the main square; they depart from the southwest corner.
Destinations San Carlos (7–8 daily; 1hr); San José (every 45min); San Ramón (every 2hr; 1hr).

ACCOMMODATION

Rancho Amalia 5.5km south of Zarcero ☎ 2463 3137, ⦿ranchoamalia.com/en. Rustic cabins (with kitchens, and sleeping up to five people) are set in neatly tended gardens at this ranch, which runs excellent horseriding trips (from US$15; available to non-guests too). U̲S̲$̲9̲0̲

Parque Nacional Volcán Poás

38km north of Alajuela • Daily 8.30am–3.30pm • US$15; parking ₡1000 • ☎ 2482 2165, ⓦ sinac.go.cr

PARQUE NACIONAL VOLCÁN POÁS is home to one of the world's most accessible active volcanoes, with a history of eruptions dating back eleven million years. Poás's last gigantic blowout was on January 25, 1910, when it dumped 640,000 tonnes of ash on the surrounding area, and from time to time you may find the volcano off-limits due to sulphurous gas emissions and other seismic activities – it was closed for a while following the **Cinchona earthquake** in January 2009 (see box, p.134), but has since reopened. It's worth checking conditions with the park before setting off, and regardless you'll still need to get to the volcano before the clouds roll in, which they invariably do at around 10am.

The park

Though measuring just 65 square kilometres, Poás packs a punch: it's a strange, otherworldly landscape, dotted with smoking fumaroles (steam vents) and tough ferns and trees valiantly surviving regular scaldings with sulphurous gases – the battle-scarred *sombrilla de pobre*, or poor man's umbrella, looks the most woebegone. The volcano itself has blasted out three craters in its lifetime, and due to the more-or-less constant activity, the appearance of the **main crater** changes regularly – it's currently around 1600m wide and filled with milky turquoise water from which sulphurous gases waft and bubble (with a pH value of 0.8, this is reputably the most acidic lake on earth). Although it's an impressive sight, you'll probably only need about fifteen minutes' viewing and picture-snapping; when you've finished you can explore one of the short trails that lead off the main route to the crater.

The trails

From the visitor centre, a few very well-maintained, short and unchallenging **trails** lead through a rare type of cloudforest called **dwarf** or **stunted cloudforest**, a combination of pine-needle-like ferns, miniature bonsai-type trees and

WATCHING WILDLIFE AT VOLCÁN POÁS

Birds ply this temperate forest, from the colourful but shy quetzal to the robin and several species of hummingbird, including the endemic **Poás volcano hummingbird**, distinguished by its iridescent rose-red throat. Although a number of large **mammals** live in the confines of the park, including wildcats such as the margay, you're unlikely to spot them around the crater; one animal you will come across, however, is the small, green-yellow **Poás squirrel**, unique to the region.

THE *CARRETA DE SARCHÍ* (P.128) >

bromeliad-encrusted ancient arboreal cover, all of which have been kept clipped by the cold weather (temperatures can drop below freezing), continual cloud cover, and acid rain from the mouth of the volcano.

The **Crater Overlook Trail**, which winds around the main crater along a paved road, is only 750m long and is accessible to wheelchairs and pushchairs. A side trail (830m; 20–30min; last access 2.30pm) heads through the forest to the pretty, emerald **Lago Botos** that fills an extinct crater and is a lovely spot to picnic. Named for the pagoda-like tree commonly seen along its way, the **Escalonia Trail** (1km; 30min) starts at the picnic area (follow the signs), taking you through ground cover less stunted than that at the crater.

ARRIVAL AND INFORMATION

PARQUE NACIONAL VOLCÁN POÁS

By bus A Tuasa bus leaves daily from Av 2, C 12/14 in San José at 8.40am, travelling via their terminal in Alajuela (9.15am) and returning from the volcano at 2.30pm (around 1hr 30min).

By car and taxi If you want to reach Poás before the tour buses and, more importantly, dense cloud cover arrive, you'll need to either drive or take a taxi.

Tours Most people visit Poás on a prearranged tour (see box, p.121) arranged through a travel agency in San José or their hotel/hostel in Alajuela. From San José a

half-day tour costs around US$60, including return transport and guide, but typically not the entry fee; similar trips from Alajuela cost around US$50.

Visitor centre The park's visitor centre (daily 8.30am–3pm) shows film of the volcano – handy if the real thing is covered by cloud – and has a couple of displays explaining the science behind it; there's also a simple snack shop, but you're probably better off packing a picnic or grabbing lunch at one of the nearby restaurants (see opposite).

ACCOMMODATION

There is **no camping** allowed in the park, but there are plenty of places to stay in the vicinity, useful if you want to get a really early start to beat the clouds. There are a couple of comfortable **mountain lodges** on working dairy farms (though you'll need a car to get to them) and other, simpler *cabinas* lining the road leading up to the volcano and reached on the bus to Poás.

Lagunillas Lodge Signposted 2km south of the park, and down a very steep 1km rutted dirt track, accessible by 4WD only ☎8389 5842. Tico-owned, high-altitude lodge offering rustic rooms and *cabinas* (sleeping up to four) with simply breathtaking views. You can even catch your dinner from the on-site trout pond, or take a guided hike or horse trot through the surrounding forest. Doubles US$41, *cabinas* US$62

Poás Lodge 6km south of the park on the road from Alajuela ☎2482 1091, ⓦpoaslodge.com. Friendly Texan owners run this pleasant little spot on the road up to Poás. The neat and tidy rooms seem to hang out over the valley; the restaurant enjoys the same superb views and makes a great lunchtime stop for cheeseburgers and the like. US$85

Poás Volcano Lodge 6km east of Poasito, which is 10km before the park, on the road from Alajuela;

THE CINCHONA EARTHQUAKE

In the early afternoon of January 8, 2009, an **earthquake** measuring 6.2 on the Richter scale struck the area just west of Volcán Poás, leaving at least 34 people dead and making thousands homeless. The worst quake to hit Costa Rica in nearly 150 years, it destroyed the village of **Cinchona** and scythed through nearby **Vara Blanca**; **Poasito** and **Fraijanes** were also damaged, while landslides affected **Parque Nacional Volcán Poás** and buried parts of **La Paz Waterfall Gardens** (see opposite), stranding some 300 tourists in the process.

The area's return to normality has been slow. Aftershocks continued in the Valle Central throughout the year – more than 2000 **tremors** were registered along the Cinchona faultline in 2009 – and workers were still repairing damage to the region's roads and buildings more than a year on; the work is now complete. The national park and gardens are open again and a new community, **Nueva Cinchona** in Cariblanco, has been built 6km from the original to house 1200 of the survivors who lost their homes in the surrounding area.

when coming from Alajuela, take a right towards Vara Blanca ☎2482 2194, ⓦpoasvolcanolodge.com. Set on a working dairy farm, on the edge of the national park, this rustic lodge is a classy place to stay. The standard en-suite rooms are nice enough, but it's better to fork out for one with a view of the volcano

(US$245). Walking trails run through the extensive grounds, and there's a restaurant, bar, library, and basement games room with pool and ping-pong tables. The lodge is 5km from the La Paz Waterfall Gardens (see below) and offers discounted tickets to the gardens. US$145

EATING AND DRINKING

La Casa del Café de la Luis 10km north of Alajuela, on the road to Poás ☎2482 1535, ⓦdokaestate.com. Roadside outlet of the Doka Estate – and thereby serving some delicious Café Tres Generaciones roasts (₡1500–3000) – this lovely little café enjoys superb views of the surrounding coffee fields from its breezy balcony. Daily 7am–5pm.

★**Chubascos** Fraijanes, 12km south of the park on the road from Alajuela ☎2482 2280, ⓦchubascos.co.cr. This extremely welcoming and relaxed restaurant, overlooking a large garden, draws crowds for its superlative local cuisine – the *gallotes*, huge tortillas heaped with various goodies (from ₡3000) take some beating – and top-notch *casados*. The area around the volcano abounds with strawberry fields, and Chubascos makes one of the best strawberry *refrescos* in the country. Mon–Fri

10.30am–5pm, Sat & Sun 9.30am–5.30pm (restricted opening hours outside the peak season).

Colbert Restaurant About 1km past the Poás Volcano Lodge, in Vara Blanca ☎2482 2776. It can come as quite a surprise to stumble upon this smart French restaurant, perched on a hill at the eastern end of Vara Blanca, just beyond the petrol station. The menu includes such Gallic delights as French onion soup, rabbit fillet in Dijon mustard, and seafood casserole à La Rochelle, the chef's former haunt. Mains ₡8000–15,000. Mon–Wed & Fri–Sun noon–9pm.

Jaulares 15km north of Alajuela, on the road to Poás ☎2482 2155, ⓦjaulares.com. Simple restaurant with *típico* dishes (from ₡25,000), using local produce cooked on a wood-burning stove (try the *sopa negra*), and a generous buffet. Live music on Sat. Mon–Thurs 7am–9pm, Fri & Sat 7am–midnight, Sun 7am–8pm.

La Paz Waterfall Gardens

15km east of Poás • Daily 8am–5pm • US$42, under-13s US$26; jungle cat exhibit US$5 extra • ☎ 2482 2720, ⓦwaterfallgardens.com

One of Costa Rica's most popular attractions, the **LA PAZ WATERFALL GARDENS** bore the brunt of the Cinchona earthquake (see box opposite), but has since been restored to its former glory. Self-guided tours meander through a pretty garden planted with native shrubs and flowers, taking in a butterfly observatory, orchid display, frog house, snake garden, hummingbird garden – home to 26 different species – and a **jungle cat** enclosure. The 35 felines here were brought to La Paz when the rescue centre housing them closed, and it is now home to five of Costa Rica's six cat species (only the oncilla is absent); it's hoped that any future offspring will be released back into the wild.

The waterfalls

Beyond the frog house, an immaculate series of riverside trails links five **waterfalls** on the Río La Paz, starting with Tempio and winding past Magia Blanca – the highest, which crashes deafeningly 40m down into swirling whitewater – before concluding at the top of the eponymous La Paz Waterfall, Costa Rica's most photographed cascade (it can also be seen from the public highway that runs below); viewing platforms at various points along the way place you above and beneath the falls.

ARRIVAL AND DEPARTURE

LA PAZ WATERFALL GARDENS

By bus Buses from San José's Terminal del Caribe (C Central, Av 15) to Puerto Viejo de Sarapiquí pass La Paz (10 daily; 1hr 30min). They travel via Heredia (30min from La Paz).

By car If you're driving, take a right at the junction in Poasito towards Vara Blanca and, on reaching the village,

take a left at the petrol station and follow the well-marked signs for about 5km.

By tour You can visit the gardens as part of an organized trip – for example, Expediciones Tropicales (see box, p.121) includes La Paz Waterfall Gardens as part of their combination tour.

ACCOMMODATION

Peace Lodge ☎ 2482 2720, ⓦ waterfallgardens.com. Luxurious but overpriced option, where the handsome rooms feature handmade canopy beds, stained-glass windows, private bathrooms, hot tubs and balconies with views over the gardens (and up to Volcán Poás). Staying in the lodge entitles you to entry to the gardens outside the official opening hours, when you can explore its lush expanses away from the otherwise constant crowds. Given the high rates, the extra charge for breakfast feels rather stingy. US$463

2

Heredia and around

Just 11km northeast of San José lies the lively city of **HEREDIA**, boosted by the student population of the Universidad Nacional (UNA), at the eastern end of town. Central Heredia is a little run-down, with the Parque Central flanked by tall palms and the **Basílica de la Inmaculada Concepción**, whose unexciting squat design – "seismic Baroque" – has kept it standing through several earthquakes since 1797. North of the *parque*, the old colonial tower of **El Fortín**, "The Fortress" (closed to the public), features odd gun slats that fan out and widen from the inside to the exterior, giving it a medieval look. Although there's not a great deal to see in town, Heredia is a natural jumping-off point for excursions to **Volcán Barva**, and many tourists also come for the **Café Britt tour**, hosted by the nation's largest and most famous coffee exporter, about 3km north of the town centre.

Casa de la Cultura

Av Central, at C Central • Daily 8am–8pm • Free

The **Casa de la Cultura**, a colonial house with a large breezy veranda, was once the home of Alfredo Gonzáles Flores, president of Costa Rica between 1913 and 1917. Today the building displays local art, including sculpture and paintings by Heredia schoolchildren.

Café Britt

Just north of Heredia on the road to Barva • Standard tour daily 9am, 11am, 1.15pm & 3.15pm; 1hr 30min • US$25 • ☎ 2777 1600, ⓦ coffeetour.com • The Heredia–Barva bus runs past the turning to Café Britt every 30min, from where it's a 400m walk; otherwise, a pick-up/drop-off shuttle bus from Heredia/San José costs US$18

A visit to **Café Britt** gives you an idea of how the modern-day coffee industry operates. The *finca* grows the country's best-known brand and is the most important exporter of Costa Rican coffee to the world at large. Guides take you through the history of coffee growing in Costa Rica, demonstrating how crucial this export crop was to the development of the country, with a rather polished presentation and thorough descriptions of the processes involved in harvesting and selecting the beans. Once you've enjoyed a **tour** of the plantation, roasting factory and drying patios, it's back for a coffee-cupping demo and, of course, the inevitable stop in the gift shop. There are also extended "Coffee Lovers", "Coffee and Adventure" and "Coffee and Waterfalls" tours.

Museo de Cultura Popular

Around 3km north of central Heredia • Sun 10am–5pm • Free • **Guided tour** Mon–Fri 8am–4pm by arrangement (groups of ten or more only); 2–3hr • US$8/person; reserve in advance; one or two cooking workshops included • ☎ 2260 1619, ⓦ www.museo.una.ac.cr

The unusual **Museo de Cultura Popular** portrays coffee-plantation life from the late nineteenth and early twentieth centuries. Set in a large house with verandas, and surrounded by coffee fields, it features rooms re-created in the style of that time. The emphasis is firmly on education, a concept that extends to the **restaurant** (Sun 8am–4pm) as well, which serves authentic food of the period, including *torta de arroz* (layered rice casserole), *pan casero* (a type of sweet bread) and *gallos picadillos* (a mixture of meat, vegetables and rice).

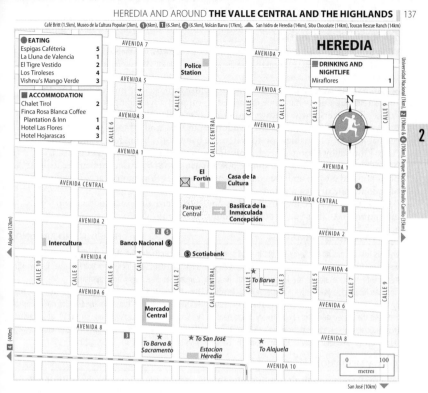

HEREDIA

■ **EATING**
Espigas Caféteria 5
La Lluna de Valencia 1
El Tigre Vestido 2
Los Tiroleses 4
Vishnu's Mango Verde 3

■ **ACCOMMODATION**
Chalet Tirol 2
Finca Rosa Blanca Coffee
   Plantation & Inn 1
Hotel Las Flores 4
Hotel Hojarascas 3

■ **DRINKING AND
NIGHTLIFE**
Miraflores 1

Finca Rosa Blanca

On the road between Barva and Santa Bárbara, 6.5km northwest of Heredia • Tours daily 9am & 1pm; 2hr 30min • US$35; book in advance • ☎ 2269 9392, ⓦ fincarosablanca.com

For an interesting alternative to large-group **coffee tours** head to **Finca Rosa Blanca Coffee Plantation & Inn**. The plantation at this fantastic hotel (see p.138) is one of the country's few **organic** setups – the beans are fertilized using rich soil from the hotel's vermiculture and compost made from their restaurant refuse, while the fields are planted with various trees and plants that help the crop's growth: *pejibaye* to deter insects, bananas to help retain moisture during the dry season, palms for shade. The resident expert passionately guides visitors through the science behind this, plus there's the chance (in season) to join in the harvesting or roasting, as well as some excellent tasting tips in the cupping sessions that finish off the tours.

Sibu Chocolate

San Isidro de Heredia, 14km northeast of Heredia • Tours Tues 10am; 1hr 30min • US$27; advance bookings required • Café & shop Tues–Sat 11am–6pm • ☎ 2268 1335, ⓦ sibuchocolate.com

For a decadent addition to the Valle Central's coffee tours, head over to **Sibu Chocolate** in the small town of San Isidro de Heredia (not to be confused with Heredia itself, a 30min drive away). This award-winning producer runs informative **tasting tours** that take you through chocolate's role in pre-Colombian, post-independence and modern Costa Rica. Among the many tasters is a hot chocolate made to a recipe dating back to the 1500s. There's also a **shop** and a **café** on site, with tasty salads, sandwiches and light meals, as well as – but of course – plenty of chocolate-flavoured cakes and desserts.

Toucan Rescue Ranch

Near San Isidro de Heredia • **Ranch tours** Mon–Sat 9am & 2pm; 2hr • US$35 • **Breakfast with the babies tours** Mon–Sat 8am; 3hr • US$60 • **Photo/artist tours** Mon–Sat (arrange a suitable time with the ranch); 2hr • US$55 • Advance bookings required for all tours • ☎ 2268 4041, ⊚ toucanrescueranch.org

Set up in 2004 to rehabilitate and release confiscated, sick or injured toucans, the **Toucan Rescue Centre** has since expanded to support a wide range of animals – including otters, owls, macaws and sloths – as well as developing breeding programmes and a visitor centre. In addition to the standard **tour**, the "Breakfast with the babies" option enables you to watch the baby sloths being fed, while the "Photo/Artist" tour allows you to sketch, paint or photograph the birds and animals. It's possible to stay on site at the simple **guesthouse** (US$165/two people; rates include breakfast and a tour) and there are also opportunities to volunteer at the rescue centre or "adopt" one of the creatures.

For security reasons, the ranch prefers not to publicize the exact address; you'll be given directions after you've booked a tour or a stay.

ARRIVAL AND INFORMATION

HEREDIA AND AROUND

By bus Heredia has no bus terminal, but instead several well-signed bus stops are scattered around town, with a heavy concentration around the Mercado Central. Buses from San José and Alajuela arrive in and leave from Heredia on Av 8, near the market. Local services to Barva (for Café Britt and the Museo de Cultura Popular) and Sacramento (for Volcán Barva) leave from stops along Av 8 and C 1.
Destinations Alajuela (every 15min; 45min); Barva (for Café Britt and the Museo de Cultura Popular; every 30min; 20min); Sacramento (for Volcán Barva; 3 daily; 1hr 45min); San José (every 5min; 30min).
By train The commuter train, the Tren Urbano (⊚ trenurbano.co.cr), runs from the Estación del Atlántico in San José to Heredia's station, on Av 10, at C Central (Mon–Fri every 30min 6–8.30am & 4–8pm; returns every 30min 5.30–8am & 3.30–7.30pm; 20min).

ACCOMMODATION

While decent **accommodation** in downtown Heredia is pretty sparse, it's unlikely, in any case, that you'll need to stay in town; San José is within easy reach, and there are several country hotels nearby, including *Finca Rosa Blanca*, one of the finest in the country.

IN TOWN

Hotel Hojarascas Av 8, C 4/6 ☎ 2261 3649, ⊚ hotelhojarascas.com. The comfortable whitewashed rooms and apartment (the latter sleeping up to four), offset by bright bed-linen, are spotless, but it's the incredibly friendly owners who make the difference at this popular spot in the southwest part of town. It's quite a pricey option for Heredia, but you get what you pay for – which includes a buffet breakfast and Café Britt coffee (and a machine) in your room, plus free luggage storage. Doubles US$90, apartment US$160

Hotel Las Flores Av 12, C 12/14 ☎ 2261 8147, ⊚ hotel-lasflores.com. Although it is a bit of a hike (or a short taxi ride) from the town centre, *Hotel Las Flores*'s simple but clean and bright rooms (with attached bathrooms and private balconies) make it a decent choice for budget travellers. US$32

OUT OF TOWN

Chalet Tirol 10km north of Heredia, well signposted on the road to Los Ángeles via San Rafael ☎ 2267 6222, ⊚ hotelchaleteltirol.com. Sitting in a lovely pine forest on the edge of Parque Nacional Braulio Carrillo, this kitsch hotel with ten alpine chalets was built to accommodate diners at *Los Tiroleses*, its renowned French restaurant (see opposite). The grounds contain a reproduction Tirol (traditional Austrian-style) village church for concerts and events. Guided walking tours also available. US$125

★ **Finca Rosa Blanca Coffee Plantation & Inn** On the road between Barva and Santa Bárbara, 6.5km northwest of Heredia ☎ 2269 9392, ⊚ fincarosablanca.com. One of Costa Rica's top hotels, this tranquil place is perched above the surrounding coffee fields and has wonderful views across the Valle Central. The thirteen unique suites, four of which can be opened up to form two villas (US$655), have been beautifully decorated with hand-painted murals and bamboo-fibre linen; some also have jacuzzis. You can relax in the fairytale-esque main lounge or take a dip in the gorgeous tiled pool, set among higuerón trees and seemingly dripping over the hillside. The restaurant (see opposite) is one of the region's best, and a sustainability tour (*Finca Rosa Blanca* has flawless eco-credentials) and a recommended tour of the organic coffee fields (see p.137) are on offer. US$373

EATING

With such a large student population, Heredia is crawling with cafés, cake shops, ice-cream joints and vegetarian **restaurants**. If you're self-catering, or fancy an inexpensive meal, head down to the **Mercado Central** (daily 5am–6pm), a clean, orderly place with plenty of fresh produce and several simple canteens.

IN TOWN

Espigas Cafetería Southwest corner of Parque Central ☎ 2237 3275. You'll find all your hangover needs at this central café; the cappuccinos, sweet pastries and filling breakfasts (₡2500–4000) should get your day off to a good start. Daily 7am–9.30pm.

Vishnu's Mango Verde C 7, Av 0/1 ☎ 2237 2526. One of a chain of vegetarian restaurants, this rustic, plant-filled place has a small garden out back and serves good food (around ₡2000–5000), including tasty *tamales*, lentil soup, fresh-fruit smoothies, and sandwiches made to order. Mon–Fri 8am–6pm, Sat 9am–6pm.

OUT OF TOWN

★**La Lluna de Valencia** Barva, 6km northwest of Heredia ☎ 2269 6665, ⓦ lallunadevalencia.com. The gregarious owner Vincente works the tables at this top Spanish restaurant on the road to Alajuela. Tapas (₡6500–8000) are decent, but the speciality is paella (₡7000–12,250 for two people), large and lip-smackingly tasty; the Valenciana, featuring rabbit, is a house favourite. There are recipes on the website, if you fancy trying to re-create the dishes when you get home. Music (acoustic

guitar sets, flamenco) at the weekends. Wed–Fri 7–10pm, Sat noon–10pm, Sun noon–5pm.

★**El Tigre Vestido** Finca Rosa Blanca Coffee Plantation & Inn, 6.5km northwest of Heredia, on the road to Barva ☎ 2269 9392, ⓦ eltigrevestido.com. The charming restaurant at this beautiful hotel (see opposite) specializes in "legacy dining", refined household cooking that celebrates the cuisine of Costa Rica and Central America in general. Eat out on the terrace with beautiful views across the twinkling lights of the Valle Central, where market-fresh food from local organic farmers is served in such dishes as pork chops stuffed with heart-of-palm and a local smoked cheese. Mains ₡8650–13,250; reserve in advance. Daily 6–10pm.

Los Tiroleses Chalet Tirol, 10km north of Heredia, well signposted on the road to Los Ángeles via San Rafael ☎ 2267 6222, ⓦ hotelchaleteltirol.com. One of Costa Rica's most acclaimed French restaurants with a Cordon Bleu-trained chef and an elegant dining area adorned with murals and a large and eclectically stocked wine cellar. Try the excellent bean-heavy cassoulet or the Chateaubriand (mains around ₡10,000). Mon noon–7pm, Tues & Wed noon–9pm, Thurs noon–10pm, Fri & Sat noon–11pm, Sun noon–6pm.

DRINKING AND NIGHTLIFE

The student-focused **nightlife** is concentrated around the four blocks immediately to the west of the Universidad Nacional, in the east of Heredia; keep your wits about you after dark, as muggings do sometimes occur.

Miraflores Av 2, C 2/4 ☎ 2260 2727. Heredians dance salsa and merengue at this lively joint – the country's longest-running club – which attracts a slightly older,

mellower crowd than some of the other venues in town. Mon–Thurs 8pm–5.30am, Fri–Sun 8pm–6am.

DIRECTORY

Banks and exchange The Banco Nacional at C 2, Av 2/4 and Scotiabank at Av 4, C Central/2 both have ATMs, and change currency.

Language school As befits a university town, Heredia is also home to the excellent Intercultura Spanish language school (C 10, Av 2/4; ☎ 2260 8480,

ⓦ interculturacostarica.com), with rates from US$275/ week (homestay from US$155/week). They have another branch by the beach in Sámara in Guanacaste.

Post office The post office (Mon–Fri 8am–5.30pm, Sat 8am–noon) is on the northwest corner of the Parque Central.

Parque Nacional Braulio Carrillo

15km northeast of Heredia • Daily 8am–3.30pm • US$12 • ☎ 2268 1039 (Quebrada González section), ☎ 2261 2619 (Volcán Barva section) • The Quebrada González ranger station is 42km northeast of Heredia; the Volcán Barva ranger station is 3km north of Sacramento

PARQUE NACIONAL BRAULIO CARRILLO covers nearly 500 square kilometres of virgin rainforest and dense cloudforest, but draws few visitors on account of its sheer size and lack of facilities – most tourists experience the majestic views of thick foliage only from the window of a bus on their way to the Caribbean coast. Those who do spend any length of time here tend to spend it tackling **Volcán Barva**, which dominates the southwest corner of the park and is accessed from the village of Sacramento.

The park is named after Costa Rica's third, and rather dictatorial, chief of state, who held office in the mid-1800s. It was established in 1978 to protect the land from the possible effects of the **Guápiles Highway**, then under construction between San José and Limón, a piece of intelligent foresight without which this whole stretch of countryside might have been turned into a solid strip of petrol stations and motels.

Note that, unfortunately, security is a problem in the park; if driving, never leave anything in your car, and always use a guide for longer hikes (see p.52).

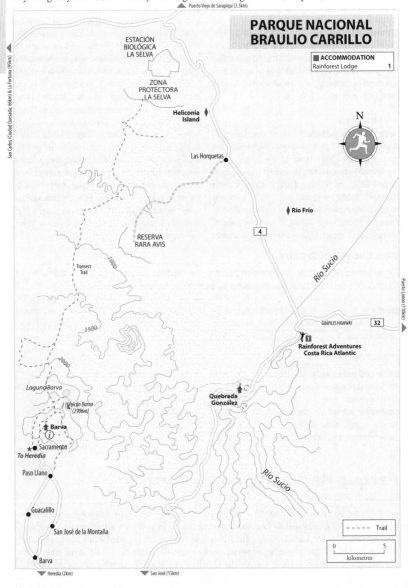

PARQUE NACIONAL BRAULIO CARRILLO

ACCOMMODATION
Rainforest Lodge   1

Puerto Viejo de Sarapiquí (3.5km)

San Carlos (Ciudad Quesada: 66km) & La Fortuna (95km)

ESTACIÓN BIOLÓGICA LA SELVA

ZONA PROTECTORA LA SELVA

Heliconia Island

Las Horquetas

Río Frío

4

RESERVA RARA AVIS

Transect Trail

1600

1500

2000

Río Sucio

GUÁPILES HIGHWAY   32

Rainforest Adventures Costa Rica Atlantic   1

Puerto Limón (110km)

Quebrada González

Laguna Barva

Volcán Barva (2906m)

Barva

Sacramento

To Heredia

Paso Llano

Guacalillo

San José de la Montaña

Río Sucio

Barva

N

Heredia (2km)   San José (15km)

- - - - - Trail

0   5
kilometres

Quebrada González

Three short, circular **trails** lead off from the ranger station at **Quebrada González**, on the Guápiles Highway, 2km east of the Río Sucio bridge – though as they are narrow, steep and often ungroomed, they can take longer than you might think to complete. **Las Palmas** (1.6km), just behind the ranger station, is a good bet for birds; directly across the Guápiles Highway, **El Ceibo** (1km) loops down to the Río Sucio, named "Dirty River" due to its discolouration by minerals; while the high-hiking route of **Botarrama** (2.5km) is more likely to provide chance encounters with some of the park's animals.

2

ARRIVAL AND INFORMATION   QUEBRADA GONZÁLEZ

By bus Hourly buses from San José's Terminal del Caribe pass the Quebrada González ranger station (about 45min; you'll need to ask the driver to drop you off there) en route to Limón and Puerto Viejo de Sarapiquí.

For the return journey, it's a case of flagging one down on the highway.

Guides Guides (around US$20–30 for 3–4hr) can be hired through the ranger station at Quebrada González.

Volcán Barva

Most people visit the more popular Barva section of the park with just one aim: climbing **Volcán Barva**, a forest-clad peak that tops out at just over 2900m. From the ranger station, **a trail** (5km; 4hr round-trip) ascends through dense deciduous cover, giving fleeting panoramic views over the Valle Central and southeast to Volcán Irazú along the way. At the summit, the striking green-blue **Laguna Barva** fills the small, pristine crater, surrounded by dense forest that is often obscured in cloud. Take a compass, water and food, a sweater and rain gear, and leave early in the morning to enjoy the clearest views of the top.

The **Transect Trail**, which leads north through the park from here as far as the Estacíon Biológica La Selva (see p.230), takes around four days to complete and is strictly for highly experienced jungle hikers only; you'd need to be totally self-sufficient, and take all your food, water and camping equipment with you.

ARRIVAL AND DEPARTURE   VOLCÁN BARVA

By bus Buses run from Heredia (Mon–Sat 6.25am, 11.45am & 3.55pm, Sun 6.30am, 11am & 4pm; 1hr 45min) to the tiny hamlet of Sacramento, from where it's a 3km walk up a steep track to the Barva ranger station; buses

back to Heredia leave at 7.30am, 1pm (12.30pm on Sun) and, most conveniently, 5pm.

By car You'll need a 4WD if driving to Volcán Barva, even in the dry season.

Rainforest Adventures Costa Rica Atlantic

Just beyond the northeastern boundary of Parque Nacional Braulio Carrillo, 1.5km from the Guápiles Highway • Daily 7am–4pm • Tram US$60, under-13s US$30; canopy tour from US$50; birdwatching and trekking tours from US$99; serpentarium and butterfly and frog garden US$10 • Various multi-activity packages available • ☎ 2257 5961, ⓦ rainforestadventure.com

The brainchild of American naturalist Donald Perry, the Rainforest Aerial Tram has now been rebranded by some marketing whizz as the **Rainforest Adventures Costa Rica Atlantic**. Funded by private investors, and the product of many years' research, the tram

---

WATCHING WILDLIFE IN BRAULIO CARRILLO

Due to its enormous size and varied altitude, Braulio Carrillo has one of the highest levels of biodiversity in Costa Rica, with over 530 species of **bird**, including the rare quetzal (mostly seen at higher elevations), toucans, trogons and eagles, and some 135 species of **mammal**, such as collared peccary, paca, jaguar and ocelot. The park, particularly the Barva area, is one of the few places in the country where the bushmaster, Central America's largest **venomous snake**, makes its home, along with the equally venomous fer-de-lance.

was, when it opened in the mid-1990s, the first of its kind in the world: there's another one in Costa Rica near Jacó on the Pacific coast (see p.340) and several elsewhere in Central America/the Carribbean. In his book *Life Above the Jungle Floor* (see p.433), Perry tells how he risked life and limb to get the project started. Committed to protecting the rainforest canopy and the jungle floor, he refused to allow the construction firm erecting the tram's high-wire towers to use tractors; they were unable to secure a powerful enough helicopter in Costa Rica, but Nicaragua's Sandinistas came to the rescue, loaning one of their MI-17 combat helicopters (minus the guns) to help erect the poles.

The tram

The tram's premise is beautifully simple: twenty overhead cable cars, each holding five passengers and one guide, run slowly (and largely silently) along the 2.6km aerial track, skirting the tops of the forest and passing between trees, providing eye-level encounters along the way. The ride (45min each way) affords a rare glimpse of birds, animals and plants, including the epiphytes, orchids, insects and mosses that live in the upper reaches of the forest – wear a hat and insect repellent, and bring binoculars, camera and rain gear. For those staying in the lodge (see below), **torchlit night rides** (until 9pm) examine the canopy's nocturnal inhabitants.

Other activities

To view the treetops at a faster pace, you can sign up for a **canopy tour** (no under-12s), which sends you whizzing through the forest along seven ziplines. More conventionally, you can also explore the park via a network of ground-level trails (included in the price), or on a number of full-day **guided tours**, such as birdwatching and trekking. A **butterfly and frog garden** and a **serpentarium** complete the attractions.

ARRIVAL AND DEPARTURE RAINFOREST ADVENTURES COSTA RICA ATLANTIC

By bus Hourly buses from San José's Terminal del Caribe to Limón and Puerto Viejo de Sarapiquí can drop you off at the turning for the Aerial Tram (about 1hr; you'll need to ask the driver to drop you off there), from where it's a 1.5km walk. To get back to San José, you'll need to flag down buses on the highway.

By tour It's much easier to take a tour, either directly with the tram's San José office on Av 7, C 5/7, or on one of the combination tours offered by several San José-based agencies (see p.54).

ACCOMMODATION

Rainforest Lodge Inside the park ⓣ 1 866 759 8736, ⓦ rainforestadventure.com. Accommodation at the tram's expensive *Rainforest Lodge* comprises a collection of luxury bungalows (sleeping up to three), all with views of the forest. Rates include two tram rides, a morning birdwatching tour, unlimited access to the trails in the company of an expert guide, and full board. **US$220**

Cartago and around

Founded in 1563 by Juan Vásquez de Coronado, **CARTAGO**, meaning "Carthage", was Costa Rica's capital for two hundred and sixty years before the centre of power was moved to San José in 1823. Like its ancient namesake, the city has been razed a number of times, although in this case by earthquakes instead of Romans – two, in 1823 and 1910, almost demolished the place. Most of the town's fine nineteenth-century and *fin-de-siècle* buildings were destroyed, and what has grown up in their place – the usual assortment of shops and haphazard modern buildings – is not particularly appealing. Nowadays, Cartago functions mainly as a busy market and shopping centre, with some industry around its periphery. The star attraction is its soaring **cathedral**, or *basílica*.

Las Ruinas

Parque Central

The ruined Iglesia de la Parroquía, known as **Las Ruinas**, dominates the dour, paved Parque Central, and is as popular with a cacophony of roosting great-tailed grackles as it is with the townsfolk. Originally built in 1575, the church was repeatedly destroyed by earthquakes but stubbornly rebuilt every time, until eventually the giant earthquake of 1910 vanquished it for good. Only the elegantly tumbling walls remain, enclosing pretty subtropical gardens; unfortunately, the gardens are locked more often than not, but you can peer through the iron gate at the fluffy blossoms flowering inside. If you inspect the sides and corners of the ruins carefully, you'll see where the earthquake dislodged entire rows of mortar, sending them several centimetres beyond those above and below.

Basílica de Nuestra Señora de Los Ángeles

Av 2, at C 16 • No fixed opening hours • Free

Cartago's cathedral, properly named the **Basílica de Nuestra Señora de Los Ángeles**, was built in a decorative Byzantine style after the previous *basílica* was destroyed in an earthquake in 1926. This huge cement-grey structure with its elaborate wood-panelled interior is home to **La Negrita**, the representation of the Virgin of Los Ángeles, patron saint of Costa Rica. On this spot on August 2, 1635, the Virgin reportedly appeared to a poor peasant girl in the form of a dark doll made of stone. Each time the girl took the doll away to play with it, it mulishly reappeared on the spot where she had found it; this was seen as a sign, and the church was built soon after. In the left-hand antechamber of the cathedral you'll see silver *ex votos* (devotional sculptures) of every imaginable shape and size, including horses, planes, grasshoppers (representing plagues of locusts), hearts with swords driven through them, arms, fingers and hands. This is a Latin American tradition stretching from Mexico to Brazil, whereby the faithful deposit representations of whatever they need cured, or whatever they fear, to the power of the Almighty.

Jardín Botánico Lankester

4km southeast of Cartago • Daily 8.30am–5.30pm, last entry 4.30pm • US$10 • ☎ 2511 7939, 🔊 jbl.ucr.ac.cr • Take the Paraíso-bound bus (every 10min or so) from Cartago; the driver will drop you on the main road, from where it's a (signposted) walk of about 500m

Orchids are the chief attraction at the University of Costa Rica's **Jardín Botánico Lankester**, a research centre southeast of Cartago. The large, attractive gardens (the oldest in the country) are covered with a bewildering array of tropical plant and flower species, including orchids, heliconias and bromeliads – ostentatious, elaborate blooms that thrust out from the undergrowth. The most rewarding time to visit is the dry season, particularly in March and April, when the garden explodes with virulent reds, purples and yellows.

> **EL DÍA DE LA NEGRITA**
>
> The celebration of the Virgin of Los Ángeles (**El Día de la Negrita**) on August 2 is one of the most important days in the Costa Rican religious calendar, when hundreds of pilgrims make the journey to Cartago to visit the tiny black statue of the Virgin, tucked away in a shallow subterranean antechamber beneath the crypt in the town's *basílica*. It is a tradition in this grand, vaulting church for pilgrims to shuffle down the aisle towards the altar on their knees, rosaries fretting in their hands as they whisper a steady chorus of Hail Marys: indeed, many will have travelled like this from as far away as San José to pay their respects.

ARRIVAL AND DEPARTURE

By bus Empresa Lumaca buses run to and from C 5, at Av 10 in San José (every 10min; 45min) and their terminal in Cartago on C 6, at Av 3, and from stops along Cartago's Av 6. Buses for Turrialba leave from a stop on Av 4, C 5/7. Local services are frequent and reliable: buses for Paraíso and Orosí use the stops on C 3, Av 2/4; buses for Cachí leave from Av 3, C 4/6. Note that local bus stops do move around town periodically, so check with a local before setting off.

Destinations Cachí (for Ujarrás; roughly hourly; 25min);

CARTAGO AND AROUND

Orosí (every 15min–1hr; 40min); Paraíso (for the Jardín Botánico Lankester; every 10min; 15min); Turrialba (every 30min–1hr; 1hr 20min).

By train The Tren Urbano commuter train (ⓦtrenurbano .co.cr) runs between Cartago's railway station, on Av 6, at C 3, and San José (Mon–Fri 13 daily during the morning and afternoon rush hours; 45min).

By taxi Cartago's taxi rank is at Las Ruinas; the journey to Jardín Botánico Lankester costs roughly ₡4000–5000.

ACCOMMODATION

Casa Aura C 1, Av 6/8 ☎2591 8161. This modest guesthouse, located a short walk from the centre of town, has just four reasonable, though pretty spartan, rooms

(they do have TV and private bathrooms), as well as a garden and a small book-swap. US$64

EATING

There are a few simple restaurants in Cartago, and a handful of low-cost **sodas**. Your best bet may be to pop into one of the pastry shops and enjoy lunch on a bench in front of the *basílica*.

Cartago Grill Av 2, C 5/7 ☎2591 5342. This popular restaurant has a no-nonsense menu of steaks, grilled chicken, burgers and the like, plus plenty of promotions,

including weekday set breakfasts (₡2950) and lunches (₡3850). Mon–Thurs & Sun 9am–9pm, Fri & Sat 9am–10pm.

Parque Nacional Volcán Irazú

32km north of Cartago • Daily 8am–3.30pm • US$15 • ☎2200 5025

The blasted lunar landscape of **PARQUE NACIONAL VOLCÁN IRAZÚ** reaches its highest point at 3432m and, on clear days, offers fantastic views all the way to the Caribbean coast. Famous for having the gall to erupt on the day President John F. Kennedy visited Costa Rica on March 19, 1963, Irazú has been more or less calm ever since. But while its **main crater** is far less active, in terms of bubblings and rumblings, than that of Volcán Poás, its deep depression creates an undeniably dramatic sight, even though the strange algae-green lake that once filled it dried up in 2013.

The volcano makes for a long and entirely uphill but scenic trip from Cartago, especially in the early morning before the inevitable **clouds** roll in (about 10am). While the main crater draws the crowds, it's worth noting that the shallow bowl to its right, the flat-bottomed and largely unimpressive **Diego de la Haya crater**, is the remnant of Irazú's first and largest eruption: when it blew in 1723, the eruption lasted ten months and showered San José in ash.

There's not much to do around here after viewing the main crater from the *mirador* – no official trails cut through this section of the park, though you can scramble among the grey ash dunes that have built up on **Playa Hermosa**, the buried, older crater that spreads to the left of the walkway and is dotted with what little vegetation can survive in this moon-like environment. Stay behind the barriers at all times, though, as volcanic ash crumbles easily, and you could end up falling in.

ARRIVAL AND DEPARTURE

By bus Only one bus runs to the park entrance, leaving from opposite San José's *Gran Hotel Costa Rica* on Av 2, C 1/3 at 8am daily (get there early in high season to get a seat; 2hr), stopping to pick up passengers in Cartago (on the corner of Las Ruinas; 45min from San José) at 8.45am; the

PARQUE NACIONAL VOLCÁN IRAZÚ

bus returns to San José at 12.30pm.

By tour You can also get to Irazú on any number of half-day tours, run by travel agencies in San José (see p.54) and Orosí (see p.146), which whisk you back and forth in a minibus for around US$45–60, excluding the entrance fee.

INFORMATION

Facilities At the crater parking area, you'll find toilets, an information board, and a reception centre with a gift shop and snack bar, which serves cakes and hot drinks. There are picnic tables out front, but make sure you keep an eye out for the many white-nosed coatis (members of the raccoon family), who can be a real pain as they scrounge for food.

What to wear It can get both cold and wet at the summit of Volcán Irazú, so bring a jumper and a waterproof jacket.

Valle Orosí

After workaday Cartago, the verdant **VALLE OROSÍ**, occupying a deep bowl just 9km to the southeast, is a veritable Garden of Eden. Passing through Paraíso, the road drops down a ski-slope-shaped hill to the pretty villages of **Orosí** and, on the other side of Lago Cachí, **Ujarrás**, each with their own lovely church; annoyingly, although they lie less than 8km apart, no bus runs between them, so without your own transport you'll have to backtrack to Paraíso. Alternatively, some of the hotels and guesthouses in Orosí (see p.146) can arrange guided tours of the valley. Southeast of these lies the little-visited **Parque Nacional Tapantí–Macizo Cerro de la Muerte**, a wildlife-rich park that's one of the closest places to the capital for rainforest hiking.

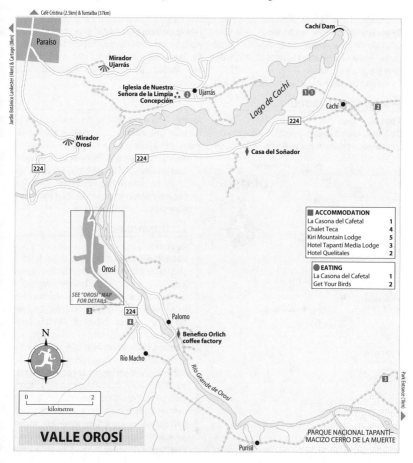

Orosí

Nestled in a little topographical bowl between thick-forested hills and coffee plantations, **OROSÍ** is one of the most picturesque villages in Costa Rica. Its bucolic charms have a way of seducing visitors, and many end up staying far longer than they intended – on a clear morning, when the lush hillsides are drenched in sunlight and with Irazú and Turrialba volcanoes hovering on the horizon, Orosí can feel like the most idyllic spot in Costa Rica.

Iglesia San José de Orosí

In the centre of Orosí • **Church** No fixed opening hours • Free • **Museum** Tues–Sat 1–5pm, Sun 9am–5pm • ₡500

While Orosí's laidback atmosphere is its top attraction, the village does also boast the **Iglesia San José de Orosí** (built in 1735), Costa Rica's oldest church still in use, which sits squat against the rounded hills behind. This simple, low-slung adobe structure, single-towered and roofed with red tiles, has an interior devoid of the hubris and frothy excess of much of Latin American religious decor.

The adjacent **religious art museum** exhibits fascinating *objectos de culto* from the early 1700s such as icons, religious paintings and ecclesiastical furniture, along with a faithful re-creation of a monk's tiny room.

ARRIVAL AND DEPARTURE   OROSÍ

By bus Regular buses leave from the stop on C 6, Av 1/3 in Cartago for the journey to Orosí (every 15min–1hr; 40min); the last service back to Cartago leaves at 10pm from the stops along the main street.

By car Take the road from Cartago to Paraíso, then turn right at the Parque Central and drive straight on until you begin to descend the precipitous hill to the village.

By taxi Taxis congregate on the north side of the football pitch, outside *Restaurante Coto* (see opposite).

INFORMATION AND TOURS

Otiac 300m south of the church ☎ 2533 3640. Run by the folks at *Montaña Linda* (see opposite), Otiac provides information on the area as well as offering a wide range of activities – from rock climbing and cooking classes to homestays and volunteer programmes – and Spanish lessons at its popular language school (US$199/week with dorm accommodation, US$300/week with guesthouse accommodation, US$305/week in a homestay). You can also buy postcards and send mail here, organize car hire, and get advice on the wide variety of hiking trails in the vicinity. Daily 10.30am–3pm.

Ujarrás (17.2km) & Cartago (20km)

OROSÍ

N

Religious Art Museum

Football Field

Iglesia San José de Orosí

Balneario de Aguas Termales

HWY 224

Banco Nacional

Otiac

Balneario de Aguas Los Patios (1km) & Parque Nacional Tapantí–Macizo Cerro de la Muerte (11km)

● EATING
Giardino	3
Orosí Lodge	4
Panaderia Suiza	5
Restaurante Coto	2
Soda Luz	1

■ ACCOMMODATION
Hotel Reventazón	2
Montaña Linda Guesthouse	4
Montaña Linda Hostel	1
Orosí Lodge	3

ACCOMMODATION

IN TOWN

Hotel Reventazón 300m south of the football pitch ☎ 2533 3838, ⊛ hotelreventazon.wordpress .com; map opposite. This low-key hotel has a collection of small, clean rooms, all of which have lovely valley vistas, private bathrooms, TVs and fridges. It's a good fallback if *Montaña Linda Guesthouse* is full up. US$40

Montaña Linda Guesthouse 25m south of Otiac ☎ 2533 3640, ⊛ montanalinda.com; map opposite. A charming, well-run guesthouse featuring spacious, light-filled rooms with private bathrooms and glorious valley views from the wraparound balcony. The communal kitchen and lounge area – complete with book exchange, noticeboard, and wonderfully detailed guides to the Orosí Valley written by the helpful Dutch owners – is a great space to relax, study or chat with

ACTIVITIES IN VALLE OROSÍ

There are two **hot springs** in Orosí: **Balneario de Aguas Termales** (☎ 2533 2156; Mon & Wed–Sun 7.30am–4pm; US$5.50), at the southern end of the village, is attractively framed by forest-clad hills and well maintained; **Balneario de Aguas Los Patios** (☎ 2533 3009; Tues–Sun 8am–4pm; US$5.50), a 15min walk south of town, has been recently renovated, and features a particularly hot adults-only pool, as well as plenty of facilities for children.

There are various ways of exploring the surrounding countryside. You can ride along the valley by **bike** – available to rent from *Orosí Lodge* (US$15/day), who can also provide you with a map of the area featuring points of interest, or *Panadería Suiza* (see below) – or by **motorbike** – with Costa Rica Moto (at *Panadería Suiza* in the village; ☎ 2533 1442, ⓦ costarica-moto.com), who rent bikes (from US$55/day) and also offer tailor-made tours (from US$100/day).

For a gentler excursion, you can take an early morning **horseriding** tour through the valley with Francisco "Pancho" Martínez (US$15/hr; ☎ 2830 6058), who can be found just left of the Balneario de Aguas Termales.

2

other travellers. The owners have recently opened a new "vacation house" sleeping up to six (US$65 for double occupancy; US$10 for each additional guest). Breakfast not included. US$30

Montaña Linda Hostel 200m south and 100m east of the football pitch ☎ 2533 3640, ⓦ montanalinda.com; map opposite. Benefiting from the same chilled-out vibe as its sister accommodation, this is one of the best budget options in the Valle Central. There is a range of quirky dorms and private rooms (with shared or attached bathrooms), plus a communal kitchen, laundry service, and several hammocks and easy chairs to relax in. Breakfast not included. Dorms US$9, doubles US$22

★**Orosí Lodge** 25m east of Aguas Termales ☎ 2533 3578, ⓦ orosilodge.com; map opposite. Lovely little hotel whose six wood-floored and -beamed rooms (the top three have volcano views; the bottom three each have an extra bed) are spacious, tastefully decorated and equipped with coffee-maker, minibar and fan. The chalet (sleeping up to five) around the back makes an excellent base, with a large high-ceilinged lounge, kitchenette and a private balcony looking across Orosí to Irazú and Turrialba, looming on the horizon. The *casita*

(sleeping up to four) is similarly well-equipped and also has great views. Breakfast (which costs extra) can be taken at the on-site café (see below). Doubles US$71, chalet/*casita* US$113

OUT OF TOWN

Chalet Teca 2km outside Orosí, on the road to Tapantí ☎ 2533 3268, ⓦ chaletorosi.com; map p.145. Good-looking wood-and-stone chalet set in compact but attractive grounds on a hill south of the village. There's a well-equipped kitchen and inviting open fireplace, plus fine views from its terrace (complete with jacuzzi). Breakfast costs extra. US$121

Hotel Tapantí Media Lodge 1km south of the church and 100m up a steep hill ☎ 2533 9090, ⓔ tapantimedia@gmail.com; map p.145. Fronted by flags flapping in the breeze and offering superb views of the valley, *Tapantí Media Lodge* has clean but modest rooms, with TV and private bathrooms. If you can score the top-floor far-corner room with two big bay windows, you've got it made. There's a cosy bar with comfy lounge chairs and fireplace – perfect for those chilly Orosí nights. US$60

EATING

Giardino 100m south and 100m east of the football pitch ☎ 2533 2022; map opposite. Facing a lush garden, this Italian restaurant has reasonable thinnish-crust pizzas (₡5000–13,500), as well as pasta dishes, bruschette and, of course, tiramisu. Opening hours are a little erratic. Daily noon–10pm.

Orosí Lodge 25m east of Aguas Termales ☎ 2533 3578, ⓦ orosilodge.com; map opposite. A delightful café serving superb all-day breakfasts (₡4500), sandwiches and home-made cakes, and its own blend of coffee (sourced from Café Cristina; see box, p.148). There's a 1950s Wurlitzer jukebox and table football to

help pass the time, and the owners are founts of local knowledge. It's also a good spot for souvenir shopping, with coffee beans, local art, world music CDs, and more for sale. Daily 7am–7pm.

Panadería Suiza 100m south of Banco Nacional ☎ 8706 6777; map p.145. This friendly, Swiss-run bakery-café is a good spot for breakfast (₡2500–3500) or a coffee and a pastry – don't miss the top cinnamon rolls. You can also rent out bikes here, and organize tours of the valley. Tues–Sat 8am–5pm, Sun 6am–3pm.

Restaurante Coto Opposite the football field

☎ 2533 3032; map p.146. Although a bit overpriced, *Coto* has a plum position bang in the centre of town, and an inviting terrace at which it's easy to while away a few hours. The menu features *típico* food (mains ₡4000–10,000), plus a good weekday lunch special (₡4000), and tempting frappes (₡2500). Daily 8am–midnight.

Soda Luz 100m north of the church ☎ 2533 3701; map p.146. This friendly little *soda*, kitted out with red-and-white checked tablecloths, has been going strong since 1942. Its concise, economical menu features a tasty *gallo pinto*, a few *arroz cons* and *casados*, and burger and fries (dishes ₡2300–3500). Mon–Fri 7am–4pm, Sat & Sun 7am–8pm.

The Lago de Cachí loop

The 30km loop-road from Orosí around **Lago de Cachí** makes for a great half-day trip, ambling through some of the most beautiful scenery in the valley. Heading north out of Orosí you pass a couple of *miradors* before arriving at the small settlement of **UJARRÁS**, 17km north of Orosí and home to the remains of a historic church. Six kilometres beyond Ujarrás, over Cachí Dam and beyond the turn-offs to Cachí itself, you'll come to the Casa del Soñador workshop. From here, the road continues along the shore of Lago de Cachí for a few more kilometres before arcing south and running alongside the Río Grande de Orosí until it reaches the hamlet of Paloma; crossing the rickety bridge just beyond here and turning right will lead you back into Orosí.

Iglesia de Nuestra Señora de la Limpia Concepción

If coming by bus, ask to be dropped at the fork for Ujarrás, from where it's a 1km walk • Daily 8am–4pm • Free

The tiny agricultural hamlet of Ujarrás boasts the evocative ruins of the **Iglesia de Nuestra Señora de la Limpia Concepción**. Built between 1681 and 1693 on the site of a shrine erected by a local fisherman who claimed to have seen the Virgin in a tree trunk, the church was abandoned in 1833 after irreparable damage from flooding; today, the sun-bleached limestone ruins are lovingly cared for, with a full-time gardener who tends the landscaped grounds. The ruined interior, reached through what used to be the door, is now a grassy, roofless enclosure fluttering with parrots; despite its dilapidated state, you can identify the fine lines of a former altar.

Casa del Soñador

Around 2km southwest of Cachí • Daily 9am–6pm • Free • ☎ 2577 1186

The charming **Casa del Soñador** is a wooden and bamboo cottage decorated with local woodcarver Macedonio Quesada's lively depictions of rural people – gossiping women, musicians and farmers – and religious scenes. Señor Quesada passed away in 1995, and his sons now use the house as a workshop, where they create and sell their wood-carvings (from US$10), mostly figures etched into coffee-bush roots.

ARRIVAL AND DEPARTURE   THE LAGO DE CACHÍ LOOP

By car The easiest way to explore the Lago Cachí loop is by car.
By bus Ujarrás and Cachí (for the Casa del Soñador) are

accessible by buses from Cartago (every 30min–1hr; 25min to Ujarrás).

COFFEE AT CRISTINA

One of the most interesting activities in the area is visiting **Café Cristina** (☎ 2574 6426, ⓦ cafecristina.com), a small-scale organic coffee farm about 9km northeast of Orosí, on the road from Paraíso to Turrialba, which has been toiled by an American family since 1977. The charismatic owners, Linda and Ernie, offer 1hr 30min tours (Mon–Sat 9am & 2pm; US$15; reservations essential) and take great pride in explaining every stage of the coffee-making process – from growing to milling to roasting. The tour culminates in one of the sweetest cups of coffee you'll taste in Costa Rica.

By jeep-taxi A tour around the lake in one of Orosí's jeep-taxis costs around US$40.

By bike If you're fit enough, cycling is a great way to tour the valley: bikes are available for rent in Orosí (see box, p.147).

ACCOMMODATION

★**La Casona del Cafetal** By the lake, around 900m northwest of Cachí ☎2577 1414, ⓦlacasonadelcafetal.com; map p.145. With an idyllic lakeside setting, it's easy to see why this hotel-restaurant is a popular spot for weddings. There are smart en-suites, and plenty of activities on offer. US$113

Hotel Quelitales 3.5km east of Cachí ☎2577 2222, ⓦhotelquelitales.com; map p.145. Gorgeous boutique hotel with a handful of modern, artfully decorated suites and bungalows (both sleeping two people), all of which have plenty of space, alfresco showers and wonderful rainforest views. On the grounds are bucolic gardens, a waterfall, and a fish-focused restaurant. Suites/bungalows US$198

EATING

La Casona del Cafetal By the lake, around 900m northwest of Cachí ☎2577 1414, ⓦlacasonadelcafetal.com; map p.145. The restaurant here is one of the best in the area, with a menu that's strong on fish dishes like tilapia *a la plancha* and locally caught trout. The all-you-can-eat Sunday buffet (₡13,000) is also something of a local institution. Mon–Sat noon–10pm, Sun noon–8pm.

Get Your Birds Ujarrás, 250m east of the church ☎8512 6315, ⓦgetyourbirds.com/gyb-ujarras; map p.145. This oddly named restaurant has a novel concept: here you can eat breakfast/lunch (US$15) or have a beer (US$6) while watching the remarkably wide range of birds that flock to the restaurant's lush garden, attracted by perches strung with fresh fruit. Daily 8.30am–4pm.

Parque Nacional Tapantí–Macizo Cerro de la Muerte

12km southeast of Orosí • Daily 8am–4pm • US$10 • ☎2206 5615

Rugged, pristine **PARQUE NACIONAL TAPANTÍ–MACIZO CERRO DE LA MUERTE** is one of Costa Rica's least-visited national parks, covering around 580 square kilometres. Altitude in this watershed area ranges from 1220m to 3490m above sea level and contains three life zones (low mountain and premontane rainforest, and paramo), habitats that provide shelter for a multitude of **bird, animal and insect life** – it's perhaps one of the easiest places in the country to spot the beautiful Blue Morpho butterfly. Flora is equally spectacular, including bromelia, heliconia and numerous ferns and mosses; it has been estimated that each 2.5-acre section contains up to 160 different species of tree. The park is divided into two sectors: **Tapantí**, accessed from Orosí (and described here), and **Macizo Cerro de la Muerte**, approached from the Interamericana.

The trails

Tapantí's three densely wooded, relatively short **trails** lead off from the main road that cuts through the park. Of the walks that skirt the Río Grande de Orosí, the easiest is the sun-dappled **Sendero La Oropendola** (1.2km), which, true to its name, is a good place to spot Montezuma oropendola – a flock can normally be seen in the trees near where the trail loops back. The slightly harder **Sendero La Pava–Catarata** (1.5km) descends, via a couple of little bridges, to a section of small rapids (Catarata) or a boulder-strewn spot along the river (Pava). On the opposite side of the main road, the steep and difficult **Sendero Natural Arboles Caídos** (2km) is a reliable birdwatching trail. Follow the road beyond the trails from the park entrance, and you'll find a turning for a **viewpoint** (*mirador*).

ARRIVAL AND DEPARTURE   PARQUE NACIONAL TAPANTÍ

By jeep-taxi From Orosí, jeep-taxis from the north side of the village square cost around US$25 each way to the park; a tour costs around US$50.

By car Follow the main road south of Orosí to the Beneficio Orlich coffee factory, where the road bends left across a small bridge; turn right (the park is signposted from here) and continue for 10km along a progressively more rugged track (you'll need a 4WD in the rainy season).

2

WATCHING WILDLIFE IN TAPANTÍ

Tapantí is chock-full of **mammals**; about 45 species live here, including the elusive tapir, as well as ocelot and margay, although you're more likely to spot paca, coati and, if you're lucky, kinkajou. **Birdlife** is abundant (260 species), particularly along the trails that wind up into the hills: look out for black guan, tinamou and chacalaca. The park's high rainfall makes it nirvana for **reptiles** and **amphibians**, too, including eyelash vipers and basilisk lizards.

INFORMATION

Facilities Despite its low numbers of visitors, the park has decent services, with a ranger station and car-parking spaces at the trailheads and toilets and drinking water at regular intervals along the trails themselves.

Climate Tapantí receives one of the highest average annual rainfalls (a whopping 7000mm) in the country. October is the wettest month, but bring rain gear whenever you go, and dress in layers – if the sun is out it can be blindingly hot, whereas at higher elevations, when overcast and rainy, it can feel quite cool.

ACCOMMODATION

Kiri Mountain Lodge 2.5km south of the park ☎ 2533 2272, ⓦ kirilodge.net; map p.145. The closest hotel to Tapantí, *Kiri Mountain Lodge* is an isolated, peaceful place with basic but comfortable rooms and a restaurant and bar, and they can also arrange guided walks and trout-fishing excursions for guests. <u>US$60</u>

Turrialba and around

The agricultural town of **TURRIALBA**, 45km east of Cartago on the slopes of the Cordillera Central, boasts sweeping views over the rugged Talamancas – and not much else. With the demise of the railroad to the Caribbean and the opening of the Guápiles Highway further north, Turrialba has faded in importance, though there are a number of worthwhile day-trips around town: most visitors come through here en route to the **Monumento Nacional Guayabo** or for a **whitewater rafting** trip on the thrilling *ríos* Pacuare and Reventazón, but there are also the excellent biological gardens at **CATIE** to explore.

CATIE

4km east of Turrialba • **Jardín Botánico** Mon–Fri 7am–4pm, Sat & Sun 8am–4pm • US$10, tours from US$25; reservations recommended • **Bird-banding** Mon, Wed & Fri 5.30–9am • US$15; reserve in advance • ☎ 2558 2000, ⓦ catie.ac.cr • Turrialba–Siquirres buses pass by CATIE; Explornatura offers guided tours for US$55 (☎ 2556 2070, ⓦ explornatura.com)

Regarded as one of the world's premier tropical research stations, the **Centro Agronómico Tropical de Investigación y Enseñanza**, thankfully otherwise known by its acronym **CATIE**, is unique in Costa Rica. For the last 65 years, the agricultural research and higher education centre has worked on marrying the needs of Latin America's rural poor with those of the environment – it was here that the technique for producing *palmito* (heart-of-palm) from the *pejibaye* was developed – and at any one time it is involved in over a hundred research and development projects, from tackling climate change to producing disease-resistant tropical crops.

Jardín Botánico

It's this expert knowledge that makes the **tours** of CATIE's landscaped **Jardín Botánico** so eye-opening. The genial guide will introduce you to some of the 472 species being preserved here, explaining the virtues of the miracle fruit (it makes sour things taste sweet) or divulging some of the 101 benefits of eating noni. The tour is very interactive, so you'll spend much of your time sniffing spices, touching tubers and munching on freshly picked tropical fruit such as mangosteen and pink ornamental bananas.

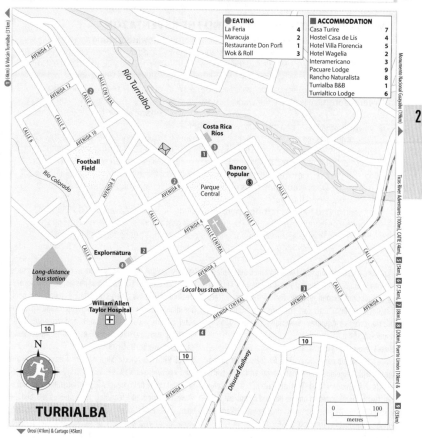

EATING		ACCOMMODATION	
La Feria	4	Casa Turire	7
Maracuja	2	Hostel Casa de Lis	4
Restaurante Don Porfi	1	Hotel Villa Florencia	5
Wok & Roll	3	Hotel Wagelia	2
		Interamericano	3
		Pacuare Lodge	9
		Rancho Naturalista	8
		Turrialba B&B	1
		Turrialtico Lodge	6

TURRIALBA

Wildlife-watching

As well as hosting a number of vital germplasm projects, including one of the most important collections of coffee and cacao plants in the world, CATIE harbours a range of **wildlife**: armadillos, coatis, sloths and caimans, and, attracted by the myriad tropical plants, 300 species of bird – the central lagoon alone is home to boat-billed heron, northern jacana and purple gallinule, and is the roosting site for a hundred or so great white herons. Keen birders can take part in the **bird-banding** research run by the Programa Monitoreo de Aves, part of an ongoing study into land-use transition – vital when so many Costa Rican farmers are replacing their coffee plantations with sugar cane. Volunteers can help with the catching, weighing and releasing of birds in various habitats across campus.

ARRIVAL AND DEPARTURE

TURRIALBA AND AROUND

By bus Buses to/from San José (every 30min–1hr; 2hr), Cartago (every 30min–1hr; 1hr 20min) and Siquerres (hourly; 2hr) use Turrialba's long-distance station, 400m west of the Parque Central, as do buses to/from Monumento

Nacional Guayabo (3 daily; 1hr). Buses to/from CATIE (8–9 Mon–Fri, 4–5 Sat; 15min) use the local bus station, one block south of the Parque Central.

ACCOMMODATION

IN TOWN

★ **Hostel Casa de Lis** Av Central, C 2/6 ☎ 2556 4933,

ⓦ hostelcasadelis.com. Welcoming Dutch-run "boutique hostel" with clean and spacious dorms, as well

2

WHITEWATER: THE PACUARE AND THE REVENTAZÓN

Turrialba is blessed with two of Central America's finest **whitewater rafting** rivers on its doorstep. Indeed, the scenic **Río Pacuare**'s adrenaline-inducing mix of open canyons and narrow passages has made it one of the best on Earth – when rapids are called "Double Drop" and "Upper Pinball", you know they've earned their names. Although a controversial hydroelectric dam project has put paid to some of the most popular sections of the **Río Reventazón**, there is still a lot of world-class water to ride, especially the technical drops that constitute the Pascua section, where you can tackle the "Corkscrew", the "North Sea" and "Frankenstein" (it's a bit of a monster), among others.

Most **day-trips** (around US$90, including lunch and transport) on the Pacuare run the 29km stretch of Class-IV rapids on the Lower Pacuare (up to 5hr on the river); trips down the Reventazón tend to hit the Class-III rapids at the Caribbean-side section of Florida (up to 2hr 30min on the river) or, for experienced rafters, the 24km of Class-IV+ rapids at Pascua (up to 3hr 30min on the water). **Multiday trips** on the Pacuare include overnight accommodation at jungle lodges along the river.

Recommended Turrialba **rafting operators** include Tico's River Adventure (☎ 2556 1231, ⓦ ticoriver.com) and Costa Rica Ríos (☎ 2556 9617, ⓦ costaricarios.com). Several specialists, including Ríos Tropicales and Exploradores Outdoors, run trips out of San José (see p.67).

---

as private en-suite rooms that wouldn't look out of place in a mid-range hotel. There's also a communal kitchen and small book exchange. Rates include tea and coffee, but not breakfast. Staff can organize horseriding trips to the scenic Aquiares waterfall. Dorms US$14, doubles US$41

Hotel Wagelia Av 4, C 2/4 ☎ 2556 1566, ⓦ hotel wageliaturrialba.com. *Hotel Wagelia* feels a bit like a motel, with beige and somewhat overpriced rooms (with attached bathrooms and TVs) set around a peaceful courtyard. There's a decent on-site bar and restaurant, and a sister hotel, *Wagelia Espino Blanco Lodge*, in Verbena village, 8km north of Turrialba. US$65

Interamericano Av 1, C Central/1 ☎ 2556 0142, ⓦ hotelinteramericano.com. Near the old train station, *Interamericano* is a strong budget option – basic but friendly and an excellent place to meet other travellers. There are a variety of private rooms on offer, and staff can organize kayaking and various other tours. Breakfast costs extra. US$22

★**Turrialba B&B** C 1, Av 6/8 ☎ 2556 6651, ⓦ turribb .com. There's a great vibe at this rafters' favourite, whose rooms come with queen-size beds and sleep up to five people. The spacious public areas include a large kitchen, courtyard with bar and jacuzzi, and a roof terrace. There's also a pool table and dartboard to keep you occupied. US$85

OUT OF TOWN

★**Casa Turire** 8km southeast of Turrialba on the road to La Suiza ☎ 2531 1111, ⓦ hotelcasaturire.com. Elegant, Swiss-owned colonial plantation mansion enfolded by Lago Angostura. Each mellow, wood-floored room has a king-sized bed, cable TV, bathtub and private

balcony, while the honeymoon-worthy master suite (US$452) runs over two floors and has jacuzzi, couches and breathtaking views. There's a dazzling swimming pool, fine-dining restaurant, bar, games room, and spa. The hotel has its own walking trails, and organizes bird-watching and kayaking, as well as trips to Monumento Nacional Guayabo. US$185

Hotel Villa Florencia 5km east of Turrialba, on the road to Siquirres ☎ 2557 3536, ⓦ villaflorencia.com. Set amid coffee fields near CATIE, the large, likeable rooms – wood-floored and featuring two queen-sized beds – open out onto lovely grounds, home to toucans, oropendolas and a variety of other chattering birdlife. There's a decent restaurant, too. US$157

Pacuare Lodge 35km northeast of Turrialba, on the Río Pacuare ☎ 2225 3939, ⓦ pacuarelodge.com. Archetypal luxury hideaway (palm-thatched river-view suites, vast canopy king-sizes dressed in Egyptian-cotton sheets) with a difference – you paddle yourself there in a raft, negotiating several kilometres of the raging Río Pacuare (see box above) in order to bed down for the night in your own private piece of paradise (it is also possible to travel to the lodge by bus, mini cable car, and electric car). Dinner can be taken in the "Nest", a platform in the branches of a kapok tree, 60m above the jungle floor. The ecolodge part-funds a nearby jaguar research project and its own conservation efforts include reintroducing howler monkeys into the surrounding area. Minimum two-night stay. US$521

Rancho Naturalista 20km southeast of Turrialba, beyond La Suiza ☎ 2554 8100, ⓦ costaricagateway .com. Rustic lodge with cosy rooms that is famed among birdwatchers (more than 400 bird species have been spotted in the area). It's not cheap, but the cost includes

PARQUE NACIONAL VOLCÁN TURRIALBA

Volcán Turrialba (3328m), around 15km north of Turrialba, erupted for the first time in 145 years on January 5, 2010, blowing a large vent in the crater's upper wall and forcing the evacuation of sixty people from local villages. There have been several further eruptions – and evacuations – since then, and at the time of publication, the park remained closed to the public.

three gourmet communal meals and guided tours – and the property has its own network of rainforest trails. Rates include full board. US$360

Turrialtico Lodge 7.5km southeast of Turrialba, on the road to Siquirres ☎ 2538 1111, ⚇ turrialtico.com. Cosy lodge, groaning under the weight of its blossoming bougainvillea. Farmhouse-style rooms are decorated with handmade bedspreads and work by local artists; some have balconies overlooking the gorgeous surrounding countryside (rooms with views of the Turrialba volcano cost US$11 extra). They organize tours to Monumento Nacional Guayabo. US$64

2

EATING

Turrialba's great range of accommodation options is sadly not matched by its dining scene, which is decidedly underwhelming. Several *sodas* around the main square offer inexpensive *típico* dishes, while fresh produce can be bought every Friday and Saturday at the **farmers' market** held alongside the disused railway tracks (7am–5pm).

La Feria Av 4, just up from Hotel Wagelia ☎ 2556 5550. Simple, friendly restaurant with a no-nonsense menu of *casados*, *gallo pinto* and *arroz cons* (₡1200–5000), as well as more expensive steak, fish and chicken dishes, and a range of salads. The walls are decorated with musical notes and photos of the town's award-winning municipal band. Mains around ₡3000–5000. Mon & Wed–Sun 11.30am–10pm, Tues 11.30am–2pm.

Maracuja C 2, Av 10/12 ☎ 2556 2021. This cheerful café feels a touch more contemporary than its competitors, with a creative selection of light meals (₡3300–3800), including club sandwiches, falafel-filled pitas, and stuffed plantains, plus good coffee, smoothies and ice cream sundaes. Mon & Wed–Sun 11am–9pm.

Restaurante Don Porfi 4km north of Turrialba, on the road to Volcán Turrialba ☎ 2556 9797. *Restaurante Don Porfi* provides the best food in town – or, rather, just outside town. The international cuisine (mains ₡4000–9000) is well prepared, and there's a good wine list, too. Mon, Tues & Thurs–Sun 11am–11pm.

Wok & Roll C 1, at Av 6 ☎ 2556 6756. Head here for a change from the norm and some pan-Asian flavours: sushi, pad thai, chop suey, and *bibimbap* (a tasty Korean rice dish) all feature, as well as some less-successful fusion options (mains ₡4000–20,000). Service is slow, but portions are huge – the "*entero*" size is big enough for two. Mon & Wed–Sun 11.30am–10pm.

DIRECTORY

Banks and exchange There are several ATMs around town, including at the Banco Popular on Av 4. Hospital William Allen Taylor Hospital (just off Hwy-10; ☎ 2558 1300).

Post office The post office (Mon–Fri 8am–5.30pm) is just north of the centre, directly above the square.

Monumento Nacional Guayabo

19km northeast of Turrialba and 84km east of San José • Daily 8am–3.30pm • US$5 • ☎ 2559 1220 • Guides (around US$10) can be hired at the entrance, though not all speak English

The most accessible ancient archeological site in Costa Rica, the **MONUMENTO NACIONAL GUAYABO** was discovered by explorer Anastasio Alfaro at the end of the nineteenth century; the remains of the town of Guayabo, believed to have been inhabited from about 300 BC to 1400 AD, were only excavated in the late 1960s. Thanks to a lack of funds and the fact that it is surrounded by privately owned land, only a fraction of the site has been excavated, but facilities are improving. The site, a dairy farm until 1968, lacks the dramatic monuments of the magnificent Maya and Aztec ruins in Mexico and Guatemala – cultures contemporaneous with Guayabo – but is nevertheless an evocative place to visit. The mosquitoes (and other biting insects) can be fierce here, so make sure you bring repellent.

2

The site

Facing the considerable difficulties posed by the density of the rainforest terrain, the Guayabo managed not only to live in harmony with an environment that remains hostile to human habitation, but also constructed a complex system of water management and social organization, and expressed themselves through the "written language" of **petroglyphs**. Other than this, little is known of them, and there are no clues as to why Guayabo was ultimately abandoned, though hypotheses include an epidemic and war with neighbouring tribes.

The mysteries of Guayabo are amplified by today's site, which lacks anything in the way of information or interpretation; it's a good idea to hire a **guide** to help you decipher what can otherwise look like random piles of stone. Either way, it's best to start at the gloomy **exhibition** space, which has a model showing how the town would have looked, before heading up to the *mirador* for an overview; the trail (1.6km) then weaves its way down among the mounds; a new wheelchair-accessible section of the trail opened in mid-2017.

Aqueducts

Most of the heaps of stones and basic structures now exposed were erected between 300 and 700 AD, though the (still working) **aqueducts** at the northwestern end of the site are some two thousand years old. Excavations have shown that the Guayabo were particularly skilled in water conducting – look out for the stone **tanque de captación** near here, where they stored water carried in these subterranean channels from nearby springs.

Mounds and tombs

At the heart of the town is the **central mound**. Of the 43 *montículos* (mounds) that make up the site, this is the tallest circular base unearthed so far, with two staircases and pottery remains at the very top. Guayabo houses were built to a hierarchial system, and it is likely that this was home to the community chief, a *cacique*, who had both social and religious power. Near the central mound, you can see some of the **tombs** (known as *tumbas de cajón*, or drawer tombs) that have been uncovered in various parts of the site. They were constructed in layers of rock (hence their name) brought from surrounding rivers; unfortunately, the tombs discovered so far were plundered by looters long ago. Beyond here, at the eastern end of the site, a paved road, the **Calzada Caragra**, runs for 200m before disappearing into thick jungle; the main entrance to town, this is believed to have once stretched for 20km.

Petroglyphs

The people of Guayabo brought stones to the site from a great distance, probably from the banks of the Río Reventazón, and **petroglyphs** have been found on 53 of these. Most are now in the Museo Nacional in San José (see p.96), but you can still see carvings of what appear to be lizard and jaguar gods, as well as an altogether more intriguingly patterned rock, the so-called **Sky Stone**. Some experts believe this represents a celestial map of the southern skies, and therefore possibly of use as an ancient calendar.

ARRIVAL AND TOURS
MONUMENTO NACIONAL GUAYABO

By bus Daily buses make the 1hr journey from Turrialba's main station (Mon–Sat departs 11.15am, 3.10pm & 5.20pm, returns 5.15am, 7am, 12.30pm & 4pm; Sun 9am, 3pm & 6.30pm, returns 7am, 12.30pm & 4pm). The inconvenient timetable means you'll probably get too long at the site, so alternatively you can walk back to the main road, a 4km downhill hike, and intercept the bus from Santa Teresita to Turrialba, which passes by at about 1.30pm (double-check the times with the *guardaparques*

at the ticket office); if you get stuck, you can always bed down at the monument's small campsite (US$5/person).
By car Driving from Turrialba takes about 30min.
By taxi Taxis charge around US$20 from Turrialba (one way).
Tours Most hotels in Turrialba run tours to the site, as do Explornatura (Av 4; ☎ 2556 0111, ⓦ explornatura .com), who offer a guided hike for US$65 (including return transport).

Limón Province and the Caribbean coast

PLAYA COCLES

Limón Province and the Caribbean coast

The Caribbean coast forms part of the huge, sparsely populated Limón Province, which sweeps south in an arc from Nicaragua to Panama. Hemmed in to the north by dense jungles and swampy waterways, to the west by the mighty Cordillera Central and to the south by the even wider girth of the Cordillera Talamanca, Limón can feel like a lost, remote place. The region features just a handful of really good beaches, mostly along the gorgeous stretch of shore south of the backpacker enclave of Puerto Viejo – other than that, it's mostly a battered, shark-patrolled coast, littered with driftwood.

Nevertheless, you can watch gentle giant sea turtles lay their eggs on the wave-raked beaches of **Tortuguero**; snorkel coral reefs at the unspoilt **Cahuita** or Punta Uva along the **southern Caribbean coast**; or go animal- and bird-spotting in the region's many mangrove swamps. The interior of Limón Province, accessed via the **Guápiles Highway**, is crisscrossed by the powerful Río Reventazón and Río Pacuare, two of the best rivers in the Americas for whitewater rafting.

Though cruise day-trippers have boosted tourism, especially around Puerto Limón, much of the region remains the domain of ecotourists and backpackers, with several laidback towns catering to the trade. Indeed, the province has the highest proportion of protected land in the country, from the **Refugio Nacional de Vida Silvestre Barra del Colorado**, on the Nicaraguan border, to the Refugio Nacional de Vida Silvestre Gandoca-Manzanillo near Panama in the extreme south.

The Caribbean coast also exudes a greater sense of cultural diversity than anywhere else in Costa Rica, thanks to its unique and complex local history. **Puerto Limón**, the only town of any size, is one of several established "black" Central American coastal cities, like Bluefields in Nicaragua and Lívingston in Guatemala. A booming Caribbean port, it has a large, mostly Jamaican-descended Afro-Caribbean population. In the south, near the Panamanian border, live several communities of **indigenous peoples** from the Bribrí and Cabécar groups.

The area's diverse microclimates mean there is no best **time to visit** the Caribbean coast. In Tortuguero and Barra del Colorado, you'll encounter wet weather year-round,

TORTUGUERO CANAL

Highlights

❶ Carnival, Puerto Limón Merrymakers in Afro-Caribbean costumes and spangly tops parade through the streets to a cacophony of tambourines, whistles and blasting sound systems. **See p.165**

❷ Tortuguero Canal Spot moss-covered sloths, chattering spider monkeys, crocodiles, caimans and local life as you float up the beautiful Tortuguero Canal. **See p.170**

❸ Snorkelling in Parque Nacional Cahuita Watch manta rays glide by and iridescent schools of fish shimmer at Costa Rica's largest coral reef. **See p.186**

❹ Playa Cocles, Playa Chiquita and Punta Uva The idyllic beaches of Cocles, Chiquita and Punta Uva dot one of the most beautiful stretches of Costa Rica's Caribbean coast. **See p.192, p.195 & p.196**

❺ Visiting indigenous reserves Learn about traditional plant remedies and indigenous history on a tour to Bribrí and Cabécar villages, led by the grassroots organization ATEC and locals whose families have been in the area since the eighteenth century. **See p.193**

❻ Jaguar Rescue Center Costa Rica's leading conservation initiative is the perfect place to spot howler monkeys, margays, sloths, owls, snakes and caimans (but not jaguars). **See p.193**

HIGHLIGHTS ARE MARKED ON THE MAP ON P.160

with somewhat drier spells in February, March, September and October. South of Limón, September and October offer the best chance of rain-free days.

Brief history

Little is known of the ancient indigenous **Bribrí** and **Cabécar** peoples who inhabited the area when Columbus arrived just off the coast of present-day Puerto Limón, on his fourth and last voyage to the Americas in 1502. Well into the mid-eighteenth century, the only white people the Limón littoral saw were British **pirates**, rum-runners and seamen from the merchant vessels of the famous Spanish Main, plying the rich waters of the Caribbean, and bringing with them commerce and mayhem. Nefarious buccaneers often found refuge on Costa Rica's eastern seaboard, situated as it was between the two more lucrative provinces of Panama and Nicaragua, from which there was a steady traffic of ships to raid. Their presence, along with the difficult terrain, helped deter full-scale settlement of Limón.

LIMÓN PROVINCE AND THE CARIBBEAN COAST

HIGHLIGHTS

1. Carnival, Puerto Limón
2. Tortuguero Canal
3. Snorkelling in Parque Nacional Cahuita
4. Playa Cocles, Playa Chiquita and Punta Uva
5. Visiting indigenous reserves
6. Jaguar Rescue Center

Railways and bananas

The province's development was inextricably linked to two things, themselves related: the **railway and bananas**. In 1871 it was decided that Costa Rica needed a more efficient export route for its coffee crop than the long, meandering river journey from Puerto Viejo de Sarapiquí to Matina (midway between Tortuguero and Puerto Limón), from where the beans were shipped to Europe. From the other main coffee port – Puntarenas on the Pacific coast – boats had to go all the way round South America to get to Europe. **Minor Keith**, an American, assumed control of construction of the railroad across the Cordillera Central from San José to Puerto Limón in 1877 (his uncle, Henry Meiggs, had initiated the project); to help pay for the laying of the track, he planted bananas along its lowland stretches. Successive waves of Chinese, Indian (still locally called Hindus) and Italian immigrant labourers, as well as highland Costa Ricans, were brought in for the gruelling construction work, only to succumb to yellow fever – at least four thousand people died while laying the track for the **Jungle Train** (including Keith's three brothers).

In the final stages, some ten thousand Jamaicans and Barbadians, thought to be immune to the disease, were contracted, many of them staying on to work on further railroad expansion or in the banana plantations. In 1890, the first Jungle Train huffed its way from San José via Turrialba and Siquirres to Limón, bringing an abrupt end to the Caribbean coast's era of near-total isolation. This also marked the beginning of Costa Rica's **banana boom**. Initially planted as a sideline to help fund the railroad, the fruit prospered in this ideal climate, leading Keith to found the United Fruit Company in 1899, whose monopoly of the banana trade throughout Central America made him far wealthier than the railroad ever could.

3

MULTICULTURALISM IN LIMÓN PROVINCE

In his book *Tekkin a Waalk*, journalist and travel writer Peter Ford uses the ingenious term "an anthropological Galápagos" to describe the ethnic and cultural oddities encountered in Limón, where the Caribbean meets Central America. There's no doubt that the province provides a healthy dose of **multiculturalism** lacking in the rest of Costa Rica's relatively homogeneous Latin, Catholic society. In Limón, characterized by intermarriage and racial mixing, it's not unusual to find people who are of combined Miskito, Afro-Caribbean and Nicaraguan ancestry.

ETHNIC DIVERSITY

Though the first black inhabitants of the province were the slaves of the British pirates and mahogany-cutters who had lived in scattered communities along the coast since the mid-1700s, the region's **ethnic diversity** stems largely from the influence of Minor Keith (see p.412), who brought in large numbers of foreign labourers to work on the construction of the Jungle Train. They were soon joined by turtle fishermen who had settled in Bocas del Toro, Panama, before migrating north to escape the Panamanian war of independence from Colombia in 1903. The settlers brought their respective **religions** with them – unlike most other Costa Ricans (who are Catholic), most Afro-Caribbeans in Limón Province are Protestant.

Regardless of race or religion, the coastal settlers were resourceful and independent. They not only planted their own **crops**, bringing seeds to grow breadfruit, oranges, mangoes and ackee, all of which flourished alongside native coconuts and cocoa, but also made their own salt, charcoal, musical instruments and shoes, and brewed their own **spirits** – red rum, *guarapo*, cane liquor and ginger beer.

Limón's diversity has never been appreciated by the ruling and economic elite of the country. Until 1949, Afro-Costa Ricans were effectively forbidden from settling in the Valle Central or the highlands, and while the **indigenous communities** have a degree of autonomy, their traditional territories have long since been eaten up by government-sanctioned mining and banana enterprises. Official discrimination against the province's Afro-Caribbean inhabitants ended in 1949 with a new constitution that granted them full citizenship. Black *limonenses* now make up around thirty percent of the province's population.

Into the modern era

The United Fruit Company kept the region booming well into the twentieth century, though conditions for workers remained harsh – a fact not lost on Jamaican-born activist **Marcus Garvey**, who worked in Puerto Limón in 1910 (see p.164). Costa Rican author and political activist **Carlos Luis Fallas** organized the major banana workers' strike of 1934, but little changed until well after World War II. In 1990, United Fruit renamed itself **Chiquita Brands International** – the company continued to invest heavily in the region, but Limón was neglected and underfunded by the government until relatively recently. The province suffered a major blow in the 1991 **earthquake**, which heaved the Caribbean coast about 1.5 metres up in the air. Already badly maintained roads, bridges and banana railroads were destroyed, including the track for the Jungle Train, one of the most scenic train rides in the world (it's still not in operation). Thanks to a burgeoning container port business and expanding ecotourism, things are much improved today, though banana and plantain exports remain economic mainstays and the southern Talamanca district, home to most of the region's indigenous population, still struggles with high levels of poverty.

3

GETTING AROUND   LIMÓN PROVINCE AND THE CARIBBEAN COAST

By plane There are daily flights from San José to Tortuguero and Limón – you can also fly between Tortuguero and Limón. Barra del Colorado is currently only served by charter flights. See relevant sections for details.

By car Between San José and Puerto Limón, you have a choice of just two roads: the Guápiles Highway (Hwy-32; see below) and the Turrialba Road (Hwy-10). Slow and narrow but well-maintained, the latter runs through Turrialba (see p.150) on the eastern slopes of the Cordillera Central before following the old switchbacking San José–Limón train tracks down to the Guápiles Highway near Siquirres. From Puerto Limón south to the Panama border at Sixaola,

Hwy-36 is the one decent route. Petrol provision is generally poor; it's best to leave San José (and Puerto Limón, if you're driving towards Panama) with a full tank, and fill up at the next station as soon as you reach half a tank.

By shuttle bus All the major shuttle bus companies serve the Caribbean coast. Interbus (ⓦ interbusonline.com) runs direct door-to-door services from San José and, very usefully, La Fortuna, to Puerto Limón and Puerto Viejo.

By bus A reliable bus network operates throughout the province south of Puerto Limón, with the most efficient and modern routes running from San José to Puerto Limón and on to Sixaola.

The Guápiles Highway

The main land route to the Carribbean coast, the **Guápiles Highway** (Hwy-32) begins in San José at the northern end of Calle 3 and climbs out of the highlands to the northeast. Some 65km northeast of San José, **Guápiles** is the first town of any size on the highway and largely functions as a supply centre for the Río Frío banana plantations and a way station for the *bananero* workers – there's little reason to stop here. From Guápiles you can continue on Hwy-32 toward Siquirres and Puerto Limón or, if your ultimate destination is Tortuguero, follow the signs left out of town (Hwy-247 to La Pavona).

Siquirres and around

As the rusted hulks of freight cars and track-scarred streets show, **SIQUIRRES** – which means "reddish colour" in a Miskito dialect – used to be a major railway hub for the **Jungle Train** that carted people, bananas and cacao to the highlands. Along with Turrialba, this is where black train drivers, engineers and maintenance men would swap positions with their "white" (Spanish, *mestizo*, European or highland) counterparts, who would then take the train into the Valle Central, where black people were forbidden from travelling until 1949. Though the Jungle Train no longer runs, trains still haul bananas and machinery to and from Siquirres, mainly servicing the innumerable banana towns or *fincas* nearby (easily recognizable on maps from their factory-farm names of Finca 1, 2, a, b and so forth).

RIVER RAFTING AROUND SIQUIRRES

Siquirres is a major centre for **whitewater rafting**, though most people come through on day-tours from San José or the coast. About 1km east of Siquirres on Hwy-32 is the Exploration Center for **Exploradores Outdoors** (see box, p.190), which runs white-knuckle trips down the Río Pacuare. Use you own transport to get here and receive a US$10 discount (they otherwise offer transport from San José, Fortuna and Puerto Viejo). The **Rios Tropicales Operations Center** also lies off Hwy-32, 6km west of Siquirres (☎2233 6455, ⊛ riostropicales .com), offering one-day river rafting on the Pacuare from US$99.

These days sleepy Siquirres is increasingly trying to pitch itself as an ecotourism destination; the mighty **Río Pacuare** is just to the south of town and **whitewater rafting** operators are based here or in Turrialba (see p.152). You won't find much in the way of sights in town itself except for the **Iglesia Católica de Siquirres**, a completely round church on the western side of the football field (C Central, Av Central/2). Dedicated to San José Patriarca and built to mirror the shape of a Miskito hut, its authentic indigenous shape shelters a plain, wood-panelled interior.

3

ARRIVAL AND DEPARTURE   SIQUIRRES

By bus Buses from San José stop at the bus terminal adjacent to the central plaza (football field), Av 2, at C 1.

Destinations Guápiles (20 daily; 40min); Puerto Limón (16 daily; 50min); San José (10–12 daily; 1hr 30min); Turrialba (14 daily; 2hr).

ACCOMMODATION AND EATING

Centro Turístico Pacuare Hwy-32, at the east edge of town ☎2768 8111, ⊛ centroturisticopacuare.com. Squat, modern facility with sixty spotless rooms that all have cable TV, a/c and wi-fi. There's an outdoor pool, a decent restaurant serving *comida típica*, burgers (₡4000) and salads, a café and a lively karaoke bar on site. As the name implies, it's possible to book trips down the Pacuare here. **US$75**

Rancho Roberto's At the intersection of Hwy-32 and Hwy-4, 13km west of Guápiles ☎2711 0146, ⊛ restauranteranchorobertos.com. This popular roadside restaurant is a welcoming spot to break up the journey from San José to the coast. The menu features heaped plates of *comida típica*, with great-value buffets at ₡3200–5600. Daily 7am–9pm.

Puerto Limón and around

The sweltering capital of the Caribbean coast, **PUERTO LIMÓN** is the country's biggest Afro-Costa Rican city, giving it a street life and cultural flavour quite unlike anywhere else. It's definitely an acquired taste: though things are looking up, Limón (as it's more often simply called) is a traffic-clogged port city that seems a very long way from the ecofriendly attractions that draw most visitors to Costa Rica, and it's principally a hub from which to get a **boat to Tortuguero** (departing Puerto Moín, 7km west), or to catch a bus south to the **beach towns** of Cahuita and Puerto Viejo. **Playa Bonita**, a small beach four kilometres northwest of the centre on the road to Moín, is the most appealing spot in which to base yourself around the city, with a clutch of decent seafront places to stay and eat. Nevertheless, spending at least a day in Limón offers a unique glimpse of contemporary Costa Rica, with its Afro-Caribbean residents speaking an English-based creole reminiscent of the West Indies, vibrant street life and a raucous bar scene that combines salsa, reggaeton, Jamaican ragga and dancehall. If you like to party, the best time to visit is during **El Día de la Raza** carnival, one of the country's most exuberant festivals (see box, p.165).

Brief history

Limón only developed as a major port and railway hub in the 1870s. Thousands of workers from **Jamaica**, Barbados, and Trinidad and Tobago were brought in, which explains the profusion of English surnames here and the accent (see box, p.161).

One of them was Jamaican-born **Marcus Garvey**, who moved to Limón in 1910 to work for the United Fruit Company – his experiences of racism and poor working conditions would inform his later career in New York, where he became a controversial activist for African-American rights. In 1922, Garvey's **Universal Negro Improvement Association** built an office in Limón; known as the **Black Star Line** building, after Garvey's short-lived shipping venture, and later a popular restaurant, it tragically burned down in 2016 (at the time of research there were plans to rebuild).

After years of neglect, Limón is beginning to shake its seedy reputation, with the city's **container port** business booming (ninety percent of the country's exports depart from here, and the new US$1 billion Moín container terminal is due to open in 2018), while its development as a **cruise ship** destination means security in the centre is much improved. Though development has already transformed the heart of town, with new shops, condos and businesses, the city is unlikely to lose its essential character anytime soon – it remains down-at-heel in parts, with sleazy bars spilling onto the streets and salsa beats wafting through the market.

Mercado Central and around

Av 2, C 3/4 • Mon–Sat 6am–8pm

Pedestrianized **Avenida 2** is Limón's main drag, a melange of contemporary stores and dilapidated buildings along both the north edge of Parque Vargas and the south side of the **Mercado Central**. At times, the market seems to contain the entire population of Limón – dowager women mind their stalls while men clutch cigarettes, chattering and gesticulating. The produce is fresh: chayotes, plantains, cassava, yucca, beans and the odd banana (most of the crop is exported) vie for space with bulb-like cacao fruit, baseball-sized tomatoes and huge carrots. For an inexpensive bite to eat, try the market's numerous *sodas* and snack bars (modern Costa Rican chains seem to have taken over on the outside – go deeper into the market to find the more traditional stalls). The market dates back to 1893 but has been remodelled several times – the latest was completed in 2017. Just across the street (Av 2, at C 4), take a look at the recently restored emerald-green **Correos y Telégrafos** (Post Office & Telegraph Building), a handsome example of the city's "Victorian Caribbean" architecture, completed in 1911.

Parque Vargas and around

C 1, Av 1/2 • Daily 24hr

Limón's lush **Parque Vargas** was opened by the United Fruit Company in 1905, and after many years of neglect is gradually being refurbished. The park's soaring royal palms, its most distinctive feature, offer a pleasantly shady respite from the chaotic streets beyond – look out for the **sloths** that lounge in the trees (locals will find them for you for ₡1000), though thanks to recent construction, their future looked uncertain at the time of writing. The park features several small monuments, notably the elegant Neoclassical bandstand of 1911 (now restored), the sculpted installation that pays homage to the many cultures that built the railroad, and a smaller shrine-like memorial to Christopher Columbus; the admiral supposedly anchored his ship off Isla Uvita in 1502, the small island visible from the scrappy **malecón** viewpoint at the eastern end of the park (at the end of Av 2). The island is uninhabited, but features a reef break popular with local surfers – swimming here is not advised, however. The *malecón* end of the park also features a now-dilapidated amphitheatre, shaped like a ship's prow and long abandoned. Opposite, also at the end of Avenida 2, lies the **Municipalidad** (town hall), a Neoclassical building that dates back to 1942, and the adjacent, beautifully restored **Centro Comunitario Expresión Artística**, a cultural centre housed in the former Capitanía de Puerto Limón (port management office), constructed out of pitch pine by the United Fruit Company in 1930.

EL DÍA DE LA RAZA CARNIVAL

Though carnivals in the rest of Latin America are usually associated with the days before Lent, the Limón carnival celebrates Columbus's arrival in the New World on October 12, 1492 (and more especially, his alleged arrival in Limón in 1502). The festival was dreamed up in 1949 by Alfred "King" Smith, a local who had been away working in Panama's Canal Zone. He was so impressed with that country's Columbus Day celebrations that he decided to bring the merriment home to Limón. Today, **El Día de la Raza** (Day of the People) basically serves as an excuse to party. Throngs of highland Ticos descend upon Limón – buses fill to bursting, hotels brim and partygoers hit the streets in search of this year's sounds and style. Rap, rave and ragga – in Spanish and English – are hot, and Bob Marley lives, or at least is convincingly resurrected, for carnival week.

Carnival can mean anything you want it to, from noontime displays of Afro-Caribbean dance to calypso music, bull-running, children's theatre, colourful *desfiles* (parades) and massive firework displays. Most spectacular is the **Grand Desfile**, usually held on the Saturday before October 12, when locals in Afro-Caribbean costumes – sequins, spangles and fluorescent colours – parade through the streets to a cacophony of tambourines, whistles and blasting sound systems.

The overall atmosphere – even late at night – remains unthreatening, with teens and grandparents alike enjoying the music around Parque Vargas. Kiosks dispense steaming Chinese, Caribbean and Tico food, and on-the-spot discos help pump up the volume. Kids can play games at small fairgrounds to win candyfloss and stuffed toys. Elsewhere, bars overflow onto the street, and the impromptu partying builds up as the night goes on.

Catedral Limón

C 4, at Av 4 • Daily 6am–7pm • ☎ 2758 0093

One of the more distinctive buildings in Limón is the Catedral del Sagrado Corazón de Jesús, aka **Catedral Limón**, a modern edifice consecrated only in 2010. Don't be put off by the dull, concrete exterior – inside there's a bank of stunning stained-glass windows, and beyond the new building there's an older section and bell tower from the 1890s, that has survived various hurricanes and the 1991 earthquake.

ARRIVAL AND DEPARTURE

PUERTO LIMÓN AND AROUND

BY PLANE

Limón's tiny Aeropuerto Internacional Pablo Zidar is on the coast, 5km south of the centre off Hwy-36. Sansa flies daily from San José (35min) – some flights go via Tortuguero (20min). Taxis charge around ₡5000 or US$10 for the ride into town. You can also flag down local buses on the road outside (₡105).

BY CAR

It can be useful and cost effective to rent a car here to explore the coast to the south: Adobe (☎ 2758 4042, ⓦ adobecar.com) has an office in the centre on Av 1, C 4/5 (daily 8am–5pm).

BY BUS

You should buy your tickets several days in advance during El Día de la Raza (see box, p.165), even though extra buses run at this time.

Terminal Caribeños Av 2, C 7/8. Grupos Caribeños (☎ 2222 0610) buses from San José, Siquirres, Liverpool (for Veragua Rainforest) and Guápiles arrive and depart here. At the same terminal you can catch a bus to Moín, which leaves only when it's full.

Destinations Guápiles (10–14 daily; 1hr 30min); Moín (hourly 5.30am–6.30pm; 30min); San José (daily every 30min; 2hr 30min–3hr); Siquirres (16 daily; 50min).

Autotransportes MEPE Terminal C 6, at Av 1 (three blocks southwest of Mercado Central), ☎ 2257 8129. Buses to/from the south – Bananito, Cahuita, Puerto Viejo, Manzanillo and Sixaola – use this modern terminal; there's an ATM and plenty of snack stalls here.

Destinations Bananito (daily 5am–6pm, every 30min; 1hr); Cahuita (daily 7.30am–4.30pm, every 30min; 1hr); Manzanillo (6 daily; 1hr 45min); Puerto Viejo de Talamanca (daily 7.30am–4.30pm, every 30min; 1hr 30min); Sixaola (daily 5am–7pm, hourly; 3hr).

BY LANCHA

A co-operative of water taxis provides a shared service from the docks at Moín to Tortuguero (3–4hr) daily at 10am (arrive before 9am to secure a spot). Expect to pay at least US$35 one way (shallow-bottomed private *lanchas* also make the trip up the coastal canal from the docks, but you'll have to pay a lot more).

BY TAXI

Taxis line up on Av 2 and around the corner from Terminal Caribeños: they do long-haul trips to Cahuita and Puerto Viejo (US$60–80) and beyond. If you're going to Moín, a taxi (around US$10) makes more sense than waiting for the bus, which won't leave until it's full.

ACCOMMODATION

Staying **downtown** puts you in the thick of things, but the truth is that most hotels in central Limón are seedy, poor value and old – if you want to stay here, try the *Park Hotel* (see opposite), which stands alone on a little promontory close to the sea and is by far the best option (book ahead). There's also a group of quieter hotels outside town (about 4km up the spur road to Moín) at **Playa Bonita**. A taxi here costs around ₡2500, and the bus to and from Moín runs along the road every

---

LIMÓN PATOIS

Limón patois combines **English phrases**, brought by Jamaican and Barbadian immigrants to the province in the last century, with a Spanish slightly different to that spoken in the highlands. Though used less these days, the traditional greeting of "What happen?" ("Whoppin?") remains a stock phrase, equivalent to the Spanish *"¿Qué pasa?"* ("What's going on?"). In Limón, you'll also hear the more laconic "Okay" or "All right" (both hello and goodbye) taking the place of the Spanish *"Adiós"* ("hello" in Costa Rica, rather than goodbye), *"Que le vaya bien"* and *"Que Dios le acompañe"*.

While English might be spoken at home, and among the older Limón crowd, Spanish is the language taught at school and used on the street, particularly among the younger generation. Older *limonenses* sometimes refer to Spanish-speakers as "Spaniamen" (which comes out sounding like "Sponyaman").

20min or so; it's not advisable to walk into town. **Hotel prices** rise by as much as fifty percent for carnival week, and to a lesser extent during Semana Santa (Easter week). Free wi-fi is included at all the recommendations below.

Hotel La Uvita Carretera a Portete (Hwy-240), Playa Bonita ☎ 2795 2583. Charming little hotel run by a friendly couple with a lovely swimming pool, clean cabins (which sleep up to three people) with a/c, sea views and breakfast delivered to your room for ₡3000. US$55

★ **Hotel Playa Westfalia** Hwy-36 (2km south of Limón airport) ☎ 2756 1300, ⓦ hotelplayawestfalia.com. If you're looking for serenity within easy driving distance of Limón, this idyllic beachfront hotel is unquestionably your best choice. The eight well-appointed rooms and suites all have a/c and cable TV, and the hotel has a pool and a pleasant restaurant serving Caribbean cuisine. US$110

Maribú Caribe Carretera a Portete (Hwy-240), Playa Bonita ☎ 2795 4010, ⓦ maribu-caribe.com. Very basic seaside hotel with thatched-roof huts, cable TV, 1960s decor, a pool and a pleasant but pricey bar-restaurant overlooking the sea – great views and friendly staff, at least. Basic breakfast included. US$78

Park Hotel Av 3, C 1/3, Puerto Limón ☎ 2758 4364, ⓦ parkhotellimon.com. Popular with Ticos and travellers alike, this comfy hotel has rooms in a range of styles, though all are a little dated (especially the bathrooms); the more expensive ones come with a sea view, while slightly cheaper rooms have a street view (which can be noisy). All are clean, and come with cable TV, and there's a good restaurant on site. It's important to book in advance, as this is considered (by far) the city's best hotel. US$110

EATING

Limón has a decent variety of places to eat, with several restaurants focusing on authentic **Caribbean and Creole cuisine** – spicy dishes such as jerk chicken, *rondón* (usually a stew) and anything with cashew nuts (look out for cashew wine, which is a speciality here). Inside the Mercado Central it's quite safe and you'll find a host of decent *sodas* serving tasty *casados* (they tend to close after lunch).

IN TOWN

Caribbean Kalisi Coffee Shop C 6, Av 3/4 (opposite the cathedral) ☎ 2758 3249. Popular buffet restaurant with an enticing spread of Limonese favourites, from Caribbean chicken (jerk-style) to red beans and rice cooked in coconut milk – each meal comes with a pasta or salad and plantains. Leave space for the Jamaican-style ginger ale, and the delicious home-made desserts such as passionfruit cheesecake. Around ₡5000 per head. Mon–Sat 7.30am–8pm, Sun 7.30am–5pm.

Gelato y Café Lemons C 6, Av 2/3 ☎ 2758 6897. Best ice cream in town, with giant scoops from ₡1200, plus frozen yoghurt, banana splits and a range of sweet toppings. Mon–Sat 11am–9pm.

Park Hotel Av 3, C 1/3 ☎ 2758 4364, ⓦ parkhotellimon.com. The only restaurant in town where you feel you might actually be in the Caribbean – warm breezes float in through large slatted windows that look out onto vistas of blue seas and clouds as far as the eye can see. Dine on excellent, though pricey, breakfast and standard Costa Rican dishes, including seafood (from ₡5870) and *arroz con pollo* (₡4300). Daily 7am–10pm.

Soda El Patty Av 5, at C 7 ☎ 2798 3407. No-frills hole in the wall celebrated locally for its tasty Jamaican meat patties (pasties stuffed with chillies and minced beef; ₡750– 1500), plus its fresh juices (from blackberry, tamarind and mango to "hiel", a sort of ginger ale). Daily 7am–7pm.

Taylor's Restaurant C 5, at Av 5 ☎ 2798 1948, ⓦ taylorrestaurant.com. Popular local diner across from the old Black Star Line building, serving classic Limonese food, such as oxtail *casado* (₡4100) and red snapper with shrimp sauce (₡10,000). Mon–Fri 6am–9.30pm, Sat & Sun 11am–6pm.

Tsunami Sushi C 1, at Av 3 ☎ 2758 8628. This casual spot across from the *Park Hotel* serves decent sushi but is best known for its lively bar, especially on Fri and Sat when DJs are supplemented by live bands (mostly ragga and reggaeton). Mon–Sat 11.30am–2am.

PLAYA BONITA

Quimbamba Bar & Restaurant Hwy-240, Playa Bonita ☎ 2795 4805. Dine on excellent Caribbean seafood dishes (try the garlic shrimp with the coconut rice-and-beans) cooked to order at this hopping split-level beach-bar. Live music at the weekend. Tends to be popular with cruise ship tours, so avoid on port days. Mains ₡3000–6000. Daily 8am–late.

DRINKING IN LIMÓN

Gringos in general and women especially should avoid most **bars** in downtown Limón, especially those that have a large advertising placard blocking your view of the interior, which is often less than salubrious. *Tsunami Sushi* (see p.167) is a safer bet for a raucous night out, while the beachside restaurants of **Playa Bonita** offer a laidback alternative for cold beers and live music.

★**Restaurante Reina's** Hwy-240, Playa Bonita ☎ 2795 0879. Stylish beachside restaurant and lounge-bar that's equally successful at delivering tasty Caribbean cuisine (particularly the seafood), smooth cocktails and energetic local live acts and DJs. Mains ₡2500–5000. Daily 10am–10pm.

DIRECTORY

Banks and exchange The Banco de Costa Rica (Av 2, at C 1) and Scotiabank (Av 3, at C 2) both offer money exchange and have ATMs that accept Visa and Cirrus.

Hospital ☎ 2758 2222. Hospital Dr. Tony Facio Castro is the largest hospital on the coast, located on the northern edge of town, along the *malecón*; to get there, just follow Av 6 and walk north along the shore.

Post office Av 2, at C 4 (Mon–Fri 8am–5pm, Sat 8am–noon). The mail service from Limón is poor – you're better off posting items from San José.

CREOLE CUISINE IN LIMÓN PROVINCE

Creole cuisine is known throughout the Americas, from Louisiana to Bahía, for its imaginative use of African spices and vegetables, succulent fish and chicken dishes and fantastic sweet desserts. Sample Limón's version at any of the locally run restaurants dotted along the coast. Sitting down to dinner at a red gingham tablecloth, with a cold bottle of Imperial beer, reggae on the boombox and a plate heaped with coconut-scented rice-and-beans is one of the real pleasures of visiting this part of Costa Rica. Note that many restaurants, in keeping with age-old local tradition, feature Creole dishes at weekends only, serving simpler dishes or the usual highland rice concoctions during the week.

TYPICAL DISHES

Everyone outside Limón will tell you that the local speciality, **rice-and-beans** (in the lilting local accent it sounds like "rizanbin"), is "*comida muy pesada*" (very heavy food). However, this truly wonderful mixture of red or black beans and rice cooked in coconut milk is no more *pesada* – and miles tastier – than traditional highland dishes like *arroz con camarones*, where everything is fried; it's the coconut milk that gives this dish its surprising lift. Another local speciality is **pan bon**, glazed sweet bread laced with cheese and fruit which is often eaten for dessert, as are ginger biscuits and plantain tarts. *Pan bon* doesn't translate as "good bread", as is commonly thought; "bon" actually derives from "bun", brought by English-speaking settlers.

Rondón (to "rundown" is to cook) is a vegetable and meat or fish stew in which the plantains and breadfruit cook for many hours, very slowly, in spiced coconut milk. It may be hard to find, mainly because it takes a long time, at least an afternoon, to prepare. Though some restaurants – *Miss Junie's* (see p.175) in Tortuguero and *Miss Edith's* (see p.184) in Cahuita – have it on their menus as a matter of course, it's usually best to stop by on the morning of the day you wish to dine and request it for that evening.

Herbal teas are also a speciality of the province and available in many restaurants: try wild peppermint, wild basil, soursop, lime, lemongrass or ginger ("huil").

THE KEY INGREDIENTS

Favoured **spices** in Limonese Creole cooking include cumin, coriander, peppers, chillies, paprika, cloves and groundspice, while the most common vegetables are those you might find in a street market in West Africa, Brazil or Jamaica. Native to Africa, **ackee** (in Spanish *seso vegetal*) was brought to the New World by British colonists, and has to be prepared by knowledgeable cooks because its sponge-cake-like yellow fruit, enclosed in three-inch pods, is poisonous until the pods open. Served boiled, ackee resembles scrambled eggs and goes well with fish. **Yucca**, also known as manioc, is a long pinkish tuber, similar to the yam, and usually boiled or fried. Local yams can grow as big as 25kg, and are used much like potato in soups and stews. Another native African crop, the huge melon-like **breadfruit** (*fruta de pan*), is more a starch substitute than a fruit, with white flesh that has to be boiled, baked or grated. **Pejiballes** (*pejibaye* in Spanish – English-speaking people in Limón pronounce it "picky-BAY-ah") are small green or orange fruits that look a little like limes. They're boiled in hot water and skinned – and are definitely an acquired taste, being both salty and bitter. You'll find them sold on the street in San José, but they're most popular in Limón. Better known as heart-of-palm, **palmito** is served in restaurants around the world as part of a tropical salad. **Plantains** (*plátanos* in Spanish), the staple of many highland dishes, figure particularly heavily in Creole cuisine, and are deliciously sweet when baked or fried in fritters.

Veragua Rainforest Research & Adventure Park

Brisas de Veragua (12km south of Liverpool) • Tues–Sun 8am–3pm • Exhibits US$38; canopy tour US$55; exhibits & aerial tram US$69; exhibits, aerial tram & canopy tour US$99 • ☏ 4000 0949, ⓦ veraguarainforest.com

Some 25km west of Limón, the **Veragua Rainforest Research & Adventure Park** provides a quick and sleek introduction to some of the region's rich biodiversity, as well as offering exhilarating ziplines and a cable car ride through the jungle canopy. On the downside it's a very pricey experience, and is now almost totally marketed to cruise-ship tours (Oct–May is the main cruise-ship season) – it's only worthwhile for independent travellers with very limited time in Costa Rica.

Owned and operated entirely by Costa Ricans, Veragua attractions include several smartly-designed animal exhibits (including a butterfly garden and frog and reptile habitats), the aerial tram, a nine-zipline canopy tour and an elevated trail through the rainforest leading to a waterfall. Given the volume of visitors passing through you are unlikely to see much wildlife, however, though the resident troupe of white-faced capuchin monkeys aren't exactly camera-shy. The real highlight for most visitors is the Foundation for Rainforest Research, where you can talk with the resident biologists and learn more about the ongoing study of the park's stunning collection of butterflies.

3

ARRIVAL AND DEPARTURE   VERAGUA RAINFOREST

By bus Buses for Siquirres leave Limón's Terminal de Caribeños hourly; get off at the Liverpool town stop, about 12km from Limón on Hwy-32 – let the bus driver know you're going to Veragua. The road leading to Veragua is signposted about 50m from the bus stop. Call in advance to arrange pick-up from here, which is possible most days.

By car If you're driving, a 4WD is necessary to negotiate the bone-rattling gravel road that covers the final 3km

to the rainforest.

By tour The Veragua Rainforest offers day-trip packages including transport from San José (US$149/person) and Puerto Viejo (US$129/person), with pick-up from your hotel (minimum four people; canopy tour US$40 extra).

By taxi You should be able to negotiate a rate of around US$50–60 (return) with taxi drivers in Limón, including the wait at the reserve; they'll ask for much more initially.

Tortuguero

Despite its isolation – **TORTUGUERO** is 254km from San José by road and water – the **Parque Nacional Tortuguero** is among the most visited national parks in Costa Rica. Though its biodiversity has few peers in the country, it is most known for its turtles, specifically the **green sea turtle**. Along with leatherback and hawksbill turtles, green sea turtles lay their eggs here between July and October in great numbers, making it one of the most important nesting sites in the world for the species.

First established as a protective zone in the 1960s, Tortuguero officially became a national park in 1970. It encompasses 770 square kilometres of protected territory (some 500 square kilometres is marine), including not only the beach on which the turtles nest, but also the surrounding impenetrable tropical rainforest, coastal mangrove swamps and lagoons, and canals and waterways. Except during the comparatively dry months of February, March, September and October, the park is fairly wet, receiving over 3500mm of rain a year.

As elsewhere in Costa Rica, logging, economic opportunism and fruit plantations have affected the parkland. Sometimes advertised by package-tour brochures as a "Jungle Cruise" along "Central America's Amazon", the journey to Tortuguero is indeed Amazonian, taking you past tracts of **deforestation** and lands cleared for cattle – all outside the park's official boundaries but, together with the banana plantations, disturbingly close to its western fringes.

Tortuguero village

The peaceful village of **TORTUGUERO**, with a population of around 1500, lies at the northeastern corner of the park, on a thin spit of land between the sea and the

ACCOMMODATION

Aracari Garden Hostel	8
Cabinas Balcón del Mar	11
Cabinas Meriscar	9
Cabinas Tortuguero	10
Casa Marbella	7
Laguna Lodge	5
Mawamba Lodge	3
Miss Junie's Lodge	6
Pachira Lodge	4
Tortuga Lodge	2
Turtle Beach Lodge	1

SEE MAP BELOW FOR DETAILS

0 — 5 kilometres

PARQUE NACIONAL TORTUGUERO

TORTUGUERO VILLAGE

EATING

Budda Café	4
Dorling's Bakery	3
Miss Junie's	2
Miss Miriam's	5
El Muellecito	6
Wild Ginger	1

DRINKING AND NIGHTLIFE

La Culebra	1
La Taberna	2

0 — 100 metres

Tortuguero Canal, the waterway that connects the port of Moín (8km north of Puerto Limón) to the national park. It was dug in the late 1960s in order to bypass the treacherous breakers of the Caribbean. The exuberant foliage of wisteria, oleander and bougainvillea imbues the village with a tropical garden feel, while tall palm groves loom over patchy expanses of grass dotted with zinc-roofed wooden houses, often elevated on stilts. This is classic Caribbean style: washed-out, slightly ramshackle and pastel-pretty, with very little to disturb the torpor until after dark.

A dirt path – the "main street" – runs north–south through the village, from which narrow paths lead to the sea and the canal. Smack in the middle of the village (near the football field, the major landmark) stands one of the prettiest churches (Iglesia Católica de Tortuguero) you'll see anywhere in Costa Rica, tiny and pale yellow, with a small spire and an oval doorway.

Natural History Museum

The northern edge of the village, near the beach • Daily 10am–noon & 2–5.30pm • US$2 • ⓦ conserveturtles.org

At the north end of Tortuguero village is the **Natural History Museum**, run by the Sea Turtle Conservancy, with a small but informative exhibition explaining the life cycle of sea turtles. You can watch a rather portentous twenty-minute video explaining the history of turtle conservation in the area and, before you leave, you'll be invited to "adopt a turtle" for US$25, for which you'll receive an adoption certificate and information so that you can track the migratory progress of your chosen beast on the internet as it makes its slow, purposeful way across the ocean.

Cerro Tortuguero

US$2 (payable to the park authorities) • Must go with a guide; accessible only by *lancha* from Tortuguero village

Cerro Tortuguero, an ancient volcanic deposit, looms 119m above the flat coastal plain 6km north of the village. A half-day climb up the gently sloping sides leads you to the "peak", where you can enjoy good views of flat jungle and inland waterways. Of the lodges, only *Laguna Lodge* (see p.175) offers the guided climb as part of its accommodation package.

Parque Nacional Tortuguero

Main entrance at the south end of the village • Daily 6am–6pm (last entry 4pm) • US$15 • ☎ 2710 2929

Most people visiting the **PARQUE NACIONAL TORTUGUERO** come for the **desove**, or egg-laying of endangered marine turtles. Few are disappointed, with the majority of tours during **laying seasons** (March–May & July–Oct) resulting in sightings of the surreal procession of the reptiles from the sea to make their egg-nests in the sand. While turtles have been known to lay in the daylight (the hatchlings wait under the cover of sand until nightfall to emerge), it is far more common for them to come ashore in the relative safety of night. Nesting can take place turtle-by-turtle – you can watch a single mother come ashore and scramble up the beach just south of the village – or, more strikingly, in groups (*arribadas*), when dozens emerge from the sea at the same time to form a colony, marching up the sands to their chosen spot, safely above the high-tide mark. Each turtle digs a hole in which she lays eighty or more eggs; the collective whirring noise of sand being dug away is extraordinary. Having filled the hole with sand to cover the eggs, the turtles begin their course back to the sea, leaving the eggs to hatch some weeks later. When the hatchlings emerge they instinctively follow the light of the moon on the water, scuttling to safety in the ocean.

Along with the **green** (*verde*) turtle, named for the colour of soup made from its flesh, you might see the **hawksbill** (*carey*), with its distinctive hooked beak, and the ridged **leatherback** (*baula*), the largest turtle in the world, which weighs around 300kg – though some are as heavy as 500kg and reach 2.4m in length. The green turtles and hawksbills nest mainly from July to October (August is the peak month), while the leatherbacks may come ashore from March to May.

El Gavilán trail and beach

The well-maintained **El Gavilán Trail** (4km round trip) starts at the ranger station at the park entrance and heads toward the coast where it turns south as the **Jaguar Trail**, following the beach for another 1.3km (this is the trail used to watch turtles). It's a mostly shaded walk, and it gives you a good chance of glimpsing macaws, lizards and monkeys. As for the long, wild **beach**, in theory you could continue to amble south for up to 24km, spotting crabs and birds along the way, and also looking for turtle tracks, which resemble the two thick parallel lines a truck would leave in its wake. Swimming is not a good idea, due to heavy waves, turbulent currents and sharks. Remember that you need to pay **park fees** to walk either on the beach or along the trail.

ARRIVAL AND DEPARTURE   **PARQUE NACIONAL TORTUGUERO**

BY LANCHA
North of Puerto Limón there is no public land transport

at all: instead, *lanchas* ply the coastal Tortuguero Canal. La Pavona, not much more than a boat dock about 50km

---

WILDLIFE IN PARQUE NACIONAL TORTUGUERO

Tortuguero is home to a staggering abundance of **wildlife** – fifty kinds of **fish**, numerous **birds**, including the endangered green parrot and the vulture, and about 160 **mammals**, some under the threat of extinction. Due to the waterborne nature of most transport and the impenetrability of the ground cover, it's difficult to spot them, but howler, white-faced capuchin and spider monkeys lurk behind the undergrowth. The park is also home to the fishing bulldog bat, which locates its underwater prey by sonar, and a variety of large rodents, including the window rat, whose internal organs you can see through its transparent skin. Jaguars used to thrive here, but are slowly being driven out by the encroaching banana plantations at the western end of the park. You may also spot the West Indian manatee, or sea cow – or much less likely, bull sharks, as good a reason as any to not try swimming here. It's the **turtles**, however, that draw all the visitors. The sight of the gentle beasts tumbling ashore and shimmying their way up the beach to deposit their heavy load before limping back into the dark, phosphorescent waves can't fail to move you.

THREATS TO MARINE TURTLES

For hundreds of years the fishermen of the Caribbean coast made their living culling the seemingly plentiful turtle population, selling shell and meat for large sums to middlemen in Puerto Limón. Initially, turtles were hunted for local consumption only, but during the first two decades of the 1900s, the fashion for turtle soup in Europe, especially England, led to large-scale exports.

TURTLE-HUNTING

Turtle-hunting was a particularly brutal practice. Spears were fashioned from long pieces of wood, and fastened with a simple piece of cord to a sharp, barbed metal object. Standing in their canoes, fishermen hurled the spear, like a miniature harpoon, into the water, lodging the spear in the turtle's flesh. Pulling their canoes closer, the fishermen would then reel in the cord attached to the spear, lift the beasts onto the canoes and take them ashore dead or alive. On land, the turtles might be beheaded with a machete or put in the holds of ships, where they could survive a journey of several weeks to Europe if they were given a little water.

CONSERVATION EFFORTS

Today, turtles are **protected**, their eggs and meat a delicacy. Locals around Tortuguero are officially permitted to take two turtles a week during nesting season for their own consumption – the unlucky green turtles are considered the most delicious. The recent sharp decline in the populations of hawksbill, green and leatherback turtles has been linked, at least in part, to **poaching**. This has prompted the national park administration to adopt a firm policy discouraging the theft of turtle eggs within the park boundaries, and to arm park rangers. Note that, should you find a turtle on its back between July 10 and September 15, you should not flip it over; in most cases it's being tagged by researchers, who work on the northern 8km of the 24km-long nesting beach.

NATURAL PREDATORS

It is not just the acquisitive hand of humans that endangers the turtles. On land, a cadre of **predators**, among them coati and racoons, regularly ransack the nests in order to eat the unborn reptiles. Once the hatching has started – the darkness giving the baby turtles a modicum of protection – the turtles must run a gauntlet of vultures and other birds on their way from the beach to the sea, while barracudas, sharks and even other turtles (the giant leatherback has been known to eat other species' offspring) snap them up once in the water. Only about sixty percent – an optimistic estimate – of hatchlings reach adulthood, and the survival of marine turtles worldwide is under question.

---

northeast of Guápiles, also provides access to the Tortuguero Canal. Expect a 3–4hr trip (sometimes longer), depending upon where you embark: if you're on a package tour, it will probably be Hamburgo de Siquirres on the Río Reventazón; travelling independently, you'll find it logistically easier to leave from La Pavona or Moín. The *lanchas* drop you at Tortuguero dock in the centre of the village, from where you can walk to the village or take another *lancha* up the canal to the lodges (see p.174).

From Moín A co-operative of water taxis (see p.166) provides a shared service from the docks at Moín to Tortuguero (daily 10am; 3–4hr; US$35). The return boat also leaves at 10am.

From La Pavona Alternatively, you can do as the locals do and take a 6.30am, 9am (best option) or 10.30am bus from San José's Terminal Gran Caribe to Cariari (1hr 30min–2hr), and then switch to either the 9am, 11.30am or 3pm bus to La Pavona (45min–1hr; pay on the bus). Note that the bus terminals in Cariari are around five

blocks apart (San José buses use the Guapileños terminal, while Pavona buses use the Coopetraca terminal), though some buses pick up from both terminals – ask when you buy your ticket. From La Pavona (also known as Rancho La Suerte; buy tickets at the restaurant of the same name) public *lanchas* depart daily along the Río Suerte to Tortuguero (7.30am, 11am, 1pm & 4.30pm; around 1hr 15min; a boat is timed to leave shortly after the bus arrives from Cariari, and it will wait if the bus is late; one-way fares around ₡2400, plus ₡1000 for each large bag). The journey is long, but you'll save money, particularly if you're travelling alone. Return boats to La Pavona leave daily at 5.45am, 9am, 11am, 2.30pm; the last bus to San José from Cariari departs at 5.30pm. Private boats are available for around US$30/₡15,000 one way.

BY CAR

The best entry point by far is La Pavona. Though the roads are in reasonable condition (the last 16km or so are gravel, but fine for normal cars in dry weather), don't rely on

TURTLE TOURS AND CANAL TOURS

Turtle tours, led by certified guides, leave at 8pm and 10pm every night from the information kiosk in the village. If you're not going with an organized group from one of the lodges, you'll need to buy park entrance tickets from the kiosk. Be sure to get there early because the number of visitors is strictly limited (no more than 200 people are allowed on the beach at any one time); visitors must wear dark clothing and refrain from smoking, and aren't allowed to bring cameras (still or video) or flashlights. Everyone must be off the beach by midnight. There are over a hundred certified guides in Tortuguero; they charge around US$10 for a turtle tour (plus the park ticket). If you haven't already sorted one out, they conveniently tend to hang around the ticket kiosk at 5pm in search of customers.

Almost as popular as the turtle tours – and with good reason – are Tortuguero's **boat tours** (from US$25) through the *caños*, or lagoons, to spot a jaw-dropping array of wildlife, including caimans, crocodiles and Jesus Christ lizards, as well as birds such as nocturnal herons with bulbous eyes, dignified-looking cranes and kingfishers. You may also glimpse immobile sloths clinging to a tree or perhaps even a troupe of spider monkeys making their leaping, chattering way through the waterfront canopy. Most lodges have **canoes** (some also have hydro-bikes) that you can take out on the canal – a great way to get around if you're handy with a paddle, but stick to the main canal, as it's easy to get lost in the complex lagoon system northwest of the village. The information kiosk has a list of locals who rent canoes.

3

signposts to drive between Guápiles and La Pavona via Cariari (where there's a petrol station) – use GPS/SatNav or a very good map. There's a covered parking area at La Pavona (US$10 or ₡5000/day). Allow at least three hours from San José. Leave no valuables in the car.

BY PLANE

Much less time-consuming, of course, is a flight from San José to the airstrip across the canal from *Tortuga Lodge* (see p.175), 4km north of the village. The trip is a spectacular one, as you rise above the mountains outside the city and are afforded a bird's-eye view of the canals as you approach the park from the south. Sansa and Nature Air fly regularly from San José, with some flights routing through Puerto Limón. Water taxis usually meet flights (US$12–15 to most hotels), though the more upscale lodges will come and pick you up; otherwise it's a long walk south on muddy paths to the village.

Destinations Limón (1–2 daily; 15–20min); San José (4 daily; 25–35min).

INFORMATION AND TOURS

The most popular way to see Tortuguero is on one of literally hundreds of **tour packages**, many of which are two-night, three-day affairs that use the expensive lodges across the canal from the village. Accommodation, meals and transport (which otherwise can be a bit tricky) are all taken care of. The main difference between tours comes in the standard of accommodation, and most importantly, the quality of your guide. Ask about your guide's accreditations, and don't hesitate to check their level of English. Budget options also tend to involve some form of bus/boat transfer, while the more expensive tours fly direct from San José.

TOURIST INFORMATION

A small, somewhat faded display on the turtles' habits, habitat and history surrounds the information kiosk (daily 9am–6pm) in the village centre. This is the official place to buy tickets for turtle tours; park rangers sell the tickets at the kiosk 5–6pm. You can also get contact info for local guides.

TOUR OPERATORS

★ **Costa Rica Expeditions** C Central, at Av 3, San José ☎ 2257 0766, ⓦ costaricaexpeditions.com. Exceedingly well-run and attentive outfit offering upscale Tortuguero packages including flights from San José, accommodation at the comfortable *Tortuga Lodge* and three meals a day. Prices start at US$625/person for a three-day, two-night package. They also offer trips to Barra del Colorado.

Ecole Travel C 7, Av 35/37, San José ☎ 2234 1669, ⓦ ecoletravel.com. One of the longest-established companies offering Tortuguero tours, Ecole has excellent budget tours popular with students and backpackers. Tours (US$219 for one night and two days) start from San José; pick-ups can be arranged by your hotel.

Jungle Tom Safaris ☎ 2221 7878, ⓦ jungletomsafaris .com. Long-running US-owned operator offering some of the more inexpensive tours to Tortuguero. They lead one-, two- and three-day trips from US$105 from San José.

Riverboat Francesca Tours ☎ 2226 0986, ⓦ tortugurocanals.com. Two-day, one-night tours of the Tortuguero canals from US$220. The price includes bus transportation from San José to Moín (where you embark on the canal portion), meals and lodging.

3

LOCAL GUIDES

There are numerous guides in the village who offer tours of the canals and national park. The ones listed below are among the best and most established (and all speak good English) – it's generally best to not immediately make arrangements with the guides who hover around the *lanchas* arriving from Moín or La Pavona. Rates tend to be a standard US$20–25 for 2–3hr.

Ballard Excursions (Ross Ballard) ☎2709 8193, ✉srossballard@gmail.com. Canadian botanist Ross Ballard leads informative 3hr tours on the canals and into the national park, as well as multiday excursions.

Castor Hunter Thomas Enquire at his restaurant, Soda Doña María ☎8870 8634. Well-respected local

guide whose father was Tortuguero's first to take paying customers out in the surrounding area.

Daryl Loth Opposite La Clínica (north end of the village, on the canal side) ☎2709 8011, ⊛casa marbella.tripod.com. Canadian naturalist and local resident Darryl Loth, who runs *Casa Marbella* (see below), can arrange tours, including boat trips and hikes up Cerro Tortuguero (see p.170).

Iguana Verde Tours Operates out of Miss Junie's Lodge ☎2231 6803, ⊛iguanaverdetours.com. Offers a number of tours, including popular canal and national park excursions, as well as a village tour (US$35) that provides an excellent introduction to local and Caribbean culture.

ACCOMMODATION

With a little planning you can get to Tortuguero independently and stay in basic **cabinas** in the village, though staying at one of the posher **lodges** can be more challenging, if comfortable (see box below). Basing yourself in the village allows you to explore the beach at leisure – though swimming is not advised – and puts you within easy reach of restaurants and bars. If you haven't booked a hotel in advance, be aware that accommodation in the village can fill up quickly during the turtle-nesting seasons (March–May & July–Oct). Unless stated otherwise, all the options below include free wi-fi.

TORTUGUERO VILLAGE

Aracari Garden Hostel South of the football field ☎2767 2246, ⊛aracarigarden.com. Run by a local family, this hostel features a clean, comfortable dorm and seven private doubles (with bathrooms), all with cold water and fan, amid a beautiful tree-filled garden. No breakfast. Dorm US$12, doubles US$36

Cabinas Balcón del Mar On the beach, 3 blocks south of the football field ☎2709 8124. One of the cheapest options in town, with simple but clean rooms with fans, shared kitchen and hammocks outside. Shared or private bathrooms available; most en-suite rooms (US$35) come with hot water, but you can save a little more by opting for cold water (US$24). US$20

Cabinas Meriscar One block south of the football field, where three dirt roads converge ☎2709 8202. Newer cabins (US$30) come with private bathrooms, while the older, slightly gloomy but clean *cabinas* have shared spick-and-span bathrooms (both types sleep up to 4 people). Communal kitchen available 6am–9pm, and free wi-fi at reception. US$20

Cabinas Tortuguero South of football field on the

canal side, towards the entrance to the national park ☎2709 8114, ⊛cabinas-tortuguero.com. Simple cabins (sleeping up to 3 people) with fans surround a lovely garden at this quiet spot. Tasty meals are offered, including Italian food, as one of the owners is from Bologna; breakfast is US$6. US$30

Casa Marbella Opposite La Clínica (north end of the village, on the canal side) ☎2709 8011, ⊛casa marbella.tripod.com. Managed by a committed Canadian environmentalist, an inexhaustible source of info on the regional flora and fauna, this friendly B&B has several large, comfortable en-suite rooms (the best rooms, on the upper floor, overlook the canal; US$65). Breakfast, included, is served on a small terrace by the water. US$45

Miss Junie's Lodge At the north end of the village, just before you reach the Natural History Museum ☎2709 8029, ⊛iguanaverdetours.com/lodge.htm. Tortuguero's most popular cook (see opposite) also offers refurbished, simply decorated, comfortable rooms with hot-water private bath and fans. Excellent breakfast included in the price. US$55

STAYING AT TORTUGUERO'S LODGES

Most of Tortuguero's **lodges** lie across the canal from the village, and though convenient, and in some cases quite luxurious, life as a lodger can be a rather regimented affair. Guests are shuttled in and out of the lodges with stopwatch precision, there's precious little nightlife and, as all meals are included in most packages, it can be tempting to never leave the grounds. If you want to explore the village and the beach on your own you have to get a *lancha* across the canal (free, but often a hassle to arrange). Note, however, that outside the turtle-watching season, most lodges don't operate their *lanchas* at night. Note also that owing to Tortuguero's perennial popularity with package tourists, the lodges don't always have space for independent travellers.

PARQUE NACIONAL TORTUGUERO

The rates below are all per-night for packages for two people sharing. Camping on the beach is not allowed, though you can set up a tent for about ₡2000 per day at the mown enclosure near the ranger station at the southern end of the village, where you enter the park. It's in a sheltered situation, away from the sea breezes, and there's drinking water and toilets. Bring a groundsheet and mosquito net, and make sure your tent is waterproof.

Laguna Lodge A little over 1km north of the village ☎ 2253 1100, ⓦ lagunatortuguero.com. This well-equipped lodge has a riverside bar, swimming pool, beach access and a conference centre (which looks like a giant turtle as envisaged by Gaudí). For some, the lodge's regime, with set meal and tour times, may be a bit too constraining. Nevertheless, the rooms are perfectly comfortable and the tour guides extremely knowledgeable. This is one of the few lodges that offers hiking trips through the jungle as well as canal tours. Includes full board and two tours. US$502

★Mawamba Lodge 1km north of the village ☎ 2709 8181, ⓦ mawamba.com. This large, ritzy lodge has a daily slide show and round-the-clock cold beers from room service. The *cabina*-style rooms come with ceiling fans and private bathroom, there's a large pool and jacuzzi, and the village and ocean are just a short walk away. Full board only. US$642

Pachira Lodge Across the canal at the north end of the village ☎ 2257 2242, ⓦ pachiralodge.com. This luxurious establishment has 88 spacious, attractive rooms in wood cabins, linked by covered walkways, with large en-suite, hot-water bathrooms and a tranquil pool. Full board only. US$430

★Tortuga Lodge Across the canal from the airstrip ☎ 2709 8136, ⓦ tortugalodge.com. Owned by Costa Rica Expeditions (see p.173), this is the plushest lodge in the area (but among the furthest from the village) with large, attractive en-suite rooms, exemplary service, excellent food, a riverside swimming pool and elegantly landscaped grounds from which several trails depart into the jungle. Meals extra. US$188

Turtle Beach Lodge About 5km north of the village ☎ 2241 1419, ⓦ turtlebeachlodge.com. The most removed of the major lodges, this secluded upmarket option has handsome and supremely comfortable rooms and an inviting pool. Being so far away from the village means you're more reliant on the lodge and what it offers, but it's an easy trade-off to make, as the food and tours (included) are top-notch, not to mention the stunning 175-acre grounds. Full board only. US$410

EATING

Tortuguero village offers homely **Caribbean food** with a wide selection of fresh fish, as well as more international options. Expect to pay more for a meal here than you would in other parts of Costa Rica, but the standard is comparatively high.

★Budda Café In the village centre (canal side) ☎ 2709 8084, ⓦ buddacafe.com. A relaxing spot with seats along the canal, *Budda* offers an assortment of tantalizing crêpes (from ₡2500), pizzas and speciality drinks, such as coffee with rum, ice cream and milk. Daily noon–9pm.

Dorling's Bakery Next to Casa Marbella ☎ 2767 0444. A very basic interior belies heavenly baked goods, gut-busting breakfasts (around ₡8000) and coffee strong enough to see you through the morning. The service is friendly, too. Mon–Sat 5am–7pm, Sun 5am–noon.

Miss Junie's North end of village path, 50m before the Natural History Museum ☎ 2709 8029. Boasting an a/c dining room, the town's most revered restaurant offers solid Caribbean food – red beans, jerk chicken, rice, *chayote* and breadfruit (mains from ₡6500), all on the same plate – dished up by Nicaraguan-born Miss Junie. Wash it down with an ice-cold beer. Daily noon–2pm & 6–9pm.

Miss Miriam's On the north side of the football field ☎ 2709 8002. A good spot to watch the village football teams in action, this cheerful restaurant serves Caribbean food, including chicken with rice-and-beans cooked in coconut milk, at very reasonable prices (most main dishes around ₡4500). Daily 7.30am–9pm.

El Muellecito In the centre of the village ☎ 2709 8104. One of Tortuguero's best breakfast spots, with tasty pancakes and fruit salad. For lunch and dinner the menu is heavy on Costa Rican regulars like grilled beef with rice and fried plantains (mains ₡4000–8000). Daily 8am–9pm.

★Wild Ginger At the north end of the village ☎ 2709 8240, ⓦ wildgingercr.com. Justly regarded as Tortuguero's best restaurant, and certainly its most cosmopolitan, this ecofriendly spot exudes an unmistakeable Californian vibe. Its inventive dishes include treats like Caribbean beef stew (₡9000) and garlic-ginger shrimp (₡9500), everything house-made with local ingredients. Mon & Wed–Sun 6–9pm.

DRINKING AND NIGHTLIFE

La Culebra Next door to the dock (on the canal) ☎ 2767 0615. This local bar with basic wooden tables has a booming nightly disco, though the clientele can be a bit rough. Daily 8pm–late.

La Taberna Next door to the Bambú supermarket. Tortuguero's best bet for a laidback sundowner, this is the place to come to kick back to a reggaeton soundtrack and drink ₡1500 beers. Daily 11am–11pm.

DIRECTORY

Banks and exchange There are no bank or money-changing facilities – bring all the cash you'll need with you (there are banks and ATMs in Cariari, but not in La Pavona), as few places take credit cards. By the end of 2017 there should be a Banco de Costa Rica ATM installed on the main street, but don't bet on it.

Internet Most hotels and restaurants offer free wi-fi, and the telecom company ICE (ⓦ grupoice.com) offers wi-fi at its office in the centre of town. Only the ICE kölbi network has mobile phone coverage in Tortuguero.

Medical services Tortuguero has a very basic public medical clinic ("La Clínica", at the north end of the village; daily 7.30am–10pm). There is no pharmacy; the nearest pharmacy and hospital are in Cariari.

Post office There is no post office in Tortuguero, though some places sell stamps; there are mail boxes but post is only collected every 15 days. If villagers are heading to Limón they might offer to carry letters for you and post them from there, which can be useful if you're staying here for any length of time.

Refugio Nacional de Vida Silvestre Barra del Colorado

Created to preserve the area's abundant fauna, the **REFUGIO NACIONAL DE VIDA SILVESTRE BARRA DEL COLORADO** lies at the northern end of Costa Rica's Caribbean coast, 99km northeast of San José, near the border with Nicaragua. This ninety-square-kilometre, sparsely populated (by humans, at least) tract of land is crossed by the Río Colorado, which meets the Caribbean Sea next to the village of Barra del Colorado. The grand Río San Juan marks the park's northern boundary, which is also the border with Nicaragua. The river continues north of the border all the way to the Lago de Nicaragua and almost all traffic in this area is by water.

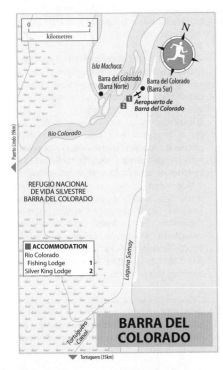

Barra del Colorado

The small, quiet village of **BARRA DEL COLORADO**, the area's only settlement of any size, is inhabited by a mixed population of Afro-Caribbeans, Miskitos, Costa Ricans and a significant number of Nicaraguans, many of whom spilled over the border during the civil war. The village is divided into two halves: Barra Sur and the larger Barra Norte, which stand opposite each other across the mouth of the Río Colorado. Tropical hardwoods are still under siege from illegal logging around here – you may see giant tree trunks being towed along the river and into the Caribbean, from where they are taken down to Limón. There are no public services in town (no post office, police station, internet café or hospital) except for a couple of public phones outside the souvenir shop next to the airport and near the *Los Almendros* bar.

It is extremely **hot** and painfully **humid** around Barra. Wear a hat and

---

ACTIVITIES IN BARRA

Very few people come to Barra on a whim. As far as tourism goes, **sportfishing** is its *raison d'être*, and numerous lodges offer packages and transportation from San José. Large schools of tarpon and snook, two big-game fish prized for their fighting spirit, ply these waters, as does the garfish, a primeval throwback that looks something like a cross between a fish and a crocodile. The sportfishing season runs from January to May, and September to October.

Because of the impenetrability of the cover, activities for non-fishing tourists are limited to **wildlife-watching** from a boat in one of the many waterways and lagoons. The usual sloths and monkeys are in residence, and you'll certainly hear the wild hoot of howler monkeys shrieking through the still air. If you are really lucky, and keep your eyes peeled, you might catch sight of a *manatí* (manatee, or sea cow) going by underneath. These large, benevolent seal-like creatures are on the brink of becoming an endangered species. This is **shark** territory so you shouldn't swim here – even though you may see locals taking that risk.

---

sunscreen and, if possible, stay in the shade during the hottest part of the day. It rains throughout the year, though February– April is the driest time.

ARRIVAL AND DEPARTURE
BARRA DEL COLORADO

By lancha In terms of the time it takes to get there, Barra is one of the least accessible places in the country. Most people arrive either by *lancha* from Tortuguero (1hr 45min) or Puerto Lindo (45min). For the latter you'll need to catch the 2pm bus from Cariari (2hr), which will drop you at the small dock in Puerto Lindo where a *lancha* will be waiting to pick up passengers for Barra (departures usually at 6am and 4pm, returning 5am and 3pm; around ₡3000 one way). *Lanchas* arrive in Barra Sur, or, if you ask, will take you directly to your accommodation.

By plane The flight (30min) from San José to Barra (landing at Barra Sur) affords stupendous views of volcanoes, unfettered lowland tropical forest and the coast; only Nature Air currently operates charter flights on this route (from US$1632 one way, for six people).

ACCOMMODATION

Because of Barra's inaccessibility and its emphasis on fishing, hardly anyone comes here for just one night. Most lodges are devoted exclusively to **fishing packages**, although you could, theoretically, call in advance and arrange to stay as an independent, non-fishing guest. The lodges can provide details on their individual packages; generally they comprise meals, accommodation, boat, guide and tackle, and most offer air transfer to/from San José, boat lunches, drinks and other extras.

Río Colorado Fishing Lodge Barra Sur ☎ 2232 4063, ⓦ riocoloradolodge.com. Built on walkways over the river, the oldest lodge in town has lots of character. Comfortable wooden rooms are homely and come with a/c, free wi-fi, cable TV and bathrooms. Enjoy good food and pretty Barra Norte views in the dining room, where local musicians often perform in the evenings. Non-fishing guests can stay for US$195 per night, including meals. Full board US$195, full board plus 8hr fishing US$575, package deal US$321

Silver King Lodge Barra Sur ☎ 2794 0139 or ☎ 1 877 335 0755, ⓦ silverkinglodge.net. Efficient, well-equipped fishing lodge, with spacious rooms, bar, restaurant, swimming pool, jacuzzi, free wi-fi and satellite TV with US channels. Closed July & Dec. Minimum stay three nights. Full board US$500, package deal US$1028

The southern Caribbean coast

Most visitors head for the rich cluster of attractions south of Puerto Limón, where the rarely visited **Reserva Selva Bananito** and the **Reserva Biológica Hitoy-Cerere** are worthy diversions on the road to the popular **Sloth Sanctuary** and resort town of **Cahuita**. Further south lies the busy backpacker hangout of **Puerto Viejo**, followed by a fifteen-kilometre stretch of coast that features some of the most enticing **beaches** on the entire Caribbean shore. **Playa Chiquita**, **Playa Cocles**, **Punta Uva** and **Manzanillo** collectively hold all the trappings of a pristine tropical paradise, with palm trees leaning over calm sands, purples, mauves, oranges and reds fading into the sea at sunset. Public transport is adequate

THE RÍO SAN JUAN AND THE NICARAGUAN BORDER

Heading to or from Barra via the Sarapiquí area in the Zona Norte entails a trip along the Río Sarapiquí to the mighty **Río San Juan**. Flowing from Lago de Nicaragua to the Caribbean, the San Juan marks most of Costa Rica's border with Nicaragua, and the entire northern edge of the Refugio Nacional de Vida Silvestre Barra del Colorado. It's theoretically in Nicaraguan territory, but Costa Ricans have the right to travel on the river – though this eastern stretch of the San Juan has been the source of a diplomatic dispute between the two countries since late 2010 (see box, p.420). There isn't, however, an official entry point between the two countries, so it's technically illegal to cross into either country along this stretch. It is possible to cross into Nicaragua 7km north of Los Chiles (see box, p.223).

One bizarre phenomenon local to this area is the migration of **bull sharks** from the saltwater Caribbean up the Río San Juan to the freshwater Lago de Nicaragua. They are unique in the world in making the transition, apparently without trauma, from being saltwater to freshwater sharks.

You'll notice much evidence of **logging** here, especially at the point where the Sarapiquí flows into the Río San Juan – the lumber industry has long had carte blanche in this area, due to the non-enforcement of existing anti-logging laws. The **Nicaraguan side** of the Río San Juan, part of the country's huge Reserva Indio Maíz, looks altogether wilder than its southern neighbour, with thick primary rainforest creeping right to the edge of the bank. Partly because of logging, and the residual destruction of its banks, the Río San Juan is silting up, and even shallow-bottomed *lanchas* get stuck in this once consistently deep river. It's a far cry from the sixteenth and seventeenth centuries, when pirate ships used to sail all the way along the Río San Juan to Lago de Nicaragua, from where they could wreak havoc on the Spanish Crown's ports and shipping.

enough down here, though with your own transport you'll be able to explore regions such as **Refugio Nacional de Vida Silvestre Gandoca-Manzanillo** with a lot more freedom.

Reserva Selva Bananito

About 8km inland from Bananito Norte • Daily 7am–6pm • Hiking and horseback tours (3hr) US$40; hiking tour with abseiling (7–8hr) US$70; birdwatching tour (2hr) US$20; zipline tours (2–3hr) US$40; day-trips including transportation from Cahuita or Puerto Viejo and one hiking or horseback tour US$120 • ☏ 2253 8118, ⓦ selvabananito.com

Twenty kilometres south of Limón, the eight-square-kilometre private **Reserva Selva Bananito** unfolds alongside the Parque Internacional La Amistad (see p.404) and protects an area of mountainous, virgin rainforest – toucans, orioles, various raptors and kingfishers have all been spotted in here. For day-trippers there is a choice of several activities on offer, from horseback tours of the reserve, to canopy tours (zipline) and a hike through the jungle to a waterfall (with abseiling). Whether or not you're planning to stay at the reserve's lodge, call or email in advance to advise of your estimated arrival time and make tour arrangements.

ARRIVAL AND DEPARTURE

By car The reserve is reached via a gravel road from the main coastal Hwy-36 that goes inland through the small town of Bananito Norte and then along a very rough track across several rivers (you'll need a 4WD).

By bus Autotransportes MEPE operates buses between

RESERVA SELVA BANANITO

Limón and the village of Bananito Norte hourly (daily 5am–6pm; less frequent on Sun); you will need to call *Selva Bananito Eco Lodge* and arrange to be picked up from the bus stop at Salon Delia in the centre of Bananito Norte (pick-up US$40 return).

ACCOMMODATION

★**Selva Bananito Eco Lodge** ☏ 2253 8118 or ☏ 8386 1005, ⓦ selvabananito.com. The reserve's wonderfully peaceful and remote lodge has eleven attractive, spacious cabins with verandas overlooking the forest; meals and drinks are served in the main ranch. Owned and run by the environmentally conscious children of a pioneering German farmer, the lodge is built from secondhand wood discarded by loggers, has solar-powered hot water and lamps (though no electricity) and donates some of its profits to the Fundación Cuencas de Limón, which helps protect the local area and develop educational programmes. Minimum stay three nights. B&B US$100, full board US$200

Sloth Sanctuary

Aviarios del Caribe, Hwy-36 • **Tours** Tues–Sun hourly 8am–2pm; 2hr • US$30 • **Insider's Tour** Tues–Sun 7.15am & 10.45am; 4hr; reserve in advance • US$150 • ☏ 2750 0775, ⓦ slothsanctuary.com

The small but controversial (see box below) **Sloth Sanctuary** sits near the mouth of the Río Estrella, on the main highway 33km south of Limón, functioning as a rehabilitation and research centre for injured and orphaned sloths – not surprisingly, it is the best place in Costa Rica to see them up close, though the experience is not cheap. Note also that this is not a wildlife park – **tours** (the only way to get in) simply visit two rooms where sloths eat and doze in cages (one room for adults and one for juveniles). The English-speaking guides are incredibly informative, however, and after an hour you'll be an expert on all things sloth, including the differences between the two-fingered and three-fingered species. The second hour of the tour is spent on a gentle canoe cruise along the creek at the back of the sanctuary, where you might see wild sloths, crocodiles, howler monkeys and all kinds of birds. The mascot of the sanctuary (once featuring in *Animal Planet* series "Meet the Sloths") is **Buttercup**, who lives in her own cage at reception. The first sloth to be rescued in 1992, she is the oldest one here (turning 25 in 2017). The **Insider's Tour** (which you must reserve in advance), includes a visit to see baby sloths and the "Slothpital", where injured sloths recover, plus breakfast or lunch.

3

ARRIVAL AND DEPARTURE   SLOTH SANCTUARY

By bus Most buses running north or south along the coast road (Hwy-36) should drop off at the sanctuary entrance, but you must tell the driver in advance; shuttle buses will also drop you off here on request.
By taxi Taxis charge around US$35 (one way) from Limón or Puerto Viejo.

ACCOMMODATION

Buttercup Inn ☏ 2750 0775, ⓦ slothsanctuary.com. The sanctuary's lodge has comfortable B&B accommodation in five spacious rooms, with a/c and private bathroom with hot water. To stay here you need to book the Insider's Tour (see above), though the tour price is not included. Tues–Sat only. US$100

Reserva Biológica Hitoy-Cerere

Off Hwy-36, 60km south of Limón • Daily 8am–4pm • US$10 • ☏ 2206 5516, ⓦ www.sinac.go.cr

A two-hour drive south of Limón is one of Costa Rica's least visited national reserves, the **Reserva Biológica Hitoy-Cerere**. Sandwiched between the Tanyí, Telier and Talamanca indigenous reservations, this very rugged, isolated terrain – ninety-one square kilometres of it – has no campsites, bathrooms or any real services to speak of, though there is a ranger station at the entrance.

In the Bribrí language, *hitoy* means "woolly" (the rocks in its rivers are covered with algae, and everything else has grown a soft fuzz of moss); and *cerere* means "clear waters", of which there are many. One of the wettest reserves in all of Costa Rica, it receives a staggering 4m of **rain** per year in some areas, with no dry season at all. Its complicated biological profile reflects the changing altitudes within the park. The top canopy trees loom impressively tall – some as high as 50m – and epiphytes, bromeliads, orchids and lianas grow everywhere beneath the very dense cover. **Wildlife** is predictably

---

> **SLOTH CONTROVERSY**
>
> Despite the Sloth Sanctuary's fine intentions, the seemingly cramped cages at the reserve might upset some visitors. In 2016, two South American veterinarians that had worked at the sanctuary claimed that the sloths were mistreated, calling it "a prison", and complained that the owners exaggerate the difficulty of releasing sloths in order to profit from tourists. The sanctuary denied the charges and claims that the cages are the only practical way to care for sloths that have been badly injured, and that most would simply die if released back into the jungle. With so little known about sloths in the wild, the dispute is unlikely to be resolved in the near future.

abundant, but most of the species are nocturnal and rarely seen, although you might spot three-toed sloths, and perhaps even a brocket deer. You'll probably hear howler monkeys, and may glimpse white-faced monkeys. Pacas and rare frogs abound, many of them shy and little-studied. More visible are the 115 species of **bird**, from large black vultures and tiny hummingbirds to trogons and dazzling blue kingfishers.

Sendero Espavel

Hitoy-Cerere's **Sendero Espavel**, a tough nine-kilometre hiking trail, leads south from the ranger station through lowland and primary rainforest past clear streams, small waterfalls and beautiful views of the green Talamanca hills. Only **experienced tropical hikers** should attempt it; bring a compass, rubber boots, rain gear and lots of water. The trail begins at a very muddy hill; after about 1km, in the area of secondary forest, you'll notice the white-and-grey wild cashew trees (*espavel*) after which the trail is named. Follow the sign here; it leads off to the right and cuts through swathes of thick forest before leaving the reserve and entering the Talamanca reservation, which is officially off-limits. At the reserve's boundary, take the trail leading up a steep hill. This ends at the Río Moín, 4.5km from the start. All you can do now is turn back, taking care to negotiate the numerous fallen trees, tumbled rocks and boulders. Many of them were felled by the earthquake in 1991; older casualties are carpeted in primeval plants and mosses. The only possible respite from very dense jungle terrain are the small dried-up riverbeds that follow the streams and tributaries of the *ríos* Cerere and Hitoy.

ARRIVAL AND DEPARTURE	RESERVA BIOLÓGICA HITOY-CERERE

By car Having a 4WD car is the most convenient way to get to Hitoy-Cerere. From Puerto Limón follow Hwy-36 towards Cahuita. After 33km take the right fork at Penshurst (4km south of the Sloth Sanctuary) and follow the signs to the reserve.

By bus and taxi Using public transport, you'll need to take the bus from Limón to Valle de Estrella (Pandora, Finca Ocho or Las Rosas), and get off at the end of the line at a

banana town called (confusingly) both Fortuna and Finca Seis. It's 15km from here to the reserve, most of it through banana plantation. A local 4WD taxi – ask at the plantation office – can take you there and return to pick you up, at a mutually agreed time, for around US$20. From Cahuita, take any bus headed north and get off at Penshurst to catch the Limón-to-Valle de Estrella bus; taxis should charge around US$60–70 for a return trip from Cahuita.

ACCOMMODATION

There is a ranger station at the entrance with a small dormitory where you can bed down for the night (US$8/ person). Beyond this, the nearest accommodation is at Cahuita (see p.182).

Cahuita

Like other settlements on the Talamanca coast, the village of **CAHUITA**, 45km south of Puerto Limón, has become a byword for relaxed, inexpensive Caribbean holidays, with a laidback atmosphere and great Afro-Caribbean food, not to mention top surfing beaches further south. In contrast to its southern neighbour Puerto Viejo however, Cahuita hasn't been completely overwhelmed by the tourist industry, with locals sitting on their verandas sharing the well-maintained streets with a handful of restaurants and bars, and overall a much more laidback vibe. Most of the inhabitants are descendants of Afro-Caribbean settlers from the Bocas del Toro area of Panama, and from Jamaican workers brought to help build the Jungle Train.

At the southern end of the village lies the main attraction, the largely marine **Parque Nacional Cahuita** (see p.186), which was created to protect one of Costa Rica's few living coral reefs; many people come here to snorkel and take glass-bottom-boat rides (there's no beach to speak of in the village itself). The main street runs from the national park's entrance at Kelly Creek to the northern end of the village, where it continues as a dirt road for three kilometres north along **Playa Negra** to the **Tree of Life**.

The beaches

Cahuita lies between two popular **beaches**: the most enticing is white-sand **Playa Blanca**, an undeveloped, palm-backed stretch just south of the village in the national park (see p.187), though swimming here can be dangerous because of riptides. At the northern end of the village, **Playa Negra** (or Black Sand Beach) is safe for swimming in most places but often littered with driftwood. Note that nude or topless bathing is definitely unacceptable at either beach, as is wandering through the village in just a bathing suit.

Tree of Life

Northern edge of Playa Negra (3km from central Cahuita) • Tours July, Aug & Nov to mid-April Tues– Sun 11am (1hr 30min) • ₡8000 • ☎ 8317 0490, 🌐 treeoflifecostarica.com

Playa Negra's **Tree of Life** is one of Cahuita's more popular outings, despite its rather restrictive visiting hours. In between towering ginger plants and below a dense canopy, this still-growing wildlife rescue centre is devoted to providing care and comfort to indigenous species from the surrounding region – and sometimes further afield – with the goal of releasing as many as possible back into the wild. The centre lovingly cares for numerous mammals, including capuchin and spider monkeys, kinkajous, peccary and coatis, and also has a walk-in enclosure teeming with brilliantly coloured butterflies. The **tours** (the only way you're allowed to visit) are an excellent source of information not only on regional wildlife, but also on flora from their natural habitats – the centre is set in the grounds of a botanical garden chock-full of endemic plants and trees. From the main road (Hwy-36), the reserve is signposted left off the passable gravel road, before you reach Cahuita; you can walk to it along the gravel coast road from Cahuita itself in around 30 to 40 minutes.

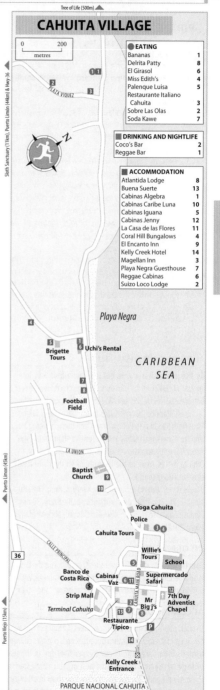

Tree of Life (500m)

CAHUITA VILLAGE

0 — 200
metres

● EATING

Bananas	1
Delrita Patty	8
El Girasol	6
Miss Edith's	4
Palenque Luisa	5
Restaurante Italiano Cahuita	3
Sobre Las Olas	2
Soda Kawe	7

■ DRINKING AND NIGHTLIFE

Coco's Bar	2
Reggae Bar	1

■ ACCOMMODATION

Atlantida Lodge	8
Buena Suerte	13
Cabinas Algebra	1
Cabinas Caribe Luna	10
Cabinas Iguana	5
Cabinas Jenny	12
La Casa de las Flores	11
Coral Hill Bungalows	4
El Encanto Inn	9
Kelly Creek Hotel	14
Magellan Inn	3
Playa Negra Guesthouse	7
Reggae Cabinas	6
Suizo Loco Lodge	2

PLAZA VIQUEZ

Sloth Sanctuary (11km), Puerto Limón (44km) & Hwy-36

Playa Negra

Brigette Tours

Uchi's Rental

CARIBBEAN SEA

Football Field

LA UNION

Puerto Limón (45km)

Baptist Church

Yoga Cahuita

Police

Cahuita Tours

CALLE PRINCIPAL

Willie's Tours

School

36

Banco de Costa Rica

Cabinas Vaz

Supermercado Safari

Strip Mall

Mr Big J's

7th Day Adventist Chapel

Terminal Cahuita

Restaurante Típico

Puerto Viejo (15km)

Kelly Creek Entrance

PARQUE NACIONAL CAHUITA

3

PIRATES AND GHOSTS

Up until the early 1800s, the coastal waters of the Caribbean crawled with pirates. Two **shipwrecks** in the bay on the north side of Punta Cahuita are believed to be pirate wrecks, one Spanish and one French. You can sometimes see the Spanish wreck on glass-bottom-boat tours to the reef although it has been (illegally) picked over and the only thing of interest that remains is encrusted manacles – an indication of the dastardly motives of the ship's crew.

In her excellent collection of local folk history and oral testimony, *What Happen*, sociologist Paula Palmer quotes Selles Johnson, descendant of the original turtle-hunters, on the pirate activity on these shores:

… them pirate boats was on the sea and the English gunboats was somewhere out in the ocean, square rigger, I know that. I see them come to Bocas, square rigger. They depend on breeze. So the pirate boats goes in at Puerto Vargas or at Old Harbour where calm sea, and the Englishmen can't attack them because they in Costa Rican water… so those two ships that wreck at Punta Cahuita, I tell you what I believes did happen. Them was hiding in Puerto Vargas and leave from there and come around the reef, and they must have stopped because in those days the British ship did have coal. You could see the smoke steaming in the air. So the pirate see it out in the sea and they comes in here to hide.

Where you find pirates you also find pirate ghosts, it seems, doomed to guard their ill-gotten treasure for eternity. Treasure from the wrecks near Old Harbour, just south of Cahuita, is said to be buried in secret caches on land. One particular spot, supposedly guarded by a fearsome headless spirit dressed in a white suit, has attracted a fair share of treasure hunters. No one has yet succeeded in exhuming the booty, however; all of them have fainted, fallen sick or become mysteriously paralyzed in the attempt.

ARRIVAL AND DEPARTURE CAHUITA

By bus The easiest way to get to Cahuita from San José (around US$12) is by bus on the comfortable, direct Autotransportes MEPE (☎ 2257 8129) service from the Terminal Atlántico that continues on to Puerto Viejo. Taking a bus from San José to Puerto Limón and then changing for Cahuita is only marginally less expensive than taking the direct bus and increases travel time by at least an hour. In Cahuita, buses arrive at the bus station on the main road into the village centre.

Destinations Puerto Limón (daily every 30min; 1hr–1hr 30min); Puerto Viejo de Talamanca (daily every 30min; 30min); San José (5 daily; 4hr–4hr 30min); Sixaola (daily every 2hr; 1hr 30min).

By shuttle bus Companies such as Interbus (ⓦ interbusonline.com) serve Cahuita daily from La Fortuna (6hr), San José (5hr) and Puerto Viejo (40min), with door-to-door service, though rates are much more expensive than public buses (at least US$52 one way from San José, for example), and the trip can actually take longer.

By car Cahuita is 43km southeast of Limón on Hwy-36. Pay attention, as the turn-off sign is by no means obvious. You can aim for the private grassy car park in the centre for ₡2000/day, or look for free spaces near the national park entrance.

INFORMATION

Tourist information The website ⓦ cahuita.cr is the best locally generated resource for information on Cahuita, with comprehensive accommodation, restaurant and tour listings. Tour companies provide the only visitor information in the village itself.

ACCOMMODATION

Though popular with budget travellers, Cahuita is not especially cheap. If you're travelling in a group, however, you can keep costs to a minimum because most *cabinas* charge per room and have space for at least three or four people. Upstairs rooms are slightly more expensive, due to the sea breezes and occasional ocean views. The **centre of the village** has several options, the best of which are listed below; staying here is convenient for restaurants, bars and the national park. There's also accommodation in all price ranges on the long (3km or so) road that runs by the sea north along **Playa Negra**. It's quieter here, and the beach is not bad, though take care walking this road at night.

You'll find several camping options in the vicinity; the most attractive is at the Puerto Vargas ranger station in the national park (see p.187). All the recommendations below offer free wi-fi.

IN THE VILLAGE

Buena Suerte Central Cahuita, 25m west of Restaurante Típico ☎ 8834 5525, ⓦ buenasuertebedbreakfast.com. Excellent, Italian-owned budget bed and breakfast near the heart of the village and the national park, with simple but clean rooms, some that feature a/c (about US$10 extra), hot water and cable TV – a great deal for the price. US$40

Cabinas Caribe Luna North of the village on the road to Playa Negra (behind El Encanto Inn) ☎ 2755 0131, ⓦ www.cabinascaribeluna.com. Set in a lush garden, this popular choice has five cosy cabins (sleeping 4–5 people), with private bathrooms (hot showers), and private terraces with hammocks. US$45

Cabinas Jenny On the waterfront ☎ 2755 0256, ⓦ cabinasjenny.com. Simple but comfy rooms (especially the more expensive ones upstairs, from US$45) with high wooden ceilings, sturdy bunks, mosquito nets, fans and wonderful sea views. Deckchairs and hammocks are provided, there's on-site parking and all doors have stout locks. US$35

La Casa de las Flores Central Cahuita (200m east of Banco de Costa Rica) ☎ 2755 0326, ⓦ lacasadelas floreshotel.com. Stylish modern rooms in the centre, with flatscreen TVs, tiled floors, immaculate bathrooms and a tiny pool in the back garden. Excellent breakfast included. US$100

★ El Encanto Inn North of the village on the road to Playa Negra ☎ 2755 0113, ⓦ elencantocahuita.com. Bright and pleasantly furnished hotel, with a gorgeous garden, pool, spa, seven beautifully decorated doubles, and a delicious breakfast included in the room rate. US$125

Kelly Creek Hotel Beside the national park beach at Kelly Creek ☎ 2755 0007, ⓦ hotelkellycreek.com. Four vast, wood-panelled rooms right by the park entrance, each with two double beds, fans and mosquito nets (which you will definitely need). Continental breakfast included (with fresh smoothies). US$70

PLAYA NEGRA

Atlantida Lodge Playa Negra, about 1km from the village ☎ 2755 0115. This friendly hotel offers rustic chic with pretty grounds, good security, and a pool, jacuzzi and poolside bar. The elegant rooms are decorated in tropical yellows and pinks, with heated water, and you get free coffee and bananas all day. Breakfast included, but free wi-fi usually available in public areas only. US$80

Cabinas Algebra 2km or so up the Playa Negra road (600m before Tree of Life) ☎ 2755 0057, ⓦ cabinas algebra.com. Run by a friendly Austrian couple, these three attractive, bargain *cabinas* (the two larger ones come with kitchens and room for three people, from US$45) are some distance from town, but the owners offer free pick-up

from the village, as well as laundry service and bike rentals. The tasty meals at its on-site restaurant *Bananas* (see p.186) are enough to keep you from wandering far for other options. Free wi-fi in public areas only. Cash only. US$25

Cabinas Iguana Calle Humphrey, inland from central Playa Negra (turn left at Reggae Bar) ☎ 2755 0005, ⓦ cabinas-iguana.com. Swiss-run lodge with six lovely wood-panelled *cabinas* on stilts set back from the beach (with room for 4–6 people; one has three double rooms that can be rented individually or as a whole from US$90), a large screened veranda, laundry service, book exchange and a swimming pool with adorable waterfall and sundeck. Doubles US$30, *cabinas* US$60

Coral Hill Bungalows C Humphrey, inland from central Playa Negra (turn left at Reggae Bar) ☎ 2755 0479, ⓦ coralhillbungalows.com. These three luxury wooden cottages (sleeping two people) are beautifully decked out with bamboo furniture, colourful fabrics, polished wood floors and ceiling fans; the bathrooms are especially artsy, with hand-painted sinks and large mosaics. Full breakfast included. US$130

★ Magellan Inn 3km up Playa Negra, on a small signposted road leading off to the left ☎ 2755 0035, ⓦ magellaninn.ticosweb.com. This comfortable, quiet hotel has beautiful gardens dotted with pre-Columbian sculptures and a small pool. The hacienda-style rooms have rattan furniture and hot water; some also have a/c and TVs. Rates include continental breakfast, and there's also a bar and an excellent French Creole restaurant, though it's only open in high season and then only to guests. Secure on-site parking. US$115

Playa Negra Guesthouse Playa Negra road (100m north of the football field) ☎ 2755 0127 ⓦ playanegra .cr. Charming cottages in lush grounds with a pool and laundry on site; rooms are all spotless and comfortably furnished, with fan, rattan furniture and kitchenettes. US$70

Reggae Cabinas Central Playa Negra ☎ 2755 0209. Budget digs (six *cabinas*, sleeping up to three people each), just off the centre of the beach, with the popular *Reggae Bar* (see p.186) on site and basic rooms that feature flatscreen cable TV, modern en-suite bathrooms and fan. US$30

★ Suizo Loco Lodge 200m down approach road to Playa Negra ☎ 2755 0349, ⓦ suizolocolodge.com. Immaculate, Swiss-run, stylish hotel built with great attention to detail and an ecofriendly focus (water is heated by solar power). The staff are particularly helpful and knowledgeable about local activities. There's a good restaurant (breakfast included) and a great pool with whirlpool. All rooms have a TV, fan, fridge and hairdryer. US$115

3

TOURS AND ACTIVITIES AROUND CAHUITA

The principal daylight activity in Cahuita involves taking a boat trip out to the Parque Nacional Cahuita's coral reef to **snorkel** – any of the town's tour companies or local guides can take you (from US$25). You can **surf** at Cahuita – Cahuita Tours rents out boards – but Puerto Viejo (see p.187) has better waves. Wherever you swim, either in the park itself or on Playa Negra, don't leave possessions unattended, as even your grubby T-shirt and old shorts may be stolen. Exploradores Outdoors in Puerto Viejo (see box, p.190) can pick up from Cahuita for their whitewater-rafting trips on the Río Pacuare. **Yoga** classes are available all over the village (usually US$15/hr); for example, *Goddess Garden* (⟐ thegoddessgarden.com) hosts various yoga and meditation retreats, usually arranged by instructors visiting from the US and Canada.

★**Brigitte Tours** Playa Negra ☎ 2755 0053, ⟐ brigittecahuita.ticosweb.com. Based at Swiss-born Brigitte's small ranch just off the beach, offering a variety of enjoyable horseriding tours around Cahuita, including a 6hr trip through the jungle to a farm and waterfall (US$85). Also rents bikes and organizes surfing lessons and kayaking on the Río Estrella. Tours of the indigenous Bribrí community of Yorkín, near the Panama border, are US$110.

Cahuita Tours 50m south of the police station in the village centre ☎ 2755 0101, ⟐ cahuitatours.com.

Specializes in snorkelling outings to the national park (US$50), but also combines them with hikes (US$60) and offers day-trips to Bribrí indigenous communities (US$65; 6hr).

Willie's Tours Cahuita main street ☎ 2755 1024, ⟐ williestourscostarica.com. Long-running, friendly company that offers a variety of tours, from snorkelling in the national park to visits to Bribrí indigenous villages, from US$60. Also acts as the unofficial village information centre.

EATING

Cahuita has plenty of places to eat fresh local food – as with accommodation, prices can be higher than elsewhere in Costa Rica, though the quality in general more than makes up for it. As you might expect, the European, US and Creole impact is strong and restaurants tend to be creative with their influences.

IN THE VILLAGE

Delrita Patty 50m off main street, near Soda Kawe. Shack selling classic Jamaican-style patties filled with either spicy beef, plantain or pineapple for just ₡600. They also sell a delicious rice-and-beans (₡3000), served with chicken and salad. Takeaway only. Sat & Sun, usually from 9.30am until sold out.

El Girasol Just off the main street, opposite Cabinas Vaz ☎ 2755 1164, ⟐ elgirasolrestaurante.com. Fine Italian restaurant – the owners are an Italian couple – with attentive staff and excellent pizzas, Mediterranean-inspired salads and wonderfully fresh veggies (mains from ₡6000). The real espresso is a treat. Mon, Tues & Thurs–Sun 6–11pm.

Miss Edith's Northern end of the village ☎ 2755 0248. Can be hit-and-miss, but on a good night *Miss Edith's* dishes up Cahuita's best Creole food. Dig into tasty rice-and-beans, "rundown" (*rondón*; coconut stew with vegetables, fish or meat; from ₡6000), *pan bon* (sweet bread) and a wide range of vegetarian dishes. Top off the meal with home-made ice cream and herbal teas. The service is notoriously slow, especially at dinner, and no alcohol is served. Mon–Sat 10am–10pm, Sun noon–6pm.

Palenque Luisa In the middle of the village, opposite

Willie's Tours ☎ 8960 3971. This popular restaurant offers an extensive menu of *casados* (from ₡5500), fish and Creole dishes. Enjoy live calypso music on Sat nights. Tues–Sun noon–8pm.

★**Restaurante Italiano Cahuita** Next to the police station ☎ 2755 0179. Justly popular, modern Italian restaurant (it's another place owned by an Italian family), specializing in superb wood-fired pizzas – big enough to share – and home-made pastas in a great location near the sea. Some outdoor seating. Mains ₡5500–8000. Mon–Wed & Fri–Sun 4–9.30pm.

Sobre Las Olas Northern end of the village (on the Playa Negra road), right on the beach ☎ 2755 0109. Atmospheric hangout serving first-rate seafood – the ceviche and seafood pasta are particularly good – with the sound of lapping waves in the background, though service can be hit-and-miss and it's easily one of the more expensive spots in the village (most mains are around ₡8000–10,000). Wed–Sun noon–10pm.

Soda Kawe Main street, 2 blocks north of the national park. Best deal in the village for classic Costa Rican breakfast and lunch, cooked over a wood fire to give the beans a smoky flavour (*casados* for ₡3000 including drink; fruit smoothies from ₡1000). Mon–Sat 5.30am–7pm.

FROM TOP PUERTO VIEJO DE TALAMANCA (P.187); SLOTH SANCTUARY (P.179) >

PLAYA NEGRA

Bananas Cabinas Algebra, 2km or so up the Playa Negra road (600m before Tree of Life) ☎ 2755 0057, ⓦ cabinasalgebra.com. Inviting, family-run restaurant serving superb Creole-Caribbean cuisine, such as roasted vegetables with rice-and-beans (₡3000). The portions are ample and there is live music some nights. Daily 8am–1pm & 5–8pm.

DRINKING AND NIGHTLIFE

Coco's Bar The centre of the village ☎ 2755 0437. The place to party in Cahuita, with a pleasant balcony over the main street, a dancefloor inside, nonstop reggae tunes and gaggles of young backpackers soaking up the atmosphere. If you're a single woman you'll inevitably be chatted up by the resident dreadlocked hustlers, though they're harmless enough. Fri is Reggae Night, though it seems like every night is reggae night. Daily 10am–2.30am.

Reggae Bar Playa Negra. Local Rasta hangout directly opposite the beach with a refreshingly laidback vibe and filling Caribbean cuisine. More inviting than some of the spots in the village and made more alluring by the sight of crashing waves. Daily noon–midnight.

Riki's At the intersection of the main road into the village and the principal cross-street ☎ 2755 0305. This place, with its large, rather dark interior and powerful sound system, operates somewhat erratic opening times but it gets heaving with live music on Wed and Sat nights. Daily 1pm–midnight.

DIRECTORY

Banks and exchange There's a Banco de Costa Rica (Mon–Fri 9am–4pm) at the strip mall attached to the bus station, but its ATM isn't very reliable for foreign cards.
Internet Most cafés offer free wi-fi.
Petrol station The nearest petrol station is about 7km south of Cahuita at Hale Creek, on the road to Puerto Viejo.

Pharmacy Farmacia Cahuita at the bus-terminal strip mall is open Mon–Sat 9am–6pm.
Police The small police station is on the last beach-bound road at the north end of the village.
Post office At the strip mall attached to the bus station (Mon–Fri 8am–noon & 1.30–5.30pm).

Parque Nacional Cahuita

Mon–Fri 8am–4pm, Sat & Sun 7am–5pm • Admission by donation • ☎ 2755 0302

One of Costa Rica's smallest national parks, 10.7-square-kilometre **PARQUE NACIONAL CAHUITA** covers a wedge-shaped piece of land that encompasses the area between Punta Cahuita and the main highway and, most importantly, the **coral reef** (*arrecife*) about 500m offshore. On land, Cahuita protects the coastal rainforest, a lowland habitat of semi-mangroves and tall canopy cover that backs the gently curving white-sand beaches of Playa Vargas to the south and Playa Blanca to the north. Resident **birds** include ibis and kingfisher, along with white-faced capuchin monkeys, sloths and snakes, but the only animals you're likely to see are howler monkeys and, perhaps, coati, who scavenge around the northern section of the park, where bins overflow with rubbish left by day-trippers.

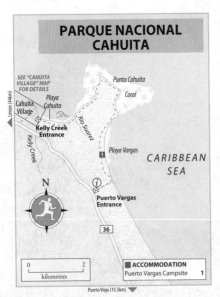

Note that **snorkelling** is not permitted on your own; you must make arrangements with a guide or go on a tour (see box, p.184).

The beach trail

The park's one **trail** begins at the Kelly Creek entrance and continues on to the Puerto Vargas ranger station 7km away.

CAHUITA CORAL

Arcing around Punta Cahuita, the *arrecife de Cahuita*, or **Cahuita reef**, comprises six square kilometres of coral, and is one of just two snorkelling reefs on this side of Costa Rica – the other is further south at the Refugio Nacional de Vida Silvestre Gandoca-Manzanillo (see p.197). **Corals** are actually tiny animals, single-celled polyps, that secrete limestone, building their houses around themselves. Over centuries the limestone binds together to form a multilayered coral reef. The coral thrives on algae, which, like land plants, transform light into energy to survive; reefs always grow close to the surface in transparent waters where they can get plenty of sun. The white-sand beaches along this part of the coast were formed by shards of excreted coral.

Unfortunately, much of Cahuita's once-splendid reef is dying, soured by agricultural chemicals from the rivers that run into the sea (the fault of the banana plantations), and from the silting up of these same rivers caused by topsoil runoff from logging, as well as the effects of global warming. The species that have so far survived are common **brain coral**, grey and mushy like its namesake; **moose horn coral**, which is slightly red; and sallow-grey **deer horn coral**. In water deeper than 2m, you might also spot fan coral wafting elegantly back and forth.

This delicate **ecosystem** shelters more than 120 species of fish and the occasional green turtle. Lobsters, particularly the fearsome-looking spiny lobster, used to be common but are also falling victim to the reef's environmental problems. Less frail, and thus more common, is the blue parrotfish, so called because of its "beak": actually teeth soldered together. Unfortunately, the parrotfish is causing a few environmental problems of its own as it uses its powerful jaws to gnaw away at the coral's filigree-like structures and spines.

It skirts **Playa Blanca** for most of its length, with a gentle path so wide it feels like a road, covered with leaves and other brush and marked by segments of boardwalk. Stick to the trail, as snakes abound here. The Río Perzoso – about 2km from Kelly Creek, or 5km from the Puerto Vargas trailhead – is not always fordable, unless you like wading through chest-high water when you can't actually see how deep it is. Similarly, at high tide the beach is impassable in places: ask the ranger at the Puerto Vargas entrance about the tide schedules. Walking this trail can be unpleasantly humid and buggy: it's best to go in the morning. Despite the dense cover of tall trees, when it rains, you'll still get wet.

The beach south of Punta Cahuita – sometimes called **Playa Vargas** – is better for swimming than those in the village. It's protected from raking breakers by the coral reef and also patrolled by lifeguards. It does, however, take some effort to reach it – you need to follow a trail for half a kilometre or so through thick vegetation and mangrove swamps that back the shore.

ARRIVAL AND INFORMATION   PARQUE NACIONAL CAHUITA

Park entry There are two entrances to the park, one just across the bridge over Kelly Creek at the southern end of Cahuita village (open during daylight hours) and another at Puerto Vargas (Mon–Fri 8am–4pm, Sat & Sun 7am–5pm), accessible off Hwy-36, 4km southeast of Cahuita.

ACCOMMODATION

Puerto Vargas campground 📞 2755 0461. You'll find good camping facilities at the Puerto Vargas park entrance, complete with barbecue grill, pit toilets and showers, but you'll need to bring your own drinking water, insect repellent and torch. Be careful, too, not to pitch your tent too close to the high-tide line; check with the rangers first. Theft can also be a problem, so don't leave anything unattended and ask the rangers for advice – they may be able to look after your belongings. <u>US$5</u>

Puerto Viejo de Talamanca

The languorous village of **PUERTO VIEJO DE TALAMANCA**, 17km south of Cahuita, has become a byword for backpacker and surf-party culture, with a vibrant nightlife and an abundance of cheap accommodation, though as always, the main attraction is the

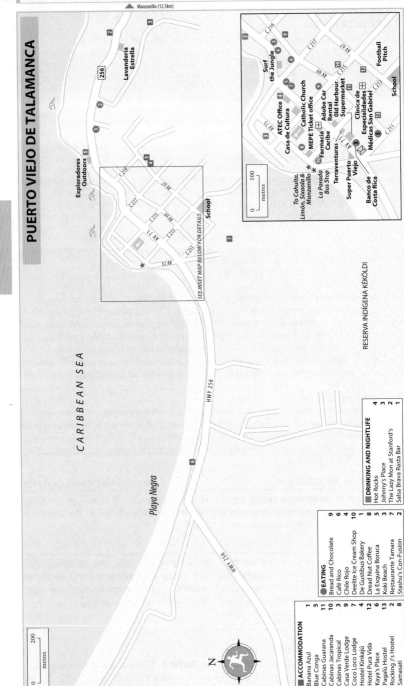

PUERTO VIEJO DE TALAMANCA

Manzanillo (12.5km)

Lavandería Estrella

256

Exploradores Outdoors

SEE INSET MAP BELOW FOR DETAILS

School

CARIBBEAN SEA

Playa Negra

HWY 256

HWY 256

RESERVA INDIGENA KÉKÖLDI

Bribri (14km) & Cahuita (15km)

0 200 metres

N

C219
C217
AV 69
C215
C113
AV 71
AV 73

Surf the Jungle

ATEC Office

Casa de Cultura

Catholic Church

MEPE Ticket office

Adobe Car Rental

Farmacia Caribe

Old Harbour

Supermarket

Clínica de Especialidades

Médicas San Gabriel

Football Pitch

School

C219
AV 69
C217
AV 69
C215
C213
C211

To Cahuita,
Limón, Sixaola &
Manzanillo

La Parada
Bus Stop

Terraventuras

Super Puerto
Viejo

Banco de
Costa Rica

0 100 metres

ACCOMMODATION

Banana Azul	1
Blue Conga	5
Cabinas Guarana	11
Cabinas Jacaranda	10
Cabinas Tropical	3
Casa Verde Lodge	7
Coco Loco Lodge	9
Hostel Kinkajú	4
Hotel Pura Vida	12
Kaya's Place	6
Pagalú Hostel	13
Rocking J's Hostel	2
Samasati	8

EATING

Bread and Chocolate	9
Café Rico	6
Chile Rojo	4
Deelite Ice Cream Shop	10
De Gustibus Bakery	7
Dread Nut Coffee	1
La Esquina Boruca	12
Koki Beach	5
Restaurante Tamara	3
Stashu's Con-Fusion	2
	8

DRINKING AND NIGHTLIFE

Hot Rocks	4
Johnny's Place	3
The Lazy Mon at Stanford's	2
Salsa Brava Rasta Bar	1

backdrop of pristine Costa Rican rainforest and a shoreline of enticing, palm-backed beaches. The village lies between the thickly forested hills of the Talamanca Mountains and the sea, where locals bathe and kids frolic with surfboards in the waves. It can be a dusty little place in daylight hours but reasonably well cared for, with bright hand-painted signs pointing the way to *cabinas*, bars and restaurants – even the streets are now labelled and numbered. The main drag through the centre (Av 71), is crisscrossed by a handful of side streets crammed with stores and tour operators. As in Cahuita, many foreigners have been drawn to Puerto Viejo, and have set up their own businesses; you'll find lots of places offering health foods, yoga and New Age remedies. Most locals, however, are of Afro-Caribbean descent and signs of **indigenous culture** are more evident here than in Cahuita, with the **Reserva Indígena KéköLdi**, inhabited by about two hundred Bribrí and Cabécar people, skirting the southern end of the town.

It's **surfing**, however, that really pulls in the crowds; the stretch south of *Stanford's* (see p.192) at the southern end of Puerto Viejo offers some of the most challenging waves in the country and certainly the best on the Caribbean coast. Puerto Viejo's famous twenty-foot wave "**La Salsa Brava**" crashes ashore between December and March and from June to July; September and October, when La Salsa Brava completely disappears, are the quietest months of the year. Then there's the **Puerto Viejo Chocolate Festival** (Ⓦpvchocolatefestival.com), held every year in October to celebrate local cacao farmers and chocolate makers, with plenty of free samples on offer.

ARRIVAL AND GETTING AROUND

PUERTO VIEJO DE TALAMANCA

By bus Autotransportes MEPE buses to/from San José stop at La Parada on Av 73, at C 213 – the ticket office is just across the street.
Destinations Cahuita (daily every 30min; 30min); Manzanillo (6 daily; 30min); Puerto Limón (daily 6.30am–6.30pm, every 30min; 1hr 30–2hr); San José (5 daily; 4hr 30min); Sixaola (daily every 2hr; 1hr).
By shuttle bus Companies such as Interbus (Ⓦinterbusonline.com) serve Puerto Viejo daily from La Fortuna (6hr), San José (5hr) and Cahuita (30–40min), with door-to-door service, though rates are much more expensive than public buses (at least US$52 one-way from San José, for example). You can buy shuttle bus tickets at the main ticket office (see above).

By bicycle The best way to negotiate the coast road beyond Puerto Viejo is by bike. You'll find several bicycle rental shops in town and many of the local hotels and *cabinas* also rent out bikes for around ₡3000/day.
By car It's an easy drive along Hwy-36 – very good condition – then Hwy-256 – surfaced but slightly less maintained – to Puerto Viejo from Cahuita (16km), Puerto Limón (60km) and points north. The road is in reasonably good condition (barring the odd pothole) all the way to Manzanillo, where it reverts to dirt track. From San José it's advisable to leave before 2pm to avoid driving at night. To rent a car, visit the Adobe Car Rental (Mon–Sun 8am–5pm; ☎ 2750 0715, Ⓦadobecar.com) office on the main street in Puerto Viejo (Av 71, at C 213).

INFORMATION

Tourist information There's no tourist information office but the village's tour operators (see box, p.190) can help with advice, maps and so on. Websites such as Ⓦpuertoviejosatellite.com can be useful but are not always updated regularly.

ACCOMMODATION

You shouldn't have any problem finding accommodation in Puerto Viejo, although it's still best to reserve a room in advance during high season and **surfing-season weekends** (June, July & Dec–March). The majority of places in the village are simple *cabinas*, some without hot water, while more upmarket establishments line the coast south of the village towards Playa Cocles (see p.192). Quieter options face **Playa Negra**, the black volcanic sand beach northwest of the village on the road back to Limón (not to be confused with the beach near Cahuita). You can camp on the beaches, but budget travellers should forsake their tents for the excellent *Pagalù Hostel*. All the options below offer free wi-fi unless stated otherwise.

IN THE VILLAGE

★ **Blue Conga** On the eastern edge of town (Hwy-256 to Manzanillo) ☎ 2750 0681, Ⓦhotelblueconga.com. One of the better choices in the village, this brightly painted hotel has breezy, pleasantly frescoed rooms, most with canopy beds. Continental breakfast is included, and you can rent bikes and snorkelling gear. **US$75**
Cabinas Guarana Av 69, C 213/215 ☎ 2750 0244,

ⓦhotelguarana.com. Run by a friendly Italian couple, this lovely small hotel has attractive rooms, tiled bathrooms, hammocks and a communal kitchen. Climb up the treehouse in the garden for great views over the village. US$45

Cabinas Jacaranda Av 67, C 215/217 ☎2750 0069, ⓦcabinasjacaranda.com. Basic but very clean option (with fans only, interiors can get hot), with rustic but immaculate *cabinas* (sleeping 2–4 people) decorated in lively Guatemalan fabrics and set amid a lush tropical garden. US$45

Cabinas Tropical Av 67, C 217/219 ☎2750 2064, ⓦcabinastropical.com. Small, quiet and clean hotel

with ten large, comfortable rooms (all with satellite TV, some with a/c), and pet birds in the garden. Owned by German-born biologist Rolf Blancke and his Costa Rican wife Juana, who offer guided jungle hikes and birdwatching tours. US$45

Casa Verde Lodge Av 69, C 217/219 ☎2750 0015, ⓦcabinascasaverde.com. Five comfortable *cabinas* (sleeping up to three people), decorated with shell mobiles and washed-up coral, with sparklingly clean showers, ceiling fans (some have a/c), mosquito nets and space to sling hammocks. Get a poolside massage or lounge in the whirlpool near the frog garden. *Cabinas* with private bathrooms are US$25 extra. US$58

TOURS AND ACTIVITIES AROUND PUERTO VIEJO

Though a lazy day on the beach is the biggest draw for most visitors to Puerto Viejo, there's no shortage of tours and activities on offer, from surfing, diving and kayaking along the coast to yoga classes, chocolate tours and day-trips to indigenous reserves. You can also arrange trips to Tortuguero (see p.171) from here (two days from around US$155). Surf lessons offered by the surf shops in the village generally cost US$25–30/hr, while half-day board rentals cost around US$25.

ATEC Av 71, C 215/217 ☎2750 0398, ⓦateccr.org. The ATEC (Asociación Talamanqueña de Ecoturismo y Conservación) office arranges not-to-be-missed hiking tours in the Reserva Indígena KéköLdi (US$32–46). They exclusively use local guides and also offer day-trips (US$93) to the Bribrí community of Yorkín, near the Panama border (overnight stays US$115), and even Afro-Caribbean cooking (US$43) and dance classes (US$37).

Caribeans Coffee & Chocolate Hwy-256, Playa Cocles ☎8836 8930, ⓦcaribeanschocolate.com. This coffee shop (see p.194) also runs excellent chocolate tours (2–3hr; US$28), which include a guided hike through their cacao forest and chocolate tastings. Tours Mon 10am, Tues & Thurs 10am & 2pm, Fri & Sat 2pm.

★**Exploradores Outdoors** Hwy-256, just north of central Puerto Viejo ☎2750 2020, ⓦexploradores outdoors.com. Excellent outfit running several tours of the local area, including a kayaking and hiking trip to Punta Uva (US$49). They also lead one of the best day-trips in the country, whitewater rafting on the Río Pacuare, which includes four hours of rafting on Class III and IV sections of the river – a total of 38 rapids – and lunch (US$99). Tours depart from their rafting centre in Siquirres, with pick-ups from Puerto Viejo, Cahuita or San José: they can drop you off at a different location than pick-up, which is handy if you're moving on to San José or Cahuita. One-way transportation to Bocas del Toro (Panama) from US$29, and Tortuguero packages from US$179. Also rents bikes.

Om Retreat & Training Center Cashew Hill Jungle Lodge, C 213 ☎2750 0001, ⓦomatcashewhill.com. Popular yoga school atop Cashew Hill, just outside

Puerto Viejo (drop-in classes US$12; US$5 on Fridays). Daily 8am–7pm.

Prancing Pony Hwy-256, Playa Chiquita ☎8307 0118, ⓦfacebook.com/pg/theprancingponycr. Relatively new stables in Playa Chiquita, offering 1hr 30min, half-day and full-day tours on horseback along the coast and deep into the jungle (especially fun for kids). Mon–Sat 9am–4pm.

Pure Jungle Spa Hwy-256, at the edge of Puerto Viejo ☎2756 8413, ⓦpurejunglespa.com. Get pampered at this incredibly lavish spa, offering massages (from US$65/hr), body treatments and facials in lush, tropical garden surroundings. Mon–Sat 10am–6pm, Sun 2–6pm (Aug–Nov closed Sun).

Punta Uva Dive Center Punta Uva (signposted off Hwy-256) ☎2759 9191, ⓦpuntauvadivecenter .com. Beachfront dive shop with highly qualified instructors offering one-tank dives from US$65 (2 tanks for US$80), PADI courses from US$235 and 3hr snorkelling trips for US$55.

Surf the Jungle Av 71, at C 217 ☎8374 6145, ⓦsurfthejungle.com. Local surf school founded by local hero Misael Brown, offering excellent surfing lessons from US$60 (2hr; includes board) – all instructors are Salsa Brava veterans. Also arranges local tours. Daily 8am–4pm.

Terraventuras Av 71, at C 213 ☎2750 0750, ⓦterraventuras.com. Runs a popular zipline canopy tour (US$58), birdwatching tour in the Reserva Indígena KéköLdi (US$75), a half-day trip to the Gandoca-Manzanillo reserve (US$55), as well as outings further afield, to destinations such as Arenal.

Coco Loco Lodge C 211, at Av 67 ☎ 2750 0281, ⓦ coco locolodge.com. Just outside the centre, this lodge is one of the better options if you want to be close to the village but a little apart from the attendant late-night partying. The charming, well-kept bungalows (for up to four people) are spread across four acres of attractive landscaped grounds and feature mosquito nets and cable TV; a/c is US$25 extra, and the breakfast buffet is US$9 extra. US$75

Hostel Kinkajú Av 67, C 217/219 ☎ 2750 0615, ⓦ hostelkinkaju.com. Spotless, locally run hostel with friendly staff, TV room, and two excellent shared kitchens. Bright, colourful dorms or small private rooms (all with fans) and three shared bathrooms. Dorms $13, doubles $32

Hotel Pura Vida Av 67, C 213/215 ☎ 2750 0002, ⓦ hotel-puravida.com. This popular budget hotel has ten pleasant rooms (private bathrooms are an extra US$10), ceiling fans, mosquito nets, a pleasant veranda and garden. It tends to fill quickly. Breakfast is an extra US$7. US$35

★**Pagalù Hostel** Av 69, C 211/213 ☎ 2750 1930, ⓦ pagalu.com. One of the more sedate of the Puerto Viejo area's hostels, immaculate and cosy *Pagalù* offers spacious doubles (some with private bathroom) and dorms with lockers. There's a shared kitchen area and the staff are quick to share their local knowledge. Dorms US$14, doubles US$30

Rocking J's Hostel On the eastern edge of town (Hwy-256 to Manzanillo) ☎ 2750 0665, ⓦ rockingjs.com. To say that *Rocking J's* has contributed its fair share to Puerto Viejo's reputation as a beachside backpacker's party paradise is an understatement, but it can be a fun hostel nonetheless (adorned with mosaics and folk art) and not always as hedonistic or hippy as you may think. As well as the slightly faded dorm rooms, which are the cheapest in town, accommodation includes hammocks in a large shed (bug spray essential; US$7), pre-erected tents (US$16 for

two people), cabins (for up to three people; US$26) and a "king" suite (US$60) with double bed and private bathroom. There's bike and surfboard rental, the infamous bar and an adequate communal kitchen. Breakfast is US$6 extra. Dorms US$11

PLAYA NEGRA AND AROUND

★**Banana Azul** Playa Negra ☎ 2750 2035, ⓦ banana azul.com. Colourful and creatively designed lodge set in gorgeous grounds a short walk from the beach. Each room is spacious with a unique style; those on the top floor have particularly impressive views, and there's also the secluded two-bedroom Tree House Apartment (US$170). The open-air lounge, restaurant and bar area look onto a pool punctuated by thatched-roof shades and vibrant flowers. US$130

Kaya's Place 200m west of town (Hwy-256) ☎ 2750 0690, ⓦ kayasplace.com. Artistic and unique 26-room lodge and craft brewery (BriBri Springs Brewery) built in rustic Afro-Caribbean style, using recycled driftwood from the beach and local materials; there's also a private cabin with three bedrooms (from US$85) and two houses (sleeping four to nine people; from US$100). Rooms with private bathrooms US$8 extra. US$27

★**Samasati** Hone Creek (6.5 km west of Puerto Viejo) ☎ 2537 3418, ⓦ samasati.com. Combining a stay in Puerto Viejo with yoga classes, *Samasati* is one of the best health-focused and ecologically minded retreats in the country. The accommodation, ranging from simple bungalows to a large wooden house (from US$253), is impeccably designed and furnished and blends in well with the surroundings: verandas provide spectacular views. The restaurant serves creatively prepared, mostly vegetarian dishes, and there's a full-service spa. A variety of packages are offered, including daily yoga classes and spa treatments. US$102

EATING

As you might expect in such a popular, international resort, Puerto Viejo offers a cosmopolitan range of places to eat, from excellent European-style bakeries owned by foreign residents to local *sodas* serving tasty Caribbean cuisine. Prices are relatively high and the quality not always good, though, especially the seafood – don't assume everything is caught locally. For a splurge the restaurants in Cocles (see p.194) and further along the coast are better value. US dollars are accepted everywhere, but even here you are likely to be given change in colones.

CAFÉS AND BAKERIES

★**Bread and Chocolate** C 215, Av 69/71 ☎ 2750 0723. People queue before this bakery opens – which, in a village of late risers, says something. A definite must-eat, run by American migrants, offering hearty breakfast in the form of cinnamon-oatmeal pancakes (from ₡2750), real bagels, and even biscuits and gravy (a US diner favourite). Everything is home-made; try the mint chocolate brownies. Cash only. Tues–Sat 6.30am–6.30pm, Sun 6.30am–2.30pm.

Café Rico Av 69, C 217/219 ☎ 2750 0510. Englishman Roger knows everything about the locality and can hook

you up with anything you need. His legendary café is hemmed in by mountains of secondhand books and serves some of the best coffee in town, made with Café Britt Arabica, as well as great fruit plates, tasty sandwiches and French toast (mains from ₡3000). Cash only. Mon–Wed & Fri–Sun 6am–2pm.

De Gustibus Bakery Hwy-256 (Av 71), leading out of town to Playa Cocles ☎ 2756 8397. Friendly, Italian-style bakery serving home-made loaves, cakes, sandwiches, salads and pastries from coconut biscuits to banana bread (pastries from ₡1500). Daily 6.45am–6pm.

3

Deelite Ice Cream Shop Av 73, at C 213 ☎ 8419 2023. Fresh gelato from this Italian-run *gelatería* opposite the bus stop. They have around twenty home-made flavours, from peanut butter to coconut, plus decent espresso. Scoops from ₡2000. Daily 7am–8.30pm.

DreadNut Coffee Av 73, C 213/215 ☎ 8703 9993. Small, high-quality coffee shop near the bus stop and the beach, serving excellent espresso drinks (from ₡1000), plus iced coffee, sandwiches, brownies and banana pancakes. Daily 7.30am–6.30pm.

RESTAURANTS

Chile Rojo Av 71, C 217/219 ☎ 2750 0025. Old standby serving tasty Asian fusion dishes from Thai-style food to fresh sushi, with main courses from ₡3000–4500. It's also a popular place for a drink, with 2-for-1 at happy hour (Mon, Tues & Thurs–Sun 5–8pm). Great balcony for people-watching. Mon, Tues & Thurs–Sun noon–11pm.

La Esquina Boruca C 217, at Av 71 ☎ 2750 0180. Best pizza in the village, with all the usual delicious toppings (pepperoni, Hawaiian, margarita; ₡8500) plus *empanadas*

(₡1000), lasagne (₡3000), roast chicken (whole bird ₡6500) and buckets of local beer for ₡5000. Daily noon–1am.

★**Koki Beach** Av 71, C 217/219 ☎ 2750 0902. Hip open-air restaurant and lounge with recycled furnishings, built around an almond tree. Serves mostly Caribbean cuisine with some international dishes (mains ₡7500–15,000). Tues–Sun 5–11pm.

Restaurante Tamara Av 71, C 215/217 ☎ 2750 0148. No-frills lunch and dinner spot serving tasty Caribbean cuisine, such as rice-and-beans with shrimp (₡6000), *rondón* (₡4500) and chicken with salsa Caribeña (₡3800). Daily 8am–10pm.

★**Stashu's Con-Fusion** Hwy-256 (Av 71), leading out of town to Playa Cocles ☎ 2750 0530. *Stashu's* devoted following is due to its consistently stellar execution of its far-reaching menu, which includes curries, jerk chicken and tandoori dishes, all well prepared and colourful (most mains ₡3500–5200). It's a lively spot with frequent evening music performances, when the inventive cocktails are particularly popular. Mon, Tues & Thurs–Sun 5–10pm; closed mid-Nov to early Dec.

DRINKING AND NIGHTLIFE

Hot Rocks Av 71, at C 217 ☎ 8708 3183. One of the town's more openly touristy places, this lively café-bar has themed nights every day of the week, from karaoke on Fri to salsa on Sun. Mon & Wed–Sun 6am–2.30am.

Johnny's Place Av 73, C 215/217 (on the waterfront) ☎ 2750 2116. Though it's a restaurant as well as a bar, this beachfront spot is best for cocktails during the week and for DJs and dancing at the weekends – skip the food, which tends to be overpriced. Mon, Thurs, Fri & Sun 11am–7pm, Wed, Fri & Sat 11am–2am.

The Lazy Mon at Stanford's Av 71, at C 219 (on the waterfront) ☎ 2750 2116, ⌨ thelazymon.com. Very popular at weekends, this sports bar serves a small range of snacks and has a large outdoor disco where you can dance to the sounds of reggae and waves crashing on the shore. Daily 1pm–late.

Salsa Brava Rasta Bar Av 71, at C 221 ☎ 8429 2929. Open for drinks during the day, then morphs into the best dance club in Puerto Viejo after 10pm; Wed, Fri and Sun feature reggae and ragga, while Sat usually features a mix of pop and dance. Daily 1pm–2am.

DIRECTORY

Bank Bank of Costa Rica (with ATM) is on Av 71, C 211/213.

Laundry Lavandería Estrella, on Hwy-256 just outside the village towards Cocles (daily 6am–10pm), will deliver and pick up; *Café Rico* (see p.191) also does cheap laundry (₡1000/kilo for wash and dry).

Medical facilities Clínica de Especialidades Médicas San Gabriel (☎ 2750 0848) is on C 213, Av 67/69.

Petrol There is a large petrol station (daily 24hr) about 5km west of Puerto Viejo in Hone Creek, at the junction of Hwy-36 and Hwy-256.

Pharmacy Farmacia Caribe is on Av 71, C 213/215.

Post office The post office (Mon–Fri 7.30am–6pm, Sat 7.30am–noon) is on Av 71, at C 211.

Playa Cocles

The first settlement you encounter heading southeast from Puerto Viejo is **PLAYA COCLES**, which straggles along Hwy-256 for a couple of kilometres either side of the Río Cocles. The main beach lies 2km from central Viejo, just off the main road, with its own collection of hostels and restaurants. The beach here is by far the best place to access the sea (it's a wide, sandy stretch, with surfboard rentals), although there are smaller, less busy stretches accessible from the road at various points further south (*Le Caméléon*, for example, has its own tiny beach; see p.194).

THE RESERVA INDÍGENA KÉKÖLDI AND ATEC

About two hundred Bribrí and Cabécar people live in the **Reserva Indígena KéköLdi**, which begins just south of Puerto Viejo and extends inland into the Talamanca Mountains. The reserve was established in 1976 to protect the indigenous culture and ecological resources of the area, but the communities and land remain under constant threat from logging, squatters, tourism and banana plantations. The worst problems arise from lax government checks on construction in the area, which, inhabitants claim, have led to several hotels being built illegally on their land. The main obstacle between the indigenous peoples and their neighbours has been, historically, their irreconcilable views of land. The Bribrí and Cabécar see the forest as an interrelated system of cohabitants all created by and belonging to Sibö, their god of creation, while the typical *campesino* view is that of a pioneer – the forest is an obstacle to cultivation, to be tamed, conquered and effectively destroyed.

The best way to visit the reserve is on one of the **tours** organized by **ATEC** (see box, p.190), a grassroots organization set up in 1990 by members of the local community – Afro-Caribbeans, Bribrí indigenous peoples and Spanish-descended inhabitants. If you're spending even just a couple of days in the Talamanca region, an ATEC-sponsored trip is a must; to reserve a tour, go to their Puerto Viejo office at least one day in advance. The organization's main goal is to give local people a chance to demonstrate their pride in and knowledge of their home territory, and to teach them how to make a living from tourism without selling their land or entering into more exploitative business arrangements. In this spirit, ATEC has trained about fifteen **local people as guides**, who get about ninety percent of the individual tour price. Whereas many of the hotel-organized excursions use cars, ATEC promotes **horseback and hiking** tours. They also visit places on a rotating roster, so that local hamlets don't deteriorate from foreigners traipsing through daily.

The Bribrí speak Spanish (as well as Bribrí) and wear Western clothes. But underneath this layer of assimilation lie the vital remains of their culture and traditional way of life. Although the area has seen some strife between the reserve dwellers, their neighbours and foreign hotel developments, these altercations remain largely on the level of policy. As a visitor, you won't see any overt ill-feeling between the groups.

Treks usually last about four hours, traversing dense rainforest and the Talamanca Mountains. The tour does not take you, as you might expect, to villages where indigenous peoples live in "primitive" conditions; they start near the road to Puerto Viejo – where **Bribrí crafts**, including woven baskets and coconut-shell carvings, are on sale – and pass cleared areas, cocoa plantings and small homesteads, before heading into secondary, and finally primary, cover. In this ancient forest the guide may take you along the same trails that have been used for centuries by Bribrís on trips from their mountain homes down to the sea, pointing out the traditional medicinal plants that reportedly cure everything from malarial fever to skin irritations. A tour may also involve discussions about the permanent reforestation programme or a visit to the iguana-breeding farm established by the local community. However, they conveniently neglect to mention one of the reasons they breed the iguanas is to eat them – especially when the females are pregnant – a major reason they are on the verge of extinction.

Jaguar Rescue Center

Punta Cocles • Entry by guided tour only Mon–Sat 9.30am & 11.30am; 1hr 30min • US$20 • ☎ 2750 0710, ⓦ jaguarrescue.foundation • Signposted off Hwy-256 in Playa Cocles

Founded in 2008 some 4km from Puerto Viejo, the **Jaguar Rescue Center** has quickly blossomed into one of Costa Rica's most successful conservation initiatives. The aim of the small sanctuary is to eventually release the rescued animals – which include howler monkeys, margays, sloths, owls, snakes and caimans (though no jaguars) – back into the wild once they reach maturity. In the meantime, the informative guided **tour** (the only way you can visit) allows you to interact with some of the monkeys and parrots that can't be released. You can also tour **La Ceiba Primary Forest**, the centre's release site, 5km further along the road (see p.195).

Finca Tierra

C Ole Caribe, Playa Cocles • Tours Fri 2pm; 2hr; by reservation only • US$50 • ☎ 8390 8348, ⓦ fincatierra.com • Signposted off Hwy-256; drive 2.8km on gravel C Ole Caribe, keep bearing left (4WD only)

Deep in the jungle above Playa Cocles, **Finca Tierra** is a working farm (solar-powered and off-the-grid) that primarily runs courses on permaculture (permanent agriculture), though it also offers fascinating guided **tours** on Fridays (including snacks), plus popular tour evenings on select Saturdays through the year, with the focus on a spectacular jungle meal. Tours – the only way you can visit – introduce the concept of permaculture with walks through their tropical "food forests", with low-maintenance food production systems such as fruit trees, medicinal plants and edible greens. Many travellers sign up for the two-week **Permaculture Design Certificate Course** (US$1300; includes meals, field trips and accommodation in bamboo cabins).

ACCOMMODATION
PLAYA COCLES

All the recommendations below offer free wi-fi.

★**Le Caméléon** Hwy-256 ☎2750 0501, ⓦle cameleonhotel.com. There's nothing on the Caribbean coast quite like *Le Caméléon*, which wouldn't feel at all out of place in Miami. This brilliant white and exceedingly chic boutique hotel has 23 luxurious rooms occupying two storeys around a tempting pool. The range of amenities doesn't disappoint and there's a first-rate restaurant on-site (*Numu*), while across the street is its own private beach club. US$220

Cariblue Hwy-256 ☎ 2750 0518, ⓦ cariblue.com. *Cariblue* has luxurious individual *cabinas* (various sizes sleeping 3–7), all with balconies and hammocks, in a well-maintained jungle setting with a top-notch Italian restaurant (*SoleLuna*), a swimming pool (with pool bar) and souvenir shop. US$160

★**La Costa de Papito** Hwy-256 ☎2750 0704, ⓦlacostadepapito.com. Run by an effusive New Yorker and an extremely friendly staff, *La Costa de Papito* offers "bungalows for the noble savage". Its pretty gardens are home to thirteen bungalows (of various sizes, sleeping 2–6 people) – all with bamboo beds, pink mosquito nets and balconies. There's a lovely spa, bike rental and an included breakfast buffet. US$109

★**Physis Caribbean Bed & Breakfast** Hwy-256 ☎8866 4405, ⓦphysiscaribbean.net. This idyllic B&B offers four brightly decorated rooms (with a/c and flatscreen TV with free Netflix and satellite cable), surrounded by lush jungle gardens and fountains. Friendly Canadian hosts Chad and Anna knock out excellent breakfasts (included). US$105

Playa 506 Hwy-256 ☎2750 2158, ⓦplaya506.com. Excellent hostel and best budget option on Playa Cocles main beach, with mixed dorm with four wooden bunks, simple private rooms, bike rentals, shared kitchen and hammocks on the sand. Quiet at night (on-site bar and restaurant closes at 10pm in high season, 6pm low season). Basic breakfast included. Dorm US$25, doubles US$75

EATING

★**Caribeans Chocolate Tasting Lounge** Hwy-256 ☎8836 8930, ⓦcaribeanschocolate.com. Friendly, open-air café serving a variety of decadent home-made chocolate treats, including bars, brownies (₡2000) and drinks. The iced coffee (₡1500), made from beans grown on their land, is a real treat. A great spot to people-watch along the Puerto Viejo–Manzanillo road, and there's free wi-fi, too. Mon–Sat 9am–6pm.

La Nena Hwy-256 ☎2537 9791. No-frills local place under a small *palapa*, serving cheap, tasty Caribeña dishes (mains from ₡3000) – be prepared for a long wait if it's busy. Mon & Wed–Sat 7am–8pm, Sun 8am–8pm.

Panadería Frances Hwy-256 (near Le Caméléon) ☎8498 3901. Tiny little bakery run by a French couple, serving stellar coffee and superb French-style pastries made with local ingredients – guava-filled tarts, their own handmade *pain au chocolat*, mini pizzas, plus baby eclairs and tasty tuna, ham and cheese baguettes (₡2500–4000). Tues–Sun 8am–5pm.

★**La Pecora Nera** Hwy-256 ☎2750 0490. This dinner-only restaurant is the best Italian in the region, helmed by a wise-cracking Italian chef and serving exquisite pastas (the gnocchi is amazing), seafood, home-made *foccacia* and *carpaccio* (many of the ingredients grown locally or flown in from Italy). Complemented by imported Italian wines, *limoncello* and grappa. Mains ₡9000–15,000. Tues–Sun 5–10pm.

DRINKING AND NIGHTLIFE

Tasty Waves Hwy-256 ☎2750 0507. Popular local bar at the north end of the main beach, a haven for surfers and beach bums, serving cold beers, cocktails and tasty tacos. Themed nights include live DJs (Tues), popular trivia quiz (Thurs) and karaoke (Fri). Tends to get crazy busy in high season. Mon, Tues & Thurs–Sun 10am–1am.

Playa Chiquita

Some 2km beyond Cocles lies **PLAYA CHIQUITA**, another small, laidback community of homes, hotels and restaurants that straggles along Hwy-256, albeit slightly inland from the shore. The beach area – white sand, but narrow here and divided into several small bays – is accessed by pedestrian-only trails (try opposite the *Shawandha Lodge*, and at the *Tree House Lodge*), and is wonderfully secluded and unspoiled.

Chocorart

Set at the end of a 400m gravel road in Playa Chiquita, signposted off Hwy-256 • **Tours** Call ahead for latest schedule, but usually: Jan–April, June–Sept & Dec Mon–Fri 3pm; Oct Mon, Wed & Fri 3pm; usually closed Nov & May; 2hr • US$24 • ☎ 2750 0075

The Swiss-owned **Chocorart** is a chocolate-lover's delight. On a **tour** (the only way to visit) round the cacao plantation, you'll see various stages of the chocolate-making process, as well as have a chance to spot wildlife that lives in the surrounding rainforest. The real treat, of course, is sampling the chocolate, which is predictably decadent, some even infused with fruit grown on the land.

La Ceiba Primary Forest

Signposted 2km off Hwy-256 at the eastern end of Playa Chiquita • Guided tours Mon–Sat 7.30am & 6.30pm (rubber boots provided); 2hr • US$60 • ☎ 2750 0710, ⓦ jaguarrescue.foundation • Accessible by 4WD only, preferably with high clearance; 4WD taxi from Puerto Viejo around US$10

Serving as the Jaguar Rescue Center's (see p.193) animal release site, **La Ceiba Primary Forest** protects a dense 111-acre swathe of humid tropical forest. The reserve is crisscrossed by several trails anchored by its namesake, the Ceiba, a massive tree that can live for over five hundred years and reach 50m in height.

After a spectacular survey of the surrounding forest from the elevated deck of the reserve's headquarters, the guided early-morning hike winds through the immediate vicinity, eventually bringing you to a massive hollowed-out tree where you can gaze up at slumbering bats. It's the **night tour** (at 6.30pm) however – when you can spot frogs, nocturnal insects and snakes, and hear the forest come alive – that should not be missed.

ACCOMMODATION   PLAYA CHIQUITA

★**La Kukula Lodge** Off Hwy-256 ☎2750 0653, ⓦ lakukulalodge.com. One of the most enticing lodges along this stretch, *La Kukula* has smartly designed rooms and bungalows (sleeping up to five people; US$190), powered by a hybrid solar/electric grid. There's a pool, bar, library and free wi-fi, and the staff go out of their way to help you with local activities. US$120

Namuwoki Lodge Hwy-256 ☎ 2750 0278, ⓦ namuwoki .com. Peaceful, Spanish-owned property with nine spacious bungalows (of various sizes sleeping 2–8 people), nestled amid thickly-wooded grounds. Popular with families and groups, the bungalows are all handsomely furnished and each has its own deck. There's a small pool and breakfast is included. Free wi-fi in common areas. US$137

Shawandha Lodge Hwy-256 ☎2750 0018, ⓦ shawandha.com. The long-running *Shawandha* was

one of the original lodges built along the Puerto Viejo–Manzanillo stretch and it still has a style entirely its own. Each spacious palm-roofed bungalow (sleeping 2–3 people) combines a Bali-esque look with comfortable furnishings; the unique tile-work in each bathroom is exquisite. The open-air restaurant (see below) is a real gem; breakfast is included. Free wi-fi. US$145

Tree House Lodge Set back from the beach, off Hwy-256 ☎2750 0706, ⓦ costaricatreehouse.com. Marked by a giant iguana sculpture at the gates on the main road, this creative hotel consists of five separate houses built around six enormous trees, connected by a steel suspension bridge. There's no TV or restaurant on the property, though there is a/c and free wi-fi in the bedrooms. The Beach Suite (US$390) bathroom resembles a colourful UFO – with a seahorse jacuzzi. US$200

EATING

Pura Gula Hwy-256 ☎8634 6404. Italian-run candlelit restaurant with deceptively simple and exceedingly tasty dishes, like fish burritos, ham and cheese crêpes and margarita pizza. Hands down one of the best-value spots on the coast (most mains under ₡10,000). Daily noon–10pm.

Wandha Restaurant At Shawandha Lodge, Hwy-256

☎2750 0018, ⓦ shawandha.com. The most elegant night out in the area, this striking open-air restaurant serves an inventive mix of delicious French and Caribbean dishes, with fresh fish and tender beef a speciality; the heart-of-palm salad is a treat, too (mains from ₡10,000). Daily 7.30–10am & 5.15–10.30pm.

Punta Uva

Serene **PUNTA UVA**, 3km beyond Playa Chiquita, is another small community along Hwy-256, with two beach areas either side of densely forested "grape point" itself. The first is accessed via a short dirt road (at the Super Punta Uva shop) that leads to the **Punta Uva Dive Center** (see p.190) and **Sloth Point**, a small craft stall selling indigenous art and cold drinks, and offering kayak rentals. The sandy beach here is set in a protected cove, making it particularly good for swimming (though there's limited parking). The other side of the headland is accessed from a dirt road a bit further along Hwy-256 (look for signposts to *Arrecife Restaurante*), where the palm-backed beach is more attractive but the sea is a lot rougher.

ACCOMMODATION   PUNTA UVA

★**Almonds and Corals** 200m off the main road (Hwy-256), and 100m from the beach in Punta Uva ☎2759 9056, ⓦalmondsandcorals.com. The *Almonds and Corals* luxury tent lodge lies amid lush rainforest in the Gandoca-Manzanillo refuge. Jacuzzi aside, the lodge does not aspire to be a luxury resort – more like an adventure. You sleep in a screened-in hut on stilts within the jungle. Wildlife is everywhere and deafening at night. Each of the huts has comfortable furniture and an adjoining bathroom. The pathways are raised wooden boardwalks and one must stay on them to avoid the undergrowth. Howler monkeys live in the canopy above and wake you every morning around dawn. Truly a primitive, revitalizing experience. US$145

Korrigan Lodge Hwy-256 ☎2759 9103, ⓦkorrigan lodge.com. Tranquil B&B just off the main road and 400m from the beach, featuring four rustic but luxuriously furnished hardwood cottages (sleeping 2–3 people). Kayaks are US$10/hr, laundry US$10/load. Excellent breakfast and free wi-fi included. US$115

EATING

★**El Refugio Grill** Hwy-256 ☎2759 9007. Set deep in the jungle, this is perhaps the best restaurant on the Caribbean coast, with a small but thoughtfully prepared menu that changes daily but always includes artfully prepared seafood and incredible Argentine-style steaks and barbecue. Most mains ₡9000–15,000. Cash only; reservations recommended. Mon, Tues & Thurs–Sun 5–10pm.

Selvin's Hwy-256 ☎2750 0664, ⓦselvinpuntauva .com. You can feast on locally caught fish served with coconut-flavoured rice-and-beans (₡3500) and especially tasty *rondón* at this perennially popular Caribeño-style restaurant-bar. Cash only. Hours can be erratic, so it's good to call ahead. Thurs–Sun noon–8pm.

Ara Project

Signposted off Hwy-256, 12km from Puerto Viejo • Guided tours daily 4pm; 1hr (reservations essential) • US$20 • ☎8971 1436, ⓦthearaproject.org • 4WD not required, but if cycling/walking note it's very steep

The wonderful **Ara Project**, tucked away in the rainforest between Punta Uva and Manzanillo, is dedicated to saving the endangered great green macaw (wild population estimated to be fewer than one thousand globally). Operated by the government-supervised nonprofit Asociación El Proyecto Ara, **tours** take you to a lookout point where the spectacular views will be matched by a chance to see frolicking macaws (most of them released since 2011 by the project), a spectacular and heart-warming sight. Guides will ensure you are a parrot and macaw expert by the end of the tour. Remember to bring bug repellent.

Manzanillo

Coastal Hwy-256 ends at the small seaside community of **MANZANILLO**, 13km from Puerto Viejo, where a scrubby beach gives access to a large shelf of coral reef just offshore that teems with marine life and offers some of the best **snorkelling** in Costa Rica. The village itself is charming and much less developed than its neighbours (its **First Baptist Church** is one of the region's oldest), with laidback locals and a couple of great places to eat and hang out (there's also a small supermarket). The main reason for a visit here is to access the Refugio de Vida Silvestre Gandoca-Manzanillo, which surrounds the village.

MANZANILLO AND PLAYAS COCLES, CHIQUITA & UVA

ACCOMMODATION	
Almonds and Corals	11
Le Caméléon	5
Cariblue	1
Casa Bongo	12
Korrigan Lodge	9
La Costa de Papito	2
La Kukula Lodge	8
Namuwoki Lodge	6
Physis Caribbean	
Bed & Breakfast	4
Playa 506	3
Shawandha Lodge	7
Tree House Lodge	10

EATING	
Caribeans Chocolate	
Tasting Lounge	1
El Refugio Grill	8
La Nena	3
La Pecora Nera	4
Maxi's	9
Panadería Frances	2
Pura Gula	5
Selvin's	6
Soda Mima	10
Wandha Restaurant	7

DRINKING AND NIGHTLIFE	
Tasty Waves	1

Nature Observatorio Manzanillo

Guided tours daily, reservations essential • Half-day tour (5hr) US$50–70; full-day tour U$70–90; overnight tour US$140–190 • ☎ 8628 2663, ⓦ natureobservatorio.com • Signposted off Hwy-256, 1km before Manzanillo village

The bizarre but totally inspiring **Nature Observatorio Manzanillo** is actually a treehouse, suspended by nylon straps 25m up in the jungle canopy (no nails were used), and accessed by climbing ropes. You can get pulled most of the way up; abseiling down is much more fun. The observation deck features hammocks and loungers, a spectacular perch from which to view the surrounding forest, where you'll spy toucans, monkeys and sloths. The upper floor features two queen-size beds for the overnight tours. There's also a small kitchen with water cooler and even a shower and toilet up here (though not with much privacy), supplied by rainwater and solar power. Half-day tours are enough to get a taster, with a guided hike through the jungle and plenty of time in the treehouse.

ARRIVAL AND DEPARTURE   MANZANILLO

By bus The Puerto Limón–Manzanillo bus (6 daily; 30min) is the only reliable public transportation that plies this route, terminating at the small plaza in front of Maxi's.

ACCOMMODATION

Casa Bongo ☎ 2759 9016, ⓦ congo-bongo.com. Just outside the village proper, this is the most comfortable option in the area, with seven individual cottages (of various sizes sleeping 3–7 people), all with full kitchens, mosquito nets, hot showers, verandas with hammocks and free wi-fi. Free bottle of red wine on arrival, plus bottled water. **US$165**

EATING

Maxi's At the end of Hwy-256, in the village centre ☎ 6045 2121. Split-level wooden veranda restaurant and bar with great views over the beach. It's renowned for its seafood (mains from ₡4500), notably red snapper – though the lobster is a bit overrated. Gets packed at the weekend. Daily 11.30am–10pm.

Soda Mima 25m behind Maxi's, set about 100m back from the beach. Simple soda with veranda seating serving heaps of Caribbean specialities, like shrimp with rice and Tico staples such as steak with rice-and-beans (from ₡3000). Daily 11am–8pm.

Refugio de Vida Silvestre Gandoca-Manzanillo

Daily 7am–5pm • Free • ☎ 2759 9100

Covering over fifty square kilometres of land and a similar area of sea, the **REFUGIO DE VIDA SILVESTRE GANDOCA-MANZANILLO** covers a vast swathe of coastline and inland

3

THE PUNTA MONA CENTER FOR REGENERATIVE DESIGN

If you are looking for an alternative to conventional tourism and even backpacking, and want to settle in a remote spot, Punta Mona is worth a visit. Founded in 1997, the **Punta Mona Center for Regenerative Design & Botanical Studies** (ⓦ puntamona.org) is an 85-acre organic farm and retreat centre located inside the Refugio Nacional Gondoca-Manzanillo. The only way to get there is by boat from Manzanillo (arranged through the centre for US$50 per boat), on horseback or a two- to three-hour hike from Manzanillo, where the coastal road ends and the rainforest begins (taxis from Puerto Viejo charge US$20 to the trailhead). The café and convenience store in the village are the last opportunity to purchase provisions until your return.

If you are feeling adventurous, you could tackle the 8km **trail** (see below) that goes south along the beach, crosses a stream and heads on towards Punta Mona. Bear in mind this trail is usually very muddy and can be slow going (allow about 2hr–2hr 30min with a pack).

Promoting a sustainable way of living through example, the gardeners who give life to Punta Mona grow their own food organically, recycle and manage all waste, use eco-technologies such as solar power, and create an amazing sense of community. You learn about the fruit, vegetables and trees, gather the food and participate in the cooking. Their architecturally impressive houses are built from fallen trees, they've constructed a complex irrigation system, solar panels provide the electricity, and they've planted a wide variety of tropical fruits, nuts, spices and herbs.

When you're not doing your share to keep the place running, you can laze on a hammock, take Spanish lessons, snorkel, kayak, hike, look for dolphins or nesting turtles (in season), play dominoes or simply surf the solar-powered satellite internet in your own pocket of paradise. Day **tours** (4hr; US$35) run daily at 10am and include lunch and snorkelling; overnight stays are US$85 per person (US$550/week) or US$185 for a private cabin for two. Cash only.

---

forest, from Cocles to Manzanillo and all the way to the Río Sixaola and the frontier with Panama. It was established in 1985 to protect some of Costa Rica's last **coral reefs** – the most accessible is **Punta Uva**, which offers great snorkelling (see p.196). There's also a protected **leatherback turtle-nesting beach** south of the village of Manzanillo (Feb–May), along with tracts of mangrove forests and the last *orey* swamp in the country. More than 350 **bird** species have been identified here, many of them rare. Other species found in the refuge include the manatee, tapir and American crocodile, who hang out along the river estuaries, though you're unlikely to see them.

Gandoca

Four kilometres from Manzanillo down a rough track (Sendero del Bosque), **GANDOCA** provides access to the Laguna Gandoca, a bird-spotter's delight with boat trips organized from the village. You can get here by walking from Manzanillo, or there's access from Hwy-36 near Sixaola – if you have a 4WD – via the banana *fincas* of Daytonia, Virginia and Finca 96. Puerto Viejo's tour companies (see box, p.190) offer guided hikes and snorkelling.

The trail to Punta Mona

Gandoca-Manzanillo has one fairly demanding but rewarding **trail** (Sendero Punta Mona; 5.5km each way), that passes primary and secondary forest as well as some pretty, secluded beaches on its way from Manzanillo to **Punta Mona** (Monkey Point). It can get extremely hot, and mosquitoes are usually out in force, so carry plenty of water, sunscreen and repellent. Beginning at the northeast end of Manzanillo village, the trail proceeds along the beach for 1km. After crossing a small creek and entering a grove of coconut trees, it becomes poorly marked and easy to lose, but should be just about visible as it climbs up a small bluff. The trail then drops to lower ground and skirts a few small beaches with shark infested waters, before heading inland. Some of these up-and-down sections are quite steep, and if it has been raining (as it invariably has) then mud and mosquitoes can make the trip unpleasant. However, the trail does offer great opportunities for spotting birds and wildlife; you're almost guaranteed a sight of chestnut-mandibled and keel-billed **toucans**. The tiny flashes of colour darting about on the ground are **poison dart frogs**; watch where you're stepping, and avoid touching them. Punta Mona, at the end of the trail, is flanked by a shady beach, from where you can see across to Panama, only about 8km to the south. From here you return to Manzanillo the same way.

Sixaola and into Panama

From Puerto Viejo, the paved road (Hwy-36) continues inland to Bribrí (an admin centre with little to see), about 10km southwest, arching over the Talamancan foothills, before continuing as a dusty gravel highway for another 34km through solid banana *fincas* to gritty **SIXAOLA**. Locals cross the border here to do their shopping in Panama, where most things are less expensive. The majority of foreigners who cross into Panama do so simply because their tourist visa for Costa Rica has expired and they have to leave the country for 72 hours, though the pristine Panamanian island of **Bocas del Toro** just over the border offers an inviting prospect even for those who don't need an extension.

The Sixaola–Guabito crossing

The torpid **Sixaola–Guabito** crossing doesn't see much foreign traffic, and for the most part formalities are simple, but you should still arrive as early in the morning as possible as lines can build up through the day. The rusty old bridge across the Río Sixaola that looks like it's about to collapse into the river at any moment has finally been replaced by a new one. There's nowhere to stay in Guabito, the tiny hamlet on the Panamanian side of Río Sixaola, so aim to take an onward bus connection as quickly as possible.

ARRIVAL AND INFORMATION THE SIXAOLA–GUABITO CROSSING

By bus Autotransportes MEPE (☎ 2758 1572) buses arrive at Sixaola regularly from Limón and Puerto Viejo. To get further into Panama from Guabito, your best option is to catch a frequent bus (behind the Panama immigration post) to the banana town of Changuinola (US$2) from where there are connections to the rest of the country as well as a bus service across the Cordillera Central to Chiriquí on the Interamericana, where you can get bus connections to Panama City and back to San José. If you're planning to visit Bocas del Toro, take a bus

to Changuinola and transfer to an Almirante bus (30min; US$1.45) from there. Once in Almirante, catch a water taxi to Bocas del Toro (last departure 6pm; around 30min; US$6).

Departures from Sixaola Limón (daily 5am–7pm, hourly; 3hr); Puerto Viejo (hourly; 1hr).

Departures from Guabito Changuinola (every 30min; 30min).

By taxi Taxis (ask at the border post) make the 30min trip to Changuinola for about US$20.

CROSSING THE BORDER INTO PANAMA

The Sixaola–Guabito border is open daily 8am–5pm Panama time (one hour ahead of Costa Rica). Tourists leaving Costa Rica need to buy an exit stamp (US$7) – you can pay by credit card at the small immigration office, though the machine is often not working, or at some of the businesses next to the office (which will charge an additional US$1 admin fee); make sure you get a receipt. You'll also need to fill in a departure form (free). In recent years locals have started charging a US$4 entry fee at the Panama end of the bridge – these are folks from Guabito, not Panama Immigration, but it's best to simply pay to avoid hassle. There is a small Panama Immigration Office after this where you can get your passport stamped; note that Panama has been quite strict enforcing its entry requirements in recent years, and most travellers will be asked to show proof of onward travel out of the country. Immigration requirements often change – check with the Panamanian Consulate (see p.115). The official currency in Panama is US dollars.

The Zona Norte

HOT SPRINGS AT BALNEARIO TABACÓN

The Zona Norte

Vast by Costa Rican standards, the Zona Norte (Northern Zone) spans the hundred-odd kilometres from the base of the Cordillera Central to just short of the mauve-blue mountains of southern Nicaragua. Historically cut off from the rest of the country, the Zona Norte has developed a distinct character, with large segments of the population consisting of independent-minded farmers and Nicaraguan refugees. Neither group journeys to the Valle Central very often, and many here have a special allegiance to, and pride in, their region; indeed, the far north, which for years was mauled by fighting in the Nicaraguan civil war, feels more like Nicaragua than Costa Rica.

Topographically, the Zona Norte separates neatly into two broad, river-drained plains (*llanuras*) stretching all the way to the Río San Juan on the Nicaragua–Costa Rica border: in the west, the Llanura de Guatusos is dominated by Volcán Arenal, while to the east the Llanura de San Carlos features the tropical jungles of the **Sarapiquí region**. Less obviously picturesque than many parts of the country, it nonetheless has a distinctive appeal, with rivers snaking across steaming plains, and flop-eared cattle languishing beneath riverside trees.

Most visitors use the bustling tourist centre of **La Fortuna** as a gateway to **Parque Nacional Volcán Arenal**, whose active but slumbering volcano looms over the eastern end of **Laguna de Arenal**. Located on the southern edge of the lake, the charming village of **El Castillo** is a more sedate place to base yourself than La Fortuna. To the **north of La Fortuna**, meanwhile, is a reserve housing one of the few remaining Maleku indigenous communities. The multitude of activities on offer in the La Fortuna region make it the most popular destination in the Zona Norte, though the Sarapiquí region, with its tropical-forest ecolodges and research stations, notably **La Selva** and **Rara Avis**, also draws significant numbers of visitors. The regional capital, **San Carlos**, lies between the two; though devoid of actual sights, its easy-going nature – and the fact that it's a transport hub – make it a decent place to break your journey. In the **far north**, the remote flatlands are home to the increasingly accessible wetlands of the **Refugio Nacional de Vida Silvestre Caño Negro**, which boasts an extraordinary number of birds. Few visitors venture any further, though a steady trickle passes through the border town of Los Chiles en route to Nicaragua.

One of the prime agricultural areas in the country, the Zona Norte is carpeted with vast banana, pineapple and sugar-cane plantations and huge dairy-cattle farms. The worst excesses of slash-and-burn deforestation are all too visible from the roadsides and riverbanks, with the matchstick corpses of once-tall hardwoods scattered over stump-scarred fields patrolled by a few cattle. Legal and illegal logging over the last twenty-five years has cleared more than seventy percent of the region's original forest, though the Refugio Nacional de Vida Silvestre Mixto Maquenque helps link protected areas in Nicaragua with the Valle Central.

VOLCÁN ARENAL

Highlights

❶ Volcán Arenal The lava flows may have stopped but the volcano remains a stunning sight (at least when you get a clear day) and the surrounding area is packed with activities. **See p.214**

❷ Laguna de Arenal Relax in one of the great lodges on the shores of this serene lake, or get out onto its sparkling waters, to fish or to try your hand at windsurfing. **See p.215**

❸ Rancho Margot Take a riverside yoga class, help milk the cows, go for a hike or take out a kayak at this groundbreaking eco-retreat and organic farm. **See p.216**

❹ Refugio Nacional de Vida Silvestre Caño Negro This spectacular seasonal floodland near the border with Nicaragua offers some of the best wildlife-watching in Central America. **See p.224**

❺ Birdwatching at La Selva Explore the vast network of trails at this renowned research station – home to nearly 500 species of bird – with some of the most informative guides in the country. **See p.230**

❻ Reserva Rara Avis The dense rainforest of the Sarapiquí region provides the perfect setting for some excellent private reserves, most notably the wonderfully remote, wildlife-rich Reserva Rara Avis. **See p.232**

HIGHLIGHTS ARE MARKED ON THE MAP ON P.204

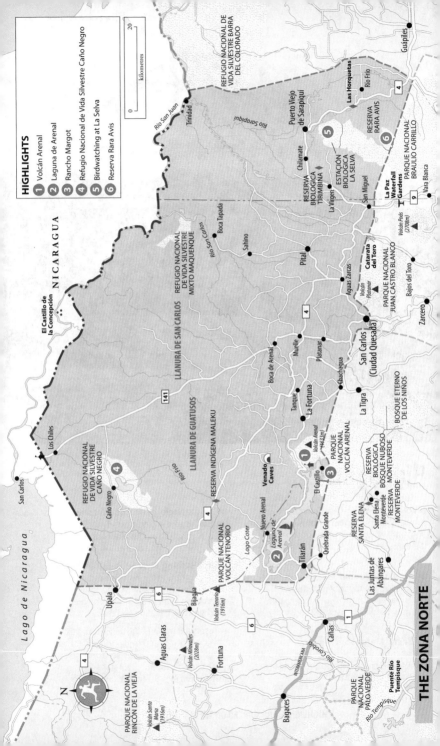

HIGHLIGHTS

1. Volcán Arenal
2. Laguna de Arenal
3. Rancho Margot
4. Refugio Nacional de Vida Silvestre Caño Negro
5. Birdwatching at La Selva
6. Reserva Rara Avis

THE ZONA NORTE

NICARAGUA

Lago de Nicaragua

PARQUE NACIONAL RINCÓN DE LA VIEJA

Volcán Santa María (1916m)

Aguas Claras

Fortuna

Volcán Miravalles (2028m)

Bagaces

Cañas

Puente Río Tempisque

PARQUE NACIONAL PALO VERDE

Río Tempisque

INTERAMERICANA

Río Corobicí

Las Juntas de Abangares

Upala

Bijagua

Volcán Tenorio (1916m)

PARQUE NACIONAL VOLCAN TENORIO

RESERVA INDIGENA MALEKU

LLANURA DE GUATUSOS

Río Frío

Los Chiles

REFUGIO NACIONAL DE VIDA SILVESTRE CAÑO NEGRO

Caño Negro

San Carlos

El Castillo de la Concepción

LLANURA DE SAN CARLOS

REFUGIO NACIONAL DE VIDA SILVESTRE MIXTO MAQUENQUE

Boca Tapada

Río San Carlos

Sahino

Pital

Aguas Zarcas

Volcán Platanar

Catarata del Toro

PARQUE NACIONAL JUAN CASTRO BLANCO

Bajos del Toro

Zarcero

Lago Coter

Nuevo Arenal

Laguna de Arenal

Tilarán

Quebrada Grande

RESERVA SANTA ELENA

Santa Elena Monteverde

RESERVA MONTEVERDE

RESERVA BIOLOGICA BOSQUE NUBOSO MONTEVERDE

BOSQUE ETERNO DE LOS NIÑOS

La Tigra

Venado Caves

El Castillo

Volcán Arenal (1633m)

PARQUE NACIONAL VOLCAN ARENAL

La Fortuna

Tanque

Muelle

Boca de Arenal

Platanar

Chachagua

San Carlos (Ciudad Quesada)

Trinidad

Río San Juan

REFUGIO NACIONAL DE VIDA SILVESTRE BARRA DEL COLORADO

Río Sarapiquí

Puerto Viejo de Sarapiquí

Chilamate

RESERVA BIOLOGICA TIRIMBINA

La Virgen

ESTACION BIOLOGICA LA SELVA

San Miguel

Las Horquetas

Río Frío

RESERVA RARA AVIS

La Paz Waterfall Gardens

Vara Blanca

Volcán Poás (2708m)

PARQUE NACIONAL BRAULIO CARRILLO

Guápiles

N

20

0

kilometres

141

4

4

6

6

4

4

1

9

1

2

3

4

5

6

Brief history

For thousands of years before the Conquest, the original inhabitants of the Zona Norte were tribal groups – chief among them the **Corobicí** and **Maleku** – who made contact with one another via the great rivers. The **Spanish presence** was first felt in the early sixteenth century, when galleons meandered up the Río San Juan and into Lago de Nicaragua, looking for a route to the east. Pirates (mainly British) soon followed, wreaking havoc on the riverside communities. It was another two hundred years before the Spanish made a **settlement** of any size, the Quesada family coming down from San Ramón in the nineteenth century to found a village at present-day San Carlos (officially named Ciudad Quesada). In the meantime, cross-border commerce carried on as it had for thousands of years via the San Juan, Frío, Sarapiquí and San Carlos rivers – the **Río Sarapiquí** in particular remained a more important highway than any road well into the eighteenth century, carrying coffee for export from Heredia out to the Caribbean ports of Matina and Limón.

INFORMATION

Getting around Although many roads in the region are seriously potholed, getting around is easy enough, and there's a good bus network linking La Fortuna and Puerto Viejo de Sarapiquí; if you plan on travelling outside these areas, however, you're better off hiring a car.

Climate The Zona Norte's climate is hot and wet, more so in the east than in the west near Guanacaste, where there is a dry season. You'll be drenched by regular downpours, but the rain always makes for an enjoyable respite from the heat.

La Fortuna and around

4

LA FORTUNA (or La Fortuna de San Carlos, as it's officially named) was once a simple agricultural town dominated by the majestic conical form of Arenal, just 6km away. True to its name, La Fortuna is now booming as a thriving base for the area's sports, activities and tours. Despite all the tour buses whizzing through town, however, it remains a pleasant, inviting community. There's nothing specific to see, as most of the streets are taken up by travel agencies, souvenir shops, guesthouses and restaurants, and visitors wander between them comparing prices, while gazing keenly towards the volcano and popping into *sodas* for much-needed *refrescos* to cope with the heat.

Looming at 1633m, **Volcán Arenal** seems to emerge directly from the town's fringes. Although still considered to be active, the volcano has been slumbering since 2010 and the famous evening lava tours are now a thing of the past. On a clear day it remains a majestic sight, but when it's rainy and foggy – which is more often than not – the volcano is almost totally obscured, its summit hidden behind a sombrero of cloud; indeed, locals estimate that one in two visitors never actually gets a glimpse of the summit.

The picturesque **Catarata de La Fortuna**, the waterfalls southwest of town, are a popular half-day diversion, while the area to the northwest offers a variety of outdoor activities, from hiking forested trails to ziplining to bathing in steaming **hot springs**.

The hot springs

A number of **hot springs** line the road from La Fortuna to Arenal, all set around a variety of pools fed by thermally heated underground streams. The majority of agencies in town sell tickets and transportation to the springs, but you can easily visit them independently. Some **hotels** have worked hot springs into their landscaped grounds, which are also open (for a fee) to non-guests.

For years, locals in the know have been enjoying a natural – and **free** – hot soak in small ponds nestled within the fast-flowing river near the bridge just after Tabacón. If you decide to take the plunge, keep in mind that the rocks here can be slippery and the river treacherous, especially during the rainy season.

LA FORTUNA

EATING
La Choza de Laurel	5
Don Rufino	2
Lava Lounge	4
Life House	6
La Parada	3
Rainforest Café	7
Restaurant Nene's	1

ACCOMMODATION
Arenal Backpackers	4
Gringo Pete's	3
HotelSan Bosco	1
Monte Real	5
Sleeping Indian Guesthouse	2

SHOPPING
| Down to Earth | 1 |

Balneario Tabacón

10km west of La Fortuna • **Hot springs** Daily 10am–10pm • Day-pass with lunch/dinner US$94, night-pass with buffet dinner US$77 • Grand Spa daily 8am–9pm • Restaurant daily 11am–4pm & 5–9pm • ☎ 2460 2020, ⓦ tabacon.com

The glitziest of the main hot springs and the destination for most tourists is **Balneario Tabacón**. Fed by a magma-boiled thermal river originating in the nether parts of Volcán Arenal – the water temperature ranges from 27°C (80°F) to about 42°C (108°F) – the complex comprises fifteen mineral-rich pools, most of which are secluded among rich vegetation. Several are set beneath waterfalls, so you can manoeuvre yourself under the cascades for a pummelling hot-water "massage". The atmosphere, with cocktail bar and bikini-clad tourists, makes you feel like you've just stepped into a 1970s James Bond film.

Given the steep admission, many people make a day of it and take lunch at one of Tabacón's on-site **restaurants**; you can choose between à la carte or a daily-changing buffet.

Grand Spa

Tabacón's award-winning **Grand Spa** offers massages and therapies (individually priced) in a cluster of treatment bungalows, tucked away at the top of the gardens and surrounded by lush foliage. If you really want to push the boat out, opt for their signature Tabacón treatment, which starts with a stretching session, and also involves a full-body massage using volcanic mud.

Baldi Hot Springs

4km west of La Fortuna • Daily 9am–10pm • Day-pass US$35, day-pass with lunch/dinner US$57; US$5 for lockers, US$10 towel deposit • ☎ 2479 2190, ⓦ baldihotsprings.cr

Baldi Hot Springs is more accessible than Tabacón for those without transport. While it lacks the classy touches of its rival, it's significantly cheaper and offers many of the same facilities, including three wet bars. Baldi boasts 25 steaming pools, including Roman-style baths and waterfall-fed pools, and – for younger soakers – has three waterslides.

Ecotermales Fortuna

4km west of La Fortuna • Daily 10am–9pm, split into three allotted sessions of 10am–1pm, 1–5pm & 5–9pm • Day-pass US$37 • ☎ 2479 8787, ⓦ ecotermalesfortuna.cr

Fronted by imposing wooden gates, the exclusive-looking **Ecotermales Fortuna** has five cascading thermal pools of varying temperatures set in idyllic forested surrounds. It's stylishly low-key, and only 100 people are allowed in during any of the allotted times, so be sure to book ahead in high season. While there's no volcano view from the pools, the rainforest setting more than makes up for it. The price includes towel, locker and access to two bars and a restaurant.

Termales Los Laureles

5.5km west of La Fortuna • Daily 9am–9pm • ₡6000 • ☏ 2479 1431, ⓦ termaleslosaureles.com

Termales Los Laureles is the least expensive official hot springs in the Arenal area and is

---

ACTIVITIES AROUND LA FORTUNA

You could spend several weeks in La Fortuna rafting, horseriding, mountain biking and ziplining and still not sample all the activities on offer. The below should keep you busy for a while, at least.

CANOPY TOURS, AERIAL TRAMS AND HANGING BRIDGES

Arenal Canopy Tour Montaña de Fuego Inn, 9km northwest of La Fortuna ☏ 2479 9769, ⓦ canopy.co.cr. La Fortuna's original ziplining operation, with nine cables (US$50), plus a 40m abseil, horseriding (US$77 for all three activities) and an aerial tram (US$81).

Canopy Los Cañones Los Lagos, 6km northwest of La Fortuna ☏ 2479 1047, ⓦ hotelloslagos.com. Based in the grounds of *Hotel Los Lagos*, this canopy system has a dozen cables and 13 platforms covering a distance of almost 3km (US$50).

Ecoglide Arenal Park 3.5km west of La Fortuna ☏ 2479 7472, ⓦ arenalecoglide.com. Thirteen cables, fifteen platforms and a Tarzan swing (US$75 for all three) in a park beneath the volcano. There's also a mini cable for practice.

Sky Adventures 23km from La Fortuna, on the road to El Castillo ☏ 2479 9944, ⓦ skyadventures.travel. Try out the aerial tram (US$46), or the hanging bridges and canopy tour (seven cables; US$81). One of the few places you can go ziplining at sunset. Also offers mountain-biking trips.

WHITEWATER RAFTING, CANOEING AND CANYONING

Canoa Aventura 1.5km west of La Fortuna ☏ 2479 8200, ⓦ canoa-aventura.com. Canoe and kayak specialists, with half-day trips on Laguna de Arenal (US$57), a full-day paddle in Caño Negro (US$108) and a family-friendly "safari float" (US$59) down the forest-fringed Río Peñas Blancas by raft or kayak.

Costa Rica Descents Av Central, opposite the southwest corner of the church, La Fortuna ☏ 2479 9419, ⓦ costaricadescents.com. Run by two brothers who got their whitewater wings rafting in the Rockies, this is La Fortuna's only Class V outfitter, with full-day trips on the Upper Balsa (US$130). They also run gentler trips on the

Class II–III Río Sarapiquí and Río Balsa (both from US$85).

Desafío Opposite the west side of the church, La Fortuna ☏ 2479 9464, ⓦ desafiocostarica.com. Well-run, efficient rafting specialist running tours on the Class II–III Balsa (from US$69) and the Class III–IV Sarapiquí (from US$85). They also offer exciting canyoning trips (from US$99), as well as paddle boarding on Lake Arenal (from US$65).

Pure Trek Canyoning Opposite the northwest corner of the church, La Fortuna ☏ 2461 2110, ⓦ puretrek.com. Four abseils (three down a series of waterfalls) in a canyon near town (US$101).

HORSERIDING

Desafío (see above). In addition to their recommended rafting trips, Desafío run horseriding tours to the Catarata de La Fortuna (US$73); their transfer to Monteverde includes a lakeside ride on well-cared-for horses (US$90; 5hr).

Don Tobías Arenal Springs Resort, 7km northwest of La Fortuna, then 450m down a signed turn-off to the right ☏ 2479 1212, ⓦ gruporiosdelarenal.com. Offers a 2hr 30min tour (from US$65) in the

fields and forests around Volcán Arenal, with some creek-crossing involved, plus an atmospheric full-moon ride (from US$120). Safety-conscious, experienced guides.

Rancho Arenal Paraíso Arenal Paraíso Resort & Spa, 8km west of La Fortuna ☏ 2460 5333, ⓦ arenalparaiso.com. The hotel's ranch runs similar trips (from US$55) to Don Tobías, mostly on mountain trails on the slopes of Arenal.

FOOD AND DRINK

Don Olivo Chocolate Tour ☏ 8302 7992, ⓦ arenalvolcanochocolatetour.com. As the name suggests, this 2hr tour takes you through the

chocolate-making process, with plenty of tasters (US$25, including transport your hotel).

4

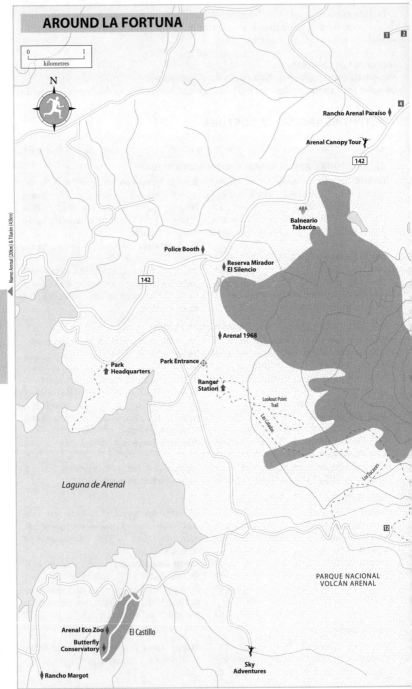

AROUND LA FORTUNA

0   1
kilometres

N

Nuevo Arenal (20km) & Tilarán (43km)

4

Rancho Arenal Paraíso

Arenal Canopy Tour

142

Balneario
Tabacón

Police Booth

Reserva Mirador
El Silencio

142

Arenal 1968

Park
Headquarters

Park Entrance

Ranger
Station

Lookout Point
Trail

Las Coladas

Las Tucanes

12

Laguna de Arenal

PARQUE NACIONAL
VOLCÁN ARENAL

Arenal Eco Zoo

El Castillo

Butterfly
Conservatory

Rancho Margot

Sky
Adventures

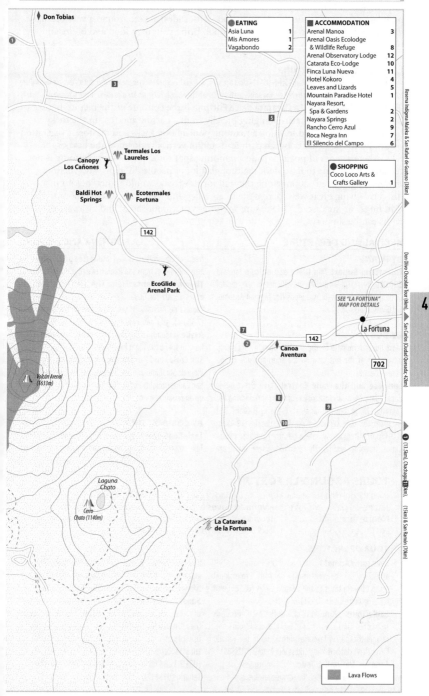

● EATING

Asia Luna	1
Mis Amores	1
Vagabondo	2

■ ACCOMMODATION

Arenal Manoa	3
Arenal Oasis Ecolodge	
& Wildlife Refuge	8
Arenal Observatory Lodge	12
Catarata Eco-Lodge	10
Finca Luna Nueva	11
Hotel Kokoro	4
Leaves and Lizards	5
Mountain Paradise Hotel	1
Nayara Resort,	
Spa & Gardens	2
Nayara Springs	2
Rancho Cerro Azul	9
Roca Negra Inn	7
El Silencio del Campo	6

● SHOPPING

Coco Loco Arts &	
Crafts Gallery	1

Reserva Indígena Maleku & San Rafael de Guatuso (38km)

Don Olivo Chocolate tour (6km)

San Carlos (Ciudad Quesada 42km)

SEE "LA FORTUNA"
MAP FOR DETAILS

La Fortuna

(13.5km), Chachagua (13km)

(15km) & San Ramón (70km)

4

Don Tobias

Termales Los
Laureles

Canopy
Los Cañones

Baldi Hot
Springs

Ecotermales
Fortuna

142

EcoGlide
Arenal Park

La Fortuna

142

Canoa
Aventura

702

Volcán Arenal
(1633m)

Laguna
Chato

Cerro
Chato (1140m)

La Catarata
de la Fortuna

	Lava Flows

popular with Ticos. Four simple pools (one with slides) are set around a very ordinary garden, but the volcano views are sensational. Bring your own food and booze and make a night of it.

La Catarata de La Fortuna

4km southwest of La Fortuna • Daily 8am–5pm • US$12 • Most agencies run tours (see box below) to the waterfall, but it's cheaper to get there by taxi (around US$10) and more fun by horseriding across the fields; Desafío (see box, p.207) runs 4hr trips (US$73) that take in the waterfalls

The dramatically sited **La Catarata de La Fortuna** is the epitome of the picture-book cascade – a tall, thin stream plunging prettily from a narrow aperture in the rocky heights 75m above, and forming a foaming pool among rocks and rainforest vegetation below. From the ticket booth, a path leads 600m vertically down to the base of the falls, where a series of pools provide a tempting spot for a quick dip; swimming is not recommended, due to flash floods, although a lot of people do it anyway. There's a *mirador* (signposted) 200m along the trail for those who would rather look from a distance, giving great views across the steep valley and its heavily forested floor to the thin finger of the cascade. Make sure you wear waterproof shoes, and be aware that the paths can be slippery.

ARRIVAL AND DEPARTURE — LA FORTUNA AND AROUND

BY PLANE

La Fortuna Airport 7km to the east of town (around ₡10,000 by taxi). Nature Air has flights to the capital (1 daily; 30min), as well as Quepos (for Manuel Antonio; 1 daily; 35min).

BY BUS

Most buses terminate at the station, though some drop passengers at the bus stop on the southern side of the Parque Central.

San José and the Valle Central Three direct buses depart daily from San José for La Fortuna (4hr), leaving the Atlántico Norte bus terminal at 6.15am, 8.40am and 11.30am; two daily services make the return run (12.45pm & 2.45pm). Alternatively, take a bus from San José to San Carlos (roughly hourly; 2hr 30min), where there are

frequent connections to La Fortuna (see p.222). There are also daily buses from San Ramón (4 daily; 2hr 30min).

Tilarán and Santa Elena (for Monteverde) Daily buses depart for Tilarán (2–3 daily; 3hr), at the head of Laguna de Arenal – if you catch the first one to Tilarán (7.30am), you can connect there with the Santa Elena service (around 12.30pm; 2hr 30min); otherwise, you'll have to spend the night in Tilarán.

San Carlos and Puerto Viejo de Sarapiquí For Puerto Viejo de Sarapiquí and the Sarapiquí region, catch a bus to San Carlos (roughly hourly; 1hr 30min), where you can pick up an onward service.

BY COMBINATION

Taxi–Boat–Taxi Many people opt for the "Taxi–Boat–Taxi" transfer to Monteverde (daily departures around

---

TOURS AROUND LA FORTUNA

Even though the sunset lava tours are a thing of the past, La Fortuna remains a prime setting-off point for trips to the **Venado Caves** and the remote wildlife refuge of **Caño Negro**; shorter tours to the latter will just take you on a scenic cruise down the Río Frío from Los Chiles, so make sure that you'll actually be visiting the refuge itself.

TOUR OPERATORS

Aventuras Arenal 150m east of the Parque Central ☏ 2479 9133, ⓦ aventurasarenal.com. Professional setup offering tours to the Venado Caves (US$85) and hikes up Cerro Chato (US$110).

Eagle Tours 325m west of the Parque Central, in front of La Choza Inn ☏ 2479 9091, ⓦ eagletours.net. Budget backpacker favourite with a trip to the Venado Caves that's dubbed "the darkest tour in town" (US$85).

Jacamar Naturalist Tours 50m southwest of the Parque Central ☏ 2479 9767, ⓦ arenaltours.com. Runs

a range of naturalist tours, including a tour to the Maleku indigenous reserve (US$119), Caño Negro trips (US$96), hiking up Cerro Chato (US$106) and ATV tours (US$90).

Sunset Tours Av Central, by the southwest corner of the church ☏ 2479 9800, ⓦ sunsettour .net. Often a little pricier than the rest but they only use professional, well-qualified guides. They run trips to Cerro Chato and the La Fortuna waterfall (US$91) and hikes along the Río Celeste near Volcán Tenorio (US$117).

8–8.30am & 2–2.30pm; around US$32; 3hr); it saves time and the boat trip across the lake is spectacular. Trips are also run in the opposite direction. Slightly different alternatives offered by some agencies, including Desafío (see box, p.207), offer a horse or bike ride on the final leg (both around US$90).

INFORMATION AND GETTING AROUND

Bike rental Bike Arenal (☎2479 9454, ⊕bikearenal .com), on Av Central, rents out mountain bikes from US$25 per day; one-day road and mountain-bike tours are around US$135.

Car rental Alamo, 200m west of the church (☎2479 9090, ⊕alamocostarica.com); Mapache, 800m west of the church (☎2479 0010, ⊕mapache.com).

By taxi There's a taxi rank on the eastern side of the Parque Central; expect to pay around ₡5000 to La Catarata de La Fortuna (one way).

Security Theft is on the rise in La Fortuna; never leave anything unattended, especially in a car, and be careful about walking around alone late at night. Note, too, that there have been a number of serious complaints (credit-card fraud and scams) from travellers about the agencies that operate out of the bus station. Also keep a close eye (and indeed a firm hand) on your bags when travelling by bus to/from La Fortuna.

ACCOMMODATION

Budget travellers usually stay in or around **La Fortuna** itself, while people with their own transport and/or a bit of money tend to head to the lodges that surround town; some of these are quite remote and local public transport is erratic or nonexistent, but many offer a free shuttle service into town. The nearby communities of **Chachagua**, 10km southeast of La Fortuna, and **El Castillo** (see p.216) are more relaxed alternatives to the main town but still close enough to the action.

LA FORTUNA

Arenal Backpackers 300m west of the church ☎2479 7000, ⊕arenalbackpackers.com; map p.206. Although it doesn't live up to its self-described "five-star hostel" billing, this flashy joint remains a good choice, particularly if you're a young American who wants to party. There's a swanky pool with volcano views, a restaurant-bar and (rather overpriced) private rooms with a/c, TVs and attached bathrooms. There are also eight- and twelve-bed mixed and female-only dorms that are rather dark but have a/c and shared bathrooms, as well as permanent dome tents (sleeping up to two) if you'd prefer to camp. Dorms US$12, tents US$35, doubles US$77

Gringo Pete's 300m east and 100m south of Parque Central ☎2479 8521; map p.206. Classic, chilled-out hostel whose super-basic dorm beds and cell-like private rooms are within even the most shoestring traveller's budget. There's a communal lounge, outdoor patio with garden and barbecue area, and handy noticeboard. There are only five rooms, so if it's full, try the sister establishment 225m west of the bus station. Dorms US$6, doubles US$16

Hotel San Bosco 100m northeast of the Parque Central ☎2479 9050, ⊕hotelsanbosco.com; map p.206. A solid, mid-range choice, this quiet little hotel is on the north side of town. Rooms, which come with a/c and spacious bathrooms, vary in price and size, so ask to see a few. You can enjoy lovely views of Arenal from the pool and hot tub as well as from the upper-level terrace. US$88

★**Monte Real** 100m south and 300m east of the Parque Central ☎2479 9357, ⊕monterealhotel.com; map p.206. Just about the best deal in town, this friendly hotel is set amid tranquil gardens and alongside a gurgling river. Stylish rooms – some with dead-on volcano views – are well equipped with a/c, fridge and private bathrooms; "premium" ones (US$99) and suites (US$111) benefit from a balcony/terrace. There's also a plunge pool. US$88

Sleeping Indian Guesthouse Opposite the church, just west of the Parque Central ☎8446 9149, ✉sleepingindianhostel@gmail.com; map p.206. Despite the dodgy name, this guesthouse is a good-value place to stay, with simple rooms with fans. There are laundry facilities, a communal lounge, and a big kitchen for guests to use. It's right in the centre of town, so try to get a non-street-facing room. US$50

AROUND LA FORTUNA

Arenal Manoa 7km west of La Fortuna, then 800m down a signed turn-off to the right ☎2479 1111, ⊕arenalmanoa.com; map pp.208–209. The welcome cocktails set the tone at this beautifully done hotel, whose brightly decorated rooms boast a/c, TVs, fridges and private patios, complete with rocking chairs. There's a pool (with wet bar), spa and restaurant, and you can also tour the resort's nearby dairy farm. US$255

Arenal Oasis Ecolodge & Wildlife Refuge 1km west of La Fortuna, then 800m down a signed turn-off to the left ☎2479 9526, ⊕arenaloasis.com; map pp.208–209. A 15min walk outside town, this lodge is located in its own nature reserve, featuring sloths, anteaters and around 200 species of bird. Accommodation is in rustic Hansel-and-Gretel-style *cabañas* (which feature carved wooden beds and sleep up to five), and a range of tours is available, including frog-spotting night walks. US$96

4

Catarata Eco-Lodge 2km southwest of La Fortuna on the road to the waterfall ☎ 2479 9522, ⊕ catarata lodge.com; map pp.208–209. Sitting on fertile farmland between La Fortuna and the waterfall, this lodge has a nice swimming pool and cosy and comfortable rooms, all with fans and private bathrooms. The restaurant serves tasty local food made with organic produce from its garden. US$95

★ **Finca Luna Nueva** 3.5km south of Chachagua, then 2.5km down a gravel road to the right ☎ 2468 4006, ⊕ fincalunanuevalodge.com; map pp.208–209. Bordering the Bosque Eterno de los Niños (see p.312), this ecolodge and organic farm is a destination in itself. Atmospheric rooms, circular adobe huts (sleeping up to three), and bungalows (sleeping up to six) made from recycled timber provide a relaxing base for learning about its sustainable practices or indulging in a number of activities, from waterfall hikes to tours of the farm (included in the rates). A range of treatments are available at the spa, including the soothing "hot rock massage" (massages from US$35/30min), and there's a yoga pavilion. Doubles/adobe huts US$121, bungalows US$136

Hotel Kokoro 8.5km west of La Fortuna ☎ 2479 1222, ⊕ arenalkokoro.com; map pp.208–209. Run by a friendly family from Taiwan who emigrated to the area thirty years ago, Hotel Kokoro has fifteen acres of grounds crisscrossed by trails, as well as a hot tub fed by hot springs, a spa and a fine restaurant. Accommodation options range from simple rooms to smarter cabins (some of them big enough to host a family). Doubles US$145, cabins US$175

Leaves and Lizards 7.5km north of La Fortuna ☎ 2478 0023, ⊕ leavesandlizards.com; map pp.208–209. Located high in the mountains above La Fortuna, this incredibly relaxing retreat has a selection of cabins (sleeping up to five; with terraces and hammocks), a great restaurant that takes advantage of home-grown, organic produce, and a range of tours (the horseriding is particularly good). Check the website for info on how to get there. Minimum three-night stay. US$190

Mountain Paradise Hotel 7km west of La Fortuna, then 500m down a signed turn-off to the right ☎ 2479 1414, ⊕ hotelmountainparadise.com; map pp.208–209. Spacious hacienda-style *casitas* dotted in pairs among beautiful grounds that are a haven for hummingbirds. They can easily accommodate two big wooden beds and come with TVs, a/c and huge bathrooms, complete with dramatic-looking "waterfall" showers. Friendly staff, pool with wet bar, and a spa complete the package. US$140

Nayara Resort, Spa & Gardens 7km west of La Fortuna, then 500m down a signed turn-off to the right ☎ 2479 1600, ⊕ arenalnayara.com; map pp.208–209. The beautiful, spacious en suites at this world-class resort feature super-comfy four-posters – think quality linens and feather duvets – and private gardens with outdoor showers and jungle or volcano views; villas (sleeping up to two; US$610) come with stunning balconies/terraces with jacuzzis overlooking the volcano. It also has extensive facilities, including several great restaurants and bars (see opposite), a spa, gym and pool, and spot-on service. Its sister hotel, the even more luxurious *Nayara Springs*, is attached by a bridge and shares facilities. US$486

★ **Nayara Springs** 7km west of La Fortuna, then 500m down a signed turn-off to the right ☎ 2479 1600, ⊕ nayarasprings.com; map pp.208–209. Attached to *Nayara Resort, Spa & Gardens* by a bridge through the rainforest, this stunning, adults-only resort is quite simply one of the most memorable places to stay in Central America. Its vast, secluded villas (sleeping up to two) feature four-poster beds, indoor and outdoor "rain" showers, and their own private plunge pools fed by natural springs. Facilities include a high-class spa, pool and gym, several of the region's finest restaurants and bars (see opposite), a coffee shop (serving Nayara's own blend), and a range of free daily activities, including yoga classes and birdwatching tours. Make reservations well in advance. US$768

Rancho Cerro Azul 1.5km southwest of La Fortuna, on the road to the waterfall ☎ 2479 7360, ⊕ rancho cerroazul.com; map pp.208–209. One of the better-value hotels around La Fortuna, with spacious wood-panelled cabins (sleeping up to four) set amid bucolic grounds close to the river. Each cabin has a/c, TV, attached bathroom, and great volcano views from the private terraces out front. US$99

Roca Negra Inn 2km west of La Fortuna ☎ 2479 9237, ⊕ hotelrocanegradelarenal.com; map pp.208–209. One of the best-value deals in – or, rather, just outside – town, Roca Negra Inn offers high-ceilinged a/c rooms with private bathrooms, terraces, fridges and TVs, plus a bird-filled garden, small swimming pool, jacuzzi and pool table. US$80

El Silencio del Campo 5km west of La Fortuna ☎ 2479 7055, ⊕ hotelsilenciodelcampo.com; map pp.208–209. Though they are quite clustered together, these tranquil villas with volcano views are perfect for families: there are two swimming pools (one for children only), a restaurant and a small hot spring. The hotel is just 300m from Ecotermales Fortuna (see p.206), and guests get discounted entry. US$215

EATING

In addition to low-cost joints serving *casados*, *platos del día* and *arroz cons*, La Fortuna has numerous (generally pretty pricey) restaurants serving imaginative international cuisine, with several **fine-dining options** on the road west of town. Virtually every restaurant in the area doubles up as a bar, too. In addition to the cafés listed below, the shop Down to Earth (see below) is also a great spot for a coffee.

LA FORTUNA

La Choza de Laurel 400m west of the Parque Central, on the main road ☎2479 7063, ⌨lachozadelaurel.com; map p.206. Very much on the tourist-bus circuit, but atmospheric nevertheless, with hefty steaks, crispy, wood-roasted chicken, and various fish and seafood options (mains ₡4000–12,000). Daily 7am–10pm.

Don Rufino 100m east of the Parque Central ☎2479 9997, ⌨donrufino.com; map p.206. The wide-ranging, rather pricey menu trots around the world, but steaks (₡10,600–16,9000) are the speciality: ribeye, sirloin, flank, New York and filet mignon are all on offer, alongside a choice of sauces ranging from green pepper to Argentine *chimichurri*. Daily 11.30am–9.30pm.

Lava Lounge 200m west of the Parque Central ☎2479 7365, ⌨lavaloungecostarica.com; map p.206. This funky restaurant-bar, particularly popular with American travellers, serves a mouthwatering mixture of burritos (around ₡5000), wraps, burgers, sandwiches, and pizza (₡5000–9000), as well as a fine selection of local craft beers (₡2500–3000); there are also regular live music performances. A share of the *Lava Lounge's* profits goes to support a street-dog rescue centre. Daily 7am–10pm.

Life House Av Central, at C2, just west of the church ☎2479 7365; map p.206. If you've overindulged, head to this health-conscious restaurant, which has plenty of vegetarian (and gluten-free and vegan) options. As well as good breakfasts, there are tasty lunch and dinner options (most dishes ₡5000–6000) like root-veg curry, falafel burgers and veggie lasagne. Daily 7am–9pm.

La Parada Directly opposite the bus stop on the Parque Central ☎2479 9098; map p.206. This popular *soda* is perfect for people-watching while you fill up on economical (for La Fortuna) *casados*, *arroz cons*, *gallo pintos*, pasta dishes and burgers (₡2200–4500), and more expensive steaks and pizzas. Daily 24hr.

Rainforest Café 75m southeast of the Parque Central ☎2479 7239; map p.206. Take your time over a cup of Costa Rica's great coffee (₡1000–25,000) in this airy café that hums along to mellow tunes. Smiling waiters serve up good breakfasts, *casados* and cakes, too. Daily 7am–10pm.

Restaurant Nene's 250m east and 50m south of the Parque Central ☎2479 9192; map p.206. This highly regarded restaurant adorned with a mural of tropical birds is known for its ceviche, but people also come from far and wide to enjoy its varied menu of sea bass, steak and pastas (mains from ₡4000) and range of cocktails. Daily 10am–10pm.

AROUND LA FORTUNA

★**Asia Luna** Nayara Resort, Spa & Gardens ☎2479 1600, ⌨arenalnayara.com; map pp.208–209. This appealing pan-Asian restaurant's menu features sushi, *sashimi*, *gyoza*, Thai curries and stir fries, plus inventive fusion dishes like sesame beef with a sweet potato aioli and a caramel reduction (mains from ₡7500). To accompany your meal, go for one of the many sakes on offer. Daily 6–10pm.

Mis Amores Nayara Springs ☎2479 1600, ⌨nayarasprings.com; map pp.208–209. Ideal for a romantic dinner, with smart service, a strong wine list (glasses from ₡5000) and a menu that ranges across Europe, with a few forays into North Africa. Try the blue crab cakes to start, followed by the lamb tagine, with the Grand Marnier soufflé to finish (mains ₡11,000–18,000). Daily 6–10pm.

Vagabondo 2km west of La Fortuna ☎2479 8087, ⌨vagabondocr.com; map pp.208–209. This attractive, open-air restaurant serves up authentic Italian wood-fired pizzas, pasta dishes and salads (₡4000–10,000). In the back, a large, convivial bar with pool tables stays open late. Daily noon–11pm (bar till 1/2am).

SHOPPING

Coco Loco Arts & Crafts Gallery 3.5km south of Chachagua ☎2468 0990, ⌨artedk.com; map pp.208–209. This excellent shop/gallery has beautiful masks, mirrors, wall-hangings, ceramics and paintings, produced by the owner and other local artists. Mon–Sat 8am–5pm.

Down to Earth Opposite the west side of the Parque Central ☎2479 7061, ⌨godowntoearth.org; map p.206. One-stop shop for your gourmet caffeine needs, specializing in coffee, chocolates and liqueurs; there's a café attached. Daily 10am–6pm.

DIRECTORY

Banks and exchange The Banco Nacional on the northeastern side of the Parque Central has an ATM.

Health care Clinica, 125m east and 50m north of the Parque Central (☎2479 9501; Mon 8am–8pm, Tues–Thurs 8am–10pm, Fri–Sun 24hr).

Laundry Lavandería La Fortuna, 125m west and 125m

north of the Parque Central (Mon–Sat 8am–9pm).

Police On Av Central, 125m east of the Parque Central (☎2479 9501); also a booth at the turning to Parque Nacional Volcán Arenal west of town.

Post office Opposite the north side of the church (Mon–Fri 8am–5.30pm, Sat 7.30am–noon).

Parque Nacional Volcán Arenal

14km west of La Fortuna • Daily 8am–4pm • US$10 • ☎ 2461 8499

Volcán Arenal was given protected status in 1995, becoming part of the national parks system as the **PARQUE NACIONAL VOLCÁN ARENAL**. Though Arenal is still technically active, it has been quiet since 2010, with no lava or explosions and only the occasional release of gas. It remains a spectacular sight, however, and the park has several good walking trails.

The trails

The park contains a few good **trails**, all accessed from the main park entrance, including the **Lookout Point Trail** (1.3km) and the **Las Coladas Trail** (2.8km), which heads southeast to a lava flow from 1992. The **Los Tucanes Trail** (4km), also accessed off the road up to the *Arenal Observatory Lodge* (see opposite), takes you to the part of the forest that was flattened by the 1968 eruption. You may see some wildlife on these hikes; birds (including oropendolas and tanagers) and agoutis are particularly common. Although the park has a simple café, it's best to take a picnic lunch and plenty of water if you intend to walk extensively.

Reserva Mirador El Silencio

5km north of the park entrance • Daily 7am–7pm • US$8 • ☎ 2479 9900, ⓦ miradorelsilencio.com

A number of hikes on the fringes of Parque Nacional Volcán Arenal are worth exploring, including those at the **Reserva Mirador El Silencio**. The four trails at this reserve lead through primary forest sheltering peccaries and spider monkeys to a lookout at the foot of the volcano.

Arenal 1968

1.2km north of the park entrance • Daily 8am–6pm • US$12 • ☎ 2462 1212, ⓦ arenal1968.com

Arenal 1968 offers taxing but highly worthwhile hikes up to the original 1968 lava flow,

---

VOLCÁN ARENAL: EXPLOSIONS AND ERUPTIONS

Volcán Arenal is the youngest **stratovolcano** – the term for a steep, conical volcano created by the eruption of thick lava flows – in Costa Rica. Geologists have determined that Arenal is no more than 2900 years old; by comparison, Cerro Chato, which flanks Arenal to the south, last erupted in the late Holocene period, around 10,000 years ago. Geologists speculate that Arenal directly taps a magma chamber located on a fault about 22km below the surface.

Arenal's growth over the ages has been characterized by massive **eruptions** every few centuries: it is thought to have erupted around 1750, 1525 and 1080 AD, and 220 and 900 BC. At the time of its most recent eruption in the late 1960s, Arenal seemed to be nothing but an unthreatening mountain, and locals had built small farms up its forested sides (take a look at Cerro Chato and you get the idea). But on **July 29, 1968**, an earthquake shook the area, blasting the top off Arenal and creating the majestic, lethal volcano seen today. Arenal killed 78 people that day, with fatalities caused by a combination of shockwaves, hot rocks and poisonous gases. The explosion created three craters, and Arenal has been active ever since, though it's currently in a quiet period.

While history would suggest that it's not due another major blowout for a few hundred years yet, and despite the recent years of slumber, Arenal is still very much an active volcano, so a few safety tips are worth bearing in mind: **never veer from trails** or guided tours, and do not attempt to hike anywhere near the crater, since lethal gases, ballistic boulders and molten rock, all of which were expelled regularly until relatively recently, can appear or change direction without warning. Indeed, technically everything between the volcano and the roads that run from La Fortuna to Laguna de Arenal and El Castillo lie in a **high-risk area** – a guide and a young girl were killed by a pyroclastic flow while walking "safe" trails (now closed) in the *Los Lagos* complex in August 2000 – so choose your trip with care.

including a 3km loop that takes you past a shrine to those who lost their lives in the eruption, as well as a longer 4.5km trail that takes you through some bird-filled forested areas.

ARRIVAL AND INFORMATION   VOLCÁN ARENAL

By car Coming from La Fortuna, the entrance to Parque Nacional Volcán Arenal is 14km west; look for the well-signed driveway on the left-hand side of the road.

By taxi Taxis head from La Fortuna to the west side of the volcano for around US$15, though you'll need to negotiate the rate if you want them to wait. Unless you're in a large group, it's cheaper – and easier – to take a tour.

By bus Buses from La Fortuna to Tilarán (2–3 daily; 15min) can drop passengers off 2km from the park entrance, though the return journey can be tricky, as you'll need to connect with the bus coming from Tilarán or Nuevo Arenal.

Tours Although the lava-spotting night tours no longer run, many operators in La Fortuna (see box, p.210) still run day-trips (around US$70).

ACCOMMODATION

★**Arenal Observatory Lodge** 5km beyond the park entrance ☎ 2479 1070, ⓦ arenalobservatorylodge .com; map pp.208–209. If you want to spend a night in the shadow of the volcano, head to this lodge, just 1.8km from the crater. Standard rooms (US$133) are rustic but comfortable, while the superior "Smithsonian" rooms (US$180) have big beds and huge windows looking out at Arenal, which seems awesomely close; the cheapest rooms are in *La Casona* farmhouse. Families renting the *White Hawk Villa* (sleeps 8; US$530), 800m from the main lodge, can soak up the finest views of the lot. The extensive grounds include primary rainforest with trails, a small museum, pool and spa. There's a US$5 charge for non-guests to enter the grounds, even if coming to eat at the overpriced restaurant (daily 11.30am–4.30pm & 6–8.30pm) – but you're really paying for the view. **US$104**

4

Laguna de Arenal

The **LAGUNA DE ARENAL** makes what would otherwise have been a pretty area into a very beautiful one – a fact exploited by the tourist board's promotional posters showing a serene Volcán Arenal rising preternaturally out of the lake. Pretty as it is, it's actually a man-made body of water created when the far smaller original lake was dammed in 1973; the resulting Arenal Dam now generates much of the country's hydroelectricity. The lake is an excellent **fishing** spot: the rainbow bass (*guapote*), an iridescent fish found only in freshwater lakes and rivers in Costa Rica, Nicaragua and Honduras, is particularly prolific here. It is similarly good for **windsurfing**; (see p.219). Tourism has brought with it a sizeable colony of foreign residents, many of them Germans or Austrians attracted by the combination of a rather European-looking landscape with year-round tropical temperatures.

LAGUNA DE ARENAL ACTIVITIES

The area's activities unsurprisingly revolve around the lake. Laguna de Arenal is the country's prime spot for windsurfing (see box, p.219), though this is done mainly out of Tilarán, on the western side of the lake. Many visitors come hoping to hook the hard-fighting *guapote*, while there are also a range of cruises and kayak trips. The agencies below can be contacted by phone/online or via your accommodation.

Arenal Kayaks ☎ 2694 4336, ⓦ arenalkayaks.com. Offers guided kayak tours (from US$40 for 2hr; longer trips available too), which can be tailored depending on how energetic you're feeling.

Captain Ron ☎ 2694 4678 or ☎ 8339 3345, ⓦ arenalfishing.com. Equipped for conventional fishing, fly-fishing and kayak-based fishing trips; expect to pay US$225 for a 5hr trip and US$295 for a 7hr trip (the fee includes a complimentary Costa Rican cigar to help you celebrate any big catches).

Enchanted Tours ☎ 2694 4731, ⓦ worldviewsintl .com. Offers a variety of fishing tours in a pontoon boat, including half-day catch-and-release fishing expeditions (US$200), as well as nature and birdwatching cruises, including a 2hr sunset trip (US$75, with snacks and soft drinks).

El Castillo

Just 23km southwest of La Fortuna but a world away in ambience, the idyllic mountain village of **EL CASTILLO** is all undulating hillsides covered with farmland and rainforest, with dead-on volcano views. The turn-off for El Castillo is 15km west of La Fortuna, on the road to Nuevo Arenal; the bumpy road that heads 8km east from here has for years kept the village off the traditional tourist trail, making it a welcome retreat from the buzzing commercial circus that is La Fortuna.

There's not much to the village itself, just one main street with a school, church, small supermarket and the Arenal Eco Zoo.

Arenal Eco Zoo

Main St • Tours daily 8am–7pm (on demand); 30min • US$23 • ☎ 2479 1059, ⓦ arenalecozoo.com

Principally a serpentarium housing more than eighty species of snake, including a monster Burmese python that's knocking on for 4m long, the **Arenal Eco Zoo** is also home to an array of rather smaller amphibians, butterflies and insects. It's enjoyable, if rather overpriced.

Butterfly Conservatory

About 800m up the road from El Castillo's school • Tours daily 8am–4pm (on demand); 30min • US$15 • ☎ 2479 1149, ⓦ butterflyconservatory.org

The enchanting **Butterfly Conservatory** is a regeneration project occupying a former cattle ranch, with six well-tended butterfly atriums, a small insect museum, medicinal herb garden and riverside trails that weave through lush regenerating rainforest.

Rancho Margot

5km west of El Castillo • Daily tours 8.30am, 10.30am, 1.30pm & 3.30pm; 2hr • US$35; book in advance • ☎ 2479 7259, ⓦ ranchomargot.com

The main reason for coming to El Castillo is to visit the extraordinary **Rancho Margot**, an organic farm, wildlife rescue centre and scenic accommodation option (see p.218) that is well on the way to becoming the poster child for ecotourism in Costa Rica. The expansive property, set in a valley of the Río Caño Negro, is a byword for sustainability: a water-powered micro-turbine generates the ranch's electricity, the outdoor pool is heated using a biodigester that converts animal waste into energy, and most of the food served in the excellent buffet-style restaurant is grown or raised on the property.

Alongside the standard two-hour **tour**, you can do horseriding, kayaking and hiking trips. There are also yoga teacher training sessions, and courses on sustainable living.

ACCOMMODATION

EL CASTILLO

Essence Arenal 2km south of the village ☎ 2479 1131, ⓦ essencearenal.com; map opposite. Ecofriendly hostel set amid 22 acres of (organic) farmland, forest and jungle with a peaceful, New Age feel. There are spots to pitch your tent (it also has permanent tents) and rooms (private or shared bathrooms), plus a vegetarian restaurant, cooking classes, yoga sessions, jacuzzi, and even a trampoline. Camping US$5, tents US$32, doubles US$32

Hotel Castillo del Arenal In the centre of the village ☎ 2479 1146, ⓦ hotelcastillodelarenal.com; map opposite. A string of compact *cabinas*, sleeping up to four (opt for one of the trio of standalone ones; US$97), staggered along a ridge directly opposite Arenal. They're all simply attired but with huge windows

that make the most of the panorama. There's also a restaurant on site. US$85

Hummingbird Nest In the centre of the village ☎ 2479 1144, ⓦ hummingbirdnestbb.com; map opposite. This delightful American-run B&B has sparkling en-suite rooms and an outdoor hot tub – all with spectacular views of the volcano. There's even a mini spa offering massages, beauty treatments and the like. US$96

★**Linda Vista del Norte** On the road into El Castillo ☎ 2479 1551, ⓦ hotellindavista.com; map opposite. Perched on a hillside, *Linda Vista del Norte* has gobsmacking lake and volcano views from the pool, hot tub or restaurant. The top-notch en suites have picture windows, attractive

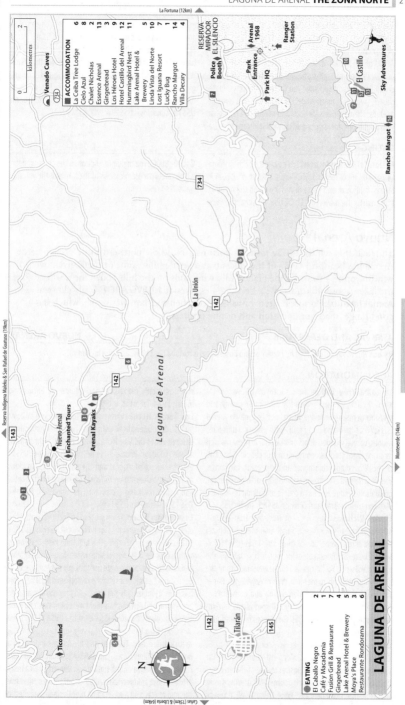

La Fortuna (12km)

● **Venado Caves**

■ ACCOMMODATION
La Ceiba Tree Lodge	6
Cielo Azul	8
Chalet Nicholas	2
Essence Arenal	13
Gingerbread	3
Los Héroes Hotel	9
Hotel Castillo del Arenal	12
Hummingbird Nest	11
Lake Arenal Hotel & Brewery	5
Linda Vista del Norte	10
Lost Iguana Resort	7
Lucky Bug	1
Rancho Margot	14
Villa Decary	4

RESERVA MIRADOR EL SILENCIO

Arenal 1968

Police Booth

Ranger Station

Park Entrance

Park HQ

El Castillo

Sky Adventures

Rancho Margot

Reserva Indígena Maleku & San Rafael de Guatuso (19km)

734

Nuevo Arenal

Enchanted Tours

Arenal Kayaks

142

Laguna de Arenal

La Unión

142

Ticowind

Montverde (14km)

Tilarán

142

145

● EATING
El Caballo Negro	2
Café y Macadamia	1
Fusion Grill & Restaurant	7
Gingerbread	4
Lake Arenal Hotel & Brewery	5
Moya's Place	3
Restaurante Rondorama	6

LAGUNA DE ARENAL

Cañas (15km) & Liberia (64km)

N

4

0   kilometres   2

wood panelling and princely bathrooms. Staff can organize a wide range of tours in the La Fortuna region. US$94

★**Rancho Margot** 5km west of El Castillo ☏2479 7259 or ☏8302 7318, ⓦranchomargot.com; map p.217. This terrific self-sufficient eco-retreat (see p.216) encourages a hands-on stay; you can milk the cows, make cheese, wine or marmalade, or help till the organic gardens. There's a riverside yoga and meditation studio, or you might opt for canyoning, kayaking, horseriding, a

massage or one of the other activities on offer – adventurous types can even hike to Reserva Santa Elena, 8km away (see p.309). Accommodation ranges from the basic dorm-style bunkhouse to honeymoon-worthy hilltop bungalows (sleeping up to five) with piping-hot showers, gigantic windows and wraparound terraces. Rates include full board, daily yoga classes and a guided farm tour. Dorm US$79, bungalows US$236

EATING

Fusion Grill & Restaurant In the centre of the village ☏2479 0336, ⓦfusiongrillrestaurant.com; map p.217. Steaks, fish, pizza and pasta dishes are all on the menu at this smarter-than-average El Castillo restaurant (mains

₡4000–8000). The highlight, though, is the open-air deck, which offers panoramic views of the lake and the volcano. Daily 7.30am–10pm.

Nuevo Arenal

The road that winds its way from La Fortuna around the northern shore of Laguna de Arenal has beautiful views of the volcano and gentle hills, some of them given over to wind-farming – look for the giant white windmills on the hills above the north edge of the lake. About 40km from La Fortuna, lies lakeside **NUEVO ARENAL**, also known as **Arenal Town** (the original Arenal was flooded when the dam was built), which has a good range of accommodation and dining options.

ARRIVAL AND DEPARTURE NUEVO ARENAL

By bus Nuevo Arenal is served by Tilarán-bound buses from La Fortuna (2–3 daily; around 1hr 30min).

ACCOMMODATION

La Ceiba Tree Lodge 4km south of Nuevo Arenal ☏2692 8050, ⓦceibatree-lodge.com. This romantic and relaxing German-run lodge just above Laguna de Arenal has *cabinas* (sleeping up to four) with private bathrooms, fridges, carved wooden doors and tasteful artwork, as well as an excellent studio sleeping up to four people. Best of all is the big, shady communal terrace, great for sunset viewing. Named after the massive 500-year-old tree in the grounds, the lodge also has a couple of walking trails and a Mediterranean restaurant. *Cabinas* US$89, studio US$165

Chalet Nicholas 2km west of Nuevo Arenal ☏2694 4041, ⓦchaletnicholas.net. Small, beautifully kept hotel with just three rooms, one of them split level (US$75), all with private bathrooms, looking out to the lake or the distant volcano. You'll get a warm welcome from the charming hosts, not to mention their massive Great Danes who have their own suite. Horseriding and birdwatching tours can be arranged, though you'll spot plenty of birds within the guesthouse grounds. Great breakfasts (included in rates), too. US$65

Gingerbread 1km east of Nuevo Arenal ☏2694 0039, ⓦgingerbreadarenal.com. Sleep off your meal at the excellent restaurant (see opposite) in one of the attached boutique hotel's five themed rooms – Butterfly, Cupid, Jungle, Garden of Eden and Wine Cellar – all boasting

spacious, locally made beds and adorned in enchanting murals by a local artist. US$130

Los Héroes Hotel 15km east of Nuevo Arenal ☏2692 8012, ⓦpequenahelvecia.com. This charming hotel perched above the lake looks transported straight from an alpine meadow. Rooms – some with balconies (US$15 extra) – are comfortable, and there are several spacious apartments (sleeping up to four) too, plus a hot tub, pool and quirky revolving restaurant (see opposite). Doubles US$95, apartments US$150

Lost Iguana Resort 18km west of La Fortuna, across the dam, then 1.5km down a signed road to the right ☏2461 0122, ⓦlostiguanacr.com. This high-end lodge has rooms with balconies offering volcano vistas, large, comfortable beds and a/c, TVs and private hot tubs, plus *Las Casitas*, two-bedroom suites set in a separate hilltop building. The resort has several jungle trails and a spa, and they can also arrange any sort of local activity. Two-night minimum stay, and good online discounts. Doubles US$305, suites US$616

★**Lucky Bug** 3km west of Nuevo Arenal ☏2694 4515, ⓦluckybugcr.net. This bed-and-breakfast overlooking a pond is truly fantastical – think Alice in Wonderland goes tropical and you're on the right track. Owned by a German artist whose rainforest-inspired work graces the five themed rooms, you'll have a fine night's sleep sprawled in the king-sized beds. There's an inviting communal lounge area and breakfast is served in the adjoining *El Caballo Negro* restaurant (see below). Non-guests should be sure to visit the on-site art gallery and gift shop. US$112

★ **Villa Decary** 2km east of Nuevo Arenal ☎ 2694 4330, ⍟ villadecary.com. Set just metres from Laguna de Arenal, the beautifully furnished rooms and *casitas* (sleeping up to four) here have big beds decorated with colourful Guatemalan fabrics, and balconies with lovely forest and lake views. The hospitable hosts (who bought the guesthouse having originally stayed here as guests) can provide a wealth of information on the area, and serve up a delicious breakfast featuring home-made jams. The lush grounds, planted with rare palms, make this a haven for birds – and, of course, birdwatchers. Doubles US$123, *casitas* US$185

EATING

El Caballo Negro Lucky Bug, 3km west of Nuevo Arenal ☎ 2694 4757, ⍟ luckybugcr.net. Outstanding spot, part of the lovely *Lucky Bug* B&B (see opposite), dishing up delicious sandwiches (including a fine Reuben), bratwurst and schnitzels, and tasty veggie options like aubergine parmigiana (most mains ₡7000–10,000). Meals are served on a patio overlooking the hotel's lake, frequented by a menagerie of birds. Daily 7am–5pm.

★ **Café y Macadamia** 6km west of Nuevo Arenal ☎ 2692 2000. Enormous sandwiches (around ₡5000–6000; try the capresa – turkey, mozzarella, avocado and pesto on home-baked bread), organic salads, soups and a great selection of cakes make this an essential pit stop en route to Tilarán or La Fortuna. Even if you're not hungry, it's worth stopping for a portion of local macadamia nuts – drenched in chocolate, coconut, cinnamon and the like – and to take in the gorgeous lake views from out the back. Daily 7.30am–5pm.

★ **Gingerbread** Gingerbread hotel, 1km east of Nuevo Arenal ☎ 2694 0039, ⍟ gingerbreadarenal.com. Fine dining courtesy of a French-taught Israeli chef, whose fusion cuisine is among the most creative in the country. The menu (mains ₡8000–12,500) changes daily, in accordance with whatever is freshest at the time, but has a big Mediterranean influence; the fish and seafood are particularly good. Dishes are large enough to share, and there's a strong wine list. Make sure you book a table, especially on Fri & Sat. You can also stay here (see opposite). Tues–Sat 5–9pm.

Moya's Place Nuevo Arenal, opposite the petrol station ☎ 2694 4001. This cool little café has a laidback vibe, serving snacks and meals (₡4000–10,000); the pizzas, burgers, wraps and burritos are particularly good. A takeaway service is available. Daily 11.30am–9.30pm.

Restaurante Rondorama Los Héroes Hotel, 15km east of Nuevo Arenal ☎ 2692 8012, ⍟ pequenahelvecia .com. It's just as much fun getting to the kitsch revolving restaurant at this alpine-esque hotel (see opposite) as it is eating there – it's reached on a miniature railway (US$10; reservations required), which whisks visitors 3km through tunnels, over bridges and up a hill, where you can feast on both the food (mains ₡5000–10,000) and the panoramic valley views. Daily 11am–3pm.

Tilarán and around

Unhurried **TILARÁN** lies 40km northwest of Monteverde and roughly 60km west of La Fortuna. The town's wide streets channel the vigorous breezes that breathe life into an otherwise lazy tropical hamlet – these same winds create the best **windsurfing and kitesurfing** conditions in the country at nearby Laguna de Arenal, 5km away. On the last weekend in April, Tilarán celebrates its ranching roots with a well-attended **rodeo festival**.

WINDSURFING AND KITESURFING

Thanks to its unusually consistent conditions, Laguna de Arenal is the best place in Costa Rica for **windsurfing and kitesurfing** – the strong winds that buffet the surface of the lake from December to April can reach speeds of up to 25mph, drawing experienced riders from around the world. The wind peaks between mid-December and February, so aim for the late-season months if you're looking to learn.

OPERATORS

Ticowind About halfway between Nuevo Arenal and Tilarán ☎ 2692 2002 or ☎ 8383 2694, ⍟ ticowind.com. Well-respected outfit with over twenty years' experience. They rent quality equipment (from US$55/US$61 for a half-day's windsurfing/kitesurfing), while windsurfing classes cater for first-timers and those looking to improve their technique (US$120/2hr 20min). Their comprehensive beginner's kitesurfing (US$590) course includes 9hr on the water.

ARRIVAL AND DEPARTURE

TILARÁN

By bus Buses from La Fortuna (2–3 daily; 3hr), Santa Elena (1–2 daily; 2hr 30min) and San José (4 daily; 4hr) arrive at and depart from 100m north of the Parque Central. There are also connections west to Cañas and the Interamericana (hourly; 30min), from where you can head north to Liberia and the Guanacaste beaches.

ACCOMMODATION AND EATING

Cielo Azul 500m northeast of town ☎2695 4000, ⓦcieloazulresort.com; map p.217. A 10min-walk from the centre of Tilarán, "Blue Sky" has en suites that are comfortable and well equipped (TVs, fridges, microwaves, etc) if a little dated – check out the super kitsch tiger-face bedspreads. There's also a pool and a small gym. __US$75__
Lake Arenal Hotel & Brewery On the lakeshore north of town ☎2695 5050, ⓦlakearenalhotel.com; map p.217. After a series of name changes (including *Tilawa* and *Minoa*), this place seems to have settled on *Lake Arenal Hotel*. It has dorms equipped with bunk beds, large doubles, and apartments sleeping up to eight people, plus a great swimming pool and a hot tub, as well as a microbrewery – it bills itself as the first in Costa Rica – and a restaurant (daily 7am–11pm; mains ₡6000–10,000). Dorms __US$23__, doubles __US$68__, apartments __US$122__

North of La Fortuna

The area north of La Fortuna, on the western fringes of the Llanura de Guatusos, is a world away from the activity-driven hubbub of town. The long road that runs from La Fortuna via Tanque sees little traffic, and peters out beyond the village of **San Rafael de Guatuso** into seemingly endless bumpy tracks that head northeast to Caño Negro or northwest to the border with Nicaragua. This is, however, one of the few places outside the Caribbean where you can interact with the country's indigenous peoples: San Rafael is the modern-day home of the **Maleku**, and visitors are welcome to call in at the **Reserva Indígena Maleku**, just south of the village. On the way here – though more often visited on a tour – the **Venado Caves** provide a rare opportunity to head underground, their labyrinthine system of bat-filled caverns proving an interesting alternative to the ubiquitous canopy tours.

Venado Caves

Around 30km northwest of La Fortuna • Nov–April daily 8am–3pm • US$25 • ☎2478 8008, ⓦcavernasdelvenadocr.com • Several travel agencies in La Fortuna (see box, p.207) run tours

Near the tiny mountain town of **Venado** ("Deer"), the **Venado Caves** are a small network of subterranean caverns. They're quite accessible, provided you aren't afraid of bats and don't mind getting wet, as you'll need to walk through waist-high water to get to some of them. Inside is a spooky and unique tangle of stalactites and smoothed-out rock formations; look out for the Papagayo Rock, shaped (with a little imagination) like a parrot. The entry fee includes a guide, rubber boots, a flashlight, and access to a swimming pool; it's worth bringing mosquito repellent with you.

Reserva Indígena Maleku

Around 40km north of La Fortuna • Several daily buses travel to Guatuso from La Fortuna (1hr–1hr 30min) and San Carlos (2hr–2hr 30min) • Agencies in La Fortuna (see box, p.207) run tours here

The village of **SAN RAFAEL DE GUATUSO** (known locally as Guatuso) lies at the heart of Costa Rica's few remaining **Maleku communities**, who live in *palenques* (straw huts) on the **Reserva Indígena Maleku**, established by the government in the 1960s. Historically part of the Corobicí tribal group, the present-day Maleku (also known as Guatuso) are a group of interrelated clans that have inhabited northwestern Costa Rica and southern Nicaragua for thousands of years. Now numbering about six hundred, their history and the story of their steady decline is a familiar one for tribal peoples in the area. Victims of disease, inter-tribal kidnapping and slavery to Spanish settlers in Nicaragua, they were dealt further blows in the 1700s and 1800s by the efforts of the Nicaraguan and Costa Rican Catholic churches to convert them to Christianity.

Though the Maleku speak their own language – broadcast by Radio Sistema Cultural Maleku and taught in schools – you won't see native dress or any outward signs of tribal identity around Guatuso. The best place to get a sense of traditional indigenous culture is at the reserve itself, set in bucolic countryside 7km south of the village.

Centro Ecológico Maleku Araraf

Tours daily 8am–4pm (on demand); 4hr • US$35; ask for Luis Denis • ☎ 8839 0540, ✉ centroecologicomalekuararaf@yahoo.es

On the excellent guided tours at the **Centro Ecológico Maleku Araraf** you'll learn about medicinal plants, get insight into local religious beliefs and burial practices (for example, the dead are buried directly beneath their homes), hike a rainforest trail and eat traditional food. There's also an on-site museum with a modest selection of artefacts and handicrafts.

Centro Ecocultura Maleku TAFA

Daily 7am–8pm • US$35 • ☎ 2464 0443 or ☎ 8838 1320, ✉ eco_cultura_maleku_tafa@yahoo.ca

The **Centro Ecocultura Maleku TAFA**, run by the family of former Maleku leader Wilson Morera Elizondo (who was known as "TAFA"), gives demonstrations of religious ceremonies and organizes language classes; some of the handmade crafts you can buy here include masks and drums constructed out of iguana skin.

San Carlos and around

4

Perched on the northern slopes of the Cordillera Central, 650m above sea level, **SAN CARLOS** (also known as **Ciudad Quesada**, or simply Quesada) has a decidedly rural atmosphere – fresh produce overflows from market stalls onto the streets, and *campesinos* with weathered faces hang out in the main square in front of the church. You're likely to pass through here on the way from or to La Fortuna; there's not much to actually do, but therein lies its charm. Strolling about town, you get a real feel for what drives Costa Rica's economy: much of the nation's milk, beef, citrus fruit and rice comes from the large-scale agricultural holdings in these parts. Positioned at the heart of cattle country, San Carlos is also something of a **saddlery** centre; it's well worth dropping by one of the expert saddlers, if only to watch them skilfully working the supple leather.

La Marina Wildlife Rescue Center

9km northeast of San Carlos • Daily 8am–4pm • US$10, children US$8 • ☎ 2474 2202, 🌐 zoocostarica.com

The family-run **La Marina Wildlife Rescue Center** houses some five hundred animals (over eighty species) that have been saved from illegal owners or areas where their habitat has been destroyed. Though acting on a very tight budget – the centre relies completely on donations from its visitors – it has established a successful breeding programme, including tapirs, spider monkeys and the endangered great green macaw, releasing a number of these into the wild. If you take a particular shine to the place, try one of the number of volunteering opportunities; see the website for details.

Muelle

The sleepy village of **Muelle**, 22km north of San Carlos, is a useful stop-off on the road between La Fortuna, Puerto Viejo de Sarapiquí and Los Chiles (there's a petrol station here, handy if you're driving). It's worth stretching your legs by the bridge across the Río San Carlos, the trees around which are a favoured basking spot for a large group of **iguanas**.

ARRIVAL AND DEPARTURE

By bus There are frequent buses from San José's La Coca-Cola terminal (hourly; 2hr 30min), stopping in San Carlos town centre before heading to the bus station, 1km north of the Parque Central. There are also services to/from La

SAN CARLOS AND AROUND

Fortuna (roughly hourly; 1hr 30min), Los Chiles (hourly; 2hr 30min), Puerto Viejo de Sarapiquí (15 daily; 2hr 30min) and Tilarán (3 daily; 3hr 30min).

INFORMATION

Tourist information The Zona Norte's tourist information centre (Mon–Fri 8am–4pm; ☎ 2461 9102, ⓦ ict.go.cr) lies at the the far southern end of Calle Central, though the sparseness of information on offer hardly warrants the hike out here.

Events As befits its setting, San Carlos hosts various horseriding shows throughout the year – the biggest is the San Carlos International Expo, a ten-day event at the end of April featuring horse parades, rodeos and cattle auctions.

ACCOMMODATION

You'll find plenty of budget options in San Carlos, but if you're looking for more luxurious accommodation, try the nearby villages of Muelle, Platanar and Aguas Zarcas, set in the beautiful countryside around town.

Hotel Don Goyo C 2, Av 4, San Carlos ☎ 2460 1780, ⓔ hoteldongoyo@hotmail.com. One of the most pleasing options in town, these clean, quiet, brightly painted rooms, all with private bathrooms and fans, are in a modern building near the centre. There's also a reputable restaurant downstairs. US$50

Tilajari Resort Hotel 800m west of Muelle, 22km north of San Carlos ☎ 2469 1212, ⓦ tilajari.com. This peaceful resort hotel sits on an out-of-the-way cattle ranch by the croc-populated Río San Carlos (which many of the rooms overlook). Double rooms have private bathrooms, a/c, terraces and TVs, and there's a restaurant,

pool, and tennis and basketball courts. Iguanas roam the landscaped grounds, and horseriding and rainforest walks can be arranged. US$119

Tree Houses Hotel 17km northwest of San Carlos ☎ 2475 6507, ⓦ treehouseshotelcostarica.com. Three cute treehouses (sleeping up to four) – or rather wooden cabins raised on stilts and with private bathrooms – surrounded by an 80-acre wildlife refuge filled with birdlife. There's a spa (massages from US$55/1hr), and plenty of guided tours on offer (including a free night hike). US$112

EATING

La Terrazza C Central, Av 5/7, San Carlos ☎ 2460 5287. Airy first-floor restaurant with a balcony overlooking Calle Central. Meat, of course, tops the list – try the Argentine

steak served with *chimichurri* sauce – but the bar's varied *boca* menu (including ceviche) takes some beating. Mains ₡4000–7000. Daily noon–11pm.

SHOPPING

Talabartería La Moderna Av 3, C Central/1, two blocks north of the Parque Central, San Carlos ☎ 2460 1761, ⓦ talabarterialamoderna.com. One of the best of the saddlers' stores (*talabarterías*) dotted around town, selling a good range of cowboy paraphernalia. While you

may not have room in your luggage for a full-sized saddle, they can normally fashion you something smaller while you wait. Cowboy boots, hats and lassos are also on offer. Mon–Fri 8am–7pm, Sat 7am–6pm.

DIRECTORY

Banks and exchange You can change cash at the Banco de Costa Rica on the southwestern corner of the Parque Central; it also has an ATM.

Hospital For medical emergencies, the Hospital de San Carlos (☎ 2401 1200, ⓦ ccss.sa.cr), 750m south of the town centre, is the best in the Zona Norte.

The far north

The **far north** of the Zona Norte is an isolated region, culturally as well as geographically, closer in spirit to Nicaragua than to the rest of the country and mostly devoted to sugar cane, oranges and cattle. Years of conflict during the Nicaraguan civil war made the region more familiar with CIA agents and arms-runners than with tourists, but it's all quiet now.

Most visitors are here to see the **Refugio Nacional de Vida Silvestre Caño Negro**, a vast wetland that makes up one of the most remote wildlife refuges in the country. Located at a key point on the migratory route between North and South America, it acts as the resting place for hundreds of migrant bird species and is considered by the Ramsar Convention on Wetlands to be the third most important wetland reserve in the world.

Caño Negro is accessed from **Los Chiles**, near the Nicaraguan border, and the only village of any size in the far north. The drive up here, along an unnervingly straight stretch of road from San Carlos, takes you through a flat landscape of rust-red soil and open pasture, broken only by roadside shacks, with the Llanura de Guatusos stretching, hot and interminable, to the west.

During the Nicaraguan civil war, Los Chiles was a Contra (US-backed right-wing militants) supply line. Nowadays, there's a climate of international cooperation, helped by the fact that many of the residents are of Nicaraguan extraction, and **crossing the border** is straightforward, as long as your documents are in order.

Los Chiles

The only reason tourists make it to **LOS CHILES**, a border settlement just 3km from the Nicaraguan frontier, is to break their journey on the way to **Caño Negro**, 25km downstream on the Río Frío (see p.224), or to cross the Nicaraguan border – although

---

INTO NICARAGUA

The **border at Los Chiles** has a turbulent history: during the Nicaraguan civil war, US-sponsored Contras were supplied through here, and it was not unusual to see camouflaged planes sitting on the airstrip on the edge of town, disgorging guns. In the past, the border was closed to foreigners, and for a period also to Nicaraguans and Costa Ricans, though it's now possible for anyone to **enter Nicaragua** from here.

4

CROSSING THE BORDER

A new **road crossing** (daily 8am–4pm) at **Tabillas**, some 7km north of Los Chiles, finally opened in 2015, which has made leaving/entering Nicaragua here a lot more straightforward. Regular buses (hourly; 15min) travel between Tabillas and Los Chiles. Few nationalities require a **visa** (see box, p.75) for Nicaragua, but there is a US$12 entry fee, as well as a US$7 exit fee to leave Costa Rica overland.

It is currently still possible to reach Nicaragua **by boat** on the Río Frío: daily services leave the docks in Los Chiles (generally around 1pm). From the border control point, it's a 14km trip up the Río Frío to the small town of **San Carlos de Nicaragua** (around US$15–20; 45min) on the southeast lip of huge Lago de Nicaragua. The Los Chiles *migración* officials are relatively friendly, and you may be able to confirm boat times with the groups of Nicas or Ticos who hang around the office. Make sure that the **Nicaraguan border patrol**, 3km upriver from Los Chiles, stamps your passport, as you will need proof of entry when leaving Nicaragua.

You'll need some **local currency** upon arrival in San Carlos de Nicaragua; change a few colones for córdobas at the bank in Los Chiles. From San Carlos de Nicaragua, it's possible to cross the lake to **Granada** and on to **Managua**, but check with the consulate in San José because this is an infrequent boat service: without forward planning you could end up stuck in San Carlos for longer than you'd hoped.

DAY-TRIPS

It is currently possible to go on **organized day-trips** from Los Chiles to Nicaraguan **San Carlos**, **Lago de Nicaragua** and even the **Islas Solentiname**. Visitors may even be able to see the fortress of **San Juan** (also called the Castillo de la Concepción or Fortaleza) on Lago de Nicaragua, one of the oldest Spanish structures (built 1675) in the Americas, built as a defence against the English and pirates – often one and the same – plying the Río San Juan, though note that all these trips can be very expensive (US$250–300). Hotels in Los Chiles (see p.224) can organize trips for you.

the majority of travellers still cross at Peñas Blancas, further west on the Interamericana. There's little to do in town other than soak up its end-of-the-world atmosphere – the highway peters out just beyond Los Chiles in the direction of the Río San Juan, leaving nowhere to go but the river – though you can while away some time wandering down to the docks, where the tumbledown houses evoke a forlorn, France-in-the-tropics feel.

ARRIVAL AND DEPARTURE   LOS CHILES

By bus Buses arrive at and depart from the small station just west of where the main road turns left down to the port. Four buses do the daily run to/from San José (Terminal Atlántico) to Los Chiles (5hr). More frequent buses run to/from San Carlos (hourly; 2hr 30min). For Caño Negro, you'll need to take one of the daily buses signed "Upala" (3 daily; 1hr 15min) from Los Chiles.

By car Driving from San Carlos, Hwy-141 heads north along a reasonable road through the tiny settlements of Florencia and Muelle, and then along the 66km stretch of virtually empty highway, potholed in places, from Boca de Arenal to Los Chiles. There are few service stations north of Muelle, so make sure you have plenty of petrol.

INFORMATION AND TOURS

Heliconia Tours & Restaurant 100m east of the docks ☎ 2471 2096 or ☎ 8307 8585. The best source of information in town, where you can check bus schedules and the times of the *colectivo* boat to Nicaragua, and get details of travelling on to Granada; they also organize

early-morning trips up the Río Frío, spotting birds, reptiles (iguanas and turtles) and monkeys en route (US$35; 3hr), and can arrange transportation to San Carlos de Nicaragua should you want to leave earlier than the public boat. Daily 7am–8pm.

ACCOMMODATION AND EATING

Heliconia Tours and Restaurant 100m south of the docks ☎ 2471 2096 or ☎ 8307 8585. *Heliconia Tours and Restaurant* cooks up a fine rainbow bass, plucked straight from the murky waters meandering just metres from the restaurant entrance. Most mains cost around ₡4000. Daily 7am–10pm.

Hotel Wilson Tulipán Opposite the migración ☎ 2471 1414. Formerly known as *Rancho Tulipán*, this modest hotel is a comfortable option, with large, freshly painted en-suite rooms with a/c, TVs and in some cases fridges, as well as an on-site restaurant (daily 7am–10pm). Staff can arrange tours to Caño Negro and Nicaragua. <u>US$50</u>

DIRECTORY

Banks and exchange You can change dollars and colones, and pick up Nicaraguan córdobas at the Banco Nacional on the north side of the football field (Mon–Fri

8am–3.30pm), which also has an ATM.
Post office The post office (Mon–Fri 8am–noon & 1–5.30pm) is opposite the bus station.

Refugio Nacional de Vida Silvestre Caño Negro

25km southwest of Los Chiles • Daily 8am–4pm • US$10, payable at the reserve authority's office (daily 8am–4pm; ☎ 2471 1309), 250m east and 300m north of the *parque* in Caño Negro

The largely pristine **REFUGIO NACIONAL DE VIDA SILVESTRE CAÑO NEGRO**, 25km southwest of Los Chiles, is one of *the* places in the Americas to view enormous concentrations of both migratory and indigenous **birds**, along with mammalian and reptilian **river wildlife**. Until recently, its isolation kept it well off the beaten tourist track, though access has improved and nowadays numerous tours are offered from San José, La Fortuna and – best of all – the adjacent village of **Caño Negro**.

The refuge is created by the seasonal flooding of the Río Frío, so depending on the time of year you may find yourself whizzing around a huge 1980-acre lagoon in a motorboat or walking along mud-caked riverbeds. There's a 3m difference in the water level between the rainy season, when Caño Negro is at its fullest, and the dry season, and while the mammalian population of the area stays more or less constant, the birds vary widely.

Caño Negro village

The sweltering, dusty village of Caño Negro is a loose collection of ramshackle houses and *sodas*. Few locals speak English, but they are a patient and welcoming bunch. Aside

WATCHING WILDLIFE IN CAÑO NEGRO

The wildlife that calls Caño Negro home includes a staggering variety of **birds** such as **storks**, **cormorants**, **kingfishers** and **egrets**. You should be able to tick off a number of the **heron** species that inhabit the riverbanks (including green, boat-billed and rufescent tiger herons), along with **northern jacana** and **purple gallinule**. The lagoon itself is a good place to spot the elegant, long-limbed **white ibis**; its shimmering dark-green cousin, the **glossy ibis**; and perhaps the most striking of all the reserve's avifauna, the **roseate spoonbill**, a pastel-pink bird that is usually seen filtering the water with its distinctive flattened beak. The most common species are the sinuous-necked **anhingas** (sometimes called "snakebirds" in English), who impale their prey with the knife-point of their beaks before swallowing, though Caño Negro is also home to the world's largest – and Costa Rica's only – colony of **Nicaraguan grackle** (*zanate*), a dark, crow-like bird.

Reptiles are abundant, particularly the large **caimans** that lounge along the river and on the fringes of the lagoon, though you'll also spot plenty of pot-bellied **iguanas**. Look out, too, for the strikingly green **emerald basilisk lizard**; **swimming snakes**, heads held aloft like periscopes, bodies whipping out behind; and the various **turtles** (yellow, river and sliding) that can be seen resting on logs at the water's edge.

Large **mammals** living in Caño Negro include pumas, jaguars and tapirs, but these shy creatures are rarely spotted. **Howler monkeys** are at least heard if not seen – it helps to have binoculars to distinguish their black hairy shapes from the surrounding leaves in the riverside trees – though it takes a good guide to pick out a **sloth**, camouflaged by the green algae often covering their brown hair. The rows of small grey triangles you might see on tree trunks are **bats**, literally hanging out during the day.

Perhaps the reserve's most unusual inhabitant (in the wet season, at least) is the **tropical garfish**, a kind of in-between creature straddling fish and reptile. This so-called living fossil is a fish with lungs, gills and a nose, and it looks oddest while it sleeps, drifting along in the water.

from tours of the refuge, the town has a couple of other attractions to keep visitors lingering for a few hours. **Criadero de Tortugas** (daily 8am–4pm; free; ☎2876 1181), 600m west of the football field, is a turtle conservation project run by local volunteers, where turtle eggs are collected and hatchlings looked after for a year and a half before being released into the wild. Fifty metres south of the refuge entrance, **Mariposa La Reinita** (daily 8am–4pm; US$5) is a lovingly tended butterfly garden behind the home of the Avalos Jiménez family.

ARRIVAL AND DEPARTURE   CAÑO NEGRO

By bus Daily buses (signed "Upala") leave Los Chiles for the village of Caño Negro at 5am, 2pm & 5pm, stopping outside *Soda La Palmera*, opposite the Parque Central, and the Coopecane Cooperativa; they return at 7am, noon and 6pm (1hr each way).

By car It's nineteen bone-shuddering kilometres from the turn-off south of Los Chiles.

INFORMATION AND TOURS

Tour practicalities You can take a tour from San José, La Fortuna (see box, p.207), Los Chiles (from where most tour boats leave) or some of the smarter Zona Norte hotels, but bear in mind that the first 25km of the trip down the Río Frío – taking an hour or more by *lancha* – does not take you through the wildlife refuge, which begins at the mouth of the large flooded area and is marked by a sign poking out of a small islet. Make sure you actually get taken into Caño Negro – some operators will skimp on the time, petrol and refuge entrance fee and take you nowhere near the real thing – or better still,

that your tour company drives all the way to Caño Negro village and starts the boat tour from there.

Real Tour Association Daily 8am–4pm; ☎2471 1621. On the southwest corner of the *parque*, near the refuge entrance, the Real Tour Association represents all official tour operators in the community and charges US$60–80/2hr (depending on the size of the group; the US$10 entrance fee is sometimes included). If you want to visit the main lagoon, you'll need to take a 2hr – or longer – tour. They can also arrange guided canoeing, horseriding and hiking. If the office is closed, your hotel or just about anyone in Caño Negro can hook you up with a local guide.

Fishing permits The reserve is hugely popular with anglers, who trawl the murky waters during the fishing season (Aug–May) for snook, tarpon and rainbow bass; you'll need a permit (US$30) from Incopesca (ⓦwww.incopesca.go.cr) – the bigger lodges and travel agencies can sort them out for you.

When to visit The best time to visit Caño Negro is Jan–March, when the most migratory bird species are in residence and you'll see scores of caimans basking on the riverbanks.

ACCOMMODATION

There are a handful of options in the village of Caño Negro, including a couple of **homestays**, and all can help arrange tours in the wildlife refuge.

Caño Negro Natural Lodge 200m east and 100m north of the Parque Central ☎2471 1000, ⓦcanonegro lodge.com. Surprisingly smart, given the modesty of the village, *Caño Negro Natural Lodge*'s elegant en suites are set in manicured gardens and come with a/c. Facilities include a good restaurant (see below) and a swanky swimming pool with wet bar. A wide range of tours is also on offer. US$147

Hotel de Campo Caño Negro Near the entrance to the village, about 100m from the Los Chiles/Upala junction ☎2471 1012 or ☎8877 1212, ⓦhoteldecampo.com. Occupying fruit-tree-filled grounds on the edge of a large lagoon, the bungalow rooms at *Hotel de Campo Caño Negro* have big beds, a/c and private bathrooms. There's a pool, and the restaurant serves up mostly organic produce. Staff can organize fishing, birdwatching, kayaking, canoeing and boat trips. US$95

Kingfisher Lodge 100m east and 400m north of the Parque Central; reception at Casa Sequera, 100m east of the Parque Central ☎2471 1116 or ☎8870 0458, ⓦkingfisherlodgecr.com. Five simple cabins that sleep up to five surrounded by groomed gardens; you can pay US$10 more for a/c. Cheaper, more basic digs (around US$25) are offered at *Casa Sequera*, which is under the same management. US$55

EATING

Restaurant Jabiru Caño Negro Natural Lodge ☎2471 1000, ⓦcanonegrolodge.com. The best place to eat in town is at the airy *Restaurant Jabiru*, which has a menu (dishes from ₡3000) that runs the gamut from burger and fries to freshly caught tilapia. Daily 7–9am, noon–3pm & 6–10pm.

The Sarapiquí region

Costa Rica's **Sarapiquí region** stretches around the top of Parque Nacional Braulio Carrillo and west to the village of San Miguel, from where Volcán Arenal and the western lowlands are easily accessible by road. Tropical and carpeted with fruit plantations, the area bears more resemblance to the hot and dense Caribbean lowlands than the plains of the north and, despite large-scale deforestation, still shelters some of the best-preserved **premontane rainforest** in the country.

The largest settlement in the area, sleepy **Puerto Viejo de Sarapiquí**, attracts few visitors and is primarily a river transport hub and a place for the plantation workers to stock up on supplies, though it can make a good base for exploring the superb **Estación Biológica La Selva**. The region's chief tourist attractions, however, are the rainforest lodges of **Rara Avis** and **Selva Verde**, which offer access to some of the last primary rainforest in Costa Rica.

Unsurprisingly, the region receives a lot of rain, though these heavy downpours help create a variety of whitewater thrills for the kayakers and rafters who flock to the area around **La Virgen** for runs on the **Río Sarapiquí**.

INFORMATION

Getting there The road between San José and the region, via Vara Blanca, has now been repaired, following the damage done to it by the Cinchona earthquake (see box, p.134).

When to visit The Sarapiquí receives up to 4500mm of rain annually, and there's no real dry season, so rain gear is essential. Less rain is recorded in the Jan–May period, so this is the best time to visit.

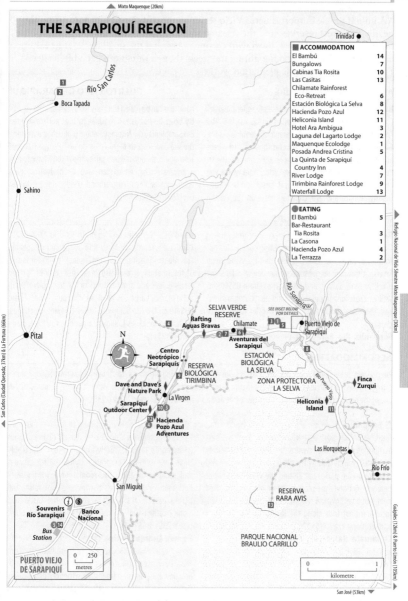

THE SARAPIQUÍ REGION

Mixto Maquenque (20km)

Trinidad ●

Boca Tapada

Sahino

Pital

San Carlos (Ciudad Quesada; 37km) & La Fortuna (66km)

Río San Carlos

N

SELVA VERDE
RESERVE
Rafting
Aguas Bravas
Chilamate
Aventuras del
Sarapiquí
Centro
Neotrópico
Sarapiquís
RESERVA
BIOLÓGICA
TIRIMBINA
Dave and Dave's
Nature Park
La Virgen
Sarapiquí
Outdoor Center
Hacienda
Pozo Azul
Adventures

SEE BELOW
FOR DETAILS
Puerto Viejo de
Sarapiquí
ESTACIÓN
BIOLÓGICA
LA SELVA
ZONA PROTECTORA
LA SELVA
Heliconia
Island
Finca
Zurqui

Río Sarapiquí

Río Puerto Viejo

San Miguel

Las Horquetas

Río Frío

RESERVA
RARA AVIS

PARQUE NACIONAL
BRAULIO CARRILLO

Refugio Nacional de Vida Silvestre Mixto Maquenque (30km)

Guápiles (12km) & Puerto Limón (105km)

San José (53km) ▼

ACCOMMODATION

El Bambú	14
Bungalows	7
Cabinas Tia Rosita	10
Las Casitas	13
Chilamate Rainforest Eco-Retreat	6
Estación Biológica La Selva	8
Hacienda Pozo Azul	12
Heliconia Island	11
Hotel Ara Ambigua	3
Laguna del Lagarto Lodge	2
Maquenque Ecolodge	1
Posada Andrea Cristina	5
La Quinta de Sarapiquí Country Inn	4
River Lodge	7
Tirimbina Rainforest Lodge	9
Waterfall Lodge	13

EATING

El Bambú	5
Bar-Restaurant Tia Rosita	3
La Casona	1
Hacienda Pozo Azul	4
La Terrazza	2

PUERTO VIEJO
DE SARAPIQUÍ

Souvenirs
Río Sarapiquí
Banco
Nacional
Bus
Station

0   250
metres

0   1
kilometre

4

Puerto Viejo de Sarapiquí and around

Just short of 100km northeast of San José, **PUERTO VIEJO DE SARAPIQUÍ** is an important hub for banana plantation workers and those who live in the isolated settlements between here and the coast. Life in Puerto Viejo is inextricably linked with the Río Sarapiquí, and most cargo, both human and inanimate, is still carried by river to the Río San Juan and the Nicaraguan border to the north, and to the canals of Tortuguero and Barra del Colorado in the east.

A humid jungle outpost, Puerto Viejo serves as a jumping-off point for visiting the nearby **rainforest reserves**, and the research station at **La Selva**; everything in town itself focuses on the main street, lined with coconut trees, and the small docks at its eastern end. Puerto Viejo plods along during the week, though things can get a bit lively on Friday evenings when the plantation workers are paid.

ARRIVAL AND DEPARTURE
PUERTO VIEJO DE SARAPIQUÍ

By bus Numerous buses leave San José's Gran Terminal del Caribe for Puerto Viejo de Sarapiquí (buses marked "Río Frío" also serve Puerto Viejo de Sarapiquí), running via the Guápiles Highway and Las Horquetas (hourly; 2hr). There are also numerous services (15 daily; 2hr 30min) between Puerto Viejo de Sarapiquí and San Carlos, from where you can connect to La Fortuna. Local buses for La Virgen (hourly; 30min) and attractions in between run on the

hour, and can be hailed from any roadside bus stop.

By boat It's possible to continue by boat north along the Río Sarapiquí to the Nicaraguan border and then east along the Río San Juan to Barra Colorado and Parque Nacional Tortuguero, though it'll be a pricey trip – you'll have to rent a private *lancha*, which can take 4–5hr (you're going upstream) and will cost around US$800 for up to ten people; ask at your hotel.

INFORMATION AND TOURS

Posada Andrea Cristina 1km west of central Puerto Viejo ☎2766 6265, ⓦposadaandrea.wixsite.com /andreacristina. The travel agencies (Ibis Tours and Green Rivers) at this popular guesthouse (see below) offer some excellent birdwatching and rafting trips (from US$50), as well as excursions to pineapple plantations, frog gardens and chocolate producers. They even offer Latin dance classes.

Souvenirs Río Sarapiquí Diagonally across from

the Banco Nacional on the main road ☎2766 6727, ⓔluisalbertosm@ice.co.cr. Run by the knowledgeable Luis Alberto Sánchez, this shop/agency is a useful source of information. It can also make reservations for the area's lodges and arrange tours to the Tortuguero/Barra del Colorado area, as well as riverboat rides (from US$40) on the Río Sarapiquí to see caimans, crocodiles, sloths and monkeys lounging around in the heat. Daily 8am–5.15pm.

ACCOMMODATION

Puerto Viejo de Sarapiquí's **accommodation** is quite varied considering the town's size, though Friday and Sunday nights can get booked up with plantation workers. To experience the region's dense rainforest, however, you may prefer to stay at one of the nearby **jungle lodges** at the Selva Verde and Rara Avis reserves (see p.233 & p.235).

El Bambú On the main street opposite the football field ☎2766 6005, ⓦelbambu.com. The swishest accommodation in the town centre, this hotel has nicely decorated rooms (all with a/c and TVs), a bar and restaurant (see p.230) set around the massive stand of bamboo that gives the place its name, and a good-sized pool and small gym. A range of tours can be arranged, including boat trips along the Río Sarapiquí. Breakfast and wi-fi cost extra. US$128

Chilamate Rainforest Eco-Retreat 6km west of central Puerto Viejo ☎2766 6949, ⓦchilamate rainforest.com. Run by a Tico-Canadian family, this delightful lodge is set in 55 acres of rainforest, right on the Río Sarapiquí, and there is a strong focus on conservation. Accommodation options range from bunk-bed dorms to private en-suite rooms, plus family suites sleeping up to five people and featuring a kitchen area and TV lounge. Rates include a guided rainforest walk. Dorms US$29, doubles US$108, family suites US$175

★**Hotel Ara Ambigua** 1.5km west of Puerto Viejo,

400m down a signed gravel road to the right ☎2766 7101, ⓦhotelaraambigua.com. Lovely rustic cottages (sleeping up to four), nicely furnished and impeccably clean. Beautifully decorated with pastel shades and pictures of birds, the rooms come with private bathrooms and a/c. There's a swimming pool, sauna and a frog garden. It's worth a visit for the tasty food alone, dished up in the hotel's rustic restaurant (see p.230). US$106

Posada Andrea Cristina 1km west of central Puerto Viejo ☎2766 6265, ⓦposadaandrea.wixsite.com /andreacristina. On the edge of town, amid lush, overflowing tropical gardens, this friendly place offers simple rooms with fans, private bathrooms and – in many cases – kitchenettes, some in A-frame cabins with high wooden ceilings, as well as more atmospheric treehouses. One of the owners, Alex Martínez, is a qualified nature guide and good source of information on the region; he runs a wide range of tours (see above). Great breakfasts included, too. Cabins US$59, treehouses US$64

WATERFALL, RESERVA RARA AVIS (P.232) >

FRUITS OF THEIR LABOUR

Despite harbouring some of the largest remaining tracts of primary rainforest in the country, the Sarapiquí region is also home to a frightening number of **banana and pineapple farms**, while south of Puerto Viejo de Sarapiquí, the land around the small town of Las Horquetas is the site of the biggest **palmito** (heart-of-palm) plantations in the world. As in the rest of Costa Rica, it's a difficult balance between preserving the rainforest (land rendered useless by monobiotic methods employed in the cultivation of pineapples, for example, can take up to fifty years to recover), and appeasing the needs of the local workers – *palmitos*, bananas and pineapples form the core of the regional economy.

For a closer look into the everyday lives of these workers (many of them Nicaraguan migrants) you can take a **tour** of the Dole banana plantation at **Finca Zurqui** (phone for tour times; US$15; 1hr 30min; ☎ 2768 8683, ⊕ bananatourcostarica.com), 5km southeast of Puerto Viejo de Sarapiquí.

EATING

There are several inexpensive *sodas* in town, with smarter restaurants attached to the hotels. For a snack, a few fruit stalls on the main street sell seasonal treats like *mamones chinos*, spiky lychees that look like sea anemones.

El Bambú On the main street opposite the football field ☎ 2766 6005, ⊕ elbambu.com. At the hotel of the same name (see p.228), this is the most formal restaurant in the town centre (not that there's much competition), with an airy dining room and vast rainforest mural across one wall. The menu has pricey steaks, and better-value *casados*, *arroz con*s and pasta dishes (all ₡3100–5700). Daily 7am–10pm.

La Casona 1.5km west of Puerto Viejo, 400m down a signed gravel road to the right ☎ 2766 7101, ⊕ hotelaraambigua.com. If you have transport or don't mind the walk, it's worth venturing 2km west of town to *La Casona*, attached to *Hotel Ara Ambigua* (see p.228), where you can sample Costa Rican standards and some mighty fine pizza in a laidback, rustic barn (mains ₡4000–9000). Call in advance to let them know you're coming. Daily 8am–10pm.

Estación Biológica La Selva

4km southwest of Puerto Viejo de Sarapiquí • Guided walks daily 8am & 1.30pm • US$35 half-day, US$45 full day; book well in advance • ☎ 2766 6565 or ☎ 2524 0607, ⊕ ots.ac.cr or ⊕ threepaths.co.cr

The fully equipped research station of **ESTACIÓN BIOLÓGICA LA SELVA**, 4km southwest of Puerto Viejo de Sarapiquí, is one of the best **birdwatching** destinations in the Sarapiquí, if not the country. You can spot over half of Costa Rica's bird species here (489 in total), including the red-capped manakin – La Selva is a regular port of call for documentary makers looking to capture the birds' energetic mating displays. An equally staggering number of tree species (some 350) have been identified, as well as 113 species of mammal, including anteaters, sloths (both two- and three-toed) and monkeys.

Leading biologists from around the world have studied here, and its facilities are extensive: a large swathe of premontane rainforest shouldering the northern part of Parque Nacional Braulio Carrillo forms the natural laboratory, while the research facilities include lecture halls and accommodation for scientists and students.

Note that only visitors staying at the complex are allowed to explore the reserve on their own; day-trippers have to take one of the two daily **guided walks**.

Trails

The terrain at La Selva extends from **primary forest** (sixty percent of the reserve's total area) through abandoned plantations to pastureland and brush, and is crossed by an extensive network of about 25 **trails** totalling just over 60km. The trails vary in length from short to more than 5km long, and some are accessible to pushchairs and to travellers with disabilities. Tourists tend to stick to the main routes within the part of La Selva designated as the **ecological reserve**, next to the

Río Puerto Viejo; these radiate from the river research station and lead through dense primary growth, the close, tightly knotted type of tropical forest that the Sarapiquí area is famous for. Most trails are in very good condition and clearly marked, though when the guides are as good as they are at La Selva, that's hardly a drawback.

Tours and activities

Twitchers may want to take a private **birdwatching tour** (daily 5.45am; 2hr; from US$50), recommended for the quality of both the guiding and the birding – you've a good chance of seeing the slaty-tailed trogon and rufous motmot. For beginner birders, the full-day **birdwatching workshop** (daily, if there is sufficient demand; 3hr; US$60) is a detailed introduction to habitats and behaviour that includes a guided walk on which you'll learn how to look for birds and then identify them.

You can also join a **night walk** (daily 7pm; 2hr; from US$50) in search of porcupines and kinkajou, or, for a glimpse of what life is like for the 350 or so researchers who study in the reserve each year, sign up for the **Scientist for a Day** workshop (daily, if there is sufficient demand; 3hr; US$60), where you'll be taught how to use scientific methodology to help record the station's flora and fauna. Book all tours/activities well in advance.

ARRIVAL AND DEPARTURE
LA SELVA

By bus Local buses from Puerto Viejo de Sarapiquí (every 30min; 15min) run past the turn-off to La Selva on their way to Las Horquetas/Guápiles; it's a 15min walk from the road. Buses from San José's Gran Terminal del Caribe to Puerto Viejo can also drop you off at the entrance. La Selva also runs shuttle buses to/from San José; book when you make your reservations.

By taxi A taxi from Puerto Viejo de Sarapiquí costs about US$15.

ACCOMMODATION

Estación Biológica La Selva ☎ 2766 6565 or ☎ 2524 0607, ⍟ ots.ac.cr or ⍟ threepaths.co.cr. The cabin accommodation (sleeping up to three) at La Selva includes private bathrooms (there are also four-person options suitable for families; US$316), three buffet-style meals a day served in the communal dining hall, and one half-day guided walk (additional guided walks from US$35/person). It's impossible to overstate the reserve's popularity – if you want to stay you need to reserve months in advance (particularly Nov–April). __US$203__

Heliconia Island

8km south of Puerto Viejo de Sarapiquí • Daily 8am–5pm • US$10, US$18 with tour • ☎ 2764 5220, ⍟ heliconiaisland.com • Local buses for Las Horquetas and Guápiles run every 30min or so from Puerto Viejo (ask to be let off at the turn-off on the main highway, then follow the signs down a dirt track before crossing a metal bridge to the island); a taxi from Puerto Viejo costs around US$15–20

Set on a five-acre island on the Río Puerto Viejo, the immaculately landscaped gardens of **HELICONIA ISLAND** boast over four hundred varieties of heliconia, and as the island's microclimate makes it blissfully cooler than Puerto Viejo, it has become a refuge for sloths, howler monkeys, river otters and more than three hundred species of **bird**, including various hummingbirds (the exclusive pollinator of the heliconia). Plant-lovers will get a kick out of the fragrant ylang ylang tree, torch gingers and Phenomenal sperm (*Phenakospermum guyannense*) – a flowering Guyana native closely related to the South American Traveller's Palm.

ACCOMMODATION
HELICONIA ISLAND

Heliconia Island ☎ 2764 5220, ⍟ heliconiaisland .com. If you want to make the most of the Dutch-run Heliconia Island, you can stay a night or two at its lodge, which offers simple rooms and apartments (the latter sleeping up to four people), both with fans and hot-water bathrooms, amid lush botanical gardens. Rates include breakfast; other meals can be taken in the restaurant. Doubles __US$82__, apartments __US$115__

Reserva Rara Avis

17km south of Puerto Viejo and about 80km northeast of San José • Only accessible to guests at the reserve's lodge

Stunningly remote **RESERVA RARA AVIS** offers one of the most thrilling and authentic ecotourism experiences in Costa Rica. Bordering the northeastern tip of pristine Parque Nacional Braulio Carrillo, the reserve features both primary rainforest and some secondary cover dating from over forty years ago, and boasts incredibly diverse rainforest **flora**. The area is home to a number of unique **palm species**, including the stained-glass palm tree, a rare specimen much in demand for its ornamental beauty, and the walking palm, whose tentacle-like roots can propel it over a metre of ground in its lifetime as it "walks" in search of sunlight. **Orchids** are also numerous, as are non-flowering bromeliads, heliconias, huge ancient hardwood trees smothered by lianas, primitive ferns and other plants typically associated with dense rainforest cover.

Established in 1983 by American Amos Bien (a former administrator of the Estación Biológica La Selva), forest ranger Robert Villalobos and biologist Carlos Gómez, Rara Avis combines the functions of a tourist lodge and a private rainforest reserve, and is dedicated to both the conservation and farming of the area. A pioneer in the country's **ecotourism** movement, its ultimate objective is to show that the rainforest can be profitable, giving local smallholders a viable alternative to clearing the land for cattle. Another significant part of the reserve's mandate is to provide alternative sources of employment in nearby Las Horquetas, where most people work for the big fruit companies or as day-labourers on local farms.

Rara Avis also functions as a **research station**, accommodating student groups and volunteers whose aims include development of rainforest products – orchids, palms and so forth – as crops, as well as the silk of the golden orb spider. It also hosts travellers in the *Waterfall Lodge* and *Las Casitas* (see opposite).

Trails and activities

Rara Avis has a 30km network of excellent **trails**, which are well marked and offer walks of thirty minutes to several hours. The informative **guided walks** are a great opportunity for spotting some of the 386 species in the reserve (see box below); they are run by knowledgeable guides, most of whom have lived at or around the reserve for some time. Guests are also welcome to go it alone: you'll be given a map at the lodge reception, but you should always let the staff know which trail you are following and about how long you intend to be. After dark you see a different side of the rainforest,

---

WILDLIFE-WATCHING AT RARA AVIS

A mind-boggling number of **bird species** (367) have been identified at Rara Avis, and it's likely that more are yet to be discovered. As well as the fearsome black, turkey and king vultures and the majestic osprey, you might see nine species of parrot, over twenty types of antbird, thirty different species of hummingbird, both chestnut-mandibled and keel-billed toucans, and the unlikely-named great potoo. The endangered great green macaw also nests here, and trogons, bare-necked umbrellabirds and the distinctive-looking three-wattled bellbird can also be spotted.

Among the more common **mammals** are opossums, monkeys, armadillos, anteaters, sloths and bats (eleven species in total). The reserve harbours five of the country's six cat species, though the closest you'll probably come to an ocelot or jaguar is discovering their tracks on a muddy trail. You may also encounter the Watson's climbing rat.

Amphibians and reptiles are abundant, ranging from the tree-climbing salamander to the white-lipped mud turtle, and including eight species of tree frog alone. Along with other vipers, the fer-de-lance and bushmaster **snakes**, two of the most venomous in the world, may lie in wait, so take extra care on the trails by looking everywhere you step and put your hand. Boa constrictors also hang out here; if you do see one, be careful, as the generally torpid boa can get aggressive when bothered.

and **night walks** (either guided or independent) offer the chance to spot a variety of insects, amphibians and nocturnal mammals, such as the arboreal four-eyed opossum.

A short walk below the *Waterfall Lodge*, the main accommodation complex in the reserve, a 50m-high waterfall plummets into a deep pool – **swimming** in the ice-cold pool, shrouded in a fine mist, is a wonderful experience, but keep an eye on the weather and check with the staff regarding approaching floodwaters, an occasional but deadly hazard up here.

ARRIVAL AND DEPARTURE — RESERVA RARA AVIS

Rara Avis is extremely isolated – it's what makes the place so special – and getting here is something of an endurance test. The reserve's office is in the village of **Las Horquetas**, just off the Guápiles Highway; here guests are kitted out with rubber boots before making the arduous 15km journey (3hr–5hr 30min) to the reserve itself.

GETTING TO LAS HORQUETAS

By bus Local buses from Puerto Viejo de Sarapiquí run to the school in Las Horquetas (hourly; 20min), 100m from the reserve's office. Puerto Viejo-bound buses from San José's Gran Terminal del Caribe (hourly; 1hr 30min) can drop you at the turn-off to the village, a 5min walk away from the reserve's office.

By taxi Taxis from Puerto Viejo cost around US$25 to Las Horquetas; the lodge can also arrange transfers from San José (US$95 for up to four people) and Puerto Viejo (US$50 for up to four people).

By car You can leave your car at the reserve's office, which is signed off the Guápiles Highway.

GETTING TO/FROM THE RESERVE

By cart A tractor-pulled cart laboriously ascends the first 12km from Las Horquetas (US$200, fits up to 14 people; 2hr–2hr 30min), leaving daily at 9am if demand is sufficient; coming from San José you'll need to catch the 6.30am bus from Gran Terminal del Caribe via the Guápiles Highway to make this connection. Remarkably, the road gets even worse after this, and travelling on the cart for the final leg (1hr) can be distinctly uncomfortable; many travellers hike on a rainforest trail (1hr 30min) to the reserve, instead.

By horse and on foot You can hire a horse for the first section of the journey (US$35; 3–4hr), then complete the final 3km to the reserve on foot (1hr 30min).

ACCOMMODATION

Rara Avis has a couple of accommodation options, neither of which has electricity: *Waterfall Lodge*, the main accommodation complex, and the more rustic, dorm-like *Las Casitas*. Rates are fully inclusive, with all meals served in the *Waterfall Lodge*'s open-air dining area (which has electricity for 3–4 hours in the evenings; you can charge your electronic devices during this period), home to a small naturalist library and board games. A **daily guided tour** is also included in the rates. Given the arduous journey here, it's worth staying at least a couple of nights.

Las Casitas Reserva Rara Avis ⓣ 2764 1111, ⓦ rara-avis.com. Five minutes from the main lodge, *Las Casitas* consists of six rooms, each sleeping four people in bunk beds. Facilities are comfortable enough, with clean, shared bathrooms, although you'll have to hike back from the dining area through dense forest at night. Dorms US$73

★**Waterfall Lodge** Reserva Rara Avis ⓣ 2764 1111, ⓦ rara-avis.com. Set 200m from a picture-perfect cascade, *Waterfall Lodge* has simple rooms with private bathrooms (with hot water), plenty of candles and spacious wrap-around balconies with hammocks and fantastic views of pristine rainforest and the hot lowland plains stretching towards the Caribbean. Less than 50m from the dining area, it's an idyllic place to stay: the only sounds heard at 5 or 6am are the echoing shrieks of birds and howler monkeys, and the light, especially first thing, is sheer and unfiltered, giving everything a wonderfully shimmering effect. US$181

Selva Verde

6km west of Puerto Viejo • Only accessible to guests at the reserve's lodge • ⓣ 2766 6800, in the US ⓣ 1 800 451 7111, ⓦ selvaverde.com

A paradise for birdwatchers, **SELVA VERDE** has two square kilometres of preserved primary rainforest alongside the Río Sarapiquí. The luxurious *Selva Verde Lodge* comprises an impressive complex of rooms, bungalows, lecture halls and a lovely riverside restaurant-bar where monkeys chatter above and the Sarapiquí bubbles below. It's set in tropical gardens rather than dense overgrowth, though the vegetation around the lodge is still home to toucans, sloths and howler monkeys, while iguanas and basilisk lizards are frequent poolside visitors. Wilder, primary

THE GREAT GREEN MACAW: BACK FROM THE BRINK?

The Sarapiquí region harbours the country's last flocks of **great green macaw** (*lapa verde*), the largest parrot in Central America. Globally endangered, it is estimated that fewer than 300 birds remain in Costa Rica (including around 30 breeding pairs), but the fact that they survive here at all – in what constitutes just ten percent of their original home range – is only due to some sterling conservation work. Continued deforestation across the Zona Norte has caused a dramatic decrease in the population of the great green macaw, whose unfortunate fate is to rely on the **almendro tree** (a popular tropical hardwood) for their existence, nesting in its boughs and feeding on the large nuts it produces.

The almendro is now, belatedly, protected, but the first major step in the fight to save this beautiful bird was the creation of the **San Juan–La Selva Biological Corridor**, which ecologically links the Reserva Biológica Indio-Maíz in Nicaragua with the Cordillera Central – great green macaws require a wide area for breeding and foraging, and the corridor acts as a vital migratory pathway. Its conservational focus is the **Refugio Nacional de Vida Silvestre Mixto Maquenque** (see p.237), which plays a vital role in sustaining Costa Rica's great green macaw population, though the bird's future depends as much on the continuity of the corridor, which can only really be achieved through the creation of private eco-reserves that provide a financial incentive for conserving their habitat.

The first of these initiatives, the **Costa Rican Bird Route** – which includes Reserva Biológica Tirimbina (see p.236), *Selva Verde Lodge* (see opposite) and Estación Biológica La Selva (see p.230) – was set up to improve bird tourism in the region, thus delivering greater economic opportunities to local communities. The development of the Bird Route (see p.71) has resulted in another fifteen square kilometres of forest being newly protected as official private reserves.

4

rainforest stretches off into the distance the other side of the river, accessed on a **guided tour**, and provides habitat for one of the region's most endangered species, the **great green macaw** (see box above).

Tours and activities

Selva Verde's expanse offers an excellent variety of walks along well-marked trails through primary and secondary forest, riverside, swamps and pastureland. The **guided walks** (daily 9am & 2pm; 2hr; US$25) through the denser section of premontane forest across the Río Sarapiquí are a must – the informative guides are top-notch and can make uncannily authentic bird calls to get the attention of trogons and toucans as well as pointing out poison-dart frogs, primitive ferns and complex lianas. You can take an early-morning (daily 6am; 2hr; US$27) or night (daily 7pm; 2hr; US$23) version of the guided walk, as well, plus a guided hike on the **Almendro Trail** to spot green macaws (daily, if there is sufficient demand; 4hr; US$56). There is also a **self-guided walk** in the section of secondary rainforest across the road from the lodge – ask for a map at the reception – which is explored in greater detail on one of the **birdwatching tours** (ask at the reception for details). Staff at the reserve's lodge can also organize whitewater rafting, horseriding and boat trips on the Río Sarapiquí for guests.

Selva Verde is heavily involved in the local community and is home to the nonprofit **Sarapiquí Conservation Learning Center** (☏ 2766 6482, ⊛ learningcentercostarica.org), which can arrange visits to local communities and schools (daily, if there is sufficient demand; 2hr; US$16), as well as tree-planting activities (daily if there is sufficient demand; 2hr; from US$20) and Latin dance classes (daily 7/7.30pm, if there is sufficient demand; 1hr; from US$10).

ARRIVAL AND DEPARTURE   SELVA VERDE

By bus Buses (hourly; around 20min) running westwards from Puerto Viejo de Sarapiquí to La Virgen can drop you at the entrance to Selva Verde.

By taxi Taxis from Puerto Viejo cost around US$15; the

lodge can arrange transport from most parts of Costa Rica.

By car Selva Verde is signed off the road near the village of Chilamate, which is 8km west of Puerto Viejo and 9km east of La Virgen.

ACCOMMODATION

All accommodation in the reserve is part of the *Selva Verde Lodge* complex.

Bungalows Selva Verde Lodge ☎ 2766 6800, in the US ☎ 1 800 451 7111, ⓦ selvaverde.com. A scenic 10–15min walk from the reception, these secluded bungalows (sleeping up to four) are the most comfortable accommodation option at the lodge, with a/c, private bathrooms, tea/coffee-making facilities, and screened balconies. The rates here include breakfast; full board options cost US$33 extra per person. US$170

★**River Lodge** Selva Verde Lodge ☎ 2766 6800, in the US ☎ 1 800 451 7111, ⓦ selvaverde.com. The comfortable a/c en suites at the *River Lodge*, from which the Sarapiquí's gentle gurglings can be heard, are connected to each other by a walkway and have dark-wood floorboards contrasting with bright walls. The rates here include breakfast; full board options cost US$37 extra per person. US$118

EATING

La Terrazza Selva Verde Lodge ☎ 2766 6800, in the US ☎ 1 800 451 7111 ⓦ selvaverde.com. The best restaurant in the region, *La Terrazza* overlooks the Río Sarapiquí, with an Italian-influenced menu that includes home-made pasta, fresh fish and a wide range of pizzas and calzones baked to perfection in the wood-fired oven (mains from ₡5000). Daily 6–10pm.

La Virgen and around

Lying on a bend in the Río Sarapiquí, the rafting hub of **LA VIRGEN** sprawls for 5km along the busy road between San Miguel and Puerto Viejo de Sarapiquí, the latter 17km to the east. The town is second only to Turrialba (see p.150) as Costa Rica's prime **rafting and kayaking centre**, and between July and December, outdoor types with well-toned arms come here by the busload to brave the variety of nearby runs.

4

WHITEWATER THRILLS ON THE PUERTO VIEJO AND THE SARAPIQUÍ

The wild Río Pacuare near Turrialba may lure adrenaline junkies to Costa Rica, but the churning waters around La Virgen also offer plenty of thrilling whitewater action. The relaxing **Class I–II** run that puts in on the **Río Puerto Viejo** is essentially a scenic float along a jungle-lined river, suitable for wildlife-watchers and small children (from age 3). Moving up a grade, the **Class III** runs, which start on the **Río Sarapiquí** around La Virgen, require good physical fitness but can be ridden by anyone over 8. If you want to tackle the ferocious and technically more demanding **Class IV** runs on the Upper Sarapiquí, you must be over 16 and have plenty of experience wielding a paddle.

TOUR OPERATORS

A number of companies in and around La Virgen offer guided whitewater rafting and kayaking tours (around US$60/half day, US$120/full day), most of which include lunch and transportation.

Aventuras del Sarapiquí Roble, 12km east of La Virgen ☎ 2766 5101, ⓦ sarapiqui.com. Offers a range of rafting, canoeing and tubing trips, as well as private full- and four-day kayaking courses. They also run mountain-biking and hiking trips and have a zipline canopy tour that shoots strapped-in victims across two rivers.

Hacienda Pozo Azul Adventures 2km west of La Virgen ☎ 2761 1360, ⓦ pozoazul.com. Rafting Class I, II–III and IV rapids is just part of the package at this one-stop-shop for outdoor adventure sports, based at the hacienda of the same name (see p.236). Other

activities include abseiling, horseriding, a nine-cable canopy tour and hiking.

Rafting Aguas Bravas Roble, 12km east of La Virgen ☎ 2766 6524 or ☎ 2992 2072, ⓦ www.aguasbravascr.com. One of the largest rafting companies in the country, Aguas Bravas runs on Class I–II, III and IV rapids. Prices include transport from La Fortuna; pick-ups from San José cost US$20 extra.

Sarapiquí Outdoor Center 1.5km west of La Virgen ☎ 2761 1123, ⓦ costaricaraft.com. Well-established rafting and kayaking company, offering trips on the Puerto Viejo and Sarapiquí.

Reserva Biológica Tirimbina

2km east of La Virgen • Daily 7am–5pm • US$17 • ☎ 2761 1579, ⓦ tirimbina.org • **Night hikes** Daily 7.30pm; 2hr • US$28 • **Frog tour** Daily 7pm; 2hr • US$28 • **Bat programme** Daily 7.30pm; 2hr • US$28 • **Birdwatching walks** Daily 6am; 3hr • US$28 • **Chocolate tour** Daily 8am & 1.30pm; 2hr • US$30

The thrilling **Reserva Biológica Tirimbina** is a small private reserve with 9km of trails weaving through primal rainforest and across a couple of suspension bridges, one of which is 272m long and straddles the gurgling Río Sarapiquí. While the trails here are well marked and maintained, this is no sanitized rainforest experience: hidden cameras have captured jaguars, margay, ocelots and Baird's tapir going about their business.

A variety of **guided and self-guided walks** (advanced bookings are required for all) are offered, including night hikes, frog tours, bird-spotting strolls and even a chocolate tour explaining the cacao fruit's journey from tree to chocolate bar. Perhaps the most interesting, though, is the **bat programme**, one of only two activities in the country dedicated to this misunderstood mammal (the other is in Monteverde); part of an ongoing research project, the programme uses bats caught in drift nets that evening to explain their physiology and feeding habits.

Centro Neotrópico Sarapiquís

1km north of La Virgen • Daily 8am–6pm • US$20 • ☎ 2761 1004, ⓦ sarapiquis.com

Part-funded by the Belgian government, the **Centro Neotrópico Sarapiquís** has a rather disjointed feel. Essentially an archeological park built on the site of a six-hundred-year-old pre-Columbian tomb, it also features a museum that explores the relationship between indigenous cultures and the rainforest, plus botanical gardens and a hotel.

Dave and Dave's Nature Park

200m north of the cemetery in La Virgen • Daily 7am–5pm • US$20 • ☎ 2761 0801, ⓦ costaricanp.com

Run by the eponymous father-and-son team from the US, **Dave and Dave's Nature Park** offers an easy introduction to the rainforest, with a short but attractive trail along the river and a garden filled with hummingbirds and toucans. Guided early-morning birdwatching and night-time nature walks (US$30; 1hr 30min) are also available, if there is sufficient demand.

ARRIVAL AND DEPARTURE

LA VIRGEN AND AROUND

By bus Buses from San José travel via the Guápiles Highway and Las Horquetas (hourly; 2hr) and terminate in

Puerto Viejo (see p.189), from where you can hop on one of the hourly local buses for the 30min journey to La Virgen.

ACCOMMODATION

In addition to the accommodation listed below, there is also local lodging at the Centro Neotrópico Sarapiquís (see above) and Selva Verde (see p.233).

Cabinas Tia Rosita 1km west of La Virgen ☎ 2761 1125. Although somewhat lacking in atmosphere, these four clean and basic cabins (sleeping up to four) – attached to the *soda* of the same name (see opposite) – are good value. Each comes with TV and private bathroom. US$30

Hacienda Pozo Azul 2km west of La Virgen ☎ 2761 1360, ⓦ pozoazul.com. Based on a 2000-acre ranch, next to the bubbling Río Sarapiquí, is this adventure sports centre (see box, p.235). *Hacienda Pozo Azul* provides accommodation in permanent tents (sleeping up to three), with comfy beds and attached bathrooms. There's also a decent restaurant, guest lounge, and kiosk. US$84

La Quinta de Sarapiquí Country Inn 5km east of La Virgen, then 1.5km up a side road on the left

☎ 2761 1052, ⓦ laquintasarapiqui.com. On the banks of the Río Sardinal, this lodge has spacious a/c *casitas* (sleeping up to four) set amid heliconia plants, so there's plenty of hummingbird activity to watch from the rocking chair or hammock on your veranda. Activities include swimming in the pool, tubing down the river and exploring the lodge's butterfly house and frog pond. US$124

Tirimbina Rainforest Lodge Reserva Biológica Tirimbina ☎ 2761 1579, ⓦ tirimbina.org. The Tirimbina reserve has comfortable flagstone-floored rooms, equipped with a/c; smarter options (US$110) come with more space and private terraces. Rates include entry to the reserve, valid for three consecutive days. Buffet-style lunches and dinners available. US$89

EATING

Bar-Restaurant Tia Rosita 1km west of La Virgen ☎ 2761 1125. The most popular *soda* around these parts, *Bar-Restaurant Tia Rosita* serves above-average Tico specialities for around ₡3000. You can also stay here (see opposite). Mon–Fri 7am–9pm, Sat 8am–9pm, Sun 8am–4pm.

Hacienda Pozo Azul 2km west of La Virgen ☎ 2761 1360, ⊚ pozoazul.com. The adventure centre at *Hacienda Pozo Azul* (see opposite) has a decent restaurant where you can munch on everything from delicious *enyucados* (filled cassava patties) to juicy steaks while taking in the view over the Río Sarapiquí from its outdoor deck. Mains from ₡4000. Daily 7am–10pm.

Refugio Nacional de Vida Silvestre Mixto Maquenque

In the far north of the Sarapiquí region, just beyond the town of Boca Tapada, and separated from Nicaragua by the San Juan River, the **Refugio Nacional de Vida Silvestre Mixto Maquenque** is a multi-use wildlife refuge encompassing more than 500 square kilometres of wetlands, lagoons and lowland Atlantic forest. This remote reserve, established in 2005, after ten years of hard lobbying, is home to an array of birdlife, and is one of the very few places in Costa Rica where you might still see the highly endangered **great green macaw** (see box, p.234), as well as a large resident colony of more common oropendolas.

ARRIVAL AND DEPARTURE ┊ RN DE VIDA SILVESTRE MIXTO MAQUENQUE

Both lodges (see below) will pick you up from Boca Tapada, or you can arrange transfers from San José, La Fortuna or Puerto Viejo de Sarapiquí.

By car To reach the reserve by car from San José or San Carlos, head east through Aguas Zarcas to Pital and then – on good gravel roads – to Boca Tapada. It's possible to drive 7.5km northeast to the *Laguna del Lagarto Lodge*; it's a reasonable road, although a 4WD is recommended.

By bus There are daily buses from San José (Terminal Atlántico; 2 daily; 3hr 45min) and San Carlos (every 30min; 1hr 15min) to Pital, from where you can connect with buses north to Boca Tapada (daily 9.30am & 4.30pm, returns 5.30am & 12.30pm; 2hr).

ACCOMMODATION

Laguna del Lagarto Lodge Inside Refugio Nacional de Vida Silvestre Mixto Maquenque ☎ 2289 8163, ⊚ lagarto-lodge-costa-rica.com. One of the most remote lodges in the country – and only 16km from the Nicaraguan border – this ecolodge is home to an incredible variety of trees, plants and animals, and offers some of the best birdwatching in the country. Rooms are rustic but comfortable, with private bathrooms and peaceful views from their balconies. There are 10km of well-marked rainforest trails to explore, as well as canoeing (included in the rates) and boat trips (US$32; 4hr) on the San Carlos and San Juan rivers. Meals cost extra (breakfast US$8, lunch US$10, dinner US$16). **US$75**

Maquenque Ecolodge Inside Refugio Nacional de Vida Silvestre Mixto Maquenque ☎ 2479 8200, ⊚ maquenqueecolodge.com. Inside Mixto Maquenque, bordering the San Carlos River and only accessible by boat (check the lodge's website for details), this lodge has a cluster of attractive bungalows (sleeping up to three) and atmospheric treehouses (sleeping up to four), a good restaurant and a range of activities – from boat trips to visits to local schools. Rates include a rainforest walk, canoeing on a lagoon, a school visit, and the chance to plant a tree in the rainforest. Lunch US$16 extra, dinner US$20 extra. Bungalows **US$131**, treehouses **US$197**

4

Guanacaste

OLIVE RIDLEY TURTLES

5

Guanacaste

For the majority of the Tico population, the province of Guanacaste, hemmed in by the mountains of the Cordillera de Guanacaste to the east and the Pacific to the west, and bordered on the north by Nicaragua, is a land apart. Guanacastecos still sometimes refer to Valle Central inhabitants as "Cartagos", an archaic term dating back to the eighteenth century when Cartago was Costa Rica's capital. Little tangible remains of the dance, music and folklore that made the region distinct, but there is undeniably something special about the place. The landscape is some of the prettiest you'll see in the country (though much of it has come about through the slaughter of tropical dry forest), especially in the wet season, when wide-open spaces, stretching from the ocean across savannah grasses to the brooding humps of volcanoes, are awash in earth tones, blues, yellows and mauves.

The dry heat, relatively accessible terrain and panoramic views make Guanacaste the best place in the country for walking and horseriding, especially around the mud pots and stewing sulphur waters of the spectacular **Parque Nacional Rincón de la Vieja** and through the tropical dry forest cover of **Parque Nacional Santa Rosa**. Beyond **Cañas**, protected areas administered by the Área de Conservación Tempisque (ACT) encompass **Parque Nacional Palo Verde**, an important site for migratory birds, Reserva Biológica Lomas Barbudal, and the deep underground caves of **Parque Nacional Barra Honda** on the Nicoya Peninsula, just across the Río Tempisque.

For many travellers, however, Guanacaste means only one thing: beaches. Most are found where the **Nicoya Peninsula** joins the mainland. Roughly two-thirds of this mountainous peninsula is in Guanacaste, while the lower third belongs to the Puntarenas Province, which is covered in Chapter 6 (see p.315). Beaches range from tranquil hideaways such as Nosara in the **central Nicoya Peninsula** to bland mega-resorts aimed firmly at the North American market, most of which are in the **northern Nicoya Peninsula**. Several beaches are also nesting grounds for marine turtles – giant leatherbacks haul themselves up onto Playa Grande, near Tamarindo, while Parque Nacional Santa Rosa is the destination for olive ridley turtles. The only towns of any significance for travellers are the provincial capital of **Liberia**, and **Nicoya**, the main town on the peninsula. If you are overnighting on the way to Nicaragua, La Cruz in **northwestern Guanacaste** makes a useful base.

PLAYA SÁMARA

Highlights

❶ Parque Nacional Rincón de la Vieja The beautiful landscapes of this park encompass terrains varying from rock-strewn savannah to patches of tropical dry forest, culminating in the blasted-out vistas of the volcano crater. **See p.251**

❷ Fiestas Lively community fiestas celebrate Guanacaste's livestock heritage with bullfights, rodeos, processions and traditional dancing. **See p.259, p.282 & p.286**

❸ Parque Nacional Santa Rosa Costa Rica's oldest national park is also one of its most popular, with good trails and great surfing, as well as plenty of turtle-spotting opportunities. **See p.260**

❹ Leatherback turtles Playa Grande is the annual destination for hundreds of leatherback

turtles, the largest of the four species of marine turtle that lay their eggs along Costa Rica's shores. **See p.276**

❺ Cowboys Skilful and self-reliant, Guanacaste's cowboys – or *sabaneros*, as they are known here – encapsulate the history of Costa Rica's vibrant rural communities. **See p.282**

❻ Parque Nacional Barra Honda Explore subterranean limestone caves filled with eerie formations, stalagmites and stalactites at this national park. **See p.285**

❼ Playa Sámara One of the Pacific coast's finest beaches, with excellent swimming, spectacular sunsets and good waves for beginner surfers. **See p.287**

HIGHLIGHTS ARE MARKED ON THE MAP ON P.242

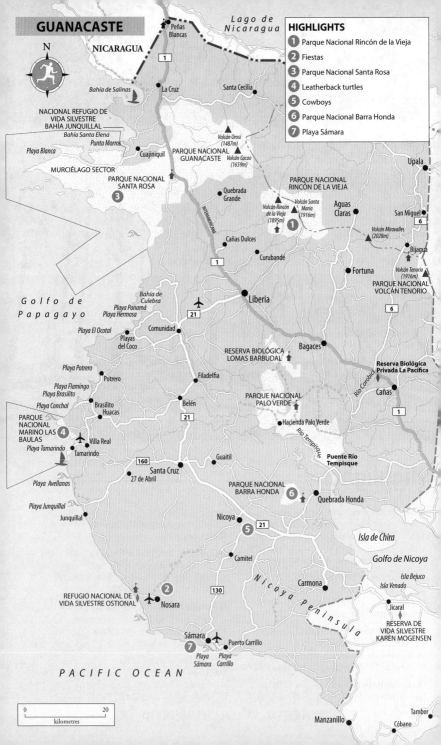

GUANACASTE

NICARAGUA

N

Lago de Nicaragua

Peñas Blancas

1

Bahía de Salinas

La Cruz

Santa Cecilia

NACIONAL REFUGIO DE VIDA SILVESTRE BAHÍA JUNQUILLAL

Bahía Santa Elena
Punta Morros

Playa Blanca

Cuajiniquil

MURCIÉLAGO SECTOR

PARQUE NACIONAL SANTA ROSA
3

PARQUE NACIONAL GUANACASTE

Volcán Orosí (1487m)

Volcán Cacao (1659m)

Upala

Quebrada Grande

PARQUE NACIONAL RINCÓN DE LA VIEJA

Volcán Rincón de la Vieja (1895m)

Volcán Santa María (1916m)

Aguas Claras

San Miguel

6

Volcán Miravalles (2028m)

Cañas Dulces

1

Curubandé

Bijagua

Volcán Tenorio (1916m)

Fortuna

PARQUE NACIONAL VOLCÁN TENORIO

Liberia

21

6

Golfo de Papagayo

Bahía de Culebra
Playa Panamá
Playa Hermosa

Playa El Ocotal

Comunidad

Playas del Coco

Bagaces

RESERVA BIOLÓGICA LOMAS BARBUDAL

Reserva Biológica Privada La Pacífica

Río Corobicí

Cañas

1

Playa Potrero

Potrero

Playa Flamingo
Playa Brasilito

Playa Conchal

PARQUE NACIONAL MARINO LAS BAULAS
4

Brasilito
Huacas

Filadelfia

Belén

21

PARQUE NACIONAL PALO VERDE

Hacienda Palo Verde

Río Tempisque

Villa Real

Tamarindo

Playa Avellanas

160

Guaitil

Puente Río Tempisque

Santa Cruz
27 de Abril

PARQUE NACIONAL BARRA HONDA
6

Quebrada Honda

Playa Junquillal

Junquillal

Nicoya

5   21

Isla de Chira

Golfo de Nicoya

Camitel

Isla Bejuco
Isla Venado

REFUGIO NACIONAL DE VIDA SILVESTRE OSTIONAL

2

Nosara

130

Carmona

Jicaral

N i c o y a   P e n i n s u l a

RESERVA DE VIDA SILVESTRE KAREN MOGENSEN

Sámara

7

Puerto Carrillo

Playa Sámara

Playa Carrillo

PACIFIC OCEAN

0   20
kilometres

Manzanillo

Cóbano

Tambor

5

These days, Guanacaste is changing fast. An enormous number of hotels, many of them all-inclusive resorts, have been built on the Pacific coast, with more in the pipeline. Inland, mass tourism is less evident, and, despite the presence of *McDonald's* in its dignified streets, Liberia itself remains one of the most charming cities in the country; the recent airport expansion and the growth of flights here from across the Americas (and beyond) means that it is more accessible than ever before. For many tourists, the province is their first – and perhaps only – glimpse of Costa Rica.

Brief history

Due to significant excavations in the area and some contemporaneous Spanish accounts, Guanacaste's **pre-Columbian** history is better documented than that of the rest of Costa Rica. Archeologists have long been interested in the **Chorotegas**, considered to have been the most highly developed of all Costa Rica's scattered and isolated pre-Columbian peoples, but whose culture predictably went into swift decline after the Conquest. In archeological terms it belongs to the **Greater Nicoya Subarea**, a pre-Columbian designation that includes some of western Nicaragua, and which continues to yield buried clues to the extent of communication between the Maya and Aztec cultures to the north and smaller groups inhabiting Mesoamerica from the fifth to the fifteenth centuries.

Following the Conquest, the region became part of the administrative entity known as the **Capitanía General de Guatemala**. Guanacaste was annexed by Nicaragua in 1787, but in 1812 the Spanish rulers about-turned and donated the province to Costa Rica, so that its territory became large enough for it to be officially represented in the Captaincy. When the modern-day Central American nations declared independence from Spain, and the Captaincy was dissolved in 1821, Guanacaste found itself in the sensitive position of being claimed by both Costa Rica and Nicaragua. In an 1824 vote the province's inhabitants made their allegiances clear: the *guanacastecos* in the north, traditionally cattle ranchers with familial ties to Nicaragua, voted to join that country, while the inhabitants of the Nicoya Peninsula wished to maintain links with Costa Rica. The peninsular vote won out, by a slim margin.

As the nineteenth century progressed, **cattle ranching** began to dominate the landscape, providing the mainstay of the economy until well into the twentieth century. Despite the continuing presence of the cattle culture and the *sabanero* (see box, p.282) in Guanacaste, however, beef prices have been dropping in Costa Rica for some years now, after the boom years of the 1960s and 1970s when deforestation was rife. In contrast, as in the rest of the country, the **tourist industry** is becoming increasingly important to the local economy, as seen by the sprawl of beach resorts along the coast.

ARRIVAL AND INFORMATION   GUANACASTE

By plane Liberia's modern airport (see p.256) is the second busiest in the country (after the capital), with an extensive range of domestic and international flights.

By car Access to most of Guanacaste from San José is

GUANACASTE'S CLIMATE

Highland Ticos tend to describe Guanacaste as a virtual desert, liberally applying the words *caliente* (hot) and *seco* (dry). Certainly it is dry, in comparison to the rest of the country: parts of it receive only 500mm of rain a year, ten times less than the Caribbean coast. To some extent irrigation has helped, but in summer (Dec–April), Guanacaste still experiences some drought. This is when you'll see an eerie landscape of bare, silver-limbed trees glinting in the sun, as many shed their leaves in order to conserve water. The province is significantly greener, and prettier, in the wet season (May–Nov), which is generally agreed to be the **best time** to come, with the added benefit of fewer travellers than at other times of the year and lighter rainfall than the rest of the country receives during these months.

5

easy – take the Autopista General Cañas (Hwy-27) to the Puntarenas turn-off, then the Interamericana (Hwy-1), which runs right through to the Nicaraguan border at Peñas Blancas. Follow the road rules, particularly on the Interamericana, which is heavily patrolled by traffic cops.

By bus Modern, comfortable buses ply the highway, with good services to Cañas, Liberia and the border. The national parks of Rincón de la Vieja and Santa Rosa are trickier to reach, however, and bus travellers may have to walk, hitch or take a taxi for part of the journey. All the beaches are accessible by

bus and car, though the roads are not in fantastic shape, and journeys from San José can take several hours.

Tourist information The Área de Conservación Tempisque (ACT) regional office in Bagaces, opposite the Interamericana turn-off to Parque Nacional Palo Verde (Mon–Fri 8am–4pm; ☎ 2671 1455), is not geared up for tourists, though staff can advise on current road conditions to Palo Verde and provide information on parks in Guanacaste. For general information, it's best to stop by the ICT offices in Liberia (see p.257) or Nicoya (see p.285).

Cañas

Sleepy **CAÑAS**, 168km northwest of San José and 50km southeast of Liberia, is the heart of agricultural commerce for the surrounding area. While a pleasant morning or afternoon can be spent **rafting** the nearby **Río Corobicí**, it's only really worth staying overnight here if you arrive late or are planning to use it as a base for a trip into Palo Verde or Tenorio.

It's a pleasant town of single- and two-storey traditional buildings, with activity decidedly at a minimum; what there is mostly takes place within a few blocks of the unremarkable grass-and-concrete **central square**. Cañas has only one real sight to speak of, the incongruous modernist **church**, on the east side of the square. The barn-like structure is replete with colourful, Gaudí-esque mosaics that reach a bright blue crescendo in the steeple, capped by an understated cross. Its interior is significantly more subdued, marked by a ceiling covered with stained wood blocks and a minimalist altar backed by a wall patterned with limestone rectangles.

Las Pumas Rescue Shelter

Hwy-1, 4.5km west of Cañas; the reserve is 500m up a side road from Safaris Corobicí (see box below) • Daily 8am–4pm • US$12 • ☎ 2669 6044, ⓦ centrorescatelaspumas.org

For over forty years, **Las Pumas Rescue Shelter** has provided a refuge for native wildlife once kept as pets, or orphaned due to human activity. Although its enclosures are relatively small, the centre cares for over sixty species of animal that cannot be released back into the wild, including five of Costa Rica's six native cats: jaguar, puma, margay, jaguarundi and ocelot.

ARRIVAL AND INFORMATION   CAÑAS

By bus Buses arrive at the terminal on Av 11, at C 1, some four blocks north of the central square.

Destinations Bagaces (every 15–30min; 1hr); Bijagua (10 daily; 1hr 5min); Liberia (every 30min; 1hr); Nicoya, via

Irma (hourly; 2–3hr); San José (every 30min–1hr; 3hr 30min); Upala (10 daily; 1hr 45min).

Tourist information The town has no tourist office, but staff at *Hotel Cañas* (see opposite) can provide local info.

RAFTING THE RÍO COROBICÍ

Five kilometres west of Cañas on the Interamericana, the long-established **Safaris Corobicí** (☎ 2669 6191, ⓦ nicoya.com) specializes in gentle floating trips on the Río Corobicí (2hr to half a day; US$37–65/person, snacks included). Knowledgeable guides row while you observe the local mammals and reptiles, including howler and spider monkeys, surprisingly large crocodiles, iguanas and caimans. The trip also provides a prime opportunity for birdwatching, as several species – including motmots, cuckoos, falcons, ospreys, herons and the endangered jabiru stork – can be spotted along the river's length.

ACCOMMODATION

Hacienda La Pacífica 5km northeast of town on the Interamericana ☎ 2669 9393, ⓦ pacificacr .com. Set in the grounds of a large cattle ranch, this hotel has country-style *cabinas* sleeping up to four and furnished with a/c, TVs, sleek bathrooms and comfortable, ornate beds; there are also a few studios with kitchenettes (US$78). The most refined meal in the area can be had at the restaurant here; most of the ingredients are grown or raised on the ranch's land (most mains ₡7500–10,000). US$66

Hotel Cañas C 2, at Av 3 ☎ 2669 0039, ⓦ hotel canascr.com. A couple of blocks from the main square, this central option has worn but acceptable en-suite rooms; some have TVs and a/c (US$50). The restaurant is not exactly memorable but serves straightforward, good-value Tico grub. US$40

EATING

Cafetería Sol Café Av 3, at C 5 ☎ 8627 9558. One of the buzzier places to eat in this low-key town, serving up first-rate coffee (₡1000–25,000), salads and sandwiches for lunch, and cakes and pastries for an afternoon pick-me-up. Daily 7am–6pm.

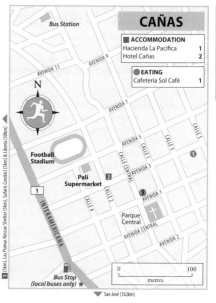

CAÑAS

■ ACCOMMODATION
Hacienda La Pacifica 1
Hotel Cañas 2

● EATING
Cafeteria Sol Café 1

Parque Nacional Palo Verde and around

23km southwest of Bagaces • Daily 8am–4pm • US$12

PARQUE NACIONAL PALO VERDE, on the northern bank of the Río Tempisque, was created in 1982 to preserve the habitat of the **migratory birds** that nest in the estuary of the Tempisque and a large patch of relatively undisturbed lowland dry forest. With a distinctive topography featuring ridged limestone hills – unique to this part of the country, and attesting to the fact that certain parts of Guanacaste were once under water – the park shelters about fifteen separate ecological habitats. From December to May, Palo Verde can dry out into baked mudflats, while in the wet season, extensive flooding gives rise to saltwater and freshwater lakes and swamps. Following the wet season, the great floodplain drains slowly, creating marshes, mangroves and other habitats favoured by migratory birds. Little visited by tourists, the park is mainly of interest to serious **birders**, but what you see depends on the time of year – by far the **best months** are at the height of the dry season, between January and March, when most of the 250 or so migratory species are in residence. In the wet season, roughly May to November, flooding makes parts of the park inaccessible.

The park is home to one of the largest concentrations of **waterfowl** in Central America, both indigenous and migratory, with more than three hundred species of bird, among them the endangered jabiru stork and black-crowned night heron. Further from the riverbank, in the tree cover along the bottom and ridges of the limestone hills, you may spot toucans, and perhaps even one of the increasingly rare scarlet macaws. At evening during the dry season, many birds and other species – monkeys, coatis and even deer – congregate around the few remaining waterholes; bring binoculars and a torch. Note, though, that you shouldn't swim in the Río Tempisque (or anywhere else), as it's home to particularly huge crocodiles – some, according to the park rangers, are as much as 5m long.

5

PRE-COLUMBIAN GUANACASTE

Greater Nicoya (modern-day Guanacaste) was an archeological and cultural buffer zone between the complex cultures of the Aztecs and the Maya to the north, and the simpler agrarian cultures to the south, which had more in common with the prehistoric peoples of the Amazon basin. Greater Nicoya was occupied from an indeterminate date by the **Nicoyans**, about whom little is known, but most of the historical and archeological facts discovered about the region relate to the peoples known as the **Chorotegas**, who arrived in Nicoya around 800 AD, fleeing social and political upheavals far to the north.

The central Mexican empire of Teotihuacán, near the Mexico City of today, had fallen into disorganization by about 650 AD, and was abandoned about one hundred years later, at the same time that the Classic Maya civilizations of modern-day Yucatán and northern Guatemala also collapsed. New **fragmented groups** were created, some of whom forged migratory, militaristic bands. In the eighth century, harassed by their territorial enemies the Olmecs, groups of Maya and Aztecs migrated south. Among them were the people who would become known as Chorotegas. The word Chorotega derives from either their place of origin, Cholula, or from two words in the Chorotegan language: *cholol* (to run or escape) and *teca* (people) – "the people who escaped".

Evidence of immediate and long-term cultural upheaval in the area after 800 AD includes a significant increase in the number of Nicoyan **burial sites** found dating from around this time. The use of objects associated with elites – like ceremonial skulls, jades and elaborate *metates* (mortars) – suddenly declined almost to the point of disappearing completely, and populations seem to have migrated from the interior toward the coasts. While this evidence could suggest a natural disaster (a volcanic eruption, perhaps) it also bears the hallmarks of what could be termed an invasion.

THE ARRIVAL OF THE SPANISH AND THE DEMISE OF THE CHOROTEGAS

The Chorotegas' first contact with the **Spanish** was calamitous. The 1522 Spanish expedition from Panama up the Pacific coast to Nicaragua brought smallpox, the plague and influenza to the indigenous people of Greater Nicoya. Imprisonment and slavery followed, with coastal peoples raided, branded and sold into slavery in Panama and Peru. The demise of the Chorotegas from the sixteenth century was rapid and unreversed.

The trails

From the Hacienda Palo Verde Research Station two **trails** lead up to the top of hills, from where you can see the expansive mouth of the Río Tempisque to the west and the broad plains of Guanacaste to the east. A number of other **loop trails**, none more than 4km long, run through the park. The shortest of the trails, at just 300m, is **Las Calizas**; others include **El Manigordo** ("ocelot"; 1.5km), **El Mapache** ("raccoon"; 2km) and **El Venado** ("deer"; 2km). You've got a good chance of seeing collared peccaries, abundant in this area, or a coati, which you may see or hear foraging in the undergrowth. White-tailed deer also live here, but they're very shy and likely to dart off at the sound of your approach.

For longer treks, try the **Bosque Primario** trail (about 7km), through, as the name suggests, primary forest cover. You can also walk the 6km (dry season only) to the edge of the Río Tempisque from where you'll see the aptly named **Isla de los Pájaros** (Bird Island). Square in the mouth of the river, the island is chock-full of our feathered friends all year, with black-crowned night herons swirling above in thick dark clouds. Many hotels and tour agencies in the province offer boat trips around the island, but landings are not permitted, so you have to content yourself with bird-spotting and taking photographs from the boat.

Check with rangers regarding **conditions** before walking on any of the trails: access is constantly subject to change, due to flooding and sometimes bee colonies. The Río Tempisque walk in particular can be muddy and unpleasantly insect-ridden in all but the driest months. You should bring plenty of water, as the heat and humidity are considerable.

BELIEF SYSTEMS AND RITUALS

Excavations in Guanacaste and the Nicoya Peninsula reveal something of the Chorotegas' **belief systems** and social arrangements. Near Bahía Culebra, anthropologists unearthed pottery shards, utensils and the remains of hearths, along with a burial ground holding twenty women, children and infants. Chorotega villages were made up of longhouse-type structures – common to many indigenous cultures of the Americas – inhabited by entire extended families, and centred on a large square, site of religious ceremonies and meetings.

Like the Maya and Aztecs, the Chorotegas had a belief system built around **blood-letting** and the **sacrifice** of animals and humans. Although it is not known if beating hearts were ripped from chests, virgins were definitely thrown into volcano craters to appease their gods, about whom little is known. Chorotegas also believed in **yulios**, the spirit alter ego that escaped from their mouths at the moment of death to roam the world forever. Although pagan, Chorotega priests shared a number of duties and functions with the Catholic priests who worked to destroy their culture. Celibate, they may also have heard confessions and meted out punishments for sins.

Few Chorotega **rituals** are documented. One known practice was the formation of a kind of human maypole of *voladores*, men suspended "flying" (actually roped) from a post, twirling themselves round and round while descending to the ground. Originating with the Aztecs, the ritual was dedicated to the Morning Star deity; the four *voladores* represented the cardinal points. You can still see it in the Mexican state of Veracruz and in certain Guatemalan villages.

SOCIETAL AND CULTURAL MARKERS

The Chorotega **economy** was based on maize (corn). They also cultivated tobacco, fruit, beans and cotton, using cacao beans as currency, and the marketplace was run by women. All land was held communally, as was everything that was cultivated and harvested, which was then distributed throughout the settlement. This plurality did not extend to social prestige, however. Three strata characterized Chorotega society: at the upper echelon were chieftains (*caciques*), warriors and priests; in the middle were the commoners, and at the bottom were the slaves and prisoners of war. The Chorotegas were the only indigenous peoples in Costa Rica to have a written **language**, comprising hieroglyphs similar to those used by the Maya. They were also skilled artisans, producing ornamental jewellery and jade, and colouring cotton fabrics with animal and vegetable dyes. It was the Chorotegas who made the bulk of the distinctive **ceramics** so celebrated in the country today, many of which can be seen in San José's Museo Nacional (see p.96).

ARRIVAL AND DEPARTURE   PARQUE NACIONAL PALO VERDE

By car Getting to Palo Verde takes a while, though it is theoretically possible year-round with a regular non-4WD vehicle. From the well-signed turn-off from the Interamericana at Bagaces (opposite the ACT regional office), it's a 23km drive to the entrance hut, and a further 7km to the Organization for Tropical Studies (OTS) Research Station. There are signs all along the road to the park, but at long intervals, and the road forks unnervingly from time to time without indicating which way to go. If in doubt, follow the tyre tracks made by the rangers.

INFORMATION AND TOURS

While it's possible from the trails to see some of the bird species for which Palo Verde is noted, travelling along the Río Tempisque offers far more opportunities. In addition to the tour operator listed below, some of those based in Liberia (see p.257) offer boat tours in the park.

Tourist information The ACT office (see p.244) is the most complete source of information on the park; the ranger station at the park entrance can also advise on the trails and where to spot wildlife.
Palo Verde Boat Tours Ortega ☎ 2651 8001, ⓦ paloverde boattours.com. With its main office in a small community just west of the national park, this locally owned and operated company leads friendly and informative 2hr tours (from US$55) on the Tempisque. Pick-ups can be arranged from several points throughout Guanacaste, with prices varying depending on the distance from the national park. Discounts are available if you make your own way to the park.

ACCOMMODATION

Hacienda Palo Verde Research Station About 7km south of the park entrance ☎ 2524 0607, ⓦ ots.ac.cr. The OTS has a rustic field station at Palo Verde, originally set up for comparative ecosystem study and research into the

5

BEWARE THE KILLER BEES

In recent years swarms of **Africanized bees** – sometimes termed "killer bees" – have taken to colonizing Palo Verde. Africanized bees are aggressive, and may pursue – in a swarm – anyone who unwittingly disturbs one of their large, quite obvious, nests. They are known to attack dark colours, so if attacked remove all dark clothing and cover dark hair. The conventional technique is to cover your head and run in a zigzag pattern so that you can dodge the cloud of pursuing bees. Although, luckily, this occurs very rarely, you should take special care if you are sensitive to stings, and ask the rangers about the presence of nests on or around trails. Bees are also found in the Reserva Biológica Lomas Barbudal (see below).

---

dry forest habitat. If it's not full of scientific researchers, you can stay there. Accommodation is in clean dormitories, and all meals are included in the rates. Dorms US$95

Ranger Station Campsite ☎ 2671 1290 or ☎ 2671

1062. It's possible to camp at the small, very basic site next to the ranger station at the park entrance, where there are toilets, but it's best to call ahead to check that there's space. US$5

Reserva Biológica Lomas Barbudal

7km north of Parque Nacional Palo Verde • Daily 7am–4pm • US$12

The **RESERVA BIOLÓGICA LOMAS BARBUDAL** is an impressive, though small-scale, initiative just north of Parque Nacional Palo Verde. Home to some of the last vestiges of true **tropical dry forest** in the region, Lomas Barbudal means "bearded hills" and that's just what they look like, with relatively bare pates surrounded by sideburns of bushy deciduous trees. Stretches of savannah-like open grassland are punctuated by the thorny-looking **shoemaker's tree** and crisscrossed by rivers and the strips of deciduous woods that hug their banks. The reserve also features isolated examples of the majestic **mahogany** and **rosewood** trees, whose deep-blood-red timber is coveted as material for furniture.

Lomas Barbudal is also rich in **wildlife**. If you don't spot a howler monkey, you'll at least likely hear one. And this is practically the only place in Guanacaste where you have a reasonable chance of seeing the **scarlet macaw**. Like Parque Nacional Santa Rosa to the north, Lomas Barbudal hosts an abundance of **insects** – over two hundred **bee species** alone, around 25 percent of the species in the entire world. Those allergic to stings or otherwise intolerant of insects might want to give Lomas Barbudal a miss; the reserve is filled with insects, including the aggressive Africanized bees (see box above).

The visitor centre and around

At the park entrance, 6km from the Interamericana turn-off • Daily 7am–4pm • ☎ 2659 9194

The **visitor centre** (called the Casa de Patrimonio) has a small museum with a few displays on the flora and fauna; from here a **short trail** (2km round trip) leads to a sizeable watering hole equally popular with wildlife which comes to cool off (particularly in the dry season), and swimmers who do the same. There are also two swimmable rivers and a small network of unmarked trails designed and cleared by local volunteers.

ARRIVAL AND INFORMATION

RESERVA BIOLÓGICA LOMAS BARBUDAL

By car Lomas Barbudal is 14km from Bagaces and is best reached with your own transport. Take Hwy-1 northwest from Bagaces, and after about 8km follow the road off to the left; note that it's in pretty bad condition. It's also possible to reach the reserve from Palo Verde via a very rough 7km track from the national park's entrance; ask at the ranger station if

the road is passable before trying this route.

By taxi It's possible to arrange a taxi from Bagaces (around ₡20,000 round trip).

Tourist information The visitor centre is on the scenic banks of the Río Cabuyo, and can provide information about the reserve.

Cordillera de Guanacaste

5

Cutting a large diagonal swathe through the region's uppermost reaches, the rugged
CORDILLERA DE GUANACASTE stretches from Volcán Arenal in the southeast to
Volcán Orosi in the northwest in Parque Nacional Guanacaste. At its heart, **Volcán
Miravalles** and **Volcán Tenorio** loom large over the hot Guanacaste lowlands.
Miravalles, at 2028m the highest volcano in Guanacaste, is home to an important
forest reserve with abundant wildlife and birds, though it's not open to the public;
while Tenorio, standing at 1916m, forms the centrepiece of an increasingly popular
national park. From **Hwy-6**, a reasonably maintained 58-kilometre stretch that runs
between the two volcanoes, you can contemplate the spectacular colour changes and
cloud shadows on their flanks.

TROPICAL DRY FOREST

With its mainly deciduous cover, Guanacaste's **tropical dry forest**, created by the combination of
a Pacific lowland topography and arid conditions, looks startlingly different depending upon the
time of year. In the height of the dry season, almost no rain falls on lowland Guanacaste, trees
denude themselves of leaves to conserve water, and the landscape takes on a melancholy, burnt-
sienna hue. In April or May, when the rains come, the whole of Guanacaste perks up and begins to
look comparatively green, although the dry forest never takes on the lush look of the rainforest.

The story of the demise of the tropical dry forests in Mesoamerica is one of nearly wholesale
destruction. In all, only about two percent of the region's pre-Columbian dry forest survives,
and what was once a carpet stretching the length of the Pacific side of the isthmus from
southern Mexico to Panama now exists only in besieged pockets. Today, dry forests cover just
518 square kilometres of Costa Rica, almost all in Guanacaste, concentrated around the Río
Tempisque and, more significantly, north in the Parque Nacional Santa Rosa. Due to
deforestation and climatic change, tropical dry forests are considered a rare life zone. Their
relative dryness means they are easily overrun by field fires, which ranchers light in order to
burn off old pasture. Hardy grasses spring up in their wake, such as the imported African
jaragua, which gives much of Guanacaste its African savannah-like appearance.

TREE SPECIES

Along with the leafy trees, tropical dry forest features **palms** and even a few **evergreens**.
At the very top of a good thick patch of dry forest you see the umbrella form of **canopy trees**,
although these are much shorter than in the tropical rainforest. The humid rainforest has about
three or four layers of vegetation, whereas dry forest is a far less complex ecosystem; like
temperate-zone deciduous forests, the tropical dry forest has only two strata. The ground
shrub layer is fleshed out by thorn bushes and tree ferns, primitive plants that have been with
us since the time of the dinosaurs. Unlike rainforest, dry forest has very few epiphytes (plants
growing on the trees), except for bromeliads (the ones that look something like upside-down
pineapple leaves). The most biologically diverse examples of tropical dry forest are in the lower
elevations of Parque Nacional Santa Rosa, where the canopy trees are a good height, with
many different species of deciduous tree. There are also some pockets of mangroves and even
a few evergreens in the wetter parts of the park.

WILDLIFE

Tropical dry forests can support a large variety of **mammal life**, as in the Parque Nacional Santa
Rosa–Parque Nacional Guanacaste corridor. Deer and smaller mammals, such as the coati and
paca, are most common, along with large cats, from the jaguar to the ocelot, provided they have
enough room to hunt. You may see the endangered **scarlet macaw** – which likes to feed on the
seeds of the sandbox tree – in a few remaining pockets of Pacific dry forest, including Lomas
Barbudal and, further south, around Río Tárcoles and Parque Nacional Carara (see p.337), itself a
transition zone between the dry forests of the north and the wetter tropical cover of the southern
Pacific coast. In addition, the staggering number and diversity of **insects** are of great interest to
biologists and entomologists: there are more than two hundred types of bee in Lomas Barbudal,
for example, and a large number of butterflies and moths in Parque Nacional Santa Rosa.

5

Parque Nacional Volcán Tenorio

3.5km southeast of Bijagua • Daily 8am–4pm (last entry 2pm) • US$12

An active volcano (1916m), although so far without spectacular eruptive displays, **TENORIO** was designated a national park in 1995. Though most people come to the park to glimpse the surreal turquoise waters of the **Río Celeste**, wildlife also thrives within the park's borders, and you may be lucky enough to spot tapirs, agoutis, armadillos, long-tailed manakins and howler monkeys.

A **trail** (6km; 4hr round trip) departs from the ranger station at the park entrance and enters the forest where it eventually splits into a few well-marked loops. Don't wander from the trails, for the area is geothermically active; there are fumaroles (little columns of hot vapour escaping from the ground) and mud pots – one false move and you could step into skin-stripping superheated volcanic soil. The main trail climbs steadily and opens up to a spectacular view of Volcán Miravalles, before eventually leading to a striking waterfall of the Río Celeste where you can take a dip. The highlights of the park, though, are a stunningly blue lagoon, the **Laguna Azul**, and similarly coloured (bright blue) sections of the river that flow alongside the trail – all created by a rare mix of sulphur, copper sulphate and calcium carbonate.

The park – and, indeed, much of this part of Guanacaste – was hit hard by Hurricane Otto in late 2016; at the time of writing it was unclear quite what impact this had had on the flora and fauna and the park's infrastructure.

ARRIVAL AND DEPARTURE PARQUE NACIONAL VOLCÁN TENORIO

By car From the Reserva Biológica Privada La Pacífica, 7km north of Cañas, turn north off the Interamericana onto the paved road towards Bijagua (Hwy-6), where there's a sign by the supermarket for the turn-off to the park.

ACCOMMODATION AND EATING

Restaurante Los Pilones Opposite the ranger station ☎ 8866 8088. The only place to eat in the national park is the friendly *Restaurante Los Pilones*, in a whitewashed building with outside seating and a pleasant overlook. It serves reasonably priced, well-made *comida típica*, such as chicken with rice-and-beans (around ₡3000). Daily 10am–8pm.

Río Celeste Hideaway 2km south of the entrance to Parque Nacional Volcán Tenorio on Hwy-4 ☎ 2206 5114, ⓦ riocelestehideaway.com. Within walking distance of the national park entrance, this striking property has elegant earth-toned *casitas* (sleeping up to four), each adorned with handsome dark-wood furnishings and four-poster beds, facing either the garden or the forest. Amenities include outdoor showers, TVs and private terraces. There's also a pretty pool with its own wet bar, as well as a classy restaurant. US$150

Bijagua

Some 40km north of Cañas, roughly equidistant to the two volcanoes, is the small hamlet of **BIJAGUA**. The impressively enterprising community is home to a number of ecotourism projects, including an ecology centre, organic farms and a collective of female artisans. Though there is little to detain you, it's a good spot to stock up on picnic supplies before venturing into the national park, or take a tour to Refugio Nacional de Vida Silvestre Caño Negro (see p.224; lodges in Bijagua can arrange day-trips), travelling via the spectacular road north to Upala, from where you can glimpse the shimmering blue waters of Lago de Nicaragua and the Islas Solentiname.

In late 2016, Hurricane Otto caused major flooding in Bijagua, killing five people and destroying a number of homes and farms, and it is likely to be some time before the town is fully back on its feet. Staying a night at one of the lodges or having a meal at a restaurant here are small ways tourists can help speed up the recovery.

ARRIVAL AND DEPARTURE BIJAGUA

By bus There's a small bus stop on the main road in the centre of the village.

Destinations Cañas (10 daily; 1hr 5min); Upala (9 daily; 40min).

ACCOMMODATION

La Carolina Lodge 7km northeast from Bijagua, in the hamlet of San Miguel ☎2466 6393, ⓦcms .lacarolinalodge.com. The rustic *La Carolina Lodge* is set on a working farm well off the beaten path amid tranquil surroundings and has rooms in the main lodge, *cabinas* (sleeping up to three) and larger, self-contained houses off the grounds (sleeping up to seven). Rates include full board and activities. By the lodge is a (swimmable) river where toucans, green parrots and hummingbirds nest, and where you might also catch a glimpse of sloths and anteaters. Horseriding, yoga, birdwatching and even cow-milking are on offer, trips to Parque Nacional Tenorio can be arranged, and the owners offer transport from Liberia; alternatively, a taxi from Bijagua to the lodge costs about ₡7500. Doubles/*cabinas* US$170, houses US$190

Casitas Tenorio About 3km east of Bijagua ☎8312 1248, ⓦcasitastenorio.com. Five charming and comfortable *casitas* on a farm with views of Volcán Miravalles. There is an outdoor kitchen, and the friendly owners can arrange guided hikes and tours of the area as well as volunteering opportunities. *Casitas* US$95

Heliconias Lodge 3km north of Bijagua on the road to Upala ☎2466 8483, ⓦheliconiaslodge.net. At 750m elevation in a private forest reserve right between the volcanoes, this beautifully sited lodge holds several hiking trails, waterfalls and natural hot springs. The accommodation consists of six cabins (sleeping up to four) with private bath, and four smartly designed, spacious cottages (sleeping up to four); there's also a restaurant and stunning views from around the grounds. The lodge can arrange walking tours of Parque Nacional Volcán Tenorio as well as trips to the Refugio Nacional de Vida Silvestre Caño Negro. Cabins US$95, cottages US$130

The Miravalles hot springs

Over 26,000 acres encircling **Volcán Miravalles** are given over to the Miravalles Protected Zone, a diverse mix of cloudforest and dry savannah, home to a wide variety of species, including peccaries, coyotes and capuchin and howler monkeys. While the Protected Zone is not open to the public the surrounding area holds numerous enticing **hot springs** and mud pools, by-products of the extensive underground geothermal activity. A handful of complexes have been erected around the more accessible hot springs, all of which are within easy reach of Bijagua, making an afternoon or evening visit ideal after a hike in Parque Nacional Volcán Tenorio.

Las Hornillas Volcanic Activity Center

4km northeast of Bagaces • Daily 8am–5pm • US$35 entry to the center, mud pools, crater walks, sauna and water-slide; waterfall US$40; everything US$55; all rates include lunch • ☎8839 9769, ⓦhornillas.com

One of the first operators in the area to capitalize on Miravalles' geothermic activity, **Las Hornillas Volcanic Activity Center** offers dips in large mud pools, soothing hot springs, swimming pools, walks to and around an active crater, a sauna, a torpedo-like ride down a never-ending water slide and a pretty hike through the forest to two nearby waterfalls. The facilities are not as well maintained as they could be, but the owners are friendly and the views – drifting clouds permitting – can be spectacular.

Yökö Termales

3km northeast of Bagaces • Daily 7am–10pm • US$10 • ☎2673 0410, ⓦyokotermales.com

If you're mainly interested in a therapeutic soak, inexpensive **Yökö Termales** is a good bet with its five hot springs surrounded by a manicured lawn near the base of Miravalles. It's not usually as busy as some of the other options in the area, and the layout is reminiscent of a water park. You can order food and drinks from a poolside bar.

Parque Nacional Rincón de la Vieja

About 25km northeast of Liberia • Tues–Sun 8am–3pm • US$15 • ☎2661 8139, ⓦacguanacaste.ac.cr

Perhaps Guanacaste's most memorable national park, the entirety of **PARQUE NACIONAL RINCÓN DE LA VIEJA** is utterly dominated by its massive and majestic namesake volcano, a perfectly proportioned conical peak. In the park's eastern sector, the crater of Volcán Santa María is impressive in its own right, even if it's not quite as

PARQUE NACIONAL GUANACASTE

PARQUE NACIONAL RINCÓN DE LA VIEJA

Quebrada Grande

ACCOMMODATION
Borinquen Mountain Resort	1
Buena Vista Lodge	3
Casa Rural Aroma de Campo	4
Hacienda Guachipelín	2
Rinconcito Lodge	5
El Sol Verde	6

Volcán Rincón de la Vieja (1895m)

Volcán Santa María (1916m)

SECTOR PAILAS

SECTOR SANTA MARÍA

Hornillas (Steam Holes)

Las Pailas

Sendero Las Pailas

Entrance

Entrance

Santa María

Pailas de Barro (Mudpots)

Sendero Bosque Encantado

N

Nicaragua (102km)

INTERAMERICANA

Cañas Dulces   Curubandé

918

- - - - - Trail

0   2
kilometres

1

Liberia (5km)   Liberia (20km)   Bagaces (35km)

visually arresting. The beautifully dry landscape encompasses terrains varying from rock-strewn savannah to patches of tropical dry forest and it's undeniably an enchanting place, with quite simply the best **hiking** and **horseriding** in the country. A variety of elevations and habitats reveals hot springs, sulphur pools, bubbling **mud pots** (*pilas de barro*), fields of *guaria morada* (purple orchids) – the national flower – plus a great smoking volcano at the top to reward you for your efforts. **Animals** in the area include all the big cats (just don't expect to see them), the shy tapir, red deer, collared peccary, two-toed sloth, and howler, white-faced and spider monkeys. There's a good chance you will see a brilliant flash of fluttering blue – this is the **Blue Morpho** butterfly, famous for its electric colours. **Birders** will enjoy the profusion of over two hundred species in residence, and may spot the weird-looking three-wattled bellbird, the Montezuma oropendola, the trogon and the spectacled owl, among others.

The local dry season (Dec–March especially) is the **ideal time** to visit the park, when the hiking trails and visibility are at their best and the heat is fairly comfortable.

From Las Pailas ranger station (see p.254), you have several walking options: some trails lead west to the *cataratas escondidas* (hidden waterfalls), another runs east to the Santa María station, along an 8km path.

Sendero Las Pailas

The most popular and least demanding trail is **Sendero Las Pailas**. It has recently been updated, with smooth, concrete pathways and a wheelchair-accessible section. The *sendero* heads east on a very satisfying 6km circuit past many of the highly unusual natural features with which the park abounds, including a mini-volcano and **mud pots** (*pilas de barro*); listen out for strange bubbling sounds, like a large pot of water boiling over.

Mud pots, which should be treated with respect, are formed when mud, thermally heated by subterranean rivers of magma, seeks vents in the ground, sometimes actually forcing itself out through the surface in great thick gloops. It's a surreal sight: grey-brown muck blurping out of the ground like slowly thickening gravy. Another feature is the geothermal **hornillas** (literally, "stoves"), mystical-looking holes in the ground exhaling elegant puffs of steam. You almost expect to stumble upon the witches of *Macbeth*, brewing spite over them. Make sure not to go nearer than a metre or so, or

5

THE FLOWERING TREES OF GUANACASTE

Guanacaste's many flowering trees dot the landscape with pastel puffs of colour. Trees blossom in a strange way in the dry lands of Guanacaste, flowering literally overnight and then, just as suddenly, shedding their petals to the ground, covering it in a carpet of confetti colours. The **corteza amarilla** bursts into a wild Van Gogh-like blaze in March, April and May, and is all the more dramatic for being set against a landscape of burnt siennas, muted mauves and sallow yellows. The **guanacaste** tree itself, also called the "elephant ear", is a majestic wide-canopied specimen and an emblem of the nation. Its cream-coloured flowers appear in May, and its curious seedpods feed the cattle and horses.

In November the deciduous **guachipelín** tree blooms, with its delicate fern-like leaves; in January it's time for the pastel-pink floss of the **poui**, followed in March by the equally pretty **tabebuia rosea**. By the end of the dry season, the red flowers of the **malinche** explode into colour.

you'll be steamed in no time. The combined effect of all these boiling holes is to make the landscape a bit like brittle Swiss cheese – tread gingerly and look carefully where you're going to avoid the ground crumbling underneath you. Many hikers have been scalded by blithely strolling too close to the holes. The trail also takes you through forest with abundant fauna and flora, and be prepared to ford a couple of streams.

The hike to the summit

The most direct approach to the crater and summit of the Rincón de la Vieja volcano is via the Las Pailas entrance, along a marked trail. This trail was **closed** in 2015 because of increased volcanic activity, which resulted in several eruptions in March 2016. However, there are hopes that it will reopen in the future, so it's definitely worth checking the latest when you visit.

When it is open, the hike to the summit is undoubtedly the **highlight of the park**; it's hard to get lost, but the top is 7.7km away, so you should start early to get up and down without hurrying too much. Low visibility and high winds are also issues to be aware of, and it's worth phoning ahead to check conditions before setting out. The trail takes you through forest similar to lower montane rainforest, densely packed, and lushly covered with epiphytes and mosses. Cool mist and rain often plague this section of the trail: if you are anywhere near the top and lose visibility, which can happen very suddenly, you're advised to stay away from the crater, whose brittle and ill-defined edges become more difficult to see, and consequently more dangerous, in cloudy weather.

At the **summit**, Rincón de la Vieja presents a barren lunar landscape, a smoking hole surrounded by black ash, with a pretty freshwater **lake**, Lago los Jilgueros, to the south. Quetzals are said to live in the forest that surrounds the lake, though you're unlikely to see them. When clear, the **views** up here are ample reward for the uphill sweating, with Lago de Nicaragua shimmering silver-blue to the north, the hump of the Cordillera Central to the southeast and the Pacific Ocean and spiny profile of the Nicoya Peninsula to the west. You can get hammered by wind at the top; bring a jumper and windbreaker.

Sendero Bosque Encantado

From the Santa María entrance, there is a more difficult and longer walk to the crater. This is also currently closed, but there are a number of other worthwhile trails, including the three-kilometre **Sendero Bosque Encantado** (Enchanted Forest Trail). It leads to a small forest and some hot springs next to a creek, which hikers love to leap into after a wallow in the springs, imitating a sauna effect. The temperature is usually just about right for soaking, but you should never jump into any thermal water without first checking current temperatures at the ranger station.

5

SAFETY IN RINCÓN DE LA VIEJA

The land here is actually alive and breathing: Rincón de la Vieja's last major eruptions took place in 1995 and 1998, and were serious enough to evacuate local residents. The danger has always been to the northern side of the volcano, facing Nicaragua (the opposite side from the two entrance points), and the most pressing **safety** issue for tourists is to be aware that rivers of lava and hot mud still boil beneath the thin epidermis of ground. While danger areas are clearly marked with signs and fences, you still have to watch your step: walkers have been seriously **burned** from crashing through this crust and stepping into mud and water at above-boiling temperatures.

If you stay at one of the lodges and take their summit tours, either by horseback or on foot, you may pass through areas not covered in this section. Also, bear in mind that Rincón de la Vieja is an active volcano, and the trails described may be altered due to periodic **lava flows**. Before setting out, you should always check current conditions at one of the ranger stations, or call the Área de Conservación de Guanacaste (ACG) headquarters at the Parque Nacional Santa Rosa. It's also advisable to carry all your **drinking water** – streams might look inviting, but often carry high concentrations of minerals (like sulphur) that can lead to extreme stomach upset if drunk.

ARRIVAL AND INFORMATION

Park entrances The park is split into two sectors: Sector Las Pailas ("The cauldrons") and Sector Santa María, each with its own entrance and nearby ranger station. The two are linked by an 8km walking trail. From Liberia most people travel through the hamlet of Curubandé, about 10km northeast, to the Las Pailas sector. The other ranger station, Santa María, lies about 25km northeast of Liberia.

By private transfer Getting here from Liberia is easy – transfers (around US$20) run by hotels such as *La Posada del Tope* and *Hotel Liberia* (see p.257) are convenient and good value.

By car To get to the Las Pailas sector by car (you'll almost certainly need a 4WD), where most of the lodges are, take

PARQUE NACIONAL RINCÓN DE LA VIEJA

the Interamericana north of Liberia for 6km, then turn right to the hamlet of Curubandé. Here you'll see signs for the *Guachipelín* and *Casa Rural Aroma de Campo* lodges. A couple of kilometres before *Guachipelín* there's a barrier and tollbooth, where you'll be charged ₡700 to use the road. The Santa María sector and the *Rinconcito Lodge* are reached by driving through Liberia's Barrio La Victoria in the northeast of the town; ask for the *estadio* – the football stadium – from where it's a signed 24km drive to the park.

On foot Both routes to the park are along stony roads, not at all suitable for walking. People do, but it's tough, uninteresting terrain, and it's really more advisable to save your energy for the trails within the park itself.

ACCOMMODATION

Borinquen Mountain Resort About 3km northwest of the Las Pailas park entrance ☎ 2690 1900, ⊛ borinquen resort.com. High-end lodge with its own spa centre, mud pools and sauna, set in a stunning landscape at the skirts of Volcán Rincón de la Vieja. Accommodation is in luxurious and fully equipped villas and bungalows (both sleeping up to five). There's a classy restaurant, disabled access and facilities for children. They also organize horseriding and ATV (all-terrain vehicle) excursions to the volcano. Villas **US$219**, bungalows **US$244**

Buena Vista Lodge 2km north of Cañas Dulces and 20km west of the Las Pailas park entrance ☎ 2665 7759, ⊛ buenavistalodgecr.com. A working cattle ranch – you can even ride with the cowhands if your horsemanship is up to it – with stupendous views over Guanacaste and some great trails through pockets of rainforest on the flanks of the volcano and up to the crater. The rooms are housed in individual bungalows, many set around a small lake in which you can swim. A restaurant serves up wholesome meals, and there are reasonably priced horseriding and hiking tours, and cookery and arts

classes available – the place even has its very own canopy tour. If you're driving here, a 4WD is recommended; alternatively, you can arrange to be picked up from Cañas Dulces (which is accessible from Liberia by bus). **US$75**

Casa Rural Aroma de Campo 2.5km northeast of Curubandé ☎ 2665 0008, ⊛ aromadecampo.com. A short drive from the national park, this idyllic B&B has a peaceful rural setting, and a blend of colourful rooms (think green and purple walls) in the main hacienda-style building and larger, artfully decorated suites in converted shipping containers (sleeping up to four; US$116). The owners are charming, and there's a friendly (and early rising) parrot named Koki, a small pool fed from a nearby river, and plenty of hammocks and easy chairs. Dinner is served "family style" on a communal table. **US$81**

Hacienda Guachipelín 5km beyond Curubandé on the edge of the park ☎ 2666 8075, ⊛ guachipelin.com. A working ranch, the *Guachipelín* looks every inch the old cattle hacienda, with comfortable en suites in the main house and a fantastic pool. There's a nearby waterfall, and also an adventure centre on-site with a wide range of activities, including nature walks, horseriding, mountain biking and hot springs. Pick-ups from Liberia can be arranged for a fee. US$118

Rinconcito Lodge In San Jorge, 3km south of the Santa María park entrance ☎ 2666 2764, ⓦ rinconcito lodge.com. The cheapest option close to the park, this farm is owned by a friendly family and has plain but good-value *cabinas*. The owners are a good source of advice on local transport, guides and directions, and can also arrange horseriding, guided tours and pick-ups from Liberia. All meals are available at an additional cost. US$58

El Sol Verde Curubandé ☎ 2665 5357, ⓦ elsolverde .com. Located on the edge of the village of Curubandé, this laidback lodge and campsite has two doubles and a quad (US$71), all with attached bathrooms and fans, plus camping spots and two permanently fixed tents (sleeping up to two; US$29.50). Meals are available – though only breakfast is included in the rates – and there's a library and collection of board games, in case you need something to keep you occupied. Staff can organize tours and transport to the national park. Camping US$10, doubles US$52

Liberia and around

True to its name, the spirited provincial capital of **LIBERIA** (from *libertad*, meaning liberty) is distinctively friendly and progressive, its wide streets the legacy of the pioneering farmers and cattle ranchers who founded it. Known colloquially as the "Ciudad Blanca" (White City) due to its whitewashed houses, Liberia is the only town in Costa Rica that seems truly colonial in style and character. Many of the white houses still have their **puerta del sol** – corner doors that were used, ingeniously, to let the sun in during the morning and out in the late afternoon, thus heating and then cooling the interior throughout the day – an architectural feature left over from the colonial era and particular to this region.

Most travellers use Liberia simply as a jumping-off point for the national parks of **Rincón de la Vieja** and **Santa Rosa**, an overnight stop to or from the **beaches** of Guanacaste, or a break on the way to Nicaragua. However, Liberia is an appealing city, particularly if you explore on foot in the shade of its numerous mango trees. The nearby international airport – which has undergone a recent expansion – delivers ever-increasing coachloads of visitors to the western beaches, but Liberia happily remains unchanged, at least for now: it's still the epitome of dignified (if somewhat static) provincialism, with a strong identity and atmosphere all its own.

5

Attractions in the city itself are pretty limited, though the old city prison was being turned into a municipal museum at the time of writing.

Parque Central

Av Central/1, C Central/2

The town is arranged around a large **Parque Central**, officially called Parque Mario Cañas Ruiz, named after a twentieth-century poet and musician whose songs paid tribute to *sabanero* culture. The *parque* is dedicated to *el mes del anexión*, the month of the annexation (July), celebrating the fact that Guanacaste is not in Nicaragua. Liberia's Parque Central is one of the loveliest central plazas in the whole country, ringed by benches and tall palms that shade gossiping locals. On the eastern edge of the *parque* is the town **church**, a contemporary structure whose startlingly modernist – some would say downright ugly – form looks a little out of place in this very traditional city.

Iglesia de la Agonía

Av Central, at C 11 • Irregular hours • Free

The colonial, gleaming white **Iglesia de la Agonía** on the eastern end of the city was long on the verge of collapse – it had a hard time in successive earthquakes – but a recent renovation has infused it with new life. It's rarely open, though it is worth giving the heavy wooden door a shove just in case. If it gives way, inside you'll see numerous remnants of the church's storied history, including ecclesiastical paintings hanging from the pillars, and imposing statues.

Calle Real

The most historic street in Liberia is the **Calle Real** (marked as Calle Central on some maps). In the nineteenth century this street was the entrance to Liberia, and practically the whole road has been restored to its original colonial simplicity. Stately white adobe homes feature large windows with ornate wooden frames and wide overhanging eaves under which locals pass the evenings in cane armchairs.

ARRIVAL AND DEPARTURE
LIBERIA AND AROUND

By plane 12km west of the town, Liberia's sizeable international airport is connected to domestic destinations by regular Sansa and NatureAir flights; there are also numerous international flights. You can take a taxi from here into town (around ₡10,000); many buses (see below) travelling between Liberia and Tamarindo also call at the airport, or you can walk 15min from the terminal to the main road, where any eastbound bus will take you to Liberia.

Destinations via Sansa Nosara (1 daily; 1hr 10min); Playa Sámara (Mon–Sat 1 daily; 1hr); San José (4–5 daily; 1hr); Tamarindo (1 daily; 20min); Tambor (1 daily; 30min).

Destinations via NatureAir Playa San José (2–3 daily; 1hr); Tamarindo (2 daily; 20min).

By bus Liberia is the main regional transport hub, providing easy access to Guanacaste's parks and beaches, the Nicaraguan border (see p.268) and San José. The city's bus terminal is on the western edge of town near the exit for the Interamericana – it's a 10min walk at most from here to the centre of town – and serves all destinations except San José. At the bus station is an elaborate list of departure times; these are pure fiction, so you must check with the ticket office. San José buses arrive at and depart from the more modern Pulmitan terminal, a block southeast of the main bus terminal.

Destinations Bagaces (every 30min; 30min–1hr); Cañas (every 30min; 1hr); La Cruz (every 45min–1hr; 40min–1hr); Nicoya (every 30min–1hr; 1hr 40min); Parque Nacional Santa Rosa (every 45min; 30min); Peñas Blancas (every 45min; 1hr 30min); Playa del Coco (hourly; 1hr); Playa Hermosa (11 daily; 1hr); Playa Panamá (8 daily; 1hr 20min); Puntarenas (9 daily; 3hr); San José (11–16 daily; 4hr 30min); Santa Cruz (every 30min; 1hr 10min); Tamarindo (every 30min–1hr; some travel via the airport; 1hr 30min–2hr).

By car If you're coming by car, you should take the exit off the Interamericana at an intersection with traffic lights and three petrol stations – known as La Esquina de las Bombas (Gas Station Corner). Turning left (if coming from the south) takes you to the beaches, while a right takes you along the town's Avenida Central, lined with floppy mango trees.

FROM LIBERIA TO SANTA ROSA AND RINCÓN DE LA VIEJA

5

For **Parque Nacional Santa Rosa** (40min), take a La Cruz or Peñas Blancas bus. You should take the earliest one possible to give yourself time for walking; ask the driver to let you off at Santa Rosa – it takes about an hour to walk from here to the park's administration centre. You can also reach the park by *colectivo* taxi (around US$20/car), shared between four or five people. Catch one at the northwestern corner of Parque Central. *Colectivo* taxis are also good value if you're heading to **Parque Nacional Rincón de la Vieja** or the lodges near Las Pailas ranger station (roughly US$30 for four people). Pretty much the best way to get to Rincón de la Vieja is to travel with one of the Liberia hotels – *La Posada del Tope*, *Hotel Liberia* and *Hotel Guanacaste* can all arrange transport to the park. All services are open to non-guests, though hotel guests get first option.

INFORMATION AND TOURS

Car rental Liberia is a useful place to rent a car, with many operators, mostly along the road to the beaches; 5km east of the airport on Hwy-21, Vamos Rent-A-Car (☏ 2665 7650, 🌐 vamosrentacar.com) is a great choice with a fleet of 4WDs. Most hotels can also arrange car rental, with *La Posada del Tope* consistently offering the best deals. It's definitely worth considering a 4WD, as the potholed roads can easily cause a flat tyre in a smaller car.

Tourist information There's an ICT office 50m west of the *guardia rural* (☏ 2666 2976, ✉ ictliberia@ict.go .cr), a few kilometres north of Liberia on the Interamericana, but staff at *La Posada del Tope* (see below) are usually better sources of information.

Travel agencies The best operator in the city is Offi Tours (☏ 8899 8149, 🌐 offitours.com), which offers fun and informative excursions to the nearby national parks and the Guanacaste beaches as well as day-trips to Monteverde and Granada, Nicaragua. Tour prices are generally per vehicle, so it makes sense to go with a group. *La Posada del Tope* (see below) run tours to attractions in the surrounding area, including Rincón de la Vieja, Palo Verde and the Guanacaste beaches.

ACCOMMODATION

Liberia has a vast range of hotels, hostels and guesthouses, but apart from a few notable exceptions standards are relatively low, while prices are on the high side across the board.

El Bramadero Av 1, at the Interamericana ☏ 2666 0371, 🌐 hotelbramadero.com. Despite an unprepossessing setting, right on the Interamericana and next to a *McDonald's*, this motel-style place is a decent choice. The a/c rooms are clean and comfy, even if they're far from stylish; noise isn't as much of a problem as you might expect, but it's wise to get one towards the rear of the property. There's a small pool and an okay restaurant. <u>US$73</u>

Hospedaje Dodero Av 1, at the Interamericana ☏ 8729 7524, 🌐 hospedajedodero.yolasite.com. A block away from the bus station, this no-frills hostel does the basics well: neat six-bed dorms; clean if tiny private rooms with TVs and shared bathrooms (plus fans or a/c); communal kitchen; friendly welcome; and a range of tour and transport options. Dorms <u>US$11</u>, doubles <u>US$26</u>

Hotel Guanacaste Av 1, 300m south of the bus station ☏ 2666 0085, ✉ guanacaste.hotel@gmail .com. Popular, HI-affiliated hostel, with a traveller-friendly cafeteria-restaurant. The dorms and rooms are simple and clean but a bit gloomy. The hostel fills up quickly, so book ahead. With an HI card you get a fifteen percent discount, and you might wangle a further ten percent with a student ID. Staff organize transfers to Rincón de la Vieja and Santa Rosa, and can arrange car rentals as well. Dorms <u>US$14</u>, doubles <u>US$36</u>

Hotel Javy C 19, at Av 19, 2km northeast of the main square ☏ 2666 9253, 🌐 hoteljavy.com. Charming, professionally run hotel with spick-and-span en-suite rooms, set around a leafy courtyard garden. The only downside is the location, northeast of the city centre in the Pueblo Nuevo neighbourhood – the walk in can be a bit of a slog in the heat of the day. <u>US$60</u>

Hotel Liberia C Central, 75m south of Parque Central ☏ 2666 0161, 🌐 hotelliberiacr.com. Well-established, friendly youth-hostel-type hotel in a colonial-era building set around a sunny courtyard restaurant. As well as reasonable dorms, there are good-value (for Liberia) private rooms with TVs and attached bathrooms; the newer ones in the annexe to the rear are the best of the bunch. Staff offer transfers to Rincón de la Vieja and the airport. It's popular, so book well ahead, especially in the high season. Dorms <u>US$15</u>, doubles <u>US$48</u>

La Posada del Tope C Central, 150m south of the Gobernación ☏ 2666 3876, 🌐 facebook.com/Hotel LaPosadaDelTope. Popular budget hotel in a beautiful historic house. The rooms (with fans and shared bathrooms) in the old part of the hotel are basic and a bit stuffy; the

5

LA COCINA GUANACASTECA: CORN COOKING

Corn is still integral to the regional cuisine of Guanacaste, thanks to the Chorotegas, who cultivated maize (corn) to use in many inventive ways. One pre-Columbian corn concoction involved roasting and grinding the maize, and then combining the meal-like paste with water and chocolate to make the drink *chicha*. Although you can't find this version of *chicha* any more you can still get **grain-based drinks** in Guanacaste, such as *horchata* (made with rice or corn and spiced with cinnamon), or *pinolillo* (made with roasted corn), both milky and sweet, with an unmistakeably grainy texture.

Corn also shows up in traditional Guanacastecan snacks such as **tanelas** (like a cheese scone, but made with cornflour) and **rosquillas**, small rings of cornflour that taste like a combination between tortillas and doughnuts. You can buy these at roadside stalls and small shops in Liberia. Served throughout the country, **chorreados** crop up on menus in Guanacaste: they're a kind of pancake made (again) with cornflour and served with *natilla*, the local version of sour cream.

more modern ones (with TVs) across the street in the annexe are set around a charming courtyard. The cleanliness isn't always as high as it should be, but there's plenty of character here. Staff (and especially the manager) are good sources of information, and transport is offered to Rincón de la Vieja, as well as trips to Palo Verde. <u>US$26</u>

EATING

Liberia has a strong dining scene with several above-average restaurants serving local dishes such as **natilla** (sour cream) eaten with eggs or *gallo pinto* and tortillas. For a real feast, try **desayuno guanacasteco**, a hearty local breakfast of tortillas, sour cream, eggs, rice-and-beans, and sometimes meat. You can get rock-bottom lunches from the **stalls** at the bus terminal or the *sodas* at the nearby covered market, and Guanacastecan **corn snacks** from stalls all over town.

★**Café Liberia** C Real, Av 2/4 ☎2665 1660, ⓦ cafeliberia.com. Wonderful café and arts centre set in a historic house that screens films and hosts occasional live performances. Long the best place in town to relax with a cup of coffee and hear locals discuss the region's latest political and arts developments, it also serves some of the area's more inspired meals: try one of the inventive salads, a ceviche or the wagyu burger (all ₡4000–5000). Mon–Sat 10am–6pm.

Cantarranas Tacos 5km down the road towards the beaches, 50m back from the road on the right. Nondescript Mexican restaurant on the road from Liberia to the beaches – and a bit of a local secret. Delicious tacos (around ₡1500–2500) are served inside or alfresco. Great atmosphere and staff. Mon–Sat 9am–6pm.

Casero Express Av 1, at C Central. Basic *soda* with counter seating and small tables churning out staples like grilled chicken with rice-and-beans and fried plantains (dishes ₡3000–4000). Though it lacks atmosphere, it's handily located, economical and popular with locals. Daily 5am–10pm.

Los Comales C Real, Av 5/7, 200m north of the northeast corner of Parque Central. A typical Costa Rican *soda*, very popular with Liberia residents for its generous portions of tasty rustic food, with *gallo pinto*s and *casados* costing around ₡3000; there are also several rice dishes on offer. Daily 7am–9pm.

Copa de Oro C Real, at Av 2 ☎2666 0532. Bang in the centre of town, this stalwart is famous for its fish and seafood. Try one of the rice dishes with octopus or prawns, the seafood soup or the grilled sea bass fillet. Mains ₡2700–10,000. Mon–Sat 11am–10pm.

Jauja Av Central, C 8/10 ☎2665 2061, ⓦrestaurante jaujacr.com. One of the better restaurants in town, though very touristy. Large and tasty pasta dishes and pizzas (₡5500–13,000), plus the usual steak, chicken and fish: the daily-changing lunch special (around ₡3300) is the best-value option. It's all served in a pleasant, outdoor garden setting, although the big-screen TV can be off-putting. Mon–Fri 7am–10pm, Sat & Sun noon–10pm.

Pizza Pronto C 1, at Av 4 ☎2666 2098. Rustic-chic local favourite where dark-wood tables are covered with topographical maps of Guanacaste. Look beyond the short selection of salads and pasta dishes, and go for one of the pizzas (₡6000–12,000), which are baked in an adobe clay oven. Some rather unusual toppings are available – octopus, smoked salmon, peach, etc – but the classic combos are the best bets. Daily 11am–11pm.

DRINKING AND NIGHTLIFE

The main evening activity at the weekend involves watching the locals parading around the Parque Central in their finery, having an ice cream, and maybe going to the movies at Multicines Liberia (ⓦmulticinesliberia.net), located in the shopping mall 1km south of the main Interamericana intersection. Beyond that, there are a couple of **clubs** that regularly teem with action.

Kurú About 200m west of the Interamericana down the road to the beaches. The town's main disco gets lively with young locals showing off their best salsa and merengue moves, especially on weekends and holidays. Tues–Sat 6pm–late.

DIRECTORY

Banks and exchange There are plenty of banks, many on Av Central, leading into town, several with ATMs, including the Banco de Costa Rica, across from Parque Central.
Hospital Just off C 13, east of the football stadium ☎ 2666 0011.

Post office Av 3, at C 8 (Mon–Fri 7.30am–6pm, Sat 7.30am–noon). The efficient post office is a bit hard to find: it's between Av 3 and Av 5 in the low-slung white house across from an empty, square field bordered by mango trees.

Ponderosa Adventure Park

10km southeast of Liberia on the Interamericana, outside the town of El Salto • Daily 8am–5pm • US$50 • ☎ 2288 1000, Ⓦ ponderosaadventurepark.com

Ponderosa Adventure Park (formerly known as Africa Mia, among other names) is one of Guanacaste's most curious and highly touted attractions. The reserve has taken the region's resemblance to the African savannah one step further by populating several hundred acres with animals endemic to the continent, such as giraffes, zebras, giant elands, ostriches and warthogs; for good measure you can spot native wildlife too, including monkeys and various bird species. All of the animals roam free (there are no predators), and your best chance of seeing them is on one of the safari vehicle tours. The somewhat curious decision to import exotic animals into a country already teeming with wildlife aside, the preserve is exceedingly well run and there's no denying the thrill of seeing animals galloping about you that you might have only previously glimpsed in the confines of a zoo.

Recently it has expanded into an adventure park, offering horseriding, canopy tours, kayaking, 4WD trips and more (from US$50). There are also cafés, a restaurant and several shops on-site.

Northwestern Guanacaste

Densely forested and comparatively little-developed, **northwestern Guanacaste** feels much more isolated than its proximity to Liberia would indicate. Much of it is given over to a triumverate of striking protected areas: **Parque Nacional Santa Rosa**, **Parque Nacional Guanacaste** and **Refugio Nacional de Vida Silvestre Bahía Junquillal**. Together they form a large part of the ecologically significant Área de Conservación Guanacaste (Ⓦ acguanacaste.ac.cr), which provides an uninterrupted wildlife corridor extending from the Pacific to the Caribbean lowlands. Not surprisingly, conservation research takes precedence over tourism in this corner of the province, but there are still plenty of trails to explore and remote beaches to savour. Much of the coast along here sees few visitors, in fact, with one notable exception: **Bahía Salinas**, whose powerful winds draw kitesurfers from around the world.

5

Parque Nacional Santa Rosa

35km north of Liberia • Daily 8am–5pm; a maximum of twenty visitors are allowed access to the nesting area each day (ask at the administration centre or call the number listed) • US$15, which includes access to the Murciélago sector; guides around US$15/person • ☎ 2666 5051, ⓦ acguanacaste.ac.cr/turismo/sector-santa-rosa

Established in 1971 to protect a stretch of increasingly rare, dry tropical forest, **PARQUE NACIONAL SANTA ROSA** (also known as the Santa Rosa sector), is Costa Rica's oldest national park. Today it's also one of the most popular in the country, thanks to its good trails, great surfing (though poor swimming) and prolific turtle-spotting opportunities. It's also, given a few official restrictions, a great destination for **campers**, with a site on the beach.

Santa Rosa has an amazingly diverse topography for its size of 387 square kilometres, ranging from mangrove swamp to deciduous forest and savannah. Home to 115 species of mammal (half of them bats), 250 species of **bird** and 100 of **amphibian** and **reptile** (not to mention 3800 species of **moth**), Santa Rosa is a rich biological repository, attracting researchers from all over the world. Jaguars and pumas prowl the park, though you're unlikely to see them; what you may spot – at least in the dry season – are coati, coyotes and peccaries, often snuffling around watering holes.

The appearance of the park changes drastically between the **dry season**, when the many streams and small lakes dry up, trees lose their leaves, and thirsty animals can be

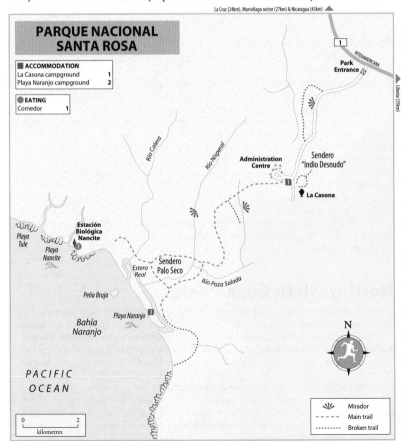

PARQUE NACIONAL
SANTA ROSA

La Cruz (24km), Murciélago sector (27km) & Nicaragua (43km)

ACCOMMODATION
La Casona campground ... 1
Playa Naranjo campground ... 2

EATING
Comedor ... 1

Park Entrance

INTERAMERICANA

Liberia (35km)

Río Colera

Río Nisperal

Administration Centre

Sendero "Indio Desnudo"

La Casona

Playa Tule

Estación Biológica Nancite

Playa Nancite

Estero Real

Sendero Palo Seco

Río Poza Salada

Peña Bruja

Playa Naranjo

Bahía Naranjo

PACIFIC OCEAN

N

0   2
kilometres

〰 Mirador
- - - Main trail
· · · · · Broken trail

seen at known water holes, and the **wet months**, which are greener, but afford fewer animal-viewing opportunities. From July to November, however, you may be able to witness hundreds of **olive ridley turtles** (*tortugas lloras*) dragging themselves out of the surf and nesting on Playa Nancite by moonlight; September and October are the months in which you are most likely to see them. Though too rough for swimming, the picturesque **beaches** of Naranjo and Nancite, about 12km down a bad road from the administration centre (see p.262), are popular with serious **surfers**. They're also great places to hang out for a while, or do a little camping and walking on the nearby trails.

La Casona

About 400m from the administration centre • Daily 8–11.30am & 1–3.30pm • Free

The formidable wooden and red-tiled homestead **La Casona** (Big House), one of Costa Rica's most famous historical sites, was for many years the centre of a working hacienda until the land was expropriated for the national park in 1972. In 2001 it was burned down by poachers, who were retaliating against arrests by park rangers. However, phoenix-like, it stands again after being lovingly (and painstakingly) reconstructed in less than a year – this time, with the addition of smoke alarms.

Information panels recount the various instances of derring-do which have occurred at La Casona, with resumés of the battles of March 20, 1856 – the confrontation between William Walker's filibusters and the Costa Rican forces (see box, p.265) – of 1919 (against the Nicaraguans), and of 1955, against another Nicaraguan, the dictator Anastasio Somoza García, who ruled the country from 1936 until his assassination in 1956. His hulk of a tank can still be seen, rusting and abandoned, along a signed road just beyond the entrance hut.

La Casona, set around a flowering courtyard, is full of rustic character. It's now entirely given over to **exhibitions**, and you are free to clamber up and down the steps and wander around the dark rooms, which have a significant population of resident bats. Many of the exhibits were destroyed in the fire, but there's some information on the life of the notorious William Walker (see box, p.265), remnants of dead animals and archeological remains. At one side of La Casona, a stair path leads up to a viewpoint with a magnificent perspective of the twin volcanoes of Parque Nacional Rincón de la Vieja.

The trails

Many of Santa Rosa's **trails** are intended for scientific researchers rather than tourists, and so are not well signed. If you do set off to walk, it's a good idea to hire a guide. If you walk only one trail in the entire park, make it the very short (1km) and undemanding *sendero natural*, which provides an introduction to the unique features of the tropical dry forest. Curving around from the road just before La Casona, it's signed as the **Sendero "Indio Desnudo"**, after the peeling-bark trees of the same name (also tongue-in-cheekily called "sunburned-tourist trees"). Along the trail you'll see acacia and **guapinol** trees, whose colloquial name is "stinking toe" on account of its smelly seedpods. Look out for monster iguanas hiding innocuously in tree branches, and for the ubiquitous bats.

From the administration centre a rough (but signposted) track leads past La Casona camping area, with several trails branching off along the way. Some of these may be restricted at any one time for research purposes; check first at the administration centre, however, as you can usually walk where you want as long as you let someone know. After about 5km you come to a fork, bearing left to Playa Naranjo, and right to Playa Nancite, both of which are about 3km further on.

Playa Nancite

Playa Nancite is a lovely grey-sand beach and when the tide has just gone out, it's as lustrous as a wet seal's skin. It is also the nesting home of the **olive ridley turtles**, a

5

BORDER CHECKS IN GUANACASTE

Driving along the Interamericana north of Liberia, don't be surprised to see a blue-suited *policía de tránsito* (traffic cop) or a light-brown-suited *guardia rural* (border police officer) leap out, kamikaze-like, into the highway directly in front of you – you'll need to stop and show your driver's licence and passport (which you must have on you at all times). These are routine checks, mainly to deter undocumented Nicaraguans from entering Costa Rica. The nearer the **border** you get, the more frequent the checks become. Make sure you drive carefully: knocking over a policeman is not a good move.

species which nests here and at Ostional near Nosara on the Nicoya Peninsula (see p.295). With none of the large tour groups you find at other Costa Rican turtle beaches, it's a great place to watch the **arribadas** (see box, p.34), during which up to eight thousand turtles – weighing on average around 40kg each – come ashore on any given evening, virtually covering the beach. According to estimates, more than eleven million eggs can be deposited by the turtles during a single *arribada*.

Due to riptides, Playa Nancite is no good for swimming but, as is usually the case, it's good for **surfers**, with huge, rolling, tubular waves.

Playa Naranjo

For the best surf you should head for **Playa Naranjo** (also known as Witch's Rock). Theoretically you can hike between the two beaches (2hr) on a narrow trail across the rocky headland, which opens out on top into hot, dry scrub cover, but you have to watch the tide, since the trail crosses the deep Estero Real, the drainage point for two rivers. Ask for the *marea* (tide times) from the administration centre before setting out.

ARRIVAL AND INFORMATION

By car Santa Rosa's entrance hut is 35km north of Liberia, signed from the Interamericana.

Maps and information After paying the park fee at the entrance hut, pick up a map and proceed some 6km or so, taking the right fork to the administration centre (daily

PARQUE NACIONAL SANTA ROSA

8am–5pm; ☎ 2666 5051), which can provide further information and also runs Guanacaste and Rincón de la Vieja national parks. You can check road conditions and get your camping/turtle-watching permits here.

GETTING AROUND

By car From the administration centre a rough road leads to the beaches; to drive to these, even in the height of the dry season, you need a sturdy 4WD. The administration discourages any driving at all beyond the main park road; nevertheless, people – surfers, mainly – insist on doing so, and survive. Most park their vehicle at the administration centre and walk. One thing is for sure: don't try to drive anywhere in the park (including the road to Cuajiniquil and the Murciélago sector to the north) in the rainy season without asking

rangers about the state of the roads. You could get bogged down in mud or stopped by a swollen creek. Before setting off for the park, you can always phone the Área de Conservación de Guanacaste (ACG) headquarters (☎2666 5051; Spanish only) to check the current state of the roads in the park.

On foot If you're walking down to the beach (8km), a ranger or fellow tourist will probably give you a ride, but on no account set out without water – you'll need a couple of litres per person, at least.

ACCOMMODATION

Camping facilities at Santa Rosa are some of the best in the country's national parks. Whichever of the two sites you pick, watch your fires (the area is a tinderbox in the dry season), take plastic bags for your food, do not leave anything edible in your tent (it will be stolen by scavenging coati) and, of course, carry plenty of water.

La Casona campground. The shady *La Casona* campground is the more comfortable of the two in the park, boasting both bathrooms and grill pits, and is open year-round. US$19

Playa Naranjo campground. This site is located right

on the beach, but is only open outside the turtle-nesting season. It isn't quite as well equipped as *La Casona*, thought it does have picnic tables and grill pits, and a ranger's hut with outhouses and showers plus, apparently, a boa constrictor in the roof. US$19

EATING

You can also buy snacks and drinks, including small bottles of water, at the administration centre. Alternatively, the petrol stations on the road from Liberia stock easy-to-carry bottles of water with plastic handles.

Comedor Adjacent to the administration centre. Make reservations at the administration centre (at least 3hr in advance) for a simple lunch in the basic comedor. The food – *casados* with fish, chicken or meat and salad (around ₡4000) – is good, and this is a great place to get talking to rangers and other tourists. Daily 11am–4pm.

Murciélago sector

9km west of Cuajiniquil • Daily 8am–6pm • US$15, which includes access to the Santa Rosa sector; surfing US$12 extra • ☎ 2666 5051,
Ⓦ acguanacaste.ac.cr/turismo/sector-murcielago

Few tourists go to ACG's **MURCIÉLAGO SECTOR**, an area of reserve to the northwest of – and entirely separate from – the Santa Rosa sector. It's a kind of reforestation laboratory in which former cattle pasture is slowly being regenerated, though there's also a campsite and a beach that's safe for swimming. Dirt roads lead from the Murciélago ranger station to a series of fine swimming beaches (this part is known as the **Área Recreativa Junquillal**), accessible by walking or by 4WD. The westernmost of these, **Playa Blanca**, a small white stretch of sand, is the prettiest and one of the most isolated and least visited in the country.

Just 30km from the border, Murciélago is home to the remains of the training grounds used by the CIA-backed **Contras** during the Nicaraguan civil war. They're overgrown and scrubby today, with no sign that anything was ever there. It was also the location of the famous "secret" airstrip built, on US National Security Council member Oliver North's orders, in direct violation of Costa Rica's declared neutrality in the conflict. Originally given the go-ahead by President Alberto Monge, the airstrip was eventually destroyed under President Oscar Arias's subsequent administration – a unilateral action that led to the US reducing its financial and political support for Costa Rica.

ARRIVAL AND INFORMATION   **MURCIÉLAGO SECTOR**

By car Drive along the Interamericana from the main Santa Rosa entrance about 10km north then take the left turn and go 8km to the hamlet of Cuajiniquil. A poor road continues here another 9km to the ranger station. Be sure to take the dirt road, not the paved one. You'll almost certainly need a 4WD, at least in the wet season, when there are two creeks to ford.

Border checks Officials are particularly vigilant in this area (see box opposite). As usual, have your passport and all other documents in order.

Ranger station 9km from Cuajiniquil (open daily 8am–7pm).

ACCOMMODATION

Murciélago Sector Campsite At the ranger station you can camp and arrange meals (at the Santa Rosa *comedor*; see above) with prior notification. Limited water and simple toilet facilities. <u>US$19</u>

Parque Nacional Guanacaste

36km north of Liberia on the Interamericana • Daily 8am–4pm • US$12 • ☎ 2666 5051, Ⓦ acguanacaste.ac.cr

Not long ago **PARQUE NACIONAL GUANACASTE** was little more than cattle pasture. Influential biologist D.H. Janzen, editor of the seminal *Costa Rican Natural History*, who had been involved in field study for many years in nearby Santa Rosa, was instrumental in creating the park virtually from scratch in 1991. Raising over US$11 million, mainly from foreign sources, he envisioned creating a kind of biological corridor in which animals, mainly mammals, would have a large enough tract of undisturbed habitat in which to hunt and reproduce.

The **Santa Rosa–Guanacaste** (and, to an extent, Rincón de la Vieja) **corridor** is the result of his work, representing one of the most important efforts to conserve and regenerate tropical **dry forest** in the Americas. Containing tropical wet and dry forests

5

PARQUE NACIONAL GUANACASTE

■ ACCOMMODATION
Cacao Field Station Lodge	2
Maritza Field Station Lodge	1

- - - - Trail

and a smattering of cloudforest, Parque Nacional Guanacaste also protects the **springwell of the Río Tempisque**, as well as the ríos Ahogados and Colorado. More than three hundred species of **bird**, including the orange-fronted parakeet and the white-throated magpie jay, have been recorded, while mammals lurking behind the undergrowth include jaguar, puma, tapir, coati, armadillo, two-toed sloth and deer. It's also thought that there are about five thousand species of moth and **butterfly**, including the giant owl butterfly.

The park is devoted to research rather than tourism, and the administration staff at Santa Rosa (see p.262) discourage casual visitors. There are three main research stations, and it is sometimes possible to stay at two of them if you show enough interest and contact the Santa Rosa administration centre well in advance. Apart from the primary rainforest that exists at the upper elevations, the park's highlight is an astonishing collection of **pre-Columbian petroglyphs** at El Pedregal on the lower flanks of **Volcán Orosí**. The Sendero de los Indios leads up to the site from the Maritza field station. In addition to the path to the petroglyphs, there's the Sendero Cacao, which connects Maritza with the Cacao station on the southwestern slope of **Volcán Cacao**.

ARRIVAL AND DEPARTURE
PARQUE NACIONAL GUANACASTE

By car Access is very difficult, unless (as usual) you've got a Range Rover or some other tank of a vehicle; if you don't have one, it's not worth the risk of being stranded along the road.

THE GREAT PRETENDER: WILLIAM WALKER

Born in Tennessee in 1824, **William Walker** was something of a child prodigy. By the age of 14 he had a degree from the University of Nashville, notching up further degrees in law and medicine just five years later before setting off to study at various illustrious European universities. However, upon his return to the US, Walker failed in his chosen professions of doctor and lawyer and, somewhat at a loose end, landed up in California in 1849 at the height of the Gold Rush. Here he became involved with the **pro-slavery** organization Knights of the Golden Circle, who financed an expedition, in which Walker took part, to invade Baja California and Mexico to secure more land for the United States. Undeterred by the expedition's failure, Walker soon put his mind to another plan. Intending to make himself overlord of a Central American nation of five slave-owning states, and then to sell the territory to the US, Walker invaded Nicaragua in June 1855 with mercenary troops. The next logical step was to secure territory for the planned eleven-kilometre canal between Lago de Nicaragua and the Pacific. Gaining much of his financial backing from Nicaraguan get-rich-quick militarists and North American capitalists who promptly saw the benefits of a waterway along the Río San Juan from the Pacific to the Atlantic, in 1856 William Walker, and several hundred mercenary troops, invaded Costa Rica from the north.

Meanwhile, Costa Rican president **Juan Rafael Mora** had been watching Walker's progress with increasing alarm and, in February 1856, declared war on the usurper. Lacking military hardware, Costa Rica was ill-prepared for battle, and Mora's rapidly gathered army of nine thousand men was a largely peasant-and-bourgeois band, armed with machetes, farm tools and the occasional rusty rifle. Marching them out of San José through the Valle Central, over the Cordillera de Tilarán and on to the hot plains of Guanacaste, Mora got wind that Walker and his band of three hundred buccaneers were entrenched at the **Santa Rosa Casona**, the largest and best-fortified edifice in the area. Although by now Mora's force was reduced to only 2500 (we can only guess that, in the two weeks that it took them to march from San José, heat exhaustion had left many scattered by the wayside), on March 20, 1856, they routed the filibusters, fighting with their *campesino* tools. Mora then followed Walker and his men on their retreat, engaging them in battle again in Nicaraguan territory, at **Rivas**, some 15km north of the border, where Walker's troops eventually barricaded themselves in another wooden *casona*. It was here – and not, as is commonly thought, at Santa Rosa – that **Juan Santamaría**, a 19-year-old drummer boy, volunteered to set fire to the building in which Walker and his men were barricaded, flushing them out, and dying in the process. Walker, however, survived the fire, and carried on filibustering, until in 1857 a US warship was dispatched to put an end to his antics, which were increasingly embarrassing for the US government, who had covertly backed him. Undeterred after a three-year spell in a Nicaraguan jail, he continued his adventuring until he was shot dead by the Honduran authorities in September 1860.

Later, Mora, no devotee of democracy himself, rigged the 1859 Costa Rican presidential election so that he could serve a second term – despite his military victories against Walker, there was strong popular opposition to his domestic policies – but he was deposed later that year. He attempted a coup d'état, but was subsequently shot in 1860, the same year that his former adversary met his Waterloo in Honduras.

To the Cacao station The road to the Cacao field station leaves the Interamericana 10km south of the Santa Rosa turn-off. It leads to the hamlet of Potrerillos; once there, head for Quebrada Grande (on some maps called García Flamenco) and continue for about 8km. It's passable most of the way, but the suspension-rattling boulders begin to appear 3km from the entrance; at this point you have to ditch non-4WD vehicles and walk.

To the Maritza station To reach the Maritza station from the Interamericana, take a right turn opposite the left turn-off to Cuajiniquil (see p.266), and continue along the poor road for about 15km.

ACCOMMODATION

Cacao and Maritza field station lodges ✆ 2666 5051. There's very basic lodge accommodation of four rooms at Cacao and Maritza field stations; each field station sleeps up to 32 people. Call the Santa Rosa sector administration centre to check if they're open. They'll try to discourage you, so make your interest clear. <u>US$20</u>

5

Refugio Nacional de Vida Silvestre Bahía Junquillal

5km north of Cuajiniquil • Daily 8am–4pm • US$19 • ☎ 2666 5051, ⓦ acguanacaste.ac.cr/turismo/sector-junquillal

Occupying five square kilometres that fan out from its namesake bay, **REFUGIO NACIONAL DE VIDA SILVESTRE BAHÍA JUNQUILLAL** holds particular significance for the variety of coastal ecosystems it protects. Thanks to its relatively remote location, it sees fewer visitors than the nearby national parks and is an idyllic spot to spend a day or two and glimpse a surprising variety of wildlife in the process, from sea urchins to spider monkeys. A few short, mostly flat **trails** depart from near the ranger station by the entrance, all of which can together be walked in under an hour. The shortest of these, **Sendero El Carao**, passes briefly through a mangrove forest before reaching an overlook, while the slightly longer **Sendero La Laguna** parallels 2km-long **Playa Junquillal** and provides a good opportunity to spot hermit crabs, sea stars and several seabirds, including frigate birds, which typically only land to breed or nest.

Most people, though, come to soak up the sun on the picturesque beach and to cool off in the calm, clear waters, which are ideal for **swimming** and **snorkelling**. *Santa Elena Lodge* (see below) in the village of Cuajiniquil can help arrange tours.

ARRIVAL AND INFORMATION
RN DE VIDA SILVESTRE BAHÍA JUNQUILLAL

By car Take the Interamericana turn-off to Cuajiniquil (Hwy-914) for 8km. Near the western edge of the village, turn north along the dirt road to the refuge entrance.

By bus It's possible to take a bus to Cuajiniquil, 5km to the south of the refuge. From there you can hire a taxi for the 15min drive to the entrance.

Destinations from Cuajiniquil La Cruz (1 daily; 45min); Liberia (2 daily; 1hr).

Tourist information The ranger station (daily 7am–5.30pm) can provide the current tide conditions and information on where to see the refuge's wildlife.

ACCOMMODATION

Santa Elena Lodge On Hwy-914 in Cuajiniquil ☎ 2679 1038, ⓦ santaelenalodgecr.com. On the left side of the main road just before the turn-off to the national refuge, this welcoming lodge has simple rooms with a/c, hot water and private bathrooms. There's an attached restaurant (the menu often features freshly caught fish), and the gregarious owner can arrange tours (including whale-watching in the Bahía Junquillal, plus snorkelling and fishing). US$95

Sector Junquillal Campsite Just west of the ranger station. This large campsite with striking views is set back a few metres from Playa Junquillal. Several of the sites have shade and there are basic services, including showers. US$19

La Cruz

Set on a plateau north of Parque Nacional Guanacaste, overlooking Bahía de Salinas and the Pacific Ocean to the west, the tiny, sleepy town of **LA CRUZ** is the last settlement of any size before the border, just 20km away. For this reason alone it makes a reasonable stopover if you're heading up to Nicaragua, though the striking views at **sunset** are certainly worth lingering for as well. There's not much else to see, though the town is pleasant enough and there are a few nice places to stay in the area.

ARRIVAL AND DEPARTURE
LA CRUZ

By bus Buses pull in at the station two blocks north of the Parque Central.

Destinations Cuajiniquil, for Reserva Nacional de Vida

Silvestre Bahía Junquillal (1 daily; 45min); Liberia (every 45min; 1hr); Peñas Blancas (every 45min; 30min); San José (9 daily; 5hr 10min).

ACCOMMODATION

Amalia's Inn About 100m south of the town's Parque Central ☎ 2679 9618. The charming *Amalia's Inn* has spacious rooms with a/c, a pool and a spectacular view over the bay. It's well worth paying a bit extra (around US$20) to secure a room with a view of the sea. US$60

Finca Cañas Castilla About 7km north of La Cruz, near the

hamlet of Sonzapote ☎ 8381 4030, ⓦ canas-castilla.com. A Swiss-run ranch on 150 acres alongside the Río Sapoa, offering homely cabins sleeping up to four and spots to pitch your tent (or park your motorhome). The farm has several groves of fruit trees, including orange and banana, while free-range chickens provide fresh eggs daily for guests and the local market. Mainly hilly terrain with thick forests as well as expansive grassland for grazing, the ranch can be explored on horseback – in addition to the livestock you might catch a glimpse of sloths and anteaters. To get to the farm from La Cruz,

head north on the Interamericana and turn right after 5km onto an unpaved road which leads to the village of Sonzapote; continue for another 2km from here and you'll see signs to the *finca*. Camping US$12, cabins US$65

DIRECTORY

Banks and exchange There's a Banco Nacional with ATM at the turn-off (Hwy-935) into town off the Interamericana.

Bahía de Salinas

To the west of La Cruz, Hwy-935 descends for about 12km to the windswept kitesurfing mecca of **BAHÍA DE SALINAS**. Prevailing conditions produce gusts throughout the year, but they tend to intensify from November to July, which is when the bay sees the most visitors. While the reliable (and often quite forceful) winds attract professional kitesurfers from around the world, it's also a good place for beginners to try their hand at the sport.

Though most of the pretty bay's **beaches** are predictably windy throughout the year, if you're looking to rest on the sand without having it blown in your face, try **Playa Jobo** on the bay's southern arm, the most sheltered spot. Just 1.5km offshore is rocky and rugged **Isla Bolaños**, an important nesting site for numerous seabirds – including the frigate bird, which rarely sets foot on land. While the island has no facilities, a number of the bay's hotels lead day-trips to it, and at low tide you can walk around the island on the beach; dense vegetation makes it just about impossible to trek into the interior.

ARRIVAL AND DEPARTURE

BAHÍA DE SALINAS

By bus Buses from La Cruz (5 daily; 40min) stop in the hamlet of El Jobo, on the southern edge of the bay.
By car Much of Hwy-935 to Bahía de Salinas can be

mud-laden at certain times of the year; check about the road's condition in La Cruz before setting out.
By taxi A taxi from La Cruz is around ₡5000.

ACCOMMODATION

Blue Dream On the left of the approach road to Bahía de Salinas ☎8826 5221, ⓦbluedreamhotel.com. *Blue Dream* has some of the most comfortable accommodation on the bay, with pleasant rooms, wooden bungalows with balconies sleeping up to three, and a dorm. Its lively on-site restaurant serves mostly Mediterranean dishes and wood-oven pizzas. It also has a windsurfing/kitesurfing school (see box below). Daily 7am–11pm. Dorm US$17, doubles US$45, bungalows US$52

Eco Playa On the right of the approach road to Bahía de Salinas, Playa La Coyotera ☎2676 1010,

ⓦwww.ecoplaya.com. Sprawling and attractive resort with a combination of rooms and more spacious villas (sleeping up to four). All have TV and a/c; the villas also have kitchenettes. The resort has its own private beach and leads a variety of tours, including day-trips to Nicaragua and snorkelling outings to Isla Bolaños. The Costa Kite kitesurfing school (see box below) is based here. Doubles US$95, villas US$125

Kite House Playa Copal ☎2676 1045, ⓦkite boardingcostarica.com. Offering clean, simple and low-cost dorms and private rooms, the sociable *Kite House* is

---

KITESURFING IN BAHÍA DE SALINAS

There are several places lining the bay where you can take **kitesurfing lessons** for as little as an hour as part of a multiday package. Most of these spots rent gear as well.

Blue Dream Kitesurfing School Blue Dream hotel. The best choice in the bay, Blue Dream is the longest-running school of its kind in the country. It rents out all the gear you'll need to get up on the water (US$50/day) and provides lessons ranging from one-hour (US$35; minimum of two people) to a four-day package (US$245).

Costa Kite Eco Playa. Costa Kite offers three-hour introductory windsurfing and kitesurfing lessons (both US$90; minimum of two people), plus a range of longer courses, as well as gear rental (US$70/day).
Kite House Kite House hotel. Offers kiteboarding lessons (from US$48/hr) and equipment rental (US$68/day for everything).

5

CROSSING THE NICARAGUAN BORDER AT PEÑAS BLANCAS

The **border crossing** is 20km north of La Cruz (daily 6am–midnight; get there well before closing time); few nationalities require a visa (see box, p.75) to cross into Nicaragua. Exit stamps are given on the Costa Rican side, where there is a restaurant and a helpful, well-organized Costa Rican tourist office (daily 6am–noon & 1–8pm). Money-changers are always on hand and can change colones, córdobas and dollars. After getting your Costa Rican exit stamp (US$7) it's a short walk north to the barrier from where you can get one of the regular shuttle buses 4km north to the Nicaraguan shantytown of Sapoa, where you go through Nicaraguan *migración*. There's a US$12 entry fee for foreigners charged on the Nicaraguan side, plus a US$2 regional fee.

Buses on both sides of the border are far more frequent in the morning. If you're arriving from Nicaragua, note that the last San José-bound bus (Transportes Deldú; ☎ 2677 0091) leaves at 5.30pm, and the last Liberia bus (Transbasa; ☎ 2677 0157) at 6.30pm. Through-buses from San José to Managua stop at the main bus terminal in Liberia, although it can be tricky to get a seat. The bus station sells tickets for this route (as does *Hotel Guanacaste*) if there is a vacant seat; otherwise it's a question of jumping on the bus, paying the driver and hoping you can grab one.

Liberia services are roughly hourly (1hr 30min), as are buses for San José (5hr 30min).

also an ideal place to learn to kiteboard or perfect your skills, thanks to its school (see box, p.267). There are regular barbecue buffet dinners (US$17). Breakfast costs extra. Dorms U̲S̲$̲1̲8̲, doubles U̲S̲$̲2̲5̲

Peñas Blancas

The main crossing point into Nicaragua, **PEÑAS BLANCAS** is emphatically a border post and not a town, with just one or two basic *sodas* and no hotels. Aim to get here as **early** as possible, as procedures are ponderous and you'll be lucky to get through the whole deal in less than ninety minutes. Costa Rican and Nicaraguan border officials are quite strict, and there are many checks to see that your paperwork is in order.

The situation is far more difficult for the two thousand **refugees** – men, women and children – who are trapped in dire conditions in a makeshift camp close to the border. In recent years, increasing numbers of migrants – most are from Africa, but there are also significant numbers of Haitians – have travelled up from South America and through Central America in a bid to reach the US and a better life. But in 2016 Nicaragua closed its border to them, leaving them stranded here in Costa Rica. The Costa Rican Red Cross (🌐ifrc.org; donations welcome) provides support, but as of early 2017 there were serious humanitarian fears about conditions in the camp.

Northern Nicoya Peninsula

The impressive expanses of playas Flamingo and Tamarindo aside, few of the **beaches** along the rocky coastline of the **northern Nicoya Peninsula** could truthfully be called beautiful, and most are actually quite small. Often located in coves or sheltered bays, they are generally ideal for swimming. Getting around can take time, as the beaches tend to be separated by rocky headlands or otherwise impassable formations, with barren hilly outcroppings coming right down to the sea, carving out little coves and bays, but necessitating considerable backtracking inland to get from one to the other.

The landscape of the Nicoya Peninsula is changing rapidly, and often not for the better. Many of the northern beaches, including Tamarindo and Playa Panamá/ Culebra, have been aggressively developed for mass tourism, leading to a proliferation of monolithic, generally characterless US-style resorts. The nearby airport in Liberia exists mainly to service the package and charter market along this coast. Within easy reach of the airport are the calm waters in the **Bahía Culebra** (marked on some maps as

5

Playa Panamá, which is actually only one of the beaches in the bay), some of the clearest and most sheltered in the country, with good snorkelling. Sprawling across nearly the entire Bahía Culebra is the **Papagayo Project**, the country's largest tourist development, consisting of hotels, condos, a mall and a golf course.

The signs of mass tourism lessen as you head further south towards **Parque Nacional Marino Las Baulas**, where droves of **leatherback turtles** come ashore to lay their eggs between October and February. The beaches here have drawn US expatriates in pursuit of paradise, and these cosmopolitan enclaves are in sharp contrast to the rest of the region, with resorty **Tamarindo** being the top spot for surfing.

ARRIVAL AND DEPARTURE
NORTHERN NICOYA PENINSULA

By plane You can travel by air from San José: both NatureAir and Sansa offer regular flights to Tamarindo (see p.103).

By bus/car It can take a long time to get to the Guanacaste coast from San José by bus or car (4hr–5hr 30min) and in some places you feel very remote indeed. From Liberia, the coast is more easily within reach, with most beaches 45min–2hr away.

GETTING AROUND

By bus Travelling from beach to beach on the peninsula by bus is tricky, and you'll have to ask locals to figure out the peninsular services, whose schedules are not formally published, but which locals will know. Shuttle buses (see p.48) are a useful, though rather pricey, alternative.

By car By far the most popular option is to rent a car, which allows you to beach-hop with relative ease. Roads are not bad, if somewhat potholed – you'll do best with a 4WD, though this can prove expensive.

Bahía Culebra

Sheltered from the full force of the Pacific, the clear blue waters around **Bahía Culebra** boast some of the best beaches in the country for swimming and snorkelling. The calm waters quietly lap at the grey volcanic sands of **Playa Panamá**, the northernmost beach of the bay. Unusually for this dry, hot zone of Guanacaste, **Playa Hermosa**, on the southern edge of the bay at the mouth of the Golfo de Papagayo, is blessed with soothing shade, calm waters and gorgeous sunset views of the Pacific and offshore islets (be aware that there are other beaches named Playa Hermosa in Costa Rica – for example, near Santa Teresa and near Jacó). The waters off Playa Hermosa are also a popular spot for **diving** (see below). Development in the bay is proceeding at a brisk pace, and while upscale shops are becoming more commonplace, the whole area still has an appealingly laidback feel to it for now.

ARRIVAL AND DEPARTURE
BAHÍA CULEBRA

By car Both Panamá and Hermosa beaches are easily accessible by car from Liberia. Take the turn-off to the right just after the hamlet of Comunidad – signposted to playas Hermosa, Panamá and Coco – and continue for several kilometres over the good paved road. Further on from Comunidad, there's another turn-off to Hermosa and

Panamá on the right.

By bus There's a bus stop on the main road at the northern edge of Playa Hermosa.

Destinations Alajuela (1 daily; 4hr 50min); Liberia (9 daily; 50min).

ACTIVITIES

Sirenas Diving On a side road toward the beach at the north end of Playa Hermosa ☎8387 4710, ⓦsirenasdivingcostarica.com. This family-run outfit offers expert trips and lessons as well as PADI courses; they also lead snorkelling tours and rent out equipment.

ACCOMMODATION

★**Hotel Bosque del Mar** On Playa Hermosa ☎2672 0046, ⓦhotelplayahermosa.com. Situated in a great spot right on the beach, with lush gardens featuring hundred-year-old trees near a large swimming pool with jacuzzi. This hotel is owned and managed by Ticos offering old-fashioned hospitality, with a stellar beachfront open-air restaurant that's also open to non-residents. All the rooms are sizeable suites, and feature a/c, TVs and views of the gardens or the sea. US$226

Iguana Inn On the northern access road to Playa Hermosa ☎ 2672 0065. A stone's throw from the beach, this pleasant budget option has simple, colourful rooms with fan and small attached bathrooms. There's also a swimming pool and a well-equipped shared kitchen. US$30

Secrets Papagayo At the end of the Playa Panamá beach road ☎ 2672 0000, ⓦ secretsresorts.com. Formerly part of the Hilton network, this high-end all-inclusive complex promises "unlimited luxury". Well, not quite, but the facilities are extensive, and include an infinity pool, spa, fitness centre and several restaurants and bars. The rooms and bungalows (the latter sleeping up to four) are elegantly furnished with a minimalist design and have a wide range of amenities. Rates include all food and drink and lots of activities. Doubles and bungalows US$687

El Velero Off the northern access road to Playa Hermosa ☎ 2672 1017, ⓦ costaricahotel.net. Friendly hotel with split-level rooms with balconies. Enjoy sea views from the lovely, bird- and lizard-filled gardens; a short path leads from the hotel down to the beach. There's also a good restaurant, a small pool, and they offer guests sunrise, sunset and full-day tours on their 38ft sail boat. US$112

EATING

★**Ginger** On the main road, 2km inland from Playa Hermosa ☎ 2672 0041, ⓦ gingercostarica.com. Chrome, glass and sharp angles cantilevered in the hills, *Ginger* is popular with the foreign resident community. The focus here is on "Asian-inspired tapas": think potstickers, *gyoza*, spring rolls, chicken tikka, Mongolian ribs, and the like. While the plates might be small, the prices are not – most dishes cost around ₡5000. Save some room for dessert: strawberry and passion fruit pavlova and ginger-and-lime cheesecake are among the options. Tues–Sun 5–10pm.

Pescado Loco Opposite El Velero. For appealing cheap (for Playa Hermosa at least) eats, head to this low-key restaurant where freshly caught fish costs around ₡5000–7000. Good cocktails, too. Daily 11am–9pm.

Playas del Coco

Some 35km west of Liberia, booming **PLAYAS DEL COCO** was the first Pacific beach to hit it big with weekending Costa Ricans from the Valle Central. Since then it has undergone a rapid transformation into a brash US-style resort, with both high-end hotels and casinos and backpacker-focused dive bars and clubs. The beach itself is nice enough and is kept clean by rubbish-collecting brigades organized by local residents. The town's accessibility and wide range of budget accommodation make it a useful base to explore the more photogenic beaches nearby. It also has a thriving eating and drinking scene, and is a good place from which to take a **snorkelling** or **diving** tour (see below). El Coco town spreads out right in front of the beach, with a tiny **parquecito** and the adjacent unmissable lime-green **Iglesia Católica** as the focal point.

ARRIVAL AND GETTING AROUND

PLAYAS DEL COCO

By car Playas del Coco is a 35min drive west of Liberia, with good road conditions along the entire route.

By bus Buses stop next door to the Banco Nacional on the main road leading to the beach.

Destinations Liberia (hourly; 1hr); San José (3 daily; 5hr 30min).

By taxi Taxis gather by the *parquecito* on the beach; trips to the nearby Playa Hermosa and Playa Ocotal cost around ₡5000.

ACTIVITIES

Deep Blue Diving On the main road diagonally across from the Banco Nacional ☎ 2670 1004, ⓦ deepblue-diving.com. Excellent dive shop with a full slate of trips on offer, including two-tank dives in the Gulfo de Papagayo (US$85), more technical excursions around the Islas Catalinas (from US$115) and PADI courses (Open Water US$435).

Rich Coast Diving On the main road about 300m from the beach ☎ 2670 0176, ⓦ richcoastdiving.com. This venerable dive shop organizes snorkelling and scuba trips (US$85 for a two-tank dive), including to Isla Murciélago (Bat Caves) in Santa Rosa sector, as well as PADI certification.

ACCOMMODATION

Coco has plenty of fairly basic *cabinas*, catering to weekending Ticos, expats and tourists. In the **high season** you should **reserve at weekends**, when the village often sees a large influx of visitors. You can probably get away with turning up on spec midweek, when rooms may also be a little cheaper. In the **low season** bargains abound.

5

B&B Villa del Sol 1km north of the village; turn right off the main road 150m before the beach ☎ 2670 0085, ⓦ villadelsol.com. Small, welcoming B&B in a quiet location with rooms set around a large grassy space – all have private bathrooms, a/c and ocean views. Pleasantly decorated by the friendly French-Canadian owners, the hotel also has a large pool, and studio apartments (US$630/week) designed for longer stays. **US$65**

Hotel Chantel On a hill about 4km from the beach ☎ 2670 0389, ⓦ hotelchantel.com. This small-scale hotel gets consistently good reviews from travellers, thanks to its neat-and-tidy en-suite rooms – all with a/c, safes and magnificent ocean views. If you want to self-cater, opt for one of the apartments sleeping up to four (from US$100), which have kitchenettes. **US$89**

Hotel Coco Palms On the beach, next to the football pitch ☎ 2670 0367. Like a motel in style, with nice and clean rooms with a/c. There's a pool as well as Coco's only sushi spot and the *Lazy Frog* sports bar. Rooms away from the pool are usually quieter. **US$30**

Pato Loco Inn On the road coming into town, about 300m before the village ☎ 2670 0145, ⓦ patolocoinn .com. The "Crazy Duck" is rather more sedate than its name might suggest, drawing a steady stream of regular guests thanks to its good-value rooms (with fans or a/c) and personal service. There are a couple of long-stay apartments sleeping up to five (from US$70) with kitchen. A big American breakfast is included in the rates. **US$58**

La Puerta del Sol Off the road leading to the right 100m before you reach the beach ☎ 2670 0195, ⓦ lapuertadelsolcostarica.com. Friendly Italian-run retreat set in quiet gardens; all rooms have a/c, phones, TV and a small terrace (or balcony) and lounge area. The thoughtfully arranged complex has a pool, gym and the *Sol y Luna* restaurant (see below), serving top-notch Italian food. **US$124**

★Rancho Armadillo On a hill about 5km from the beach ☎ 2670 0108, ⓦ ranchoarmadillo.com. Run by an easy-going American former chef, this stunning hilltop estate with centuries-old sculptures spread throughout the grounds is quite unlike anything else in the area. The rooms are exceedingly comfortable, well appointed and decorated with striking wood furnishings, the communal areas invite extended lingering, the pool is beautiful and the views of the Pacific are unmatched. That said, what truly makes the place memorable is the care and attention of the staff, who make you feel right at home. **US$244**

EATING

Coco has two very distinct types of places to eat and drink: those catering to Ticos and those that attempt a cosmopolitan vibe to hook the gringos; the latter, as you might suspect, are generally much more expensive. The biggest supermarket within walking distance of the beach is Luperón (☎ 2670 0950), next to the Banco Nacional.

Andre's Beach Bar On the beach just northeast of the main road ☎ 2670 2052. A low-key spot favoured by expats and worth a stop for filling, US-style hot dogs and decent pizzas (₡10,000 will get you a big one). Daily 7am–11pm.

Le Coq On the main drag, near the bus station ☎ 2670 0680, ⓦ facebook.com/LeCoqCostaRica. The lime-green-T-shirted staff at this Lebanese joint serve up a steady stream of quality falafel wraps, hummus, chicken shawarmas and beef kebabs, all of which are competitively priced (₡2500–5000). Mon–Sat 11.30am–10pm.

Papagayo On the main drag, 100m before the beach ☎ 2670 0298. If it's fresh and available, you'll find it on the menu at Coco's best seafood restaurant, run by the family of the big shot of the local fishing fleet. The "catch of the day" will set you back ₡5000–7000, while the delectable mixed seafood platter is a fine option. The fish is prepared in a wide variety of styles, but the quality is consistently excellent. Daily noon–10/11pm.

Sol y Luna La Puerta del Sol hotel. An attractive setting where you can sample well-prepared Italian food, including home-made pasta (₡5000–8500). The owners make a big effort to import authentic ingredients, and there's also a decent wine selection. Mon & Wed–Sun 5–10pm.

DRINKING AND NIGHTLIFE

Coco has over two dozen bars, and nightclubs rock through the night. Much of it emanates from *La Vida Loca* and its neighbours on the main street, which offer up plenty of cocktails, shooters and moody bass beats.

Coconutz On the main road, a block and a half from the beach ☎ 2670 1982, ⓦ cocnutz-costarica.com. Popular sports bar with plenty of outside seating where you can watch live US and (to a lesser extent) global sports. There's also standard bar food, movie nights (Wed; US$9 with all-you-can-eat pizza), regular live music (check the website for the latest listings) and plenty of food and drink promotions. Daily 11am–midnight.

La Vida Loca On the beach south of the main road just past the wooden pedestrian bridge ☎ 2670 0181. Popular with Coco's foreign residents, this American-owned beachfront bar with a buxom mermaid out front is a good spot for an afternoon drink, and can get pretty lively later on when most other places close for the night. Daily 11am–1am.

DIRECTORY

Banks and exchange The Banco Nacional, on the main road as you enter town, will change dollars and has an ATM.

Post office There's a miniscule post office (Mon–Fri 7.30am–5pm) across from the *parquecito*.

Playa Ocotal

Past the rocky headland south of Coco, the high-end enclave of **PLAYA OCOTAL** is reached by taking the signed turn-off to the left 200m before reaching the beach at Coco. Ocotal and its surroundings have lovely views over the ocean and across to the Papagayo Gulf from the top of the headland, and the small beach is better for swimming than Coco. But the real attractions are the marlin and other "big game" fish that glide through these waters: many of Ocotal's **hotels** are tied in with sportfishing packages.

ACCOMMODATION   PLAYA OCOTAL

Bahía Pez Vela Signposted off the road to Ocotal Beach Resort ☎ 2670 0129, ⓦ bahiapezvela.com. Top-end resort with forty two-storey villas (sleeping up to eight people) in beautiful grounds, with a trio of pools and a gorgeous lawn area above a nice private beach ideal for swimming. If you want to be near the beach, ask for a villa on the grounds' lower end. The bar and restaurant *Picante* is open-air, casual and by the pool, but pricey by local standards. US$339

Villa Casa Blanca Signposted off the road to Ocotal

Beach Resort ☎ 2670 0448. A small, quiet and very accommodating B&B that offers boat tours, deep-sea fishing, scuba diving to the Islas Murciélagos near Santa Rosa, and horseriding trips. The Spanish-style villas (sleeping up to four) feature colourful and bright canopy beds, plus there's a charming bridged pool and a tennis court in the grounds, and rates include breakfast. There's no restaurant as such, but the owner can prepare meals with a little advance notice. US$125

EATING

Father Rooster Take the road past Ocotal Beach Resort's gate, then take the first right and continue to the end ☎ 2670 1246, ⓦ fatherrooster.com. In a historic hacienda dating back to 1917 and situated right on the beach, *Father*

Rooster has long been a favourite in these parts. Snack on light bites like buffalo wings, opt for one of the many tacos (₡7400–8400) or go for one of the mains (₡7900–12,000), which include a tasty shrimp kebab. Daily 11.30am–9.30pm.

Playa Flamingo and around

Despite its name, there are no flamingoes at the pricey gringo enclave of **PLAYA FLAMINGO**, a place that feels more Cancún than Costa Rica. Some of the big beach houses lining the white sands are even owned by the odd film star. It does, however, have the best beach on this section of the coast, with white sand, gentle breakers and picturesque rocky islets offshore. Flamingo is also known as a top spot for **sportfishing**: almost all the resort-style hotels in the area cater to fishing enthusiasts or sun-worshippers on packages. It's approached via the road to the small, unappealing **Playa Brasilito**, a scruffy beach with darkish sand, which lies about 5km before Playa Flamingo's marina.

To escape the rather static and standoffish atmosphere of Flamingo, head 3km north to **Playa Potrero**, a small cove that opens onto a decent crescent-shaped beach with secluded camping and calm waters good for swimming.

The most southerly of the four beaches, **Playa Conchal** ("Shell Beach") is set in a steep, broad bay a couple of kilometres south of Playa Brasilito. Protected by a rocky headland, it has appealing pink-coloured sand, with mounds of tiny shells and quiet waters that are good for swimming and snorkelling.

ARRIVAL AND DEPARTURE   PLAYA FLAMINGO AND AROUND

By car To reach the beaches by car, take the Liberia–Nicoya road to Belén, then turn right off the main road and follow a side road to the hamlet of Huacas, 25km beyond Belén, from where the beaches are signposted. To get to Conchal from Flamingo, you have to backtrack inland, turning right

at the village of Matapalo. It's quicker to drive along the sand from Brasilito to Conchal, but you'll need a 4WD or a tug-of-war team.

By bus Buses arrive in Playa Flamingo on the main road at the stop diagonally opposite *Mariner Inn*, and in Playa

5

Brasilito at the stop on the main road next to the Super Brasilito. Playa Concha's stop is on the main road next to the Banco Costa Rica, and Playa Potrero's stop is by the plaza set back from the beach. Note that the destinations below reflect times from Playa Flamingo; add 5–15min to the times for the other beaches.

Destinations Liberia (every 1–2hr; 1hr 30min); Santa Cruz (roughly hourly; 1hr 40min).

ACCOMMODATION

Cabinas Cristina Playa Potrero ☎ 2654 4006, ⓦ cabinascristina.com. Bright, comfortable rooms and apartments (the latter sleeping up to four people) with kitchenettes, TVs and a/c. There's a pool, and the helpful owners rent boats and can arrange tours. Doubles US$57, apartments US$79

Flamingo Beach Resort Playa Flamingo ☎ 2654 4444, ⓦ resortflamingobeach.com. Although this monolith of a resort is rather characterless, it does boast a pretty setting across from the beach, a large pool, a restaurant and bar, a casino, a spa and spacious en suites. The hotel can arrange charter flights and will pick you up from the nearby airstrip. US$186

Hotel Brasilito Playa Brasilito ☎ 2654 4237, ⓦ brasilito.com/hotel.html. The best budget option in the area and right on the beach. The sizeable rooms are sparsely furnished but do have large beds and attached bathrooms. The cheapest options only have fans; a/c options cost from US$20 more than the rates quoted below. There's a pleasant restaurant, and kayaks are available for hire. US$40

Westin Golf Resort & Spa Playa Conchal ☎ 2654 3500, ⓦ westinplayaconchal.com. Set back from the beach between *playas* Brasilito and Conchal is this mega complex, whose arrival dramatically changed the character of an area that was once a sleepy low-key beach community. The exclusive resort is nothing if not brash, boasting hundreds of suites, tennis courts, an 18-hole golf course, spa and a beautiful pool. The rates are all-inclusive. US$640

EATING

El Oasis Playa Brasilito ☎ 2654 4237, ⓦ brasilito.com /restaurant-menu.html. Inside *Hotel Brasilito* (see above), this reasonably priced (for the area, at least) restaurant serves typical regional cuisine such as shrimp with rice and red snapper, as well as more international choices (most mains ₡5000–10,000). Daily 7.30am–9pm.

Parque Nacional Marino Las Baulas

4km west of Matapalo • Daily 6am–6pm • US$12 • **Night tours** Open in nesting season • US$30 (includes admission price; call ahead to check frequency and duration) • ☎ 2653 0470

On the Río Matapalo estuary between Conchal and Tamarindo, **PARQUE NACIONAL MARINO LAS BAULAS** is less a national park than a reserve, created in 1995 to protect the nesting grounds of the critically endangered **leatherback turtles**, which come ashore here to nest from November to February. Leatherbacks have probably laid their eggs at **Playa Grande** for millions of years, and it's now one of the few remaining such nesting sites in the world. The beach itself offers a beautiful sweep of light-coloured sand, and outside laying season you can surf and splash around in the waves, though swimming is rough, plagued by crashing waves and riptides. Despite its proximity to an officially protected area, developers were given carte blanche to build: the *Rancho Las Colinas Golf and Country Club*, which includes an eighteen-hole golf course and over two hundred villas, is symptomatic of the lack of planning, the short-termism and the plain daftness (the golf course is located in an area with a long, hot dry season and a history of water shortages) that characterizes so much recent tourist development in Costa Rica. There are serious concerns about the impact of the development on the ancient nesting ground of the turtles.

In the past Playa Grande was a magnet for tour groups from top-end Guanacaste hotels as well as day-trippers from Tamarindo and Coco. Nowadays, however, **visitor numbers are regulated** and you are no longer allowed to walk on the beach during nesting season (get the rangers to tell you stories of what people used to do to harass the turtles and you'll see why).

Turtle-watching tours

Turtle nesting takes place only in season and at **night**, with moonlit nights at high tide being the preferred moment. Note that you are not guaranteed to see a nesting turtle on any given night, and it's definitely worth calling in at El Mundo de la Tortuga (see below) before your visit, both to see the informative exhibition and to ask if tides and weather are favourable – alternatively you could ask the rangers at the entrance hut.

Those who see a nesting are often moved both by the sight of the turtles' imposing bulk, and also by their vulnerability, as they lever themselves up on to the beach. Each female can nest up to twelve times per season, laying a hundred or so eggs at a time, before finally returning to the sea – after which she won't touch land again for another year. Eggs take about sixty days to hatch, and the female turtle **hatchlings** that make the journey from their eggs to the ocean down this beach will (if they survive) return here ten to fifteen years later to nest themselves.

While it's worth seeing a nesting, it's difficult not to feel like an intruder. Groups of up to fifteen people are led to each turtle by guides (some of them "rehabilitated" former poachers), who communicate via walkie-talkie – and if it's a busy night there might be several tour groups after the same turtle. When the guide locates a turtle ready to lay her eggs you trudge in a group along the beach and then stand around watching the leatherback go through her procreative duty, while from time to time the turtle will cast a world-weary glance in the direction of her fans. It's hard not to think it would be better for the turtle if everyone just stayed away, although the viewing is well managed and fairly considerate, and the revenue does help to protect the turtles' habitat.

El Mundo de la Tortuga

200m from the park entrance • Daily 8am–1pm & 2–4pm, or much later when turtles are nesting • Covered by entry fee • ☎ 2653 0471

The impressive and educational **El Mundo de la Tortuga** exhibition includes an audio-guided **tour** in English and some stunning photographs of the turtles. You'll gain an insight into the leatherbacks' habitats and reproductive cycles, along with the threats they face, and current conservation efforts. There's also a souvenir shop and a small café where groups on turtle tours are often asked to wait while a nesting turtle is located. It's open late at night – often past midnight – depending on demand and nesting times.

ARRIVAL AND INFORMATION   PARQUE NACIONAL MARINO LAS BAULAS

There are two official entrances to Playa Grande, though tickets to enter the reserve can only be bought at the **southern entrance**, where the road enters the park near the *Villa Baula*. There are no bus services to the park.

By car To drive to Las Baulas, take the road from Huacas to Matapalo, and turn left at the football field (a 4WD is recommended for this stretch during the wet season).

By boat Most people visit the park by boat with a Tamarindo tour operator (see p.278), entering at the southern end.

ACCOMMODATION

Bula Bula At the southern end of the Playa Grande ☎ 2653 0975, ⓦ hotelbulabula.com. In a splendid setting between Playa Grande and the river that runs behind the beach, this brightly coloured hotel offers ten rooms, plus some bungalows (sleeping up to six people), all with a/c and TVs. Excursions include kayaking, sportfishing, horseriding and mountain biking. The restaurant serves fantastic food, particularly the large continental and Costa Rican breakfasts (included in rates). **US$150**

★**Indra Inn** On the main road at the entrance to Playa Grande ☎ 2653 4834, ⓦ playagrandehostel.com. Appealing family-run guesthouse with modern, super-clean, if rather sparsely furnished a/c rooms, gardens filled with fruit trees, delicious breakfasts (included in rates), and regular live music in the evenings. The owners are well informed and helpful, too. **US$65**

RipJack Inn Centre of Playa Grande ☎ 2653 1636, ⓦ ripjackinn.com. The focus is on surfing (board rental and classes are available) and yoga (drop-in classes US$15; see website for schedule) at this well-established hotel, which also has two pools and an excellent restaurant (see p.276). The en-suite rooms themselves are light and airy, with a/c, coffee-makers and private terraces. **US$113**

Las Tortugas Hotel Centre of Playa Grande ☎ 2653 0423, ⓦ lastortugashotel.com. The area's longest established hotel, with a pool, restaurant and a combination of eleven standard and more luxurious rooms and suites. The conscientious owners have kept the light the hotel reflects onto the beach to a minimum (turtle hatchlings are confused by light coming from land), and designed the building so that it will block light from any future developments to the north. They also rent surfboards, can advise on turtle tours and horseriding and have hillside apartments (sleeping up to five; US$100) available for extended stays. **US$60**

THE LEATHERBACK TURTLE

Leatherback turtles (in Spanish, *baulas*) are giant creatures. Often described as a relic from the age of the dinosaurs, they're also one of the oldest animals on Earth, having existed largely unchanged for 120 million years. The leatherback's most arresting characteristic is its sheer size, reaching a length of up to 2.4m and a weight of 500kg. Its front flippers are similarly huge – as much as 2.7m long – and it's these which propel the leatherback on its long-distance migrations (they're known to breed off the West Indies, Florida, the northeastern coast of South America, Senegal, Madagascar, Sri Lanka and Malaysia). Leatherbacks are also unique among turtles in having a skeleton that is not firmly attached to a shell, but which consists of a **carapace** made up of hundreds of irregular bony plates, covered with a leathery skin. It's also the only turtle that can regulate its own body temperature, maintaining a constant 18°C even in the freezing ocean depths, and withstanding immense pressures of over 1500 pounds per square inch as it dives to depths of up to 1200m.

Since the 1973 **Convention on the International Trade of Endangered Species**, it is illegal to harvest green, hawksbill, leatherback and loggerhead turtles. Unlike olive ridleys or hawksbills, leatherbacks are not hunted by humans for food – their flesh has an unpleasantly oily taste – though poachers still steal eggs for their alleged aphrodisiac powers. Even so, leatherbacks still face many human-created hazards. They can choke on discarded plastic bags left floating in the ocean (which they mistake for jellyfish, on which they feed), and often get caught in longline fishing nets or wounded by boat propellers – all added to a loss of nesting habitats caused by beachfront development and the fact that, even in normal conditions, only one in every 2500 leatherback hatchlings makes it to maturity.

The number of nesting females at Las Baulas alone dropped from 1646 in 1988 to 215 in 1997, although numbers have since increased to over 800. At Las Baulas, authorities have established a hatchling "farm" to allow hatchlings to be born and make their trip to the ocean under less perilous conditions than would normally prevail, though this will not affect adult mortality, which is believed to be the root cause of the drop in leatherback numbers. While the population is healthier than it was fifteen years ago, it continues to be plagued by longline fishing, large-scale rubbish dumping, ocean contamination and other factors contributing to fertility problems.

Earthwatch (⊛earthwatch.org) have run conservation holidays on *playas* Grande and Langosta for a number of years, documenting numbers of nesting turtles and their activity patterns.

EATING

El Huerto Centre of Playa Grande ☏ 2653 1259, ⊛ elhuertodeplayagrande.com. The wood-fired pizzas (₡6000–10,000) have been drawing the crowds to *El Huerto* for over two decades. Paella, steaks, fresh fish, and tempting desserts like passion fruit cheesecake are also well worth a look. Daily 10am–10pm.

RipJack Inn Centre of Playa Grande ☏ 2653 1636, ⊛ ripjackinn.com. One of the top restaurants in the area, attached to the hotel of the same name (see p.275), *RipJack*'s menu features dishes like sea bass in a panko-coconut crust (mains around ₡10,000). There's a daily happy hour (4–6pm), while the Sunday brunch (which includes French toast with rum-poached mango) is not to be missed. Daily 8am–9pm.

Playa Tamarindo and around

A sprawling tourist hotspot, **TAMARINDO** enjoys a lively beach culture and raucous nightlife, at least during high season. Many come here to learn to surf – indeed, the gentle breakers are an ideal training ground – or simply to laze on the beach, which is undeniably gorgeous. Tamarindo is, however, the least Costa Rican of places: locals are easily outnumbered by tourists and immigrants, and the town has a rather artificial, US feel, with its mini-malls, numerous estate agents and flashy (but often bland) restaurant-bars. The constant development gives the area an unsettled air and it all feels a bit characterless.

Though fishing still plays a small part in the local economy, Tamarindo's transformation from village to booming beach resort has been rapid, with the usual associated worries about drugs and the loss of community. The village loop at the end of the main road effectively constitutes Tamarindo's small centre and is lined with places to eat, souvenir stalls and surf shops. **Swimming** isn't great around Tamarindo, because of choppy waters and occasional riptides. Most people are content to paddle in the rocky coves and tide pools south of the town. Tamarindo is, however, an ideal **surf** spot because of the reliable, but relatively gentle, waves and the beach attracts a combination of enthusiastic surfers and well-to-do Costa Ricans, who own holiday houses in the vicinity.

In the evening, the main activity here is watching the typically opulent **sunsets**, as the sun disappears into the Pacific just beyond the rocky headland that marks the southern end of the beach, but attention soon shifts to the bar with the cheapest drinks specials.

North of the Tamarindo river estuary begins the long sweep of Playa Grande (see p.274), where **leatherback turtles** lay their eggs. Turtles also come ashore at Tamarindo, but in much smaller numbers. Officially, Tamarindo is within the boundaries of Parque Nacional Marino Las Baulas, insofar as the ocean covered by the protected area extends out in an arc, encompassing Tamarindo beach. The Las Baulas park authorities have also bought up the beach south of Tamarindo to Playa Langosta, preventing further hotel development and allowing turtles to continue coming ashore along this entire stretch.

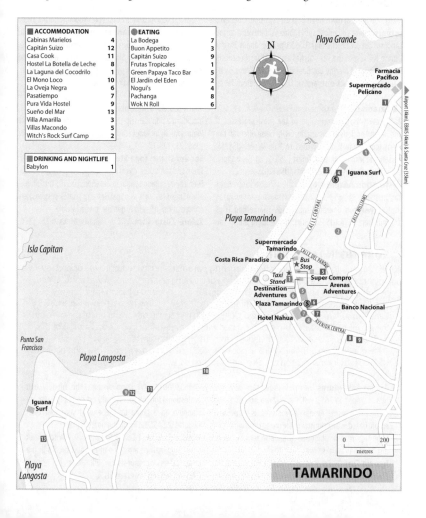

ACCOMMODATION	
Cabinas Marielos	4
Capitán Suizo	12
Casa Cook	11
Hostel La Botella de Leche	8
La Laguna del Cocodrilo	1
El Mono Loco	10
La Oveja Negra	6
Pasatiempo	7
Pura Vida Hostel	9
Sueño del Mar	13
Villa Amarilla	3
Villas Macondo	5
Witch's Rock Surf Camp	2

EATING	
La Bodega	7
Buon Appetito	3
Capitán Suizo	9
Frutas Tropicales	1
Green Papaya Taco Bar	5
El Jardín del Eden	2
Nogui's	4
Pachanga	8
Wok N Roll	6

DRINKING AND NIGHTLIFE	
Babylon	1

TAMARINDO

ARRIVAL AND DEPARTURE

By plane NatureAir (☎2653 1452) and Sansa (☎2653 0012) fly to the small airport 4km north of the village off Hwy-152. Both companies have offices in town.
Destinations via NatureAir Liberia (2 daily; 15min); San José (2–3 daily; 50min).
Destinations via Sansa San José (3 daily; 50min).

PLAYA TAMARINDO AND AROUND

By bus Buses arrive by the village loop. Connections along the coast aren't great, so you may want to take one of the shuttle services run by Interbus and Gray Line (see p.48).
Destinations Liberia (every 30min–1hr; 2hr); San José (4 daily; 5hr 30min–6hr); Santa Cruz (9 daily; 1hr).

GETTING AROUND

By car, scooter or bike For getting around the area – and out to Playa Langosta, the beach just south of the village – you can rent a scooter or mountain bike from CR Paradise (see below), among other places. Numerous places rent cars, including Alamo (☎2242 7733,

ⓦalamocostarica.com), which is on the main road at the northern entrance to the village.
By taxi Taxis congregate on the loop across from the bus stop. Trips to Las Baulas and Playa Avellanas each cost US$20–30.

TOURS AND ACTIVITIES

Many operators in town run a popular two-hour boat excursion (around US$50/person) that takes you around the **river estuary** where you might spot monkeys, birds and crocodiles. In **leatherback nesting season** (Nov to mid-Feb), you can head out on a turtle tour (US$30/person; about 2hr); trips leave in the evening, the exact hour depending on the tide. During the rest of the year, turtles also nest further south at Refugio Nacional de Vida Silvestre Ostional (see p.295) and Parque Nacional Marino Las Baulas (see p.377), usually only on a couple of days each month, depending on the moon. A trip there and back costs around US$50. Numerous Tamarindo operators run these and other trips.

CR Paradise Centro Comercial Plaza Conchal ☎2653 2251, ⓦcrparadise.com. One of the most professional and helpful options in Tamarindo, CR Paradise offers all the usual tours as well as day-trips to Palo Verde (US$95), horseriding into dry tropical forest (US$35; 2hr) and short, but exhilarating gyrocopter flights (US$120).
Destination Adventures On the village loop, near the bus stop ☎2653 3842, ⓦdestinationadventures .net. A well-run operator that leads snorkelling trips around Tamarindo (US$55; 3hr), horseriding along the

beach (US$45; 2hr 30min) and day-trips further afield, including a popular trip to Parque Nacional Rincón de la Vieja which includes climbing, abseiling and ziplines (US$125; 12hr).
Ser Om Shanti Yoga Studio Plaza Tamarindo, second floor ☎8346 8005, ⓦseryogastudio.com. Daily Vinyasa, Hatha and Ashtanga yoga classes (from US$10; 1hr 15min–1hr 45min), as well as yogalates and pilates sessions, are offered at this friendly Argentine-owned studio.
Xplore Costa Rica Plaza Tamarindo ☎2653 4130,

SURFING IN TAMARINDO

The Tamarindo area has always been a **surfing paradise**, and its credibility was upped several notches when Bruce Brown's seminal surfing docudrama *Endless Summer II* was partly filmed here. Most surfers ride the waves at Tamarindo, Playa Grande and adjacent Playa Langosta, an excellent surf beach a couple of kilometres south. There are some hazards, however: in 2015 a Canadian surfer was attacked by a crocodile, which had apparently swum out of the river into the sea in search of food. The surfer escaped with relatively minor injuries, and attacks of this nature are very rare, but nevertheless still something to be aware of.

All schools rent surfboards; typical prices are US$10–30 for a day's rental of a long board, or US$100 plus for a week. You can also rent bodyboards, windsurfing equipment, and masks and snorkels.

Arenas Adventures On the village loop, near the bus stop ☎2653 0108, ⓦaa.arenascr.com /tamarindo.html. Arenas Adventures is a popular school based in an unmistakeable round building with a huge sign reading "hightide". They also rent out ATVs, dirt bikes and kayaks.
Iguana Surf On Calle Central, about 100m north of Plaza Conchal; also along the road to Playa Langosta

☎2653 0613, ⓦiguanasurf.net. The friendly and professional Iguana Surf will almost certainly have you standing on a board by the end of your first class (around US$45/2hr, including board rental).
Witch's Rock Surf Camp See opposite. Witch's Rock Surf Camp, named after one of the best breaks in the area, offers non-guests a full slate of lessons (US$45/2hr) and board rentals.

ⓦxplorecostarica.com. This popular company has a strong reputation for reliable service and knowledgeable guides. They offer a long list of local and long-distance tours, from snorkelling and kayaking combo tours off nearby beaches (from US$60; 2hr 30min) to day-trips to Granada, Nicaragua (US$185; 13hr).

ACCOMMODATION

Many of Tamarindo's hotels are very good, if expensive, with plenty of options for all budgets. While staying in the **village** places you steps from the heart of the action, **Playa Langosta**'s swish B&Bs and hotels offer an all-too-necessary retreat from the hectic Tamarindo beachside scene, and are a quiet 15–20min walk away.

IN THE VILLAGE

Cabinas Marielos C Central ☎2653 0141, ⓦcabinasmarieloscr.com. One of the lower-cost options in town, *Marielos* has no-frills rooms with fans and private bathrooms (rooms with a/c cost around US$11 extra) in pleasant grounds set back from the main road. There's a small communal kitchen for guests to use, and the owner is a helpful source of local info. US$57

★**Hostel La Botella de Leche** Just off Av Central ☎2653 2061, ⓦlabotelladeleche.com. Excellent hostel with comfortable bunk-bed dorms and private rooms. It has a/c, a small pool and a well-equipped communal kitchen as well as spick-and-span shared bathrooms. It's designed with surfers in mind – you can rent and repair boards here, as well as arrange classes (there are plenty of surf-and-accommodation packages – check the website for details). It's very popular, and although the super-friendly owner will do her utmost to squeeze you in, you'd be wise to reserve ahead. Dorms US$18, doubles US$50

La Laguna del Cocodrilo C Central ☎2653 0255, ⓦlalagunadelcocodrilo.com. With a prime beachfront spot at the northern end of the village, *Laguna del Cocodrilo* offers a more tranquil stay than the more central spots and has large and airy rooms, apartments (the latter with kitchenettes and sleeping up to four), and generous suites with views of the ocean and a pretty garden; each comes with a/c and TVs. The excellent on-site French bakery and restaurant will keep you happy at mealtimes. Doubles US$77, apartments US$99, suites US$141

La Oveja Negra Av Central ☎2653 0005, ⓦlaovejanegrahostel.com. Chilled-out hostel and surf camp, with a large communal area, rowdy bar, and well-stocked surf shop. The simple bunk-bed dorms and en-suite cabins (the latter sleeping up to four) aren't bad for the price, though if you're after a quiet night's sleep, look elsewhere. Good-value surf-and-accommodation packages start at US$260/person for three days. Dorms US$15, cabins US$80

Pasatiempo Av Central ☎2653 0096, ⓦhotelpasatiempo.com. Rightly popular hotel with a homely atmosphere, bright and spacious en suites (all with a/c and their own private terraces), hammocks shaded by mango and royal palm trees, and a swimming pool. There's also a lively restaurant and bar; it's good fun, but can be pretty loud in the high season. US$112

Pura Vida Hostel Av Central ☎2653 2464, ⓦpuravidahostel.com. "Come as a guest, leave as a friend" is the motto at this welcoming hostel, which offers bright bunk-bed dorms, private rooms (with shared or attached bathrooms), more spacious apartments (sleeping up to four and equipped with kitchenettes) and regular live music performances, plus perks like free surfboard and bike hire. Dorms US$15, doubles US$50, apartments US$80

Villa Amarilla C Central ☎2653 0038, ⓦhotelvillaamarilla.com. A favourite spot for a quick beer on the beach between catching waves, *Villa Amarilla* also has seven *cabinas* and a communal kitchen. Rooms are decked out in wood; the simpler ones have fridge, fan and shared bathroom, while the en-suite rooms have a/c and TVs. There's an economical restaurant, too. US$136

★**Villas Macondo** ☎2653 0812, ⓦvillasmacondo.com. Tamarindo hotels are generally overpriced, but this quiet, welcoming spot is a refreshing exception to the rule. The colourful *cabinas*, set around an enticing swimming pool, have comfortable beds (for up to four people), wooden ceilings and a little terrace strung with hammocks; the more expensive ones (US$85) include TVs, a/c and fridges. There are also a/c apartments with one or two bedrooms. Guests have access to a kitchenette. *Cabinas* US$60, apartments US$125

Witch's Rock Surf Camp ☎2653 1262, ⓦwitchsrocksurfcamp.com. The best choice in the village for all-in daily surf lessons, unlimited board rentals and accommodation. The breezy, brightly coloured rooms vary in size, though all have a/c, private bathrooms and ocean views; some also have balconies. Packages typically start at seven nights though shorter stays can be arranged. There's an open-air restaurant, *Eat at Joe's*, and an on-site surf shop. Per person US$124

PLAYA LANGOSTA

Capitán Suizo On the road to Playa Langosta ☎2653 0075, ⓦhotelcapitansuizo.com. Popular, top-end Swiss-run hotel set in spacious, landscaped grounds on the beach. The gorgeous *cabina*-style rooms all have a balcony or terrace, fridge, ceiling fans or a/c, bathtub, and an outside shower. The palm-shaded pool is bigger than most, and the atmosphere friendly and relaxed. There's also a cocktail bar and restaurant (see p.280), spa, and beautiful beach views. US$288

5

★**Casa Cook** On the road to Playa Langosta ☎ 2653 0125, ⊕ casacook.net. Small, beautiful hotel with beachfront *cabinas*, a *casita* and an apartment (sleeping up to four), each well-furnished and with a full range of amenities, including kitchenettes, a/c, TVs and safes. There's a small pool, and the affable staff are an excellent source of information on the area. Apartment US$198, *cabinas* and *casita* US$289

El Mono Loco About 300m up the road to Playa Langosta ☎ 2653 0238, ⊕ hotelmonoloco.com. Run by a relaxed Tico family, this clean little hotel is set around a tranquil garden with a small plunge pool. There are dorms as well as simple private rooms with a/c – try to get room 1, which receives considerably more sunlight than the others. Some rooms sleep up to seven, so it's good value for groups. The owners also rent bikes and can prepare meals for guests. Dorms US$20, doubles US$40

Sueño del Mar Playa Langosta ☎ 2653 0284, ⊕ sueno -del-mar.com. Swing in a hammock on the ocean-facing veranda of this B&B, which is based in a beautiful Spanish hacienda-style building, with tiled roofs and adobe walls. The charming and luxurious rooms and *casitas* (the latter sleeping up to four) all come with pretty tiled showers. Doubles US$237, *casitas* US$277

EATING

IN THE VILLAGE

★**La Bodega** Hotel Nahua, diagonally opposite the Banco Nacional ☎ 8395 6184, ⊕ labodegatamarindo .com. This organic café and shop serves some of the best breakfasts (₡1500–3000) in town: try the "chino omelette" with spinach, bacon, cheese and tomatoes, or the smoked trout with goat's cheese. Sandwiches, house-made banana bread and lemon poppy seed scones are fine options for later in the day. Top coffee, too. Daily 7am–3pm.

Buon Appetito Across from Zullymar ☎ 2653 0598, ⊕ facebook.com/BuonAppeti. Italian-owned café serving sandwiches (₡3000–5000) on fresh ciabatta bread as well as thin-crust pizzas, hearty breakfasts, refreshing fruit shakes, and superior coffee. Daily 7am–10pm.

Frutas Tropicales On the main road, at the north end of town. One of the few genuinely cheap places in Tamarindo. The name says it all: all kinds of tropical fruit are on offer, including delicious fruit *refrescos*. They also serve good *casados* (around ₡3000) and hamburgers. Daily 8am–10pm.

★**Green Papaya Taco Bar** 50m down the road from Pasatiempo hotel ☎ 2653 0863, ⊕ facebook.com /Gr33nPapaya. Attractive café and taco bar with reclaimed wood furnishings, terrace seating and plenty of natural light. There's a nice selection of coffee and teas, and the tacos (₡2800–4900) and burritos (₡3500–4200) are full of flavour and made from organic ingredients; the shrimp tacos are highlights. Daily 7am–9pm.

El Jardín del Eden El Jardín del Eden hotel ☎ 2653 0137, ⊕ jardindeleden.com. Romantic, swish (but reasonably priced) restaurant in tropical gardens that serves high-quality French and Italian cuisine made with top-notch ingredients. The lobster and the seafood kebabs are both recommended; or go for the three-course set dinner (US$34). Daily 6.30am–10pm.

Nogui's On the Tamarindo loop ☎ 2653 0059, ⊕ noguistamarindo.com. Long-running favourite where you can dine well throughout the day. For dinner, try the smoked pork chops with a pineapple salsa (₡7300), the shrimp kebab (₡12,000) or the lobster tacos (₡9700). Whatever you choose for your main, don't miss the divine coconut, chocolate or banana cream pies (₡2000). Mon, Tues & Thurs–Sun 6am–10pm.

Pachanga Near the Pasatiempo hotel; turn left up towards Playa Langosta; as the road bends right, go straight ahead ☎ 2653 0406. Intimate, candlelit restaurant, tastefully decorated and with a French-influenced menu (mains around ₡8000). The snapper fillet is a reliable choice, but it's also worth considering one of the daily specials. Mon–Sat 11am–10pm.

Wok N Roll Right in the centre of town, next to Essence Day Spa and across from the Tamarindo Plaza ☎ 2653 0156. The menu here ranges right across Asia, and also offers up plenty of fusion dishes – think Korean *bulgogi* beef wraps and Peking duck tacos. The sushi (₡4500–7000), though, is the real standout. Service isn't exactly hurried but the food is enticing. Daily 4.30–11pm.

PLAYA LANGOSTA

Capitán Suizo Capitán Suizo hotel ☎ 2653 0075, ⊕ hotelcapitansuizo.com. Popular, inviting open-air restaurant fronted by the hotel's gorgeous pool and with views of the ocean. Though the menu changes regularly, it features creative and reasonably priced, healthy dishes prepared with sustainable ingredients. Expect dishes like grilled sea bass on barley risotto and beef tenderloin with a ginger and tamarind sauce (mains ₡8000–20,000). Happy hour daily 4–5.30pm. Daily 11am–10pm.

DRINKING AND NIGHTLIFE

Babylon In the village centre, about 100m from the beach ☎ 8939 3588. Drawing tourists and locals alike, this reggae bar remains the place to be as the week draws to a close. There's frequent live music, particularly at the weekend, and though it's often packed it never feels sweltering thanks to ocean breezes. Daily 11am–3am.

DIRECTORY

Banks and exchange There are many banks in town, several with ATMs, and you'll be hard-pressed to find anywhere in Tamarindo that doesn't accept dollars.
Medical services EBAIS (☎ 2653 0736), the nearest public health clinic, is located 4km away in the hamlet of Villareal. There's a pharmacy, Farmacia Pacífico, on the beach side of the main road as you enter the village from the north.

Playa Avellanas

The waves at the **surfing** hotspot of **PLAYA AVELLANAS**, 11km south of Tamarindo, can be, at times, every bit as enticing as those in Tamarindo; that you won't be threading through crowds to get on them makes them that much more appealing. The **beach** itself is wide and long with a pleasantly isolated feel to it. There are a few surfers' hangouts where you can stay at Avellanas, with spartan but good-value accommodation; though if you're not a surfer, you might feel a bit out of it.

ARRIVAL AND DEPARTURE   PLAYA AVELLANAS

By car It's not possible to continue straight down the coast from Tamarindo: to pick up the road south you have to return a couple of kilometres inland to the hamlet of Villareal. Don't head south in the rainy season without a 4WD, and not at all unless you like crossing creeks – there are plenty on this stretch, and they can swell worryingly fast in the rain.

ACCOMMODATION AND EATING

Cabinas Las Olas Set back from the beach ☎ 2652 9315, ⓦ cabinaslasolas.co.cr. A smarter option than some of the other accommodation options catering to surfers, *Cabinas Las Olas* has pleasantly bright bungalows sleeping up to four, plenty of board games to keep you occupied and swinging hammocks among mangroves. It also has a surf shop where you can rent equipment as well as kayaks and mountain bikes. <u>US$110</u>
★**Lola's** On the beach ☎ 2652 9097, ⓦ facebook.com /playaavellanas. Named after a (sadly departed) pet pig, *Lola's* is rightly revered up and down the coast. Its Asian-Californian fusion dishes take advantage of fresh local ingredients, and it's tough to find something you won't like on the menu, though the fish tacos are particularly delicious. It's also a popular spot to relax with a few afternoon cocktails and take in the action out on the waves. Arrive early if you want to grab a table at lunchtime. Tues–Sun 11am–5pm.

Playa Junquillal

Ten kilometres beyond Avellanas, lovely **PLAYA JUNQUILLAL** has a long, relatively straight beach. It's ideal for **surfing**, pounded by breakers crashing in at the end of their thousand-kilometre journeys, but far too rough for swimming. If you're looking for seclusion and quiet, however, it's a great place to hang out for a few days – there's precious little to do, and nothing at all in the way of nightlife.

ARRIVAL AND DEPARTURE   PLAYA JUNQUILLAL

By bus Buses arrive at the centre of the hamlet on the side road off Hwy-160 from Santa Cruz. Destinations San José (2 daily; 6–7hr); Santa Cruz (3 daily; 1hr 30min).

ACCOMMODATION

El Castillo Divertido On a hillside about a third of a mile from the beach ☎ 2658 8428, ⓦ castillodivertido .com. Enchanting, small, white turreted "castle" run by entertaining hosts. The rooms have fans, some have an ocean view (US$50) and there's a bar, restaurant and rooftop terrace. Kayak tours can be organized here. <u>US$34</u>
Guacamaya Lodge 2km south of Junquillal ☎ 2658 8431, ⓦ guacamayalodge.com. Swiss-run hotel in a serene setting with comfortable, semicircular rooms, villas (sleeping up to four), lovely views, friendly management and a pool. There's also an on-site bar and restaurant serving Swiss specialities and a few Tico staples. Doubles <u>US$85</u>, villas <u>US$158</u>

Hotel Iguanazul 3km north of Playa Junquillal ☎ 2658 8123, ⓦ hoteliguanazul.com. Friendly hotel in a great setting overlooking the sea: it has bright rooms decorated with indigenous art (those with a/c have a US$30 surcharge), plus a pool, bar and restaurant with a lovely view of the beach. It offers fishing, diving and horseriding tours, as well as excursions to Las Baulas. <u>US$119</u>
Los Malinches About 5km south of Hotel Iguanazul ☎ 8628 5920, ⓦ facebook.com/pg/Campinglos malinches. Pleasant campground with shaded sites, located just a few steps from the beach. Facilities include water, showers and electricity. <u>US$6</u>

5

Santa Cruz

Generally regarded by travellers as little more than somewhere to pass through on the way from Liberia or San José to the beach, the sprawling town of **SANTA CRUZ**, some 30km inland from Tamarindo and 57km south of Liberia, is actually "National Folklore City". Much of the music and dance considered quintessentially Guanacastecan originates here, like the various complex, stylized local dances, including the "Punto Guanacasteco" ("*el punto*"), which rivals Scottish country dancing for its complexity and has been adopted as the national dance. That said, they're not exactly dancing in the streets of Santa Cruz; life is actually rather slow, much of it lived out in a contemplative fashion on the wide verandas of the town's old houses.

Unless you arrive during the **Fiesta Santa Cruz** (mid-Jan), when the town comes alive with bullfights and fireworks and the streets overflow with revellers, Santa Cruz offers little reason to linger longer than it takes to catch the bus out. There are few facilities too, apart from the **Banco Nacional** on the way into town.

ARRIVAL AND DEPARTURE   SANTA CRUZ

By bus Santa Cruz is a regional transport hub, with good connections inland and to the coast. Tralapa (☎ 2221 7202) and Alfaro (☎ 2222 2666) run daily buses to San José which depart more or less hourly from the bus terminal on the west side of the central plaza. There are also numerous local bus services to Liberia. A number of buses head to Tamarindo, including a direct service. You can also get to playas Flamingo and Brasilito, via Tamarindo.

Destinations Liberia (every 30min; 1hr 10min); Nicoya (every 30min–1hr; 30min); Playa Brasilito (hourly; 1hr 30min); Playa Flamingo (hourly; 1hr 45min); Playa Junquillal (3 daily; 1hr 30min); San José (hourly; 4hr 30min); Tamarindo (every 1–2hr; 1hr).

ACCOMMODATION AND EATING

★Coope-Tortillas Just off the central plaza. For food, join the locals at this popular barn-sized tortilla-making co-operative with its own restaurant that serves chicken, Guanacastecan *empanadas* and sweet cheese bread, as well, of course, as tortillas (most dishes ₡3000–5000). Daily 7am–5pm.

Hotel Paraje del Diriá 3km north of town ☎ 2680 1826. Located just outside Santa Cruz, *Hotel Paraje del Diriá* makes a decent choice, with modest a/c rooms (all with private bathrooms) plus a couple of small swimming pools. **US$60**

COWBOY CULTURE IN GUANACASTE

Much of Guanacaste remains cattle country, and a huge part of the region's appeal is its **sabanero** (cowboy) culture. As in the US, the *sabanero* has acquired a mythical aura – industrious, free-spirited, monosyllabic, and a skilful handler of animals and the environment – and his rough, tough body, clad in jeans with leather accoutrements, symbolizes "authenticity" (women get assigned a somewhat less exciting role in this rural mythology: the *cocinera*, or cook). In reality, however, the life of the *sabaneros* is hard; they often work in their own smallholdings or as *peones* (farmworkers) on large haciendas owned by relatively well-off ranchers.

To witness the often extraordinary skills of the *sabaneros*, head for the smaller towns – particularly on the Nicoya Peninsula – where during the months of January and February weekend **fiestas** are held in the local *redondel de toros* (bullring). More a rodeo than a bullfight, unlike in Spain, no gory kills are made: the spectacle comes from amazing feats of bull riding and roping. You'll see cowboys riding their horses alongside the Interamericana highway, too, often towing two or three horses behind them as big transport trucks steamroll past on their way to Nicaragua.

This dependence on cattle culture has its downside. Much of Guanacaste is **degraded pastureland**, abandoned either because of its exhaustion by grazing or as a result of continually poor domestic and foreign markets for Costa Rican meat. Although impressive efforts to regenerate former tropical dry forest are ongoing – at Parque Nacional Santa Rosa and Parque Nacional Guanacaste, for example – it is unlikely that this rare habitat will recover its original profile.

FROM TOP FIESTA SANTA CRUZ; PARQUE NACIONAL RINCÓN DE LA VIEJA (P.251) >

5

CHOROTEGA POTTERY

The chief characteristics of **Chorotega pottery** are the striking black and red on white **colouring**, called *pataky*, and a preponderance of panels, decorated with intricate anthropomorphic snake, jaguar and alligator motifs. Archeologists believe that pieces coloured and designed in this way were associated with the elite, possibly as mortuary furniture for *caciques* (chiefs) or other high-ranking individuals. In the Period VI (an archeological term for the years between 1000 BC and 500 AD) the *murillo appliqué* style emerged, an entirely new, glossy, black or red pottery with no parallel anywhere else in the region, but curiously similar to pottery found on Marajó Island at the mouth of the Amazon in modern-day Brazil, thousands of kilometres away.

After the Conquest, predictably, pottery-making declined sharply. The traditional anthropomorphic images were judged to be pagan by the Catholic Church and subsequently suppressed. Today you can see some of the best specimens in San José's Museo Nacional (see p.96) or watch them being faithfully reproduced in **Guaitíl**, where potters use local resources and traditional methods little-changed since the days of the Chorotegas. To make the clay, local rock is ground on ancient *metates*, which the Chorotegas used for grinding corn. The pigment used on many of the pieces, *curiol*, comes from a porous stone that has to be collected from a natural source, a four-hour walk away, and the ceramic piece is shaped using a special stone, also local, called *zukia*. *Zukias* were used by Chorotega potters to mould the lips and bases of plates and pots; treasured examples have been found in Chorotega graves.

Guaitíl

The only town in Guanacaste where you can still see crafts being made in the traditional way is **GUAITÍL**, 12km east of Santa Cruz, famous throughout Costa Rica for its **ceramics**. On the site of a major Chorotega potters' community, the present-day artisans' co-operative (*cooperativo artesanía*) was founded more than twenty years ago by three local women whose goal was to use regional traditions and their own abilities as potters and decorators for commercial gain. Today the artisans are still mainly women, keeping customs alive at the distinctive, large, dome-shaped kilns, while the men work in agricultural smallholdings.

Every house in Guaitíl seems to be in on the trade, with pottery on sale in front of people's homes, on little roadside stalls and in the **Artesanía Cooperativa** on the edge of the football field. Some of the houses are open for you to wander inside and watch the women at work. Wherever you buy, don't haggle and don't expect it to be dirt cheap, either. A large vase can easily cost US$35 or more. Bear in mind, too, that this is decorative rather than functional pottery, and may not be that durable.

ARRIVAL AND DEPARTURE   GUAITÍL

By bus The main bus stop is in the centre, adjacent to the church, and has regular Santa Cruz services (2 daily; 20min).

By car Guaitíl is on the old road to Nicoya; to get there from

Santa Cruz, head east on the smaller road instead of south on the new road; turn off to the left where you see the sign for Guaitíl.

By taxi Taxis from Santa Cruz cost about ₡10,000.

Central Nicoya Peninsula

The **central Nicoya Peninsula** is marked by the contrast between the traditional Tico character of the pastoral interior and the expat-favoured coast. Though they are easier to reach than they once were, the laidback surfing towns of **Sámara** and **Nosara** feel far removed from the glitz and encroaching resorts along the coast to the north. The peninsula's principal town, **Nicoya**, remains little changed and is still a quiet base from which to make forays into the otherworldly caverns of nearby **Parque Nacional Barra Honda**.

Nicoya

Bus travellers journeying between San José and the beach towns of Sámara (see p.287) and Nosara (see p.290) generally need to make connections at the country town of **NICOYA**, inland and northeast of the beaches. Set in a dip surrounded by low mountains, Nicoya is the peninsula's major travel and agricultural centre. It's also Costa Rica's oldest city and one that retains a strong indigenous presence alongside a significant Chinese community, with many of the town's restaurants, hotels and stores owned by descendants of Chinese immigrants.

The town is permeated by an air of infinite stasis but is undeniably pretty, with a lovely **Parque Central**, cascading bougainvillea, colourful plants and a white adobe church, the **Parroquia San Blas**. Founded in 1644, this mission-style church is the oldest in the country; it's survived multiple earthquakes and has recently undergone extensive renovation.

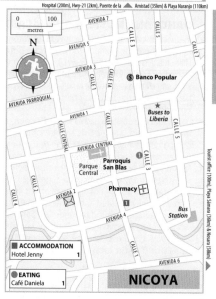

ARRIVAL AND INFORMATION

By bus Most buses arrive at Nicoya's bus station on the southern edge of town, a short walk from the centre; the Liberia service pulls in across from the *Hotel Las Tinajas*.
Destinations Cañas, via Irma (hourly; 2–3hr); Liberia (every 30min–1hr; 1hr 40min); Nosara (6 daily; 1hr 30min); Playa Sámara (8–12 daily; 45min–1hr); San José (10 daily; 4hr); Santa Cruz (every 30min–1hr; 30min).

By taxi Taxis line up by the Parque Central (or call Coopetico on ☎ 2658 6226).
Tourist information The ICT office (Mon–Fri 10am–5pm; ☎ 2685 3260, ⌨ ict.go.cr), a few blocks south of the centre on Hwy-150 across from the national university, provides a wealth of information and maps on the peninsula as well as most of Guanacaste.

ACCOMMODATION

Hotel Jenny C 1, at Av 4 ☎ 2685 5050. Few tourists stay in Nicoya, but if you need a bed for the night, head to this no-frills hotel near the Parque Central. The rooms are musty and tired, but okay for a night, with TVs and a/c. Staff are a useful source of local info, and can help arrange tours. **US$30**

EATING

Café Daniela 100m east of Parque Central ☎ 2686 6148. If you need a quick meal while waiting for your transport connection, head to this pleasant *soda*, which doles out straightforward *comida típica* (around ₡3000) all day long; try the chicken *casado*. Daily 7am–9pm.

DIRECTORY

Banks and exchange There's a Banco Popular with an ATM at C3, Av 1/3.

Hospital Seven blocks north of Parque Central is Hospital La Anexion (☎ 2685 8400), C 3, Av 11/15.

Parque Nacional Barra Honda

3km northeast of the hamlet of Santa Ana • Daily 8am–4pm • US$12

Parque Nacional Barra Honda, about 13km west of the Río Tempisque, is popular with spelunkers for its forty-odd subterranean **caves**. A visit to Barra Honda is not for

5

DANCE AND MUSIC IN GUANACASTE

In their book *A Year of Costa Rican Natural History*, Amelia Smith Calvert and Philip Powell Calvert describe their month on Guanacaste's **fiesta** circuit in 1910, starting in January in Filadelfía, a small town between Liberia and Santa Cruz, and ending in Santa Cruz. They were fascinated by the formal nature of the functions they attended, observing: "The dances were all round **dances**, mostly of familiar figures, waltzes and polkas, but one, called '*el punto*' was peculiar in that the partners do not hold one another but walk side by side, turn around each other and so on."

At Santa Cruz, "All the ladies sat in a row on one side of the room when not dancing, the men elsewhere. When a lady arrived somewhat late, then the rest of the guests of the company, if seated, arose in recognition of her presence. The **music** was furnished by three fiddles and an accordion. The uninvited part of the community stood outside the house looking into the room through the open doors, which as usual were not separated from the street by any vestibule or passage." The Calverts were also delighted to come across **La giganta**, the figure of a woman about 4m high; actually a man on stilts "with a face rather crudely moulded and painted". What exactly *La giganta* represented isn't known, but she promenaded around the streets of Santa Cruz in her finery, long white lace trailing, while her scurrying minders frantically worked to keep her from keeling over. *La giganta*, along with other oversized personalities, still features in nearly every large village fiesta, usually held on the local saint's day.

claustrophobes, people afraid of heights (some of the caves are more than 200m deep) or anyone with an aversion to creepy-crawlies.

The landscape around here is dominated by the **limestone plateau** of the Cerro Barra Honda, which rises out of the flat lowlands of the eastern Nicoya Peninsula. About seventy million years ago this whole area – along with Palo Verde, across the Río Tempisque – was under water. Over the millennia, the porous limestone was gradually hollowed out, by rainfall and weathering, to create caves and weird karstic formations.

The caves

The caves form a catacomb-like interconnecting network beneath the limestone ridge, but you can't necessarily pass from one to the other. Kitted out with a rope harness and a helmet with a lamp on it, you descend with a **guide**, who will normally take you down into just one. The **main caves**, all within 2km of each other and of the ranger station, are the Terciopelo, the Trampa, Santa Ana, Pozo Hediondo and Nicoa, where the remains of pre-Columbian peoples were recently found, along with burial ornaments and utensils thought to be over two thousand years old. Most people come wanting to view the huge needle-like **stalagmites** and **stalactites** at Terciopelo, or to see subterranean wildlife such as bats, blind salamanders, insects and even birds. Down in the depths, you're faced with a sight reminiscent of old etchings of Moby Dick's stomach, with sleek, moist walls, jutting rib-like ridges and strangely smooth protuberances. Some caves are big enough – almost cathedral-like, in fact, with their vaulted ceilings – to allow breathing room for those who don't like enclosed spaces, but it's still an eerie experience, like descending into a ruined subterranean Notre Dame inhabited by crawling things you can barely see. There's even an "organ" of fluted stalagmites in the Terciopelo cave; if knocked, each gives off a slightly different musical note.

The trails

Above ground, three short **trails**, not well marked, lead around the caves. It's easy to get lost, and you should walk them with your guide or with a ranger if there is one free, and take water with you. In the early 1990s, two German hikers attempted to walk the trails independently, got lost and, because they were not carrying water, died of dehydration and heat exhaustion.

CAVE ARCHITECTURE

Created by the interaction of water, calcium bicarbonate and limestone, the distinctive cave formations of stalagmites and stalactites are often mistaken for each other. **Stalagmites** grow upwards from the floor of a cave, formed by drips of water saturated with calcium bicarbonate. **Stalactites**, made of a similar deposit of crystalline calcium bicarbonate, grow downwards, like icicles. Both are formed by water and calcium bicarbonate filtering through limestone and partially dissolving it. In limestone caves, stalagmites and stalactites are usually white (from the limestone) or brown; in caves where copper deposits are present colours might be more psychedelic, with iridescent greens and blues. They often become united, over time, in a single column.

The endangered **scarlet macaw** sometimes nests here, and there are a variety of ground mammals about, including anteaters and deer. As usual, you'll be lucky to see any, though you'll certainly hear howler monkeys. Note that anyone who wants to follow the trails at Barra Honda has to tell the rangers where they are intending to walk and how long they intend to be gone for.

ARRIVAL AND INFORMATION

PARQUE NACIONAL BARRA HONDA

By bus Buses from Nicoya arrive at 8.30am, 1pm and 4pm in Santa Ana (two travel in the opposite direction, departing at 1pm & 6pm; 30min), 3km from the park entrance. From there it's sometimes possible to find a ride to the park, though you can go on foot; the walk is pleasant and not taxing.

By car Driving to Barra Honda is possible even with a regular car. From the Nicoya–Tempisque road, the turn-off, 13km before the bridge, is well signed. It's then 4km along

a good gravel road to the hamlet of Nacaome (also called Barra Honda), from where the park is, again, signed. Continue about 6km further, passing the hamlet of Santa Ana, until you reach the ranger station, where most people arrange to meet their guide.

By taxi It's possible to arrange a taxi in Nicoya to drive you to the entrance, usually for around ₡10,000.

Information The ranger station at the entrance (8am–4pm; ☎ 2659 1551) can provide information and maps.

TOURS AND ACTIVITIES

Spelunking You need to be pretty serious about caves to go spelunking in Barra Honda. Quite apart from all the planning, what with the entrance fee, and the payment to the guide and equipment rental (US$30), costs can add up. It's obligatory to go with a guide, who will also provide equipment; to do otherwise would be foolhardy, not to mention illegal. Sometimes the ranger station can supply a guide, but to save a trip, it's worth checking conditions and availability of guides first, either at the

ACT regional headquarters (see p.244) on the Interamericana or in Nicoya.

Bat tour Witnessing the mass exodus at dusk of the thousands of bats who reside in the Pozo Hediondo cave and hearing the flapping of their wings in the air is one of the park's clear highlights. Guided tours (US$10) to the cave depart from the ranger station daily at 4pm and return by 8pm.

Playa Sámara

One of the peninsula's more peaceful coastal villages, **SÁMARA** is a great place to relax, and its distance from the capital makes it much quieter than the more accessible Pacific beaches. Even at the busiest times, there's little action other than weekenders tottering by on stout *criollo* **horses** and the occasional dune buggy racing up the sand. On Sundays, the town turns out in force to watch the local **football** teams who play on the village field as if they're Brazil and Argentina battling it out for the World Cup – even weekending Ticos shun the beach for the sidelines.

Sámara boasts some of the calmest waters, making it ideal for **swimming**. The long, gorgeous stretch of sand is protected by a reef about a kilometre out, which takes the brunt of the Pacific's power out of the waves. The effect also makes the beach one of the best spots on the Pacific coast to learn to **surf**; the waves are strong enough without being too unforgiving on beginners.

5

THE FRIENDSHIP BRIDGE

Opened in 2003, the 780m **Puente Tempisque** connects the mainland with the Nicoya Peninsula, spanning from near Puerto Moreno (17km east of the Nicoya–Carmona road) on the peninsula to a point 25km west of the Interamericana on the mainland. The bridge replaced a time-consuming ferry connection and saves at least two hours on the journey between San José and Sámara. The US$26 million bridge was financed by Taiwan in exchange for commercial fishing rights in Costa Rican waters, which were quickly rescinded due to abuses. It's partly held up by suspension cables connected to towers that, at 80m, make it the tallest structure in Costa Rica.

ARRIVAL AND INFORMATION

By plane Sansa (☎ 2656 0765) planes from San José arrive at the airstrip 6km east of town at Carrillo, from where 4WD taxis make the trip to Sámara for about ₡5000.

By bus Buses stop at the village's northern edge, where the roads to Nicoya and Nosara meet. You can buy tickets for some bus services from the Transporte Alfaro

PLAYA SÁMARA

office (daily 7am–5pm) in the centre of the village.
Destinations Nicoya (8–12 daily; 45min–1hr); Nosara (3 daily; 40min); San José (1–2 daily; 4hr 45min).

By car Hwy-150 runs the 35km between Nicoya and the coast at Sámara.

Information ⓦisamara.co is a useful website, with lots of info on local restaurants and bars.

ACTIVITIES AND TOURS

Sámara Adventure Company In the middle of the beach ☎ 2656 0920, ⓦsamara-tours.com. Choose from a host of tours at this enthusiastic operator, including stand-up paddle boarding (US$60; 3hr) and mountain biking (US$60; 3hr 30min). One of the most enjoyable excursions is the kayaking-and-snorkelling tour (US$50;

3hr) to scenic Isla Chora, a tiny island south of the village.

Fit Xtreme 100 back from the beach ☎8997 9357, ⓦfitxtremevacations.com. Based at *Tico Adventure Lodge* (see opposite), this surf shop offers group classes (from US$39/1hr 30min), as well as more focused one-to-one private classes (US$65/1hr 30min).

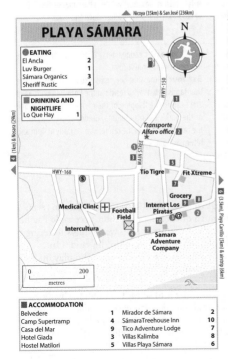

▲ Nicoya (35km) & San José (236km)

PLAYA SÁMARA　N

● EATING
El Ancla	2
Luv Burger	1
Sámara Organics	3
Sheriff Rustic	4

■ DRINKING AND NIGHTLIFE
| Lo Que Hay | 1 |

(1km) & Nosara (29km)

HWY-150

Transporte Alfaro office

MAIN STREET

HWY-160

Tío Tigre　Fit Xtreme

Medical Clinic ✚　Football Field

Grocery

Internet Los Piratas @

Interculta

Samara Adventure Company

(3.5km), Playa Carrillo (5km) & airstrip (6km)

0　　200
metres

ACCOMMODATION

Belvedere 100m down the road to Carrillo ☎ 2656 0213, ⓦbelvederesamara.net. This pleasant hotel has ten rooms and two larger apartments sleeping up to four with either a/c or fan, and all are brightly furnished in light wood, with mosquito nets and solar-heated water. There's also a jacuzzi and a pair of swimming pools, and a good German-style breakfast (included in the room rates). Doubles US$85, apartments US$110

Camp Supertramp 1.4km west of town ☎ 2656 0373, ⓦcampsupertramp.com. A 15min walk outside town, this bohemian, decidedly eccentric, utterly charming backpacker dive offers low-cost, well-kept dorms and camping spots (bring your own tent), a sociable attitude, welcoming staff, and bird- and animal-filled gardens strung with hammocks. No breakfast. Camping US$8, dorms US$15

Casa del Mar 50m north of the entrance to beach on the left ☎ 2656 0264, ⓦcasadelmarsamara.net. Large, good-value rooms (although a bit sparsely furnished) close to the beach. Those on the ground-floor rooms are clean, but rather dark, so ask for one upstairs, which will have palm-fringed sea views. US$55

Hostel Matilori 125m back from the beach ☎ 2656 0291, ⓦisamara.co/matilori. A strong alternative to *Camp Supertramp*, this backpacker favourite has colourful four- and six-bed dorms and a trio of private rooms; both share clean bathrooms. No breakfast, but free coffee in the mornings. Dorms US$15, doubles US$40

Hotel Giada About 100m before you come to the beach, on the left ☎2656 0132, ⓦhotelgiada.net. Small hotel set around a compact pool, with spotless banana-yellow rooms, good beds, overhead fans, private bathrooms and tiled showers – the upstairs rooms are better for views and breeze. There's also an attached Italian restaurant. US$95

Mirador de Sámara First left as you come into Sámara and 100m up the hill from the Marbella ☎2656 0044, ⓦmiradordesamara.com. Huge apartments (each sleeping up to 7 people; the rates below are based on double occupancy) with large bathrooms, bedrooms, living rooms, kitchen and terrace, all with panoramic views of the town and beach, as well as more straightforward hotel-style rooms. The bar is in an impressive tower with spectacular sunset views, and there's a small pool with wooden sundecks. Good low-season and extended-stay discounts. Doubles US$90, apartments US$120

★**Sámara Treehouse Inn** On the beach ☎2656 0733, ⓦsamaratreehouse.com. The atmospheric bungalows (sleeping up to four) here are made of tropical hardwood and raised up on tree-trunk stilts, with strung hammocks beneath them; four face the beach while the other faces the pool. They have modern ceramic-tiled bathrooms, there's a shady open patio with a barbecue, and the beach is just a few steps away.

There are also some simpler en-suite rooms. Doubles US$124, bungalows US$158

★**Tico Adventure Lodge** 100 back from the beach ☎2656 0628, ⓦticoadventurelodge.com. A fantastic deal, this smartly designed US-run hotel has a collection of cheerful rooms (including good-value singles; US$35), many with a/c and balconies, and for larger groups a house (sleeping up to six; US$150) set alongside the pool and an upstairs apartment (sleeping up to four; US$120). There's an on-site spa offering massages, daily yoga classes, and even acupuncture. The personable owner is a great source of local information, and staff can arrange surfing lessons (see opposite). US$85

Villas Kalimba On the road to Carillo ☎2656 0929, ⓦvillaskalimba.com. The six earth-toned villas (sleeping up to four) are set around a pool and jacuzzi and have handcrafted wooden windows and furniture, kitchenettes and a/c. There's also a lovely pool with a mini waterfall and a jacuzzi. US$186

Villas Playa Sámara On the road to Carrillo ☎2656 1111, ⓦvillasplayasamara.com. High-end resort, very popular among wealthy Costa Rican families, with both all-inclusive and bed and breakfast-only tariffs (we list the latter below). The villas (sleeping up to six) come with large, spacious kitchens and sitting rooms, plus outside terraces and hammocks. Though the whole effect is a bit artificial, service could be more efficient, and prices are a bit high, the beachside setting at the quiet, south end of the beach is lovely. US$385

EATING

El Ancla Cabinas El Ancla ☎2656 0254, ⓦisamara.co /ancla. Brightly painted waterside restaurant with an extensive menu of fish dishes that attracts plenty of holidaying Ticos who know good seafood when they smell it. The catch of the day served up with a shrimp sauce is hard to beat (around ₡5500). Daily 11am–11pm.

★**Luv Burger** Near Hotel Giada ☎2656 3348, ⓦluvburger.com. Forgive the spelling of the name and the fact that they have a so-called "manifesto" – this vegetarian, mostly organic joint delivers the goods (dishes ₡3000– 9000). Flavoursome, plant-based (often vegan) burgers, featuring things like "coconut bacon" and "cashew cheese" – both tastier than they sound – plus wonderful falafel, sweet potato fries, and tempting desserts like tiramisu.

There's another branch in the capital. Daily 9am–9pm.

Sámara Organics On the main road in the centre of the village ☎2656 3056, ⓦsamaraorganics.com. Run by a Californian couple, this delightful café attached to a health-food market offers great coffee and guilt-free breakfasts, brunches and lunches (including home-made veggie burgers). Most dishes ₡3000–7000. The owners organize regular farmers' markets (Tues 8–11am & Fri 2–5pm). Mon–Sat 8am–7pm.

Sheriff Rustic On the beach. Right on the sand, this no-frills *soda* has been serving up generous portions of *comida típica* for years. The menu features fresh fish dishes, *casados* and various *arroz cons* (₡2500–6000). Daily 7am–10pm.

DRINKING

Lo Que Hay On the beach ☎2656 0811, ⓦisamara.co /loqhay. Appealing beach bar with live sports on the big screen, cold beers (from ₡1300), well-mixed Bloody Marys

(₡3000), and tasty tacos and pizzas. Head down for "Taco Tuesday", for food deals and live music. There's also a delivery service, ideal if you're feeling lazy. Daily 7am–midnight.

DIRECTORY

Banks and exchange There's a Banco Nacional (with an ATM) located down the first road to the right off the main street as you enter the village.

Medical services For non-emergency medical attention, visit the medical clinic (Mon–Fri 8am–4pm; ☎2656 0166) a few blocks north of the main street near

5

the beach. For emergencies, contact the Red Cross on ☎ 2685 5458.

Post office Sámara's small shack of a post office (☎ 2656 0368), 50m before the entrance to the beach, offers minimal services.

Spanish classes The excellent Intercultura Spanish language school (near the beach; ☎ 2656 3000, ⓦ interculturacostarica.com) offers classes from US$275/week (homestay from US$155/week). There's another branch in Heredia (see p.139).

Playa Carrillo and around

Aficionados of Pacific sunsets will want to head 6km east of Sámara to **PLAYA CARRILLO**, a ninety-minute walk along flat sands. Known for its spectacular evening light and colours, beautiful palm-fringed Carrillo is also safe for swimming, though the fact that more and more people are setting up hotels and restaurants means the beach no longer has the sleepy, end-of-the-line feel it once had.

Hwy-160 east of Carillo

The stretch of **Hwy-160 east of Carillo** is for off-road driving nuts only, and should not be attempted without a 4WD (make sure the clearance is high). You need a good **map**, because roads go haywire in this part of the peninsula, veering off in all directions, unsigned and heading to nowhere, some ending in deep creeks (impassable at high tide even in the most sturdy of 4WDs). The further south you go, the tougher it gets, as dirt roads switch inland and then through the hamlets of Camaronal, Quebrada Seca and Bejuco, all just a few kilometres apart but separated by frequent creeks and rivers. It's best not to drive down here alone, as there's a very good chance you'll get stuck (rising to a virtual certainty in the rainy season, whatever vehicle you have) and settlements are few and far between. There is a **petrol station** in Cóbano: bring a spare can with you just in case, because the distance between here and Sámara (see p.287), in total, is about 70km. Also, be sure to carry lots of drinking water and food, and, if possible, camping gear.

ACCOMMODATION AND EATING   PLAYA CARRILLO AND AROUND

Cabinas El Colibrí 200m back from the beach ☎ 2656 0656, ⓦ cabinaselcolibri.com. Run by super-friendly Argentines, "The Hummingbird" offers good budget accommodation: the rooms have a/c, TV, attached bathrooms, and comfy beds, though breakfast isn't included in the rates. The steakhouse on site (open to non-guests) serves huge slabs of expertly grilled beef, best consumed with tangy *chimichurri* sauce. Daily 7–10am & 7–10pm. US$70

Hotel Guanamar On the beach in front of the hamlet ☎ 2656 0054, ⓦ hotelguanamar.com. Solid option, high on a hilltop, with spacious rooms overlooking a garden or the ocean; it's well worth paying more for a sea view. There's a pleasant open-air restaurant that catches nice

breezes, plus a swimming pool, and the staff organize a handful of tours in the bay, including kayaking and snorkelling. Breakfast included. US$140

Hotel Punta Islita 8km east of Playa Carrillo ☎ 2231 6122, ⓦ hotelpuntaislita.com. The most luxurious option in the area is the isolated *Hotel Punta Islita*, part of the Marriott group, with hillside villas and rooms boasting majestic views and elegant furnishings. The atmosphere is exclusive and facilities include a gorgeous infinity pool, spa, golf driving range, tennis courts, restaurants, bars and a canopy tour, while snorkelling, mountain-biking, horseriding and fishing trips can also be arranged. Breakfast included. Doubles US$305, villas US$625

Nosara and around

The scenic drive from Sámara 25km northwest to the village of **NOSARA** runs along shady, secluded dirt and gravel roads punctuated by a few creeks. It's passable with a regular car (low clearance) in the dry season (though you'll still have to ford two creeks except at the very driest times of year), but you'll need a 4WD or high clearance in the wet. The road follows a slightly inland route; you can't see the coast except where you meet the beach at **Garza**, about ten minutes before Nosara. This little hamlet is a good place to stop for a *refresco* at the *pulpería*, and perhaps take a dip in the sea.

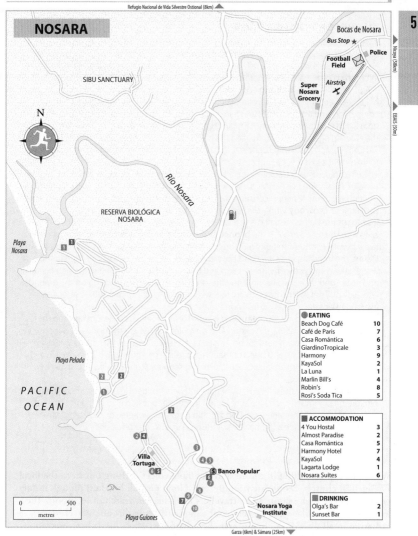

NOSARA

Refugio Nacional de Vida Silvestre Ostional (8km)

Bocas de Nosara
Bus Stop
Police
Football Field
Super Nosara Grocery
Airstrip

Nicoya (58km)
EBAIS (50m)

SIBU SANCTUARY

N

Río Nosara

RESERVA BIOLÓGICA NOSARA

Playa Nosara

Playa Pelada

PACIFIC OCEAN

Villa Tortuga

Banco Popular

Nosara Yoga Institute

Playa Guiones

Garza (6km) & Sámara (25km)

metres 0 500

EATING	
Beach Dog Café	10
Café de Paris	7
Casa Romántica	6
GiardinoTropicale	3
Harmony	9
KayaSol	2
La Luna	1
Marlin Bill's	4
Robin's	8
Rosi's Soda Tica	5

ACCOMMODATION	
4 You Hostal	3
Almost Paradise	2
Casa Romántica	5
Harmony Hotel	7
KayaSol	4
Lagarta Lodge	1
Nosara Suites	6

DRINKING	
Olga's Bar	2
Sunset Bar	1

In contrast to Sámara, the vast majority of people who come to Nosara are North Americans and Europeans in search of quiet and natural surroundings. Indeed, the two main tourist attractions hereabouts are nature reserves: the bird-rich **Reserva Biológica Nosara** and the **Refugio Nacional de Vida Silvestre Ostional**, famed for its *arribadas* of olive ridley turtles. Yoga and surfing are also popular pursuits, with many lodges offering classes in either or both.

Bocas de Nosara

Nosara is more of a widely scattered community than a village as such; it spreads along three beaches and the hinterland behind them. The centre, if you can call it that, is known as **Bocas de Nosara** and is set about 5km inland, backed by a low ridge of hills. The atmosphere in Bocas de Nosara itself is shady and slow, with the

5

THE RECORRIDO DE TOROS

If you're in Nosara on a weekend in January or February, or on a public holiday such as the first of May, be sure not to miss the **recorrido de toros** (rodeo). *Recorridos*, held in many of the Nicoya Peninsula villages, are a rallying point for local communities, who travel long distances in bumpy communal trucks to join in the fun.

Typically, the village **bullring** (*redondel*) is no more than a rickety wooden circular stadium, held together with bundles of palm thatch. Here local radio announcers introduce the competitors and list the weight and ferocity of the bulls, while travelling bands, many of them from Santa Cruz, perform oddly Bavarian-sounding oom-pah-pah music at crucial moments in the proceedings. For the most fun and the best-seasoned rodeo jokes, sit with the band – usually comprising two saxophones, a clarinettist, a drummer and the biggest tuba known to man – but avoid the seat right in front of the tuba.

The *recorrido* usually begins in the afternoon, with "Best Bull" competitions, and gets rowdier as evening falls – after dark, a single string of cloudy white light bulbs illuminates the ring – and more beer is consumed. The *sabanero* tricks on display are truly impressive: the mounted **cowboy** who gallops past the bull, twirls his rope, throws it behind his back and snags the bull as casually as you would loop a garden hose, has to be seen to be believed. The grand finale is the **bronco bull-riding**, during which a sinewy cowboy sticks like a burr to the huge spine of a Brahma bull who leaps and bucks with increasing fury. During the intervals, local men and boys engage in a strange ritual of wrestling in the arena, taking each other by the forearm and twirling each other round like windmills, faster and faster, until one loses his hold and flies straight out to land sprawling on the ground. These displays of macho bravado are followed by mock fights and tumbles, after which everyone slaps each other cordially on the back.

The *recorrido* is followed by a **dance**: in Nosara the impromptu dancefloor takes up the largest flat space available – the airstrip. The white-line area where the planes are supposed to stop is turned into a giant outdoor bar, ringed by tables and chairs, while the mobile disco rolls out its flashing lightballs and blasts out salsa, reggae and countrified two-steps. Wear good shoes, as the asphalt is super-hard: you can almost see your soles smoking after a quick twirl with a hotshot cowboy.

The atmosphere at these events is friendly and beer-sodden: in villages where there's a big foreign community you'll be sure to find someone to talk to if your Spanish isn't up to conversing with the *sabaneros*. **Food** is sold from stalls, where you can sample the usual *empanadas* or local Guanacastecan dishes such as *sopa de albóndigas* (meatball soup with egg).

---

sweet smell of cow dung in the air and excitable voices drifting out from the local Evangelical church. People are friendly, and Nosara is still low-key, though it does get busy in the high season when travellers flock here in search of seclusion. The area around the village can be very confusing, with little dirt and gravel roads radiating in all directions. To counter the lost-tourist effect locals have erected copious signs – though there are so many at certain intersections that they simply add to the confusion. Resign yourself to driving around looking lost at least some of the time.

The beaches

The three beaches in the area – **Guiones**, **Pelada** and **Nosara** – are fine for **swimming**, although you can be buffeted by the crashing waves, and there are some rocky outcrops. Playa Guiones is the most impressive of the beaches: nearly 5km in length, populated by pelicans, and with probably the best swimming, though there's precious little shade. It's also popular for **surfing**, though not so suitable for beginners as Sámara (see p.287). One of the favourite local pastimes is watching the mass of surfers at sunrise and sunset – that is, if you're not among those out on the waves. The whole area is a great place to beachcomb for shells and driftwood, and the vegetation, even in the dry season, is greener than further north. Some attempts have been made to limit development, and a good deal of the land around the Río Nosara has been designated a wildlife refuge.

5

SIBU Sanctuary

5km north of Nosara • Tours daily 10.30am; 2hr • US$65; advance reservations essential • ☎ 8413 8889, ⓦ sibusanctuary.org

The not-for-profit **SIBU Sanctuary** rescues injured and orphaned animals, provides veterinary care and rehabilitation, and – when the time is right – releases them back into the wild. Howler and white-throated capuchin monkeys, coatimundi, porcupines, collared anteaters and tree skunks are among the species you can spot on the guided **tours**. There's also a souvenir shop and an adopt-a-monkey scheme, as well as opportunities to volunteer.

ARRIVAL AND INFORMATION

By bus There's a daily direct bus from San José as well as several from Nicoya and Playa Sámara: all pull in at/depart from the stop adjacent to the Super Nosara Grocery.

Destinations Nicoya (5 daily; 1hr 30min); Playa Sámara (3 daily; 40min); San José (1 daily; 5hr 30min).

By plane NatureAir (☎ 2682 0181) and Sansa

NOSARA AND AROUND

(☎ 2682 0856) fly daily to Nosara from San José, landing at the small airstrip by the village centre and the namesake river.

By bike It's well worth paying a visit to The Frog Pad (☎ 2682 4039, ⓦ thefrogpad.com), in the Villa Tortuga complex about 150m back from Playa Guiones, where you can rent a bike (from US$15/day), as well as quad bikes and golf carts.

ACTIVITIES AND INFORMATION

Surfing The Frog Pad (see above) rents out surfing equipment and offers classes to help you get up to speed (1hr group lesson US$30).

Snorkelling You can hire snorkelling gear at The Frog

Pad (see above).

Information ⓦ nosara.com is a useful website, with lots of handy listings, while ⓦ surfingnosara.com has the latest surf reports (and more).

ACCOMMODATION

Nosara has some **excellent beachside accommodation** if you've money to spend, and the owners and managers tend to be more **environmentally conscious** than at many other places on the peninsula. Indeed, a local civic association keeps a hawkish eye on development in the area, with the aim of retaining Nosara's natural charms and preventing it from becoming another Tamarindo or Montezuma. The cheaper accommodation options are in or near the village, but you'll need to rent a bike or count on doing a lot of walking to get to the ocean.

PLAYA GUIONES

4 You Hostal About 250m back from the beach ☎ 2682 1316, ⓦ 4youhostal.com. This hostel has a touch more style than most of its competitors in the region, with many of the furnishings sourced from Bali. The dorms, private rooms and bungalows (the latter sleeping up to four) are all clean, comfortable and good value. No breakfast. Dorms US$20, doubles US$44, bungalows US$60

Casa Romántica On a side road near the beach ☎ 2682 0272, ⓦ casa-romantica.net. Clean, well-kept family-run hacienda-style hotel right on the beach. The bright rooms have fans, fridges and terraces; some have a/c. There's also a pool and a fantastic restaurant. If you fly or take the bus, the owners will pick you up if you let them know in advance. US$105

★ Harmony Hotel About 150m from the beach ☎ 2682 4114, ⓦ harmonynosara.com. A model of sustainability, this luxury boutique hotel is integrated seamlessly within a tropical garden and lies a short walk from the beach. The

rooms are supremely comfortable with king-size beds, a/c, coffee-makers, and inside and alfresco showers. Service is attentive but not over-the-top, while facilities include a juice bar, yoga studio and spa. The striking pool is just a few steps from the open-air restaurant, which serves some of the best food in Nosara (see p.294). US$360

KayaSol Playa Guiones, about 100m back from the beach ☎ 2682 1459, ⓦ kayasolsurfhotel.com. One of the better budget choices in Nosara, this relaxing spot has simply furnished, brightly painted dorm rooms, doubles and suites. There's a nice pool, kitchen access and an excellent restaurant serving healthy dishes (see p.294). Dorms US$25, doubles US$65, suites US$105

★ Nosara Suites At the entrance to Playa Guiones ☎ 2682 1036, ⓦ nosarasuites.com. Five immaculate and positively enormous, themed ("Buddha", "Fun", "Zen", "Design" and "Modern") suites with a/c, TV, coffee-maker and fridge. There's also a fine restaurant and bakery attached. US$150

5

PLAYA NOSARA

★ **Lagarta Lodge** Signposted from the village near the mouth of the Río Nosara ☎ 2682 0035, ⊛ lagartalodge .com. Set on the edge of the Reserva Biológica Nosara (see opposite) southwest of the village, this high-end lodge has excellent birdwatching and stunning coastal views. The stylish en suites above the pool overlooking the ocean boast one of the best panoramas in the country. There's a spa, and a great restaurant-bar. US$275

PLAYA PELADA

Almost Paradise 150m back from the beach ☎ 2682 0172. One of the better budget options in Nosara, this friendly hostel has a couple of basic dorms (opt for the ocean-facing one, which has more light), a couple of private rooms (one with an ocean-facing terrace) and a few camping spots. It's clean and well organized and there's a decent restaurant and bar on-site. Camping US$5, dorms US$14, doubles US$40

EATING

The Nosara area has a profusion of very good restaurants given the area's relative isolation. There are a number of places in the village, most of them on and around the road leading to the beach or on the road into town, though many of the better restaurants are huddled together near **Playa Guiones**, where the majority of tourists eat.

PLAYA GUIONES

Beach Dog Café About 25m from the beach ☎ 8337 5317, ⊛ facebook.com/beachdogcafe. An expat favourite, this open-air café is the closest spot to the beach for a meal (₡3500–8000). The menu features American-style breakfasts, burritos and tacos, sandwiches and salads, along with good fruit smoothies and coffee. Lots of veggie, vegan and gluten-free options as well. Mon–Sat 8.30am–1pm, Sun 8.30am–3.30pm.

★ **Café de Paris** At the southern entrance to the beach ☎ 2682 1038, ⊛ cafedeparis.net. The brioches, croissants and pain au chocolats confirm this bakery as a bona fide overseas *département* of France, while the pleasant poolside restaurant serves sandwiches and pizzas for lunch (dishes ₡3000–10,000). Daily 7am–5pm.

Casa Romántica Casa Romántica hotel ☎ 2682 0272, ⊛ casa-romantica.net. Some of the most ambitious food in town, featuring a changing menu of fish, steak and pasta dishes (₡6000–12,000). There's a great wine list, too. Dining is in a small outdoor area, lit with candles at night. Daily 11am–11pm.

Giardino Tropicale South end of Nosara, on the road towards Sámara ☎ 2682 4000, ⊛ giardino tropicale.com. Superior-quality authentic pizza cooked in a wood oven and served in a pretty plant-festooned dining area (₡4000–9000). Similarly good pasta dishes are also available, and there's a takeaway service. Daily 5–10pm.

Harmony Harmony Hotel ☎ 2682 4114, ⊛ harmony nosara.com. Taking advantage of fresh produce from the hotel's (see p.293) own farm, this restaurant is hard to beat. Try the passion fruit French toast (₡6000) for breakfast, the smoked mushroom sandwich with a bitter chocolate barbecue sauce and sweet potato chips (₡8000) for lunch, and the sushi (₡5000–7500) for dinner. There's a strong cocktail list, too. Daily 7am–10pm.

KayaSol KayaSol hotel ☎ 2682 1459, ⊛ kayasol surfhotel.com. Inventive restaurant, at the hotel of the same name (see p.293), serving some of the best food in Nosara, with a distinct US–Mexican focus. Highlights include the seafood burrito, the "blackened chicken" sandwich and the deep-fried plantains with a black-bean dip (mains ₡5000–7000). There are plenty of daily specials to choose from, too, and live music on Thurs and Sat nights (from 7pm). Daily 7am–10pm.

Marlin Bill's On the main road ☎ 2682 0458. With a terrace dining area at the entrance to Playa Guiones, head here for calorific crowd-pleasers like bacon-mozzarella burgers (₡4850), jumbo fried shrimp (₡12,500), and Key lime pie (₡2500). Daily 11am–2pm & 6–11pm.

Robin's On the main road towards the beach ☎ 2682 0617, ⊛ robinscafeandicecream.com. Cute café serving top breakfasts, sandwiches, wraps, and sweet and savoury crêpes, plus daily soup, salad and veggie specials. The main draw for many, though, is the selection of sorbet and ice cream (₡1700–3500): flavours include Mayan chocolate, caramel oatmeal cookie, and pineapple-ginger, and the waffle cones are home-made. Mon–Fri 7.30am–7pm, Sat & Sun 7.30am–5pm.

★ **Rosi's Soda Tica** On a small hill above the road leading into Playa Guiones ☎ 2682 0728. Small, friendly, family-run restaurant (one of the few in the area run by locals) serving excellent *comida típica*, including *gallo pinto* for breakfast and *casados* for lunch (₡2500–4000). Mon–Sat 8am–3pm.

PLAYA PELADA

★ **La Luna** On the beach ☎ 2682 0122. A loveable spot right on Playa Pelada, with tranquil terrace tables overlooking the sea. The constantly changing menu features lip-smacking international dishes and seafood (mains ₡4000–13,000). Highlights include salads, home-made bread, and Thai soups and curries. The cheerful owners dream up some sinful desserts, including vanilla toffee pudding and chocolate fudge cake. Daily 11am–10/11pm.

DRINKING

In addition to the options below, the vast majority of restaurants in the Nosara area double up as bars, with many offering later afternoon/early evening **happy hours**.

PLAYA NOSARA

Sunset Bar Lagarta Lodge ☎ 2682 0035, ⦿ lagartalodge.com. Although the changing menu is perfectly fine – and the breakfast buffet makes for a filling start to the day – it's the setting rather than the food that makes this place special, as you drink (and/or dine) to the sound of the Pacific crashing gently below. The sociable seating arrangement has all guests sitting around a big mahogany table – a good way to meet people. Mon & Wed–Sun 7.30–9.30am, noon–2pm & 4.30–8pm.

PLAYA PELADA

Olga's Bar On the beach ☎ 8404 6316, ⦿ facebook.com/BarOlgas. Skip the so-so food and settle down for a cold beer (from ₡1000) at this restaurant-bar, which is one of the best spots to watch the setting sun. Daily 7am–11pm.

DIRECTORY

Banks and exchange Banco Popular (☎ 2682 0011) is on the left side of the main road to Playa Guiones. **Medical services** There's an EBAIS public health clinic (☎ 2682 0266) a block east of the airstrip. **Post office** There's a small post office (Mon–Fri 8am–4pm) next to the airstrip.

Reserva Biológica Nosara

Behind *Lagarta Lodge* on the northern edge of Playa Nosara • Daily 8am–4pm • US$10 • Guides US$10 • ☎ 2682 0035, ⦿ lagartalodge.com

Accessed through the *Lagarta Lodge* (see opposite), the **RESERVA BIOLÓGICA NOSARA** protects nearly one hundred acres of mangroves and dense forests that are home to a bewildering number of bird species, such as blue-footed boobies, ospreys and peregrine falcons, plus innumerable monkeys. There is quite a bit of terrestrial wildlife too, including crocodiles and caimans. An **elevated walkway** (2hr round trip) passes through a beautiful section of mangrove swamp where the calls of birds and frogs seem jarring against the often ghostly silence. Consider hiring a **guide** at the *Lagarta Lodge* for the chance to learn more about the fascinating reserve; you're likely to spot far more animals than you would on your own. Boat and kayak trips are also available, in case you want to explore further.

Refugio Nacional de Vida Silvestre Ostional

8km northwest of Nosara • Check in advance for *arribada* timings • US$12 • Guide (required) US$8 • ☎ 2682 0400

The tiny community of **Ostional** and its chocolate-coloured beach make up the **REFUGIO NACIONAL DE VIDA SILVESTRE OSTIONAL**, one of the most important nesting grounds in the country for **olive ridley turtles**, who come ashore to lay their eggs en masse from July to December. If you're in town during the first few days of the *arribadas* (see box, p.34), you'll see local villagers with horses, carefully stuffing their big, thick bags full of eggs and slinging them over their shoulders. This is quite legal: villagers of Ostional and Nosara are allowed to harvest eggs, for sale or consumption, during the first three days of the season only. Don't be surprised to see them barefoot, rocking back and forth on their heels as if they were crushing grapes in a winery; this is the surest way to pick up the telltale signs of eggs beneath the sand. You can't swim comfortably at Ostional though, since the water's very rough and is plagued by sharks, for whom turtle-nesting points are like all-you-can-eat buffets.

ARRIVAL AND INFORMATION   REFUGIO NACIONAL DE VIDA SILVESTRE OSTIONAL

By car It takes about 15min to drive the bumpy gravel-and-stone road from Nosara to the refuge.

By taxi There is no local taxi service, but if you ask at your hotel, they will arrange for a local to drive you for about US$10–15.

Tourist information There's a ranger station at the southern end of the village. To arrange a guide you can enquire here or stop by the Asociación de Guías Locales (☎ 2682 0428), in the centre of Ostinal, who can make arrangements for you.

The Central Pacific and southern Nicoya

PARQUE NACIONAL MANUEL ANTONIO

The Central Pacific and southern Nicoya

6

Costa Rica's Central Pacific region stretches from the Isla de Chira and the northern boundary of Puntarenas Province to the mouth of the Río Savegre, a languid strip of coastline rich in rainforest reserves and popular beach resorts. Southern Nicoya, effectively cut off by bad roads and a provincial boundary from the north of the peninsula (covered in Chapter 5), is also part of Puntarenas Province, whose eponymous capital, a steamy tropical port across the Gulf of Nicoya, is the only city of any size in the entire area. In stark contrast, the northernmost section of the province is home to the far cooler climes of the hilly Monteverde region.

Here you'll find the country's number-one attraction, the **Reserva Biológica Bosque Nuboso Monteverde** (the Monteverde Cloudforest Biological Reserve), draped over the ridge of the Cordillera de Tilarán. Along with nearby **Reserva Bosque Nuboso Santa Elena**, Monteverde protects some of the last remaining pristine cloudforest in the Americas. Across the gulf from **Puntarenas**, the **southern Nicoya Peninsula** itself is home to the wildlife haven of the **Reserva de Vida Silvestre Karen Mogensen** as well as some of Costa Rica's best-known beaches. Each offers a distinct experience, from the coves of chilled-out Montezuma, a former fishing village that has been transformed into a traveller hub, to the forest-flanked coastline of **Mal País** and **Santa Teresa**, to the untouched sands of the **Islas Tortuga**, just offshore. The beaches on the other side of the gulf are more easily accessed from San José on the Caldera Highway and include the waves of Jacó and Playa Hermosa, two of the country's most popular places to surf. Further south, **Parque Nacional Manuel Antonio** has several extraordinary beaches, with white sands and azure waters, while the surrounding area is packed with hotels, restaurants and tourist services.

Monteverde and around

One of Costa Rica's most magical destinations, the **MONTEVERDE** area is primarily associated with the pristine **Reserva Biológica Bosque Nuboso Monteverde**, the last sizeable pocket of primary cloudforest in Mesoamerica. Straddling the hump of the Cordillera de Tilarán between Volcán Arenal and Laguna de Arenal to the northeast and the low hills of Guanacaste to the west, this highland zone is rich in flora and fauna, as well as a host of generally low-key tourist attractions from ziplines and botanical gardens to butterfly farms and coffee shops. Along with the reserve, you'll

SANTA TERESA

Highlights

❶ Reserva Santa Elena Search for the elusive quetzal in this lush reserve that protects one of Costa Rica's most perfect cloudforests. **See p.309**

❷ Monteverde night walk The jungle comes alive after dark – take an eerie hike through Monteverde's dense rainforest on the lookout for bats, frogs and tarantulas. **See p.312**

❸ Reserva de Vida Silvestre Karen Mogensen Follow puma tracks to waterfall pools on the Nicoya Peninsula's most ecologically important nature reserve. See p.321

❹ Islas Tortuga Take a boat ride to some of the best beaches in Costa Rica, with white sands, palm trees and a lush jungle backdrop. See p.323

❺ Mal País and Santa Teresa Ride the waves at these popular surfing hangouts on the southwest Nicoya Peninsula. **See p.331**

❻ Parque Nacional Manuel Antonio Relax on palm-fringed beaches and explore tangled tropical forests and mangroves abundant with wildlife, from sloths to rare squirrel monkeys. See p.349

HIGHLIGHTS ARE MARKED ON THE MAP ON PP.300–301

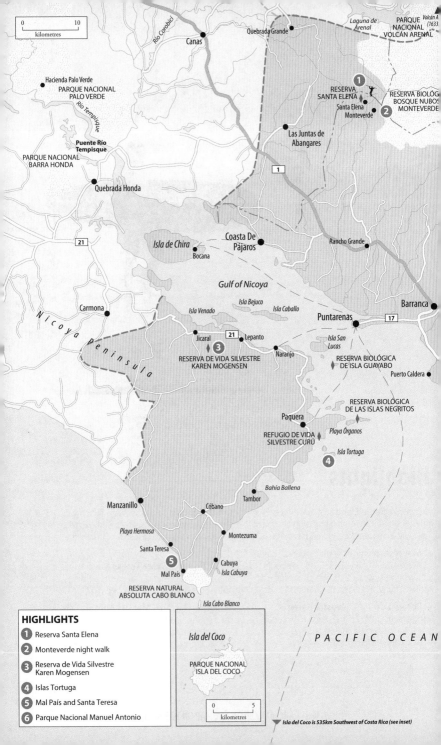

HIGHLIGHTS

1. Reserva Santa Elena
2. Monteverde night walk
3. Reserva de Vida Silvestre Karen Mogensen
4. Islas Tortuga
5. Mal País and Santa Teresa
6. Parque Nacional Manuel Antonio

Isla del Coco

PARQUE NACIONAL
ISLA DEL COCO

0   5
kilometres

▼ Isla del Coco is 535km Southwest of Costa Rica (see inset)

PACIFIC OCEAN

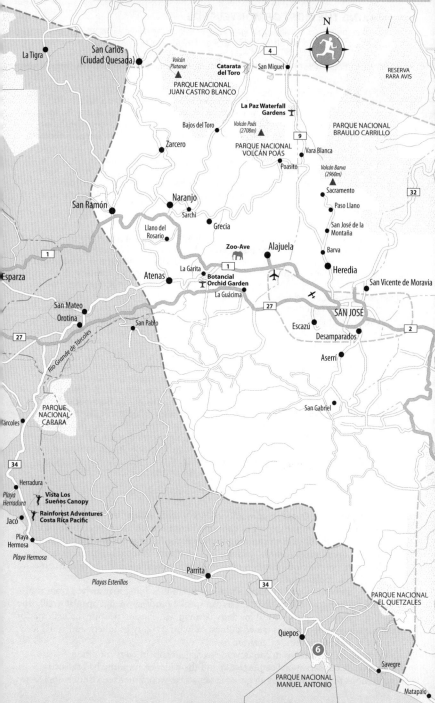

THE CENTRAL PACIFIC AND SOUTHERN NICOYA

N

La Tigra

San Carlos
(Ciudad Quesada)

Volcán
Platanar

4

San Miguel

Catarata
del Toro

RESERVA
RARA AVIS

PARQUE NACIONAL
JUAN CASTRO BLANCO

La Paz Waterfall
Gardens

Bajos del Toro

Volcán Poás
(2708m)

PARQUE NACIONAL
BRAULIO CARRILLO

9

Zarcero

PARQUE NACIONAL
VOLCÁN POÁS

Vara Blanca

Poasito

Volcán Barva
(2960m)

32

Naranjo

Sarchí

Grecia

Sacramento

Paso Llano

San Ramón

Llano del
Rosario

San José de la
Montaña

Barva

Zoo-Ave

Alajuela

Heredia

1

San Vicente de Moravia

Esparza

Atenas

La Garita

Botanical
Orchid Garden

La Guácima

27

SAN JOSÉ

San Mateo

Orotina

San Pablo

Escazú

Desamparados

2

27

Río Grande de Tárcoles

Aserri

PARQUE
NACIONAL
CARARA

San Gabriel

Tárcoles

34

Herradura

Playa
Herradura

Vista Los
Sueños Canopy

Rainforest Adventures
Costa Rica Pacific

Jacó

Playa
Hermosa

Playa Hermosa

Playas Esterillos

Parrita

34

PARQUE NACIONAL
EL QUETZALES

Quepos

6

Savegre

PARQUE NACIONAL
MANUEL ANTONIO

Matapalo

6

MAKING THE MOST OF MONTEVERDE

The sheer number of activities and sights on offer in Monteverde can be a little overwhelming at first, but attractions are relatively expensive and there's a lot of overlap. You won't miss much by being focused on just a handful of sights; visit at least one of the reserves (guided tours are best at Monteverde; see p.305), opt for just one of the canopy tours (try Selvatura; see p.305), and take in one or two of the area's private natural attractions (the Ranario frog pond is a good one; see p.306), perhaps adding on a chocolate/coffee tour (see p.307) if you have time. Note that the reserve's famed birds, orchids and frogs are hard to spot without a guide (it also depends on the time of year, weather and time of day; generally, the best time to see wildlife is at night) – but it's really the cloudforest itself that is the main event, a tranquil, mist-shrouded slice of primeval jungle. The dry season runs December to March – expect rain throughout the rest of the year, with an average temperature of 16–18°C (61–64°F), though in the sun it often feels more like 22–25°C. Note that the Monteverde reserve imposes a quota on the number of people allowed in the cloudforest at any given time (450 total, with 250 on the trails), so it's a good idea to arrive at 7am (opening time). Serious birders, wildlife spotters and those who would prefer to walk the trails in peace should avoid the peak hours of 9–11am, when tour groups pour in.

WHAT YOU MIGHT SEE...

Ever since *National Geographic* declared that Monteverde might just be the best place in all of Central America to see the **resplendent quetzal**, spotting one has become almost a rite of passage, and many zealous, binocular-toting birders come here with this express purpose in mind. This slim bird, with a sweet face and tiny beak, is extraordinarily colourful, with shimmering green feathers on the back and head, and a rich, carmine stomach. The male quetzal is the more spectacular, with a long, picturesque tail and fuzzy crown. About a hundred pairs of quetzals mate at Monteverde, in monogamous pairs, between **March and June**. During this period, they descend to slightly lower altitudes than their usual stratospheric heights, coming down to about 1000m to nest in dead or dying trees, hollowing out a niche in which to lay their blue eggs. Your best chance of seeing one is on a guided tour; alternatively arrive on your own just after dawn, the most fruitful time to spot birds.

Another bird to look out for, particularly in Santa Elena from March to August, is the bizarre-looking **three-wattled bellbird**, whose three black "wattles", or skin pockets, hang down from its beak; even if you don't see one, you'll almost certainly hear its distinctive metallic call, which has been likened to a pinball machine. The far rarer **bare-necked umbrella bird** can only be seen in Santa Elena, and not very often at that, but those lucky enough to witness its spectacular mating routine will never forget it.

Several types of endangered **cat**, including puma, jaguar, ocelot, jaguarundi and margay, live in the reserve, which provides ample space for hunting. You're unlikely to come face to face with a jaguar, but if you're lucky, you may hear the growl of a big cat echoing around the dense forest – usually unnerving enough to cure you of your desire to actually see one.

find the spread-out **Quaker** community of **Monteverde village**; the neighbouring town of **Santa Elena** – with the majority of the area's amenities and budget accommodation – and, further afield, its own cloudforest reserve, the **Reserva Bosque Nuboso Santa Elena** and several small hamlets, including **Cerro Plano**. Throughout the region, the enchantment of the cloudforests is magnified by a combination of tranquil beauty and (mostly) wet, cooler weather.

Seeking autonomy and seclusion, the Quaker families living here arrived from the United States in the 1950s (most locals can speak both English and Spanish well). The climate and terrain proved ideal for **dairy farming**, which soon became the mainstay of the economy – the region is famed domestically for its dairy products, and you'll see a variety of its cheeses in most *supermercados*.

Until recently the roads to Monteverde were generally in poor condition – the **Monteverde Conservation League** (MCL) and the wider community had resisted suggestions to pave them, arguing that easier access would increase visitor numbers to

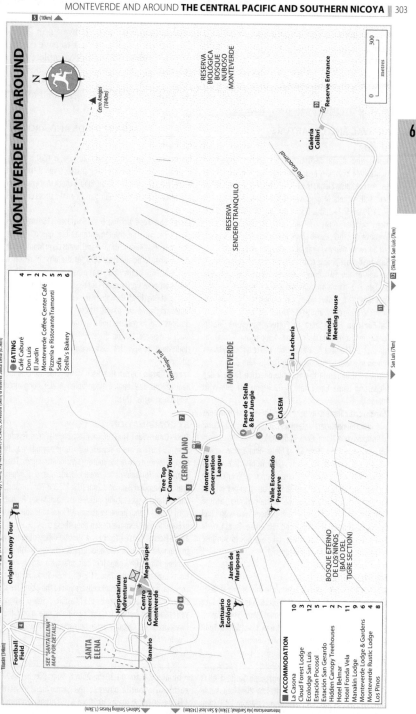

MONTEVERDE AND AROUND

N

RESERVA
BIOLÓGICA
BOSQUE
NUBOSO
MONTEVERDE

Cerro Amigos
(1840m)

Reserve Entrance 10

Galería
Colibrí

Río Guacimal

RESERVA
SENDERO TRANQUILO

Cerro Amigos Trail

MONTEVERDE

La Lechería

Paseo de Stella
& Bat Jungle

Friends
Meeting House

CASEM

Tree Top
Canopy Tour

CERRO PLANO

Monteverde
Conservation
League

Valle Escondido
Preserve

Original Canopy Tour

Mega Super

Herpetarium
Adventures

Centro
Comercial
Monteverde

Ranario

SANTA
ELENA

Jardín de
Mariposas

Santuario
Ecológico

BOSQUE ETERNO
DE LOS NIÑOS
(BAJO DEL
TIGRE SECTION)

San Luis (7km)

SEE "SANTA ELENA"
MAP FOR DETAILS

Football
Field

San Luis (7km)

12 (5km) & San Luis (7km)

11

0   300
metres

Interamericana (vía Las Juntas) &
Tilarán (34km)

1 100% Aventura (3km), 2 (3.5km), Monteverde Extremo Canopy (4km), Sky Adventure (4.5km), Selvatura (6km) & Reserva Santa Elena (6.5km)

Interamericana (vía Sardinal; 33km) & San José (143km)

Sabine's Smiling Horses (1.3km)

Interamericana (vía Sardinal; 33km) & San José (143km)

EATING

Café Caburé	4
Don Luis	1
El Jardín	2
Monteverde Coffee Center Café	7
Pizzería e Ristorante Tramonti	5
Sofía	3
Stella's Bakery	6

ACCOMMODATION

La Casona	10
Cloud Forest Lodge	3
Ecolodge San Luis	12
Estación Pocosol	5
Estación San Gerardo	1
Hidden Canopy Treehouses	2
Hotel Belmar	7
Hotel Fonda Vela	11
Manakin Lodge	9
Monteverde Lodge & Gardens	6
Monteverde Rustic Lodge	4
Los Pinos	8

6

unsustainable levels and threaten the integrity of local communities. However, in 2013 a steep decline in tourism revenue precipitated a U-turn, and the project to pave the main access road (Hwy-606) from the Interamerican highway should be complete by the end of 2017 – though at the time of research funding delays, red tape and poor weather conditions had hampered the work. Whatever the future holds, it's unlikely that Monteverde will be ruined: the community is too outspoken and organized to let itself be overrun by its own success.

6

ARRIVAL AND DEPARTURE   MONTEVERDE AND AROUND

BY BUS

Buses arrive at and depart from the Centro Commerical Monteverde complex, near the MegaSuper supermarket, just east of Santa Elena (the Transportes Monteverde office here sells tickets Mon–Sat 5–11.30am & 1–4pm, Sun 5–11.30am & 1–3pm). It's worth buying tickets for the more popular routes in advance at the Transportes Monteverde office, especially if you're heading to San José, but be aware that the timetable changes periodically.

San José Most people coming by bus from San José arrive on one of the two direct services (departing San José 6.30am & 2.30pm; 4hr 30min); demand is high, so book your tickets a few days in advance in high season. Buses for San José leave daily, also at 6.30am & 2.30pm.

La Fortuna Buses from La Fortuna travel via Tilarán (departing La Fortuna daily 8am & 4.30pm; 3hr 30min), on the shores of Laguna de Arenal, from where two daily buses run on to Santa Elena (departing Tilarán 7am & 4pm; 2hr 30min). Buses run in the opposite direction twice a day (departing Santa Elena 4am & 12.30pm; 2hr 30min to Tilarán).

Puntarenas Three daily buses travel between Puntarenas and Santa Elena (from Puntarenas 8am, 1.30pm & 2.10pm; to Puntarenas 4.20am, 6am, 3pm; 3hr).

Guanacaste The 4.20am Santa Elena–Puntarenas service stops in Las Juntas de Abangares (2hr), from where you can travel on to Liberia and points north in Guanacaste; otherwise, take any San José-bound bus and get off just after the bus turns onto the Interamericana, at the intersection for Chomes, from where you can hail northbound buses to Liberia and elsewhere. From Liberia and other points in Guanacaste, take any bus to San José and ask to get off at the same junction.

BY SHUTTLE

Monteverde is well served by shuttle bus outfits such as Interbus, with daily services to: Fortuna (1pm; 4hr); Jacó (8am; 3hr); Mal País & Montezuma (8am; 5hr 30min); Playa Flamingo (9am; 4hr 30min); San José (8am & 1pm; 4hr 30min); and Tamarindo (9am; 4hr 30min).

BY CAR

Regardless of what route you take here, a 4WD is highly recommended during the rainy season (even if the main access road is paved), and you should check that your hotel has parking, as it's impossible to park on the street once you arrive.

From San José Driving from San José (150km) takes about 3hr via the Interamericana. The quickest route branches off at Rancho Grande and heads up to Monteverde via Sardinal (officially Hwy-606). At the time of research the first 19km of Hwy-606 was a paved road in excellent condition, reverting to gravel for the last 18km beyond the village of Guacimal, though by the end of 2017 the whole highway should be paved (check in advance for road closures due to construction). In Santa Elena itself most roads are paved, but on the way to Monteverde and the cloudforest reserve it's very rough and bumpy (4WD advised).

From Tilarán You can also reach Monteverde from Tilarán, near Laguna de Arenal, a 40km uphill judder along often very rough roads (2hr).

BY COMBINATION

Taxi–Boat–Taxi These immensely popular transfers to/ from La Fortuna are a superb (and time-saving) way to travel between two of the country's major attractions. They depart La Fortuna daily around 8.30am and 2.30pm, returning around 8am and 2pm (US$25; 2hr 30min–3hr), and include a spectacular ride across Laguna de Arenal, with Volcán Arenal looming above. All local tour operators in Fortuna and Monteverde can book these trips.

Taxi–Boat–Horse–Taxi For a slightly different journey to/from La Fortuna, Desafío Expeditions and Sabine's Smiling Horses (see opposite) can arrange a taxi–horse–boat–taxi trip (daily 7am; US$85; 3.5–5hr). From La Fortuna, a taxi (20–30min) delivers you to the Lake Arenal Dam for the boat ride across to El Castillo (15min), where you switch to horses for the two-hour ride along the lakeshore to Río Chiquito. From here it's a 1.5hr taxi ride to Monteverde.

GETTING AROUND

By bus Shuttle buses run from near Santa Elena's Chamber of Tourism (see opposite) to the Monteverde reserve (daily 6.15am, 7.30am, 1.20pm & 3pm, returning 6.45am, 11.30am, 2pm & 4pm; 30min; ₡600 each way). Shuttle buses to the Santa Elena reserve (daily 6.30am, 8.30am, 10.30am & 12.30pm, returning

6

CANOPY TOURS AND HANGING BRIDGES

The **canopy tours** that now seem an obligatory part of any activities centre in Costa Rica were pioneered in Monteverde, using techniques developed by cavers and canyon abseilers to let visitors experience the rainforest from a bird's-eye view. For a different – but no less exhilarating – forest adventure, take a hike along one of the **hanging bridges**, which thread through the treetops for several kilometres; bring binoculars, for here's your chance to spot birds and howler monkeys at their own level. Most of the operators run shuttle buses from hotels in the area, though only three or four times a day.

100% Aventura Office near the police station in Santa Elena; canopy site 3.5km north of Santa Elena ☎ 2645 6959, ⊛ aventuracanopytour.com. A dozen ziplines (one is a whopping 1.59km long), interspersed with a Tarzan swing, rope bridge and abseiling (all included in canopy tour price; US$45), plus quad-bike tours through the jungle (US$60; 3hr).

Monteverde Extremo Park 4.5km north of Santa Elena ☎ 2645 6058, ⊛ monteverdeextremo.com. Offers adrenaline-fuelled tours of fourteen ziplines through secondary forest (US$53), the longest 1030m; the Superman requires adopting an arms-out, legs-up pose down a kilometre-long wire hanging 180m above the trees. Bungee jumps (US$73), Tarzan swing (US$42) and buggy tours (US$100) also on offer.

Original Canopy Tour Near Cloud Forest Lodge ☎ 2645 5243, ⊛ canopytour.com. They're not fibbing: the first canopy tour in Monteverde (and therefore the world) may be smaller than its competitors, but it's more in harmony with its surroundings – stepladders run up the trees themselves (and even through one old

fig tree), and the platforms barely get beyond poking out from their boughs. Tours (US$45; 2–3hr) include an abseil and a Tarzan swing.

Selvatura Office opposite the church in Santa Elena; reserve located 6.5km north of Santa Elena ☎ 2645 6616, ⊛ selvatura.com. The best overall outfit, with a thirteen-cable canopy tour (US$50) – the longest zip is 1km – and a network of eight hanging bridges (US$30, or US$91 combined with a canopy tour and three wildlife exhibits), plus a number of wildlife exhibits (hummingbirds, reptiles and amphibians, butterflies; US$15 each), the most interesting of which is one of the largest collections of insects in the world. Packages can bring the cost down through their website.

Sky Adventures Office on the northern corner of the Santa Elena triangle; reserve located 5km north of Santa Elena ☎ 2645 5238, ⊛ skyadventures .travel. The Sky Limit tour (US$81) comprises ziplining, abseiling and a jungle swing. Hanging-bridge canopy walks (US$39) and Sky Tram gondolas (US$46) offer more relaxed excursions through the trees.

11am, 1pm, 3pm & 4pm; 30min; ₡1500/US$3 each way) must be booked in advance; you'll then be picked up and dropped off at your hotel.
By taxi Jeep-taxis charge around US$12 one-way from

in and around Santa Elena to the Monteverde reserve or US$15 to the Santa Elena reserve. It's around US$6/₡3000 to go between Santa Elena and central Monteverde village.

INFORMATION AND ACTIVITIES

Tourist information For information in Santa Elena, try the Chamber of Tourism (daily 8am–8pm; ☎ 2645 6565) in the centre of the village.
Website For a preview of the area, ⊛ monteverdeinfo.com has details on the cloudforest's flora and fauna, tours and nearby hotels.
Horseriding Tours with Desafío, in Santa Elena (☎ 2645 5874 or ☎ 8379 9827, ⊛ monteverdetours.com), come in a

variety of forms, including "mountain and farm view" (US$49; 2hr 30min); there's also an all-day "cowboy tour" (US$85; 6hr). Sabine's Smiling Horses (☎ 8385 2424, ⊛ smilinghorses.com) arranges trips that stop at various panoramic views of the Pacific and the Nicoya Peninsula (9am, 1pm & 3pm; 2hr for US$45, 3hr for US$65), as well as monthly full-moon rides (US$60; 3hr).

Santa Elena and around

As well as being the region's transport and commercial centre, **SANTA ELENA** is also home to several good nature museums. In the centre of town, the **Jardín de Orquídeas** (entry by tour only: daily 8am–5pm, approx every 30min; 30–45min; US$12; ☎ 2645 5308, ⊛ monteverdeorchidgarden.net) contains more than 460 species of **orchid**, all of

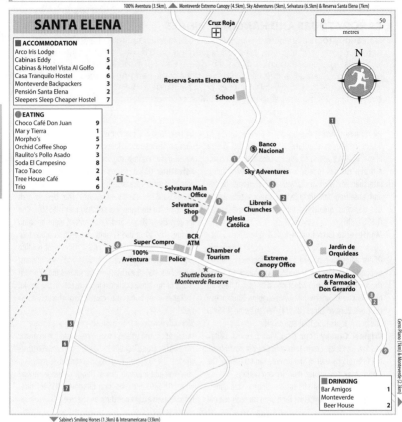

100% Aventura (3.5km), ▲ Monteverde Extremo Canopy (4.5km), Sky Adventures (5km), Selvatura (6.5km) & Reserva Santa Elena (7km)

SANTA ELENA

ACCOMMODATION
Arco Iris Lodge	1
Cabinas Eddy	5
Cabinas & Hotel Vista Al Golfo	4
Casa Tranquilo Hostel	6
Monteverde Backpackers	3
Pensión Santa Elena	2
Sleepers Sleep Cheaper Hostel	7

EATING
Choco Café Don Juan	9
Mar y Tierra	1
Morpho's	5
Orchid Coffee Shop	7
Raulito's Pollo Asado	3
Soda El Campesino	8
Taco Taco	2
Tree House Café	4
Trio	6

DRINKING
Bar Amigos	1
Monteverde Beer House	2

Sabine's Smiling Horses (1.3km) & Interamericana (33km)

them local to the region, including the world's smallest, which can be observed with a magnifying glass. On the road to Monteverde village is **Herpetarium Adventures** (aka the Serpentario; 130m south of the Jardín de Orquídeas; daily 9am–8pm; US$15, multiple entries allowed; ☎ 2645 6002), home to 23 species of slithering **snake**, including deadly pit vipers, along with various other reptiles. The serpents tend to be more active in the evenings.

Ranario (Frog Pond)

Just outside Santa Elena, accessed off the main road down to the Interamericana • Daily 9am–8.30pm; tours on demand 9am–7pm • US$13.50 (two entries) • ☎ 2645 6320

The remarkable **Ranario (Frog Pond)** is home to around 28 species of colourful amphibian (housed in glass terrariums, not actually a pond). These include poison-dart frog, the celebrated **red-eyed tree frog** (the species featured in virtually every promotional campaign for Costa Rica), and the incredible translucent glass frog. Guided **tours** are included in the price – your ticket is valid for two entries, and though staff prefer you take a tour on your first visit, you are welcome to wander around freely on the second. It's well worth making a visit during the day and one at night, when different species emerge from beneath their lily pads. You can also look around the attached **Museo de Insectos** (same hours/admission) with dead and live exhibits from stick insects to scorpions and tarantulas; there's also a small butterfly garden.

6

COFFEE IN THE CLOUDFOREST

Monteverde is probably the best place outside the Valle Central (see box, p.122) to learn about Costa Rica's golden beans. Several companies here offer **tours** of their coffee fields and processing plants, enabling you to follow the journey from bush to bag. The following are especially recommended.

Café Monteverde 4.2km northwest of Santa Elena (400m south of Iglesia de Cañitas) ☎2645 7550, ⓦcafedemonteverde.com. The country's first sustainable coffee producer offers a hands-on tour of an organic plantation, plus their coffee mill (daily 8.30am & 1pm; 2hr 30min; US$30); you can sample their beans without leaving town, at the *Monteverde Coffee Center Café* (see p.313), where the tours start and end.

Don Juan Coffee Tour Carretera Monteverde a Tilarán ☎2645 7100, ⓦdonjuancr.com. With an office on the Santa Elena triangle, this outfit runs trips to a small farm 2km northwest of Santa Elena (1hr

30min; US$35); the tour includes a look at coffee, chocolate and sugar cane processing. Tours usually run at 8am, 10am, 1pm and 3pm – free pick-ups start at around 30min before that, but you need to make reservations for these at your hotel.

El Trapiche Carretera Monteverde a Tilarán ☎2645 7650, ⓦeltrapichetour.com. This is a smaller scale and family-owned producer; their tour (2hr; US$35) also takes you through coffee, chocolate and sugar cane processing, from raw crop to final product (you get to taste at every stage). Tours usually run Mon–Sat 10am & 3pm, and Sun 3pm.

ACCOMMODATION   SANTA ELENA AND AROUND

Santa Elena has the area's lowest-priced accommodation – it's generally simple but you'll get heated water to go with a warm welcome, and the owners usually offer an array of services, from home-cooking and laundry to horse hire. All the recommendations below offer free wi-fi.

IN TOWN

★**Arco Iris Lodge** Up a side street just east of the town centre ☎2645 5067, ⓦarcoirislodge.com; map p.306. Relax in spacious, well-appointed cabins (sleeping up to 6 people) amid quiet landscaped gardens near the town centre. You can also stay in cheaper rooms with double- or bunk-beds. The delicious breakfast of hearty German bread, granola, fresh fruit and eggs is also available to non-guests (daily 7–9am; US$7.50). Doubles US$44, cabins US$91

Cabinas Eddy 100m southwest of the supermarket ☎2645 6618, ⓦcabinas-eddy.com; map p.306. The well-scrubbed rooms here (some with private bath) can accommodate up to seven people and are a cut above most of the other budget options in town. Combine this with friendly owners, free tea, coffee and mountain views from the wraparound balcony, and you're onto a winner. Breakfast is usually included. US$55

Cabinas & Hotel Vista Al Golfo 300m southwest of the church ☎2645 6682, ⓦcabinasvistaalgolfo.com; map p.306. One of the best budget options in Santa Elena, boasting bright, clean dorms and rooms, some with bathroom, plus fully equipped apartments (sleeping 4–5 people) with private balconies. Enjoy fantastic views of the Gulf of Nicoya and relax with fellow travellers in the sociable shared kitchen. The helpful owners can organize tours. Breakfast included with dorm bed only. Dorms US$14, doubles US$29, apartments US$50

Casa Tranquilo Hostel 100m downhill from the supermarket ☎2645 6782, ⓦcasatranquiloback packers.com; map p.306. This cheerful terracotta-coloured hangout buzzing with seasoned travellers has clean, bright rooms (some with private bathrooms), mixed dorm and comfortable mattresses to boot. The on-site laundry service is a bonus. Breakfast of fruit, home-made banana bread and *gallo pinto* included. Dorm US$11, doubles US$24

Monteverde Backpackers 50m southwest of supermarket (central Santa Elena) ☎2645 5844, ⓦmonteverdebackpackers.com; map p.306. Centrally located hostel with the cheapest dorm beds in the area, plus basic private rooms, all with access to well-maintained bathrooms with piping-hot showers. Free coffee. Dorms US$10, doubles US$30

Pensión Santa Elena 25m downhill from the Banco Nacional ☎2645 5051, ⓦpensionsantaelena.com; map p.306. Perennially popular central hostel – the helpful staff can share a wealth of information – offering four-bed dorms with shared hot-water bathrooms, some decent doubles (with private bathroom) out back and attractive suites big enough for families. Amenities include a kitchen, free breakfast and a large communal area where you can yap the night away with fellow backpackers. Dorms US$14, doubles US$32, suites US$60

Sleepers Sleep Cheaper Hostel 200m southwest of Santa Elena centre ☎2645 7133, ⓦsleeperssleep cheaperhostels.com; map p.306. Simple accommodation in clean (mixed) dorms and rooms (sleeping up to four people) that ticks all the boxes for backpackers: inexpensive lodgings, communal atmosphere, shared kitchen and free tea, coffee and breakfast. Dorms U̲S̲$̲1̲0̲, doubles U̲S̲$̲2̲5̲

OUT OF TOWN

Cloud Forest Lodge 500m northeast of Santa Elena ☏ 2645 5058, ⓦ cloudforestlodge.com; map p.303. Set in seventy acres of primary and secondary forest high above Santa Elena, this secluded, surprisingly low-priced hotel is one of the classiest in the area. The well-appointed wood-panelled cabins have cable TV, large private bathroom and terraces with dizzying views, and the hotel has its own 5km system of trails. Breakfast included. U̲S̲$̲1̲1̲0̲

★**Hidden Canopy Treehouses** 4km north of Santa Elena, on the road to the reserve ☏ 2645 5447, ⓦ hiddencanopy.com; map p.303. Fantastic treehouses, the sort you dreamed of as a child, perched up in the canopy, with oversized beds and huge windows that make the most of the superb views down to the Gulf of Nicoya. Bathrooms have waterfall showers, and the two (split-level) treehouses even have jacuzzis on their balconies. There are also rooms in the main house. Two-night minimum stay and no children under 16. Breakfast included. Doubles U̲S̲$̲2̲4̲5̲, treehouses U̲S̲$̲2̲9̲5̲

Monteverde Rustic Lodge C 6, at C 3, north end of the village ☏ 2645 6256, ⓦ monteverderusticlodge.com; map p.303. Small but comfortable rooms near the centre, all with private bathrooms and surrounded by lush gardens. Includes tasty breakfast with fresh fruit, eggs and local coffee. U̲S̲$̲7̲5̲

EATING

Santa Elena is home to a number of inexpensive *soda*-style cafeterias as well as a number of classier options; several of these are hotel restaurants that are open to non-guests. You can pick up fresh fruit and vegetables, home-baked bread, cheese and pickles from the **farmers' market** (Sat 6am–noon), aka "La Feria", inside the high-school gym just north of central Santa Elena.

★**Choco Café Don Juan** Near the Serpentario, on the road to Monteverde village ☏ 2479 4100; map p.306. Excellent coffee shop operated by Don Juan (see box, p.307), serving espresso drinks (from ₡950) and scrumptious cakes (torta Guinness ₡2000), but also sandwiches (₡4500), pastas (from ₡6000) and *empanadas* (₡1200). Daily 9am–8pm.

Mar y Tierra Opposite the Banco Nacional ☏ 2645 6111; map p.306. As the name suggests, *Mar y Tierra* has a good range of tempting meat and fish dishes, including shrimp ceviche and sesame-breaded mahi-mahi, served with organic vegetables from their garden. Mains ₡5000–7500. Daily 11am–10pm.

Morpho's Next to the Jardín de Orquídeas ☏ 2645 5607; map p.306. This stylish split-level restaurant decorated with hanging model butterflies and an extravagant wraparound mural serves inventive mains (₡5000–10,000) like passion fruit chicken and Monteverde blue-cheese tenderloin, as well as less expensive soups and subs. Daily 11am–9.30pm.

Orchid Coffee Shop Next to the Jardín de Orquídeas ☏ 2645 6850; map p.306. Charming café with a breezy terrace out front that's good at any time of the day. The menu features no fewer than 28 types of coffee, plus teas, crêpes (sweet and savoury; ₡2000–6000), panini and salads. Daily 7am–7pm.

★**Raulito's Pollo Asado** Central Santa Elena, next to church ☏ 8308 0810; map p.306. Sit at this casual blue-tiled lunch counter right in the centre of town and feast on mouth-watering rotisserie chicken, one of the best deals in the area; plates of chicken, rice and beans plus tortillas are around ₡2500. Daily 8am–11pm.

Soda El Campesino On the southern side of the Santa Elena triangle ☏ 8704 1867; map p.306. The menu at this unassuming *soda* holds few surprises (the usual *casados*, *arroz cons*, etc), but everything is well prepared, portions are sizeable, and service is friendly. Mains ₡5000–8000. Daily 6am–8pm.

★**Taco Taco** Pensión Santa Elena, 25m downhill from the Banco Nacional ☏ 2645 7900; map p.306. Small takeaway counter attached to the hostel (see p.307), knocking out excellent Tex-Mex style tacos, burritos and quesadillas stuffed with fish, seasoned chicken and slow-roasted short rib, topped with home-made salsas (tacos from ₡550, burritos ₡3200). Cash only. Daily 7am–8pm.

Tree House Café Opposite the church, central Santa Elena ☏ 2645 5004; map p.306. The eclectic menu includes huge platters, but you're better off opting for something simpler – pancakes and granola for breakfast, a creamy *batido* (around ₡2000) or a cocktail (₡3000–5000) – as you're really here for the huge fig tree that grows right through the centre of the restaurant. Daily 11am–10pm.

Trio 50m west of the supermarket ☏ 2645 7254; map p.306. Cool restaurant from the Karen Nielsen stable (the brains behind Cerro Plano's *Sofía*), with food served on an attractive terrace. The innovative menu features dishes such as ribs with sugar-cane syrup and beer, and sea bass with spiced watermelon sauce (mains ₡5500–10,000). Daily 11.30am–9pm.

DRINKING

Bar Amigos Down a side street opposite the church ☏ 2645 5071, ⓦ facebook.com/BarAmigosMonteverde. Most of Santa Elena's nightlife centres on *Bar Amigos*, which has live bands (every Fri night), DJs, big-screen sports events and locals and visitors slinging back beers (from ₡1500). Daily noon–2am.

Monteverde Beer House 50m from the bus station ☎ 2645 7675. Santa Elena's very own microbrewery, offering 4–6 types of decent craft beers, from IPA to stout and chilli-flavoured ales (₡2500), plus Middle Eastern food (the owners are Israeli). Brewery tours available. Daily 10am–10pm.

DIRECTORY

Banks and exchange The Banco Nacional (Mon–Fri 8.30am–3.45pm; ☎ 2212 2000) with an ATM (daily 5am–10pm), sits at the northern apex of the triangle in Santa Elena (50m north of the church); there's also a Banco de Costa Rica ATM next to the Super Compro supermarket in the centre of Santa Elena.

Bookshops Librería Chunches (Mon–Sat 8am–6pm; ☎ 2645 5147) book- and coffee shop, just south of Banco Nacional, sells espresso, snacks and secondhand paperbacks.

Laundry Chunches (see above) charges US$5/load.

Medical care The local Centro Médico (☎ 2645 7080) is on the main road to Monteverde village, just east of central Santa Elena; the Farmacia Don Gerardo is next to it.

Post office 150m east of the bus station (Mon–Fri 8am–5pm, Sat 8am–noon).

Reserva Bosque Nuboso Santa Elena

7km northeast of Santa Elena • Daily 7am–4pm • US$14 • ☎ 2645 5390, ⓦ reservasantaelena.org • Daily shuttles run from Santa Elena at 6.30am, 8.30am, 10.30am & 12.30pm, returning at 11am, 1pm, 3pm & 4pm (₡1500/US$3 each way; 30min; book in advance via ☎ 2645 6332) • A taxi costs about US$15

Less touristed than Monteverde, the **RESERVA BOSQUE NUBOSO SANTA ELENA**, 7km northeast of Santa Elena, offers an equally memorable cloudforest experience. Poised at an elevation of 1650m, the three-square-kilometre reserve is higher than Monteverde and boasts steeper, more challenging trails and a slightly better chance of seeing quetzals (and three-wattled bellbirds) in season. Established in 1992, the self-funded reserve is supported by entrance fees and donations and depends largely on volunteers, particularly foreign university students. It's run by the local high-school board, whose students help maintain the trails year-round.

The **visitor centre** at the reserve entrance has a small interpretive display documenting the life of the cloudforest ecosystem and the history of the reserve itself, and hands out a helpful leaflet on cloudforests, epiphytes and some of the mammals you might see here. It also rents out rubber boots and has a **cafeteria** that provides coffee, cold drinks and sandwiches.

The trails

Guided walks daily 7.30am, 9am, 11.30am & 1pm; 3hr • US$32

Santa Elena's 12km network of **trails** is confined to an area just east of the entrance – some are surfaced with cut wood and mesh, while others are rough tracks. The easiest is the hour-long **Youth Challenge Trail** (1.4km) with an observation tower halfway along, from where it's possible to see Volcán Arenal on clear days; for the best chance of spotting the volcano, arrive early before cloud, mist and fog roll in to obliterate views. The longest, the **Caño Negro Trail** (4.5km), named after the river that flows from here north to the border with Nicaragua, takes about four hours to complete and crosses two streams en route.

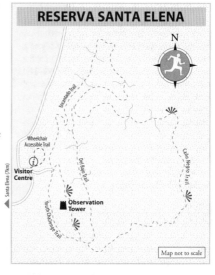

RESERVA SANTA ELENA

You'll see plenty of hummingbirds – strung along the entrance path is a line of feeders that draws many of the multicoloured birds – but for a better chance of viewing all the wildlife that lives here, sign up for one of the highly recommended **guided walks**.

Cerro Plano

The village of **CERRO PLANO**, up the road from Santa Elena, has several attractions. A signposted side street off the main road between Elena and Monteverde leads to the **Jardín de Mariposas** (daily 8.30am–4pm; tours on demand; 1hr; US$15, cash only; ☏ 2645 5512, ⓦ monteverdebutterflygarden.com), the oldest butterfly farm in the country, with four individual butterfly gardens and a leafcutter ant colony; the butterflies are at their most active on sunny mornings. The entry fee includes a **guided tour**, which begins in the on-site natural history museum.

Several private reserves in Cerro Plano offer walks along well-maintained trails in search of sloths, monkeys and birds. Just 100 metres beyond the butterfly garden, trails in the **Valle Escondido Preserve** (daily 7am–4pm; US$15; US$45 with private tour, on demand; 2hr; ☏ 2645 6601, ⓦ valleescondidopreserve.com), 27 acres of former farming land, run past a cascading waterfall and afford panoramas of the Pacific; their night walk (daily 5.30pm; US$25, includes transport from your hotel; 2hr) allows free access to the reserve during the day (before or after the tour).

Off the same side road, the **Santuario Ecológico** (daily 7am–5pm; US$15; US$30 with guided tour, 7.30am & 1.30pm; 2hr 30min; ☏ 2645 5869, ⓦ santuarioecologico.com) encompasses a swathe of transition forest and can be a good place to spot a diverse range of species; night walks (daily 5.30pm and 7.30pm; US$27, includes transport from your hotel; 2hr) head out each evening to spot porcupines, kinkajous and bats.

ACCOMMODATION   CERRO PLANO

In contrast to Santa Elena, hotels in and around the **Cerro Plano** community generally aspire to European mountain-resort facilities – large rooms, orthopedic mattresses and even saunas and hot tubs are the norm – and tend to be expensive, appealing to those who like their wilderness deluxe. These hotels often have a restaurant and meals may be included. Aside from illustrated nature talks, nightlife within the hotels is low-key to nonexistent – some have a small bar, and that's about it. All the recommendations below offer free wi-fi.

Hotel Belmar 2km east of Santa Elena ☏ 2645 5201, ⓦ hotelbelmar.net; map p.303. The oldest of the area's many Swiss-style hotels, the perennially popular (book months ahead) and very ecofriendly *Belmar* sits on a hillside above Cerro Plano, with sweeping views of the gulf. The pricier chalet double rooms (US$199–349) come with spectacular floor-to-ceiling windows and fans. Free breakfast (and coffee) plus local calls, but there are no TVs. __US$190__

Manakín Lodge 1.3km east of Santa Elena ☏ 2645 5080, ⓦ manakin.hostel.com; map p.303. This family-run lodge with the forest as its backyard offers some of the friendliest budget accommodation in the area, including family rooms that almost disappear into the trees. Breakfast is US$5 extra. __US$51__

★ **Monteverde Lodge & Gardens** 400m southeast of Santa Elena ☏ 2521 6099, ⓦ monteverdelodge.com; map p.303. Tasteful rooms with super-comfy beds and corner windows overlooking dense forest, plus three cheaper doubles/twins. After a walk in the reserve, settle down in the cosy bar (with open fire) for afternoon tea and cake. Staff are exceedingly helpful, and the on-site restaurant is superb (see opposite). __US$136__

Los Pinos 1.5km east of Santa Elena ☏ 2645 5252, ⓦ lospinos.net; map p.303. A terrific family hideaway, these great-value self-catering cabins set amid forested gardens are far enough from each other to guarantee privacy. The family cabins (for up to 6 people) are a good deal (from US$180) and come with large kitchens and lounge area. Guests can pick their own dinner from the hydroponic greenhouse. __US$95__

EATING

Don Luis 900m southeast of the bus station in Santa Elena ☏ 2645 5452, ⓦ donluiscr.com; map p.303. Happening restaurant with live music (marimba) most nights, excellent staff and a menu of Costa Rican fusion

favourites, from delicious steaks to sea bass with passion fruit sauce and beef tenderloin with wild berries (mains from ₡12,000). It also has a well-earned reputation for desserts, such as the sensational

THE QUAKERS OF MONTEVERDE

Quakerism (*cuáquerismo*), also called the Society of Friends (**ⓦ** quaker.org), is an altruistic, optimistic belief system founded by Englishman **George Fox** (1624–91), who instilled in his followers the importance of seeing God in everybody. From the beginning, Quakers placed themselves in opposition to many of the coercive instruments employed by the state and society – a philosophy that subjected them to severe discrimination when they first arrived in the New World in 1656 – and they continue to embody a blend of the conservative with an absolute resistance to state control.

In the early 1950s, a group of Quakers from Alabama fled the US, having been harassed to the point of imprisonment for refusing the draft (**pacifism** is a cornerstone of Quaker beliefs). Attracted by the fact that Costa Rica had abolished its army in 1948, they settled in Monteverde. At the time, the remote village was home to only a few Costa Rican farming families; there was no road, only an ox-cart track, and the journey to San José took several days. The Quakers bought and settled some twelve square kilometres of mountainside, dividing the land and building their houses and a school.

Quakerism doesn't impose any obvious standards of dress or appearance upon its followers – you're not going to see the jolly old man from the oatmeal box sauntering by – nor does it manifest itself in any way that is immediately obvious to visitors, except for the area's relative lack of bars. The Quakers manage their **meeting houses** individually, with no officiating minister and purely local agendas. Gatherings focus on meditation, but anyone who is moved to say a few words or read simply speaks up – all verbal offerings in context are considered valid. The meeting houses welcome outsiders, who are never subject to being converted. In Monteverde, visitors can attend meetings at the **Friends Meeting House** (**☎** 506 2645 5098; **ⓦ** monteverdequakers .org), held on Wednesdays at 9am (with schoolchildren) and Sundays at 10.30am.

gorgonzola chocolate truffles. Daily 11am–10pm.
★El Jardín Monteverde Lodge & Gardens, 400m southeast of Santa Elena **☎** 2645 5057, **ⓦ** monteverde lodge.com; map p.303. Beautifully presented dishes such as succulent *bife de chorizo* steak and tuna with garlic and macadamia flakes (mains ₡8000–10,000) hit the spot every time. Considering the quality, prices aren't too high and the imaginative salads are tremendous value. The wine list (from ₡3500/glass) is strong too, with especially good

Argentine options, and the first-rate service manages to combine efficiency with friendliness. Daily 7am–10pm.
Sofía On the main Santa Elena–Monteverde road, just past the turn-off to Jardín de Mariposas **☎** 2645 7017; map p.303. The creative "Nuevo Latino" cuisine (mains ₡7500–12,500) at this stylish restaurant with a candlelit interior won't disappoint. Sweet-and-sour fig-roasted pork loin is a real hit, and the cocktail list is top-notch. Mon–Sat 11.30am–10pm.

Monteverde village and around

Just off the main road east of Santa Elena sprawls the settlement of **MONTEVERDE**, a timeless place where modest houses perch above splendid forested views, and farmers trudge along the muddy roads in sturdy rubber boots. The closet the village has to a centre is the small park 2km from Santa Elena, dominated by *Stella's Bakery*. Here you'll find the arts and crafts collective **CASEM** (Mon–Sat 8am–5pm, Sun 10am–4pm; free; **☎** 2645 5190), which holds exhibits and sells the work of local artists. Founded in 1982 by eight women artists, the CASEM (Cooperativa de Artesanas de Santa Elena y Monteverde) has long played an important role in this small community and currently supports over a hundred local female artisans. Next door is the *Monteverde Coffee Center Café*, where you can sample and buy the local beans, plus Monteverde Whole Foods (daily 8am–6pm), an organic grocery.

Bat Jungle

Opposite *Tramonti Restaurant*, near *Stella's Bakery*, central Monteverde • Daily 9am–7.30pm, feeding times 9am, noon & 3pm • US$7 •
Tours Daily 9am–6pm, hourly; 1hr • US$14 • **☎** 2645 7701, **ⓦ** batjungle.com

High above central Monteverde, the **Bat Jungle** aims to dispel stereotypes of bats as bloodthirsty, disease-ridden creatures of the night. The guided **tour** takes visitors through a simulated tropical rainforest to view ninety cute little Monteverde bats (eight of the region's sixty species) going about their business – roosting, munching on bananas and flying around.

Bosque Eterno de los Niños

Southwest of Monteverde village • **Bajo del Tigre** Daily 8am–4pm • US$14 (US$12 at Pocosol and San Gerardo entry points) • **Guided tours** US$30 • **Night walks** Daily 5.30–7.30pm • US$22 • **Trek to Pocosol** Around US$350 • ☎ 2645 5305, ⓦ acmcr.org

Costa Rica's largest private reserve, the vast **Bosque Eterno de los Niños** ("Children's Eternal Rainforest") stretches over 225 square kilometres. The reserve was largely created thanks to the Children's Rainforest Movement, a funding initiative for eco-projects established in 1987 by Swedish schoolchildren (which quickly went global). Today the reserve is run by the **Monteverde Conservation League** – their information office is opposite the petrol station in Cerro Plano – and encompasses cloudforest, rainforest and montane evergreen forest, harbouring over fifty percent of Costa Rica's known vertebrate species. The most accessible section is at **Bajo del Tigre**, between CASEM and La Lechería, which has 4.4km of easy trails and offers birdwatching **tours** and guided day and night walks, the latter a memorable trek through transition forest, with a good chance of spotting tarantulas, frogs and roosting birds.

You can also access the reserve at two field stations; **Estación San Gerardo**, 7km north of Santa Elena, has access to 5km of trails and is a good spot for birdwatching; while **Estación Pocosol** is on the far eastern fringes of the reserve (13km from Santa Elena), with 10km of trails leading to a natural lagoon and bubbling mud pots. San Gerardo is a 3.5km hike from the Reserva Santa Elena (or a US$40 quad-bike ride), but to get to Pocosol – on the road between San Ramón and La Fortuna – you'll need to arrange private transport at Bajo del Tigre (one-way US$70/person) or embark on a two-day trek from the Monteverde reserve, overnighting at a refuge along the way. This is real bushwhacking stuff, on unmarked trails (pumas have been spotted around the refuge), and each trip is escorted by two fully equipped rangers trained in first aid; you'll need to carry all your food in, plus a sleeping bag.

La Lechería

Southeast of Monteverde village, on the road to Reserva Biológica Bosque Nuboso Monteverde • Shop Mon–Sat 8.45am–4.45pm, Sun 8am–4pm • ☎ 506 2645 7090

Established in 1954 by the original Quaker settlers (see box, p.311), **La Lechería** (aka Monteverde Cheese Factory) is no longer locally owned but remains an economic mainstay of the community. The cheese factory produces a range of European-style cheeses, of which Monte is the best known, along with yoghurts and cream. You can buy fresh cheese (and ice cream) at **La Lechería's shop** and take a peek inside the factory through observation windows here (they don't offer tours). Note that the factory/shop is not clearly marked from the road; look for a sign showing a cow's head, near a warehouse-like building beyond the central Monteverde park.

ACCOMMODATION   MONTEVERDE VILLAGE AND AROUND

As well as the options below, you could try the excellent Finca Luna Nueva (see p.212), which borders the Bosque Eterno de los Niños but is only really accessible from the La Fortuna side.

Ecolodge San Luis San Luis town (UGA Costa Rica Campus), a 15min drive south of Monteverde village ☎ 2645 7363, ⓦ externalaffairs.uga.edu/costa_rica; map p.303. Located on a reserve owned by the University of Georgia, this ecolodge offers accommodation in dorm-like bunkhouses and more comfortable bungalows (sleeping up to 4 people) and cabins (sleeping up to 5 people). Rates for all include three daily meals and a variety of activities ranging from cow-milking to birdwatching. The reserve has an extensive network of wildlife-filled trails, as well as a botanical garden. Dorms US$54, bungalows US$154, cabins US$202

Estación Pocosol and Estación San Gerardo Bosque Eterno de los Niños ☎ 2645 5003, ⓦ acmcr.org; map p.303. You'll be vying for space with scientists and researchers at these two lodges in the heart of the Bosque

Eterno de los Niños. Both provide simple, dorm-style accommodation (each has space for 32 people) and private rooms, and rates include three meals a day. Dorms US$65, doubles US$100

Hotel Fonda Vela About 1.5km before the entrance to the Monteverde reserve ☎2645 5125, ⓦfondavela. com; map p.303. Near the reserve amid quiet grounds, this old-fashioned, family-run hotel is expertly managed by attentive staff. Junior suites aim for deluxe, with huge bathrooms and beautiful furniture, while the standard rooms have attractive wood-panelled walls and large windows – the better to enjoy the astonishing views, particularly at sunset. Breakfast included. Doubles US$105, junior suites US$145

EATING

Café Caburé In the Paseo de Stella complex above the road to the Reserva Biológica Bosque Nuboso Monteverde ☎2645 5020, ⓦcabure.net; map p.303. Relish the coastal sunset views from the lofty balcony over a glass of Malbec at this great little Argentine restaurant and *chocolatería*. There's a range of mains (from ₡7500) on offer, but the highlights are the sweet treats, which include *alfajores* (*dulce de leche*-filled biscuits), green mango strudel, and sumptuous home-made truffles and chocolates. Mon–Sat 9am–9pm.

Monteverde Coffee Center Café Facing the main park in Monteverde ☎2645 7550, ⓦcafedemonteverde. com; map p.303. Best espresso drinks in town, plus you can sample all their coffees, then buy the beans or packets of ground coffee. Also serve excellent pastries (like fresh blackberry pie). Daily 8am–5pm.

★**Pizzería e Ristorante Tramonti** Opposite the Paseo de Stella complex on the road to the reserve ☎2645 6120, ⓦtramonticr.com; map p.303. Don't leave Monteverde without dining at this divine Italian restaurant. Many of the ingredients are sourced from Italy and you can taste the Mediterranean in everything from the *caprese* salad to the wood-fired pizzas (₡5000–9000), which are the highlights. Daily 11.30am–9.45pm.

★**Stella's Bakery** Opposite CASEM ☎2645 5560; map p.303. Pleasant little coffee shop whose walls are adorned with Stella Wallace's artwork (the late founder was born in England and migrated here with the Quakers in 1947); the freshly baked bread, cakes and pastries (from ₡2500) are delicious – keep an eye out for the carrot cake and banana loaf, local favourites. Tasty breakfasts from ₡4300 and smoked trout sandwiches from ₡5900. Daily 6.30am–6pm.

Reserva Biológica Bosque Nuboso Monteverde

Daily 7am–4pm • US$20 • ☎2645 5122, ⓦcloudforestmonteverde.com

Attracting visitors in their droves, the **RESERVA BIOLÓGICA BOSQUE NUBOSO MONTEVERDE** (Monteverde Cloudforest Biological Reserve) is a rare tract of primary cloudforest. At an altitude of 1440m and straddling the Continental Divide, the reserve was established in 1972 by American biologist George Powell and Wilford Guindon, a local Quaker, to protect the country's rapidly dwindling pristine jungle. Today, it encompasses forty square kilometres of protected land (though only three percent of the reserve is open to the public), and is administered by the nonprofit Centro Científico Tropical (Tropical Science Centre), based in San José.

The reserve's sheer diversity of **terrain** – from semi-dwarf stunted forest on the wind-exposed areas to thick, bearded cloudforest vegetation elsewhere – supports six different **life zones**, or eco-communities, hosting an estimated 3000 species of plant, more than 100 types of mammal, some 490 species of butterfly and over 400 species of bird, including the resplendent quetzal and the three-wattled bellbird. The cloudforest cover – dense, low-lit and heavy – can make it **difficult to spot wildlife**, though the

VOLUNTEERING IN THE RESERVES

Both the Santa Elena and Monteverde reserves depend significantly on **volunteer labour**. Volunteers are assigned tasks according to their experience – activities include trail maintenance, teaching English and helping with conservation projects. At **Monteverde**, volunteers are expected to work Monday to Friday from 7am to 4pm and Saturday from 7am to 11.30am, for a minimum of two weeks. The reserve charges US$30 per day, which includes accommodation with a local family, three meals a day and laundry (packages are also available with accommodation at *La Casona* from US$46–83/day). For more information on volunteering at **Santa Elena** (see p.309), email ✉reservaciones@reservasantaelena.org.

RESERVA BIOLÓGICA BOSQUE NUBOSO MONTEVERDE

amazing diversity of tropical plants and insects more than makes up for this, with guided walks leading past thick mosses, epiphytes, bromeliads, primitive ferns, leaf-cutter ants and poison-dart frogs.

The trails

Twelve well-marked **trails** wind through the portion of the reserve open to the public, most contained in a roughly triangular pocket known as **El Triángulo**. They're easily walkable (at least in the dry season), and many of them are along wooden or concrete pathways that help prevent slipping and sliding on seas of mud.

If you're keen to plunge straight into the cloudforest, make for the **Sendero Bosque Nuboso** (just over 2km). The forest canopy along this route is literally dripping with moisture, each tree thickly encrusted with moss and epiphytes. You'll probably hear howler monkeys and the unmistakeable "boink" of the three-wattled bellbird, but it's difficult to spot either in this dense cover – your best bet for birdwatching is at the beginning of the hike.

At the end of the trail, a small *mirador*, **La Ventana**, looks out over vistas of the thickly forested hills on the other side of the Continental Divide. It's reached via a staircase of cement-laid steps that leads to a lookout point suspended over an amazingly green expanse of hills – a surreal place, with only the sound of wind as company.

From here you can loop back to the entrance on the **Sendero Camino** (2km). This is higher in elevation than the other trails, stony, deeply rutted in spots and often muddy – however, as the path is wider, it gets more sunlight, attracting greater numbers of birds and butterflies. To extend your hike, you can take the **Sendero Roble** where it branches off the Camino, then **Sendero Wilford Guindon**, which features a 100m suspension bridge that takes you high up into the trees for great bird's-eye views of the cloudforest canopy. The Wilford Guindon takes you back to the exit, or you can continue on the **Sendero Tosi** and **Sendero Cuecha** to a small cascade in a densely forested gorge, before heading back.

The longest loop and quite steep (often closed in rainy season) starts with the **Sendero Pantanoso** (1.8km), which passes through sun-dappled swamp forests and leads past magnolias and the rare podocarpus – the reserve's only conifer. It links with **Sendero El Río** (1.2km) to bring you, in a long arc, back to the park's entrance.

6

The tours

Guided tours Daily 7.30am, 11am & 1pm; 2–3hr • US$17 (plus admission); US$20 for private tour guide (plus admission); book a day in advance through your hotel or the reserve office • **Birdwatching tours** Daily 6am, 7.30am, 11.30am & 1.30pm; 4hr 30min • US$64 per person (min 3 people; admission included) • **Night walk** Daily 5.45pm; 2hr • US$20 (plus admission) • Transport to the reserve visitor centre for the night walk (additional US$5) leaves from Santa Elena at 5.15pm • ☏ 2645 5122, ⓦ cloudforestmonteverde.com

The reserve runs excellent **guided tours**, with knowledgeable guides who have a knack for spotting wildlife you'd never see on your own, as well as early-morning **birdwatching tours** and a fascinating if eerie **night walk**. Many of the reserve's animals are nocturnal, and your chances of seeing one, albeit only as two brilliant eyes shining out of the night, are vastly increased after dark – you may spot tarantulas, toucans with their beaks tucked between their feathers, and some guides will even catch bats. Although the guides carry a powerful flashlight, it's useful to bring your own for the night walks, as well as rain gear.

ARRIVAL AND DEPARTURE   BOSQUE NUBOSO MONTEVERDE

By bus Public buses make the 6km run from Santa Elena to the reserve entrance (daily 6.15am, 7.30am, 1.30pm & 3pm, returning 6.40am, 11am, 2pm & 4pm; ₡600 each way; 30min); they depart from the southern road of the triangle in Santa Elena.
By taxi About US$12 from Santa Elena (one way).

ACCOMMODATION

La Casona ☏ 2645 5122, ⓦ cloudforestmonteverde .com/lodging.html; map p.303. Accommodation is in basic dorms and six private en suites at this lodge, which is located just inside the reserve and has an infectious environmental buzz. It's often packed with researchers and students (both get cheaper rates); tourists are second priority, so advance reservations are essential. Rates include entrance to the reserve and three meals a day, including dinner at *Pizzería e Ristorante Tramonti* (see p.313). Free wi-fi in public areas only (hallways and the dining room). Dorms US$81, doubles US$162

Puntarenas and around

Heat-stunned **PUNTARENAS**, poised on a thin, island-like finger of sand pointing out into the Gulf of Nicoya 115km west of San José, has the look of raffish abandonment that haunts so many tropical port cities. It's hard to believe now, but until the 1970s this was a booming harbour town – the export point for much of Costa Rica's coffee to Europe – and a popular resort for holidaying Ticos. Today, most vacationing Costa Ricans have abandoned its dodgy beaches, and foreign tourists, who never spent much time here anyway, come only to catch a ferry across to southern Nicoya.

More importantly, this working port remains a jumping-off point for the pristine **Islas Tortuga** (see p.323) and two of Costa Rica's least-explored islands: **Isla de Chira** (see p.318) and **Isla del Coco** (see box, p.320).

The docks and around

Puntarenas's streets do exude a certain melancholy charm, and the local economy is starting to improve. The southerly promenade is optimistically called **Paseo de los Turistas** (Av 4), from the eastern end of which the old dock crooks out into the gulf. This is where bananas and coffee were loaded, before all the big shipping traffic shifted

6

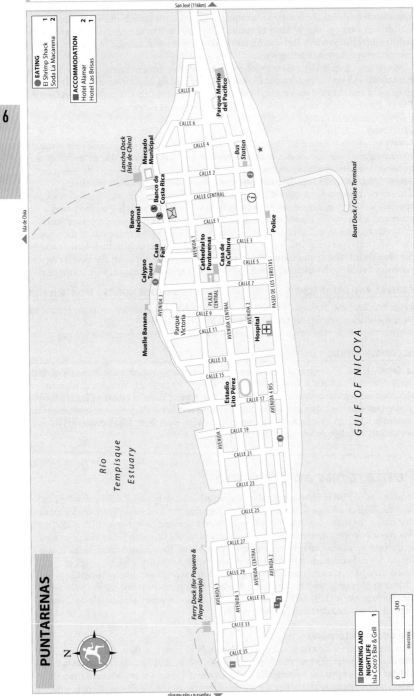

PUNTARENAS

San José (116km)

EATING
El Shrimp Shack 1
Soda La Macarena 2

ACCOMMODATION
Hotel Alamar 2
Hotel Las Brisas 1

DRINKING AND NIGHTLIFE
Isla Coco's Bar & Grill 1

Isla de Chira

Lancha Dock (Isla de Chira)

Mercado Municipal

CALLE 8

CALLE 6

CALLE 4

Bus Station

CALLE 2

Banco de Costa Rica

CALLE CENTRAL

Banco Nacional

CALLE 1

Police

Parque Marino del Pacífico

Casa Fait

AVENIDA 1

Cathedral to Puntarenas

Casa de la Cultura

CALLE 3

CALLE 5

Boat Dock / Cruise Terminal

Calypso Tours

CALLE 7

PASEO DE LOS TURISTAS

Muelle Banana

AVENIDA 3

PLAZA CENTRAL

Parque Victoria

CALLE 9

AVENIDA CENTRAL

AVENIDA 2

CALLE 11

Hospital

CALLE 13

GULF OF NICOYA

CALLE 15

Estadio Lito Pérez

CALLE 17

AVENIDA 4 BIS

Río Tempisque Estuary

AVENIDA 1

CALLE 19

CALLE 21

CALLE 23

CALLE 25

CALLE 27

CALLE 29

AVENIDA CENTRAL

AVENIDA 2

Ferry Dock (for Paquera & Playa Naranjo)

AVENIDA 3

AVENIDA 1

CALLE 31

CALLE 33

CALLE 35

Paquera & Playa Naranjo

N

0   300
metres

18km down the coast to Puerto Caldera; it's now used by giant cruise ships and lined with street vendors. The docks on the northern, **estuary** side, are a jungle of ketches and sturdy mini-trawlers testifying to a thriving fishing industry. Despite the aura of hot lassitude, plenty of business is conducted in the few blocks surrounding the docks, especially in the hectic **Mercado Municipal** (Av 3, at C 2; daily 6am–4pm), which dates back to 1907. One block west (Av 3, at C 3), the **Casa Fait** is the city's most attractive building, a delicate Art Nouveau home completed in 1925. Though safe enough during the day, it's best to avoid the docks at night.

Casa de la Cultura and Museo Histórico Marino

Av Central, at C 5 • **Casa de la Cultura** Mon–Fri 8am–4pm • Free • ☎ 2661 1394 • **Museo Histórico Marino** Tues–Sun 9.45am–noon & 1–5.15pm • Free • ☎ 2661 1394

In the centre of town, the orange colonial-style **Casa de la Cultura** (the former police headquarters and jail) exhibits evocative *fin-de-siècle* photographs documenting Puntarenas's former prosperity. Sepia images of tough fishermen hang alongside photos of white-clad ladies whose husbands made their wealth from coffee exports. The Casa's **Museo Histórico Marino** has a rundown of the region's archeology, biology and history, focusing on the town's relationship with the sea that virtually surrounds it.

Parque Marino del Pacífico

Paseo de los Turistas, C 6/14 • Tues–Sun 9am–4.30pm • US$10, under-12s US$5 • ☎ 2661 5272, ⊛ parquemarino.org

Two blocks east of the bus station, **Parque Marino del Pacífico** is a small aquarium and rescue centre dedicated to Costa Rica's marine life. Among the species here are clown fish, nurse sharks, seahorses, eels and anemones. There's also a (marine life-free) swimming pool for children (Fri–Sun; free with admission).

ARRIVAL AND DEPARTURE   **PUNTARENAS**

BY BUS

Services to and from San José use the bus station on the corner of C 2 and Paseo de los Turistas, just southeast of the Casa de la Cultura, as do services from Liberia. Buses from Santa Elena/Monteverde pull in at the bus stop on the opposite side of the *paseo*. If you're heading south along the coast to Manuel Antonio, you'll need to take the Quepos service from the bus station; most buses run via Jacó.

Destinations Jacó (7 daily; 1hr 30min); Liberia (9 daily; 3hr); Santa Elena/Monteverde (daily 8am, 1.30pm & 6pm; 3hr); Quepos (8 daily; 3hr); San José (hourly; 2hr 20min).

BY FERRY

Ferries dock at the northwestern end of Puntarenas, a 15min walk from the city centre; buses (labelled "FERRY") run up and down Av Central. It can be a slow process buying a car ticket, so in high season arrive at least an hour before departure and park in the queue before purchasing your ticket.

Paquera Navieras Tambor (☎ 2661 2084, ⊛ naviera tambor.com) runs to Paquera (6 daily 5am–8.30pm; ₡810/ person, ₡11,400/car; US dollars accepted; 1hr 15min), from where buses run on to Montezuma (2hr), via Tambor (50min) and Cóbano (1hr 30min); the 5pm ferry is the last one that connects with this service. You'll need to change buses in Cóbano for Mal País and Santa Teresa (daily 10.30am & 2.30pm; 30min).

Playa Naranjo COONATRAMAR (☎ 2661 1069, ⊛ coonatramar.com) runs to Playa Naranjo (4–6 daily 6.30am–8.30pm; ₡1005/person, ₡9000/car; US dollars accepted; 1hr), from where buses travel on to Nicoya (4 daily; 2hr).

ACCOMMODATION

If you're catching an early ferry to Paquera or Playa Naranjo, you may find the **budget hotels** around the north-shore docks quite handy, though be warned that at night this area can be seedy, and at some of the more dismal hotels the clientele may not be there for sleeping. Even considering Costa Rica's tropical climate, Puntarenas stands out as an exceptionally hot town – wherever you stay, make sure your room has a **fan** (or even better a/c) that works, otherwise you'll be as baked as a ceramic pot by morning.

Hotel Alamar Paseo de los Turistas, C 31/33 ☎ 2661 4343, ⊛ alamarcr.com. One of the better options on the seafront strip, the spacious rooms in this family-friendly hotel have a/c, free wi-fi, cable TV and private bathrooms. There are two pools, a hot tub, secure parking and a restaurant (breakfast included). **US$85**

Hotel Las Brisas Paseo de los Turistas, at C 33 ⓣ 2661 4040, ⓦ lasbrisashotelcr.com. Relax at this cheerful, clean waterfront hotel on the peninsula's southwestern tip. Rooms come with TVs, phones, free wi-fi and a/c; some also have balconies overlooking the Gulf of Nicoya. Splash about in the swimming pool and enjoy Greek food at the breezy café (breakfast included). **US$90**

EATING

Puntarenas is known for its seafood, best experienced at the beachside *sodas* near the old dock. Alternatively, pick up an inexpensive meal in the market (see p.317), but avoid drinking anything made with the local water.

El Shrimp Shack Av 3, C 3/7 (350m west of Mercado Municipal) ⓣ 2661 0585, ⓦ elshrimpshack.com. This *camarones* specialist offers high-quality seafood, and is especially well known for its buffalo shrimp in blue cheese sauce, ceviche, curry coconut shrimp and hefty shrimp burgers (mains from ₡6000). Serves as the base for Islas Tortuga (see p.323) operator Calypso Cruises. Daily 11am–5.30pm.

Soda La Macarena Opposite the bus station, on Av 4 ⓣ 2661 1415. This small *soda* with ocean views serves up cheap, delicious dishes (from ₡2500), from fruit plates to toasted sandwiches; try their "Churchills", similar to a crushed-ice *granizado* but made with ice cream. Mon & Wed–Sun 11am–6.30pm.

DRINKING AND NIGHTLIFE

Some of the larger hotels in Puntarenas have nightclubs that draw crowds on Saturday nights and holiday weekends, and you can always enjoy drinks at the open-air **bars** along the Paseo de los Turistas.

Isla Coco's Bar & Grill Av 3, at C 35 (100m west of the ferry dock) ⓣ 4700 3142. This lively restaurant and beach bar serves decent seafood but is best known for its cocktails and live music, from salsa and merengue to Costa Rican karaoke classics. Service can be hit-and-miss. Tues–Fri 6–11pm, Sat noon–11pm, Sun noon–10pm.

DIRECTORY

Banks and exchange The Banco de Costa Rica (Mon–Fri 9am–4pm) and Banco Nacional (Mon–Fri 8.30am–3.45pm, Sat 9am–1pm), virtually next to each other on Av 3 (between C Central and C 1), have ATMs and currency exchange.

Post office Av 3, C Central/C 1, just a few blocks northwest of the bus station (Mon–Fri 8am–5pm, Sat 8am–noon).

Isla de Chira

Shaped like a dinosaur skull and surrounded by crocodile-infested mangrove swamps, untouristed **ISLA DE CHIRA** is like stepping back in time to Costa Rica three decades ago. At 42 square kilometres, it is the largest island in the Gulf of Nicoya, home to three thousand Ticos who eke out a simple existence through small-scale fishing and subsistence farming. Inhabited since pre-Columbian times, more than a third of the island is mangroves, the remainder essentially farmland and tropical dry forest. Electricity was only installed in 1987 and running water didn't arrive until 2000, and you can still count on one hand the number of vehicles that pass daily along the island's rough main road.

On the surface it seems there would be little to entice visitors, but one of Costa Rica's most inspiring rural ecotourism projects is underway here. In 2000, with overfishing impacting on the island's traditional economy, a group of local women resolved to generate an alternative income based on promoting the responsible use of Isla de Chira's natural resources. Their decision to establish the island's first proper tourism initiative (consisting of a small hotel, restaurant and nature tours) was met with scepticism by the community, but with international funding, the **Asociación de Damas de la Isla de Chira** soldiered on, buying a small plot of forested land and the materials to build a lodge, restaurant and small fibreglass boat.

Hiking trails lead from *La Amistad* to lookout points, and you can borrow bikes to explore the island. Boat tours are offered to mangrove swamps and to Isla Paloma, a tiny aquatic bird sanctuary that is an important nesting site for pelicans, frigates, great egrets

CANOPY TOUR, SANTA ELENA (P.305) >

and cormorants. About 2km east of the lodge an association of female artisans have a shop dubbed **Las Artesanas**, where they make and sell locally produced jewellery and crafts.

ARRIVAL AND TOURS
ISLA DE CHIRA

By lancha The easiest way to get to Isla de Chira is from Puntarenas (₡4000 one way): a *lancha* usually leaves from the dock near the Mercado Municipal (Mon–Sat noon, Sun 7am; returning 6am daily; 2hr), and is met by a public bus at Bocana dock (₡1000), which can stop on request at *La Amistad* lodge. Check Transportes Isamar (☎6292 2545)

PARQUE NACIONAL ISLA DEL COCO

Rising dramatically out of the Pacific Ocean 535km southwest of the Costa Rican mainland, **PARQUE NACIONAL ISLA DEL COCO** is revered among divers, biologists and treasure-hunters. Gigantic waterfalls plunge off jungle-strewn cliffs straight into an underwater world that has made this national park a veritable "Costa Rican Galapagos". It's the only island in this part of the Pacific that receives enough rain to support the growth of rainforest and is home to 150 endemic species that are found nowhere else in the world, including the Cocos flycatcher and the Cocos gecko. In addition, more than 250 species of fish – including one of the world's largest concentrations of hammerhead and white-tipped reef **sharks** – patrol the surrounding waters. The rugged, mist-shrouded volcanic island itself appeared as "Dinosaur Island" in **Jurassic Park**: in the opening frames of the film, a helicopter swoops over azure seas to a remote, emerald-green isle – that's Coco.

Nearly 25 square kilometres in size, Isla del Coco is one of the world's largest uninhabited islands, yet few would be able to locate it on a map. Perhaps that's why pirates found it such a perfect hideout during the seventeenth and eighteenth centuries. Legend has it the golden spoils from fruitful church-looting expeditions to Lima were buried here; known as the "Lima Booty", the stories sparked a frenzy of treasure-seeking missions. More than five hundred tried their luck (and failed) before Isla del Coco was declared a national park in 1978, ending all gold-digging expeditions. Though evidence suggests that the island was known by pre-Columbian seagoing peoples from Ecuador and Colombia, in the modern age it was "discovered" by the navigator and sea captain Joan Cabezas in 1526. Attempts were made to establish a colony here in the early twentieth century, and nowadays wild descendants of the would-be settlers' pigs and coffee plants have upset the island's ecosystem.

Today, however, conservation is the order of the day on this **UNESCO World Heritage Site**, although illegal fishing, shark-finning in particular, within the 15km restriction zone is rife, and park rangers and marine organizations lack the resources to bring it under control. Despite this, Isla del Coco is an increasingly coveted destination for experienced **scuba divers**. More than three thousand a year brave the gut-wrenching **36-hour boat journey** from Puntarenas to spend a week or so moored in the island's sheltered harbour on liveaboard boats (it's forbidden to stay on the island itself). The subterranean treasures range from underwater caves and technicolour coral reefs to schools of manta rays and, off the northeastern side of the island, the occasional whale shark. The main danger here is **strong currents**, and divers often wear gloves so they can grip onto rocks to stop themselves from drifting away. Water temperatures are a balmy 22–26°C and the best time of year for seeing sharks is the rainy season (May–Nov). Two sheltered bays provide access to the island itself, and during the day visitors can venture onshore to hike the steaming tropical forests; trails extend from Base Wafer to Chatham Bay, and up to the highest point on the island, Cerro Yglesias.

INFORMATION AND DIVING COMPANIES

Tourist information Contact the national park itself (☎2258 8570, ⦿isladelcoco.go.cr) or Fundación Amigos de la Isla del Coco (☎2256 7476, ✉info @cocosisland.org), which was founded in 1994 to help preserve the unique terrestrial and marine biodiversity of Coco. There is a US$25/day fee to dive or visit the park's accessible areas on land (usually included in diving packages).

Aggressor Fleet ☎2289 2261 or US ☎1 800 438 2628, ⦿aggressor.com. This diving and liveaboard operator runs eight- to ten-day trips (packages from US$4099) from Puntarenas.
Undersea Hunter ☎2228 6613 or US ☎1 800 203 2120, ⦿underseahunter.com. Runs similar expeditions to Aggressor, also departing Puntarenas, with ten- to twelve-day trips (from US$4295).

for the latest *lancha* times. *Lanchas* also run between Costa de Pájaros, 33km northwest of Puntarenas (daily 7.50am & 2pm; return 6am & 1pm; 45min) and Isla de Chira; to get there take any bus heading towards Cañas from Puntarenas, and transfer in Chomes for a bus to Pájaros. The morning service is met by the public bus, whereas if you take the 2pm service you'll need to get a taxi (₡10,000).

ACCOMMODATION AND EATING

Posada Rural La Amistad 📞 2661 3261, 🌐 inchira .com. This lodge is the fruit of the labour of Asociación de Damas de la Isla de Chira, consisting of partially open basic bungalows (bring a mosquito net). Rates include breakfast and free wi-fi. Tours can also be organized through the lodge website. **US$45**

The southern Nicoya Peninsula

Most visitors' first sight of the **southern Nicoya Peninsula** is from the slow-paced ferry from Puntarenas: you'll see its low brown hills rising up in the distance, ringed by a rugged coastline and pockets of intense jungly green. Much of the region, though, has been cleared for farming or cattle grazing, or, in the case of the surf towns on its far southwestern tip, given over to tourism.

The area's main town is workaday **Cóbano**, a dull transport hub with two petrol stations, two supermarkets, a post office and a Banco Nacional with an ATM, a rare convenience in these parts. Most tourists pass straight through on their way to the thriving coastal resort towns of **Mal País**, **Santa Teresa** or **Montezuma**, comprising one of Costa Rica's most popular beach enclaves. Though traditionally regarded as a backpacker haven, these days all three spots offer a range of accommodation and dining options to fit every budget, with yoga studios and wellness spas complementing the more established surf schools.

Reserva de Vida Silvestre Karen Mogensen

Entrance near the village of San Ramón de Río Blanco · Daily 8am–4pm · US$7 · 📞 2650 0607, 🌐 asepaleco.com

The wildlife-rich **RESERVA DE VIDA SILVESTRE KAREN MOGENSEN** offers the most rewarding ecotourism experience on the southern Nicoya Peninsula. This nine-square-kilometre patch of primary and secondary dry-humid tropical forest functions as both a private reserve and tourist lodge, and has become the most crucial link in an expanding biological corridor that runs between the Reserva Natural Absoluta Cabo Blanco, 85km south at the end of the peninsula (see p.330), and Parque Nacional Barra Honda, 50km north in Guanacaste (see p.285). Named after the late Karen Mogensen, the Danish conservationist who was instrumental in

GETTING TO/FROM THE NICOYA PENINSULA

The quickest way to get to the southern Nicoya Peninsula is to fly to Tambor Airport (see p.324). Failing that, the most direct route is on one of the daily ferries from Puntarenas to Paquera or, less usefully, Playa Naranjo (see p.262). Buses generally meet these ferries and travel on to Cóbano and Montezuma.

Driving here from northern Guanacaste and Liberia is relatively straightforward (from San José it's still faster to take the ferry), with Hwy-21 maintained all the way to Lepanto (137km from Liberia and 116km from Tamarindo). The highway reverts to a narrower, bumpier road for another 9km to Playa Naranjo, before becoming a bone-shaking gravel track for the remaining 24km to Paquera – normal cars can usually pass this section, but it's not advisable in heavy rain. From Paquera the road is surfaced again to Cóbano, though it remains narrow and pot-holed throughout. The road between Cóbano and Montezuma is only partly surfaced and south of Montezuma the roads are all rough dirt tracks, best tackled in 4WD vehicles only.

6

creating Cabo Blanco, the reserve was established in 1996 by the local not-for-profit ASEPALECO – a name that references the peninsula's three main towns, Paquera, Lepanto and Cóbano.

Fence removal, tree planting and natural regeneration has returned this former patch of farmland into a fully functioning jungle ecosystem. Endangered **plant species** such as rónrón, mahogany, teak and ebony grow in the reserve, while white-faced and howler **monkeys** abound, and deer roam the forest, preyed on by elusive pumas. More than 240 species of **bird** have been spotted, including great curassow, motmot, long-tailed manakin, spectacled owl and three-wattled bellbird.

Around 22km of well-maintained **hiking trails** run through the reserve, leading to lookouts with jaw-dropping views of the Gulf of Nicoya as well as to one of the most breathtaking waterfalls in the country – the 18m **Cascada Velo de la Novia** (Bridal Veil Falls), which plummets down a rounded cliffside before dropping to a deep, turquoise swimming hole.

ARRIVAL AND DEPARTURE   RESERVA DE VIDA SILVESTRE KAREN MOGENSEN

The reserve is best accessed from the town of Jicaral, 127km southeast of Liberia and 45km northwest of Paquera.

By ferry/bus Buses for Jicaral meet the ferries at Playa Naranjo (4 daily) and Paquera (departing the docks at 11am & 4.30pm). Alternatively, there are three daily (4–5hr) Transportes Arsa buses to and from San José's Terminal 7/10 (see p.104). From Jicaral, regular buses run back to Paquera (daily 7am & 2pm; 1hr) and Playa Naranjo

(4 daily; 30min).
By car You can take a local taxi in Jicaral or organize a 4WD vehicle via ASEPALECO (both around US$25), to drive to the reserve entrance, 16km southwest by rough road. If driving yourself, there is a petrol station in Jicaral; load up on groceries here also.

ACCOMMODATION

★**Cerro Escondido Lodge** ☎ 2650 0607, ⦿ asepaleco .com. Remote but comfortable, featuring four solar-powered cabins with private bathrooms and wide balconies; the adjacent open-air restaurant serves delicious buffet-style meals, and at night local musicians provide entertainment. Rates include three meals and the services

of a local guide, and profits are reinvested in purchasing more land and planting trees. Due to the effort involved in getting here (it's a 3km uphill hike from San Ramón de Río Blanco, or a 1hr horse ride from the town of Montaña Grande, 6km northeast), visitors are encouraged to stay at least two nights. U̲S̲$̲6̲6̲

Paquera and around

The northern side of the Nicoya Peninsula is anchored by **PAQUERA**, a small town that acts as an important service centre for this largely rural region. The town centre lies 4km southwest of the ferry terminal (the "Embarcadero"), and features a Mega Super supermarket, Banco de Costa Rica (with ATM), petrol station and plenty of cheap places to eat. Other than that, it's largely just a base from which to visit the natural attractions in the area.

Playa Órganos

Wild and undeveloped **Playa Órganos** is an off-the-beaten-path beach favoured by a handful of locals, accessed via a 2.5km dirt track – 4WD recommended – off the road to the Paquera ferry (it's 5km from Paquera itself). It's a dark, volcanic sand beach, but safe enough for swimming, with some shade back in the palms and a fine view of the Islas Tortuga.

Refugio de Vida Silvestre Curú

5km south of Paquera • Daily 7am–4pm • US$12 • ☎ 2641 0100, ⦿ curuwildliferefuge.com

The small, semi-privately owned **REFUGIO DE VIDA SILVESTRE CURÚ** protects a wide variety of fauna and flora, including herds of white-tailed deer, deciduous forest and many endangered mangrove species, though the main attraction for most visitors is the chance to take a boat across to the beaches of **Islas Tortuga** (see p.323), just offshore. The reserve was carved out of an estate established in 1933 by one Frederico Schutt de la Croix (a Costa Rican of mixed German and American Cajun heritage), with logging and cattle farming the main focus. The Schutt family eventually converted their land into a nature reserve in 1983 – incredibly, this was the first in the country.

The park entrance lies around 5km south of Paquera on the road to Montezuma, where you pay the entry fee and get a very basic map. From here a dirt road leads 2.5km to **Playa Curú**, which acts as the park headquarters and where you can get boats to the Islas Tortuga and rent kayaks (see p.324). Curú beach itself is a dark-coloured, generally empty stretch of sand with little shelter beyond the nearby forest, and like most of the beaches around here, it's often littered with flotsam. You can hike to the more attractive **Playa Quesara** from here via the 5km Sendero Quesara, but allow four hours for the round trip.

The interior of the park can be accessed by a series of trails (from Playa Curú or from the access road), with your best chance of seeing some of the reserve's great variety of **wildlife** just after opening at 7am. The 2km **Sendero Finca de los Monos** passes through mangroves and is a good place to spot animals, including northern tamanduas, iguanas and agoutis, while the **Sendero Ceiba** offers a 2km jaunt through dense jungle. The longer trails (such as 2.25km Killer and 3.5km Avispero) require proper hiking footwear and plenty of insect repellent. You are likely to spot racoons, coatis, anteaters, crocodiles and monkeys – the white-faced capuchin, howler and squirrel species, the latter reintroduced a few years ago after being driven to extinction on the Nicoya Peninsula. Of the many bird species in evidence, the most exciting to spot are the **scarlet macaws**, which can sometimes be seen foraging for almonds along the coast. Extinct locally since the late 1960s, they were reintroduced to Curú in 1999 and have successfully bred in the years since.

Islas Tortuga

One of the most popular day-trip destinations in Costa Rica, the uninhabited **Islas Tortuga** (officially Isla Tolinga and its neighbour Isla Alcatraz) span over three square kilometres in total, just off the coast of the Nicoya Peninsula, near Paquera. Characterized by its two poster-perfect white-sand, palm-lined beaches and lush, tropical deciduous vegetation, Isla Tolinga is an enchanting place. It offers real tranquillity (during the week, at least), and sheltered swimming and snorkelling. At the weekend, however, boatloads of passengers come ashore, somewhat marring the islands' image as an isolated pristine tropical paradise (you can even rent jet skis for US$60/hr; kayaks are US$10/hr). There's plenty of opportunity for spotting **marine animals**, including large whale sharks, depending upon the season.

ARRIVAL AND DEPARTURE PAQUERA AND AROUND

By bus Paquera is connected by bus with Cóbano, Jicaral, San José and the beach resorts to the south. All buses between Montezuma/Cóbano and Paquera pass by the Refugio de Vida Silvestre Curú entrance (you ask the bus driver to stop), from where it's a 2.5km walk to the beach.

Destinations Cóbano via Tambor (7 daily; 1hr 30min); Jicaral (daily 11am & 4.30pm; 1hr); Montezuma

(7 daily; 2hr); San José (2 daily; 4hr); Santa Teresa (7 daily; 2hr).

By ferry Ferries for Puntarenas depart six times daily (5.30am–8pm) from the Embarcadero 5km northeast of town (buses meet incoming boats); there's not much at the ferry dock apart from the reasonable *Soda Paquera*. Get here one hour early if driving. For Tortuga, boats depart Playa Curú twice a day.

ACTIVITIES AND TOURS

Calypso Tours ☎ 2256 2727, ⊕ calypsotours.com. Offers day-trips to Tortuga (US$145 from San José, Jacó or Quepos).

They also run slower-paced, cheaper tours from Montezuma (see p.325), and Mal País and Santa Teresa (see p.331).

6

★**Seascape Kayak Tours** ☎8314 8605, ⓦseascapekayaktours.com. This Canadian outfit runs excellent small-group kayak trips in the waters off Playa Curú, with an emphasis on wildlife-watching and learning about the local environment; you're likely to see dolphins, turtles and spotted eagle rays on route. The half-day (3–4hr; US$85) or full-day (6–7hr; US$150, including gourmet lunch and snorkelling) tours run Nov–April and include entrance to Refugio de Vida Silvestre Curú.

Turismo Curú Playa Curú ☎2641 0014, ⓦturismocuru.com. Runs daily boat departures (10min) to Islas Tortuga (US$30 return, plus US$10 for lunch) at 9am and 12.30pm. Also offers kayak rentals (US$10–15/hr), paddleboards (US$15/hr), sportfishing and scuba diving.

ACCOMMODATION

Cabinas Playa Curú ☎2641 0100, ⓦcuruwildliferefuge.com. You can stay in the reserve at some very basic cold-water *cabinas*, which are located on the beach; they're popular with students and researchers, so you'll need to book in advance. Meals (US$10 each) are available at the on-site comedor. **US$60**

Hotel Vista las Islas ☎2641 0817, ⓦvistalasislas.com. Enjoy sensational views from this luxurious jungle lodge; each a/c room comes with a balcony overlooking the bay and the islands, and there's a pool and excellent restaurant on site. Wi-fi and breakfast included. Accessed by a very steep and bumpy track off the dirt road to Playa Órganos. **US$170**

Tambor

Since 1992, when Spanish hotel group Barceló unveiled its four-hundred-room *Hotel de Playa Tambor* (followed by the Los Delfines Golf & Country Club in 1999), the small village of **TAMBOR** has become synonymous with large-scale tourist-resort development. Despite the presence of the mega-hotel and condos – set off by themselves, with their own roads, grounds and guards – the whole area remains rather remote, and the village (on the main highway), hemmed in by thickly forested hills, exudes a friendly, laidback vibe missing in some of the peninsula's more touristed resorts (it's got a small supermarket and little else). Its grey/brown sandy beach – down a short side-road from the village centre and backed by a rather incongruous strip of manicured grass – stretches along a narrow horseshoe strip at the western end of the sheltered **Bahía Ballena** where, true to its name, you can sometimes spot *ballenas* (whales).

ARRIVAL AND DEPARTURE   TAMBOR

By plane NatureAir (ⓦnatureair.com) and Sansa (ⓦflysansa.com) flights from San José to Tambor (12 daily; 25min) land at the small airstrip about 4.5km north of town, in between the Los Delfines development and Barceló resort, right on the main coastal highway. Budget rents cars at the airport – the depot is nearby – and in Mal País. Note that the airport levies a US$2.50 departure and arrival fee.

By bus The Transportes Cóbano bus that runs between Montezuma and Paquera (7 daily; 50min) stops in Tambor.

ACCOMMODATION AND EATING

Cabinas Cristina A block back from the beach ☎2683 0028, ⓔcabinascristina@ice.co.cr. This chilled-out place is the best budget accommodation in Tambor, with basic but clean rooms, most with private bathrooms and one with kitchen. The helpful Tico owners (Cristina and Eduardo) dish up lovingly prepared meals at the popular on-site restaurant and can arrange tours. **US$60**

★**Henry's Pizza (Pizza Express)** Playa Tambor ☎2683 0070. Henry Mora has developed a cult following for his crisp, delicious pizzas (large ₡9500; slices ₡1000), with his "Pizza Express" delivery (Mon & Thurs–Sun 5–10pm) also popular. Daily 2–10pm.

Hotel Tambor Tropical Playa Tambor ☎2683 0011, ⓦtambortropical.com. The most luxurious place to stay in town, set in palm gardens facing languid Playa Tambor, with an inviting pool, hot tub and beautiful wooden *cabinas* with large kitchens; no under-16s are allowed. It's also the base for Seascape Kayak Tours, which runs recommended trips to nearby Curú (see above), and arranges birdwatching tours. **US$210**

★**Vista Hermosa Boutique Bed & Breakfast** Lot 14, Villas del Mar ☎2683 0551, ⓦvistahermosabedandbreakfast.com. Friendly Canadian owners run this boutique resort set around a pretty pool area and tropical gardens, where rooms have a/c and flat-screen satellite TV. There's an excellent restaurant (open for breakfast and dinner) and free transfers from Tambor Airport. Free wi-fi in public areas. **US$160**

Montezuma

The popular seaside village of **MONTEZUMA** lies about 40km southwest of Paquera, near the southern tip of the Nicoya Peninsula. Some three decades ago, a handful of foreigners seeking solitude fell in love with Montezuma and decided to stay. In those days, it was just a sleepy fishing village, largely cut off from the rest of the country, but today Montezuma draws tourists galore, and virtually every establishment in town offers gringo-friendly food and accommodation and sells tours. Nevertheless, it still feels like a village because large-scale development has been kept to a minimum – and it's still a bit of an effort to get here. The main draw is some of Costa Rica's loveliest **coastline**: leaning palms and jutting rocks dot the wild, sandy beaches, with uninterrupted views of the Pacific. Inland, thickly forested hills, including rare Pacific lowland tropical forest, dominate the landscape. In high season (Dec–May) there's a festive atmosphere to the place, with performers (from drum troupes to fire-eaters) entertaining the crowds every night.

Playa Montezuma

Other than hanging out and sipping smoothies, there's not much to do in Montezuma itself, and most visitors surf, swim, take a trip to Tortuga (see p.323) or simply lounge on the area's palm-fringed **beaches** (these are mostly of greyish, volcanic sand). **Playa Montezuma** itself comprises the small bay at the village, and the far more attractive stretch immediately to the north – though it features clean, almost golden sands, there are lots of rocky outcroppings, some hidden at high tide, and the waves are rough and currents strong. The gravel road ends just before the *Ylang Ylang Beach Resort* (see p.328), which sits at the northern end of the beach, facing its own protected cove.

6

Northern beaches

From the *Ylang Ylang Beach Resort* it's possible to walk along the coast to a series of wonderfully secluded beaches, with plenty of squawking parakeets and turtle-nesting sites along the way. The trail first cuts across a headland and down to **Piedra Colorada**, a protected cove with a small beach and an odd assortment of sculptures (basically piles of stones) at the northern end, across the creek; the tradition is said to have been started by a local artist, who used to come here every morning to maintain his rock garden. From here the trail cuts through the **Nicolas Wessberg Natural Reserve** onto the first, rocky section of **Playa Grande** – walk a bit further and you'll come to a gorgeous stretch of untrammelled sands, very broad at low tide (allow 45min from Playa Montezuma, and bring plenty of water). The jungle behind the beach is part of the semiprivate **Refugio Nacional Mixto de Vida Silvestre Romelia**. Olive ridley turtles nest along this stretch – egg-laying and -hatching season is August through January.

Continue walking beyond the next headland and you'll reach **Playa Cocolito** (allow 2hr from Montezuma), another remote beach that features **El Chorro** at the far end, a picturesque waterfall that tumbles straight into the ocean; you can swim in the waterhole here. No camping is allowed on any of the beaches.

Southern beaches

South of Montezuma a bumpy gravel road runs 7km to Cabuya (see p.329), lined with several small but enticing coves. The first is **Playa Las Palmeras**, around 300m beyond the parking for Las Tres Cascadas (see p.326), while the similar **Playa Las Manchas** lies half a kilometre further on. Experienced surfers head to **Playa Cedros**, a left-hand reef break 3km south of Montezuma, and, a kilometre further on, the right-hand point break at the mouth of the **Río Lajas** (**Playa Lajas** lies just to the south), a very rocky spot best surfed at high tide. From here it's possible to walk up the relatively gentle course of the Río Lajas through pristine jungle, to the sizeable **Lajas Falls** (allow 2hr each way from the river mouth).

Las Tres Cascadas

A number of **waterfalls** lace Montezuma and its environs; the closest and most popular is **Las Tres Cascadas** – or just Cascadas de Montezuma – on the Río Montezuma, a short walk south down the road towards Cabo Blanco (you can park here for ₡1000/ day, opposite the *Amor de Mar*). This is one of the most popular sights in the region, and while visiting can be a fun adventure and the falls themselves are very pretty, it's important to note that two to three tourists **die on the falls** every year, and many more are injured (most have to fly back to San José for treatment). Don't believe the local hype – it is not an easy and accessible hike. Trails are not marked and are slippery, muddy and very steep, and flash floods can strike in rainy season. Proper footwear is essential, though locals usually go barefoot (some will offer to guide you for ₡1000, not a bad investment). In the high season (dry season, Jan–May) the water is clear and low but the site is often crowded and the upper falls are quite feeble. The rest of the year, the water tends to be an unappealing muddy brown colour.

Hiking the falls

The first modest cascades are just a short walk from the road, but these are not one of the three main falls. You need to cross the river here, to reach a muddy path on the right bank; if the current looks strong when you get here, it's advisable to simply turn back (walking up the precipitous left side of the river is very difficult). From here it's no more than twenty minutes to the first and tallest of the falls (at around 15m), which has a lovely swimming hole at its base. Continuing on, it's a very steep and dangerous scramble up the rocks to the second and third falls – most accidents occur here, and it's advisable to visit the upper falls via the Sun Trails Canopy Tour (see opposite) instead.

The second and third falls (both around 6m) are back-to-back further up the slope, with swimming holes at the base of each; the third also has a rope-swing. If you do get this far, you can take the safer Sun Trails steps from the second to third falls, but you'll probably have to pay.

Upper Falls area

A steep road runs up the side of the Río Montezuma valley, reaching the *Cocina Clandestina* restaurant (see p.329) and the cheery **Mariposario Montezuma Gardens** (daily 8am–4pm; ₡3000; ☎2642 1317, ⊛montezumagardens.com), a butterfly reserve manned by informative volunteers. It's possible to access the upper falls of Las Tres Cascadas from nearby **Sun Trails**, where there is proper path access (₡4000). Sun Trails itself offers a range of ziplines and canopy tour options (see below).

6

ARRIVAL AND DEPARTURE
MONTEZUMA

By bus Buses stop at the dedicated area behind *El Sano Banano Hotel* in the centre of Montezuma. Local buses also head to Cabo Blanco and Cabuya (see p.329). Transportes Cóbano (☎2642 1112) runs the Montezuma to San José buses via Cóbano, Tambor and Paquera. For Mal País and Santa Teresa take the 10am or 2pm bus to Cóbano to connect with onward services there (departs Cóbano daily 10.30am & 2.30pm; 30min).

Destinations Cóbano (8 daily; 30min); Paquera (for the ferry; 6 daily; 2hr); San José (daily 6.20am & 2.20pm; 5hr).

By shuttle Montezuma is well-connected to Costa Rica's tourist shuttle network, with daily departures to San José, Monteverde and Fortuna, Manuel Antonio and

Dominical (all usually at 9am), plus Sámara/Tamarindo (usually 8.15am). All local tour operators and most hotels can arrange tickets, which cost substantially more than local buses. Most hotels can book you local shuttle bus rides to Tambor (US$15) and Mal País/Santa Teresa (US$10).

By taxi A taxi to/from Mal País/Santa Teresa costs around US$40; for Tambor Airport it should be US$40–50.

By taxi-boat The Zuma Tours (see below) taxi-boat from Playa Herradura, 7km north of Jacó (minibus between Herradura and Jacó included), is by far the quickest way of getting between Montezuma and the Central Pacific (1hr; US$40). Boats depart Herradura daily at 10am and depart Montezuma beach daily at 8.30am.

ACTIVITIES AND TOURS

ATV Rentals Other than walking, the most popular way to get around the area is by quad bikes/ATV rentals from vendors in the centre of the village, or outside *Amor de Mar* (see p.328). Rates are not cheap, starting at around US$60 for six hours (US$80 for 12hr).

Cocozuma Traveler In the centre of town, next door to *El Sano Banano Hotel* ☎2642 1011, ⊛cocozumacr .com. Offers horseback rides to El Chorro Falls (US$40), day-trips (with snorkelling) to Islas Tortuga (US$55) and sportfishing trips (from US$250).

Sun Trails 1.5km northwest of Amor de Mar hotel ☎2642 0808, ⊛montezumatraveladventures.com.

Offers a canopy tour comprising nine ziplines that also stops at the Tres Cascadas for a quick dip (from US$45).

Zuma Tours In the centre of town, near El Sano Banano Hotel ☎2642 0024, ⊛zumatours.net. The helpful, multilingual folks at Zuma Tours offer information and the largest range of tours in town, such as day-trips to Islas Tortuga (US$60, including lunch and snorkelling tour), diving (US$60), horseriding to the Florida Waterfall (US$45; 4hr) and guided trips to Refugio de Vida Silvestre Curú with a qualified naturalist (US$75; 5hr).

ACCOMMODATION

While convenient, staying in the **village** can be noisy due to traffic and the shenanigans at *Chico's Bar*. Elsewhere, you'll find it peaceful, with choices out on the **beach**, on the road that heads southwest to the Reserva Natural Absoluta Cabo Blanco, and on the sides of the steep hill about 1km above the village. **Camping** is prohibited on the beach, but there are a couple of campsites on the edge of town. All the options listed here offer free wi-fi.

IN THE VILLAGE
Cabinas Mar y Cielo By the beach, down a lane behind Super Mamatea ☎2642 0261. The clean rooms in this rambling wooden house come with fridge, private bathroom and – if you're upstairs – a balcony with ocean

views and sea breezes. The hammock-filled garden is a great place to relax, though nearby *Chico's Bar* can be noisy. U̲S̲$̲5̲5̲

★**Downtown Montezuma Hostel** 500m south of the village ☎2642 0284, ⊛dtmontezuma.com. Fun

6

hostel right in the heart of town, with clean dorms and private rooms, shared kitchen, sociable lounge, free yoga and plenty of information on local surf spots. Includes breakfast (make-your-own pancakes). Dorms US$14, doubles US$35

Hotel El Tajalín Just west of Hotel Montezuma Pacífico ☎ 2642 0061, ⓦ tajalin.com. On the main road just northwest of the centre, this hotel – named after the purple-clawed crabs that frequent the hillside behind the village – has attractively simple wood-floored rooms with a/c; the airier ones on the top floor have sea views. They also have a communal lounge with television, books and coffee. US$60

Luna Llena Hotel 200m north of the village, on the road to Paquera ☎ 2642 0390, ⓦ lunallenahotel .com. This surfer-friendly hostel sits peacefully on a forested hillside (it's a steep walk up from the centre), with a regular troupe of monkeys as visitors. Attractive rooms, one of which is en suite, have fans and sleep up to five; most are a combination of double beds and bunks (extra guests after first person US$10 each). There are two shared kitchens, a BBQ and a sociable TV lounge. Free wi-fi works well in common areas only. Dorms US$15, doubles US$38

Luz de Mono At the eastern end of the village, 50m from the beach ☎ 2642 0090, ⓦ luzdemono.com. Set between the jungle and the beach, with en-suite rooms for two to three people (queen beds, satellite TV) or *casitas* (jacuzzis, terraces) for up to five people. There are two pools, one for children, a restaurant and a bar (serving wine from their Playa Grande vineyard). Doubles US$75, casitas US$140

El Sano Banano Hotel Main street, in the centre of the village ☎ 2642 0636, ⓦ elsanobanano.com. This is a good central option if you manage to score a room without a brick-wall view. Mexican bedspreads brighten up the small and clean rooms, all with private hot-water bathrooms, a/c and a TV. The price includes breakfast at the on-site restaurant (see opposite) and guests can use the pool at *Ylang Ylang Beach Resort* (see below). US$75

AROUND THE VILLAGE

Amor de Mar 600m southwest of the village on the beach, just across the bridge ☎ 2642 0262, ⓦ amordemar.com. Rustic seafront hotel with its own tide pool sitting in pretty landscaped gardens on a rocky promontory. Hammocks hang between giant palm trees, and a nice selection of a/c rooms come with and without bathroom; those upstairs and facing the sea are best, most of which have a veranda and ocean views. The Casa Luna villa (US$270) can sleep up to seven people and is a great deal for families. US$130

★**Anamaya Resort** 500m up the hill, accessed on the road next to Amor de Mar ☎ 2642 1289, ⓦ anamayaresort.com. Yoga-centric wellness hotel set high up on the cliffs behind Montezuma, and offering a stylish women-only dorm and individually designed *cabinas*, most with superb ocean views, and a gorgeous saltwater infinity pool. The mostly organic, mostly local restaurant is also open to non-guests. Rates include three daily meals, but not activities (you can buy week-long packages of classes and activities, which include everything from aerial yoga to surfing; US$95–395/person). Minimum stay one week (bookings start Sat only). Dorm US$20, *cabinas*/person US$28

Horizontes de Montezuma 1.8km before Montezuma, on the road from Paquera ☎ 2642 0625, ⓦ hotel-horizontes-montezuma.com. Perched in the hills above Montezuma, this small, distinctive, tropical-Victorian-style hotel has spacious, airy rooms with balconies overlooking the jungle and hot-water private bathrooms. There's a nicely lit pool, and an exceptional breakfast (which features home-made German wheatbread and jams) is included. US$95

Hotel Los Mangos 500m south of the village ☎ 2642 0076, ⓦ hotellosmangos.com. Split-level hotel set amid mango trees, with brightly decorated rooms (sleeping 2–4 people), plus expensive-looking but slightly dark Balinese-style bungalows (sleeping up to 3 people); some have their own verandas and rocking chairs. There's also a pool and hot tub, and regular yoga classes are held in an airy wooden pavilion. Doubles US$75, bungalows US$90

Nature Lodge Finca Los Caballos 4km before Montezuma, on the road from Paquera ☎ 2642 0124, ⓦ naturelodge.net. Set in tropical gardens with a small pool, this casual lodge has twelve good-value rooms with hot-water private bath and a restaurant serving gourmet international cuisine – the more romantic rooms (US$146) come with huge beds, views of the ocean and either a balcony or an outdoor shower. US$86

★**Ylang Ylang Beach Resort** A 10min walk along the beach from the village (your bags will be taken care of) ☎ 2642 0638, ⓦ ylangylangresort.com. This truly romantic retreat offers secluded circular bungalows (US$195) all with beachfront verandas and outside showers. The newer split-level apartment rooms, perfect for families (sleeping up to 6 people; US$465), boast beach views, and there are also luxury tents (for 2 people; US$135; breakfast included) in the dry season. There's a lovely freeform swimming pool with a waterfall, beautifully landscaped gardens and an on-site spa. Rates for the standard doubles (all facing the beach) include breakfast and candlelit dinner at the seafront restaurant. US$220

EATING

Montezuma's varied menus offer not just *comida típica* but a slew of tourist favourites, though you can still find a couple of (relatively) low-cost *sodas* too. Self-caterers can stock up at Super Montezuma on the main street (daily 7am–10pm) or sample the organic produce at the Saturday-morning market in the park opposite (10am–12.30pm).

Bakery Café Opposite Luz de Mono ☎ 2642 0458. Stop by for the fruit shakes (₡2000), tasty home-made sandwiches (₡3300–3800), cakes and pastries (from ₡850) served on a soothing, shady terrace – perfect for lunch (*casados* ₡3600–3900). Tourists like to have their pictures taken feeding the local coatis or white-faced monkeys next to a sign that reads "Please don't feed the monkeys". The monkeys (and blue jays) will snatch bags/food lying around, so keep an eye on them. Daily 6am–10pm.

★Cocina Clandestina 750m up the hill (at the Mariposario), accessed on the road next to Amor de Mar ☎ 8315 8003. Delicious Hispanic-American fusion cuisine (from chicken enchiladas and tacos to home-made sourdough), plus tasty microbrews by Butterfly Brewing Co (only available on the premises), way up at the top of the waterfalls. Mains from ₡5000. Tues–Sat noon–9pm.

Cocolores Diagonally opposite Bakery Café ☎ 2642 0348. This intimate restaurant in a garden by the beach serves generous portions of fajitas, kebabs and fish dishes (mains ₡4000–11,000), plus some good vegetarian options and a selection of beers, ales and porters from a local microbrewery. There's a happy hour (Tues–Sun 5–6pm), but you'll have to arrive early to secure one of the prime beachfront tables. Tues–Sun 4.30–10pm.

Ice Dream Opposite Chico's Bar ☎ 2640 1005. Modern *heladería* serving tip-top gelato (from ₡1000/scoop) – the fresh fruit (banana, dragonfruit), peanut butter and Nutella flavours are among the highlights – as well as frappes (₡2300), plus fine espressos. Mon–Sat 8am–8pm.

Organico Just east of the church ☎ 2642 1322, ⓦ facebook.com/organicocostarica. Wholesomeness doesn't come at the expense of taste at this charming restaurant, with appealing salads, snacks, mains (₡4900–6500) like veggie lasagne, and treats such as chilli, rum and chocolate gelato; vegans are particularly well catered for. There's live music most nights. Mon–Sat 11am–9pm.

★Playa de los Artistas 500m south of the village ☎ 2642 0920. Beachside dining doesn't get any better – an unhurried candlelit dinner of fresh fish and lobster, vegetable dishes and delectable sushi (Fri only) at hewn-wood tables or on cushions on the sand. Main courses hover around ₡8000–10,000, and the tuna and snapper are particularly recommended. Wed–Fri 5–9pm, Sat noon–3.30pm.

Puggo's Just beyond the main turning down into the village ☎ 2642 0325. This mellow place with substantial tables fashioned from tree trunks serves up excellent Middle Eastern-inspired cuisine (the chef is Israeli), including hummus and falafel, and a top Moroccan fish stew, plus home-baked focaccia and excellent sushi (most mains ₡5000–8000). Mon & Wed–Sun noon–10pm.

El Sano Banano El Sano Banano Hotel ☎ 2642 0636. Although it's a little pricey for local food (most dishes ₡5500–7000), this is a great spot for a smoothie (₡2000–3300) or something alcoholic, especially if you catch the daily happy hour (4–7pm). There's always sport from around the world on the TVs. Daily 7am–11pm.

Soda Típica Las Palmeras 1km south of the village ☎ 2642 0269. Just up the slope from the coast road, beyond the falls, this rustic spot offers great home-cooking (most mains ₡4000), from grilled red snapper to chicken curry. Wed–Fri 5–9pm, Sat noon–3.30pm.

DRINKING AND NIGHTLIFE

Chico's Bar Next to Super Mamatea. Nightlife in Montezuma centres on *Chico's Bar*, where a heady mix of local kids – who arrive packed in the back of pick-ups – and tourists guzzle from a wide choice of alcohol (beer from ₡1500). At closing time people tend to adjourn to the beach for some alfresco drinking. Daily 11am–2am.

DIRECTORY

Banks and exchange Montezuma has a Banco de Costa Rica ATM (right in the centre), but the nearest bank branch is in Cóbano, 7km away. Dollars are accepted everywhere (but as always, you won't get a good exchange rate, and your change will usually be in colones).

Internet Zuma Tours (see p.327) operates an internet café (₡20/min).

Laundry *Lavandería Flory* is up the road opposite the bus stop (daily 7am–5pm; ₡1500/kg).

Medical care The nearest clinic is in Cóbano (☎ 2642 0208).

Cabuya

Laidback **CABUYA**, 7km south of Montezuma on a very bumpy dirt road, is a pleasant village that draws a growing community of permanent foreign residents who enjoy the slow pace of life, relative isolation and unspoiled scenery. It's everything its neighbour isn't, so if you're looking to escape the crowds and loll on secluded beaches, this is the place to come; it's also the home of the popular Spanish, yoga and surf classes at **La Escuela Del Sol** and just a short walk from the nearby **Reserva Natural Absoluta Cabo Blanco**.

El Higuerón

Just south of the Río Lajas bridge you'll see a giant banyan tree on the right, known as **El Higuerón** – it's quite a sight, with a mass of aerial roots, vines and thick woody trunks like something out of *Avatar*.

Isla Cementerio Cabuya

When the tide is low, it's possible to walk on a stony trail out to the uninhabited **Isla Cementerio Cabuya**, a small island that principally serves as the local cemetery. With the emergence of an expat community in Cabuya in recent years, foreign residents have also been laid to rest here, often with customized grave markers such as old propellers. The island is a great spot for snorkelling but bear in mind that the path is covered by the ocean during high tide.

To get there, turn left at the second major intersection on the main (Cabo Blanco) road in Cabuya. There's a small parking area for a few cars at the fishing-boat dock area at the end of the road – the trail leads out to the island from here.

ARRIVAL AND DEPARTURE   **CABUYA**

By bus The bus from Montezuma to Cabo Blanco (see below) runs through Cabuya.

By car The road from Montezuma is rough, so you'll need a 4WD if driving yourself. Another rough, and hilly, 7km road links Cabuya with Mal País (the first intersection in the village); it's only driveable in a 4WD and three water crossings often make the road impassable in the rainy season.

ACCOMMODATION AND EATING

The following places are listed in the order you encounter them heading south from Montezuma; all offer free wi-fi.

Hotel Celaje Near the entrance to the village, 200m south of the Río Lajas ☎ 2642 0374, ⓦ celaje.com. Belgian-owned beachside beauty with A-frame, palm-roofed bungalows that come with two beds (with mosquito nets) and small bathrooms. There's an inviting swimming pool, a pirate-themed bar and a restaurant (breakfast buffet included). US$80

Cabuya Resort On the road to Mal País ☎ 8531 2693, ⓦ cabuyaresort.com. Extremely chilled out hotel run by a Canadian/Tico couple, with lovely cabins featuring an artsy, Asian theme, yoga deck, pool and outdoor showers. Troupes of monkeys live in the surrounding jungle. US$100

★**Café Nimbu** 125m south of the Mal País intersection ☎ 6076 8383. Wonderful restaurant and café with a menu of varied dishes, from tacos to pizza, plus excellent coffee and pastries (cookies from ₡500). Tues–Sun 11am–9pm (closed June).

Restaurante Marvin South of Isla Cementerio Cabuya intersection ☎ 6076 8383. Popular local *soda* known for its friendly owners, home-style Costa Rican food (try the shrimp *casado*) and fresh fish. Mains from ₡4000. Tues–Sun 11am–9pm.

★**La Escuela Del Sol** 700m west of Super Chicho in centre of the village ☎ 8884 8444, ⓦ laescueladelsol .com. This popular surf, yoga and Spanish school can organize homestays in the village, with simple but private accommodation, or stays in on-site villas, which have ocean views, a/c, TVs and porch swings. Rates include class packages and meals. Minimum one-week stay. US$99

Reserva Natural Absoluta Cabo Blanco

9km south of Montezuma • Wed–Sun 8am–4pm • US$12 • Ranger station daily 8am–4pm • ☎ 2642 0093

RESERVA NATURAL ABSOLUTA CABO BLANCO is Costa Rica's oldest protected piece of land, established in 1963 by Karen Mogensen, a Danish immigrant to Costa Rica, and her Swedish husband Olof Wessberg (the latter was murdered in Corvocado in 1975 by locals opposed to his conservation work). Until 1989, no visitors were allowed into the

WATCHING WILDLIFE IN CABO BLANCO

The best time for animal spotting is around 8am, or on Wednesday mornings, after the reserve has been closed for two days. The heat chases a lot of the wildlife into the more heavily forested sections of the reserve, which are off-limits to visitors, but you're still likely to see **howler monkeys**, **white-faced capuchin monkeys** and **white-tailed deer**; **agoutis** and **coati** are also common. Harder-to-spot mammals include the **margay**, **northern tamandua** and **collared peccary** – Cabo Blanco has what is thought to be the last herd of these boar-like creatures on the Nicoya Peninsula. Birdlife is astonishingly plentiful, in the forest itself (where you might catch a glimpse of a **long-tailed manakin** or a **sulphur-winged parakeet**) but particularly down by the shore – you'll often see scores of **pelicans** and clouds of **magnificent frigatebirds**, while Costa Rica's largest community of **brown boobies** nests on Isla Cabo Blanco, the guano-encrusted island that lies 2km offshore (the island itself is off limits).

6

twelve square kilometres of reserve, which covers nearly the entire southwestern tip of the Nicoya Peninsula. Though hard to believe today, most of the reserve was pasture and farmland until the early 1960s. Since its inauguration, Cabo Blanco has been allowed to regenerate naturally; a small area of original forest that had escaped destruction served as a "genetic bank" for the re-establishment of the complex tropical forest that now fills the reserve.

The trails

You can pick up a trail map (there are only two trails) at the ranger hut (Casa de Guardaparques, signposted to the left of the entrance), which outlines the history of the reserve and the species living here. The **Sendero Sueco** (4.2km; 2hr; the "Swedish Path", named in honour of Wessberg) leads from the entrance through tropical deciduous forest to **Playa Cabo Blanco**, a lovely, lonely beach (in low season, anyway). Swimming, however, isn't great around here; due to the high tide (*marea alta*), you'll need to walk back along Sendero Sueco rather than the coast. Ask the ranger at the entrance when and where you'll likely get cut off if you want to venture along the beach. Note that it's very hot: 30°C is not uncommon, so, if possible, hike the trails early, and bring a hat, suncream and plenty of water.

ARRIVAL AND DEPARTURE   RESERVA NATURAL ABSOLUTA CABO BLANCO

By bus A minibus (₡500) runs along the rough road from Montezuma to the reserve (30min), leaving the village's bus stop daily at 8.15am, 10.15am, 12.15pm, 4.10pm & 6pm, returning from Cabo Blanco at 7.20am, 9.20am, 11.20am & 3.20pm, although it may not always run in the rainy season.

By jeep-taxi Jeeps make the trip from Montezuma for around US$15/person one way.

By car You'll need a 4WD to get there yourself, except at the very driest time of year, and even then you'll need to keep an eye out for the two creeks, which are deep at high tide.

Mal País and Santa Teresa

Just over a decade ago, the long grey-sand surf beaches fronting the virtually seamless towns of **MAL PAÍS** ("Bad Land") and **SANTA TERESA**, 12km southwest of Cóbano, began luring an increasing number of travellers. First came the surfers, then the hippies, and not long after, curious hipsters, celebrities and families started trickling in. A building boom over the past decade, particularly in Santa Teresa, has transformed this formerly sleepy stretch of Pacific coast into a trendy beach resort, and foreigners now outnumber Tico residents. The developers, banks and car rental chains show no signs of leaving town, and even though the main road is slowly being paved, the area seems certain to retain its laidback charm; and in the rainy season at least, you can still walk along jungle-flanked surf beaches for hours and see few other people.

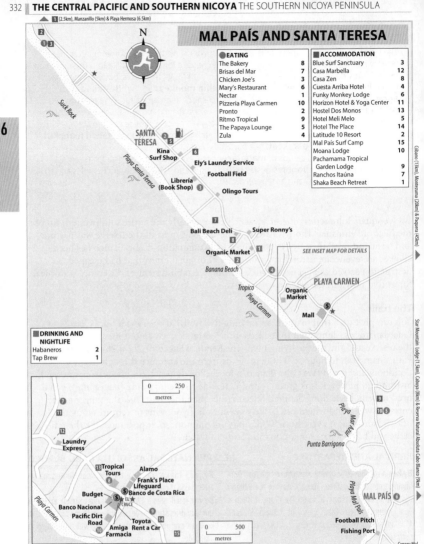

MAL PAÍS AND SANTA TERESA

EATING
The Bakery	8
Brisas del Mar	7
Chicken Joe's	3
Mary's Restaurant	6
Nectar	1
Pizzeria Playa Carmen	10
Pronto	2
Ritmo Tropical	9
The Papaya Lounge	5
Zula	4

ACCOMMODATION
Blue Surf Sanctuary	3
Casa Marbella	12
Casa Zen	8
Cuesta Arriba Hotel	4
Funky Monkey Lodge	6
Horizon Hotel & Yoga Center	11
Hostel Dos Monos	13
Hotel Meli Melo	5
Hotel The Place	14
Latitude 10 Resort	2
Mal País Surf Camp	15
Moana Lodge	10
Pachamama Tropical Garden Lodge	9
Ranchos Itaúna	7
Shaka Beach Retreat	1

DRINKING AND NIGHTLIFE
Habaneros	2
Tap Brew	1

The straggly oceanfront communities are spread along 8km and three separate **beach zones** – Mal País, Carmen and Santa Teresa. The intersection by the hotel *Frank's Place*, known as "**El Cruce**", is the traditional centre of the area.

Playa Mal País

Turning south at El Cruce takes you along the **Playa Mal País** section of the strip, which is much quieter and more peaceful than Santa Teresa. The beaches here are smaller and usually rougher; the first bay is known as Playa Mar Azul, while the second is Playa Mal País proper. Beyond the small fishing dock at the southern end of Mal País village the road becomes barely passable for 4WD vehicles, with pristine **Playa Cuevas** just around the headland. **Canopy Mal País** (see opposite) lies just up the hill from here.

Playa Carmen to Manzanillo

Across the El Cruce intersection lies **Playa Carmen**, which stretches several kilometres north and blends into **Playa Santa Teresa**, though most of the access points are pedestrian only. The main road behind the beach is lined with restaurants and lodgings all the way through **Santa Teresa**. These start to thin out once you reach popular **Playa Hermosa** (follow the signs for *Couleur Café*; a very rough track leads to the beach), some 6.5km north of El Cruce. A couple of kilometres beyond here lies the sleepy village of **Manzanillo**, with another long stretch of rocky beach and a couple of point breaks on the western side of the peninsula.

Despite the long stretches of sand, all the beaches here are prone to riptides and not ideal for **swimming**, though there are often good tidal pools for splashing about in. They are, however, excellent for **surfing** (see box, p.334).

6

ARRIVAL AND DEPARTURE

By bus Buses arrive at/depart from El Cruce. Transportes Cóbano (☎ 2642 1112) runs to San José, but usually with a change of bus in Cóbano.

Destinations Cóbano (where you can get a connection to Montezuma or Paquera for the ferry; 4–6 daily; 30min); San José (daily 6am & 2pm; 5hr).

By car If you're driving from Montezuma, you can get here

MAL PAÍS AND SANTA TERESA

via Cóbano (on a paved but pot-holed road) or, with a 4WD, take the very rough gravel road through Cabuya (crossing three small fords). There's a petrol station 2km from El Cruce on the road from Cóbano.

By taxi A taxi from Cóbano to Mal País or Santa Teresa will set you back around US$25–30.

GETTING AROUND

ATV rental Most locals bounce along the roads on ATV/quad bikes, which you can rent from various points along the main coast road for around US$70/24hr (US$50/8hr). Try Pacific Dirt Road, 75m from El Cruce on the road to the beach (☎ 8875 8452, ⊛ quadtourscostarica.com), which also rents 125cc motorbikes (US$40/24hr).

Bike rental Most hotels and hostels rent bikes (around US$10–15/day).

Car rental Budget (Mon–Sat 8am–5pm, Sun 8am–4pm; ☎ 2640 0500, ⊛ budget.co.cr) and Toyota Rent a Car (Mon–Sat 7.30am–5pm, Sun 8am–4pm; ☎ 2105 3400, ⊛ toyotarent.com) are both housed in the white strip-mall at El Cruce; Alamo is east of *Frank's Place* (daily 7.30am–5.30pm; ☎ 2640 0526, ⊛ alamocostarica.com).

ACTIVITIES AND TOURS

Canopy Mal País 1km inland from Playa Mal País ☎ 2640 0360, ⊛ canopymalpais.com. A canopy/zipline tour (US$50; 2hr) that affords blurry Pacific views as you whizz through treetops adjoining the Reserva Natural Absoluta Cabo Blanco. Transportation is US$10 extra (round trip).

Star Mountain Lodge 2km inland from Mal País (on the road to Cabuya) ☎ 2640 0101, ⊛ starmountaineco .com. If you fancy horseriding along the beach or in the surrounding jungle, try this B&B, which runs 2hr trots (non-guests allowed) through the waves at Playa Carmen (US$45).

Tropical Tours Shuttles Opposite Budget, near El Cruce ☎ 2640 0811, ⊛ tropicaltourshuttles.com.

Arranges a variety of tours, including day-trips to Islas Tortuga (US$55), plus 5hr guided tours of the Reserva Natural Absoluta Cabo Blanco (US$75). Also runs a taxi-boat to Montezuma (US$40; 50min) and shuttles 3 times daily from Santa Teresa to Liberia Airport, Sámara, Tamarindo, Nosara and San José (from US$50).

Yoga and pilates Daily classes (Mon–Sat 9am & 5pm, Sun 7am & 5pm; US$15; 1hr 30min; ☎ 2640 0524, ⊛ horizon-yogahotel.com) are held on the panoramic deck at *Horizon Hotel* (see p.335). *Casa Zen* (see p.334) also offers yoga classes (Mon, Wed & Fri 8.30am, 9.30am, 3.30pm & 6.30pm, Tues, Thurs, Sat & Sun 9.30am, 3.30pm & 6.30pm; 1hr 30min; US$9), as does *Shaka Beach Retreat* (see p.335).

ACCOMMODATION

The recent construction boom has brought with it a smorgasbord of boutique **hotels** and even the budget options here are surprisingly modern. The majority of the accommodation is set along the shores of Playa Carmen and Playa Santa Teresa; as it can be hot day and night, it's well worth splashing out on a/c. **Camping** is officially prohibited on the beach, but you can pitch a tent at the *Mal País Surf Camp* (see p.335). Most places, like the towns themselves, shut down during September and October. All the options listed offer free wi-fi.

6

SURF'S UP

Surfing put Mal País and Santa Teresa on the map, and the two communities still very much revolve around the rollers just offshore. **Playa Carmen** is an excellent beach for beginner and intermediate surfers, with a long right and a shorter left breaking over sand. More experienced types head north to the steeper waves at **Playa Santa Teresa**, where there are beach breaks and point breaks; on high swells (particularly between March and July) **Suck Rock**, at its northern end, peels into long, right-handed tubes. Only pro surfers and masochists ride **Sunset Reef** (also known as Playa de los Suecos), an extremely dangerous shallow reef-break with a fast take-off at the far southern end of Mal País; rocky outcrops along the rest of **Playa Mal País** render it uninviting for both swimmers and surfers, though **Punta Barrigona**, a slow, long left-hander halfway between Sunset Reef and the intersection, works well on a high-tide swell.

EQUIPMENT AND TUITION

The **shops** listed below all rent boards, organize surfing lessons and sometimes even run multiday regional tours; surfer-centric **hotels** such as *Blue Surf Sanctuary* (see p.334) and the *Mal País Surf Camp* (see p.335) and schools such as **La Escuela Del Sol** (see p.330) in Cabuya also offer lessons.

Del Soul Surf School 2.5km north of El Cruce ☎ 8878 0880, ⓦ surfvacationcostarica.com. Highly rated surf lessons (US$60; 1hr 30min) with maximum three students per instructor. Private lessons also offered (US$80; 1hr 30min). Daily 8.30am–6.30pm.

Jobbie's Longboards 100m towards the beach from El Cruce ☎ 8525 7430. This surf camp and yoga retreat is especially good for beginners (classes from US$50/hr) or for those a little intimidated by the waves, with super-friendly, knowledgeable instructors. Daily 9am–5pm.

Kina Surf Shop Plaza Solar #3, 2.2km north of El Cruce ☎ 2640 0627, ⓦ kinasurfcostarica.com. Wide range of boards for rent (from US$15/day); beginner, intermediate and advanced lessons (US$50; 1hr 30min); plus clothing, accessories and general surfing advice. Daily 9am–5pm.

Nalu Surf Shop Next to Super Ronny's, 300m north of El Cruce ☎ 2640 0391, ⓦ nalusurfschool.com. Rents out boards for US$10–20/day, runs professional surf classes (US$50/day), and leads three- and five-day courses (US$135–200). Also buys and sells boards. Daily 9am–6pm.

SANTA TERESA

★**Blue Surf Sanctuary** 3.9km north of El Cruce ☎ 2640 1001, ⓦ bluesurfsanctuary.com. Top-end surf camp, sponsored by Billabong and appealing to boardriders with bigger budgets – their four swanky bungalows (sleeping up to 4 people) have luxurious bathrooms and treetop views from their balconies. Surf lessons (US$60/2hr 30min) and board rental are available, of course. Cash only on-site. **US$155**

Casa Zen 1.5km north of El Cruce ☎ 2640 0523, ⓦ zencostarica.com. This stylish wooden guesthouse features Asian-inspired trimmings and plenty of space. Just 50m from the beach, accommodation options include a well-maintained dorm, doubles and an apartment (that can sleep up to 14 people). There are morning yoga classes, movie nights and a professional kitchen for guests to use. Dorm **US$18**, doubles **US$40**, apartment **US$60**

★**CasaMarbella** 550m north of El Cruce ☎ 2640 0749, ⓦ casamarbel.la. Justly popular hotel, perched on the jungle hillside off the main road, with captivating views and a small but gorgeous infinity pool. Each of the

eight rooms (all with a/c) has an ocean view and access to the pool, from the minimalist but elegant standard rooms (some with kitchenettes) to luxurious suites (US$170). **US$105**

Cuesta Arriba Hotel 2.9km north of El Cruce ☎ 2640 0607, ⓦ cuestaarriba.com. Mixed dorm beds are arranged 4–8 to a room in this sparkling budget hotel, ideally located for the Playa Santa Teresa breakers. Rooms are cleaned daily and come with lockers, fan and a bathroom with hot shower (per room). There are also a range of private doubles, including a cute, split-level loft (US$55). There's plenty of space in the upstairs TV lounge or downstairs communal kitchen. Free coffee and toast in the morning, but no breakfast per se. Dorms **US$18**, doubles **US$50**

Funky Monkey Lodge 2.3km north of El Cruce ☎ 2640 0272, ⓦ funkymonkeylodge.com. This hillside lodge with a pool and sushi restaurant is part boutique hotel, part swish backpacker hangout. Whether staying in a bamboo bungalow (for 2 people) with outdoor shower, renting a self-contained apartment (sleeping 6–10 people) with ocean views or bunking down in a dorm ("budget room") with cold-water bathroom and ceiling fan, you can enjoy the lodge's excellent facilities and mingle with other travellers in the barside communal area. There's also a yoga and dance studio. Dorms US$30, bungalows US$110, apartments US$180

Horizon Hotel & Yoga Center 750m north of El Cruce ☎2640 0524, ⊕horizon-yogahotel.com. Staggered 50m up the hillside overlooking jungle and Playa Carmen, these romantic bungalows on stilts are small but have expansive views that make up for it. Rooms come with a/c, firm mattresses, bathrooms and balconies adorned with hammocks and bamboo wind chimes. You can munch vegetarian food, bliss out in the intimate triangular pool or stretch yourself in an outdoor yoga class (see p.333). Breakfast is US$15 extra. Closed Sept & Oct. US$150

Hostel Dos Monos 220m north of El Cruce ☎2640 1199, ⊕hosteldosmonos.com. One of the newest hostels on the strip and definitely one of the best maintained, with simple but stylish doubles (with bathroom and a/c), plus a couple of spotless but slightly cramped dorms (also with a/c) and large, communal kitchen. Dorms US$25, doubles US$65

Hotel Meli Melo 2.4km north of El Cruce ☎2640 0575, ⊕hotelmelimelo.com. This fabulous B&B is a great deal and subsequently often full – book ahead. The simple but colourful rooms come with a/c, private bathrooms, shared kitchen and free bike rental, with on-site surf lessons easily organized (packages available). US$60

★**Latitude 10 Resort** 4.6km north of El Cruce ☎4001 0667, ⊕latitude10resort.com. Set amid wildlife-rich forest, this ultra-exclusive boutique hotel manages to retain a relaxed and welcoming ambience. The five suites are beautifully furnished and completely open, allowing them to benefit from the sea breezes. There's a lovely little chemical-free pool, excellent restaurant (guests only, breakfast included), and surf- and bodyboards for use on the secluded stretch of beach out front. US$420

Ranchos Itaúna 1.6km north of El Cruce ☎2640 0095, ⊕ranchos-itauna.com. This beachfront property lies smack bang in the middle of the surf breaks of Playa Carmen and Playa Santa Teresa. With just four comfortable octagonal rooms (two have kitchens and all have a/c and bathrooms), this place oozes tranquillity. The owners can arrange massages and surf lessons, and Brazilian food is served in the restaurant (breakfast US$15 extra). The lively bar hosts regular DJ sets, live music and full-moon beach parties. US$100

Shaka Beach Retreat Playa Hermosa access road, 6.6km north of El Cruce ☎2640 1118, ⊕shakacostarica.com.

This relaxed surf camp just off pristine Hermosa beach is beyond the main strip and subsequently much quieter. The spacious villas (for 1–2 people; all a/c) feature a bright, local style, blending local woods and tiled floors, and the food served on site is superb, starting with hearty breakfasts. Rent by the week via yoga or surf packages. Closed Sept & Oct. US$160

MAL PAÍS

Hotel The Place 260m south of El Cruce ☎2640 0001, ⊕theplacemalpais.com. Crisply furnished, standard double rooms, chic beach-hut-style bungalows (sleeping up 4 people) and spacious villas (sleeping up to 5) set around a chill-out lounge and garden pool. Movies are played on a big screen hanging over the pool on Tues & Fri at 7pm. Doubles US$85, bungalows US$155, villas US$320

★**Mal País Surf Camp** 450m south of El Cruce ☎2640 0031, ⊕malpaissurfcamp.com. There's good community vibe at this surfer centre, thanks to its mix of guests – accommodation ranges from dorms through to *cabinas* (for 2 people) dotted around a nice pool – and chilled-out restaurant area. Stacks of magazines and on-loop surfing films should get you in the mood. Daily lessons and surf-and-accommodation packages (from US$60/day, including three meals) available too. Camping/person US$15, dorms US$20, *cabinas* US$45

★**Moana Lodge** 1.9km south of El Cruce ☎2640 0230, ⊕moanacostarica.com. Run by chatty Irishman Aidan and his Tica wife Vicky, this boutique hotel is one of the area's most romantic and stylish. Set on a forested slope, the lovely rooms have been tastefully decorated with African-inspired trimmings and come with a/c, bathrooms and large beds draped with silk throws. Try to score one of the higher ones with a balcony for nice ocean breezes, or – if your budget allows – the superb honeymoon suite (US$275), right at the top of the hill, with panoramic views from the jacuzzi and a private deck. You can while away the day in suspended beds by the pool before taking sunset drinks in *The Papaya Lounge* (see p.336). US$120

Pachamama Tropical Garden Lodge 1.6km south of El Cruce ☎2640 0195, ⊕pacha-malpais.com. Bungalows (for 2 people) and a two-storey house (with two bedrooms and full kitchen) set in lush gardens (often visited by monkeys and coatis), perfect for families and groups. Bungalows come with mosquito net, kitchen, fridge and fan (it's US$10 extra for a/c), and a full range of activities is on offer. Bungalows US$70, house US$160

EATING

Mal País and Santa Teresa's large population of foreign residents translates into a wide range of **restaurants**, and increasingly, cafés and coffee shops, though spots tend to come and go with alarming frequency.

6

Self-caterers can make use of several well-stocked supermarkets, including Super Ronny's, 400m north of El Cruce (daily 7am–10pm).

SANTA TERESA

★ **The Bakery** 120m north of El Cruce ☎ 2640 0560. An appealing stop-off at any time of the day, with delicious pastries for breakfast (₡4500–5500), light meals like soups, pasta, sandwiches (from ₡4500) and salads for lunch, and top pizza for dinner (from 6pm). Daily 7am–10pm.

★ **Brisas del Mar** Hotel Buenos Aires, 700m north of El Cruce ☎ 2640 0941. It's at the top of a very steep hill, but fish restaurants don't come much better than this – fresh, creative and with spectacular views. Sample the spread of seafood tapas or tuck into tuna in port or delicious shrimp with bourbon-spiked Cajun cream (most mains ₡8000–10,000). Mon–Sat 8–10pm.

Chicken Joe's 1.9km north of El Cruce ☎ 02640 1110. Delicious rotisserie chicken, enhanced with home-made hot sauce, but this joint also has a cult following for its authentic ceviche (one of the owners is Peruvian), fish tacos (from ₡1000) and craft beer selection. Daily noon–9pm.

★ **Nectar** Hotel Florblanca, 4.3km north of El Cruce ☎ 2640 0232, ⓦ florblanca.com. Artistic fusion cuisine with Latin, Mediterranean and Asian influences, heavily focused on seafood: dishes range from ginger, coconut and coriander ceviche to suga-cane-skewered jumbo prawns (dinner mains ₡13,200–16,500). The strong sushi menu (served 3.30–9.30pm; ₡6050–9350) is matched by some high-quality sakes. Daily 8am–9.30pm.

Pizzeria Playa Carmen 100m towards the beach from El Cruce ☎ 2640 0110, ⓦ restaurantepizzeriaplaya carmen.com. The best pizza in town is served in an open-front restaurant overlooking the beach (it's rare for a restaurant to be so close to the water here), though it also has a well-earned reputation for seafood and inventive cocktails, best enjoyed at sunset. Mains ₡8000–10,000. Daily 11am–10pm.

Pronto 2.4km north of El Cruce (Plaza Kahuna) ☎ 8479 4888, ⓦ prontocr.com. Fabulous and authentic Italian food from Bari-born chef Giuseppe Morisco, with virtually everything on the carefully curated menu worth trying, from the aubergine parmigiana (₡5000) and lasagnas (from ₡5500), to the sensational tiramisu (₡3000). Tues–Fri 11.30am–8.30pm, Sat & Sun 11.30am–4.30pm.

Zula 700m north of El Cruce ☎ 2640 0614. A buzzing local restaurant that serves up Costa Rican and Israeli favourites (mains around ₡4500–6500) like falafel, shakshuka, kebabs and creamy bowls of hummus (from ₡2500) to dunk your pitta in. Mon–Fri & Sun 8am–10pm.

MAL PAÍS

Mary's Restaurant 3.1km south of El Cruce ☎ 2640 0153, ⓦ maryscostarica.com. Locals pack the tables and booths at this buzzing restaurant to tuck into a wide variety of Mexican dishes (nachos, tacos and burritos) and wood-fired pizzas (₡5000–7000). Mon, Tues & Thurs–Sun 5–10pm.

★ **The Papaya Lounge** Moana Lodge (see p.335), 1.9km south of El Cruce ☎ 2640 0230, ⓦ moanacostarica.com. The home-made Latin food changes daily but usually includes some mouthwatering fish dishes (think sea bass in coconut broth or peanut-encrusted mahi-mahi in ginger) as well as meaty mains like tamarind BBQ ribs. The great views – as far as Punta Islita – can also be enjoyed over sunset drinks and bocas. Dinner mains around ₡6000–10,000. May–Nov daily 7.30–10am; Dec–April Mon & Wed–Sun 7.30–10am & 5–10pm, Tues 7.30–10am.

Rítmo Tropical 190m south of El Cruce ☎ 2640 0174, ⓦ hotelritmotropical.com. Soak up your antipasti with five types of focaccia – though the real draw is the tasty thin-crust pizzas that dominate the menu (around ₡6000). Daily 5.30–10.30pm.

DRINKING AND NIGHTLIFE

Habaneros 1.2km north of El Cruce (Playa Cielo Resort) ☎ 2640 1105, ⓦ playacielo.com/en/habanero. This beachfront Mexican grill and bar serves decent food (lobster tacos and guacamole are especially good), but is best known for its killer margaritas, which range from tamarindo ginger and mango jalapeño to a beautifully crafted classic with lemon (₡3500/glass, ₡14,000/pitcher).

Daily noon–10pm.

Tap Brew 1.1km north of El Cruce ☎ 2640 1220. Craft beer has arrived in Santa Teresa and it's top-notch – sample some of the best microbrews in the country at this friendly bar. Country, rock, blues and alternative music dominate Mon–Fri 7 Sun, with DJs spinning techno and house on Sat. Daily 5pm–midnight.

DIRECTORY

Banks and exchange Both the Banco Nacional (Mon–Fri 1–7pm), next door to Budget, and the Banco de Costa Rica (Mon–Fri 9am–4pm), at El Cruce, have ATMs (both 24hr).

Internet access Virtually every hotel and restaurant

offers free wi-fi access; Tropical Tours (see p.333) has a few computers too.

Laundry Try Laundry Express (₡1000/kilo; ☎ 8313 4501), 400m north of El Cruce.

Medical care There is a private emergency ambulance service and clinic, Lifeguard (☎ 2640 1062, �🖱 lifeguardcostarica.com), at El Cruce. For more serious medical emergencies, San José is 40min by helicopter. **Pharmacy** Amiga Farmacia (Mon–Fri 8am–8pm, Sat 8am–7pm) in the mall at El Cruce.

South of Puntarenas

On the mainland **south of Puntarenas**, the coast road (eventually Hwy-34, sometimes signposted as the **Costanera Sur**) leads down to Quepos and continues to Dominical (covered in Chapter 7). At first, the landscape is sparse and hilly, with the coast coming into view only intermittently, but things improve considerably once you're past the huge trucks heading to the container port and refineries at **Puerto Caldera**, the terminus of the toll road linking San José and the Pacific (Hwy-27). About 30km southeast of Puerto Caldera, just across the wide crocodile-ridden mouth of the Río Tárcoles, **Parque Nacional Carara** encompasses a range of habitats and is known for its rich birdlife. Just to the south, the village of **Tárcoles** is close to the Catarata Manantial de Agua Viva, one of the country's most spectacular waterfalls. Beyond here is the resort of **Jacó**, which thanks to its relative proximity to San José is more popular than it might otherwise be. Better beaches (and surf) lie further south, particularly at **Playa Hermosa** and **Playas Esterillos**.

Parque Nacional Carara

Hwy-34, 90km west of San José • Daily: May–Nov 8am–4pm; Dec–April 7am–4pm • US$10 • ☎ 2637 1080

Ecologically vital **PARQUE NACIONAL CARARA** occupies a transition area between the hot tropical lowlands of the north and the humid, more verdant climate of the southern Pacific coast. Consequently, the park teems with **wildlife**, from monkeys to margays and motmots to manakins.

Carara's well-maintained **trails** are split between the heavily canopied area near the park's ranger station and visitor centre and the more open terrain around Laguna Meándrica, an oxbow lake that is home to crocodiles and often smothered in water lilies and other aquatic plants. The visitor centre is clearly marked, 2.5km south of Río Tárcoles Bridge (see p.338); from here the fully accessible and paved **Sendero Universal** loop (1.2km) links up with two rougher loop trails, the **Sendero Quebrada Bonita** (1.5km) and **Sendero Las Aráceas** (1.2km), with the latter also accessible from the main highway 3.5km south of the visitor centre. Both trails take in primary and transitionary forest and are reliable places to spot agouti and other small rodents; you can also often see great tinamou on the paths here, and sometimes even catch the spectacular leks of orange-collared manikins. Birdwatching is perhaps even better along the rivers and in

---

WATCHING WILDLIFE IN CARARA

Much of Carara's bounty of wildlife is of the unnerving sort: huge **crocodiles** lounge in the bankside mud of the Río Tárcoles ("carara" means "crocodile" in the language of the pre-Columbian inhabitants, the Huetar), while **snakes** (19 out of Costa Rica's 22 poisonous species) slither about. Mammals include **monkeys** (mantled howler and white-faced capuchin), **armadillos**, **agoutis** (commonly seen), aggressive **collared peccaries** and most of the large cats, including **jaguars** and **ocelots**. Birding is excellent, and this is one of the best places in the country to see the brightly coloured **scarlet macaw** in its natural habitat – at dawn and dusk, they migrate between the lowland tropical forest areas and the swampy mangroves, soaring over in a burst of red and blue against the darkened sky. Other birds that frequent the treetops include **trogons** (five species), **toucans** (both chestnut-mandibled and keel-billed) and **guans**, while riverside birds include **anhingas** (or snake birds), the coot-like **purple gallinule** and **storks**.

the clearings on the **Sendero Laguna Meándrica** (4.3km; 2–4hr), where the wide range of avifauna includes boat-billed herons – this trail is accessible from Hwy-34, 2km north of the visitor centre.

ARRIVAL AND TOURS

PARQUE NACIONAL CARARA

By bus Buses between Puntarenas and Jacó pass by the visitor centre for Parque Nacional Carara (8 daily; around 1hr from Puntarenas, 30min from Jacó).

By car To get to Carara from San José, take the toll Caldera Highway (Hwy-27; around ₡2000 one

way) then well-maintained Hwy-34 south towards Jacó and Quepos.

Tours Several agencies offer tours from San José; try Costa Rica Birding Journeys (☎8889 8815, ⓦ costaricabirding journeys.org; US$75; 11hr).

INFORMATION

Information Staff at the visitor centre (see p.337) have basic maps and can answer questions about the reserve's wildlife.

Guides It's worth hiring a guide (around US$25/person for 2hr) from the visitor centre, as they can also take you into areas where tourists aren't allowed on their own.

Security There have been thefts and robberies in the area, so leave your vehicle in sight of the guards at the visitor

centre (even if walking the Laguna Meándrica trail), and check the latest situation before setting off.

When to visit Note that it's extremely hot in Carara, so hit the trails early (the wildlife will be much less evident by 10am); if you want to stay overnight to get an early start, go with one of the accommodation options in nearby Tárcoles and the surrounding area (see p.340).

Tárcoles and around

The village of **TÁRCOLES**, 2km south of Parque Nacional Carara and a further 1km west along a rough road, sprawls along a dusty street and parallels a beach that is too polluted for even the briefest of toe-dippings. The main attraction here – apart from visiting the nearby national park – is the **Río Tárcoles**, or more correctly the huge **crocodiles** that bask on its muddy banks. You can spot them at the estuary just northwest of town and from the **Río Tárcoles Bridge** on the main highway (Hwy-34) – it's one of the best free attractions in Costa Rica (you can park on either side) – or take to the water and view them from the comfort of a boat.

Catarata Manantial de Agua Viva
Hwy-320, 5km east of Hwy-34 (the road is paved) • Daily 8am–3pm • US$20 • ☎ 2645 1017

Set amid a pristine rainforest valley is the **Catarata Manantial de Agua Viva**; at 200m high, this cascading waterfall, also known as Catarata Bijagual, is one of the highest in the country. The 3km hike downhill to the base can be treacherous (depending on conditions and your fitness level; 3–4hr round trip), and has often resulted in injuries (and several deaths), though the trail is relatively easy to follow, cutting through gorgeous scenery and affording glimpses of frogs, snakes and giant butterflies. Once at the bottom, you can take a dip in a series of natural swimming pools (the water can be cloudy in the rainy season). Hiking sticks are handed out at the entrance, which is on private property and is clearly marked at a small parking area; take plenty of water and wear proper hiking shoes.

Pura Vida Gardens and Waterfalls
Hwy-320, 6km east of Hwy-34 (the road is paved) • Mon–Sat 8am–5pm • US$20 • ☎ 2645 1001, ⓦ puravidagarden.com

The jungle has been tamed into submission at the **Pura Vida Garden and Waterfalls**, but as Parque Nacional Carara is next door, visitors are very likely to see scarlet macaws, toucans and poison-dart frogs while strolling the manicured nature trails at this private botanical reserve. A paved trail leads to an easily accessible viewpoint (from where the Catarata Manantial de Agua Viva is relatively distant), and a restaurant, *Adventure Dining*; in the other direction a more challenging loop trail runs through the jungle and past four small waterfalls.

ACTIVITIES AND TOURS

Costa Rica Birding Journeys ☎8889 8815, ⓦcostaricabirdingjourneys.org. Birdwatching tours explore the Carara national park and mangroves at the mouth of the Tárcoles river in search of herons, egrets and the endemic mangrove hummingbird; the price includes return transfer from hotels in San José (US$105; 11hr).

Jungle Crocodile Safari ☎2637 0338, ⓦjunglecrocodilesafari.com. Insightful crocodile tours on the Río Tárcoles – though the boats get scarily close, crocodile feeding is now banned (4 daily; US$35; 2hr).

ACCOMMODATION

There are a number of decent accommodation options around Tárcoles. Most lodges can meet you off the bus from San José; some also offer transport from the capital, or from nearby Jacó or Quepos.

Cerro Lodge 3km down a side road, signed off Hwy-34 3km north of the Río Tárcoles Bridge ☎2427 9910, ⓦhotelcerrolodge.com. This lodge offers good-value rooms and bungalows (sleeping up to 4 people) on a quiet working farm (trails run through the property): it's set in lush surrounds, with a pool to cool off in after a walk in Carara. Start the day watching scarlet macaws feeding in the trees opposite the on-site restaurant. Doubles <u>US$80</u>, bungalows <u>US$99</u>

Hotel Carara C Principal, Tárcoles ☎2637 0178, ⓦfacebook.com/hotel.carara. On the beach, this hotel has clean, modest rooms with TVs and private bathrooms, set around a small pool; US$15 more buys you more space, a/c and sea views. It's on the flight path between Carara and the coastal mangroves, so sightings of macaws are almost guaranteed in the early morning and late afternoon. <u>US$75</u>

Villa Lapas 500m east of the turn-off to Tárcoles, signed from Hwy-34 ☎2203 3553, ⓦvillalapas.com. Set in landscaped gardens near the river, this well-equipped hotel has large a/c rooms, a pool and – rather oddly – a replica of an old Costa Rican "town", complete with church, *cantina*, large restaurant and even larger souvenir shop. There's also a Sky Walk, canopy tour and small network of trails in their nearby private reserve. <u>US$99</u>

Jacó and around

Just over two hours from San José, **JACÓ** sits in a hot coastal plain behind the broad **Playa Jacó**, the closest beach to the capital. An established seaside attraction, the resort draws a mix of surfers, holidaying Ticos and retired North American baby-boomers, along with a less salubrious selection of drug dealers and prostitutes. Jacó has seen some of the most excessive development along the Pacific, but the partying crowd don't seem to mind too much. And as a base from which to explore the surf beaches along this stretch of coast, its multitude of amenities takes some beating.

The beaches

Jacó's appeal is its long, spacious **beach** – when covered in mist and backed by a spectacular Pacific sunset, the wide sands look quite attractive. It's popular with novice surfers (though the water isn't the cleanest and you do have to watch out for riptides), while more advanced riders head for the beaches nearby, including **Playa Herradura**, 7km north, a calm spot in front of the *Los Sueños Marriot Ocean and Golf Resort* complex (see p.343) and frequented by Ticos, and **Playa Hermosa** (see p.344) and **Playas Esterillos** (see p.345), wild, untamed stretches to the south of town.

Rainforest Adventures Costa Rica Pacific

5km northeast of Jacó • Mon 9am–4pm, Tues–Sun 6.30am–4pm • Gondola (Aerial Tram) US$60; Tranopy Tour US$75; various multi-activity packages available • ☎2257 5961, ⓦrainforestadventure.com • Prices include free transport from Jacó and Playa Hermosa

The catchily titled **Rainforest Adventures Costa Rica Pacific** lets you view the rainforest canopy from the surrounds of a slow-moving gondola (1hr); the price includes access to nature trails and a serpentarium. You can combine the ride with a ten-cable canopy tour – the **"Tranopy Tour"** – to pick up the pace a little, or hit the trails with a naturalist guide before taking a closer look at the canopy dwellers from the comfort of the tram.

6

TOURS AND ACTIVITIES IN AND AROUND JACÓ

Although **surfing** is the be-all-and-end-all for many visitors to Jacó, there are plenty of other activities on offer, from **kayaking** to ziplining, as well as tours to nearby **Parque Nacional Carara** or **Islas Tortuga** (see p.323).

CANOPY TOURS AND CANYONING

Costa Rica Waterfall Tours Edificio Crystal (1st Floor), Av Pastor Díaz, Jacó ☎2643 1834, ⓦcostaricawaterfalltours.com. Offers canyoning and abseiling jaunts down local cascades, plus ziplining (from US$99). Daily 7am–9pm.

Vista Los Sueños Canopy Playa Herradura (1.7km east of Hwy-34) ☎2637 6020, ⓦcanopyvistalos suenos.com. Features a twelve-cable canopy tour (including the longest zipline in the area), accessed by tractor-pulled cart. Two-hour tours from US$65. It also offers horseriding tours (US$70; 2hr) and ATV tours (US$90; 2hr). Daily 8am–5pm.

KAYAKING

Kayak Jacó Playa Agujas, 16km north of Jacó ☎2643 1233, ⓦkayakjaco.com. Runs daily kayak excursions (8am & 1.30pm; US$85 with transport from Jacó, US$65 without; 3hr 30min), which can include snorkelling and fishing if desired, plus a fresh fruit buffet on the beach. Daily 7.30am–8pm.

SAILING AND DIVING

Herradura Divers Ocean Plaza, C Principal, Playa Herradura ☎6042 0856, ⓦherraduradivers.com. Runs two-tank local dives for US$120, and more rewarding dive-trips to Islas Tortuga from US$190. PADI courses from US$405. Closed in rainy season (mid-May–Nov).

Joy Ride Sailing Tours Puesta del Sol Restaurant, Playa Herradura (beachfront) ☎2643 7129, ⓦjoyridesailing.com. This outfit runs morning and afternoon cruises (both US$90/person; both 3hr) on the sailboat *Reliant*, with snorkelling and swimming.

SURFING

Chuck's W.O.W. Surf Plaza Palma (Av Pastor Díaz), at the northern end of Jacó ☎2643 3844, ⓦwowsurf .com. Offers free tide tables and an excellent free "surf treasure map": board hire here is pricier at US$15–40 a day, and a three-hour lesson will set you back US$65. Mon–Sat 8am–8pm, Sun 8am–6pm.

Walter Surf Shop Av Pastor Díaz, opposite Budget in Jacó ☎2643 1056, ⓦwaltersurfshop.com. Staff here can match you with the right board and offer rentals for US$10–20 a day and two-hour lessons for US$40. Daily 9am–6.30pm.

ARRIVAL AND INFORMATION

JACÓ AND AROUND

By bus Buses to and from San José, Puntarenas and Quepos stop at Plaza Jacó at the north end of Av Pastor Díaz, the 3km road that constitutes the town's main drag. If you're travelling at a weekend in high season, buy your ticket at least 3 days in advance. A local bus runs between Jacó's main drag and Playa Herradura, 7km north, hourly (5am–10pm; 20–30min).

Destinations Puntarenas (8 daily; 1hr 30min); Quepos (8 daily; 1hr 30min); San José (7 daily; 2hr 30min).

By taxi-boat A Zuma Tours (ⓦzumatours.net) taxi-boat from Montezuma runs to Playa Herradura at 7.30am each day (1hr; US$40, including transfer to/from Jacó, add US$10 for Santa Teresa/Mal País; returns at 10am); it's a fast-paced trip that offers the possibility of spotting dolphins, turtles and other marine life, but note that the outward leg is a beach landing, so wear shorts and water shoes.

Security Locals advise against walking on the beach at night: hold-ups have been reported. Although bike-riding police officers patrol the streets, it is worth taking care around town at night. Part of the police's mandate is to crack down on the use of recreational drugs, and stop-and-searches are not uncommon.

GETTING AROUND

Bike and ATV Many places rent out bikes (about US$10/ day); try Jaguariders on Av Pastor Díaz (☎2643 0180, ⓦjaguariders.com) for ATV bikes (US$50/hr).

Car rental All the major agencies have offices along the main strip, including local outfit Zuma Rent A Car (daily 7am–5pm; ☎2643 1528, ⓦzumarentacar.com) and Economy (daily 8am–6pm; ☎2299 2000, ⓦeconomyrentacar.com).

Taxis Charge by the meter (starting fare ₡535) in Jacó, with most rides under ₡1000. Longer trips to Playa Herradura (US$15–20), Playa Hermosa (US$15–20) and Esterillos (US$30) should be negotiated in advance and are usually calculated in dollars.

6

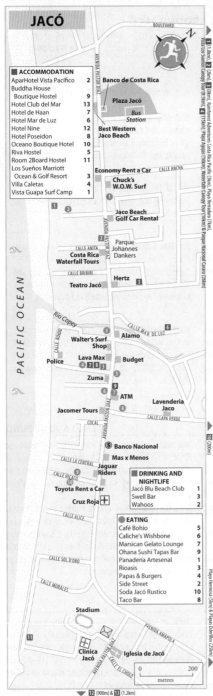

JACÓ

ACCOMMODATION

AparHotel Vista Pacífico	2
Buddha House Boutique Hostel	9
Hotel Club del Mar	13
Hotel de Haan	7
Hotel Mar de Luz	6
Hotel Nine	12
Hotel Poseidon	8
Oceano Boutique Hotel	10
Riva Hostel	5
Room 2Board Hostel	11
Los Sueños Marriott Ocean & Golf Resort	3
Villa Caletas	4
Vista Guapa Surf Camp	1

DRINKING AND NIGHTLIFE

Jacó Blu Beach Club	1
Swell Bar	3
Wahoos	2

EATING

Café Bohío	5
Caliche's Wishbone	6
Marsican Gelato Lounge	7
Ohana Sushi Tapas Bar	9
Panaderia Artesenal	1
Rioasis	3
Papas & Burgers	4
Side Street	2
Soda Jacó Rustico	10
Taco Bar	8

ACCOMMODATION

Jacó's cheapest *cabinas* generally cater to weekending *josefinos* or surfers; much of the mid-range accommodation is self-catering, useful if you're in town for more than a couple of days, and there are also a number of smarter places. Staying on the main road can mean traffic noise, particularly on busy weekends.

JACÓ

★AparHotel Vista Pacífico On the hill at the far north end of town, signed off the Boulevard ☎ 2643 3261, ⌨ vistapacifico.com. An intimate hideaway, this tranquil hotel has it all: sweeping coastal views, mountaintop breezes and an attractive garden setting. Clustered around a sparkling blue pool, the studios and suites are bright and spotless and come with private bathrooms, a/c and TVs. You'll need to drive or take taxis to the beach. US$80

★Buddha House Boutique Hostel Av Pastor Díaz, facing C Bohío ☎ 2643 3615, ⌨ hostelbuddha house.com. A relaxed vibe pervades this deluxe hostel with a tropical and (very slight) Asian theme, bright dorms and comfy private rooms (amenities range from fan and shared bathroom, to a/c and private bathroom for US$10 extra). Small pool, shared kitchen and BBQ area, but breakfast not included. Dorms US$12, doubles US$40

Hotel Club del Mar 1.5km south of Jacó, off Hwy-34 ☎ 2643 3194, ⌨ clubdelmarcostarica.com. Set on a quiet stretch of beach, these British-owned luxury rooms and apartments have a family-friendly atmosphere and a huge range of amenities, including pool, restaurant, spa, small library and games room. US$167

Hotel de Haan C Bohío ☎ 2643 1795. Run by a Dutch-Tico couple, this budget spot is popular with surfers. It has simple dorms and private rooms, a pool, and a party atmosphere, with guests socializing until the early hours most nights. Surf lessons are available too. Dorms US$12, doubles US$35

Hotel Mar de Luz C Mar de Luz, 100m off Av Pastor Díaz (north side of Río Copey) ☎ 2643 3000, ⌨ mardeluz.com. This well-kept, family-friendly hotel sits amid soothing, landscaped grounds. Colourful modern apartments (sleeping up to six; from US$200) surround two large pools and a garden. Large rooms are crammed with furniture and come with TV, a/c, microwave and kitchenette, plus there's a lounge and small library. US$93

Hotel Nine C Hidalgo ☎ 2643 5335, ⌨ hotelnine .com. This elegant contemporary property features an enticing pool, stylish rooms with balconies, a pool table and super-efficient staff. Tico breakfast included. Book months in advance. US$118

Hotel Poseidon C Bohío, just off Av Pastor Díaz ☎2643 1642, ⓦhotel-poseidon.com. The rooms at this two-storey, white stucco hotel are elegantly decorated and come with smart bathrooms and all modern conveniences, including TV and DVD player. There's a tiny pool, handy if you can't face the 30m walk to the beach, and a hearty breakfast is included. US$95

Oceano Boutique Hotel C Lapa Verde (500m inland from Pastor Díaz) ☎2643 0420, ⓦoceanojaco.com. Plush, contemporary hotel, with compact but luxurious a/c rooms (most with balconies), an enticing pool and a decent café (there's also a cheaper *soda* next door). US$85

Riva Hostel Off Av Pastor Díaz, 100m behind Plaza Coral/KFC ☎2643 4332, ⓦrivajaco.com. This friendly hostel with basic but spotless dorms and tents for two (hooked up with electricity and fans) is a good deal; no breakfast but free coffee/tea, shared kitchen and free access to the pools at surfside Jacó Blu Beach Club. Dorms US$12, camping US$30

★**Room2Board Hostel** C Morales (on the beachfront), 200m west of Clínica Jacó ☎2643 4949, ⓦroom2board.com. This attractive backpacker resort and surf school in a funky modern building offers yoga classes (US$7) on the roof terrace and daily surf lessons (US$30–35; board hire US$10/day). The dorms and private rooms are simple but stylish, all with fans (a/c available for a surcharge), and there are lots of common areas, though the kitchen can get crowded in high season. Dorms US$18, doubles US$65

Vista Guapa Surf Camp At the far north end of town, signed 500m off the main road ☎2643 2830 or ☎8364 3155, ⓦvistaguapa.com. As the name implies, this surf

hangout located high on the hill overlooking Jacó enjoys handsome views, so you can check out the breaks over breakfast. It's run by former national champion David Solano – the staff are always on hand for surfing advice – while the smart bungalows themselves have a/c and hot-water bathrooms. Week-long packages start at US$1250/person (based on two people sharing), including lessons, board hire and two meals daily. US$146

PLAYA HERRADURA

Los Sueños Marriott Ocean & Golf Resort ☎2630 9000, ⓦmarriott.com. Overlooking Playa Herradura, *Los Sueños* is an expansive resort set amid 4.5 square kilometres of neatly-tended grounds. Many of the spacious rooms come with sea views, and some have private terraces and hammocks. Among the attractions are a beautiful series of interconnected pools, plenty of activities for children and families, several restaurants and bars, a spa and gym, and a world-class eighteen-hole golf course, plus highly professional service. It's a US$15 taxi ride from Jacó. US$214

★**Villa Caletas** 15km north of Jacó, signed off Hwy-34 ☎2637 0505, ⓦhotelvillacaletas.com. Perched on a clifftop above the Pacific, this is one of Costa Rica's most extravagant boutique hotels. Beautifully decorated villas sit amid landscaped grounds that resemble a film set, with a small Greek theatre and Doric columns surrounding the pool; there are stunning views all round, especially at sunset. The restaurant serves gourmet cuisine with prices to match. A shuttle takes guests down a precipitous 1km trail to the private beach. US$365

EATING

★**Café Bohío** Av Pastor Díaz, at C Bohío ☎2643 5915, ⓦcafebohio.com. Best coffee in town, with a range of espresso drinks from the on-site roaster (from₡1000) and local beans from Finca Higuerón Arriba in nearby Tarrazú. Daily 7am–9pm.

Caliche's Wishbone Av Pastor Díaz ☎2643 3406. Running the gamut from sushi to Mexican, stuffed pitta sandwiches to *casados* and pizzas to potato salads, this recommended restaurant has just about all your cravings covered (mains ₡5500–15,000). Mon, Tues & Thurs–Sun noon–10pm.

Marsican Gelato Lounge Centro Comercial II Galeone, Av Pastor Díaz ⓦfacebook.com/pg/marsicangelato. Handmade, authentic Italian gelato and sorbet, with incredible flavours – try the pistachio. Named after the Italian Marsican brown bear, with Italian items scattered throughout – check out the 1970s Vespa inside the elegant premises. Cash only. Mon & Wed–Sun noon–10pm.

★**Ohana Sushi Tapas Bar** C El Hicaco (towards the beach) ☎2643 2226. Get your chopsticks round

wonderfully prepared sushi, sashimi, tempura rolls and salmon teriyaki in a rustic-chic dining room (candlelit at night). The produce is top-notch – expect to pay ₡1600–5000 for sushi, and ₡4800–8000 for mains. Mon, Tues, Thurs & Sun noon–9pm, Fri & Sat noon–10pm.

Panadería Artesenal Av Pastor Díaz ☎2643 6413. This little bakery and café near Chuck's W.O.W. Surf serves a good range of breads, pastries and cakes (including croissants and baguettes), as well as *empanadas* (₡1000) and light meals to eat in or take away. Mon, Tues & Thurs–Sun 6.30am–6pm.

Papas & Burgers C Bohío ☎2643 5251. Satisfy that burger craving or just take a break from rice and beans at this small but popular spot, which uses custom-ground high-quality beef and locally baked buns (from ₡2750). Cash only. Mon–Thurs 8.30am–9pm, Fri & Sat 8.30am–10pm, Sun 8.30am–8pm.

Rioasis Av Pastor Díaz (next to Río Copey bridge) ☎2643 3354. Wood-fired pizzas and Mexican favourites (around ₡4000–8000) are dished up with fervour at this

6

cavernous restaurant by the river; there's a relaxed outdoor area and an indoor bar that throbs with loud music. Mon, Tues & Thurs–Sun noon–10.30pm.

Side Street Just off Av Pastor Díaz (on street to Jacó Blu Beach Club) ☎ 2654 2724. Expect high quality from this bistro and sandwich shop, with tasty pastrami sandwiches and meaty burgers washed down with cocktails and craft beers (₡2500–4000). Tues–Sat 11am–10pm, Sun 9am–9pm.

Soda Jacó Rústico C Hicaco ☎ 2643 2727. Join the queue of hungry locals and load your plate with Tico standards at this inexpensive, buffet-style *soda*, where you can have a good feed for around ₡3000. Ask for

takeaway and eat your feast on the beach just 50m away. Mon–Wed, Fri & Sat 7am–7pm, Thurs 7am–5pm.

★Taco Bar C Lapa Verde, just off Av Pastor Díaz ☎ 2643 0222. Top lunch spot: order your taco (from ₡4000) – fish (mahi-mahi, wahoo, snapper, tuna) is the speciality – get it grilled or fried, and then smother it in BBQ, spicy or coconut sauce before scoffing it in one of the bar-side swings. Also huge burritos and hummus combos; a good all-you-can-eat salad bar is included with most dishes. Offers popular ₡1500 breakfast specials Tues–Sun 7–11am. Mon noon–10pm, Tues–Sun 7am–10pm.

DRINKING AND NIGHTLIFE

Nightlife is predictably hedonistic in Jacó, with young holidaymakers jostling for bar space with prostitutes and their clientele, especially in the *Hotel Cocal & Casino*. Clubs are definitely of the meat-market variety, but there are plenty of fun, safe places to drink along the strip.

Jacó Blu Beach Club Off Av Pastor Díaz (100m north of Parque Johannes Dankers) ☎ 2643 4372, ⓦ jacoblu.com. Exuding a South Beach Miami vibe, this spot on the waterfront is a great a place to chill and admire the sunset, with large pools and day-beds for lounging, menus of light bites, DJs and sensational cocktails. Day-pass US$24 (includes US$10 voucher to be used for drinks or food). Mon–Fri & Sun 10am–midnight, Sat 10am–3am.

Swell Bar C Bohío, just off Av Pastor Díaz ☎ 2643 5251.

One of the best bars in town, with a decent selection of drinks, a pool table, darts and table football. It's tiny, but the action spills out onto the street at weekends, when it gets especially fun. Tends to be frequented by surfers. Daily 7pm–2.30am.

Wahoos Av Pastor Díaz ☎ 2643 1876. This restaurant-bar draws in tourists and foreign residents with its long cocktail list, karaoke nights (in English and Spanish), live music, and big-screen sports. The food's pretty good, too. Daily 11am–2.30am.

DIRECTORY

Banks and exchange Several on Av Pastor Díaz, including a Banco Nacional (Mon–Fri 8.30am–3.45pm, Sat 9am–1pm) that accepts foreign-issued credit cards.

Laundry Lava Max, Av Pastor Díaz (Mon–Fri 8am–7pm, Sat & Sun 8am–5pm).

Medical care Clínica Jacó, opposite the post office (☎ 2643 1767).

Post office At the southern end of town (Mon–Fri 8am–4.30pm, Sat 8am–noon).

Supermarkets Más x Menos, Av Pastor Díaz, is smack in the centre of Jacó (daily 8am–10pm).

Playa Hermosa

Grey-sand **Playa Hermosa**, 5km south of Jacó, has long been a playground for hotshot surfers. Pummelled by powerful waves, the 10km-long strip rivals Dominical for having the most consistent **beach breaks** on Costa Rica's Pacific coast. Given its proximity to Jacó, it was inevitable that the development craze would reach here, too, and condos have gradually colonized the beachfront. The area is being sold as a smarter version of Jacó: a coastal getaway without the noise, pollution, drugs and sex work so prevalent in its neighbour – at least for now.

Hermosa is definitely not a beach for a casual dip (the riptides here are formidable), nor for novice surfers. Steep sandbars cause waves to break hard, fast and close to the shore, most impressively during the rainy season between May and August – with the best breakers in front of *Terraza del Pacífico* and the *Backyard Hotel*. On Friday and Saturday afternoons, you can watch how it should be done, when local surfers and gung-ho visitors tackle the waves as part of the Backyard Surf Series competition (4pm; free to enter; US$500 top prize).

Refugio Nacional de Vida Silvestre Playa Hermosa y Punta Mala

South of the hotel strip, the **Refugio Nacional de Vida Silvestre Playa Hermosa y Punta Mala** protects a nesting site for olive ridley turtles, which come ashore to lay their eggs between August and December. It's off limits to the public, but you can visit the turtle hatchery at the ranger station, a gridded block of beach being used to monitor the species' reproduction rates in this part of the Pacific.

ARRIVAL AND DEPARTURE
PLAYA HERMOSA

6

By bus You can get to Playa Hermosa from Jacó by catching a Quepos-bound bus (8 daily; 15min from Jacó) – just ask the driver to let you off close to your hotel (anywhere along Hwy-34).
By taxi Taxis from Jacó cost around US$15–20.

ACCOMMODATION

Backyard Hotel 500m south of the football field ☎ 2643 7011, ⓦ backyardhotel.com. The top choice for surfers with money, the sprightly rooms in this beachfront hotel have a/c, TVs and bathrooms. You can do laps in the swimming pool, just outside your balcony, party at the popular bar and restaurant next door (see below) and enjoy one of Hermosa's best surf breaks on your doorstep. U̲S̲$̲1̲3̲5̲

Cabinas Brisas del Mar Just south of the football field ☎ 2643 7023, ⓦ cabinasbrisadelmar.com. The cheapest option on the strip, this hostel buzzes with friendly surfers who congregate in the outdoor communal kitchen to cook after a hard day battling Hermosa's tubes. The private en-suite doubles have good facilities for the price – including a/c and cable TV– and there are low-cost bunks in the dorms. Three-night minimum. Dorms U̲S̲$̲1̲5̲, doubles U̲S̲$̲4̲0̲

Hermosa Surf Vacations 1.6km southeast of the football field ☎ 2440 6862, ⓦ hermosasurfvacations .com. Popular surf camp featuring elevated beachfront bungalows (sleeping up to 6 people), also marketed as *Hermosa Bungalows*, with wooden verandas, a/c, free wi-fi and full kitchens. There's a minimum three-night stay, and there are seven day/six night packages that include various combos of transportation, food and lessons from US$1090. U̲S̲$̲2̲2̲0̲

Outback Hermosa Next to the football field (on the beachfront) ☎ 2643 7096, ⓦ surfoutback.com. Surf lodge run by surfers with local knowledge, offering accommodation that's a cut above average; simple but modern dorm rooms (sleeping 5–6 people) with cable TV, hot showers, a/c and balconies with ocean views. U̲S̲$̲3̲0̲

EATING AND DRINKING

Backyard Bar and Restaurant Next to the Backyard Hotel (see above) ☎ 2643 7011, ⓦ backyardhotel.com. A great spot to watch the sun melt into the horizon over sunset happy-hour drinks (daily 4.30–7.30pm; there's also a second happy hour daily 9–11pm). At the weekend, live music shakes up the joint, while ladies' night (Wed) draws a large and boisterous crowd. Restaurant daily 8am–11pm; bar often stays open until 1am.

Las Olas Restaurant Las Olas Hotel, 300m south of the football field ☎ 2643 4398, ⓦ lasolashotelc ostarica.com. At lunchtime, a young surfer crowd congregates beneath the palm-fringed roof of this beachfront restaurant to scoff enormous portions of burgers and fries (around ₡3500–5000) while watching their fellow surfers get barrelled just metres away. Tues–Sat 7am–10pm, Sun 7am–6pm.

Playas Esterillos

South of Playa Hermosa, some 25km from Jacó, palm-fringed **Playas Esterillos** fulfils the archetypal image of a tropical paradise beach: a long wedge of chocolate-brown sands, backed by jungle and stretching into the spray-shrouded distance. Rocks and river split the coastline here into three sections, each accessed by a different side-road off the Costanera Sur; the most attractive beaches are **Esterillos Centro** and **Esterillos Este**, 3km apart by road, the latter home to one of the coolest hotels on the Central Pacific. The waves that pummel Esterillos' shores break further out than at Jacó and Playa Hermosa, and like Hermosa, will appeal to more advanced **surfers** than those who ride the rollers further north.

ARRIVAL AND DEPARTURE
PLAYAS ESTERILLOS

By bus Quepos–Jacó buses (8 daily; around 25min from Jacó, 55min from Quepos) can drop you off on the highway, from where it's just under a kilometre to Playas Esterillos.

ACCOMMODATION

★Alma de Pacifico Esterillos Este ☏2778 7070, ⓦalmadelpacifico.com. This fantastic beachfront boutique hotel put Esterillos on the map. It has an array of classy touches – unique architecture, artworks by the owner – along with personal plunge-pools in the swankier deluxe beachfront villas (sleeping up to 4 people; US$565). There's also a top-notch spa (massages from US$90/hr) and the on-site restaurant is superb. <u>US$305</u>

Hotel Pelican Esterillos Este ☏2778 8105, ⓦpelicanbeachfronthotel.com. Small beachfront hotel with tiled-floor rooms featuring a/c and attached bathrooms. Guests have free use of bodyboards, and the hotel also rents out surfboards (US$10/day) and runs lessons (US$50–60/hr); after tackling the waves, hit the on-site restaurant for sandwiches or ceviche (rates include breakfast). <u>US$96</u>

Quepos and around

Arriving in **QUEPOS** from San José, Puntarenas or Jacó, it's immediately apparent that you've crossed into the lush, wetter, southern Pacific region. The vegetation grows thicker and greener than further north, and more often than not it has just started or finished raining. With a polluted beach in front (obscured by the seaside road out to the old dock), Quepos can look pretty ramshackle, though the **Marina Pez Vela**, a newish dock built on reclaimed land southwest of town, adds a glossier sheen. What Quepos does enjoy is close proximity to **Parque Nacional Manuel Antonio** and its beaches, as well as the very different, and much more low-key, **Reserva Los Campesinos**; Quepos's range of (affordable) hotels, bars and restaurants and frequent bus services make it the most useful base for the park.

Once a banana-exporting town, Quepos (the name is derived from the indigenous language of the Quepoa people, who occupied this area before the arrival of the Spanish in 1563) was severely hit by the Panama disease, a devastating banana virus,

which prompted United Fruit to pull out in the 1950s. With the establishment of the nearby African palm oil plantations, though, the area has gone through something of a resurgence in recent decades, and thanks to the bounty of big fish (sailfish, marlin and wahoo) occupying its waters offshore, has also developed into one of the country's prime **sportfishing** destinations.

Reserva Los Campesinos

Quebrada Arroyo, Hwy-616, 25km east of Quepos (20km off Hwy-34; 4WD advised) • US$8; abseiling and hanging bridges US$61 • ☎ 2248 9470, ⊛ actuarcostarica.com

6

If you want to experience an authentic Costa Rican *campesino* lifestyle, **Reserva Los Campesinos**, 25km east of Quepos along a rough road (4WD preferable), offers a memorable day-long eco-adventure or overnight stay in its rustic *Los Campesinos Ecolodge* (☎ 22065009, ⊛ loscampesinosecolodge.com). The reserve is managed by the Quebrada Aroyo community, an association of local vanilla producers who are creating a biological corridor to Parque Nacional Manuel Antonio, and activities involve an abseiling and hanging bridge tour.

ARRIVAL AND GETTING AROUND

QUEPOS AND AROUND

By plane Sansa and Nature Air flights to Quepos from San José tend to be heavily booked, so reserve early. The Quepos airstrip lies 5km east of town on Hwy-34; a taxi costs around US$10 to Quepos and US$20 to Manuel Antonio. Note that Quepos Airport levies a US$3 arrival and departure fee.

Destinations Arenal/La Fortuna (1 daily; 20min); San José (7 daily; 30min).

By shuttle bus Companies such as Interbus run minibuses all the way to the national park entrance, picking up at hotels along the way; it's convenient but pricier than public buses, with two daily services to Jacó (1hr 15min), San José (4hr 30min) and La Fortuna (5hr 30min), plus one afternoon departure to Monteverde (4hr 30min).

By bus All buses stop at Quepos's busy terminal, which doubles as the *mercado*, one block east of the town centre.

Not all the buses that run from San José continue on to Manuel Antonio (check when you buy your ticket). On weekends, holidays and any time during the dry season, buy your bus ticket at least three days in advance, and your return ticket as soon as you arrive.

Destinations Dominical (6 daily; 1hr 30min); Manuel Antonio (7am–7pm, every 30min; 20min); Puntarenas (8 daily; 3hr) via Jacó (1hr 30min); San José (9–11 daily; 3hr 30min–4hr 30min).

By taxi Taxis line up at the rank at the south end of the *mercado*; the journey to Manuel Antonio costs around US$15.

By car You can rent cars in Quepos; Adobe (daily 8am–5pm; ☎ 2777 4242, ⊛ adobecar.com), opposite the football field on Av 2; and Alamo (daily 7.30am–5.30pm; ☎ 2777 3344, ⊛ alamocostarica .com), near the Palí supermarket.

ACTIVITIES AND TOURS

Amigos del Río Just outside Quepos, on the road to Manuel Antonio ☎ 2777 0082, ⊛ amigosdelrio.net. Runs whitewater-rafting tours on the Class II–III Río Savegre (year-round; US$95/6hr) and Class III–IV Río Naranjo (May–Dec; US$70/4hr).

Costa Rica Jade Tours ☎ 2777 0932, ⊛ costarica jadetours.com. Highly rated local operator led by naturalist guides; Manual Antonio tours (US$50) include transport, and they also do trips to the Isla Damas mangroves (US$60).

Iguana Tours Just south of the church ☎ 2777 2052, ⊛ iguanatours.com. Iguana Tours offers horseriding and whitewater rafting, plus hiking in Parque Nacional Manuel Antonio (US$59, includes entrance fee) and boat and kayak trips around Isla Damas, a wildlife-rich mangrove estuary just north of Quepos (both US$65).

MASS Just south of Quepos, on the road to Manuel

Antonio ☎ 2777 4842, ⊛ manuelantoniosurfschool .com. MASS offers surfing lessons (US$65/3hr) on Playa Espadilla in Manuel Antonio.

Oceans Unlimited Marina Pez Vela, just south of the centre ☎ 2777 3171, ⊛ scubadivingcostarica.com. If you'd rather see the fish than catch them, try one of Oceans Unlimited's scuba-diving excursions (around US$150) and multiday PADI courses.

El Santuario Canopy Adventure Tour 4km south of Quepos, on the road to Manuel Antonio ☎ 2777 6908, ⊛ elsantuariocanopyadventure.com. El Santuario is the canopy/zipline tour company of choice for adrenaline junkies (tours US$75), with the longest twin lines (1.3km) in Costa Rica, and ten lines in total over 3.6km.

Skydiving Costa Rica 3km south of Quepos Airport ☎ 8406 8544, ⊛ skydivingcostarica.com. Take that once-in-a-lifetime skydive with this reputable local outfit;

a 20min scenic flight followed by a tandem jump at 2743m up (US$339). Maximum weight 95kg/195lb.

Titi Canopy Tour Hwy-34, 5km northeast of Quepos ☎2777 3130, ⓦtiticanopytour.com. Slower and more suitable for families than El Santuario (tours US$80, children 4–12 US$65; night tours US$90 for all).

ACCOMMODATION

Cabinas Hellen Av 2, at C 1 ☎2777 0504. These secure *cabinas* at the back of a family home are equipped with private bathroom, fridge and fans. They offer decent single rates (US$20), and there's also free wi-fi, a small patio and parking. US$30

Hotel Kamuk Av Central, C 2/4 ☎2777 0811, ⓦkamuk .co.cr. Part of the Best Western chain, *Kamuk* offers rooms around a small pool, with a/c and TVs in the pricier ones – balconies with sea views. The restaurant centres on seafood – they'll cook up the fish you catch. US$77

★**Hotel Sirena** Av 3, C Central/2 ☎2777 0572, ⓦlasirenahotel.com. Pretty little hotel, whose charming blue-and-white rooms – those upstairs receive more light – come with private bathrooms and a/c. The small pool is flanked by a bar and restaurant; the bountiful breakfast served here is all either home-made or locally sourced. US$79

Wide Mouth Frog Av Central, C 1/3 (150m east of the bus station) ☎2777 2798, ⓦwidemouthfrog.org. The best place to stay on a budget. The efficient Kiwi–British owners at this sociable hostel offer a swimming pool, TV lounge, breakfast, free wi-fi and tight security. The dorms are a bit institutional, but the private rooms are much nicer (en-suite bathrooms cost US$15 extra). Dorms US$13, doubles US$35

EATING

The Mercado Municipal sells fish and fresh fruit and veg (Mon–Sat 6.30am–5pm); there's also a weekend *feria* (Fri 6am–9pm, Sat 6am–2pm) offering fruit, veg and home-made bread.

L'Angolo 25m west of the bus station ☎2777 4129. Make up your own panini (from ₡2000) using the range of Italian meats and cheeses on offer at this deli, or try one of the salads or fresh pasta dishes from the extensive menu. Mon–Sat 10am–10pm.

★**Café Milagro Coffee Roasters** C 4, Av 3 (facing the sea wall) ☎2777 0794, ⓦcafemilagro.com. The coffee (₡1000–2000) here is among the best in the country; try the delicious Queppuccino. They also serve *refrescos* (in flavours like vanilla nut chill or iced raspberry mocha) and cakes, as well as selling English-language newspapers and magazines. The breakfasts are creative and hearty, and by night it turns into a quality restaurant serving Latin-influenced cuisine, from pulled-pork corn cakes to coconut rum shrimp (mains ₡4000–10,000). Mon–Sat 7am–5pm.

★**Gabriella's** Marina Pez Vella ☎2519 9300, ⓦgabriellassteakhouse.com. Popular steakhouse and seafood restaurant overlooking the marina (book ahead for dinner), with dishes such as sizzling scallops (₡16,500), garlic shrimp (₡13,500) and Black Angus steaks (from ₡15,000), accompanied by a pricey but well-curated wine list. Daily 4–10pm.

El Gran Escape Av 1, C 4 (at the sea wall) ☎2777 0395. Decent, if fairly pricey, salads, burgers (from ₡5500) and seafood (₡3500–12,000) and a good selection of drinks at the bar (happy hour 5–7pm) draws an overwhelmingly American fishing crowd. The pleasant, plant-filled seating area opens to the street – and weekend nights can get rowdy. Mon & Wed–Sat 8am–10pm.

Soda La Costa de Oro C 2, Av Central/2 ☎2777 2655. The best and cheapest *soda* in town, *Soda La Costa de Oro* serves up tasty chicken *casados* (from ₡2500) to a busy lunchtime (or early evening) crowd of locals and tourists. Daily 6am–7pm.

NIGHTLIFE

Midweek, **nightlife** in Quepos is more or less limited to excited fishermen debating the merits of different tackle; at the weekends, several bars in the centre get lively with a mix of tourists, foreign residents and locals who hang out until fairly late at night.

Cuban Republik Av 3, at C 4 ☎8345 9922. Quepos's premier nightclub, *Republik* is a little smarter than the others in town, and draws a fun mix of locals and visitors. Expect dance, Latin and reggaeton. Tues–Sat 8pm–4.30am.

DIRECTORY

Banks and exchange Banco Nacional (Mon–Fri 8.30am–3.45pm) just northwest of the bus station on C 2, changes money and has an ATM; also Banco de Costa Rica (Mon–Fri 9am–4pm), opposite the bus station on C Central. Most businesses in town accept and change dollars.

Laundry Vera Lav, 100m west of the football field (Mon–Sat 8am–5pm).

Medical care Hospital Dr Max Terán Valls (☎ 2777 0922) near the airport on Hwy-34, or the Red Cross (Cruz Roja; ☎ 2777 0116) between the bus station and the football field (Av Central).

Post office The post office (Mon–Fri 8am–noon & 1–4.30pm, Sat 8am–noon) is near the football field, at the eastern end of town (Av Central, C 3/5).

Parque Nacional Manuel Antonio and around   6

Small but perfectly formed, **PARQUE NACIONAL MANUEL ANTONIO** ranks among the top tourist destinations in the country – visitors descend in droves to experience its stunning, picture-postcard setting, with spectacular white-grey sandy beaches fringed by thickly forested hills. The striking *tómbolo* formation of **Punta Catedral**, jutting out into the Pacific, accounts for much of the region's allure, and as you watch a lavish sunset flower and die over the ocean, it does seem as though Manuel Antonio may be one of the more charmed places on earth. That said, the huge tourist boom has undeniably taken its toll on the area, especially the small corridor of land between the old banana-exporting town of **Quepos** and the park itself.

Quepos to Manuel Antonio

Southeast of Quepos, a 7km stretch of road (officially Hwy-618) winds over the surrounding hills, through the village of **Manuel Antonio** (now largely indistinguishable from the adjacent development) and pitching up at the entrance to the Parque Nacional Manuel Antonio. This area was one of the first places in the country to feel the effects of the 1990s tourist explosion – drawn by its lavish beauty, hoteliers and businesses rushed to the area, and these days the entire, well-maintained highway is one of the most crowded pieces of real estate in the country, featuring an unbroken line of hotels and restaurants that run right down to the park's perimeter.

Playa Espadilla
6km south of Quepos

Just north of the park entrance lies **Playa Espadilla**, one of the most popular beaches in Costa Rica, and boasting wide, smooth, light-grey sands and stunning sunsets; MASS (see p.347) has an outlet here, offering surf lessons. The beach is plagued by **riptides** (travelling up to 10kph), though lots of people do also swim here – or rather, paddle and wade – and live to tell the tale. Lifeguards now patrol in high season, so it's considerably safer, but avoid weekends when it gets overwhelmed by day-trippers.

ARRIVAL AND DEPARTURE   QUEPOS TO MANUEL ANTONIO

By bus The Tracopa bus from San José (8–12 daily; 5hr) drops people off at their hotel along the road between Quepos and the park entrance; local buses from Quepos to Manuel Antonio village (every 30min; 20min; ₡295) depart from the bus terminal between 7am and 7pm.

ACCOMMODATION

The most exclusive – and expensive – **hotels** are hidden away in the surrounding hills, with lovely ocean and sunset views. Though you'll find some affordable places in Manual Antonio village, and the occasional low-season discount, prices are high compared to the rest of the country. Reserve well in advance if visiting in the peak season (Dec 1–Jan 15).

★ **Arenas del Mar** 1.6km off Hwy-618 (6km south of Quepos) ☎ 2777 2777, ⓦ arenasdelmar.com. Set over large grounds on the headland at the northern end of Playa Espadilla (golf carts whizz you about), this sumptuous resort has spacious en suites, with huge bathrooms, flat-screen TVs and tasteful design; some also have outdoor jacuzzis and great views down over Punta Catedral. The hotel incorporates everything from solar-powered hot water to recycled roof tiles – and the owners spent twenty years replanting the area (it was

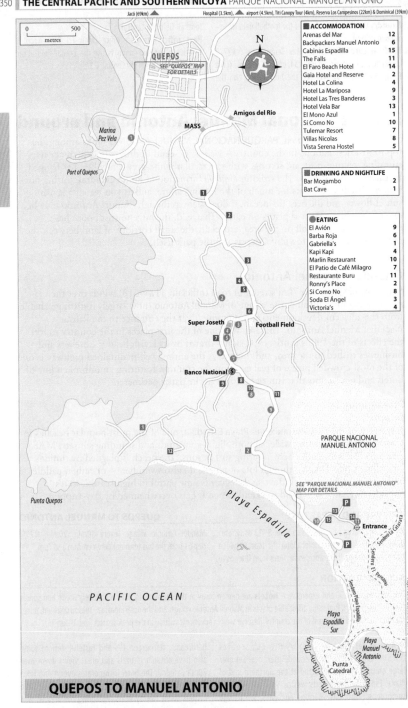

Jacó (69km) ▲   Hospital (3.5km), ▲ airport (4.5km), Titi Canopy Tour (4km), Reserva Los Campesinos (22km) & Dominical (39km)

0   500
metres

QUEPOS
SEE "QUEPOS" MAP
FOR DETAILS

N

Amigos del Rio

MASS

Marina
Pez Vela

Port of Quepos

Super Joseth   Football Field

Banco National $

Punta Quepos

PARQUE NACIONAL
MANUEL ANTONIO

SEE "PARQUE NACIONAL MANUEL ANTONIO"
MAP FOR DETAILS

Playa Espadilla

Entrance

Sendero La Catarata

Sendero El Perezoso

Sendero Playa Espadilla

Playa Puerto Escondido (600m) ▶

PACIFIC OCEAN

Playa
Espadilla
Sur

Playa
Manuel
Antonio

Punta
Catedral

QUEPOS TO MANUEL ANTONIO

ACCOMMODATION

Arenas del Mar	12
Backpackers Manuel Antonio	6
Cabinas Espadilla	15
The Falls	11
El Faro Beach Hotel	14
Gaia Hotel and Reserve	2
Hotel La Colina	4
Hotel La Mariposa	9
Hotel Las Tres Banderas	3
Hotel Vela Bar	13
El Mono Azul	1
Sí Como No	10
Tulemar Resort	7
Villas Nicolas	8
Vista Serena Hostel	5

DRINKING AND NIGHTLIFE

Bar Mogambo	2
Bat Cave	1

EATING

El Avión	9
Barba Roja	6
Gabriella's	1
Kapi Kapi	4
Marlin Restaurant	10
El Patio de Café Milagro	7
Restaurante Buru	11
Ronny's Place	2
Sí Como No	8
Soda El Ángel	3
Victoria's	4

formerly a plantain farm), so there's plenty of wildlife on-site, from howler monkeys to black iguanas. There's also an excellent restaurant, plus two pools, and direct access to secluded sections of beach. US$350

Backpackers Manuel Antonio Hwy-618 (3.4km south of Quepos) ☎2777 2507, ⌨backpackers manuelantonio.com. This family-run hostel is one of the cheapest options on the road to the park, offering a mix of cell-like dorms and private rooms (some with a/c), all with shared hot-water bathrooms. It's also one of the most sociable, whether you're teaming up on the table football or grilling meat on the patio out back (there's a good butcher's just across the road). Dorms US$16, doubles US$39

Cabinas Espadilla Off Hwy-618 (6.8km south of Quepos) ☎2777 2113, ⌨espadilla.com. Set in attractive gardens with a pool, these pleasant, airy cabins (sleeping up to 4 people) have large beds, hot-water private bathrooms, a kitchen and fan or a/c, though are better value for groups of three to four people. Guests have use of the tennis court at the nearby sister hotel (*Hotel Playa Espadilla*), and there's easy access to Playa Espadilla. US$118

The Falls Hwy-618 (4.7km south of Quepos) ☎2777 1332, ⌨fallsresortcostarica.com. Individually designed suites offering comfortable four-poster beds, large bathrooms and a pleasant patio with views of the tropical gardens – plenty of animals, including toucans and sloths, can be spotted in the waterfall-laced grounds. There's also a small infinity pool that seems to "hang" out over the foliage. US$155

El Faro Beach Hotel Near the park entrance (7km south of Quepos) ☎2777 4025, ⌨elfarobeachhotel .com. Has the dubious distinction of being the nation's only "container hotel"; the compact rooms are literally converted shipping containers, piled like a giant hive on the hillside, with stunning views, a/c, flat-screen TV and pool access. US$130

★**Gaia Hotel and Reserve** Just off Hwy-618 (2.3km south of Quepos) ☎2777 9797, ⌨gaiahr.com. This ultra-chic boutique hotel takes style and service to the next level. Well-appointed terraced suites and villas, decked with natural flooring, come with huge, cloud-soft beds, flat-screen TVs and rainforest views. There are two pools, one cascading into the other, and you could quite easily eat all your meals at the fine restaurant, with its varied menu and globetrotting wine list. Room rates include breakfast and a free treatment at the on-site spa. No under-13s. US$320

Hotel La Colina Hwy-618 (3km south of Quepos) ☎2777 0231, ⌨lacolina.com. Set on an incline locals call "Cardiac Hill", this lovely hotel offers comfortable rooms with private bath and a/c. The rooms higher up boast a fantastic 180-degree view of the jungle and sea. A

sparkling pool flows over two levels, and there's also an on-site restaurant. US$116

Hotel La Mariposa Just off Hwy-618 (3.4km south of Quepos) ☎2777 0355, ⌨lamariposa.com. Villas set in lovely gardens around a pair of swimming pools. You can see Punta Catedral from many of the luxurious rooms or treat yourself to the unsurpassed views from the penthouse suite, complete with floor-to-ceiling glass walls and private hot tub. Enjoy excellent meals at the prestigious Mediterranean restaurant or settle for a sunset cocktail. US$202

Hotel Las Tres Banderas Hwy-618 (2.9km south of Quepos) ☎2777 1871, ⌨hoteltresbanderas.com. Set in a quiet wooded area, this welcoming hotel has large double rooms that open onto a terrace or balcony overlooking the forest. Spacious suites have a kitchenette and sofa bed, while the apartments feature two bedrooms (which sleep up to 7 people; from US$200)– if you can find them amid the foliage. There's a swimming pool and a restaurant that sometimes serves tasty Polish specialities. Doubles US$80, suites US$120

Hotel Vela Bar Near the park entrance (6.8km south of Quepos) ☎2777 0413, ⌨velabar.com. This small hotel, near the beach and surrounded by tropical gardens, has basic, pleasant rooms with private bathrooms and fan or a/c. Rustic *casitas* (for two people; US$160) come with lounge, kitchenette and terrace. Good restaurant, too. Adults only. US$110

El Mono Azul Hwy-618 (2km south of Quepos) ☎2777 2572, ⌨hotelmonoazul.com. Small but bright rooms come with a fan or a/c and a terrace, centred round lovely swimming pools. The on-site restaurant is popular for its down-to-earth, good honest grub. US$70

Sí Como No Hwy-618 (4.4km south of Quepos) ☎2777 0777, ⌨sicomono.com. Enjoy beautiful views of the Pacific and Punta Catedral from this award-winning complex set high on a hill. Lovely, brightly furnished rooms vary from well-appointed doubles to fully equipped villas; extensive facilities include a hot tub, two pools, swim-up bar, spa and a small cinema with nightly screenings. The two restaurants (see p.352) serve excellent food. US$299

Tulemar Resort Hwy-618 (3.9km south of Quepos) ☎2777 0580, ⌨tulemarresort.com. This vast luxury complex comprises several properties, from rooms and villas, perched among the treetops, to the rustic Tulemar bungalows (sleeping up to 4 people), which still feature a/c and cable TV, and stylish Jungle House (sleeping up to 6 people), two separate units that can be rented as a whole. There are three pools (one for families) and an exclusive beach complete with (free) bodyboards and kayaks. Doubles US$260, bungalows US$280, Jungle House US$300

Villas Nicolas Hwy-618 (4.4km south of Quepos) ☎2777 0481, ⌨villasnicolas.com. Set high above the surrounding greenery, these classy villas (sleeping 2–4) come with hot-water private bathrooms and ceiling fans; some have kitchens, and there's also a small pool. Villas with full sea views go for US$20 more. No children under 6. U͟S͟$͟1͟4͟1͟

★**Vista Serena Hostel** Hwy-618 (3km south of Quepos) ☎2777 5162, ⓦvistaserena.com. Clean, welcoming hostel offering million-dollar views and plenty of dorm beds full of gringo students looking for a good time; the private ocean-view bungalows with shared bathroom can sleep three people. Watch the sunset from the hammock-strung balcony or cook with fellow travellers in the communal kitchen. Extras include BBQ nights and a TV/DVD lounge. Dorms U͟S͟$͟1͟2͟, bungalows U͟S͟$͟5͟0͟

6

EATING

Eating along the Quepos–Manuel Antonio road is notoriously expensive, and the area's few reasonably priced **restaurants** are understandably popular.

El Avión Hwy-618 (4.8km south of Quepos) ☎2777 0584, ⓦelavion.net. Dine or drink inside a US aircraft used in the 1980s for Nicaraguan Contra arms-trafficking at this appropriately named restaurant. In truth, dining is more enjoyable in the open-air section, with sensational views, but the whole place exudes character. The menu includes average burgers, pastas and fajitas (dishes from ₡5500). Daily noon–11pm (low season 1–10pm); bar open till 2am.

Barba Roja Hwy-618 (4km south of Quepos) ☎2777 5159, ⓦbarbarojarestaurant.com. This friendly, popular restaurant dishes up quality American cuisine (₡7500–10,000), including grilled fish, tenderloin steaks, chunky burgers and lip-smacking BBQ ribs. Come and nurse a quiet drink while watching the sunset (happy hour 4.30–6.30pm), or crank things up a gear on Saturday nights, when live music is on the menu (from 8pm). Tues–Sun 3–10.30pm, Sat 3–11pm.

Kapi Kapi Hwy-618 (3.8km south of Quepos) ☎2777 5049, ⓦrestaurantekapikapi.com. The select menu at this fine-dining restaurant specializes in seafood and also offers meat dishes, such as grilled chicken with miso and honey and macadamia-encrusted mahi-mahi (mains from ₡10,000). Sinful desserts include a one-is-not-enough chocolate soufflé. Tues–Sun 4–10pm.

Marlin Restaurant Near the park entrance (7km south of Quepos) ☎2777 1035. One of the cheaper places to eat in Manuel Antonio, this cheerful terrace restaurant serves up fresh seafood, Tex-Mex sandwiches and salads (mains ₡4000–5000) to crowds of hungry tourists. Daily 7am–9pm.

El Patio de Café Milagro Hwy-618 (4.1km south of Quepos) ☎2777 2272, ⓦcafemilagro.com. Pop by for one of the best breakfasts around, or drop in any time to enjoy delicious home-made pastries washed down with excellent locally roasted coffee (₡1000–2000) or a perfect cappuccino. Live music daily 7–9pm. Daily 7am–10pm.

Restaurante Buru Near the park entrance (7km south of Quepos) ☎2777 4521. Considering the location next to the park, this is a reasonable deal, though it can get busy – the food is usually of a high standard, with fresh fish, a decent cheeseburger and tacos (reckon on around ₡10,000 for lunch, including drinks). Daily 11am–9.30pm.

Ronny's Place Off Hwy-618 (3.4km south of Quepos) ☎2777 5120, ⓦronnysplace.com. Simple food – grilled chicken, steaks and pricey seafood specials (₡6500–12,500) – but sensational sunsets, the real reason you've come to this rustic place perched on the edge of the coast. Order a jug of headachingly strong *sangría* and plop yourself down at the tables lined up along the ridge. Daily noon–10pm.

Sí Como No Hwy-618 (4.4km south of Quepos) ☎2777 0777, ⓦsicomono.com. This hotel features two excellent dining options; succulent fish brochettes and other grilled treats are on offer at the *Rico Tico Jungle Grill*, which has a good children's menu and features nightly live music. More upmarket dining is served at the poolside *Claro Que Sí Seafood & Grill*, a Caribbean-influenced seafood restaurant dishing up coconut shrimps and the like (mains ₡7000–14,000). Rico Tico daily 6.30am–9.30pm; Claro Que Sí daily 5–10pm.

★**Soda El Ángel** Hwy-618 (3.5km south of Quepos). Fill up with the cheapest and best *casados* on the hill – five types are on offer, including liver (from ₡2500) – at this charming and unpretentious *soda*, home to just a few tree-trunk tables. Daily 9am–9pm.

Victoria's Hwy-618 (3.8km south of Quepos) ☎2777 5143, ⓦvictoriasgourmet.com. Upscale Italian restaurant with delicious, though pricey, pizzas (₡7000–12,500) with ingredients like home-made pesto and house mozzarella, as well as similarly priced American-Italian-style pasta dishes such as spaghetti and meatballs. Daily 4–11pm.

DRINKING AND NIGHTLIFE

Bar Mogambo Hwy-618 (5.3km south of Quepos) ☎7104 5226, ⓦfacebook.com/bar.mogambo. Cool LGBT (though hetro-friendly) lounge bar-club with anything from pop tunes to electro tracks on the sound system. It's a good opportunity to dress up. Thurs is the big night. Mon & Thurs–Sun 4pm–1am.

Bat Cave La Mansion Hotel, off Hwy-618 (5.1km south of Quepos) ☎ 2777 3489, ⊛ lamansioninn.com. For something different, if a little claustrophobic, head down a winding staircase to the *Bat Cave*, an underground bar housed in a natural grotto that has real bats flittering around the ceiling. Daily 7pm–midnight.

Parque Nacional Manuel Antonio

Tues–Sun 7am–4pm • US$16 • ☎ 2777 5185

PARQUE NACIONAL MANUEL ANTONIO may be Costa Rica's smallest national park, but it's also its most popular. One can easily imagine the fate that might have overtaken its limestone-white sands had it not been designated a national park in 1972. Even so, the park suffers from a high number of visitors – it's best to avoid weekends altogether, when Costa Rican families descend en masse to hit the beaches. The park does close on Mondays, however, to give the animals a rest and the rangers and trail maintenance staff a chance to work.

Covering an area of only 6.8 square kilometres, Manuel Antonio preserves not only the lovely **beaches** and the unique *tómbolo* formation of Punta Catedral (Cathedral Point), but also **mangroves** and humid tropical **forest**. Visitors can only explore the part of the park that faces the sea – the eastern mountain section, off-limits to the public, is regularly patrolled by rangers to deter poaching, which is rife in the area, and incursions into the park from surrounding farmers and *campesinos*.

The trails

Manuel Antonio has a tiny system of short **trails** – all easy, except in rainy conditions, when they can get slippery. From the park entrance the main trail, **Sendero El Perezoso**, runs for 1.4km down to Playa Manuel Antonio, providing, as the name suggests, a fair

PARQUE NACIONAL MANUEL ANTONIO

6

6

chance of spotting sloths in the guarumo trees along the way, as well as squirrel and howler monkeys. About 400m in, the short **Sendero La Catarata** (900m) branches off to the pretty little waterfall after which it's named.

At the end of Sendero El Perezoso, most people continue straight down to **Playa Manuel Antonio**, the park's best swimming beach and, predictably, its most crowded – both with people and with white-faced capuchin monkeys, who seem to be running a competition with the local racoon population as to who can steal the most backpack snacks. At the southern end of the beach, low tide reveals a pile of stones believed to have been used as **turtle traps** by the area's indigenous peoples – green turtles have probably nested in Manuel Antonio for thousands of years. Beyond here, it's worth embarking on the **Sendero La Trampa** (1.4km), an energetic loop around the Punta Catedral offering wonderful views of the Pacific, dotted with jagged-edged little islands; like all *tómbolos*, Punta Catedral was once an island that, over millennia, has been joined to the mainland through accumulated sand deposits.

Instead of turning right to Playa Manuel Antonio at the end of Sendero El Perezoso you can turn left for more rainforest hiking. Head inland on the **Sendero Mirador** (1.3km), which concludes at a viewpoint overlooking Playa Puerto Escondido, or take the **Sendero Playas Gemelas y Puerto Escondido** (1.6km), which heads through relatively dense, humid tropical forest cover, crossing a small creek before eventually reaching the southern end of Playa Puerto Escondido; a turn-off halfway along leads to rocky **Playas Gemelas**. You can clamber along Playa Puerto Escondido at low tide between the two trails – but check tide times with the rangers before leaving to avoid getting cut off.

ARRIVAL AND DEPARTURE

PARQUE NACIONAL MANUEL ANTONIO

By bus Buses from Quepos (7am–7pm, every 30min; 20min; ₡295) and San José (5–6 daily; 5hr) drop passengers off 200m before the park entrance.

By car If you're driving, note that you'll be charged ₡3000/day to leave your car at one of the supervised car parks on the road near the entrance, or anywhere on the main street.

MANUEL ANTONIO BEACHES

The **beaches** around Parque Nacional Manuel Antonio can be confusing, since they're called by a variety of different names. It's important to know which beach you're on, however, because some are unsafe for swimming; check with the rangers about conditions. From north to south, the beaches are as follows:

Playa Espadilla (also called Playa Primera or Playa Numero Uno). This long, popular curve of sand fronting Manuel Antonio village runs down to the park exit, just outside the park itself (see p.349).

Playa Espadilla Sur (also called Playa Dos or Playa Segunda). Espadilla Sur is the last beach you come to inside the park – the main trail towards the exit runs along the back of the beach. It's on the north side of Punta Catedral, and while usually fairly calm, it's also the most dangerous in rough conditions – beware the currents.

Playa Manuel Antonio (also called Playa Tres or Playa Blanca). Immediately south of Playa Espadilla Sur (on the other side of Punta Catedral), and in a deeper and more protected bay than the others, Manuel Antonio is by far the best swimming beach, though you can still get clobbered by the deceptively gentle-looking waves as they hit the shore. Unfortunately, it's quite narrow and can get crowded (the best time to come is before 10am).

Playa Puerto Escondido (also called Playa Cuatro). Reached along the Sendero Puerto Escondido, this is a pretty, white horseshoe-shaped beach. Don't set out without first checking with the rangers about the *marea* (tide), because at high tide you can't get across the beach, nor can you cross it from the dense forest behind. At best, it'll be a waste of time; at worst, you'll get cut off on the other side for a few hours. Rangers advise against swimming here, as the currents can be dangerous.

WATCHING WILDLIFE IN MANUEL ANTONIO

Manuel Antonio is one of the few remaining natural habitats of the **squirrel monkey**, the smallest of Costa Rica's primates, with close-set bright eyes and a delicate, white-haired face. You might spot them springing through the canopy above the park trails or outside the park in the Manuel Antonio area in general – local schoolchildren have set up a project to build overhead wooden "bridges" for the monkeys to cross the increasingly busy road from Manuel Antonio to Quepos; ask at *El Mono Azul* (see p.351) for details.

You also have a good chance of seeing other smaller **mammals**, such as coati, agouti, two- and three-toed sloths and white-faced capuchin monkeys. The abundant **birdlife** includes the shimmering green kingfisher, the brown pelican, which can often be seen fishing off the rocks, and the laughing falcon. Big **iguanas** hang out near the beaches, often keeping stock-still for ten minutes at a time, providing good photo opportunities. Beware the **snakes** that drape themselves over the trails and look like vines – be careful what you grab onto.

Due to the park's high visitor numbers, some of the wildlife is unnervingly familiar with humans, and white-faced capuchin monkeys in particular have no qualms raiding backpacks in the hope of finding a bite to eat. You can **help the animals** by not feeding them (for which you can be fined), being quiet as you walk the trails and not leaving any litter.

INFORMATION

Guides You can take informative tours with guides at the park entrance (US$15–25/person; 2hr), all of whom carry telescopic lenses to see wildlife more clearly. You may be approached by "guides" offering their services in the village, so check their ICT (Costa Rican Institute of Tourism) photo ID first.

What to bring Whether you walk the trails guided or not, make sure you take plenty of water – the climate is hot, humid and wet, all year round, with temperatures easily climbing to 30°C and above.

Tours Iguana Tours (see p.347) offer a range of day-trips in and around the national park, including hiking and kayaking.

The Zona Sur

CERRO CHIRRIPÓ SUMMIT

The Zona Sur

Costa Rica's Zona Sur (southern zone) is the country's least-known area, both for Ticos and for visitors, though tourism is increasing at a steady pace. It's a geographically diverse region encompassing the high mountain peaks of the Cordillera de Talamanca at its northern edge, the agricultural heartland of the Valle de El General, the river-cut lowlands of the Valle de Diquís around Palmar and the coffee-growing Valle de Coto Brus, near the border with Panama. The coast provides much of the allure, as elsewhere in the country, with wonderful beaches and pristine diving opportunities culminating at remote Isla del Caño.

7

The Zona Sur is particularly popular with hikers, who are spoiled for choice between the cloudforest trails around **San Gerardo de Dota** in the north and the epic multiday jungle treks of **Parque Nacional Corcovado** in the south – the latter's soaring canopy trees constitute the last chunk of tropical wet forest on the entire Pacific side of the Central American isthmus. Many come to climb **Cerro Chirripó** in the Talamancas – one of the highest peaks in Central America – set in the chilly, rugged terrain of the **Parque Nacional Chirripó** and best accessed from the pleasant city of **San Isidro de El General**. The interior also offers the chance to interact with the country's indigenous **Boruca people**, primarily in the Reserva Biológica Dúrika and Reserva Indígena Boruca, accessible from the town of **Buenos Aires**.

Along the Pacific coast, Playa Dominical was originally a surfing destination, but its tropical beauty now draws an ever-increasing number of visitors (not to mention property developers), especially since the paved **Costanera Sur** has made this entire stretch of coast accessible without a 4WD. Further south, the **Península de Osa** is home to the remote and picturesque **Bahía Drake**, while on the opposite side of the Golfo Dulce, near the **border with Panama**, is **Golfito**, the only town of any size in the region and a Tico tourist attraction after being made a tax-free zone for manufactured goods from Panama. Golfo Dulce also holds two of Costa Rica's best surfing beaches, Playa Zancudo and **Playa Pavones**, the latter the site of one of the most-sought-after waves in the world.

Despite the region's profusion of basic, inexpensive **accommodation**, you may find yourself spending more money than you bargained for simply because of the time, distance and planning involved in getting to many of the region's more beautiful spots – this is particularly true if you stay in one of the very comfortable private **rainforest lodges** in the Osa and Golfo Dulce areas. Many people prefer to take a package rather than travel independently, and travellers who stay at the rainforest lodges often choose to fly in.

RESPLENDENT QUETZAL

Highlights

❶ San Gerardo de Dota Set off in search of quetzals or try your hand at fly-fishing at this remote mountain village with a jaw-dropping setting. **See p.362**

❷ Climb Cerro Chirripó The hike up Costa Rica's highest peak is a long but varied ascent through cloudforest and paramo to rocky mountaintop. **See p.368**

❸ Nauyaca Waterfalls Hike or ride on horseback through the jungle to one of Costa Rica's most enchanting cascades. **See p.375**

❹ Bahía Drake Explore the stunning natural scenery and marine life of remote Bahía Drake. **See p.382**

❺ Isla del Caño Snorkel among coral beds and spot dolphins, manta rays and whales at Costa Rica's premier dive spot. **See p.385**

❻ Parque Nacional Corcovado Strike out into the heart of the visually and biologically magnificent coastal rainforest at Corcovado and you'll understand why it draws comparison with the Amazon basin. **See p.390**

HIGHLIGHTS ARE MARKED ON THE MAP ON PP.360–361

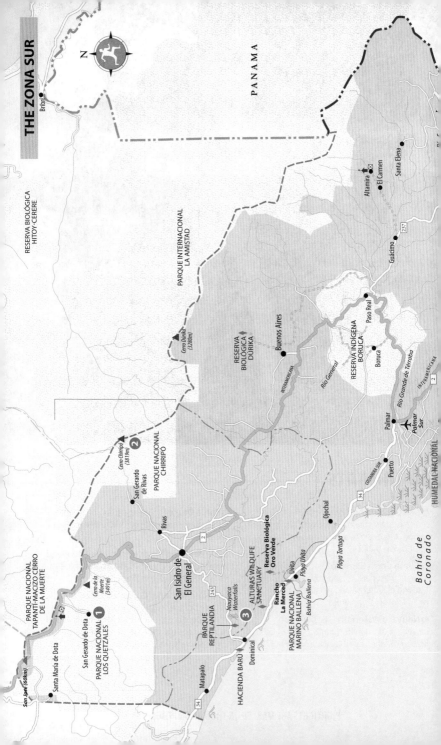

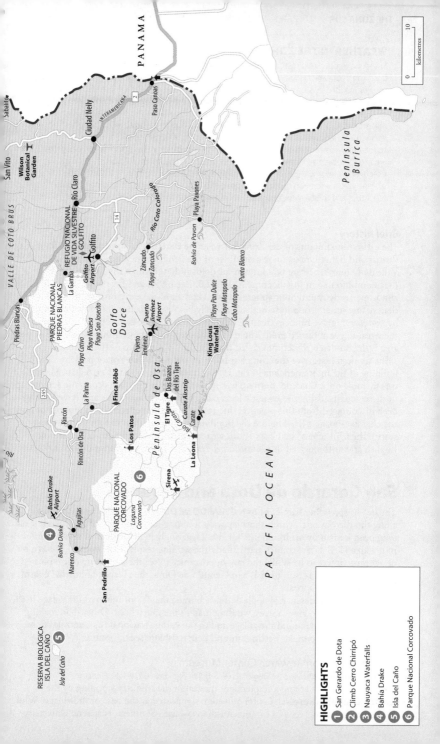

PANAMA

Sabalito

San Vito

Wilson Botanical Garden

VALLE DE COTO BRUS

Ciudad Neily

INTERAMERICANA

2

Paso Canosas

Río Claro

REFUGIO NACIONAL DE VIDA SILVESTRE GOLFITO

Golfito

Golfito Airport

14

Piedras Blancas

PARQUE NACIONAL PIEDRAS BLANCAS

La Gamba

Playa Cativo

Playa Nicuesa

Playa San Josecito

Golfo Dulce

Zancudo

Playa Zancudo

Río Coto Colorado

Playa Pavones

Bahía de Pavón

Peninsula Burica

Puerto Jiménez

Puerto Jiménez Airport

La Palma

Finca Kóbö

Península de Osa

265

Rincón

Rincón de Osa

Los Patos

Dos Brazos del Río Tigre

El Tigre

Carate Airstrip

Río Coyote

Carate

Playa Pan Dulce

Playa Matapalo

Cabo Matapalo

Punta Blanco

King Louis Waterfall

Aguilitas

Bahía Drake Airport

Bahía Drake

Marenco

PARQUE NACIONAL CORCOVADO

Laguna Corcovado

Sirena

La Leona

6

San Pedrillo

PACIFIC OCEAN

RESERVA BIOLÓGICA ISLA DEL CAÑO

Isla del Caño

5

4

Río

0   10
kilometres

WEATHER IN THE ZONA SUR

The Zona Sur has two distinct **climatic regions**. The first comprises the Pacific lowlands, from south of Quepos (covered in chapter 6) roughly to the Río Sierpe Delta at the top of the Península de Osa, and the upland Valle de El General and the Talamancas, both of which experience a dry season from December to April. The second region – the Península de Osa, Golfito and Golfo Dulce – does not have so marked a dry season (although the months from December to April are less wet) and, due to localized wind patterns from the Pacific, gets very wet at other times, receiving up to 5000mm of rain a year, with spectacular seasonal thunder and lightning storms cantering in across the Pacific from around October to December. In the rainy season, some parts of Parque Nacional Corcovado become more or less unwalkable, local roads become impassable due to surging rivers and everything gets more difficult. This makes it a good time to come if you want to avoid the crowds, but you'll need a 4WD and lots of patience.

7

Brief history

The earliest inhabitants of the Zona Sur were the **Diquis**, who lived around modern-day Palmar and Bahía Drake, on the shoulder of the Península de Osa – a region still called Valle de Diquis. They are best known for **goldsmithing**, which the Museo de Oro Precolombino in San José documents in detail (see p.92), and for their crafting of almost perfectly round **lithic spheres**. Less is known of the early history of the Diquis than of any other group in Costa Rica, chiefly because their burial sites were plundered by *huaqueros* (grave robbers/treasure hunters), who in some cases dynamited tombs in their zeal to get at buried gold. These days the only indigenous group of any size in the area is the **Boruca** – sometimes called the Brunka – a subgroup of the Diquis.

The modern history of the Zona Sur has been defined by its isolation. Before the building of the **Interamericana** in the 1950s, transport across the Cerro de la Muerte was by mule only. **Charcoal-burning** was until the 1980s the main economic activity up in these heights, using the majestic local oaks, but *campesinos* in the area have largely been discouraged from this practice, due to its deforesting effects. For a glimpse of how the charcoal-burners lived before the building of the Interamericana, read the short story "The Carbonero" by Costa Rican writer Carlos Salazar Herera, translated into English and anthologized in *Costa Rica: A Traveller's Literary Companion* (see p.434).

San Gerardo de Dota and around

The lovely, sprawling hamlet of **SAN GERARDO DE DOTA** enjoys a spectacular setting along the Río Savegre, with lush valley walls looming on either side of it. Though it has long been known by ornithologists for the staggeringly high number of species found in the area (178 at last count), particularly the striking **resplendent quetzal**, it has a bit of a forgotten feel to it. While the rare opportunity to see the almost mythical bird is for many the main reason to visit San Gerardo de Dota, the village's unhurried charm has an undeniable appeal.

Beyond a preponderance of apple and peach trees, there's not much to the village itself, which spreads 9km down a steep winding road to the valley floor. Other than making guided hikes in and around the village and to the **Parque Nacional Los Quetzales** to see the bird, the most popular pastime around here is **fishing** (see opposite).

Quetzal Education Research Center Museum

On the main road in the village centre, at the *Savegre Hotel* • Mon–Fri 9am–5pm • Free • ☎ 2740 1010, ⓦ qerc.org

If you have no luck seeing a resplendent quetzal in the wild, try stopping by the **Quetzal Education Research Center Museum**, signposted at the base of the village. While the centre mainly serves as a campus for the US-based Southern Nazarene University

THE DIQUIS

Very little is known about the history of the **Diquis region** before 1000 BC, though culturally it appears to have formed part of the Greater Chiriquí region, which takes its name from the province in southwestern Panama. Archeologists date their famous **lithic spheres** (see box, p.378) from sometime between 1000 BC and 500 AD; between around 700 and 1600 AD the Diquis began fashioning **gold** pendants, breastplates, headbands and chains, becoming master goldsmiths within a hundred years or so. Between 500 and 800 AD drastic changes occurred in the culture of the Diquis. Archeologists attribute them to the impact of the arrival of seagoing peoples from coastal Colombia or possibly further south in the Andes – a theory borne out by their *metates* and pottery, which show llama or guanaco figures, animals that would have been unknown on the isthmus. In the Diquis' own art, both the ingenious – often cheeky – goldwork and the voluptuous pottery display a unique humour as well as superlative attention to detail.

The Diquis appear to have been in a state of constant **warfare** among themselves and with foreign groups. Like the Chorotegas to the north in Greater Nicoya, they seem to have engaged in sacrifice, ritually beheading war captives. Huge *metates* unearthed at Barilles in Panama show images of these rituals, while smaller crucible-like dishes – in which coca leaves, yucca or maize may have been crushed and fermented – suggest ritual inebriation.

The indigenous peoples of Zona Sur first met the Spaniards in 1522 when the *cacique* (chief) of the Térraba group graciously hosted Captain **Gil González** for a fortnight. González was on his way from near the present-day Panama border, where his ship had run aground, to Nicaragua. Despite infirmity (he was in his fifties), he was walking all the way. The Diquis seem to have declined abruptly after this initial contact, most likely felled by influenza, smallpox, hepatitis and other diseases brought by Spanish settlers.

7

and works to protect the Río Savegre watershed, it has a stuffed male quetzal (which died of natural causes) on display, as well as examples of other local wildlife, including moths and snakes.

ARRIVAL AND DEPARTURE

By bus There are no buses to San Gerardo de Dota, though hourly San José (MUSOC or Tracopa) buses bound for San Isidro de El General will stop for you at the turn-off at Km80 on the Interamericana (2hr 30min from San José), 9km from the village centre. Make arrangements in advance for your hotel to pick you up from there. Heading back, you'll need to get a lift to the turn-off and flag buses down.

SAN GERARDO DE DOTA AND AROUND

By car The turn-off to San Gerardo de Dota is about 80km south of San José; normal cars can usually make the trip, though you'll feel safer in a 4WD, since the 9km part-gravel, part-paved road down from the Interamericana is treacherously steep in parts.
By taxi San José taxis charge US$150–170 to San Gerardo de Dota (one way), usually for up to four people.

ACTIVITIES

Birdwatching All hotels arrange early morning tours to see the quetzal, usually for around US$25/2hr.
Fishing Lure-fishing is Dec–March and fly-fishing mostly May & June. Most of the village's lodges can arrange fishing

outings on the Savegre with local guides (from US$50–75/ half-day, including equipment); make arrangements in advance of your stay.

ACCOMMODATION

For such a small village, there are some absolutely **wonderful places to stay** in San Gerardo de Dota, as well as the surrounding area. Bear in mind that although it's set in a valley, the village lies at around 2200m; it can get **chilly** at night.

Cabinas El Quetzal In the village ☎2740 1036, ⊕cabinaselquetzal.com. A relative bargain, these clean and nicely furnished cabins (sleeping 2–6) on the main road near the river are a great option if you're on a budget. Includes breakfast and dinner. Per person US$70
★**Dantica Cloud Forest Lodge** 4km from the Interamericana on the road to the village centre ☎2740

1067, ⊕dantica.com. Striking, modern lodge and art gallery with seven villas (sleeping 2–4) and a suite, all of which have south-facing terraces, comfy furnishings, jacuzzi, satellite TV and floor-to-ceiling windows with jaw-dropping views. Breakfast is included and there's a restaurant attached to the gallery where you can dine on creative beef and pork dishes, as well as locally caught trout. US$117

★**Mirador de Quetzales** Turn-off at Interamericana Km70, 10km north of the San Gerardo exit ☎2200 4185, ⓦmiradorquetzalescr.com. Set in a cloudforest reserve run by a local family, this guesthouse is cosy and very reasonably priced, comprising an eight-room lodge (shared bathrooms) and several wooden *cabinas* (sleeping 2–5) with private bathrooms overlooking a misty valley. Bedside electric heaters warm you through near-freezing night-time temperatures. Included in the rate is a guided hike along El Robledal, the *finca's* 4km trail, which offers good chances to spot the resplendent quetzal. Breakfast and dinner included. Per person US$82

Savegre Hotel In the village ☎2740 1028, ⓦsavegre.com. Long-running ecolodge, well-known among birdwatchers for the number of quetzals that nest on or near its land. The rooms are straightforward and comfortable (standard rooms come with two double beds), with homely furnishings. They have trail maps, can arrange guides (which cost extra) and offer birdwatching trips and horseriding on their 400-hectare private reserve. Breakfast included. US$152

Trogón Lodge In the village ☎2293 8181, ⓦtrogon lodge.com. Comfortable heated cabins (sleeping 2–4), though they can still get chilly at night, and beautifully landscaped grounds with several trout ponds, marked trails through the woods and a zipline tour. There are normally many quetzals to be seen around here. US$136

EATING

Café Kahawa Near the end of the village road, alongside the river ☎2740 1081, ⓦkahawa.co. Wonderful open-air restaurant with scenic river views and friendly owners. The menu features a variety of fish dishes (mostly using rainbow trout, introduced to the Río Savegre in the 1950s), such as a smoked trout sandwich (₡4500) and trout tacos (₡3000), but is also known for its tasty black bean soup (₡3000). Daily 7.30am–6pm.

Comida Típicas Miriam About 300m or so uphill from Dantica ☎2740 1049, ⓦmiriamquetzals.com. This inviting, family-run *soda* serves hearty Costa Rican staples throughout the day. Highlights include a trout *casado* (₡4500) and linguine with trout (₡6000). Daily 7am–7.30pm.

Parque Nacional Los Quetzales

About 4km north of the turn-off to San Gerardo de Dota (Km76 marker on the Interamericana) • Daily 7.30am–3.30pm • Nominally US$10 • ☎2514 0403

Opened in 2008, **Parque Nacional Los Quetzales** covers an area of over 48 densely forested square kilometres. Set higher in elevation – between 2000 and 3000m – than many of the other national parks, Los Quetzales consists mostly of cloudforest, an ideal habitat for numerous wildlife, including coyotes, jaguars, Baird's tapirs and, of course, quetzals. The quetzals feed on the reserve's abundant aguacatillo trees, and the best time to spot them is during their nesting season, from March to June.

Currently the park has just basic facilities for tourists, so is best visited on a tour with one of the lodges in San Gerardo de Dota (see p.362). At the time of research there were eight (poorly maintained) **trails** in the park, with the most rewarding a 3–4hr loop from the park entrance – following the Sendero Ojo de Agua and then the Camino Público – north of the turn-off to San Gerardo de Dota. By the end of 2017, however, the park is expected to open a brand-new and much better 2km loop trail, plus **visitor centre** – until then visitors tend not to pay the entrance fee (though tours may "include" it), as there is usually no one around to collect it.

ARRIVAL AND INFORMATION   PARQUE NACIONAL LOS QUETZALES

By car The park entrance is just past the Km76 marker on the Interamericana (4WD unnecessary).

Information Until the new visitor centre is completed, the ranger station is unlikely to be staffed, though there are displays in English that provide park information, and usually trail maps.

San Isidro de El General

After a chilly ride over Cerro de la Muerte, a spectacular descent into **SAN ISIDRO DE EL GENERAL**, 702m above sea level, brings you halfway back into tropical climes. In Costa Rica, San Isidro is regarded by foreign residents and Ticos alike as an attractive place to live, with its clean, country-town atmosphere, bustling commercial centre and full

THE ROAD TO CERRO DE LA MUERTE AND BEYOND

Though the **Interamericana** (Hwy-2) south of San José heaves with international transport trucks and other large vehicles, the road is well maintained and is no longer an intimidating drive (depending on your driving experience, obviously). Yellow-topped kilometre markings line the highway, and villages and hamlets are often referred to by these numbers. The ease of travel from the capital, via Cartago, to San Isidro de El General depends a lot on the weather. The views can be impressive along this stretch, but they're not often easy to appreciate given the need to keep one's eyes glued to the road – make use of the stopping places on route. It's not a good idea to drive at night – not just because of the chance of robbery, but more crucially because of reduced visibility, particularly on the ride up **Cerro de la Muerte** and the descent that ensues. Fog, mist and rain are a constant threat at all times, though the biggest problem you'll likely face are the long tailbacks caused by lack of overtaking opportunities. Ticos frequently risk life and limb passing large trucks on blind corners, but don't be tempted to follow suit – Costa Rica has one of the world's highest road-accident rates.

7

range of services. Though there's not much in the way of sights beyond the modern **Catedral San Isidro** on the Parque Central (just off the Interamericana), the town is close to Costa Rica's tallest mountain, Cerro Chirripó, and boasts several exuberant festivals associated with local agriculture (pineapples grow particularly well here). The town hosts an **agricultural fair** in the first week in February on the Parque Central, when farmers don their finery, put their produce up for competition and sell fresh food in the streets. May is the **month of San Isidro** – patron saint of farmers and animals – and is celebrated with fiestas, ox-cart parades, dog shows and the erection of gaudy Ferris wheels. The twice-weekly indoor **Farmers' Market** (known simply as the *feria*) is one of the region's biggest, with over two hundred vendors (Feria del Agricultor; Av 6, at C 5; Thurs 6am–4pm, Fri 7am–noon).

ARRIVAL AND DEPARTURE   SAN ISIDRO DE EL GENERAL

By bus San Isidro's main bus terminal is adjacent to the town's central market at Av 6, C Central/2, but most buses from here head to local destinations such as San Gerardo de Rivas. To and from San José and most other destinations further afield, Tracopa (☎ 2221 4214) buses stop at the terminal on the Interamericana and C 3, while the MUSOC station (☎ 2771 0468) is at Av 3, C 2/4. If you're travelling south from San Isidro to Palmar, Golfito or Paso Canoas, it's better to get a bus that

originates in San Isidro rather than one that's coming through from San José, as they're often full and you could find yourself standing all the way to Panama.
Destinations Dominical (6 daily; 1hr 30min); Golfito (2 daily; 4hr); Palmar (14 daily; 2hr 30min); Paso Canoas (4 daily; 4hr 30min); Puerto Jiménez (5 daily; 5hr); Quepos (3 daily; 3hr 30min); San Gerardo de Rivas (3–6 daily; 1hr); San José (every 30min; 3hr); Uvita (4 daily; 1hr 50min).

ACCOMMODATION

Some of the area's best accommodation lies northeast of town, 6km or so along the road to Rivas (see p.369). There are few recommended options in the centre of San Isidro itself.

Bosque del Tolomuco Interamericana (Hwy-2), Km118 (14km north of San Isidro) ☎8847 7207, ⓦ bosquedeltolomuco.com. Friendly B&B nestled in the cloudforest above San Isidro, popular with birders and hikers, with five comfortable cabins and friendly Canadian owners. US$65

Hotel Chirripó C 1, Av 2/4 ☎2771 0529. Of the budget choices in town, the best is the large *Hotel Chirripó*, which has simple rooms with private bathroom and hot shower; some rooms have a/c (from US$60). There's a decent restaurant on-site and free parking. Breakfast included. Shared bathroom US$25, private bathroom US$45

EATING AND DRINKING

La Casa del Marisco C Central, at Av 20 ☎2772 2862. It doesn't look like much, but this central spot serves up some of the best – and freshest – seafood in San Isidro,

with ceviche (₡7000) being one of its specialities. The portions are huge, making this one of the better deals around. Mon–Sat 11am–10pm, Sun 10am–6pm.

KapiBlu C 1, Av 4/6 (160m south of Parque Central) 📞2771 8598. There's not a lot of choice when it comes to cafés in San Isidro, but this is the best, serving decent espresso drinks and a variety of well-prepared light bites from delicious pastries to soup and sandwiches (from ₡3000). The free wi-fi is a bonus. Mon–Sat 8am–8pm, Sun 9am–5pm.

Urban Farm Cafe C Central, Av 14/18 (750 south of Parque Central) 📞2771 2442. The best place for breakfast is this contemporary, vegan-friendly café, serving tasty breakfast wraps, larger plates such as *huevos rancheros* and macadamia pancakes, plus delicious organic fruit smoothies (mains ₡2500–4000). Tues–Fri 7am–7pm.

DIRECTORY

Banks and exchange The Banco Nacional (Mon–Fri 8.30am–3.45pm) on the north side of the Parque Central changes travellers' cheques and has an ATM (daily 5am–10pm), as does the Banco de Costa Rica on Av 4, at C Central (Mon–Fri 9am–4pm).

Medical services The most central hospital is Hospital Dr Escalante Pradilla (📞2771 3122), C 1, at Av 12.
Supermarket MegaSuper is at C 1, Av 6/8, across from Palí, 400m south of the Parque Central.

Parque Nacional Chirripó

About 20km northeast of San Isidro • Park open 24hr; trailhead open daily 5–10am only, so you cannot start the climb after 10am • US$18 • 📞2742 5083

PARQUE NACIONAL CHIRRIPÓ is named after Cerro Chirripó, which looms at its centre – at 3820m (12,533ft) the highest peak in Costa Rica (and indeed all of Central America, south of Guatemala). Ever since the conquest of the peak in 1904 by a missionary priest, Father Agustín Blessing (local indigenous peoples may of course have climbed it before), visitors have been flocking to Chirripó to do the same, finding accommodation in the nearby villages of **San Gerardo de Rivas** and **Rivas** (see p.369).

PARQUE NACIONAL CHIRRIPÓ

■ ACCOMMODATION	
Albergue El Páramo	4
Casa de los Celtas	5
El Descanso	3
Rancho La Botija	6
Roca Dura	2
Talari Mountain Lodge	7
Hotel Urán	1

The park's terrain varies widely, according to altitude, from cloudforest to rocky mountaintops. Between the two lies the interesting alpine **paramo** – high moorland, punctuated by rocks, shrubs and hardy clump grasses more usually associated with Andean heights. The colours here are muted yellows and browns, with the occasional deep purple. Below the paramo lie areas of **oak forest**, now much depleted through charcoal-burning. Chirripó is also the only place in Costa Rica where you can observe vestiges of the **glaciers** that scraped across here about thirty thousand years ago: narrow, U-shaped valleys, moraines (heaps of rock and soil left behind by retreating glaciers) and glacial lakes, as well as the distinctive **crestones**, or heavily weathered fingers of rock, more reminiscent of Montana than Costa Rica. The land is generally waterlogged, with a few bogs – take care where you step, as sometimes it's so chilly you won't want to get your feet wet.

Many **mammals** live in the park, and you may see spider monkeys as you climb from the lower mountain to the montane rainforest. Your best bet for **bird-spotting** is in the lower elevations: along the oak and cloudforest sections of the trail you may spot hawks, trogons, woodpeckers and even quetzals, though in the cold and inhospitable terrain higher up, you'll only see robins and hawks.

The **weather** in Chirripó is extremely variable and unpredictable. It can be hot, humid and rainy between May and December, but is clearer and drier between January and April (the peak season for climbing the mountain). Even then, clouds may roll in at the top and obscure the view, and rainstorms move in very fast. The only months you can be sure of a dry spell are March and April. **Temperatures** may drop to below freezing at night and rise to 20°C during the day, though at the summit, it's so cold that it's hard to believe you're just 9° north of the equator. The park is now open all year round.

ARRIVAL AND INFORMATION   PARQUE NACIONAL CHIRRIPÓ

Though it's a short 1.25km walk from San Gerardo de Rivas along the dirt road that leads east from the centre and over the river, it's also possible to reach the park trailhead by car via the same route. As for parking, your best bet is *Hotel Urán* (see p.369) or in front of a local's house for a varying fee.

Guides and porters The services of a guide can be helpful and illuminating in helping to identify local species and interpreting the landscapes you pass through. Ask at the ranger station at the entrance for recommendations or check ⓦ sangerardocostarica.com/activities/hire-a-guide, which has a list of guides currently leading hikes to the summit. Consorcio Aguas Eternas (see below) can also arrange guides and porters (₡2086/kilo).

Maps The staff at the ranger station (see below) can supply you with an adequate map of the park, showing some altitude markings.

Ranger station By the bus stop in San Gerardo de Rivas (daily 6.30am–noon & 1–4.30pm; ☏ 2200 5348), 2km from the trailhead.

Reservations Visiting the Parque Nacional Chirripó requires advance planning, and at the time of research, was a little time-consuming; hotels in San Gerardo de Rivas offer packages that will take care of the paperwork for you – not a bad idea if your Spanish is poor. First you have to reserve admission to the park (no more than 52 hikers are allowed to make the climb to the summit per day, and demand far outstrips capacity in the popular travel seasons, around March and April, especially Easter, and Christmas). Reservations can be made online only at SINAC Reservations (ⓦ www.sinac.go.cr; click on "on-line booking"). You will need to create an account first – the website is in English and fairly easy to navigate. Choose "Sector San Gerardo" when booking your Chirripó reservation. Tickets are sold on a quarterly basis, so from the first week of July bookings are open for visits Sept–Nov, and from the first week of Oct bookings are open for visits Dec–Feb, etc. All hikers must report to the Ranger Station (see above) in San Gerardo to acquire their actual entry permit before entering the park (up to one day prior to hiking).

ACCOMMODATION

Once you have confirmed and paid for your park admission online (see above), you have ten days to book your accommodation. To do this, contact Consorcio Aguas Eternas (Mon–Fri 8am–noon & 1–4pm; ☏ 2742 5097, ⓦ chirripo .org); send your SINAC deposit receipt to ⓔ info@chirripo.org with your reservation number, and the Consorcio will then confirm your spot at the *albergue*.

CLIMBING CERRO CHIRRIPÓ

Almost everyone who climbs Chirripó goes up to the *Albergue El Páramo* first, rests there overnight, and then takes another day or two to explore the summit and surrounding peaks – it's not really feasible to climb Chirripó in one day. During high season, you'll have company on the path up the mountain, and the trail is well marked with signs stating the altitude and the distance to the summit. Watch out for **altitude sickness**, though; if you have made a quick ascent from the lowland beach areas, you could find yourself becoming short of breath, experiencing pins and needles, nausea and exhaustion. If this happens, stop and rest; if symptoms persist, descend immediately. The main thing to keep in mind is **not to go off the trail** or exploring on your own without telling anyone, especially in the higher areas of the park. Off the trail, definite landmarks are few, and it's easy to get confused.

To ensure you have a spot on the trail, make an advance reservation (see p.367) for your hike. It's also worth considering hiring a porter as well as a guide (see p.367), both of which can make your experience that much more enjoyable.

THE HIKE

The **hike** begins at 1520m and ends at 3820m, the summit – you must set off between 5am and 10am. It's almost entirely uphill and so exhausting that you may have trouble appreciating the scenery. On the first day most hikers make the extremely strenuous 14.5km trek to the *Albergue El Páramo* at 3350m – reckon on a minimum of six hours if you're very fit (and the weather is good), twelve hours or more if you're not. On the second day you can make the *albergue* your base while you hike to the summit and back, which is easily done in a day, perhaps taking in some of the nearby lagoons.

The **trailhead** is well marked about 100m uphill from *Hotel y Restaurante Urán*, a little over a kilometre northeast and on the opposite side of the river from the centre of **San Gerardo de Rivas**. The walk begins in a cow pasture, before passing through thick, dark cloudforest, a good place to spot **quetzals** (March–May are the best months). You pass into the Parque Nacional Chirripó proper after 4km, and after a relatively flat stretch of several kilometres, where you're likely to be plagued by various biting insects, you'll arrive at a **ranger station** halfway to the accommodation huts (**Refugio de Llano Bonito**, at 2519m, with potable water and a small snack shop). The **Cuesta de los Arrepentidos** ("Hill of the Repentants", meaning you're sorry at this point that you came) is the real push, all uphill for 1km to the **Albergue El Páramo**, at 3350m. At the *albergue*, the land looks like a greener version of Scotland: bare moss cover, grasslands and a waterlogged area where the lagoons congregate. There are no trees, and little wildlife is in evidence.

THE SUMMIT

The **rangers** based up here are friendly, and in the high season (Jan–April) you can ask to accompany them on walks near the summit to avoid getting lost. Do not expect this, however, as it is not their job to lead guided walks. It's just two hours' hike (5.1km) from the lodge along a well-marked trail to **the summit** – there's a bit of scrambling involved, but no real climbing. You'll need to set off by dawn, as clear weather at the peak is really only guaranteed until 9 or 10am. From the top, if it's clear, you can see right across to the Pacific. However, you're above the cloud line up here, and the surrounding mountains are often obscured by drifting, milky clouds.

PREPARING FOR THE HIKE

While Chirripó is hot at midday, it frequently drops to freezing at the higher altitudes at night. You should bring warm clothing (temperatures can fall to -7°C at night) and a proper sleeping bag (though these can be rented on site), a blanket, water, food and a propane gas stove. A short list of clothing and other essentials might include a good pair of boots, socks, long trousers, T-shirt, shirt, jumper, woolly hat and jacket, lots of insect repellent, sunglasses, first aid (for cuts and scratches), gloves (for rocks and the cold), binoculars and a torch – the *albergue* only has electricity between 6pm and 8pm.

Albergue El Páramo About 14.5km from the trailhead ☎2770 8040. The only accommodation in the park itself is this basic lodge (also known as *Albergue Base Crestones*) at the Valle de Los Crestones, which has fifteen rooms (each sleeping four people; includes sheet, pillow, blanket and sleeping bag). There's intermittent free wi-fi, potable water, eight shared bathrooms with cold showers, a cooking area, a big sink where you can wash clothes and electricity (and lighting) 6–8pm only. Buffet-style meals are served 5.30–8am (₡5000), noon–2.30pm (₡6250) and 6–7pm (₡6250); pay in cash on-site. Note that the price tends to increase year on year; payment must be made via bank transfer, or on site if within three days of reserving your park entrance fee (cash or credit card). Usually charges in colones; equivalent <u>US$34</u>

San Gerardo de Rivas

At the doorstep of the Parque Nacional Chirripó, the small community of **SAN GERARDO DE RIVAS** caters to a steady stream of hikers intent on making the trek up the mountain. Both it and to a lesser extent the village of **Rivas**, eight kilometres to the south, hold a few pleasant places to stay and eat, though there's not much other than the park and a stunning backdrop to detain you.

ARRIVAL AND DEPARTURE

SAN GERARDO DE RIVAS

By bus Buses from San Isidro de El General central bus station for San Gerardo de Rivas (1hr) depart at around 5.45am, 8.30am, 11.30am, 2.30pm, 5.30pm and 8pm (Mon–Sat only; Sun 9.30am, 2pm & 6pm), and arrive at the stop on the central square, adjacent to the church. Buses return 5.15am, 7am, 10am, 1pm, 4pm & 6.45pm (Mon–Sat only; Sun 7am, 11.30am & 4pm).

By car San Gerardo de Rivas can be reached via a well-maintained road that connects with San Isidro de El General, 18km to the southwest; follow the signs for Rivas. The final stretch from Rivas, about 9km to the southwest, is unpaved; a 4WD is not necessary at most times, but if in doubt about current road conditions call the ranger station in advance (see p.367).

By taxi It's possible to hire a 4WD taxi from the bus terminal in San Isidro de El General to San Gerardo de Rivas for around US$35–40 (one way).

ACCOMMODATION

San Gerardo de Rivas is home to several very reasonably priced, friendly places to stay – try to get somewhere with hot water, though, as it can get very cold at night. There are also a couple of attractive family-run hotels a few kilometres further back down the road towards San Isidro in the village of Rivas. Most of the hotels listed below have restaurants serving food well suited to loading up on before starting a hike to the summit.

SAN GERARDO DE RIVAS

El Descanso 200m beyond the ranger station ☎2742 5061, ⊕hoteleldescansocr.com; map p.366. Private house close to the ranger station with basic rooms, some with shared bathrooms, others with private bathroom. It also has an excellent restaurant (daily 5am–9pm) serving Costa Rican comfort food and offers various packages that include national park entry and accommodation. Shared bathroom <u>US$44</u>, private bathroom <u>US$61</u>

Hotel Urán 50m from the Chirripó trailhead ☎2742 5003, ⊕hoteluran.com; map p.366. Thirteen neat, small rooms come with shared bathrooms and eight slightly bigger ones have private bathrooms; all have hot water. They offer a variety of packages – which include the overnight hike to the Chirripó summit – and free pick-up from the ranger station. The on-site restaurant (daily 4.30am–8pm) serves up big platefuls of good, solid Tico food – the perfect preparation for a long day's hike. Shared bathroom <u>US$34</u>, private bathroom <u>US$57</u>

Roca Dura On the central square (la plaza deportiva) ☎2742 5071, ⊕hotelrocadura.com; map p.366. Six smallish but clean rooms – one is built into the large slab of rock after which this rustic hotel is named – all of which have private bathrooms and hot water. The bar and restaurant (daily 8am–2am) are a hive of activity. The hotel offers free transport to the park entrance and breakfast included. <u>US$40</u>

AROUND RIVAS

Casa de los Celtas 1.7km south of Rivas (Hwy-242) ☎2770 3524, ⊕casaceltas.com; map p.366. Quaint hilltop British-owned B&B with a cottage (sleeping two people) and a double room. Both are clean and comfortably furnished; the cottage also has a kitchenette. The grounds include an orchid garden, while the views are sensational. Lunch and dinner offered at an additional cost. Double <u>US$70</u>, cottage <u>US$70</u>

Rancho La Botija 2km south of Rivas (Hwy-242) ☎2770 2146, ⊕rancholabotija.com; map p.366. Eleven unfussy rooms, plus a freshwater swimming pool, a viewing tower overlooking the farm's coffee and banana plantations, and *La Hacienda* restaurant (Tues–Sun

9am–5pm). Several large petroglyphs carved with pre-Columbian indigenous patterns have been discovered on the property and can be seen on a 1hr tour (Tues–Sun 9.30am; US$6). **US$72**

Talari Mountain Lodge 2.4km south of Rivas (Hwy-242) ☎ 2771 0341, ⓦ talari.co.cr; map p.366. Eight brightly coloured rooms, all of which offer private bathroom with solar-heated shower, mosquito nets, fridge and a small terrace, set in a tranquil riverside forest, with walking trails and a pool. An excellent restaurant prepares dishes according to local market availability (breakfast is included), with a three-course evening meal costing US$18. They also offer guided packages to Chirripó and birdwatching outings. **US$85**

DIRECTORY

Banks and exchange There is no bank or ATM in San Gerardo – the nearest is in San Isidro. The *pulpería* (see below) will change US dollars for colones.

Food market There's a *pulpería*, Abastecedor Las Nubes (daily 6.30am–8pm; ☎ 2742 5045), across from the bus stop, where you can stock up on supplies (credit cards accepted).

Cloudbridge Nature Reserve

2.5km northeast of San Gerardo de Rivas • Daily 8am–5pm • Free, donation suggested • **Tours** Daily 8am (2–4hr) • US$20–30 • ⓦ cloudbridge.org

Adjoining the Parque Nacional Chirripó, the private **Cloudbridge Nature Reserve** protects two square kilometres of lush cloudforest on the lower flanks of Cerro Chirripó. Focused on studying reforestation and habitat recovery as well as the numerous mammals that live in the reserve, Cloudbridge offers an excellent primer to the flora and fauna that lies just beyond in the national park. It also holds a few short **trails**, **waterfalls** that cascade into the Río Chirripó Pacífico, and a thriving **botanical garden**.

ARRIVAL AND DEPARTURE   CLOUDBRIDGE NATURE RESERVE

By car You'll need a 4WD to negotiate the rough dirt track that leads from the football field in the centre of San Gerardo de Rivas to the reserve; otherwise it is a long uphill hike.

The Costanera Sur

The 35km segment of **THE COSTANERA SUR** highway (Hwy-34) from **Dominical** in the north to **Ojochal** in the south parallels one of the more tranquil and scenic stretches of the central Pacific coast. Among the highlights is the lovely **Bahía Ballena**, 20km south of Dominical, and the bay's twin tiny hamlets of **Bahía** and **Uvita**. Rather than hotels and glitzy shops you'll find a string of gloriously empty beaches washed by lazy breakers, palms swaying on the shore, and a hot, serene and very quiet atmosphere. Offshore is the **Parque Nacional Marino Ballena**, 56 square kilometres of water around Uvita and Bahía created to safeguard the ecological integrity of the local marine life and breeding humpback whales, while 15km south is the lovely shallow bay at **Playa Tortuga**, one of the most pristine in Costa Rica.

Outside of comparatively bustling Dominical, there's not a great deal to do along this portion of the Costanera Sur. That said, if you like hanging out on the beach, **surfing**, walking along rock ledges and spotting **dolphins** frolicking in the water, you'll be happy. You can also take **boat tours** around Bahía Ballena and to the Isla del Caño (see p.385) or, if you have your own equipment, you can **snorkel** to your heart's content directly off the beaches.

Matapalo

Some 14km north of Dominical, **MATAPALO** is a sleepy village stretching for less than a kilometre along a sweeping grey-sand surf beach. Backed by mountains, the straggly seaside community is a blissfully underdeveloped blip on the Pacific coast and provides a rare glimpse hereabouts of the Costa Rica of yesteryear. Sunbathing iguanas share the dusty street with children on bicycles, while a growing community of foreigners lives alongside a small Tico population. The **beach**, which enjoys monster waves and strong currents, has a dedicated team of local lifeguards patrolling.

ARRIVAL AND DEPARTURE   MATAPALO

By bus Buses chugging between Quepos and Dominical can drop you off at the turn-off to the village, from where it's a 2km walk to the ocean and hotel strip.

Destinations Dominical (5 daily; 30–40min); Quepos (5 daily; 1hr 30min–2hr).

INFORMATION AND ACTIVITIES

Charlie's Jungle House 40m from the beachfront ☎ 2787 5005, ⓦ charliesjunglehouse.com. Charlie Berghammer, the helpful American owner of *Charlie's Jungle House* (see below), is the area's unofficial source of tourist information. He can also arrange horseriding on the beach and in the surrounding jungle, as well as sportfishing, canopy tours, snorkelling and whitewater rafting excursions.

ACCOMMODATION

Casa Aba Matapalo Beachfront, Beach Rd ☎ 8783 3447. Swish, wooden guesthouse with lovely pool and rooms equipped with kitchens, ceiling fans and mosquito nets. The affable owners can arrange horseriding and other activities. <u>US$77</u>

Charlie's Jungle House Beachfront, Beach Rd ☎ 2787 5005, ⓦ charliesjunglehouse.com. Four bright, stylish suites right on the beach, all with kitchens, a/c, hot water and satellite TV, plus cheaper doubles with kitchenette and fan. Breakfast is US$5. Doubles <u>US$40</u>, suites <u>US$80</u>

Dreamy Contentment Beachfront, Beach Rd ☎ 2787 5223, ⓦ dreamycontentment.com. This beachside whitewashed colonial property set in landscaped tropical grounds has three self-contained bungalows (sleeping 2–4 people) with kitchenettes and a/c. There's also a spacious beachfront villa that can sleep up to six people and has a kitchen, lounge area, bathtub and washing machine. Bungalows <u>US$75</u>, villa <u>US$230</u>

Rafiki Beach Camp Beachfront, Beach Rd ☎ 2787 5014, ⓦ rafikibeach.com. This really is a camp right on the beach, featuring luxury African safari tents with tiled floors and huge bathrooms, and fans and ocean breezes to cool you at night. Delicious breakfasts included. Offers packages with sister resort *Rafiki Safari Lodge*, 11km up the Río Savegre. <u>US$115</u>

EATING

La Langosta Feliz Hwy-34, at the turning to Playa Matapalo ☎ 2787 5214. The "Happy Lobster" offers excellent seafood at reasonable rates (most mains ₡4000–7000), from shrimp rice to exceptional seafood pasta. Daily 11am–9.30pm.

Tico Gringo On the beach ☎ 2787 5023. Those craving a hamburger or perhaps some fried calamari (₡4000) and buffalo wings should drop by this friendly surfside spot, where Eddie (the gringo) and his Tica wife Betty will set you up with an ice-cold beer under a thatch roof. Daily 11am–10pm.

Dominical and around

The laidback but ever-expanding surfing town of **DOMINICAL**, 44km southeast of Quepos and 25km southwest of San Isidro, is made up of 4km of rainforest-backed beach – still largely unspoilt, despite the arrival of hordes of expats and a spate of hotel and property building in the last decade. It's nothing like Jacó, however, with development for the most part relatively low-key, and Dominical remains a good place to chill out by the beach and visit the nearby **Hacienda Barú National Wildlife Refuge** and **Nauyaca Waterfalls**.

Dominical village consists of a dusty or muddy, unpaved, unnamed main street (where you'll find most of the town's bars and restaurants) leading south off Hwy-34, and a connecting beachfront road heading southeast from the Río Barú lined with hotels and surf schools.

Whatever the village might be lacking, it more than makes up for it with its main draw: **surfing**. Thousands flock here every year to ride the big waves that crash onto the town's dark-sand beach. As is usual with surfing beaches, the **swimming** varies from not great to downright dangerous, and is plagued by riptides and crashing surf. About

7

ACTIVITIES AND TOURS AROUND DOMINICAL

Dominical offers a good range of tours and is home to half a dozen **surf schools** offering lessons for around US$50 per person for a two-hour session.

Bamboo Yoga Play Studio Danyasa Eco-Retreat, on the right side of the main road towards the beach ☎ 2787 0229, ⓦ danyasa.com. Highly regarded yoga studio and eco-resort offering some of the finest classes in the area (US$14) in an open-air studio space. Classes held Mon–Sat 10am & 6.30pm, Sun 9am, 11am & 6.30pm.

★ **Costa Rica Surf Camp** On a side street towards the beach off the main road ☎ 8812 3625, ⓦ crsurfschool.com. Excellent surf school with experienced and patient instructors and a friendly atmosphere. They offer a variety of six-night packages (US$1027–1245) that include accommodation, daily lessons, area tours, meals and transportation as well as private instruction for all levels.

Green Iguana Surf Camp Just back from the seafront ☎ 8825 1381. ⓦ greeniguanasurfcamp.com. The longest-running surf school in Dominical, and still going strong. As well as lessons and rentals, they offer multi-night packages that include accommodation at a nearby hotel, tours, and airport transfers (6 nights from US$935).

★ **Nauyaca Waterfalls Horseback Riding Tour** Hwy-243 (10km towards San Isidro) ☎ 2787 0541, ⓦ cataratasnauyaca.com. Away from the water, the best way to pass a half-day is on Don Lulo's horseback waterfall tour (US$70/person including breakfast and lunch; Mon–Sat 8am–2pm). The tour begins with a 1hr horse ride to Don Lulo's home (where you have breakfast and visit his small private zoo), before continuing on horseback with knowledgeable guides through lush rainforest, to the two cascades that make up the Cataratas Nauyaca – the principal one drops 46m into a sparkling pool where you can swim. A *típico* lunch cooked over an open flame on the return trip completes the day.

Southern Expeditions On the main road into the village ☎ 2787 0100, ⓦ southernexpeditionscr.com. Southern Expeditions specialize in kayak and snorkelling trips (from US$80/person) to the Parque Nacional Marino Ballena (see p.377) and Isla del Caño (see p.385), and trips further afield to Parque Nacional Corcovado (see p.390).

---

twenty minutes' walk south along the beach brings you to a small cove, where the water is calmer and you can paddle and snorkel.

As seasons can often pass between major cultural events in Dominical, the collective enthusiasm on display at the excellent **Envision Festival** (ⓦ envisionfestival.com) is that much more pronounced. Held over four days in late February or early March, this nascent festival features a compelling slate of concerts, dance, multimedia performances and yoga classes.

ARRIVAL AND DEPARTURE   DOMINICAL AND AROUND

By bus Buses usually make three stops in Dominical; outside *Patron's* coming into the village; in the centre south of the football field (opposite *Restaurante El Coco*); and further along the beach, where the bus turns around. From San José you'll need to go to Quepos or San Isidro and change, or get one of the two daily Tracopa buses to Uvita (6am and 3pm) and ask to be dropped off at Dominical; heading back to San José you can flag the Tracopa buses down on the main road (Hwy-34) at around 6am and 1.30pm.

Destinations Matapalo (5 daily; 30–40min); Quepos (6 daily; 1hr 30min); San Isidro de El General (7 daily; 1hr 30min); San José (2 daily; 5–6hr); Uvita (9 daily; 20min).

By shuttle bus Most of the nation's shuttle bus operators (see p.48) run direct routes between Dominical hotels and San José (4hr) and other major tourist hubs such as Jacó (2hr), La Fortuna (6hr), Montezuma (5hr) and Puerto Jiménez (4hr). Monkey Ride (ⓦ monkeyridecr.com) offers one-way shared rides from San José airport to hotels in Dominical for US$45 (or US$55 from downtown San José).

By car While you can get to Dominical via San Isidro de El General or Quepos in any car, it makes sense to have a 4WD if you want to explore the surrounding area.

By taxi Taxis in San Isidro de El General will make the drive to Dominical for about US$40–50; they usually gather around the central bus terminal.

INFORMATION

Tourist information The village's small information centre (irregular hours; ☎ 2787 0454, ⓦ dominical information.com) lies on the main street, just after the turn-off from Hwy-34. It has a good deal of information on the area and the beaches further south and offers internet access.

ACCOMMODATION

In Dominical itself, most lodgings are basic and cater to the surfing community, but you'll also find a number of more upmarket places, usually owned by foreigners. There are also a string of increasingly lavish hotels and B&Bs along the coast road south towards Uvita (Hwy-34), a number of which are in the hamlets of Dominicalito and Escaleras.

DOMINICAL

Cool Vibes Beach Hostel 200m southeast on main street from Restaurante El Coco/bus stop, then turn left for 75m ☎ 8353 6428, ⓦ hosteldominical.com. Aging but cosy hostel run by a French couple, with clean, comfy dorms, private rooms with fan and bathroom (a/c is US$20 extra), free wi-fi (which can be slow), well-stocked kitchen, free coffee all day (no breakfast) and surfboard rental for US$10/day. Cash only. Dorms US$13, doubles US$38

★**MAVI Surf Hotel de Dominical** 500m southeast on main street from Restaurante El Coco/bus stop, then turn left for 70m ☎ 2787 0429, ⓦ mavi-surf.com. The surf resort for surfers with a little more cash to spend, this plush boutique features tranquil gardens, pool and eight spacious and fully equipped studios (with terrace, solar-heated hot water, kitchenette and a/c). US$130

Piramys Life Hostel On main street, close to the beach, 100m southeast from the bus stop ☎ 2787 0196, ⓦ piramys.life. Old surfer hostel with a hippy vibe – it's very cheap and next to the beach at the quieter end of the village, with surf lessons and surfboard rentals easily arranged. Private cabins (sleeping up to 4; with bathrooms and fan) and basic dorm with fans; the dorm is above *La Palmas* bar, while the cabins are through the back. Generally Spanish-speaking only. Dorm US$9, cabins US$30

Que Nivel On the main street, next to the bus stop ☎ 2787 0127, ⓦ qndominical.com. Aimed squarely at the surfing community, with seven basic private rooms (some with a/c; US$15 extra), a simple but bright dorm, communal kitchen, pool table and popular bar (with decent DJs, and free drinks for ladies Tues 10pm–midnight) – it's one of the major post-surf hangouts. Dorm US$10, doubles US$30

Río Lindo Resort Just south of Hwy-34 on the main street into Dominical, on the Río Barú ☎ 8857 4937. Eight comfortable rooms (upgraded by new owners in 2017) with private bathroom and a/c, some with satellite TV. There's also a lovely round pool, bar and whirlpool on the grounds and they offer horseriding, fishing and ATV tours. Price includes breakfast. US$110

AROUND DOMINICAL

★**Costa Paraíso** Rocas de Amancio Rd, 2km south of Dominical ☎ 2787 0025, ⓦ costa-paraiso.com. Set in beautifully landscaped grounds spreading down to a rocky coastline, this eye-catching hotel has just five exceedingly comfortable rooms, all with either a queen- or king-size bed, a/c and free wi-fi; four also have kitchenettes. Breakfast (not included) is served in the open-air restaurant, with both a pool and the ocean a few steps away. US$140

★**Hotel Cuna del Angel** Hwy-34, 9km south of Dominical ☎ 2787 4343, ⓦ cunadelangel.com. Gorgeous hotel high above the coast, with lavish rooms decorated with a Colonial and Asian theme or in rustic Caribbean style (all with a/c, cable TV, free wi-fi), plus an infinity pool and an excellent restaurant, *La Palapa*. US$112

Pacific Edge Pacific Edge Rd, 5km south of Dominical (follow the signed left-hand fork off Hwy-34 at Km148) ☎ 2200 5428, ⓦ pacificedge.info. Secluded, simple and comfortable, on a ridge 600m above the sea, with beautiful views of Cerro Chirripó and Playa Dominicalito. The four roomy chalets (sleeping 4–8) each have a private shower and hammocks. Delicious breakfasts (for an additional cost) are prepared daily. A 4WD is necessary to reach the property. No children under 13. US$70

Roca Verde Hwy-34, 1.5km south of Dominical ☎ 2787 0036, ⓦ rocaverde.net. Small, ritzy hotel in a wonderful position right on the beach. All ten rooms have en-suite bathroom, a/c, free wi-fi and balcony, and there's also a swimming pool, table tennis and a restaurant serving Tex-Mex and seafood. US$129

Villas Río Mar 700m north of Hwy-34 (at the Dominical turn-off), on the Río Barú ☎ 2787 0053, ⓦ villasriomar.com. Comfortable, swish rooms in individual chalets with free wi-fi and satellite TV; some have a/c. The rooms front extensive terraced gardens with a swimming pool, bar, spa, tennis court and jacuzzi. US$110

EATING

Café Ensueño Next to Cool Vibes Beach Hostel (see above) ☎ 2787 0105. Best breakfast spot in the village, with fresh, tangy fruit smoothies (*batidos*) such as orange and mango, and sublime *gallo pinto* (with beef) that have garnered a cult following. Daily noon–9pm.

★**Cafe Mono Congo** Just off Hwy-34 at the turn-off into the village, on the Río Barú ☎ 8384 2915, ⓦ cafe monocongo.com. Popular riverside spot with swing chairs and rustic decor, known for its tasty, organic, vegan-friendly menu, which runs from totally addictive toasted cinnamon rolls and fruit smoothies (₡1500) to real bagels and high-quality Costa Rican coffee (₡1000). Daily 6.30am–9pm.

★**Del Mar Taco Shop** Main street, 50m south of police station ☎ 8428 9050. Tiny taco shop with some outdoor seating, knocking out delicious fish, beef and chicken tacos, hefty burritos and lip-smacking pit barbecue – on "Taco Tuesdays" tacos are just ₡1000. Daily 11am–9pm.

Phat Noodle just off Hwy-34, at the turn-off into the village ☎ 2787 0017. Take a break from Costa Rican/American/Italian food at this Thai joint. It's not strictly authentic, but the dishes are fresh and tasty nonetheless, with all the classics – green curry, phad Thai, satay and

pineapple fried rice from ₡3500 – on the menu. The restaurant is open-air, with food prepared in a truck. Tues–Sun 11am–2.30pm & 5–9pm.

Soda y Restaurante Nanyoa On the main street opposite Posada del Sol ☎ 2787 0195. This pleasant, airy Costa Rican diner serves all the usual classics at low prices – *gallo pinto* and *casados* are ₡2500–3500 – and you can bring your own beer. Daily 6–10pm.

DRINKING AND NIGHTLIFE

The division between restaurant and bar and even impromptu live venue and club is blurry in Dominical, but there are definitely some places better known for their **nightlife** than their food. Note that the restaurants and bars at *Roca Verde* (see p.373) and *Que Nivel* (see p.373) are also fun places to spend the evening.

La Palma Beach Club At Piramys Life Hostel (see p.373) ☎ 2787 0033. This bar and club on the beachfront gets fairly lively at weekends, though the party has to end (legally) by 10.30pm, because of the location. Crafted cocktails, snacks and a mix of locals, visitors and the no-shoes, no-shirt surfer crowd. Daily 7am–10.30pm.

Patrón's On the main street, 300m south of the turn-off into the village ☎ 8404 5572, ⓦ patronscostarica.com. This bar, grill (it does pricey but good-quality steaks) and coffee shop comes alive at night, with an extensive wine list, a couple of craft beers on tap and live music Fri–Sun, and

plenty of room to dance. Also shows most international sports events on big TV screens. Daily 5am–2am.

Rum Bar On the main street, just south of the Hwy-34 turn-off into the village ☎ 2787 0287. This no-frills sports bar and grill offers live music (often reggae) and DJs most nights. Cash only. Daily 5pm–2.30am.

Tortilla Flats Northwest end of the beach road (200m west of the central bus stop) ☎ 2787 0033. The best of the beachfront bars and restaurants, this expat hangout offers fish tacos (₡3500) and cocktails to go with fine sunset views over the Pacific, live music and DJs. Cash only. Daily 7am–11pm.

DIRECTORY

Banks and exchange There's a Banco de Costa Rica (Mon–Fri 9am–4pm) in Plaza Pacífica on Hwy-34, just

to the east of the turn-off into Dominical village.

Hacienda Barú National Wildlife Refuge

About 2km north of Dominical (on Hwy-34) • Daily 7am–5pm • Self-guided walks US$8 • **Canopy and climbing tours** Daily 8am, 11am & 2pm (2–3hr) • US$45 • **Overnight hiking tours** Mon–Sat from 3pm to 10am next day • US$135 • ☎ 2787 0003, ⓦ haciendabaru.com

The private reserve at **Hacienda Barú National Wildlife Refuge** comprises over three square kilometres of rainforest, mangroves and protected beach. There's enough here to occupy the better part of a day, with climbing trips where you winch yourself up extremely tall trees, hiking trails and an exhilarating canopy tour, which involves swooping from platform to platform through primary rainforest on long steel cables, accompanied by guides who impart a wealth of forest folklore; a nineteen-hour overnight hiking tour is also available (which includes sleeping at their jungle cabins with showers and toilets, everything provided). A great spot for birders and orchid lovers – 250 varieties of orchid grow in the reserve; there's also a butterfly enclosure, plus an observation tower set high in the forest canopy.

ACCOMMODATION AND EATING	HACIENDA BARÚ NATIONAL WILDLIFE REFUGE

Hacienda Barú Lodge By the refuge entrance ☎ 2787 0003, ⓦ haciendabaru.com. You can stay on-site in one of the comfortable self-catering cabins or in one of the lodge's

rooms that face the pool. The attached restaurant serves mostly *comida típica* (breakfast included) and a smattering of seafood dishes. U̲S̲$̲8̲5̲

Parque Reptilandia

8km north of Dominical (on Hwy-243 to San Isidro) • Daily 9am–4.30pm • US$12, under-15s US$6 • ☎ 2787 0343, ⓦ crreptiles.com

Kids will love the **Parque Reptilandia**, a series of landscaped gardens containing reptile habitats of all kinds, from giant tortoises and komodo dragons to the venomous snakes of Costa Rica.

Nauyaca Waterfalls

Entrance 8km north of Dominical (off Hwy-243 to San Isidro) • Daily 7am–5pm • US$8 • ☎ 2787 0541, ⓦ cataratasnauyaca.com

A short walk beyond Parque Reptilandia, the gorgeous **Nauyaca Waterfalls** (Cataratas Nauyaca) are comprised of two cascades – the upper falls are 43m high, while the lower, tiered falls are 18m – with a smattering of refreshing swimming holes at the base. You can hike from the entrance (which is the office of Don Lulo, the company that owns the property), but it's a 12km, often muddy, return trip. You can also drive the first 2km then walk, leaving your 4WD at the bridge (parking is free), but the best way to visit is as part of a Don Lulo horseback-riding tour (see box, p.372).

Alturas Wildlife Sanctuary

Alturas de San Martín Norte, 7km south of Dominical (signposted off Hwy-34) • Tours Tues–Sun 9am, 11am, 1pm & 3pm; 1hr 30min • US$25, under-13s US$15 • ☎ 2200 5440, ⓦ alturaswildlifesanctuary.org

One of a growing number of nonprofit rescue centres for injured animals in Costa Rica, the **Alturas Wildlife Sanctuary** does an excellent job caring for around 75 to 100 creatures at any one time, from sloths and monkeys to macaws and toucans. **Tours** highlight the centre's rehabilitation techniques and provide encounters with some of the current guests.

Uvita and the Costa Ballena

Some 20km south of Dominical, the village of **UVITA**, straggling along either side of the Río Uvita, marks the beginning of the **Costa Ballena**, where the famous "whale tail", a giant sandbar shaped like a whale fin, juts into the ocean. Uvita's centre lies inland, but the coastal district known as Bahía (1.5km off Hwy-34) abuts some of the most beautiful beaches in the country, and allows access to the **Parque Nacional Marino Ballena** (see p.377).

Aside from **Playa Uvita** that sweeps southeast of the sandbar, and the offshore national park, the main natural attraction is the **Catarata Uvita** (daily 8am–4pm; ₡1000), a waterfall that drops into a deep and thoroughly inviting pool in a pretty jungle setting. To get there, follow the signs from the Banco de Costa Rica in Uvita village centre northeast of Hwy-34 for about 1.5km.

ARRIVAL AND DEPARTURE
UVITA AND THE COSTA BALLENA

By bus From San Isidro de El General, buses leave from the Transportes Blanco bus station, C 1, Av 4/6, daily at 7am, 11.30am and 3.30pm, heading for Uvita via Dominical. From San José, direct Tracopa buses for Uvita

depart daily at 6am & 3pm.
Destinations Ciudad Neily, for Panama (3 daily; 3hr); Dominical (9 daily; 20min); Quepos (2 daily; 3hr); San Isidro (3 daily; 1hr 50min); San José (2 daily; 7hr).

TOURS AND ACTIVITIES

Bahía Aventuras Next to the elementary school in Bahía ☎2743 8362, ⓦbahiaaventuras.com. Friendly and professional tour operator leading a number of guided outings, from a whale-watching and snorkelling half-day trip (US$90) to sea-kayaking in the national park (US$78) and a boat trip through the labyrinthine mangrove forests and wetlands of the Humedal Nacional Térraba-Sierpe to the south (US$85).

Uvita 360 100m north of Parque Nacional Marino Ballena entrance in Bahía ☎8586 8745, ⓦuvita360.com. Offers a full range of surfing lessons (US$65/2hr) and

stand-up paddleboarding tours (US$75/3hr 30min), plus rentals, including surfboards (US$20/day), kayaks (US$40/day) and SUP boards (US$40/day).

Uvita Information Center Across from the Banco de Costa Rica on Hwy-34 at the northern edge of Uvita ☎8843 7142, ⓦuvita.info. The extremely helpful staff can book a wide assortment of tours, both on the water and further inland. Boat trips include snorkelling and sportfishing, while on land there are outings on horseback (from US$45) and evening hikes (US$35). Mon–Sat 9am–6pm.

ACCOMMODATION

★**La Cusinga Lodge** 5km south of Uvita (La Cusinga Rd, off Hwy-34) ☎2770 2549, ⓦlacusingalodge.com. One of the country's best ecolodges, occupying a gorgeous

rainforest setting overlooking the Parque Nacional Marino Ballena. Its seven *cabinas* (sleeping 2–4) are all made of wood from the lodge's sustainable teak plantation;

electricity is provided by solar and hydro power (there are fans, no a/c); and there's an education centre where local children can learn about the area. It has an excellent restaurant as well as trails leading through rainforest inhabited by howler and white-faced monkeys to a beautiful stretch of quiet beach, Playa Arco. US$168

★**Flutterby House** Bahía, near Playa Uvita ☎2743 8221, ⓦflutterbyhouse.com. Sustainable, ecofriendly hostel (everything is recycled) steps from Playa Uvita, with private *cabinas* (fans only) sleeping 2–5 people, open-air dorms and cabin-like treehouses (sleeping two people and constructed with local materials), plus a shared kitchen, free wi-fi, table tennis and surfboard and bike rental. Cash only. Dorms US$14, *cabinas* US$40, treehouses US$60

Hostel Cascada Verde C Bejuco, Uvita ☎2743 8191, ⓦcascadaverde.eu. A short walk north of Uvita centre will bring you to *Cascada Verde* (2km; taxi ₡2000), a great place for the nature-loving budget traveller. 5min on foot from beautiful waterfalls and swimming holes, it's like a

giant treehouse with rustic private rooms and a dormitory loft. It also offers vegetarian food, organic gardens, a kitchen, an ocean-view yoga deck and classes, body and mind workshops, tours and free wi-fi. Breakfast is US$5. Dorm US$15, doubles US$38

El Paraíso de Cristian 600m east of Banco de Costa Rica, Uvita ☎8682 3358, ⓦcostaricavacanze.com. Delightful B&B managed by Italian boxing instructor Cristian, featuring just two immaculate wooden chalets (sleeping up to three people) with a/c, private bathrooms, flatscreen TV, free wi-fi, coffee-maker and fridge. Get a boxing lesson for US$15/hr. US$70

Tucan Hotel Main street in Uvita, just north of Hwy-34 ☎2743 8140, ⓦtucanhotel.com. The budget-oriented *Tucan Hotel* offers backpacker-style dormitories as well as spartan private rooms, a campsite and hammocks. Free wi-fi is available throughout and they can arrange surfing lessons (US$30; 2hr). Camping and hammock US$10, dorms US$13, doubles US$34

EATING

Across the street from the Banco Nacional on Hwy-34 in Uvita is Supermercado BM (daily 7am–9pm; ☎2743 8031), the best place to stock up on food.

★**Bar Restaurant Los Laureles** 400m east of Banco de Costa Rica in Uvita ☎2743 8008. First-rate family-owned restaurant serving up the most satisfying meals in the area: dishes such as fish and shrimp tacos, veggie and beef *patacones* and passion fruit flan are moderately priced (from ₡4000) and mostly made from locally grown or caught ingredients. Tues–Sat 7am–9pm, Sun 7.30am–8pm.

Pura Vida Cristal Ballena Hotel, Playa Ballena, 7km south of Uvita ☎2786 5354, ⓦcristal-ballena.com. Enjoy the magnificent ocean views and poolside terrace at this classy restaurant, serving international and Costa Rican cuisine "with an Austrian touch" – think curry chicken with pineapple and *Wiener schnitzel* (from ₡5500). Daily 7am–9.30pm.

DIRECTORY

Banks and exchange There's a Banco Nacional (Mon–Fri 8.30am–3.45pm) on Hwy-34 just south of the Río Uvita (ATM open daily 5am–10pm), and a Banco de Costa Rica (Mon–Fri 9am–4pm) with ATM just off Hwy-34 in Uvita itself.

Medical services There's a government clinic in the centre of Uvita (EBAIS Uvita; ☎2743 8170), while the Hospital de Osa Tomás Casas Casajús (☎2786 8148) is 30km southeast in Puerto Cortés.

Rancho La Merced National Wildlife Refuge

3km north of Uvita (Km159, Hwy-34) • Daily 7.30am–5pm • US$6 • **Night walks** Daily 7pm; 2hr • US$35 • **Horseriding tours** Daily 9am; 2–3hr • US$45–50 • ☎2743 8032, ⓦrancholamerced.com

The privately operated **Rancho La Merced National Wildlife Refuge** protects a lush swathe of primary and secondary tropical wet forest, as well as mangroves along the Río Morete and the beach. Laced with hiking trails, it's a tranquil place to take in the local fauna and flora, as well as offering **horseriding tours** to Playa Hermosa and a local waterfall. You can wander the trails solo or arrange in advance for a guide, which will guarantee a lot more wildlife sightings; the **night walk** (two people minimum) is especially good.

Reserva Biológica Oro Verde

Turn off Hwy-34, 3km north of Uvita, then drive along dirt road for another 3.5km • Open by appointment only • Guided hikes (2–3hr) US$20–35; night tours (6–9pm) and birdwatching tours (6–9am) US$35; reservations required • ☎8843 8833

Ornithologists should check out the **Reserva Biológica Oro Verde,** a smaller private reserve a few kilometres from Rancho La Merced (the turning is on the other side of Hwy-34), celebrated for its rich birdlife. You'll need a 4WD to drive up the dirt entrance road.

Parque Nacional Marino Ballena

Beach entrances at Uvita, Colonia, Ballena and Piñuelas • Daily 7am–4pm • US$12 (valid for 1 day at all 4 entrances) • ☎ 2786 5392

Created in 1989, the **PARQUE NACIONAL MARINO BALLENA** protects a large area of ocean and coastline south of Uvita that contains one of the biggest chunks of **coral reef** left on the Pacific coast. It's also the habitat of **humpback whales**, who come here from the Arctic and Antarctica to breed – although they are spotted very infrequently (Dec–April is best) – and **dolphins**. The main threats to the ecological survival of these waters is the disturbance caused by shrimp trawling, sedimentation as a result of deforestation (rivers bring silt and pollutants into the sea and kill the coral) and dragnet fishing, which often entraps whales and dolphins.

On land, the sandy and rocky beaches fronting the ocean are also protected, as is **Punta Uvita** – a former island connected to the mainland by a narrow sandbar. At **low tide**, you can walk for 1km over the sand to the rocks, tide pools and reefs at the end, which stretch out into the sea and resembles a whale's tail. At certain times of the year (usually May–Oct), olive ridley and hawksbill **turtles** may come ashore to nest, but in nowhere near the same numbers as at other turtle nesting grounds in the country. If you want to see the turtles, talk first to the rangers (see below) and, whatever you do, remember the ground rules of turtle-watching: come at night with a torch, watch where you walk (partly for snakes), keep well back from the beach and don't shine the light right on the turtles.

Other than spotting nesting turtles or dolphins and whales frolicking from the shore, the best way to take in the park's abundant marine life is either **snorkelling**, on a **boat** or in a **kayak**; tours of each type can be arranged in Uvita (see p.375).

7

INFORMATION
PARQUE NATIONAL MARINO BALLENA

Tourist information The park has four beach entrances and designated sectors to match, from north to south at *playas* Uvita, Colonia, Ballena and Piñuelas, with a ranger station at each entrance. All the ranger stations provide information about the park, nearby picnic areas, as well as provide basic shower and toilet facilities, except at Uvita. Note that the ranger stations are not always staffed.

ACCOMMODATION

Camping It is possible to camp at sectors Colonia, Ballena and Piñuelas (which have potable water, toilets and showers), but only at spots well away from the high-tide line; ask a ranger first. Per person US$20

Ojochal

About halfway between Dominical and Palmar (and 16km south of Uvita), **OJOCHAL** sees more visitors than it once did, but it's still very much a pleasant and unhurried Tico town. Unlike most settlements along this stretch of the coast, it's on the inland side of Hwy-34. The walk to the town's beach, **Playa Tortuga**, is therefore just a tad further than elsewhere, but you'll be rewarded with one of the cleanest and most idyllic stretches of sand in the country.

ARRIVAL AND DEPARTURE
OJOCHAL

By bus Buses arrive at the dusty stop in the centre of town. For San José you'll need to change in Dominical and often San Isidro.
Destinations Dominical (3 daily; 40min); Palmar (3 daily; 50min).
By taxi Taxis charge around US$25 from Palmar Sur airport, and US$75 from Quepos airport.

ACCOMMODATION AND EATING

★**Villas Gaia** Hwy-34, 500m north of entrance to Playa Tortuga ☎ 2786 5044, ⓦ villasgaia.com. Proudly sustainably operated, *Villas Gaia* offers fourteen brightly coloured *casitas* (sleeping up to 4) – most with a/c – a pool and an inviting restaurant. It also runs a range of tours including snorkelling at Isla del Caño and boat trips around the local mangrove swamps. US$82

Villas de Oros Hwy-34, 200m north of entrance to Playa Tortuga ☎ 2786 5170, ⓦ villasdeoros.com. Five attractive and comfortable villas (sleeping 2–4) with balconies overlooking the ocean, plus kitchenettes and a/c. The villas occupy a lush, sprawling site, which is crisscrossed by a small network of trails. US$85

★**Ylang Ylang** C Estrellas, in the town centre ☎ 2786 5054. The fragrant aromas wafting from this cute open-air restaurant hint that you're in for a different sort of

meal, but they still don't quite prepare you for the explosion of flavours soon to follow. Count on mouthwatering Indonesian seafood and well-spiced vegetarian dishes (most mains ₡7000–16,000), and be sure you get a reservation – there are only ten seats and they fill up fast. Wed–Sat 5–9pm.

Palmar

Wedged in where Hwy-34 joins the Interamericana, 30km southeast from Ojochal, the small, prefab town of **PALMAR** serves as the hub for the area's banana plantations. The town is divided in two by the Río Grande de Térraba: **Palmar Sur** contains the airport, while most of the services, including hotels and buses, are in **Palmar Norte**. The town is a good place to see **lithic spheres** (see box below), and it also makes a useful jumping-off point for visiting the nearby **Reserva Indígena Boruca** (see opposite), where you can buy local crafts from the indigenous population.

ARRIVAL AND DEPARTURE
PALMAR

By plane The tiny airport in Palmar Sur is currently served by three daily flights (47min) to/from San José with Sansa (☎ 2290 4100).

By bus Tracopa (☎ 2786 6511) buses from San José and San Isidro run to the station in the centre of Palmar Norte, at the junction of Hwy-2 (Interamericana) and Hwy-34, while Transportes Térraba (☎ 2732 2306) buses for Puerto Jiménez,

Sierpe and Costanera Sur destinations leave Palmar Norte from in front of the Banco Coopealianz on the main street (Hwy-2). Destinations Buenos Aires (2 daily; 1hr 10min–1hr 30min); Dominical (3 daily; 1hr 30min); Golfito (2 daily; 1hr 40min); Ojochal (3 daily; 50min); Puerto Jiménez (3 daily; 2hr 40min–3hr); San Isidro (14 daily; 2hr 30min); San José (8 daily; 6hr); Sierpe (7 daily; 40min).

ACCOMMODATION

Brunka Lodge A block and a half south of the Interamericana (Hwy-2), on C 149 (Palmar Norte) ☎ 2786 7489. The 25 cabins (sleeping 2–4) are pleasantly furnished and have cable TV, a/c and wi-fi, and there are two pools and a restaurant. US$46

Hotel El Teca Interamericana (Hwy-2), at C 147 (Palmar Norte) ☎ 2786 8010, ⓦ hotelelteca.com. Best budget choice in town, with spotless, modern rooms with kitchenettes and a/c (though usually cold-water showers). Free wi-fi. US$35

DIRECTORY

Banks and exchange Banco Nacional (Mon–Fri 8.30am–3.45pm; ☎ 2786 6263), on the Interamericana (Hwy-2), one block east of the Costanera Sur intersection.

Medical services Hospital de Osa Tomás Casas Casajús (☎ 2786 8148) is 12km northwest in Puerto Cortés.

LITHIC SPHERES

Aside from goldworking, the Diquís are known for their precise fashioning of large stone **spheres**, most of them exactly spherical to within a centimetre or two – an astounding feat for a culture without advanced technology. Thousands have been found in southwestern Costa Rica and a few in northern Panama. Some are located in sites of obvious significance, like burial mounds, while others are found in the middle of nowhere; they range in size from that of a tennis ball up to about two metres in diameter.

The spheres' original function and meaning remain obscure, although they sometimes seem to have been arranged in positions mirroring those of the constellations. In many cases the Diquís transported them a considerable distance, rafting them across rivers or the open sea (the only explanation for their presence on Isla del Caño), indicating that their placement was deliberate and significant. (Ironically, some of the posher Valle Central residences now have stone spheres – purchased at a great price – sitting in their front gardens as lawn sculpture.)

You can see lithic spheres in and around **Palmar** (there are a few sizeable ones in the Parque Las Esferas across from the airport) and also on **Isla del Caño**, which is most easily accessed on a tour run by one of the lodges in Bahía Drake (see p.382).

Buenos Aires and around

BUENOS AIRES, a nondescript pineapple-growing town 62km northeast of Palmar via the Interamericana (Hwy-2), provides access to two little-visited sites: the remote **Reserva Biológica Dúrika** and **Reserva Indígena Boruca**, home to the Boruca people. Beyond the austere concrete angularity of the modern **San Pedro Apóstol church** on the central square, the town itself is not likely to hold your interest longer than the time it takes to drive through it. It is, however, a good place to stock up on supplies or withdraw money before continuing on.

ARRIVAL AND DEPARTURE
BUENOS AIRES AND AROUND

By bus Buses pull into the terminal in Buenos Aires on Av Central, at C 6.

Destinations Boruca (2 daily; 2hr); Palmar (2 daily; 1hr

10min–1hr 30min); San Isidro de El General (every 1hr 30min; 1hr 20min); San José (2 daily; 4hr 10min–4hr 20min).

DIRECTORY

Banks and exchange The Banco de Costa Rica (Mon–Fri 9am–4pm), one block east of the central square on C 6, has an ATM.

Medical services Centro Médico Buenos Aires is on C 6, Av

1/2 (☎ 2730 0515).

Supermarket There's a Palí (Mon–Sat 7am–7pm) supermarket on Av 5, at C Central.

Reserva Biológica Dúrika

17km northeast of Buenos Aires • US$72/day, includes all tours • ☎ 2730 0657, ⓦ durika.org

Completely off the beaten track, the isolated **Reserva Biológica Dúrika** is a compelling mix of an agricultural-based community and private reserve where you can go on hikes and explore a working farm. Nestled within 85 square kilometres of largely untouched and unexplored wilderness, it consists of only thirty or so permanent residents (though it also is home to over a hundred semipermanent residents and visitors). The community's farm has enabled them to be entirely self-sufficient, and they offer **tours** (reserve in advance; 2hr) where you can learn first-hand about their organic approach to farming. Members also lead guided **hikes** (reserve in advance; 2–4hr) to nearby Cabécar villages and into the wildlife-rich reserve, where a variety of habitats are home to several endangered species, including Baird's tapir. If arranged well in advance, local guides can also lead five-day **treks** (Nov–Feb only; call for prices) up one of Costa Rica's highest peaks, Cerro Dúrika (3280m), part of the Cordillera Talamanca, which cuts through the reserve.

ARRIVAL AND INFORMATION
RESERVA BIOLÓGICA DÚRIKA

By car The reserve is 17km northeast from Buenos Aires on a gravel road. A 4WD is recommended to navigate the bumps and the incredibly steep section at the end.

By taxi From Buenos Aires it is possible to hire a jeep taxi to the reserve for US$35–40.

Information The Dúrika Foundation's office in Buenos Aires (Mon–Sat 8am–5pm; ☎ 2730 0657), C 1, at Av 6, can make reservations and provide information on the various tours and extended stay possibilities (call well in advance if you're considering the latter).

ACCOMMODATION

Dúrika cabins At the centre of the community. The reserve has nine simple, cosy cabins available for visitor stays, each with private bath and sweeping valley views.

Vegetarian takes on *comida típica* are served in the centre's restaurant (three daily meals included). Per person US$70

Reserva Indígena Boruca

28km south of Buenos Aires • ⓦ boruca.org

About 28km south of Buenos Aires lies the village of **BORUCA**, within the **Reserva Indígena Boruca**, home of Costa Rica's indigenous Boruca (or Brunka) people. The village is known for its local **crafts**, with the women making small tablecloths and purses on home-made looms, while the men fashion balsa-wood masks, some of which are expressly intended for the *diablitos* (little devils) ceremony (see box below) and procession that take place on New Year's Eve. You can buy either from the artisans themselves or from the local women's co-operative, La Flor de Boruca – it'll help if you have at least a working knowledge of Spanish. Local people have little other outlet for their crafts (you won't find them in the San José shops), so a visit can be a good way of contributing to the local economy. The small **Museo Comunitario de Boruca** (Tues–Sun 8am–3pm; free, but donations encouraged; ☏2514 0045) in the centre of the village contains displays and artefacts charting the history, legends and culture of the Boruca people.

ARRIVAL AND INFORMATION
RESERVA INDÍGENA BORUCA

By bus Buses for Boruca depart Buenos Aires daily at 11.30am and 3.30pm (2hr). As the return buses leave Boruca at 6am and 1pm, it's not feasible to visit as a day-trip if travelling by bus. See contact below for information on homestays.

By car To reach the reserve by car from Palmar, head 24km east on the Interamericana (Hwy-2), and then take the signed turn-off for another 8km north. You will need a 4WD to get here, and if it's raining heavily, the road can become impassable. From Buenos Aires (14km south on the Interamericana, and then a further 15km on gravel roads), the drive is slightly longer but more manageable in a non-4WD.

Tourist information Mileni González (☏2730 5178, ✉laflordeboruca@gmail.com), president of the long-running local artisans group La Flor de Boruca, is the best source of information about the village and the reserve, including homestays.

Península de Osa

In the extreme south of the country, the **PENÍNSULA DE OSA** is an area of immense biological diversity, somewhat separate from the mainland, and few will fail to be moved by its beauty. Whether you approach the peninsula by *lancha* from Sierpe or Golfito, on the Jiménez bus, driving in from the mainland, or – especially – by air, you'll see what looks like a floating island – an intricate mesh of blue and green, with tall canopy trees sailing high and flat like elaborate floral hats. A surfeit of natural wonder awaits, from the sweeping arc of **Bahía Drake** in the northwest and the world-class diving and snorkelling spots of nearby **Isla del Caño** to one of the planet's most biologically rich pockets, **Parque Nacional Corcovado**, which covers the bulk of the peninsula.

THE FIESTA DE LOS DIABLITOS

Many indigenous peoples throughout the isthmus, and all the way north to Mexico, enact the **Fiesta de los Diablitos**, a resonant spectacle that is both disturbing and humorous. In Costa Rica the Borucas use it to celebrate New Year and to re-enact the Spanish invasion, with Columbus, Cortez and his men reborn every year. The fiesta takes place over three days and is a village affair: foreigners and tourists are not encouraged to come as spectators.

On the first day a village man is appointed to play the bull; others disguise themselves as little devils (*diablitos*), with burlap sacks and masks carved from balsa wood. The *diablitos* taunt the bull, teasing him with sticks, while the bull responds in kind. At midnight on December 30 the *diablitos* congregate on the top of a hill, joined by musicians playing simple flutes and horns fashioned from conch shells. During the whole night and over the next three days, the group proceeds from house to house, visiting everyone in the village and enjoying a drink or two of home brew (*chicha*). On the third day, a ritual killing of the "bull" is enacted. The symbolism is indirect, but the bull, of course, represents the Spaniard(s), and the *diablitos* the indigenous people. The bull is always vanquished and the *diablitos* always win – which of course is not quite how it turned out, in the end.

It's long been Costa Rica's wild frontier. In the early years of the twentieth century, Osa was something of a penal colony, a place to which men were sent forcibly, to be forgotten about – others went, machete in hand, to forget. Consequently, a violent, frontier-lands folklore still permeates the whole peninsula, and old-time residents of **Puerto Jiménez** are only too happy to regale you with hosts of gory tales. Some may be apocryphal, but they certainly add colour to the place. The road to **Cabo Matapalo**, at the tip of the peninsula, and further on to sleepy **Carate**, the southeastern gateway to Corcovado, retains an end-of-the-world feel, with the jungle pressing against much of it.

You could feasibly explore the whole peninsula in four days, but this would be rushing it, especially if you want to spend time walking the trails and wildlife-spotting at Corcovado. Most people allot five to seven days for the area, taking it at a relaxed pace, and more if they want to stay in and explore Bahía Drake. Hikers and walkers who come to Osa without their own car tend to base themselves in Puerto Jiménez – a place where it's easy to strike up a conversation, and people are relaxed, environmentally conscientious and not yet overwhelmed by tourism.

Bahía Drake and around

BAHÍA DRAKE (pronounced "Drah-kay") is named after Sir Francis Drake, who is said to have anchored here in 1579 and, much to the bemusement of Brits, is unequivocally known throughout Latin America as a "pirate". Today a favourite spot for sailors, the calm waters of the bay are dotted with flotillas of swish-looking yachts. This is one of the most stunning areas in Costa Rica, with the blue wedge of **Isla del Caño** floating 20km off the coast, and fiery-orange Pacific sunsets. The bay is rich in marine life, and a number of **boat trips** offer opportunities for spotting manta rays, marine turtles, porpoises and even whales. The bay's lone settlement of any size is the sprawling village of **Agujitas**, which acts as the area's main transport hub.

Bahía Drake and Agujitas make a good base to explore Parque Nacional Corcovado (see p.390) as the park's San Pedrillo entrance is within a day's walk. Visitors can combine serious trekking with serious comfort by staying at one of the region's upmarket rainforest ecolodge-type hotels. Note that there are very few facilities at Bahía Drake. As there are **no banks or ATMs**, bring all the cash you will need with you.

ARRIVAL AND DEPARTURE   BAHÍA DRAKE AND AROUND

Like many other places in Zona Sur, getting to Bahía Drake requires some planning. There are four options: the really tough way, **hiking** in from Corcovado; the cheap way, **by bus** from San José to Sierpe and then **by boat** along the Río Sierpe (possible in a day if you leave San José at 5am); the bumpy way, **by 4WD** along the gravel and dirt road between Rincón and Agujitas (which is impassable at various times of the year); and the luxury way, **flying** from San José to Bahía Drake Airport, and taking one of the many packages offered by hotels in the area. If you choose this last option, transport to your lodge is taken care of.

BY BUS/CAR AND BOAT

By bus to Sierpe From Palmar (see p.378) you can get a local bus (daily 4.30am, 7am, 9.30am, 11am, 1.30pm, 2.30pm & 5pm; 40min) or taxi to Sierpe (about US$20), where there are a few *cabinas*. Transportes Álvarez (☎8703 2121, ✉transportes.aym@hotmail.com) runs shuttle buses direct from San José (5.30am; 4hr 50min) to Sierpe via Jacó, Quepos and Dominical in time for the first boat; a bus leaves the dock at Sierpe in the other direction at 8.40am.

By car to Sierpe If you're driving to Sierpe, note that it's possible to park your car near *Restaurante Oleaje Sereno* during your stay at Drake, but it costs ₡3000/day.

By boat from Sierpe From the waterfront at *Restaurante Oleaje Sereno*, boats (1hr 15min) normally depart for Bahía Drake at 11.30am (US$15) and 3.30/4pm (US$20). It's first-come, first-served, so get here early. The boats return to Sierpe at 7.15am (US$15) and 2.30pm (US$20). It's sometimes possible to hire a boatman to take you on demand, but this will be at least US$100 (maximum usually eight people).

BY PLANE

Both NatureAir (☎8897 9393) and Sansa (☎2815 5191) operate daily flights to Bahía Drake Airport from San José (with one NatureAir flight travelling via Puerto Jiménez,

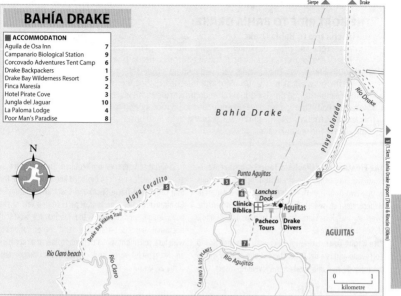

BAHÍA DRAKE

ACCOMMODATION	
Aguila de Osa Inn	7
Campanario Biological Station	9
Corcovado Adventures Tent Camp	6
Drake Backpackers	1
Drake Bay Wilderness Resort	5
Finca Maresía	2
Hotel Pirate Cove	3
Jungla del Jaguar	10
La Paloma Lodge	4
Poor Man's Paradise	8

7

but only in one direction). Be sure to arrange transport to your lodge in advance of your arrival at the tiny airstrip, 7km north of Agujitas.

Destinations via NatureAir Puerto Jiménez (1 daily; 15min; from Jiménez to Bahía Drake only); San José (2 daily; 35min–1hr 10min).

Destinations via Sansa San José (2 daily; 45min).

BY CAR/TAXI
Rainfall can make the road into Agujitas impassable at just about any time of year (there are three river crossings); if you plan on driving to your lodge, call first to find out the latest conditions. The roads are unpaved from Rincón de Osa, where you turn off Hwy-245, and a 4WD will be essential. Taxis will charge around US$120 between Puerto Jiménez and the Bahía Drake region.

BY BUS
There aren't many bus services to Agujitas. Your best bet

would be to connect with the daily 11am or 4.30pm bus (₡5000 one way) that departs from the hamlet of La Palma (buses to Puerto Jiménez will stop here if you ask) and passes through Rincón de Osa; the bus terminates at the end of the road in Agujitas by the beach (it's a bumpy 1hr 30min ride from La Palma). The bus returns to La Palma daily at around 4am and 1.30pm. This bus does not always run, so check with your hotel first.

ON FOOT
To hike between Bahía Drake and Corcovado, follow the 17km-long beachside Drake Bay Hiking Trail from Agujitas via Marenco to the San Pedrillo entrance of Parque Nacional Corcovado, a walk of around 8–12hr. You can camp at San Pedrillo ranger station (see p.393), though you should inform SINAC in advance by contacting the Puerto Jiménez office (☎ 2735 5036). If you are staying at any of the Bahía Drake lodges, they should be able to contact the Puerto Jiménez office and make a reservation on your behalf.

INFORMATION AND TOURS

All of the bay's *cabinas* and lodges offer a wide variety of tours, from guided hikes to Corcovado (from US$90/person) and boat rides to Isla del Caño (from US$100/person; see p.385), to snorkelling and diving trips (US$80–135).

Corcovado Canopy Tour ⓦ corcovadocanopytour.com. Fly through the forest via 12 ziplines, each 190–400m in length. Offers various horseriding, whale-watching and snorkelling combos, or just ziplining for US$95 (which includes the horse-ride to the site). Ziplining tours depart

Agujitas daily 7.30am, 10.30am, 1.30pm & 4pm.
Drake Divers ⓦ drakediverscr.com. Runs snorkelling (US$80) and diving (US$135) trips to Caño, as well as dolphin and whale-watching tours (from US$95). Daily 7.30am.

7

THE BOAT RIDE TO BAHÍA DRAKE

The **lancha trip to Bahía Drake** from Sierpe (see p.382) down the scenic mangrove-lined Río Sierpe is serene and provides plenty of opportunity to spot monkeys, sloths and sometimes kingfishers. The journey's tranquility dissolves abruptly when you see the Pacific rolling in at the mouth of the river. The Sierpe is very wide where it meets the sea, and huge breakers crash in from the ocean, making it a turbulent and treacherous crossing (sharks reportedly wait here for their dinner). If the tide is right and the boatman knows his water, you'll be fine. All the *lanchas* used by the lodges have powerful outboard motors, and there's little chance of an accident; all the same, some find this part of the trip a little unsettling. Once you are out in Bahía Drake the water is calm.

The Floating Tour (Pacheco Tours) ⓦ pachecotours .com/floating.html. One of the best local tours begins with a two-hour hike through the jungle to a waterfall (where you can swim), followed by a float down the river to the Río Claro beach (around 1hr 30min). US$65. Daily 8am.

The Night Tour ⓦ thenighttour.com. Beyond trips to Corcovado and Isla del Caño, there is one activity not to be missed in Bahía Drake: the evening insect tour

(US$40/person; reservations required; 2hr 30min) led by an enthusiastic American biologist known as "Tracie the Bug Lady" (aka Tracie Stice) and Costa Rican naturalist Gianfranco Gómez. The tour departs from a few of the bay's lodges and explores the fascinating world of nocturnal insects, arachnids and other animals; with luck you might spot a trapdoor spider or a caecilian, an extremely rare and little-known amphibian. Daily 7.30pm.

ACCOMMODATION

Most accommodation is clustered either in the tiny village of **Agujitas** itself, or on **Punta Agujitas**, the rocky point on the other side of Río Agujitas. Virtually all the ecolodges listed below offer a range of tours, from guided excursions to Corcovado to boat trips around Bahía Drake and out to Isla del Caño. The larger lodges often bring visitors on **packages** from San José, sometimes including transport from the capital, Palmar or Sierpe. The packages usually include three meals a day – there are few eating options in Bahía Drake otherwise – and all the prices given below include full-board and free wi-fi (unless stated otherwise). Although hoteliers say you can't **camp** in the Drake area, people do – if you want to join them, pitch your tent considerately and be sure to leave no litter.

★**Aguila de Osa Inn** At the end of the village on Río Agujitas ☎ 2296 2190, ⓦ aguiladeosa.com. Very posh sportfishing lodge with a high-quality restaurant, landscaped gardens and thirteen beautifully decorated rooms nestling into the hillside. All have large Italian-tiled bathrooms and cathedral-style ceilings with fans. The lodge has its own marina and free use of kayaks. Minimum two nights. Per person US$253

Campanario Biological Station About 150m north of the San Pedrillo entrance to Corcovado ☎ 2289 8694, ⓦ campanario.org. This remote field station offers courses in tropical ecology and tour "packages" for hardy ecotourists not fazed by its isolation. There are dorms, plus five simple but private cabins (sleeping 4–6) with cold-water bathrooms. Tours consist of short walks, long hikes or all-day expeditions to Parque Nacional Corcovado as well as trips to deforested and impacted areas to talk to local communities. No TVs, telephones or wi-fi/internet. Three nights minimum. Per person US$170

Corcovado Adventures Tent Camp Playa Las Caletas, 2km west of Agujitas ☎ 8386 2296, ⓦ corcovado.com. En route to Parque Nacional

Corcovado, this collection of well-screened and furnished tents (sleeping up to 4), complete with beds, tables and electricity, sits on platforms on an isolated beach facing the sea. Three meals included (transport US$40 round-trip). Per person US$75

★**Drake Backpackers** El Progreso, 6km from Agujitas ☎ 8981 5519, ⓦ drakebaybackpackers.com. Tucked away up in the hills above the coast in the small village of El Progreso, this nonprofit hostel is the place to really get off the tourist trail. Run by the Corcovado Foundation and working with and supporting the community, they offer local tours and shuttles to Agujitas. Basic but spotless dorms and private rooms (with or without bathroom), as well as campsites. Includes breakfast and dinner only, plus use of shared kitchen. Camping/person US$5, dorms US$15, doubles US$40

Drake Bay Wilderness Resort Punta Agujitas ☎ 2775 1715, ⓦ drakebay.com. The most established lodge in the area, providing a buffer zone between tourist and wilderness with rustic, comfortable *cabinas* or, if you want to rough it a bit, economy cabins with shared bathroom – both options (sleeping 2–4) are well screened. There's hearty local food available, and the camp also has its own solar-heated water supply, 24hr electricity, and excellent snorkelling and canoeing. Two-night minimum. Per person US$298

★**Finca Maresía** 1.8km south of Agujitas ☎2775 0279, ⊛fincamaresia.com. Seven charming, raised bungalows (sleeping 2–4) spread along a hillside in the midst of the jungle. All have open, contemporary designs, attractive furnishings and ceiling fans. The welcoming owner has a wealth of information on the Osa Peninsula, and the staff lead a full slate of tours in and around the bay. The meals are a revelation and are served in a pleasant communal setting; breakfast is included, with lunch (US$8) and dinner (US$15) extra. Cash only. US$45

Hotel Pirate Cove About 1.7km north of Agujitas ☎2234 6154, ⊛piratecovecostarica.com. Three comfortable en-suite *cabinas* (sleeping up to 5), three newer rooms (with a/c) in the main building and two tent-like bungalows (sleeping 3–4), with fans and hot water, all set in lush rainforest overlooking a pristine 2km stretch of beach (free kayaks). The excellent restaurant serves Costa Rican and European cuisine. Doubles/bungalows US$230, *cabinas* US$270

Jungla del Jaguar About 150m north of the San Pedrillo entrance to Corcovado ☎2231 5806, ⊛jungladeljaguar.com. Remote, solar-powered hostel that really is surrounded by jungle, with open-air dorms and simple private cabins (sleeping up to 4) with tiled floors, plus access to a network of trails, yoga lessons and guided tours. Meals offered but not included (free coffee); cash only. Dorms US$15, cabins US$50

La Paloma Lodge Punta Agujitas ☎2293 7502, ⊛lapalomalodge.com. Beautiful, well-appointed rooms in hilltop bungalows, with king-size beds, private bath, balconies and hammocks. The airy, two-storey bungalows (sleeping 5–6) are best, surrounded by forest and boasting spectacular views, particularly at sunset. Kayaks, bodyboards and snorkelling gear are available for guests to explore the Río Agujitas behind the lodge, and there's an attractively tiled swimming pool. No phones or wi-fi (internet in clubhouse only). Three nights minimum. Per person US$360

Poor Man's Paradise About 1km north of the San Pedrillo entrance to Corcovado ☎2771 9686, ⊛poormansparadiseresort.com. One of the most secluded lodges in what is, after all, a pretty secluded area. The basic *cabinas* (sleeping 2–4) with private bathrooms (no wi-fi, mobile phone coverage or hot water) are set in pretty gardens and have ocean views. Meals are served in the lodge's lovely indigenous-style thatched-roof restaurant (lunch and dinner are US$10 extra). US$105

DIRECTORY

Medical services Your best bet is Clínica Bíblica (Mon–Thurs 7am–3.45pm, Fri 7am–2.45pm; ☎2786 6273), located just off the beach in Agujitas.

Reserva Biológica Isla del Caño

Daily 7am–3pm • US$10 • ☎2735 5036 • A tour is usually included in the package price (from US$80) from Bahía Drake lodges or local operators (see p.383)

The tiny **RESERVA BIOLÓGICA ISLA DEL CAÑO** sits placidly in the ocean some 20km due west of Bahía Drake (1hr by boat). Just 3km long by 2km wide, the uninhabited island is the exposed part of an underwater mountain, thrown up by an ancient collision of two tectonic plates, one on either side of Costa Rica. It's a pretty sight in the distance, and going there is even better – if you can afford it.

The island is thought to have been a burial ground of the Diquis, who brought their famed **lithic spheres** here from the mainland in large, ocean-going canoes. Visits are now restricted to the beach-landing area, so day-trips focus on the island's prime **snorkelling** and **diving** opportunities, with five dive sites around the island. There's a daily cap on the number of visitors (100 people 7–11am, another 100 11am–3pm) and divers (only ten are allowed in the water at a time). Underwater you'll see coral beds and a variety of **marine life**, including spiny lobsters and sea cucumbers, snappers, sea urchins, manta rays and the occasional barracuda. On the surface, porpoises and olive ridley turtles are often spotted, and less frequently there are sightings of humpback and even sperm whales.

Puerto Jiménez

The Osa Peninsula's biggest town, relaxed **PUERTO JIMÉNEZ** – known locally as Jiménez – has plenty of places to stay and eat, and good public transport connections. Traditionally it has catered to the budget end of the spectrum, and though that may change, for now its basic *cabinas* remain in a whole different class and price range from the luxury lodges lining the road to Carate, 43km southwest (see p.389). From Jiménez, you can also take a *colectivo* truck, which serves as public transportation to Corcovado national park.

Jiménez itself is a relatively small, languid place with little to see (other than a few craft shops), but despite its down-at-heel appearance, it welcomes a constant flow of visitors throughout the year, and its mostly unpaved streets are enhanced by hordes of tropical birds (especially scarlet macaws), squawking in the almond trees. The **main street**, which runs for just a few hundred metres from the football field in the north to the petrol station in the south, represents the rather dusty heart of town. Note that almost everything shuts down after lunch for siesta and many businesses remain closed throughout October and November (the rainy season). Jiménez is not especially known for its beaches either, though if you venture 5km east to **Playa Platanares**, you'll find a pleasantly secluded stretch of sand, an ideal spot to recover after a strenuous hike in Corcovado.

7

ARRIVAL AND DEPARTURE

PUERTO JIMÉNEZ

By plane You can fly to Puerto Jiménez with Sansa (☏ 2735 5890) or NatureAir (☏ 2735 5428), landing at the sliver of an airstrip ten minutes' walk from the centre (taxis charge around ₡2000). It's also possible to fly between Jiménez and the tiny airstrip at Carate (for Corcovado; 7–10min), with Alfa Romeo Aero Taxi (☏ 2755 1515, ⓦ alfaromeoair.com), for around US$185 each for up to five people (the charter flight runs on

Jetty for Lanchas to Golfito

La Playa

Golfo Dulce

■ ACCOMMODATION
Cabinas Jiménez	1
Hostel Oro Verde	3
Hotel Inn Jiménez	2
Lunas Hostel	5
Iguana Lodge	4

● EATING
Cafetería Monka	4
Il Giardino	1
Marisquería Corcovado	2
Panadería Monar	5
Pearl of the Osa	8
Pizzamail.it	3
Restaurante Carolina	7
Soda Johanna	6

HWY 245

Football Field (Plaza de Deporte)

Red Cross

Transportes Blanco bus station

Clínica Médica

Police Station

Colectivos

Family Mart

Jaguar Tours

Interamericana (75km) & San José (335km)

Alamo

Solid/NÜ

Airstrip

Farmacia Hidalgo

MAIN STREET

Oficina de Área de Conservación Osa

Jagua Artesanías

Iglesia Católica

Airport Terminal

Banco Nacional

Banco de Costa Rica

Osa Tropical

Carate (43km) & Parque Nacional Corcovado (45km)

BM Supermercado

Osa Wild

0   100
metres

PUERTO JIMÉNEZ

(4km), ⑧ (4.3km) & Playa Platanares (5km)

demand); flying into the park at Sirena with Alfa Romeo is around US$385 per plane.

Destinations via NatureAir Golfito (1–2 daily; 5min); San José (3–4 daily; 50min).

Destinations via Sansa San José (6 daily; 55min).

By bus The Transportes Blanco bus station (open daily 7–11am & 1–5pm; ☎ 2735 5189) is one block west of the football field. San José buses usually depart at 5am & 9am. Buses also run to Ciudad Neily (for onward connections to Panama) at 5.30am & 2pm.

Destinations Buenos Aires via Palmar Norte (2 daily; 3hr 40min); Ciudad Neily (2 daily; 3hr); San Isidro de El General (1 daily, 1pm; 5hr); San José (2 daily; 8hr).

By boat Regular *lanchas* depart for Golfito (35min; ₡3000) from the pier (*muelle*) on the north side of town. Boats depart Mon–Fri 6am, 8.45am, 11.30am, 2pm & 4.20pm; Sat 6am, 8.45am, 11.30am, 2pm & 4.20pm; and Sun 6am, 11.30am & 2pm. *Lanchas* return from Golfito just as regularly (see p.396).

By car Note that Puerto Jiménez has the only petrol station on the entire Península de Osa – be sure to fill up before you leave (it's open 24hr). Hwy-245 runs for 75km from the Interamericana at Piedras Blancas to Jiménez

(allow 1hr 30min) – the turning is 32km south of Palmar Sur. For car rental in Jiménez, Alamo (daily 7.30am–5.30pm; ☎ 2735 5175) and Solid/NÜ (daily 7am–4pm; ☎ 2735 5777, ⊛ solidcarrental.com) both have offices next to the airfield.

By colectivo The main form of local public transport, the *colectivo* (a modified 4WD truck with two rows of seating), normally departs from one block south of the bus station in Jiménez for Carate (US$9; in theory 2hr), twice daily at about 6am and 1.30pm, returning at 8.30am & 4pm. Note that it's an achingly bumpy drive and involves the careful negotiation of at least half a dozen small (or in the rainy season, not-so-small) rivers. In Oct and Nov it's often not possible to go further than Matapalo because of the rain; at this time buses only run once a day Tues–Thurs & Sun at 6am, returning at 3pm. The *colectivo* will drop you off at any of the lodges between Jiménez and Carate, and will also pick you up on its way back to town if you arrange this in advance – ask the driver (☎ 8832 8680).

By taxi A number of local taxi drivers have 4WDs; the average rate for a ride to Carate is about US$80/car (for up to four people; 1hr 30min), and US$40 to Matapalo (30min).

7

INFORMATION

There is no tourist office in town, but all of the tour operators (see box, p.388) can provide local information.

Oficina de Área de Conservación Osa Facing the airstrip (nominally Mon–Fri 8am–noon & 1–4pm, but usually closed to walk-ins until 11am; ☎ 2735 5036).

Staffed by friendly rangers who can answer questions (generally Spanish only) and arrange accommodation and meals at Sirena (see p.396).

ACCOMMODATION

Hotels in town are reasonably priced, clean and basic. There are a few comfort-in-the-wilderness places **between Jiménez and Carate** around the lower hump of the peninsula, a couple of which make great retreats or honeymoon spots. These tend to be quite upmarket; backpackers usually stay in Jiménez.

Cabinas Jiménez One block north of the football field ☎ 2735 5090, ⊛ cabinasjimenez.com. Quiet *cabinas* (sleeping 2–4) next to the waterfront, with simple, nicely furnished and spotlessly clean rooms. They're well screened, with bathroom, fans, a/c and free wi-fi, though some can be dark – ask to see a few before you choose. **US$60**

Hostel Oro Verde On the main street, 200m south of police station ☎ 2735 5241. Ten basic, clean second-storey rooms right in the middle of town, with restaurant, laundry service and friendly owners. Ask for one of the five front rooms with streetside terraces. **US$30**

★ **Hotel Inn Jiménez** 50m west of the main street ☎ 2735 5431, ⊛ hoteljimenez.com. Delightful modern inn with just three, comfortable rooms (one with private bathroom), and a tiny pool in lush gardens that attract macaws. There's free coffee, strong free wi-fi, and friendly

owners (a Tica/American couple). Room TVs feature Netflix on demand rather than the usual cable channels. **US$80**

★ **Iguana Lodge** Playa Platanares (follow the signs for 5km east of Jiménez) ☎ 8848 0752, ⊛ iguana lodge.com. Wonderful hotel run by very friendly Americans Toby and Lauren, with luxurious "club" rooms and four two-storey *casitas* (sleeping up to 4 people and priced per person) in lovely gardens right on the beach – all rooms face the sea and are attractively decorated. Breakfast is included in the clubroom rate, while breakfast and dinner are included in the *casita* rate. Club rooms **US$188**, casitas **US$229**

Lunas Hostel 100m west of BM Supermarket ☎ 2735 6007, ✉ abaldi.28@gmail.com. Clean, comfy dorm beds, great shared kitchen and super-fast, free wi-fi. Kind and friendly owner Alex is a font of local knowledge. Dorms **US$12**

ACTIVITIES AND TOURS FROM PUERTO JIMÉNEZ

Puerto Jiménez is increasingly catering to outdoor adventurers, with a growing list of tour operators leading all manner of trips across the peninsula, though itineraries are often very similar (and resources/guides often pooled). If you're planning a **trip to Corcovado** you could also contact the Oficina de Área de Conservación Osa (see p.387). Most outfits provide trips to Corcovado for US$85, including guide, park entrance fee and transport, though staying the night is a far better option if you have time (it takes around 2hr 40min to just reach the park). Other highlights are the chocolate tours (from US$32) of **Finca Köbö** (ⓦfincakobo.com), which include a visit to a cacao plantation and the chocolate-processing plant, with tasting along the way; and tours of the indigenous **Ngäbe (Guaymí) village** (from US$65), right in the heart of the Osa Peninsula.

TOUR OPERATORS

Osa Aventura ☎2735 5670, ⓦosaaventura.com. Knowledgeable tours led by affable biologist Mike Boston with a strong focus on the fauna and flora of Corcovado, including three-day hikes to Sirena (see p.392) and back (from US$545) and four- to five-day, more gruelling treks to San Pedrillo (from US$657).

Osa Tropical On Hwy-245 (main street), 50m north of the petrol station ☎2735 5062, ⓦosa -tropical.com. Offers a bewildering range of tours; chances are if there's a remote corner of Osa you want to see, they can take you there. Options include hiking in the Matapalo area (from US$30 for half-day), horseback riding (US$40 for 2.5hr, US$60 for

4–5hr) and dolphin and whale-watching trips (4hr; US$340 for maximum four people).

Osa Wild Opposite BM Supermercado ☎2735 5848, ⓦosawildtravel.com. With an emphasis on trips that benefit rural communities, this Costa Rican-owned and ecologically minded operation provides expertly led, intimate tours. Their informative trips to chocolate *fincas* (2hr; US$35) provide a glimpse of Osa that not many see; they also offer tours into Corcovado (three-day package US$245; includes guide, entrance, transport, camping fee and tents, but not meals), and rent bikes for US$10/day.

EATING

There's a BM Supermercado (Mon–Fri 7am–9pm, Sun 8am–8pm) across from the petrol station, which also contains a decent espresso bar, and a smaller but more convenient Family Mart (daily 5am–10pm) on the main street, just south of the police station.

Cafetería Monka Across from the police station, on the main street ☎2735 5051. Small pavement café serving piping-hot coffee as well as *comida típica* breakfasts (from ₡2500), bagels and especially good smoothies and freshly squeezed juices, from orange to papaya. Daily 7am–noon.

★**Il Giardino** On the waterfront road by the jetty ("La Playa") ☎2735 5129. For the most refined dining in town check out this quaint Italian restaurant that, strangely enough, also boasts an excellent sushi menu. Most people come for the pizza or fresh pasta dishes (₡5000–8000), slathered with home-made sauces. Daily 8am–10pm.

Marisquería Corcovado On the waterfront road by the jetty ("La Playa") ☎2735 5659. Huge covered hall on the bayfront specializing in fresh seafood (Peruvian-style ceviche, lobster bisque, tuna steaks, sushi and more), plus free wi-fi and satellite TV screens to beam in those all-important sports events. Mains ₡5000–15,000. Daily 6am–10pm.

Panadería Monar Next to the police station, on the

main street. Tasty pastries and fresh bread on the main street. Opens very early, and is usually where all the tour groups and guides meet for coffee before heading out (it just has a few tables, all outside). Mon–Fri & Sun 4.30am–5.30pm, Sat 4.30am–6pm.

Pearl of the Osa 5km east of Jiménez at Iguana Lodge, Playa Platanares. Lively open-air restaurant and bar serving international dishes and solid Costa Rican favourites (dinner mains ₡6850–12,000), plus craft beers. Their beach barbecue nights (Tues) and salsa dinner parties (with free dance lessons; Fri) are well known throughout the area. Daily 11am–10pm.

Pizzamail.it On the west side of the football pitch ("Plaza de Deporte") ☎2735 5483. Best place for pizzas in town – the large, tasty, thin-crust, wood-fired delights are around ₡5000. Daily 4–10.30pm.

Restaurante Carolina On the main road, 1 block south of the police station ☎2735 5696. A popular spot among locals, this no-frills open-air restaurant has a slightly more expensive but good-quality *comida típica* menu (most mains ₡2000–4000), plus free wi-fi. Try to find a spot beneath one of the ceiling fans, as it can get absolutely sweltering inside. Daily 7am–10pm.

★**Soda Johanna** Opposite Hotel Inn Jiménez ☎8303 0186. Tiny but popular local spot, especially for breakfast, when huge plates of eggs, *gallo pinto*, meat and tortillas plus fresh juice and coffee only cost around ₡2500. Daily 7am–8pm.

DIRECTORY

Banks and exchange The Banco Nacional, just north of the petrol station, changes dollars, as does the Banco de Costa Rica, diagonally opposite (both Mon–Fri 9am–4pm).

Medical services The Red Cross (☎2735 5109) and medical clinic (☎2735 5203) are opposite each other on the side road that leads to the bus station. Farmacia Hidalgo (Mon–Sat 8am–7.30pm) is two blocks south of the police station on the main street; there's another pharmacy diagonally opposite Banco Nacional where English is spoken, open similar hours.

Petrol station The peninsula's lone petrol station, Bomba Osa (daily 24hr), is at the bend of the main road at the south end of the centre.

Police On the main road, 50m south of the football field.

Post office Opposite the football field on the main road (typically Mon–Fri 8–11.45am & 1.30–5pm, though hours can be erratic).

7

Cabo Matapalo

Occupying Osa's southern edge about 17km from Puerto Jiménez, **Cabo Matapalo** was for many years the exclusive domain of surfers, who still come here for some of the country's best breaks. Nowadays, it's become increasingly popular as a place to build holiday homes and for its excellent wilderness lodges hidden in the primary rainforest.

The first beach on the cape, **Playa Pan Dulce** is the best one for swimming and has long breaks for surfers. The most southerly, **Playa Matapalo** provides the hardest tests for surfers and is a great spot to watch if your own skills aren't quite up to the challenge. Nearby is the largest **waterfall** in the area, 90m "King Louis", which can be reached on a short hike from the trailhead off the Playa Matapalo road.

TOURS
CABO MATAPALO

Everyday Adventures ☎8353 8619, ⓦpsychotours .com. Biologist Andy Pruter takes people on high-adrenaline "psycho" tours that include climbing 45m-tall fig trees, abseiling waterfalls and ocean-kayaking (US$65–95). They also lead short hikes into the rainforest (US$50). Closed Aug–Nov.

ACCOMMODATION

Bosque del Cabo Above Playa Matapalo, down a private road to the left off the Carate road ☎2735 5206, ⓦbosquedelcabo.com. Run by a friendly American couple, this grand lodge has ten luxurious hardwood and stucco *cabinas* (sleeping 2–4 and priced per person), several with magnificent ocean views, plus two even more luxurious houses that sleep up to six. The lodge sits in landscaped grounds of rainforest and is very ecofriendly; all the electricity is supplied by solar and hydro power. There's also a very good restaurant and several tours are available. All meals are included in the *cabina* rates. *Cabinas* U̲S̲$̲2̲0̲0̲, houses U̲S̲$̲5̲9̲5̲

Lapa Ríos Signposted 20km south of Puerto Jiménez ☎2735 5130, ⓦlaparios.com. One of the country's most comfortable and impressive jungle lodges, set in a large private nature reserve with excellent birdwatching and beach access. Rooms have big beds and mosquito nets, and, being built of locally sourced materials (bamboo furniture, hardwood floors, palm-thatched roofs), blend nicely with the surrounding forest. There's also a huge thatched restaurant, complete with spiral staircase, and a swimming pool. All meals included. Per person U̲S̲$̲4̲8̲7̲

Carate

About 25km west of Cabo Matapalo and 43km from Puerto Jiménez, **CARATE** is literally the end of the road – the beach is just steps from where the road terminates, with the Parque Nacional Corcovado a little further to the west via hiking trail – which is the overwhelming reason why people make the journey here. There's nothing in the tiny hamlet to detain you, save for the **mini-grocery** (*pulpería*) just off the beach, where you can stock up on expensive basic foodstuffs before entering the park. You can pitch your **tent** right outside the grocery (a charge of US$5/tent per night covers the use of toilets and showers), but for those requiring more comfort, there are a few idyllic **lodges** in the area that are well worth considering.

ARRIVAL AND DEPARTURE   CARATE

By colectivo The *colectivo* from Puerto Jiménez (see p.387) terminates at the car park at the end of the small landing strip – from here you must wade across the Río Carate and walk another 45min along the beach to the Corcovado park entrance at La Leona.

ACCOMMODATION

★**Lookout Inn** Just off Playa Carate ☎ 2735 5431, ⓦ lookout-inn.com; map opposite. Kick off your shoes and relax – there's a barefoot policy and an informal, fun atmosphere at this beach house set on a rainforested hillside with large open-air rooms, secluded bungalows (sleeping up to 6 people) and open-air A-Frame "tiki huts" (sleeping two), swimming pool and beautiful ocean views. Wildlife is abundant, with plenty of scarlet macaws, hummingbirds, coatis and monkeys around. Several tours are offered, including kayaking, dolphin boat cruises and hiking on area trails. Rates include three wonderful buffet meals daily (open to non-guests for a fee). All rates are per person.

Doubles US$135, huts US$125, bungalows US$150
★**Luna Lodge** Set in the hills above Carate ☎ 2206 5859, ⓦ lunalodge.com; map opposite. Remote, tranquil and beautiful lodge with welcoming owners and staggering views over the surrounding virgin rainforest. The eight thatched-roof bungalows (sleeping 2–4) each have private gardens, large windows, high ceilings and are handsomely furnished; there are also sturdy, comfortable tents (sleeping two people) in heavily forested settings. Yoga classes take place on a specially built platform overlooking the jungle and three healthy, home-cooked meals daily are included in the rate. Tents US$137, bungalows US$275

Parque Nacional Corcovado

Southwestern Osa Peninsula • Daily 7am–4pm • US$15/day; entry with licensed guide only • ☎ 2735 5036

Created in 1975, **PARQUE NACIONAL CORCOVADO** protects an undeniably beautiful and biologically complex area of land, with deserted beaches, some laced with waterfalls, high canopy trees and better-than-average wildlife-spotting opportunities. Many people come with the sole purpose of spotting **margay**, **ocelot**, **tapir**, **puma** and other rarely seen animals. Of course, it's all down to luck, but if you walk quietly and there aren't too many other humans around, you should have a better chance of seeing some of these creatures here than elsewhere.

Serious hiking in Corcovado is not for the faint-hearted. Quite apart from the distances and the terrain, **hazards** include insects (*lots* of them, especially in the rainy season: take a mosquito net, tons of repellent and all the precautions you can think of), herds of peccaries – who have been known to menace hikers – rivers full of crocodiles (and, in one case, sharks) and nasty snakes, including the terciopelo and bushmaster, which can attack without provocation. That said, most of these are present elsewhere in the country anyway, and everybody seems to make it through Corcovado just fine – but you must at least be prepared to get wet, dirty and incredibly hot. Bear in mind that there are **sharks** in the sea here, though everyone swims and no attacks have ever been recorded.

The **terrain** in Corcovado (literally "hunchback") varies from beaches of packed or soft sand, riverways, mangroves and *holillo* (palm) swamps to dense forest, although most of it is at lowland elevations. Hikers can expect to spend most of their time on the beach trails that ring the outer perimeters of the peninsular section of the park. Inland, the broad, alluvial Corcovado plain contains the **Corcovado Lagoon**, and for the most part the cover constitutes the only sizeable chunk of tropical **premontane wet forest** (also called tropical humid forest) on the Pacific side of Central America. The Osa forest is as visually and biologically magnificent as any on the subcontinent: biologists often compare the tree heights and density here with that of the Amazon basin cover – practically the only place in the entire isthmus about which this can still be said.

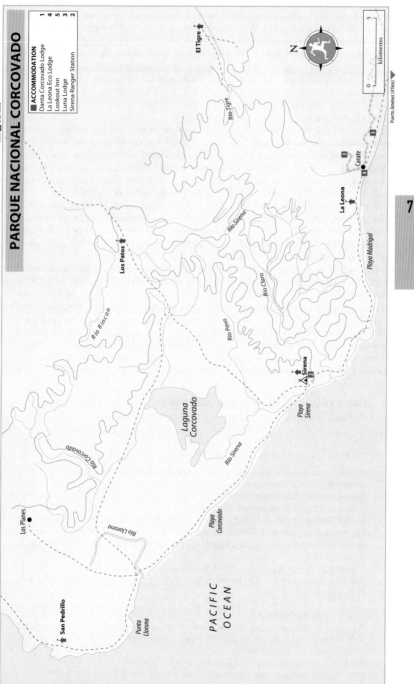

PARQUE NACIONAL CORCOVADO

ACCOMMODATION
Danta Corcovado Lodge	1
La Leona Eco Lodge	4
Lookout Inn	5
Luna Lodge	3
Sirena Ranger Station	2

N

0   5
kilometres

▲ **1** & La Palma

El Tigre

Río Tigre

Puerto Jiménez (41km) ▶

Carate

La Leona

Playa Madrigal

Río Sirena

Río Claro

Los Patos

Río Pavo

Río Rincon

Sirena

Playa Sirena

Laguna Corcovado

Río Sirena

Río Corcovado

▲ Bahía Drake (15km)

Los Planes

Río Llorona

San Pedrillo

Playa Corcovado

Punta Llorona

PACIFIC OCEAN

7

The coastal areas of the peninsular section of the park receive at least 3800mm of **rain** a year, with precipitation rising to about 5000mm in the higher elevations of the interior. This intense wetness is ideal for the development of the intricate, densely matted cover associated with tropical wet forests; there's also a dry season (Dec–April), which tends to be the peak season for visitors. The inland lowland areas, especially those around the lagoon, can be amazingly **hot**, even for those accustomed to tropical temperatures.

Trails in the park

It's suggested that you come in a group of at least two people, that you bring your own mosquito net, sleeping bag, food and water – though you can fill up at the beachside waterfalls and at the ranger stations – be fairly experienced with hiking this kind of terrain. At the time of research, **hiring a guide was mandatory** (see box below). Guides will ensure you stick to the trails – they sometimes can be tricky to follow after a heavy rain – but they will also dramatically improve your chances of spotting the recalcitrant wildlife.

When you enter the park, make sure you jot down the details of the **marea** (tides) that are posted in prominent positions at all the ranger stations. You'll need to cross most of the rivers at low tide – to do otherwise is dangerous. Rangers can advise on conditions. You should plan to **hike** early in the day – though not before dawn, due to snakes – and take shelter at midday.

The park's three longest **trails** all lead from the four peripheral ranger stations (see p.394) to **Sirena**, where you can stay for a day or two in the simple lodge (see p.394), exploring the local trails around the Río Sirena. Though there is some overlap in the type of flora and fauna you might see along the way on the different trails, each offers a distinct hiking experience. For this reason, and if your schedule permits, it's a good idea to walk into Sirena on one trail and back out via another. If you plan to spend a few days in the park, consider hiking in from Los Patos, spending a night or two in Sirena and then hiking back out to La Leona; it's much easier to move on from La Leona at the end of a hike than from Los Patos.

CORCOVADO RULES AND REGULATIONS

Park officials have tightened the **rules** governing visits to Corcovado in recent years – while these may change again (local tour operators are generally in favour of much looser restrictions), this was the situation at the time of writing – always check the current policies in advance. It's much easier to go with a tour operator (see box, p.388) that will handle all this for you.

- All park visitors must be accompanied by a **professional guide** (email the park for a current list) even for one-day tours; rates start at around US$60/day per person, but you can sometimes negotiate lower prices.
- You must apply for entry permits, up to 30 days in advance (but *after* you have arranged a guide). Tediously, payment must be made via an international wire transfer or at the Banco Nacional in Puerto Jiménez, within two days of SINAC's confirmation (email the receipt to ✉ reservaciones@parquecorcovado.org). You cannot pay at the park office in Jiménez or at the park itself.
- All overnight guests at Sirena must purchase meals from the on-site restaurant in advance (see p.394) – you can no longer cook your own food (though you can choose to snack on cold food you bring instead).
- The trail from San Pedrillo to Sirena is normally open Dec–April only, but is sometimes closed during this period also.
- It is no longer possible to rent canoes on the Río Sirena – check the latest with local guides.
- Visits to Los Patos, La Leona, Sirena and El Tigre are restricted to 80 people/day (a maximum of 40 people can camp at Sirena at any one time).
- San Pedrillo is restricted to 100 people/day.
- Night tours are not available.

LOCAL GUIDES IN OSA

In recent years, a programme to train local men and women between the ages of 18 and 35 as **naturalist guides** has been initiated at Rincón de Osa, a village about 35km northwest of Jiménez, snug in the curve of the Golfo Dulce. The programme is typical in Costa Rica – Rara Avis and Selva Verde in Sarapiquí, among others, have similar schemes – enabling people not only to make a living from their local knowledge, but also to appreciate the many ways in which a rainforest can be sustainable. Guides are taught to identify some of the 367 or more species of bird recorded in the area, the 177 amphibians and reptiles, nearly 6000 insects, 140 mammals and 1000 trees – Corcovado's biodiversity makes for a lot of homework. They are also given lectures in tourism and tutored by working professional guides. If you wish to hire a local guide, ask in Rincón or at the Oficina de Área de Conservación Osa office in Puerto Jiménez (see p.387) for details. This arrangement works best if you are planning to hike the Los Patos–Sirena trail, as this has the nearest entrances to Rincón.

Los Patos to Sirena

The reasonably marked 25km inland **trail from Los Patos to Sirena** is, for many, the holy grail of Corcovado hikes, a thoroughly intoxicating jungle adventure with opportunities to glimpse tapirs, peccaries, margay or the tracks of jaguars. This is a trail for experienced rainforest hikers. You'll want to start your hike from Los Patos to Sirena early, so plan on arriving at Los Patos soon after dawn or, preferably, the night before (allow 9hr for the hike).

From Los Patos the trail takes you steeply uphill for some 5km into high, wet and dense rainforest, after which the rest of the walk is flat. It's a gruelling trek, especially with the hot inland temperatures (at least 26°C, with 100 percent humidity) and the lack of sea breezes. Although there are crude shelters en route where you can rest in the shade (but not camp), they're not really suited for anything beyond catching your breath or waiting for torrential downpours to pass.

La Leona to Sirena

A 16km trail runs from the ranger station at **La Leona to Sirena** just inland from the beach, making it easy to keep your bearings. You can only walk its full length at low tide; if you do get stuck, the only thing to do is wait for the water to recede. If you can avoid problems with the tides, you should be able to do the walk in five to six hours, taking time to look out for birds. The walking can get a bit monotonous, but the beaches are uniformly lovely and deserted, and you are virtually guaranteed to spot a flock of **scarlet macaws** in the coastal trees. You will probably see (or hear) monkeys, too. Take lots of sunscreen, a big hat and at least five litres of water per person – the trail gets very hot, despite the sea breezes.

San Pedrillo to Sirena

Hikers and tour groups coming from the Bahía Drake area enter the park at the **San Pedrillo** ranger station, from where there are a few well-marked and short trails leading into the forest. The ranger station itself can be a good spot to see foraging wildlife, as there are several fruit trees within close proximity to it.

Corcovado's most heroic walk, all 25km of it, is from **San Pedrillo to Sirena**, the stretch along which you'll see the most impressive trees. It's a two-day trek, so you need a tent, sleeping bag and mosquito net, and you mustn't be worried by having to set up camp in the jungle. Fording the **Río Sirena**, just 1km before the Sirena ranger station, is the biggest obstacle: this is the deepest of all the rivers on the peninsula, with the strongest out-tow current, and has to be crossed with care, and at low tide only – **sharks** come in and out in search of food at high tide. Be sure to get the latest information from the San Pedrillo rangers before you set out.

The first half of the walk – a seven-hour stint – is in the jungle, just inland from the coast. Much of the rest of the hike is spent slogging it out on the beach, where the sand is more tightly packed than along the La Leona–Sirena stretch. Some hikers do the beach section of the walk well before dawn or after dark; there are fewer dangers (like snakes) at night on the beach and as long as you have a good torch with lots of batteries and/or the moon is out, this is a reasonable option.

Around Dos Brazos del Río Tigre

El Tigre ranger station, at the eastern inland entrance to the park near the tiny village (the population's just a little over 300) of **Dos Brazos del Río Tigre**, is a decent place to take breakfast or lunch with the ranger(s) before setting off on the local trails. In 2015 the **Sendero El Tigre** opened here, a potentially challenging, up-and-down, 7km loop known for its birdwatching. Ranger tours leave every hour from 5am to 11am (US$65–75; 5–6hr). The village itself boomed in the 1970s as a gold town, and small-scale panning for gold continues today.

ARRIVAL AND INFORMATION

Entry and reservations Unless you're coming as part of a tour, you must reserve several days in advance at least – the maximum is thirty days in advance – with SINAC (☏ 2735 5036, ✉ pncorcovado@gmail.com). You'll have to specify your group size and dates, plus any meals you require at Sirena (see box, p.392); it's possible to do all this via email or at the Oficina de Área de Conservación Osa office in Jiménez (see p.387), but you must arrange a guide before you contact SINAC. Incidentally, it's especially important when coming to Corcovado to brush up on your Spanish. You'll be asking the rangers for a lot of crucial information and few, if any, speak English. Bring a phrasebook if you're not fluent. Note that heavy rains can close the park, especially in Oct & Nov – if you've purchased tickets in advance there's no refund if this happens, and you cannot transfer/re-book your entry date.

Ranger stations All the ranger stations (daily 8am–4pm) have drinking water, information, toilets and telephone or radio-telephone contact. Visitor numbers are strictly controlled at Corcovado, so that the rangers at each station always know how many people are on a given trail, and how long they are expected to be (see box, p.392). If you are late getting back, they will go looking for you. This gives a measure of security but, all the same, take precautions.

PARQUE NACIONAL CORCOVADO

Always check with the rangers or ask around in Jiménez regarding current conditions.

La Leona It's a 45min–1hr walk (3.5km) across the Río Carate and along the beach from the village of Carate (see p.389) to the La Leona ranger station. Refreshments are available en route at the *La Leona Eco Lodge* (see p.394).

Los Patos The small hamlet of La Palma, 24km northwest of Puerto Jiménez, is the gateway to the Los Patos ranger station. It's a 12km walk from here to the park, much of it through hot lowland terrain (allow 4–5hr). A much more sensible idea, however – given the hike that awaits you in the park – is to try and arrange for a taxi in La Palma to take you as far as water levels on the bumpy dirt track will allow.

San Pedrillo Most people travelling to the San Pedrillo ranger station do so on a boat tour with one of the Bahía Drake lodges (see p.384). From Agujitas you can also follow the 17km trail to San Pedrillo (see p.393).

El Tigre To get here from Puerto Jiménez, drive 10km north and take the second left, a dirt track, signed to "El Tigre" and "Dos Brazos". A *colectivo* runs the 12km to Dos Brazos from Puerto Jiménez main street, just south of the police station (Mon–Fri 11am & 4pm; around ₡1300). Taxis charge US$25–30.

ACCOMMODATION

It's possible to **camp** within the park (at La Sirena) for a maximum of four nights; *La Leona Eco Lodge* is otherwise the closest accommodation to the park, with the options at Carate not far away (see p.390).

★ **Danta Corcovado Lodge** 8km from Los Patos ☏ 2735 1111, ⊚ dantalodge.com. If you want to begin the Los Patos hike early, this is an outstanding choice. A friendly, family-run lodge outside La Palma, *Danta* was built entirely from sustainable materials and features intricate woodwork and handmade furniture throughout. Accommodation is in attractive rooms or bungalows (sleeping up to three people) the latter 200m from the main lodge. Rates include breakfast; hearty lunches (US$12) and dinners (US$15) are served in the communal open-air dining area, where there is free wi-fi. They rent out horses for the 2hr trip to Los Patos and lead

several well-run tours in the area including kayaking in Golfo Dulce and night walks in their 70 hectares. Doubles US$110, bungalows US$140

La Leona Eco Lodge Just south of La Leona ranger station ☏ 2735 5705, ⊚ laleonaecolodge.com. Striking a balance between comfort and convenience, the *La Leona* complex of rustic-style tent *cabinas* (sleeping two) is set right on the beach just a short walk from the entrance to Parque Nacional Corcovado. Though they can get uncomfortably hot, the tents are well equipped and there's a very good restaurant (the price includes three meals a

WHAT TO SEE IN CORCOVADO

Chances are you'll have read much about Corcovado's unparalleled **biodiversity** before your arrival, but that does little to prepare you for the sheer scope of it when you step into the park. Suffice it to say, there is much to feast your eyes on in Corcovado.

PLANTS AND TREES

Walking through Corcovado you'll see many lianas, vines, mosses and spectacularly tall trees – some of them 50 or 60m high, and a few more than 80m high. All in all, Corcovado's area is home to about a quarter of all the tree species in the country, including the **silkwood** (or *Ceiba pentandra*), characterized by its height – it's thought to be the largest tree in Central America – and smooth grey bark. One silkwood, along the Río Llorona–San Pedrillo section of the San Pedrillo-to-Sirena trail, is over 80m high and 3m in diameter. You'll also notice huge **buttresses**: above-ground roots shot out by the silkwoods and other tall canopy species. These are used to help anchor the massive trees in thin tropical soil, where drainage is particularly poor.

MAMMALS

7

Corcovado supports a higher volume of **large mammals** than almost any other area of the country, except perhaps the wild and rugged Talamancas. **Jaguars** need more than 100 square kilometres each for their hunting; if you are a good tracker you may be able to spot their traces within the park, especially in the fresh mud along trails and riverbeds. Initially they look identical to those made by a large dog, but the four toes are of unequal size (the outermost one is the smallest) and the fore footprint should be wider than its length. You might, too, see the **margay**, a spotted wildcat about the size of a large domesticated house cat, which comes down from the forest to sun itself on rocks at midday. The **ocelot**, a larger spotted cat, is even shyer, rarely seen for more than a second, poking its head out of the dense cover and then melting away into the forest again immediately.

With a body shape somewhere between a large pig and a cow, the **Baird's tapir** is an odd-looking animal, most immediately recognizable for its funny-looking snout, a truncated elephant-type trunk. Tapirs are very shy – and have been made even more so through large-scale hunting – though you stand a reasonable chance of spotting one crossing the clearing at Sirena's airfield. More threatening are the packs of white-lipped **peccaries**, a type of wild pig; in Corcovado they typically group themselves in packs of about thirty. They are often seen along the trails and should be treated with caution, since they can bite you. The accepted wisdom is to climb a tree if they come at you threateningly, clacking their jaws and growling, though this, of course, means you have to be good at climbing trees, some of which have painful spines.

More common mammals that you'll likely spot include the ubiquitous **agouti**, foraging in the underbrush. Essentially a large rodent with smooth, glossy hair, the agouti looks similar to a large squirrel. The **coati**, a member of the racoon family, with a long ringed tail, is also sure to cross your path. Another mammal found in significant numbers in the park – and all over the peninsula – is the **tayra** (tolumuco), a small and swift mink-like creature. They will in most cases run from you, but should not be approached, as they have teeth and can be aggressive.

BIRDS

Among Corcovado's resident **birds** is the **scarlet macaw**, around 300 of which live in the park – more, in terms of birds per square kilometre, than anywhere else in the country. Macaws are highly prized as caged birds and, despite the efforts of the park authorities, poaching is still a problem here, as their (relative) abundance makes them easy prey. Around the Río Sirena estuary, especially, keep an eye out for the **boat-billed heron**, whose wide bill gives it a lopsided quality. The big black **king vulture** can also be found in Corcovado; a forager rather than a hunter, it nevertheless looks quite ominous. There are many other smaller birds in Corcovado including, perhaps, the fluffy-headed **harpy eagle**. Though the harpy is thought to be extinct in Costa Rica, ornithologists reckon there's a chance that a few pairs still live in Corcovado, and in the Parque Internacional La Amistad on the Talamanca coast.

day). The lodge also offers a range of tours including crocodile-spotting, night hikes and abseiling. Shared bathroom US$110, private bathroom US$148

Sirena Ranger Station You can sleep in the no-frills accommodation block at Sirena ranger station, renovated in 2016, which has hot water showers (with soap provided but no towels). Accommodation now comprises dorm-like cabins with mosquito nets, bedding, pillows and mattresses. Meals are offered at designated times and it is now mandatory to purchase these in advance (you cannot cook your own food, but you can bring in cold food); breakfast costs US$20, while lunch and dinner each cost US$25. There is intermittent wi-fi (free), while lockers are US$4/day. Lights off at 8pm sharp. Per person US$30

Golfito and the far south

The only town of any real size in the far south, **Golfito** has a dramatic setting on the **Golfo Dulce**, one of the deepest gulfs of its size in the world and a major hotspot for **sportfishing** (the Pacific sailfish is the main target). It's an oddly attractive place, despite the incessant rain and lack of traditional sights, and it makes for a good base to explore the nearby **Parque Nacional Piedras Blancas**, whose dense interior is home to many of the country's signature mammals and birds, as well as the region's burgeoning **ecolodge** scene. South of Golfito, well off the road to Panama, are a couple of Costa Rica's most isolated – and most alluring – beaches, **Playa Zancudo** and **Playa Pavones**.

Golfito

Created in 1938, the former banana port of **GOLFITO**, some 50km north of the Panamanian border, straggles for over 6km along the bay of the same name (*golfito* means "little gulf"). The town's setting is spectacular, backed up against steep, densely forested hills to the east, and with the glorious Golfo Dulce to the west. The low shadow of the Península de Osa shimmers in the distance, and everywhere the vegetation has the soft, muted look of the undisturbed tropics – toucans and other colourful birds frolic in the palms along the main street. Indeed, with its distinctive wooden, clapboard **tropical architecture** Golfito has plenty of down-at-heel charm – it's definitely not a tourist town. Most buildings retain their red tin roofs and wide verandas, painted in bright, if sun-bleached, colours, with huge screens and sun canopies – it sometimes feels like a colonial outpost in the South Pacific (or a dilapidated Key West). It is also very **rainy**; even if you speak no Spanish, you'll certainly pick up the local expression *va a caer baldazos* – "it's gonna pour". The **Paseo Marino Golfito** project is an ambitious beautification programme that will transform the waterfront in the coming years (the plush Golfito Marina Village is expected to be complete in 2019), though a huge tourist influx seems unlikely; the developers are primarily hoping to attract "gigayacht" owners.

The Zona Americana

Golfito is split into several sections, with the northwestern end containing the airport and the old **Zona Americana**, where the banana company executives (the *bananeros*) used to live and where better-off residents still keep beautiful hardwood houses shaded by dignified palms. Here you'll find the **Depósito Libre** (Tues 8am–3.30pm, Wed–Sat 8am–4.30pm, Sun 7am–3pm; free to look around), a bizarrely incongruous duty-free mall of around sixty stalls ringed by a circular concrete wall (see box opposite). The souvenir trinket stalls and *sodas* in front of the main complex (where all local buses terminate) are mildly diverting but the market itself is unlikely to excite foreign visitors (unless you want to buy and ship a flatscreen TV). There's little else to see other than some photogenic **old homes** and the local campus of **Universidad de Costa Rica** (UCA), which features especially attractive stilt buildings and neat, tropical clapboard huts.

Pueblo Civil

Some 4km to the southeast of the Depósito, the **Pueblo Civil** (civilian town), is a smaller, tight nest of streets – hotter, noisier and generally more crowded than the *zona*, but still featuring the same, attractive wooden housing (beyond the main road). It's here you'll find the *lancha* to Puerto Jiménez, the post office, some decent supermarkets and a handful of basic *sodas*, as well as Golfito's no-frills (and generally seedy) local bars.

Playa Cacao

Less than 1km from Golfito across the bay • Water taxis (around ₡2000) depart to the beach from the *muellecito* (ferry dock) just north of the petrol station (on demand). In the dry season, you can drive there along a rough unfinished track from the turn-off right in front of the police post, bearing left, but you need a 4WD

Despite lining Bahía de Golfito, Golfito doesn't exactly have the kinds of beaches you might be hoping for. The one beach worth spending an afternoon on, **PLAYA CACAO**, is across the bay. It has good swimming and a number of decent bars and restaurants nearby, although the beach itself is a little grimy. If you eat at the decent *Restaurante Playa Cacao* (daily 9am–10pm; ☎8886 8362), call ahead and their boat will pick you up from and drop you back to Golfito's *muellecito* for free.

7

ARRIVAL AND DEPARTURE

GOLFITO

By plane You can fly here with both Sansa and NatureAir; the airstrip is in the Zona Americana, a short walk or taxi ride (₡800–1500) from any hotel in town.

Destinations via NatureAir Puerto Jiménez (1 daily; 10min); San José (1–2 daily; 40min).

Destinations via Sansa San José (3–4 daily; 1hr).

By bus Buses to/from San José depart/terminate at the Tracopa ticket office (☎2775 0365) at the southern end of the Pueblo Civil (in front of the fire station or "Estación de los Bomberos"), with two services daily (5am & 1.30pm), plus an extra 2pm departure on Sun. Buses to Playa Pavones (daily 10am & 1pm) – where you can get onward transport to Zancudo – depart the bus stop in front of

Golfito Hospital in the Zona Americana, but the buses also stop along the main street (5–10min later at the *muellecito*), as do local buses to Ciudad Neily and Río Claro (where there are more through-buses along the Interamericana).

Destinations Ciudad Neily (hourly; 1hr); Playa Pavones (2 daily; 2hr 30min–3hr); San José (2–3 daily; 7hr).

By boat The ferry pier is known as the *muellecito*, at the centre of the Pueblo Civil; the only scheduled service is to Puerto Jiménez (35min; ₡3000); Mon–Fri 7am, 10am, 11.30am, 1pm, 3pm & 5pm, Sat 7.30am, 10am, 1pm, 3pm & 5pm, Sun 10am, 1pm & 3pm. *Lanchas* return from Jiménez just as regularly (see p.387). Always

UNITED BRANDS ("LA YUNAI")

Golfito's history is inextricably linked with the giant transnational **United Brands** (later the United Fruit Company and now Chiquita), which first set up in the area in 1938, twenty years before the Interamericana hit town. The company – known locally as "La Yunai" – built schools, recruited doctors and police and brought prosperity to the area, though "problems" with labour union organizers began soon afterwards, and came to characterize the relationship between company and town. What with fluctuating banana prices, a three-month strike by workers and local social unrest, the company eventually decided Golfito was too much trouble and pulled out in a hurry in 1985. The town declined and, in the public eye, became synonymous with rampant unemployment, alcoholism, abandoned children, prostitution and general unruliness.

Today, **tourism** and a growing **palm oil industry** have combined to help revive the local economy. Many visitors come to Golfito because it's a good base for getting to the Parque Nacional Corcovado by *lancha* or plane, and also a major **sportfishing** centre. The real rescue, though, came from the Costa Rican government, who in 1990 established a **Depósito Libre** – or tax-free mall – in the town, where Costa Ricans can buy all sorts of goods (clothing, kitchen appliances, booze and home electronics) imported from Panama without the 100 percent tax normally levied. Ticos (and anyone else) who come to shop here have to buy their tickets for the Depósito 24 hours in advance, obliging them to spend at least one night, and therefore colones, in Golfito. You can browse the market for free, but to buy you must have completed the paperwork (which involves committing to how much you want to spend).

check the current schedule before making plans. Make sure your boat has lifejackets on board: the Golfo Dulce is usually calm, but winds can come up suddenly, causing unexpectedly high waves.

By car Central Golfito lies 22km off the Interamericana at the busy junction town of Río Claro, via the well-maintained Hwy-14 (the drive takes just over 1hr from

Palmar Sur). There's a potentially faster, unsurfaced road, that runs just 12km to Golfito from the Interamericana (there's a small signpost) via the village of La Gamba and comes in from the northwest (past the airport) – saving 24km coming from the north. This route can be rough going, however, and dangerous in wet weather (normal cars can otherwise make it).

GETTING AROUND

By bus/colectivo Local buses (₡200) cruise up and down the main drag all the way to the Depósito around every hour during the day (look for the bus shelters); you can also hail red minivan *colectivos* that zip between the Depósito and Río Claro (at the Interamericana), but they

charge ₡750 for any distance.

By taxi Taxis tend to charge just ₡800–1500 for trips within town; hail them in the street (red cars) or call Cooperativa de Los Taxistas de Golfito (☎ 2775 1170).

INFORMATION

There is an official tourist information centre at the *muellecito* (Mon–Fri 8am–5pm; ☎ 2775 0349) run by the local chamber of commerce (CATUGOLFO), usually with

English-speakers, which can provide local bus and ferry timetables; Tierra Mar is another capable stand-in for area information (see p.400).

ACCOMMODATION

Much of Golfito's accommodation is **basic and inexpensive**, catering to Costa Ricans visiting the Depósito Libre, though there are a couple of slightly smarter hotels too. Be warned that the sheer number of people coming to Golfito to shop, especially at Christmas, means that rooms are often booked in advance – if you don't have reservations, try to get to town as early in the day as possible.

IN TOWN

Cabinas Princesa del Golfo Opposite the Banco Nacional on Hwy-14 ☎ 2775 0442. Small and friendly

with pleasantly decorated, good-value rooms that have a/c and free wi-fi. US$40

Casa Roland Golfito Resort C 4, Zona Americana

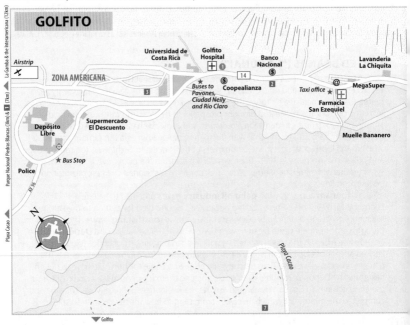

GOLFITO

☎ 2775 0180, ⊛ casarolandgolfito.com. The best hotel in town, with a lovely pool, bar and restaurant. Rooms are comfortable, with wooden beds, tiled floors, a/c and cable TV, though they (and the dimly-lit corridors) tend to be a little dark. $\overline{\text{US\$100}}$

Mar y Luna Hwy-14 (waterfront) at the southern entrance to town ☎ 2775 0192, ⊛ marylunagolfito .com. Good-value waterside hotel, with bare-bones but adequate standard rooms (with free wi-fi, cable TV, a/c and hot shower). $\overline{\text{US\$53}}$

Samoa del Sur On the main street (Hwy-14) between the Zona Americana and the Pueblo Civil ☎ 2775 0233, ⊛ samoadelsur.com. Fourteen spacious but slightly gloomy rooms on the waterfront, with a large and rather raucous boat-shaped bar-restaurant (see p.400). $\overline{\text{US\$85}}$

AROUND GOLFITO

★ **Esquinas Rainforest Lodge** La Gamba, about 7km from Km37 on the Interamericana ☎ 2741 8001, ⊛ esquinaslodge.com. Friendly ecolodge, originally funded by Austria's government – all profits go to the local community. It's set in primary rainforest, with resident wildlife and on-site hiking and horseriding trails leading into Parque Nacional Piedras Blancas. The fourteen pleasantly rustic rooms have ceiling fans and private bathrooms and are adorned with textiles crafted by local indigenous artisans. There's also a roomy jungle villa set off from the main lodge that can accommodate four. A wide range of packages is available and three fantastic meals a day are included in the room rate. Per person $\overline{\text{US\$135}}$

Ka'Kau Jungle Cabinas Playa Cacao ☎ 8583 2899, ⊛ todocontento.com. Indigenous-styled, thatched-roof mountaintop *cabinas* with pretty views of the bay. Though simply furnished, they're very comfortable (fans, but no a/c) and there's a communal dining area. Jungle walks and dolphin-watching boat trips are also available. Breakfast included. $\overline{\text{US\$45}}$

La Purruja Lodge 4km south of Golfito towards the Interamericana ☎ 2775 5054, ⊛ purruja.com. Small family-run hotel set in lovely gardens, with spacious bungalows (sleeping 2–3 and with cold-water showers and ceiling fan), a basic dorm, a campsite and a pool. Good choice if you have a car. Breakfast is US\$6 extra. Cash only. Camping/person $\overline{\text{US\$4}}$, dorms $\overline{\text{US\$10}}$, bungalows $\overline{\text{US\$35}}$

7

EATING

Golfito has plenty of decent places to eat. For **casados** and **platos del día** there are several groups of simple **sodas**: one near the Depósito Libre, and another, slightly better-value cluster on the main drag of the Pueblo Civil and in the surrounding streets. A Pearson Supermercado (Mon–Sat 7am–7pm, Sun 7am–6pm) is located on the main street in the Pueblo Civil. Further north there's a MegaSuper (daily 6am–9pm), near fresh fruit stalls and a bakery. Be wary of entering any bar with a sign positioned outside so that you can't see in, as these tend to be the haunt of local prostitutes.

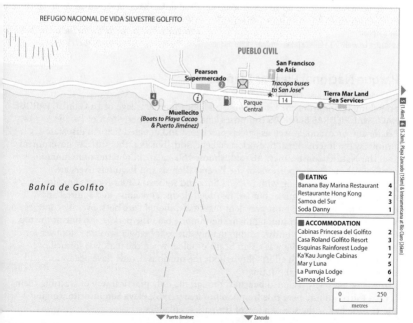

REFUGIO NACIONAL DE VIDA SILVESTRE GOLFITO

PUEBLO CIVIL

San Francisco de Asís

Pearson Supermercado

Tracopa buses to San José

Tierra Mar Land Sea Services

Muellecito
(Boats to Playa Cacao & Puerto Jiménez)

Parque Central

Bahía de Golfito

Puerto Jiménez Zancudo

EATING
Banana Bay Marina Restaurant	4
Restaurante Hong Kong	2
Samoa del Sur	3
Soda Danny	1

ACCOMMODATION
Cabinas Princesa del Golfito	2
Casa Roland Golfito Resort	3
Esquinas Rainforest Lodge	1
Ka'Kau Jungle Cabinas	7
Mar y Luna	5
La Purruja Lodge	6
Samoa del Sur	4

0   250
metres

ACTIVITIES AND TOURS IN GOLFITO

If you're in Golfito to **sportfish**, the larger hotels can help arrange tours and tackle – the area is particularly rich in marlin and sailfish. **Swimming** is no good, however, as the bay is polluted, and you'll see oil in the water and various bits of floating refuse all around Golfito. Your best bet for a swim is to head across to Playa Cacao (see p.397), or to move south towards the Península Burica.

Tierra Mar Land Sea Services On the waterfront, next to Banana Bay Marina (☎ 2775 1614, ⓦ golfitocostarica.com). As well as leading a variety of tours around Golfo Dulce, including horseriding and boat trips to the beaches at Parque Nacional Piedras Blancas, jungle hikes, panning for gold and cave exploration, as well as *lanchas* to Playa Zancudo. Costs are competitive, but you'll get a much better price if you gather a group together (from US$50 for up to six people).

Banana Bay Marina Restaurant On the main street (Hwy-14) at the southern end of town ☎ 2775 0003, ⓦ bananabaymarinagolfito.com. Pricey but atmospheric spot right on the water, perfect for watching sunsets and sipping cocktails, with a menu of straightforward but tasty gringo favourites such as chargrilled burgers, club sandwiches, steaks and the like (mains from ₡3000). Daily 6am–10pm.

Restaurante Hong Kong Pueblo Civil ☎ 2775 2383. Renowned for its excellent (and cheap) chow mein dishes (from ₡3000) and a magnet for expat yachters: despite the completely forgettable interior, it serves up some of the best Chinese food to be found in the south. Daily 11am–10pm.

Samoa del Sur On the main street (Hwy-14) between the Zona Americana and the Pueblo Civil ☎ 2775 0233, ⓦ samoadelsur.com. The beachside bar and restaurant at the *Samoa del Sur* hotel (see p.399) is a pleasant spot for an evening beer or meal, with a menu featuring seafood, such as ceviche (₡7000), and pizza (₡3000–5000). Bear in mind that it can get rowdy later in the evening (it's the bar of choice for US marines on shore leave). Daily 11am–midnight.

Soda Danny On the main street, next to the hospital ☎ 2775 0270. No-frills canteen next to the hospital, offering superb-value *casados* for just ₡2500 (chicken, rice-and-beans, salad, plantain). There are no menus, and the staff speak basic English. Daily 11am–10pm.

DIRECTORY

Banks and exchange The Banco Nacional (Mon–Fri 8.30am–3.30pm; ☎ 2775 1101) changes money and has an ATM; there's also an ATM at the Coopealianza opposite the hospital.

Laundry Lavandería La Chinita (Mon–Fri 7am–4pm) on the main street between the Zona Americana and the Pueblo Civil.

Medical services Golfito Hospital is in the Zona Americana (☎ 2775 7800).

Post office Right in the centre of the Pueblo Civil (Mon–Fri 7.30am–5pm, Sat 8am–noon; ☎ 2775 1911).

Parque Nacional Piedras Blancas

3km north of Golfito • Daily 8am–4pm • US$10 • ☎ 2775 2620

Stretching inland from the Golfo Dulce and abutting the village of La Gamba, **PARQUE NACIONAL PIEDRAS BLANCAS** comprises land that was formerly part of Parque Nacional Corcovado, as well as parcels purchased and donated by such disparate entities as the international hydroelectric behemoth Tenaska, the Austrian government and The Nature Conservancy. All told, almost 150 square kilometres of mountainous rainforest, beaches and portions of the Piedras Blancas and Esquinas rivers are protected, an area teeming with tropical flora and some of Costa Rica's signature **mammals**, including jaguars, pumas, two-toed sloths, kinkajous, and squirrel and capuchin monkeys. The most prevalent mammals, though, are **bats**: over fifty species have been observed here, among them the vampire bat. The park is also one of the top spots in the country for birdwatching, mainly due to it being a favoured stopover for **migrating birds**. Poaching was a significant problem when the park was formed over two decades ago, though efforts throughout the previous decade have been successful in greatly reducing illegal hunting.

The park has a few secluded **beaches**, though the only practical way of reaching them is on a thirty-minute boat ride from Golfito (see p.396). **Playa San Josecito**, ringing a pretty little bay, is the site of a few of the park's ecolodges.

PARQUE NACIONAL PIEDRAS BLANCAS

The park has a few, somewhat difficult to reach, access points; your best bet is to enter from *Esquinas Rainforest Lodge* (see p.399) in La Gamba, where you can make arrangements for a guide to lead you through the forest. Book any of the accommodation in advance and you'll be picked up by *lancha* from Golfito.

ACCOMMODATION

Dolphin Quest Playa San Josecito ☎8811 2099, Ⓦdolphinquestcr.com. This secluded ecolodge has a range of accommodation, from spacious dormitory rooms to private *cabinas* (sleeping up to three) to a small house that sleeps four. The lodge's extensive grounds are wedged between the ocean and dense rainforest crisscrossed by a network of trails. Between periods of lazing about in a hammock, you'll find plenty of activities and tours to keep you occupied, from snorkelling and kayaking to horseriding and fishing. Three-night minimum; all prices are per person, and include meals and boat transfers from Golfito. Dorms and *cabinas* U̲S̲$̲7̲5̲, house U̲S̲$̲9̲0̲

Golfo Dulce Lodge Playa San Josecito ☎8821 5398, Ⓦgolfodulcelodge.com. This Swiss-run ecolodge is surrounded by the undisturbed primary rainforest of Parque Nacional Piedras Blancas. There are three standard rooms as well as five posher detached wooden bungalows (sleeping 3 people) named after local wildlife, each with private veranda with hammocks. A thatched restaurant, nearby observation platform and a small freshwater pool are also in the grounds. Three-night minimum stay; all prices per person, with meals included (boat transfers US$30 return from Golfito). Doubles U̲S̲$̲1̲0̲5̲, bungalows U̲S̲$̲1̲3̲0̲

★**Playa Nicuesa Rainforest Lodge** Playa Nicuesa ☎2258 8250, Ⓦnicuesalodge.com. Owners Michael and Donna go the distance to welcome guests to the jungle at this nature retreat, adventure camp and all-inclusive resort. A model of sustainability, the lodge offers spectacular ocean and forest views from private verandas and the treetop bar. Hit the beach for kayaking, snorkelling, fishing and sailing or let a resident naturalist guide you to a nearby waterfall. All meals included, plus return transfer from Golfito or Puerto Jiménez. U̲S̲$̲4̲9̲0̲

Playa Zancudo

15km southeast of Golfito

Ask anyone in Golfito where you can swim, and they'll direct you to black-sand **PLAYA ZANCUDO**, 15km southeast of Golfito, facing the Golfo Dulce and bordered on one side by the Río Coto Colorado. On summer weekends from December to April, Playa Zancudo fills with Zona Sur Ticos taking a beach break, but otherwise it's fairly low-key, except for a small colony of mainly US foreign residents. There are a couple of professional **sportfishing** outfits, while other local activities include **surfing** and **boat trips** along the Río Coto.

ARRIVAL AND DEPARTURE

PLAYA ZANCUDO

By bus Buses to Zancudo depart Golfito daily at 10am and 3pm (1hr 45min), but schedules often change, so check with your hotel before making plans. Buses return at 5am and 12.30pm.

By boat You can reach Zancudo from Golfito by a *lancha* that departs the *muellecito* at noon and returns at 7am (Mon–Sat; around ₡4000) or via private water taxi (30–40min). Zancudo Boat Tours (Ⓦloscocos.com /boattours.htm) will take you for US$20/person (US$60

minimum). *Lanchas* arrive at the boat dock at the northern end of the beach.

By car/taxi Driving to Zancudo takes about 1hr 30min from Golfito, a trip shortened by the building of a bridge in 2010 over the Río Coto (it's all dirt roads after the bridge). You need a 4WD, whatever time of year; during the wet season it's worth checking the levels of the creeks and fords that you'll have to pass before you set out. Taxis charge around US$75 from Golfito (1–2hr).

ACCOMMODATION

Cabinas Los Cocos On the northern half of the spit ☎2776 0012, Ⓦloscocos.com. Pretty, well-equipped *cabinas* (sleeping 2–3) – each with kitchen, fridge, screens, fans and hammocks – surrounded by dense tropical foliage and steps from the beach. Bikes, kayaks, bodyboards and beach chairs are available for guests. They also lead a few boat tours (from US$50), including along the Río Coto. U̲S̲$̲7̲5̲

Sol y Mar About 25m from the boat dock ☎2776 0014, Ⓦzancudo.com. Five groovy, screened cabins in a garden by a wide section of the beach, each with fans, hot showers and free wi-fi. They offer sportfishing outings and boat trips through the mangrove swamps of the Río Coto and serve gourmet French cuisine at their restaurant. The bar is usually a hive of activity and is the site of popular volleyball competitions on Saturday afternoons. Camping is also allowed (with access to showers included). Camping/person U̲S̲$̲4̲, cabins U̲S̲$̲4̲5̲

7

Playa Pavones

About 12km south of Playa Zancudo is **PLAYA PAVONES**, famed among surfers for having one of the **longest continuous waves in the world** – a pointbreak gem that is said to offer up to three-minute rides. The waves are inconsistent, however – they tend to be at their biggest and best from May to November. Needless to say, the water's usually too rough for anything else and, though tourism is mushrooming around Pavones, the community here still largely consists of avid surfers. Not surprisingly, most of the services cater to them as well, and there are the requisite surf camps and surf shops and just about every one of the many lodges around the beach offers lessons. Regardless of the pull the waves exert on you, the hamlet has a palpable end-of-the-road charm all its own, with its breezy dirt roads and all-round welcoming air.

ARRIVAL AND DEPARTURE
PLAYA PAVONES

By bus Two buses depart daily for Pavones from in front of the hospital in Golfito (10am & 3pm; return to Golfito at 5.15am & 12.45pm; 1hr 45min–2hr).

By boat You can hire a private water taxi in Golfito to the beach (about 1hr 15min) for around US$140, but if the waves are rough, landing can be dangerous.

By car/taxi Driving to Pavones takes just under 2hr from Golfito; a 4WD is recommended, especially in wet season. Taxis from Golfito charge around US$75.

ACCOMMODATION AND EATING

★**Castillo de Pavones** In the hills above Pavones, about a 5min walk to the beach ⓦ castillodepavones .com. Fashioning itself as a jungle castle, this bold, intimate property is marked by stunning design throughout and very reasonable rates. The four stately rooms all have attractive furnishings and a full range of high-end amenities, including king-size beds, a/c, wi-fi and hot tubs overlooking the sea. The rooftop split-level restaurant and lounge delivers panoramic views and some of the finest meals in the Zona Sur, all with organic ingredients. There's a long list of tours to choose from, such as horseriding, as well as yoga classes; surfboards are included in the rate. US$141

La Manta On the main road ☎ 2776 2281. Cavernous, thatched-roof restaurant exuding cool, and a popular hangout spot throughout the day, thanks in no small part to its excellent sound system and movie showings on a massive screen. The menu is full of crowd-pleasers like burgers, burritos and fish tacos, all nicely prepared and boosted by home-grown spices (mains ₡4000–7500). Daily 10am–midnight.

★**Tiskita Lodge** Punta Banco, 10km south of Playa Pavones ☎ 2296 8125, ⓦ tiskita.com. This extremely comfortable rainforest lodge (which doubles as a biological research station) has nine cabins with a total of 17 rooms overlooking the beach and a swimming pool on the grounds. Trails weave through the surrounding forest and the birdwatching is good. You can also tour their fruit farm (the owner is an agronomist). They offer good-value packages that include guided hikes and three high-quality meals a day. Three-night minimum stay; all prices per person. US$207

Towards the Panama border

At Palmar, travellers heading south face a choice: most people intent on the quickest route to Panama stick to the Interamericana, which heads south for the final 100km to border. This section of the trip down to the **Paso Canoas** border crossing is through an empty, featureless, frontier region, with the refuelling stop of **Ciudad Neily** the only point of minor interest.

The alternative route is to head east along the Interamericana instead of south, in which direction it switchbacks its way to the small, sleepy town of **Paso Real**, 20km away, following the wide and fast-running **Río Grande de Térraba** as it cuts a giant path through the almost unbearably hot lowland landscape, its banks coloured red with tropical soils. Rainstorms seem to steamroll in with the express purpose of washing everything away, and you can almost see the river rise with each fresh torrent. This stretch is prone to landslides in the rainy season, after which you can find yourself stranded in a sea of mud.

At Paso Real, you can pick up the paved **Hwy-237**, which takes you south through some spectacularly scenic country. Steep and winding, with beautiful views, it is little used by tourists except those few heading to the pretty mountain town of **San Vito**, the jumping-off point for the **Wilson Botanical Garden, Parque Internacional La Amistad** and the **Río Sereno** border crossing. Even though the roads around here have improved, it's much easier with a 4WD to deal with occasional washouts and landslides, especially from May to November.

San Vito

Settled largely by post-World War II immigrants from Italy, **SAN VITO** is a prosperous agricultural town with a lovely setting in the Talamancas. At nearly 1000m above sea level it has a wonderfully refreshing climate, as well as great views over the Valle de Coto Brus below. The town is growing as more and more Costa Ricans discover its qualities, though there's not much to do in San Vito itself – the nearby **Wilson Botanical Garden** provides the principal diversion in the area.

7

ARRIVAL AND DEPARTURE
SAN VITO

By bus Tracopa (☎2221 4214) buses stop 25m east of Hwy-237, in the centre of town.

Destinations Ciudad Neily, for buses to Panama border and Golfito (9 daily; 1hr 40min); San José (6 daily; 6hr).

ACCOMMODATION

★**Casa Botania** Hwy-237, 5km southeast of San Vito ☎2773 4217, ⓦcasabotaniabedand breakfast.com. This eye-catching B&B, run by a young Costa Rican and Belgian couple, is full of individual touches that make a stay here feel like a real treat, from ornate wood furnishings to a superb design that's harmonious with the surrounding countryside. The understated rooms and bungalows (sleeping 2–4, each with a private terrace) exude class, and superb meals are served in an open-air dining area with striking valley views. A real bargain for the rate. Rooms/small bungalows US$75

Wilson Botanical Garden

Hwy-237, 6km south of San Vito • Daily 7am–5pm • US$10 • **Tours** Daily 5.30–7.30am, 7.30–9.30am & 7–9pm; advance reservations essential; US$30–40 • ☎2773 4004, ⓦ ots.ac.cr

The **Wilson Botanical Garden**, operated by the Organization for Tropical Studies at their Las Cruces Biological Station, is among the best in Central America – it was designed by famous Brazilian landscape architect Roberto Burle Marx in the 1960s. The gardens are home to over two thousand native plant species, including orchids and heliconias as well as several hundred endemic trees such as palms, ferns and massive bamboo. Resident biologists lead guided **tours** along the large network of paths that wind through the meticulously laid out garden, which is also primate habitat for numerous **butterfly** species; the sight of dozens of vibrantly coloured butterflies fluttering about within a couple of feet can be mesmerizing. **Bats** are common too, but aside from the tropical flora, perhaps the biggest draw is the hundreds of resident and migrating **bird** species, making this one of the country's top birdwatching spots. The highlight is the 15-metre tall **Canopy Tower**, affording expansive views of the jungle and mountains in the far distance.

THE RÍO SERENO BORDER CROSSING

Four buses daily trundle east of San Vito (departing San Vito at 7am, 10am, 1pm & 4pm; 30min) along Hwy-613 to the **Río Sereno border crossing** (daily 8am–5pm; ☎2784 0130) and into Panama. Ask the driver to drop you off at the Costa Rican *migración* to avoid walking up a hill with your bags: after clearing customs, you can walk to Panama's *migración*; few nationalities require a visa (see box, p.75). Once in Río Sereno on the Panamanian side, walk down the main street to the bus station at the street's end. From here you can catch a bus that will take you on to David and La Concepción.

ACCOMMODATION   **WILSON BOTANICAL GARDEN**

Las Cruces Biological Field Station Cabinas On a loop road off the main entrance road ☏ 2773 4004, ⊕ ots.ac.cr. You can stay at the gardens in comfortable *cabinas* (sleeping 2–3) with private bathroom and floor-to-ceiling windows. You can opt for just bed and breakfast, or three meals a day (US$95); make reservations in advance. Per person US$62

Parque Internacional La Amistad

Main entrance 25km north of San Vito • Daily 8am–4pm • US$10 • ☏ 2200 5355

Created in 1982 as a biosphere reserve, the **PARQUE INTERNACIONAL LA AMISTAD** is a joint venture by the governments of Panama and Costa Rica to protect the Cordillera de Talamanca on both sides of their shared border. Amistad also encompasses several **indigenous reserves**, the most geographically isolated in the country, where Bribrí and Cabécar peoples are able to live with minimal interference from the Valle Central. It is the largest park in the country, covering 2070 square kilometres of Costa Rican territory.

In 1983 Amistad was designated a **World Heritage Site**, thanks to its immense scientific resources. The Central American isthmus is often described as being a crossroads or filter for the meeting of the North and South American eco-communities; the Amistad area is itself a "biological bridge" within the isthmus, where an extraordinary number of habitats, life zones, topographical features, soils, terrains and types of animal and plant life can be found. Its **terrain**, while mainly mountainous, is extremely varied on account of shifting altitudes, and ranges from wet tropical forest to high peaks where the temperature can drop below freezing at night. According to the classification system devised by L.R. Holdridge (see p.421), Amistad has at least seven (some say eight or nine) **life zones**, along with six transition zones. Even more important is Amistad's function as the last bastion of some of the species most in danger of **extinction** in both Costa Rica and the isthmus. Within its boundaries roam the jaguar and the puma, the ocelot and the tapir. Along with Corcovado on the Península de Osa, Amistad may also be the last holdout of the **harpy eagle**, feared extinct in Costa Rica.

Trails in the park

Its rugged terrain limits access to much of the park, but there are two **trails** that depart from the Altamira ranger station (see opposite). If you're hiking solo, your only option is the **Gigantes del Bosque** trail, a 3km-long round-route that meanders through mostly primary rainforest. There are two towers along the way, the first of which is ideal for **birdwatching**, particularly just after daybreak, the best time to see some of the four hundred species that live in the park. The path is reasonably well marked, but not always maintained, and tall grass often grows over parts of the latter half of the trail: allow 2–3hr to make the loop.

Much longer and far more exhausting is the **Valle del Silencio** trail, which is 20km long and provides an excellent introduction to the varied habitats found in La Amistad. The trail climbs steadily to a campsite on a flat ridge near the base of Cerro Kamuk (3549m), offering stunning vistas of the park and further afield en route. There's a good chance of spotting **wildlife** along the way, possibly including quetzals and Baird's tapirs, the latter of which are thought to have larger populations here than anywhere else in the country. The trail takes about 8–10hr (return) and you cannot hike it without a **guide**; the park ranger at the Altamira station can make arrangements.

ARRIVAL AND INFORMATION   **PARQUE INTERNACIONAL LA AMISTAD**

By car Due to rough and unpredictable road conditions, the only reliable way to reach the Altamira ranger station is by car. From San Vito, head 27km north on Hwy-237 to Guácimo. From there turn onto a dirt road for about 17km through the village of El Carmen. 3km past El Carmen turn onto a dirt road that leads to Altamira.

Tourist information The small hamlet of Altamira functions as the park headquarters, with a nearby ranger station maintained by a full-time ranger who can provide information. The ranger station, 2km outside the village, is signposted from the centre.

ACCOMMODATION

Altamira Ranger Station 2km from Altamira. You can camp or stay in a spartan dorm room at the ranger station, where there are shower and toilet facilities as well as a small picnic area. Camping/dorms U̲S̲$̲6̲

Ciudad Neily

If you're making your way south to the Paso Canoas border crossing, soporific **CIUDAD NEILY** makes a good spot to stock up on any last-minute supplies before you cross into Panama (18km away). Though it is one of the largest towns in the southern third of the country and the point where the Interamericana and Hwy-237 converge, there's not much to detain you and chances are you'll pass through it quickly en route to Panama. Hwy-237 runs right down the middle of Ciudad Neily, before ending at the Interamericana; all the town's services are within a couple of blocks either side of it.

ARRIVAL AND DEPARTURE CIUDAD NEILY

By bus Buses arrive at Terminal Tracopa (☏ 2221 4214), a couple of blocks uphill and east of Hwy-237 in the centre of town.
Destinations Paso Canoas (daily every 30min 6.30am– 11.30pm; 30min); Puerto Jiménez (2 daily; 3hr); San Isidro de El General (10 daily; 4hr); San José (6 daily; 7hr); San Vito (9 daily; 1hr 40min).

ACCOMMODATION

Hotel Andrea ☏ 2783 3784. If you need to stay overnight, make a beeline for the pretty *Hotel Andrea*, just west of the bus terminal, which has comfortable rooms with fans or a/c and an open-air restaurant that serves hearty and inexpensive *comida típica* meals. U̲S̲$̲5̲5̲

DIRECTORY

Banks and exchange Theres a Banco de Costa Rica (Mon–Fri 9am–4pm) just off Hwy-237 in the centre of town and a Banco Nacional (Mon–Fri 8.30am–3.45pm) branch a few blocks north (both branches have ATMs).

Supermarket The biggest supermarket in Ciudad Neily (and surely all of southern Costa Rica) is the Supermercado Hermanos Loaiza (daily 6am–8.45pm), a block northeast of the Banco Nacional.

THE PASO CANOAS BORDER CROSSING

Duty-free shops and stalls start to line the Interamericana 17km southeast of Ciudad Neily, announcing the approach to **Paso Canoas border crossing** (usually open daily 6am–10pm; ☏ 2732 2150). As you come into town you'll pass the Costa Rican customs *migración*, next to the Tracopa bus terminal, where everybody gets a going-over. Foreigners don't attract much interest, though; customs officials are far more concerned with nabbing Ticos coming back over the border with unauthorized amounts of bargain consumer goods. You'll have to wait in line, especially if a San José–David–Panama City Ticabus comes through, as all international bus passengers are processed together. Arrive early to get through fastest.

The Paso Canoas crossing is generally quicker than the Río Sereno one (see box, p.403), if much less scenic. For changing money, there's a Banco de Costa Rica (Mon–Sat 9am–4pm, Sun 9am–1pm) on the Costa Rican side of the border and, beyond that, plenty of money-changers (Panama uses US dollars as its currency). Few nationalities require a visa for Panama (see box, p.75).

ARRIVAL AND DEPARTURE

The Tracopa (☏ 2221 4214) bus terminal is a block from the border crossing on the Costa Rican side. There are regular services to Ciudad Neily (daily every 30min 6.30am–11.30pm; 30min), Golfito (11 daily; 1hr 30min), San Isidro de El General (5 daily; 4hr 30min) and San José (5 daily; 7hr 30min).

Buses run from the terminal on the Panamanian side to David, the first city of any size in Panama (roughly hourly until 5pm; 1hr 30min). From David it's easy to pick up local services, including the Ticabus to Panama City, which you can't get at the border.

SPANISH MAP OF COSTA RICA (1850)

Contexts

History

Costa Rica was first inhabited sometime around 10,000 BC, about 25,000 years after the first Homo sapiens had crossed the Bering Strait into what is now the Americas (though the only thing to support this tentative date is a single flint arrowhead excavated in the 1890s in Guanacaste). Archeologists know almost nothing of the various peoples of what is now Costa Rica before about 1000 BC. Certainly no written records were left, and what little knowledge we do have stems mostly from limited excavations of the Monumento Nacional Guayabo in the southeastern Valle Central.

Costa Rica before the Spanish

Pre-Columbian Costa Rica was a **contact zone** – a corridor for merchants and trading expeditions – between the Mesoamerican empires to the north and the Inca Empire to the south. Excavations of pottery, jade and trade goods, and accounts of cultural traditions, have shown that the pre-Columbian peoples of Costa Rica adopted liberally from both areas.

When the Spaniards arrived in Costa Rica at the beginning of the sixteenth century, it was inhabited by as many as 27 different **indigenous groups** or clans. Most clans were assigned names by the invaders, which they took from the **cacique** (chief) with whom they dealt. The modern-day Zona Norte was home to the **Catapas**, the **Votos** and the **Suerres**; the extreme south of the Talamancas held the **Cabécars** and the **Guayamís**, whose influence spread south to the Osa Peninsula. In the nearby Valle de Diquís and Valle de El General were the **Térrabas** and their subgroup, the **Boruca**. The Valle Central contained the **Huetars**, while modern-day Guanacaste – the most heavily populated and farmed area in pre-Columbian Costa Rica – was home to the **Chorotegas** and the older Nicoyan peoples. The Chorotegas, in particular, showed signs of cultural inheritance from the Olmec peoples of southern Mexico, while those of the extreme south and the Osa Peninsula had affinities with peoples in Panama and Colombia.

Clan society

Most of these groups existed in a state of almost constant **warfare**. However, unlike in the Mesoamerican states and in the Inca Empire, where victorious campaigns had led to the establishment of complex, far-reaching empires, in Costa Rica no one group gained ascendancy, and the political position of the clans seemed to remain more or less constant throughout the ages – like the forest-dwelling tribes in Amazonia to the south, these pre-Columbian peoples waged war not to increase their territory but to capture slaves, victims for potential sacrifice or marriage partners, or simply for revenge.

The clans were, however, highly complex when it came to **religion**. Shamans were respected members of society, officiating at funerals, which were the most important rites of passage, especially in the Talamancan groups. Some clans had animal taboos that

c.4 million BC	c.10,000 BC	c.1000 BC
The collision of tectonic plates results in the creation of the Central American Isthmus	The first known peoples arrive in what is now Costa Rica	The Guayabo establish the town of the same name near modern-day Turrialba

prevented them from hunting and killing certain beasts, and which neatly complemented each other. For example, hunting tapir might have been a major activity for one group, but prohibited for a neighbouring clan. This delicate balance played itself out on various levels, promoting harmony between man and nature. Like everywhere from southern Mexico to Brazil, the jaguar was much revered among all the groups, and only hunted to provide shamans with pelts, teeth and other ritualistic articles.

Gender divisions were, to an extent, along familiar lines: men made war and performed religious duties, while women were confined to domestic roles. However, women of the Boruca group in the southwest fought alongside men, and the Votos of the Zona Norte regularly had female chiefs. In many clans, the inheritance of names and objects was matrilineal.

People lived **communally** in stockaded villages, called **palenques** by the Spaniards. Whole groups, not necessarily related by kin, would live kibbutz-like in a village big-house. They organized work "gangs" who would tackle labour projects, usually agricultural. In most cases, land was held communally and harvests shared to ensure the survival of all. **Social hierarchy** was complex, with an ascending scale of *caciques* and shamans occupying the elite positions.

The Chorotegas in Guanacaste in particular developed a high level of **cultural expression**, possessing a written, symbol-based language, and harvesting and trading such diverse products as honey, natural dyes and cotton.

Costa Rica "discovered"

On September 18, 1502, on his fourth and last voyage to the Americas, **Christopher Columbus** sighted Costa Rica. Battered by a storm, he ordered his ships to drop anchor just off Isla Uvita, 1km offshore from present-day Puerto Limón. The group stayed seventeen days, making minor forays into the heavily forested coast and its few villages. The indigenous peoples Columbus met – as he could not fail to notice – were liberally attired in gold headbands, mirrored breastplates, bracelets and the like, convincing him of potential riches. In fact, the **gold** worn by those first welcoming envoys would have been traded or come to the peoples of the Caribbean coast through inter-tribal warfare. There was very little gold on this side of the country; rather, it came from the Valle de Diquis, in the southwest, the other side of the near-impenetrable hump of the Cordillera de Talamanca. With dreams of wealth, Columbus sailed on, charting the entire coastal region from Honduras to Panama, and naming it **Veragua**.

In 1506, King Ferdinand of Spain despatched **Diego de Nicuesa** to govern what would become Costa Rica. From the start, his mission was beset by hardship, beginning when their ship ran aground on the coast of Panama, forcing the party to walk up the Caribbean shore. There they met native people who, unlike those who had welcomed Columbus tentatively but politely with their shows of gold, burned their crops rather than submit to the authority of the Spanish. This, together with the impenetrable jungles, the creatures that lived in them and tropical diseases, meant that the expedition had to be abandoned.

Next came **Gil González Davila**, in 1521, who concentrated on Costa Rica's Pacific coast, which offered safer anchorage. González and his men covered practically the entire length of Pacific Costa Rica on foot, baptizing as they went: the expedition priest

c.800 AD	1400	1502	1506
The Chorotegas arrive in Greater Nicoya (present-day Guanacaste)	The town of Guayabo is mysteriously abandoned	Columbus "discovers" Costa Rica	Spain send their first governor to Costa Rica

GOLD, LAND AND SOULS

The first Spanish accounts of Costa Rican **indigenous peoples** were made in the sixteenth century by "**chroniclers**", the official scribes who accompanied mapping and evangelical expeditions. In general, these were either soldiers or missionaries who showed almost no talent for ethnography. Rather, they approached the pre-Columbian world as inventory-takers or suspicious accountants, writing terse and unimaginative reports liberally spiced with accounts of **gold** (although they found almost none). It was they who started the trend of portraying the cultures of the indigenous peoples of Costa Rica as "low" and underdeveloped; what they in fact meant was that there was little that could be expropriated for the Crown. One of the narratives which stands out is by **Columbus** himself, who described the small welcoming party he received in 1502 in vivid and rather romanticized prose in his *lettera rarissima*, meant for the eyes of his sovereign.

Another, more important, account is by **Gonzalo Fernández de Oviedo**, whose comprehensive, nineteen-volume *Historia General de las Indias, Islas y Tierra Firme del Mar Oceano* was first published in 1535. Oviedo spent only ten or twelve days with the **Chorotega** peoples, but he had a fine eye for detail, and recorded many aspects of their diet, dress and social customs. He also noticed that they spoke a form of Nahua, the language of the Aztecs and the lingua franca of Mesoamerica, an observation that has since convinced most historians of a direct cultural link between the empires to the north and the peoples of pre-Columbian Costa Rica and Nicaragua.

One of the first things the Spanish chroniclers noticed was that the indigenous peoples in the **Talamancas** in the southeast and the **Greater Chiriquí** in the southwest practised **ritual sacrifice**. Every full moon, prisoners captured in the most recent raid would be ritually beheaded. The Spanish, of course, were repelled, and so began the systematic baptism campaigns, and the destruction of indigenous "idolatry".

later claimed that some 32,000 souls had been "saved" in the name of the King of Spain. The indigenous peoples, meanwhile, began a campaign of **resistance** that was to last nearly thirty years, employing guerrilla tactics, infanticide, attacks on colonist settlements and burning their own villages. There were massacres, defeats and submissions on both sides, but by 1540 Costa Rica was officially a **Royal Province of Spain**, and a decade later, the Conquest was more or less complete. Most of the key areas of the country had been charted or settled, with the exception of the Talamanca region, which remained largely unexplored for centuries.

Indigenous people in the colonial period

During the first years of the Spanish invasion, those indigenous Costa Ricans who grouped themselves in large settlements, like the Chorotegas, proved more easily subjected, and were carted off by the Spanish to work in the mines or build the first Costa Rican towns, or co-opted to general slavery in the guise of farm work. The more scattered groups fared better, in the main exiling themselves to the rugged Talamancas. By then, however, the real conquerors of the New World had arrived: smallpox, influenza and measles. In the seventeenth and eighteenth centuries, huge pandemics swept the country, among them the so-called **Great Pandemic** of 1611–60, in which whole towns and villages disappeared virtually overnight. Although colonial censuses

1524	1540	1563	1569
Francisco de Córdoba founds Spain's first settlement, Villa Bruselas, on the Gulf of Nicoya	Costa Rica declared a Royal Province of Spain	Juan Vásquez de Coronado founds Cartago, the country's first capital	The ruling Spanish establish the *encomienda* system

are notoriously inaccurate, in 1563 it is reckoned that an estimated 80,000 indigenous peoples lived in Costa Rica; by 1714, the official count was 999. Today, in a country of over 4.8 million, under two percent are indigenous (see box, p.418).

In 1560, **Juan de Cavallon** and **Juan Vásquez de Coronado** – the first true conquistadors of Costa Rica – succeeded in penetrating the Valle Central, the area that would become most significant in the development of the nation. As Cortés had done in Mexico, the Spaniards of Costa Rica took advantage of existing rivalries among the native groups and played them off against each other; in this way, they managed to dominate the groups of the Pacific coast with the help of tribes from the Valle Central.

The encomienda

In the early years of the colony, the Spaniards quickly established the **encomienda**, a system widespread in the Spanish Crown's Central American possessions that gave the conquistadors and their descendants the right to demand tribute or labour from the indigenous population. The *encomienda* applied to all indigenous males in Costa Rica between the ages of 18 and 50, and to a lesser extent to women, with quotas set for the donation of foods such as cacao fruit, corn, chicken, honey and chilli peppers.

Costa Rica's indigenous peoples, however, resisted servitude to the colonials quite fiercely. Sections of colonial society also challenged the treatment of the indigenous peoples during this period. High-ranking clergymen protested to their Spanish overlords – as early as 1542, the **New Laws**, influenced by the passionate appeals of Fray Bartolomé de las Casas, decreed that colonizers had a duty to "protect" the indigenous peoples, and in 1711 the Bishop of Nicaragua, Fray Benito Garret y Arlovi, informed on the governor of Costa Rica for his brutal policies. These decrees assuaged the conscience of the Spanish Crown, but what happened on the ground in the colonies was, of course, quite a different matter.

The early settlers

In 1562, **Juan Vásquez de Coronado**, renowned for his favourable treatment of the indigenous peoples, became the second governor of Costa Rica. It was under his administration that the first settlement of any size or importance was established, and **Cartago**, in the heart of the Valle Central, was made capital of the colony. During the next century, settlers confined themselves more or less to the centre of the country. The Caribbean coast remained the haunt of buccaneers – mainly English – who put ashore and wintered here after plundering the lucrative Spanish Main; the Pacific saw its share of pirate activity, too, most famously when Sir Francis Drake came ashore briefly in Bahía Drake in 1579.

This first epoch of the colony is remembered as one of unremitting **poverty**. Within a decade of its invasion Costa Rica was notorious throughout the Spanish Empire for its lack of gold. The settlers and their descendants, unlike those to the north and the south, who became wealthy on the gold of the Aztecs and Inca, did not achieve their dreams of instant aristocracy. Instead, they were confronted with almost insuperable obstacles, including tropical fever, hunger and belligerent native peoples. The Valle Central was fertile, but there was uncertainty as to what crops to grow. Coffee had not yet been imported to Costa Rica, nor had tobacco, so it was to subsistence agriculture

1579	1611	1723	1737
Sir Francis Drake lands at Bahía Drake on the Osa Peninsula	The start of the Great Pandemic, which lasts for nearly fifty years	Volcán Irazú erupts, virtually destroying Cartago in the process	San José, then known as Villa Nueva de la Boca del Monte, is founded

that most settlers turned, growing just enough to live on. Spanish fabrics, manufactured goods and money itself became so scarce that by 1709 Valle Central settlers were forced to adopt cacao beans as currency; goat's hair and bark were used as clothing fabrics. In 1719, the governor of Costa Rica famously complained that he had to till his own land. With the emphasis on agriculture, and with little industry or trade, Costa Rica was unsurprisingly slow in founding urban settlements: in 1706, Cubujuquí (present-day Heredia) was established; in 1737, Villa Nueva de la Boca del Monte (later shortened, thankfully, to San José) was founded; and in 1782, it was the turn of Villa Hermosa (present-day Alajuela).

Beginnings of a national identity

The tough yeoman **settler farmers** who survived in these conditions are the most distinct figures in Costa Rica's early colonial history, and their independent, though impoverished, state is widely believed to be the root of the country's modern-day egalitarianism. Recent historical works, however, concede that while everybody in the early days of the colony may have been equally poor, social distinctions still counted, and where they did not exist, were manufactured: indeed, there is evidence to show that, had economic conditions permitted, a system of indentureship would have been imposed on the local *mestizo* (mixed-race) population, as happened in the highlands of Nicaragua, El Salvador and Guatemala.

Two other crucial factors went into the making of the modern nation: one was **coffee**, eventually to become Costa Rica's main export, a crop that requires many smallholders rather than large hacienda systems; the other was **ethnic** as, quite simply, the vast majority of peasants in Costa Rica were descendants of the Spanish colonists, rather than **indigenos** or **mestizos**, and as such were treated as equals by the ruling elite, who saw them as **hermaniticos**, or "little brothers".

Independence and prosperity

The nineteenth century was the most significant era in the development of Costa Rica. Initially, after 1821, when Central America declared **independence** from Spain, freedom made little difference to Costa Ricans. Although granted on September 15, 1823, the news did not reach Costa Rica until a month later, when a mule messenger arrived from Nicaragua to tell the astonished citizens of Cartago the good news. Rather than rejoicing in being freed from the Spanish – Spain had not paid much attention to the poor and isolated province anyway – a **civil war** promptly broke out among the inhabitants of the Valle Central, dividing the citizens of Alajuela and San José from those of Heredia and Cartago. The Alajuela–San José faction triumphed, and **San José** became the capital city in 1823.

Coffee kicks in

Costa Rica made remarkable progress in the latter half of the nineteenth century, constructing roads, bridges and railways, and filling San José with neo-Baroque, European-style buildings. Virtually all this activity was fuelled by the **coffee trade**, bringing wealth that the settlers just a century earlier could hardly have dreamed of. Coffee beans were introduced to Costa Rica in 1779, though it was only when beans

1775	1779	1782	1821	1823
Costa Rica's first conservation laws, an attempt to limit the impact of brush-burning, are passed	Coffee is introduced to Costa Rica	Alajuela (then called Villa Hermosa) is founded	Costa Rica gains independence from Spain	San José becomes the capital

BANANA REPUBLIC: THE UNITED FRUIT COMPANY AND RACE RELATIONS

The history of **banana growing** (see p.161) in Costa Rica is inextricably linked to the creation of the railroads. The San José–Puerto Limón railway – the "Jungle Train" – was designed by American capitalist **Minor Keith** to establish an easy route for Valle Central coffee to reach the Caribbean coast; previously, the beans were transported via the Río Sarapiquí to Puntarenas, then around Cape Horn. The railway took twenty years to build – its labour provided by an uneasy coalition of highlanders, imported Chinese "coolie" labour, Italians and Jamaicans fleeing economic difficulties in their home countries – and finally puffed its way out of the capital in 1890.

Minor had ingeniously planted bananas along the tracks in order to help pay for the route's construction, and as the fruit flourished and new markets opened up in Europe and the US, it became an exportable commodity: Costa Rica was the first Central American republic to grow bananas in bulk. In 1899, Keith and a colleague founded the **United Fruit Company**. The company – **Yunai**, as it was called locally – came to transform the social, political and cultural face of Central America – and of all the countries in which it operated, it had the biggest dealings in Costa Rica. Opinions of Yunai oscillate between capitalist scourge and saviour of the nation. Almost from the beginning, the Company – from 1970 known as the **United Brands Company** and since 1990 **Chiquita** – gained a reputation for **antiunion practices**, deserting entire areas once the workforce showed any signs of being organized. While the banana companies have always generally offered high salaries, workers would often spend their income – for many years given in redeemable scrip instead of cash – on drink and dissipation. To a degree, this was a deliberate plan by the Company to have their labour force continuously in hock and therefore pliable.

As long as the Company provided a steady flow of jobs, there was no real temptation for the **Jamaican population** (some 11,000 arrived in Costa Rica between 1874 and 1891) to leave the Caribbean coast, where they had effectively transported their own culture intact. In isolated Limón, they could retain their traditional food and religion and play West Indian games like cricket, preserving their culture in the face of a much larger highlands majority. They could also use their ability to speak English to their advantage – often Afro-Caribbeans attained high-ranking positions in the *bananeros* because they could communicate with the American foremen in their own language.

When the plantations began to close down in Limón in 1925 (as a result of the dreaded banana maladies Black Sigatoka and Panama disease), their fortunes began to change. The Company started to look for locations elsewhere in the country, acquiring land and planting

from Jamaica were first planted in the Valle Central in 1808 that the coffee story really begins. The plants thrived in the highland climate, and by 1820 citizens of Cartago were being encouraged – ordered, even – to plant coffee in their backyards. But most significant in its early history was the arrival in 1844 of English merchant **William Le Lacheur**. His ship, the *Monarch*, had emptied her hold of its cargo, and Le Lacheur arrived in the Pacific port of Puntarenas looking for ballast to take back to Liverpool. He travelled to the Valle Central, where he secured a cargo of coffee beans, which he bought on credit, promising to return and pay in two years' time.

Until that point, most of Costa Rica's coffee had made its way to Chile, where it was mixed with a lower-grade South American bean, packaged for export under the brand

1824	1856	1869	1890
Guanacaste secedes from Nicaragua, though residents in the north of the province vote against it	William Walker invades Costa Rica but is routed at La Casona	General Tomás Guardia Gutiérrez establishes free (and compulsory) primary education for all	The San José–Puerto Limón railway, or "Jungle Train", opens, connecting the Valle Central with the Caribbean

bananas in the area around modern-day Quepos in the central Pacific, and Golfito in the Zona Sur, and unbeknown to its Afro-Caribbean workers signed a contract with the government stipulating that **employment preference** be given to Costa Rican citizens. It was not the first time the country's leaders had displayed such institutional racism. It is generally held that for the first half of the nineteenth century a law existed prohibiting the migration of Afro-Caribbeans to the Valle Central, while in 1933 the government had petitioned Congress to prohibit the entry of black people into the country "because they are of a race inferior to ours" – and when the contract became public in September 1930, racial tensions rose to boiling point in Limón.

Afro-Caribbeans were trapped, unable to afford the passage home to Jamaica on the one hand and prohibited from working elsewhere in the country on the other, and in 1934 the most virulent **strike** yet seen in the Costa Rican *bananeros* began. It was organized by **Carlos Luis Fallas**, labour activist and novelist, who had been exiled to Limón as a result of his militancy on behalf of labour organizations in the Valle Central. Fallas proved a brilliant organizer, though initially the proposals he put forward to the Company were quite mild, requesting things like malaria drugs, snakebite serum and payment in cash rather than scrip. Nonetheless, the Company refused to recognize these proposals, and in August 1934 the strike began in earnest, tenaciously holding on in the face of physical harassment by the Company and police forces. For the next four years, strikes and worker opposition raged on, and in 1938 the Company pulled out of Limón Province for good, deserting it for the Pacific coast.

Left behind in the economic devastation and still unable to migrate within the country in search of work, the Afro-Caribbean population either took up cacao cultivation, hacked out their own smallholdings or took to fishing or other subsistence activities. Overnight, the schools, bunkhouses, US dollars, scrip economy, liquor and cigarettes disappeared, as did the US foremen and the ample plantation-style homes they had occupied. From about the start of the strike up until 1970, the region was virtually destitute, without much of a cash economy or any large-scale employers. It is only now beginning to recover in terms of banana production – under the aegis of the national banana-franchise operators **Dole** – and only at considerable cost to the environment, as more tropical forests are felled and more rivers polluted with pesticides.

You can get a flavour of the overwhelming presence of Dole and Chiquita in the banana towns of Limón's Valle Estrella and on the road from Jacó to Quepos, where you pass through a long corridor of African palm-oil plantations, its only major remaining investment in Costa Rica. The Company also left its mark on the collective consciousness of the region – Carlos Luis Fallas's **novels** *Mamita Yunai* (see p.433) and *Gentes y gentecillas*, Gabriel García Márquez's *One Hundred Years of Solitude* and Guatemalan Asturias's masterly *El Papa Verde* all document its power in the everyday life of the *pueblitos* of Central America.

of **Café de Valparaíso** and sent to England, taking the long way around Cape Horn. With Le Lacheur's shipment, however, British taste buds were won round to the mellow, high-quality bean, and so began a trading partnership that saw the Costa Rican upper classes using Sheffield steel cutlery and Manchester linens for most of the nineteenth century.

The **coffee bourgeoisie** played a vital role in the cultural and political development of the country, and in 1848 the newly influential **cafetaleros** elected to the presidency their chosen candidate, Juan Rafael Mora. Extremely conservative and pro-trade, Mora came to distinguish himself in the battle against the American-backed filibuster William Walker in 1856, only to fall from grace and be executed in 1860 (see box, p.265).

1895	**1897**	**1899**
Forest rangers, the forerunners of *guardaparques*, are established	Edward Porter Alexander officially defines the border between Costa Rica and Nicaragua, though the exact demarcation remains a bone of contention today	Minor Keith founds the United Fruit Company (now known as Chiquita)

The early twentieth century

The first years of the **twentieth century** witnessed a difficult transition towards democracy in Costa Rica. Universal male suffrage had come into effect during the last years of the nineteenth century, but class and power conflicts still dogged the country, with several **caudillo** (authoritarian) leaders, familiar figures in other Latin American countries, hijacking power. In general, however, these characters ended up in exile, and neither the army nor the church gained much of a foothold in politics. A number of radical labour initiatives were created during the 1920s, inspired by the Russian Revolution, though for much of the twentieth century Costa Rica's successive administrations, whatever their political colour, proved no friend of labour relations, beginning in 1924 when most **strikes** were outlawed. In 1931 the Communist Party was formed, followed quickly by the National Republican Party in 1932. The latter dominated the political scene for most of the 1940s, with the election in 1940 of the Republican (PRN) candidate **Rafael Calderón Guardia**, a doctor educated in part in Belgium and a devout Catholic.

It was Calderón who instigated the social reforms and state support for which Costa Rica is still almost unique in the region. In 1941, he established a new **Labour Code** that reinstated the right of workers to organize and strike, and a social security system providing free schooling for all. Calderón also paved the way for the establishment of the University of Costa Rica, health insurance, and income security, and thus won the support of the impoverished and the lower classes – and the suspicion of the governing elites. One of those less than convinced by his policies was the man who would come to be known as **"Don Pepe"**, the coffee farmer **José Figueres Ferrer**, who denounced Calderón and his expensive reforms in a radio broadcast in 1941 and was then abruptly forced into exile in Mexico, from where he plotted his return.

The "revolution" of 1948 and after

The **elections of 1948** heralded the most eventful year of the twentieth century for Costa Rica. Constitutionally, Costa Rican presidents could not serve consecutive terms, so the election battle that year was between **Teodorico Picado**, widely considered to be a Calderón puppet, and **Otilio Ulate Blanco**, an ally of Figueres, who during two years in exile had become a heroic figure in some circles, returning to Costa Rica to play a key part in the **Acción Democrática**, a loose group of anti-Calderonistas. Ulate won the presidency, but the PRN won the majority in Congress – a fact that effectively annulled the election results.

Figueres, back on the scene and intent upon overthrowing Picado, who had stepped in and declared himself president in the face of the annulment, soon formed an opposition party, ideologically at odds with the PRN. In March, **fighting** around Cartago began, culminating in an attack by the Figueres rebels on San José. To a degree, the battles were fought to safeguard the system of democratic election in the face of corruption, and in order to stem the clannishness and personality cults that had dogged all Costa Rican political parties and presidential campaigns up until then.

Don Pepe takes control

While Figueres' rebel forces were well equipped with arms, some supplied through CIA contacts, the militia defending President Picado was not: the national army consisted of

1910	1938	1940	1940
An earthquake near Cartago kills 1750 people	The United Fruit Company cease operations in Limón, plunging the province into economic decline	Rafael Calderón Guardia, the founder of Costa Rica's regionally enlightened social policies, is elected president	*Marmita Yunai*, Carlos Luis Fallas' novel about the banana plantations of Limón Province, is published

only about three hundred men at the time, and had to be supplemented by machete-wielding banana workers. Two thousand people were dead by mid-April, when hostilities ceased. In May, the **Junta of the Second Republic** was formed, with Figueres as acting president, despite an after-the-fact attack from Nicaraguan Picado supporters in December.

Figueres wanted above all to engineer a complete break with the country's past, and especially the policies and legacies of the Calderonistas. Seeing himself as fighting both communism and corruption, he not only outlawed the PVP, the Popular Vanguard Party – formerly known as the Communist Party – but also nationalized the banks and devised a tax to hit the rich particularly hard, thus alienating the establishment. The new **constitution** drawn up in 1949 gave full citizenship to Afro-Caribbeans and full suffrage to women, as well as codifying the **abolition of the army** fitted with political precedents in Costa Rica. Nearly thirty years before, in 1922, former president Ricardo Jiménez Oreamuno had given a famous speech in which he said: "The school shall kill militarism, or militarism shall kill the Republic… We are a country with more teachers than soldiers… and a country that turns military headquarters into schools". Although the warming sentiment behind Jiménez's words is oft-repeated in Costa Rica, the truth is somewhat darker. Figueres' motives were not utopian but rather pragmatic: he was attempting to limit the political instability that had been the scourge of so many Latin American countries, and save valuable resources. Today, while the country still has no army, the police forces are powerful, highly specialized and, in some cases, heavily armed. Paramilitary organizations have existed, chief among them the Free Costa Rica Movement (MCRL); formed in 1961 and active until the mid-1980s, the MCRL was allegedly involved in a number of deeds more reminiscent of the Guatemalan army's death squads than the spirit of a harmonious and army-free Costa Rica.

In 1951, Figueres formed the **National Liberation Party**, or **PLN**, in order to be legitimately elected. He was a genius in drawing together disparate strands of society: when the elections came around the following year, he got the agricultural smallholder vote, while winning the support of the urban working classes with his retention of the welfare state. At the same time, he appeased the right-of-centrists with his essentially free-marketeering and staunch anti-communist stance.

The 1960s and 1970s

The **1960s and 1970s** were a period of prosperity and stability in Costa Rica, when the welfare state was developed to reach nearly all sectors of society. In 1977, the **Indigenous Bill** established the right of aboriginal peoples to their own land reserves – a progressive measure at the time, although indigenous peoples today are not convinced the system has served them well (see box, p.418). At the end of the 1970s, regional conflicts deflected attention from the domestic agenda, with the Carazo (1978–82) administration announcing its support for the FSLN revolutionary movement in Nicaragua, who, in dispatching President Anastasio Samoza into exile, had finally managed to end the family's forty-year dictatorship.

Storm in the isthmus: the 1980s

Against all odds, Costa Rica in the 1980s not only saw its way through the serious political conflicts of its neighbours, but also successfully managed predatory US

1948	**1963**
After a six-week civil war, CIA-backed José Figueres Ferrer assumes the presidency from Teodorico Picado, and disbands the country's army	Thanks largely to the efforts of Karen Mogensen and Olof Wessberg, Reserva Absoluta Cabo Blanco becomes Costa Rica's first officially protected area

interventionism, economic crisis and staggering debt. Like many Latin American countries, Costa Rica had taken out bank and government **loans** in the 1960s and 1970s to finance vital development. But in the early 1980s, the slump in international coffee and banana prices put the country's finances into the red. In September 1981, Costa Rica defaulted on its interest payments, becoming the first developing country to do so and sparking off a chain of similar defaults in Latin America that threw the international banking community into crisis. Despite its defaults, Costa Rica's debt continued to accumulate and by 1989 had reached a staggering US$5 billion, one of the highest per-capita debt loads in the world at the time.

Involvement in Nicaragua

To compound the economic crisis came the simultaneous escalation of the **Nicaraguan Civil War**. Throughout the decade, Costa Rica's foreign policy – and to an extent its domestic agenda – would be overshadowed by tensions with Nicaragua and the US. Initially, the Monge PLN administration (1982–86) more or less capitulated to US demands that Costa Rica be used as a supply line for the Contras (US-backed right-wing rebels), and Costa Rica also accepted military training for its police force from the US. At the same time, the country's first agreement for a structural adjustment loan with the IMF was signed. It seemed increasingly clear that Costa Rica was on the path to both violating its declared neutrality in the conflicts of its neighbours and condemning its population to wage freezes, price increases and other side-effects associated with the IMF restructuring.

In May 1984, the situation escalated with the events at the **La Penca** press conference, held by the US-backed Contra leader Edén Pastora in a simple hut on the banks of the Río San Juan. A bomb was apparently carried into the hut by a "Danish" cameraman, concealed within an equipment case, and was intended to kill all. Miraculously, an aide of Pastora's accidentally kicked the case over, so that when it was detonated the force of the blast went up and down instead of sideways, thus saving the lives of most of those within, including Pastora himself. Although nobody is quite sure who was behind the bombing – both the CIA and freelance Argentine terrorists have been implicated – it seems that the point of the carnage was to implicate Nicaragua, thus cutting off international support and further destabilizing the government formed by the Sandinistas, the left-wing rebel group that had overthrown the brutal dictatorship of Anastasio Somoza. The immediate effect was to shock the Costa Rican government and the international community into paying more attention to the deadly conflicts of Nicaragua and, by association, El Salvador and Guatemala.

The Arias peace plan

In 1986, PLN candidate **Oscar Arias Sánchez** was elected to the presidency, and Costa Rica's relations with the US and Nicaragua took a different tack. The former political scientist began to play the role of peace broker in the conflicts of Nicaragua, El Salvador and, to a lesser extent, Honduras and Guatemala, mediating between these countries and also between domestic factions within them. In October 1987, just eighteen months after taking office, Arias was awarded the Nobel Prize for Peace, attracting worldwide attention.

1968	1975	1977	1981
Volcán Arenal erupts, killing 78 people	Olof Wessberg is murdered on the Osa Peninsula	A network of 24 indigenous reserves is created	Costa Rica kick-starts a banking crisis by defaulting on its interest payments

Arias's **peace plan** focused on regional objectives, tying individual and domestic conflicts into the larger picture: the stability of the isthmus. It officially called for a ceasefire, the discontinuation of military aid to the Contra insurrectionists, amnesties for political prisoners and for guerrillas who voluntarily relinquished the fight, and, lastly and perhaps most importantly, intergovernmental negotiations leading to free and fair elections. The peace plan began, rather than ended, with the awarding of the Nobel Prize, dragging on throughout 1987 and 1988 and running into obstacles as, almost immediately, all nations involved charged one another with noncompliance or other violations. The situation deteriorated when the US stationed troops in southern Honduras, ready to attack Nicaragua. Meanwhile, Washington continued to undermine Costa Rica's declared neutrality, requesting in April 1988 that Arias approve Costa Rican territory as a corridor for "humanitarian aid" to the Contras. The same month, Arias met with US President George Bush in Washington, his diplomatic credibility enabling him to secure millions of dollars' worth of American aid for Costa Rica without compromising the country politically. For its part, the last thing the US wanted was internal unrest in Costa Rica, its natural (if not entirely compliant) ally in the region.

However, while Arias had stalled on the US using Costa Rica's northern border as a base from which to attack Nicaragua, he seemed to have fewer quibbles about what was happening in the south, in **Panama**. In July 1989, CIA-supported anti-Noriega guerrilla forces (many of them ex-Contras) amassed along the Costa Rica–Panama border in preparation for the US invasion of Panama that would take place in December. Though Arias had gained the admiration of statesmen around the world, he proved to be less than popular at home. Many Costa Ricans saw him as neglecting domestic affairs, while increasing prices caused by the IMF's economic demands meant that by the end of the decade conditions within the country had not improved much.

The 1990s

In 1990, the mantle of power fell to **Rafael Ángel Calderón Fournier** (son of Calderón Guardia), who, in the 1980s, had been instrumental in consolidating the opposition that became the free-marketeering Partido Unidad Social Cristiana, or PUSC. A year later, Costa Rica was rocked by its most powerful **earthquake** since the one that laid waste to most of Cartago in 1910. Centred in Limón Province, the quake killed 62 people and caused extensive structural damage. At the same time, nationals of El Salvador, Honduras, Guatemala and especially Nicaragua were looking to Costa Rica – the only stable country in the region – for asylum, and tension rose as the **refugees** poured in. In 1992, Costa Rica faced more trouble as it was brought before the US courts for its failure to abide by international **labour laws**, a continuing black mark on the country's copybook for most of the twentieth century.

Until 1994, elections in Costa Rica had been relatively genteel affairs, involving lots of flag-waving and displays of national pride in democratic traditions. The elections of that year, however, were probably the dirtiest to date. The PLN candidate – the choice of the left, for his promises to maintain the role of the state in the economy – was none other than **José María Figueres**, the son of Don Pepe, who had died four years previously. During the campaign, Figueres was accused of shady investment rackets and influence peddling. His free-market PUSC opposition candidate, Dr Miguel Ángel

1985	1987	1991
The US builds a secret airstrip in northern Costa Rica to aid the CIA-backed Contras in Nicaragua	Oscar Arias receives the Nobel Peace Prize	An earthquake devastates much of Limón Province

INDIGENOUS PEOPLES IN MODERN COSTA RICA

You won't see much evidence of **native traditions** in Costa Rica today. Less than two percent of the country's population is of aboriginal extraction, and the dispersion of the various groups ensures that they frequently do not share the same concerns and agendas. Contact between them, apart from through bodies such as CONAI – the national indigenous affairs organization – is minimal.

The government set up a series of **reserves** in 1977, which gave indigenous peoples the right to remain in self-governing communities. However, titles to the reserve lands were withheld: this means that the communities don't actually own the land they live on. This has led to government contracts being handed out to, for example, mining operations in the Talamanca area, leading to infringements on the communities themselves, which are further hampered by the presence of missionaries in settlements like Amubrí and San José Cabécar. The 24 so-called "Indian reserves" scattered around the country are viewed by their inhabitants with some ambivalence. As in North America, establishing a reservation system has led in many cases to a banishing of indigenous peoples to poor-quality land where enclaves of poverty soon develop.

In the last few decades, there has been a growing recognition of the importance of **preserving indigenous culture** and of providing reserves with increased services and self-sufficiency. In 1994, the first **indigenous bank** was set up in Suretka, Talamanca, by the Bribrí and Cabécar groups, to counter the fact that major banks have often refused indigenous businesses and initiatives credit; in the same year, indigenous people earned the **right to vote** in the country's elections for the first time. Political participation has been slow in coming, however, and basic rights such as control over their own land and its natural resources, and access to healthcare and an education that reflects their view of the world, are still wilfully disregarded. In 2008, the government amended the Biodiversity Law without consulting the communities whose land it affected; Laura Chinchilla's **National Development Plan 2011–2014** was seen as another missed opportunity, failing to recognize indigenous rights when at one point it was hoped the plan might even include a long-mooted law granting autonomy to indigenous communities.

In 2015 the Inter-American Commission on Human Rights urged the Costa Rican government to "protect the life and physical integrity" of members of the Bribrí community in the Salitre reserve, who have been fighting for years to reclaim land illegally occupied by outsiders.

Rodríguez, fared no better, having admitted to being involved in a tainted-beef scandal in the 1980s. Figueres won, narrowly, though his term in office was plagued by a series of scandals. On a more positive note, in January 1995 a Free Trade agreement was signed with Mexico in order to try to redress the lack of preference given to Costa Rican goods in the US market by the signing of the North American Free Trade Agreement (NAFTA), while Costa Rica's economy received a further shot in the arm in 1996 when the communications giant INTEL chose the country for the site of their new factory in Latin America, creating thousands of jobs.

In February 1998, PUSC candidate **Dr Miguel Ángel Rodríguez** was elected president, thus continuing the trend in Costa Rican politics for the past half-century, wherein power had been traded more or less evenly between the PLN and the PUSC. The new government committed itself to solving Costa Rica's most pressing problems, making improvements to the country's dreadful road system the top priority, but financing this and other major public works by private (usually foreign) investment.

2003	2009	2009	2010
Taiwan funds the Friendship Bridge, which connects the Costa Rican mainland to the Nicoya Peninsula	Costa Rica enters CAFTA	The Cinchona earthquake ravages the Poás region	Laura Chinchilla becomes the country's first female president

The new millennium

Rodríguez was succeeded in April 2002 by Abel Pacheco de Espriella, a psychiatrist also from the PUSC; it was the first time the party had been re-elected. One of the key issues Pacheco faced was **CAFTA**, the Central American Free Trade Agreement, a proposed agreement with the US that Costa Ricans feared would erode the country's advanced social system. Pacheco added Costa Rica's name to those of all the other Central American nations, but fierce debate within the country would continue to stall its ratification. Meanwhile, in 2004, Costa Rica's (generally) squeaky-clean regional image was shattered by a series of **corruption** charges aimed at three of the country's former presidents: Rafael Ángel Calderón Fournier, José María Figueres and Miguel Ángel Rodríguez, all of whom were accused of accepting illegal financial kickbacks from foreign sources.

Promising to clamp down on government corruption, **Oscar Arias Sánchez** was elected president for the second time in February 2006, only narrowly beating rival Ottón Solís of the Partido Acción Ciudadana or Citizens' Action Party (PAC), founded just six years previously. The main issue dividing the candidates was CAFTA (Arias was strongly for it); post-election, the trade agreement continued to split the country, sparking fiery nationwide protests and leading to a first national referendum in October 2007. The "*Sí*" vote eventually scraped through with just over 51 percent, though continued opposition to the agreement meant that Arias spent the majority of his second term in office trying to push the deal through. Costa Rica finally **officially entered CAFTA** in January 2009 – the same month that the most powerful **earthquake** in more than 150 years struck the Valle Central (see box, p.134) – though wrangling over the wording of individual bills meant that it wasn't until May 2010 that the final piece of legislation, a controversial copyright law, was approved.

Laura Chinchilla and the drugs cartels

It was the PLN candidate, **Laura Chinchilla**, who triumphed in the February 2010 election, and in doing so became Costa Rica's **first female president**. A former vice president, Chinchilla had pledged to continue the free-market policies of her predecessor, claiming 47 percent of the vote ahead of regular rival Ottón Solís. More important, perhaps, were her promises to tackle **violent crime**, an escalating problem in a country better known for its peaceful disposition. This alarming rise has been linked with the growing presence of **drug trafficking**, as Colombian and Mexican cartels increasingly use the country as a convenient pick-up point – the situation had grown so bad, so quickly, that in 2010 the US added Costa Rica to its "Top Twenty" list of major drug-trafficking countries. The fight against the cartels is a regional issue, and Chinchilla was quick to show her commitment to the Central American Integration System (or **SICA**) by touring Guatemala, El Salvador, Honduras and Nicaragua shortly after her victory, while the major impetus behind her visit to Mexico the following year was to improve cooperation against organized crime. Chinchilla's commitment to tackling the drug-supply route in Costa Rica was a hallmark of her presidency, so it was with bitter irony that less than a month after lobbying President Obama for Washington's help during his trip to Costa Rica in May 2013, she found herself embroiled in a drugs-related scandal. The fallout from her use of a jet with alleged links to drugs trafficking resulted in the

2010	2012	2013
Mauricio Boraschi named as the country's first anti-drugs commissioner, in an effort to tackle its growing drug-trafficking problem	Costa Rica becomes the first Latin American country to ban hunting	5000 new species are added to the country's biodiversity list

INVASION BY INTERNET

On October 18, 2010, a group of Nicaraguan soldiers set up base on **Isla Calero**, an island on the south side of the Río San Juan, as part of an ongoing operation to dredge the river. With the centre of the San Juan serving as the historical border between Costa Rica and Nicaragua, the soldiers were technically occupying Costa Rican territory, but their commander had a simple, one-word justification for their apparent incursion: Google.

On their global mapping project, the internet giant **Google Maps** had bestowed the island (some 1.7 square kilometres of land at the river's eastern end) to Nicaragua – wrongly according to Costa Rica, who believe that the border should follow the demarcation laid out in the **1897 Alexander Award**, but rightly according to Nicaragua, who feel that the **1858 Cañas–Jereüz Treaty**, which states that Isla Calero is in their territory, still holds true.

The "occupation" of Isla Calero is just the latest footnote in a dispute over the Río San Juan that stretches back over two hundred years, the arguments growing ever more intense as the river's delta dries out and the border shifts further northwards. In 2013 the International Court of Justice (ICJ) ordered Nicaragua to withdraw entirely from the area, but controversy continues. Nicaraguan President Daniel Ortega agreed to pay compensation for the environmental damage caused by the illegal dredging, but dismissed the US$6.7 million requested by Costa Rica as "exaggerated".

resignation of, among others, Mauricio Boraschi, the head of Costa Rica's intelligence and security department and, ironically, the country's first anti-drugs commissioner.

The 2014 elections and beyond

So far, CAFTA has enabled the privatization of the state-run insurance and telecoms industries and greatly increased trade with the US – by the end of 2013, Costa Rica counted for forty percent of CAFTA exports to the States. Chinchilla's term in office, however, was less triumphant, and following a series of scandals and failed infrastructure projects, her administration bowed out with the lowest approval rating in two decades.

Perhaps understandably, fighting corruption was a key theme during the run-up to the 2014 elections, and a strong stance on this – along with a promise to address the country's growing social inequality, among the worst in Latin America – helped PAC's **Luis Guillermo Solís** to a surprise run-off victory over PLN candidate Johnny Araya.

Solís faced a daunting in-tray: the growing influence of the drugs cartels (combined with the country's undersized and underfunded security forces and Coast Guard), a protracted border dispute with Nicaragua (see box above), increasing numbers of migrants transiting through the country en route to the US, and public debt of over fifty percent of GDP. His attempts to tackle these problems – by and large – have not proved popular: by mid-2016 his approval ratings were the lowest of any Costa Rican president for almost forty years.

Yet, for the country as a whole, there are more positive signs. The economy was predicted to grow by 4 percent in 2016, bolstered by the continued recent growth in **tourism**, with visitors reaching a record 2.6 million in 2015. Costa Rica also maintained its strong performance on sustainable development: in 2016 it ratified the Paris agreement on climate change and the country's electricity grid was powered entirely by renewable energy for over a hundred days.

2014	2016
Historian Luis Guillermo Solís of the centre-left Citizens' Action Party (PAC) wins presidential election, breaking the decades-long two-party system	Nicaragua agrees to compensate Costa Rica for the illegal dredging of the Isla Calero, but the two sides fail to agree on the amount; renewable energy powers the electricity grid for well over a hundred days

Landscape and habitat

Although smaller than West Virginia, Costa Rica has nearly as many habitats as the whole of the US, including forests, riverside mangroves, seasonal wetlands and coral reefs. Within this relatively small area there is a remarkably varied terrain, ranging from the plains of Guanacaste, where there is often no rain for half the year, to the Caribbean lowlands, thick-forested and deluged with a liberal 6000mm of precipitation annually. In terms of elevation, too, the country possesses great diversity: from the very hot and humid lowlands of Corcovado, the terrain rises within just 150km to the chilly heights of Cerro Chirripó, at 3819m the country's highest point.

Because Costa Rica's territory is almost bewilderingly varied, with similar geographical features found in many different places, it is often considered in terms of **life zones**, a detailed system of categorization developed in 1947 by biologist L.R. Holdridge to describe particular characteristics of terrain, and climate, and the life they support. Although he conceived the system in Haiti, with temperature and rainfall being the main determinants, this system has been used to create ecological maps of various countries, including Costa Rica.

Tropical dry forest

The most endangered of all the life zones in Costa Rica is the **tropical dry forest** (see box below), which needs about six dry months a year. Most trees here are deciduous or semi-deciduous; some lose their leaves near the end of the dry season, primarily to conserve water. They are less stratified than rainforests, with two layers rather than three or four, and appear far less dense. Orchids flower in the silver and brown branches, and bees, wasps and moths proliferate. Animal inhabitants include iguana, white-tailed deer and some of the larger mammals, including the jaguar. The best examples are in the northwest, especially **Guanacaste and Santa Rosa national parks**.

Tropical wet forest

The **tropical wet forest** is home to the greatest density of species of flora and fauna, including the bushmaster snake and tapir, along with the jaguar and other wild cats. Here, the canopy trees can be very tall (up to 80m) and, true to its name, it receives an enormous amount of rain – typically around 6000mm per year. Found in lowland areas, tropical wet forest is now confined to large protected blocks, chiefly the **Sarapiquí–Tortuguero** area and the large chunk preserved as **Parque Nacional Corcovado** on the Osa Peninsula.

ANATOMY OF A RAINFOREST

Rainforests can feature **primary forest**, which has not been disturbed for hundreds, or even thousands, of years, and what's known as **secondary growth**, which is the vegetation that springs up in the wake of some disturbance, such as cutting, cultivation or habitation. A tropical rainforest is characterized by the presence of several **layers**, each interconnected by a mesh of horizontal lianas and climbers. At its most complex, it will be made up of four layers: the **canopy**, about 40–80m high, at the very top of which are emergent trees, often flat-topped; the **subcanopy**, beneath the emergent trees; the **understorey** trees, typically 10–20m in height; and finally the **shrub**, or ground layer.

Premontane wet forest

Premontane wet forests are found upon many of Costa Rica's mountains. Some trees are evergreen and most are covered with a thick carpet of moss. These forests typically exist at a high altitude and receive a lot of rain: the cover in **Parque Nacional Tapantí–Macizo Cerro de la Muerte** in the southeast Valle Central is a good example, as is **Parque Nacional Braulio Carrillo**, which has all five of the montane life zones within its boundaries. Many of the same animals that exist in the tropical wet forest live here, along with brocket deer and peccary.

Cloudforest

Perhaps the most famous of Costa Rica's life zones are the tropical lower montane wet forests, or **cloudforests**, which occur in very isolated patches, mainly south of Cartago and on the Pacific slopes of the Cordillera de Tilarán (most famously at **Monteverde**). They're produced when the northwesterly trade winds from the Caribbean drift across to the high ridge of the Continental Divide, where they cool to become dense clouds that create a perennial near-one-hundred-percent humidity. The primeval-looking cloudforest hosts many bromeliads, including orchids, and has an understorey thick with vines, ferns and drooping lianas; its animal life includes tapirs, pumas and quetzals.

Tropical montane rainforest

Tropical montane rainforest occurs at the highest altitudes; the tops of **Poás** and **Irazú volcanoes** are good examples. Although large mosses and ferns can be seen, much of the vegetation has a shrunken or dwarfed aspect, due to the biting wind and lofty altitude. Animals that live here include the Poás squirrel (endemic to that volcano) and some of the larger birds, such as raptors and vultures.

Tropical subalpine rain paramo

In and around the country's highest elevation, near **Cerro Chirripó**, is the only place you'll find **tropical subalpine rain paramo**, an inhospitably cold environment with almost no trees. Costa Rica is the northern frontier of this particular Andean type of paramo. Except for hardy hawks and vultures, birds tend to shun this cold milieu, although at lower elevations you may spot quetzals.

Mangroves

The **mangrove** is an increasingly fragile and endangered ecosystem that occurs along tropical coastlines and is particularly vulnerable to dredging: among others, the *Hotel de Playa Tambor* in the central Pacific (see p.324) has been accused of irresponsibly draining mangroves. With their extensive root system, mangrove trees are unique for their ability to adapt to the salinity of seaside or tidal waters, or to areas where freshwater rivers empty into the ocean. Because they absorb the thrust of waves and tides, they act as a buffer zone behind which species of aquatic and land-based life can flourish unmolested. Meanwhile, the beer-coloured mangrove swamp water is like a nutritious primordial soup where a range of species can grow, including crustaceans, shrimp and fish as well as the turtles, caimans and crocodiles that feed on them, and their banks are home to a variety of birdlife.

Wetlands

Birds and reptiles are especially abundant in the country's remaining **wetlands**, which are typically seasonal, caused by the flooding of rivers with the rains, and shrinking back to pleated mudflats in the dry season. The lagoons of the **Caño Negro** and **Mixto Maquenque** wildlife reserves in the Zona Norte, and the Río Tempisque, within the boundary of **Parque Nacional Palo Verde** in Guanacaste, are the prime wetlands in Costa Rica.

Rivers

Despite increasing silting and pollution caused largely by banana plantations, Costa Rica's **rivers** support a variety of life, from fish (including snook and tarpon) to migratory birds, crocodiles, caimans and freshwater turtles. The waterways that yield the best wildlife-watching are the **Tortuguero canals** and the *ríos* San Juan, Frío and Sierpe, as well as the **Río Tárcoles** in Parque Nacional Carara on the central Pacific coast.

Coral reefs

Costa Rica's **coral reefs**, never as extensive as those in Belize, are under threat. Much of the **Caribbean coast** was seriously damaged by the 1991 earthquake, which heaved the reefs up above the water. The last remaining ones on this side of the country are at **Cahuita** and a smaller one further south at **Manzanillo** in the Refugio de Vida Silvestre Gandoca-Manzanillo. Though the Cahuita reef has been under siege for some time from silting caused by the clearing of land for banana plantations, and from the pesticides used in banana cultivation, you can still see some fine (extremely localized) specimens of moose horn and staghorn coral. On the **Pacific coast**, the most pristine reef is at **Bahía Ballena**, protected within Costa Rica's first marine national park, and also the reef that fringes Isla del Caño, about 20km offshore from the northwest coast of the Osa Peninsula. Lying 535km southwest of Costa Rica's Pacific coast, **Parque Nacional Isla del Coco** remains the country's marine treasure, a coveted destination for experienced divers whose waters are home to more than thirty species of coral.

Conservation and tourism

Costa Rica is widely seen as being at the cutting edge of worldwide conservation strategy, an impressive feat for a tiny Central American nation. At the centre of the country's internationally applauded efforts is a complex system of national parks, wildlife refuges and biological reserves, which protect more than 25 percent of its territory, one of the largest percentages of protected land in the world. Additional areas, meanwhile, are protected by private and indigenous reserves; Rara Avis (see p.232) is an excellent example of the former. These statistics are used with great effect to attract tourists and, along with Belize, Costa Rica has become virtually synonymous with ecotourism in Central America.

On the other hand, the National Parks Service is underfunded and these areas are under constant pressure from logging and agricultural encroachment, and to a lesser extent from mining interests. In addition, the question uppermost in the minds of conservationists and biologists is what, if any, damage is being caused by so many feet walking through the rainforests.

Conservation in the New World tropics

The **traditional view** of conservation is a European one of preserving, museum-like, pretty animals and flowers: an idea conceived and upheld by relatively wealthy Old World countries in which the majority of the forests have long-since disappeared. Today this definition of conservation no longer works, and certainly not in the New World tropics, besieged as they are by a lack of resources, huge income inequities, legislation that lacks bite and the continual appetite of the world market for tropical hardwoods, not to mention the Old World zeal for coffee and picture-perfect supermarket fruits.

There's a left-wing perspective on conservation that sees an imperialistic, bourgeois and anti-*campesino* agenda among the large conservation organizations of the North. Indigenous critiques, meanwhile, challenge the impact conservation can have on traditional ways of life; for example, by banning hunting and/or forcing groups to leave their ancestral lands. By this reckoning, saving the environment is all very well but does little for the day-to-day realities, say, of the twenty-one percent of Costa Rica's population who live below the poverty line. These people have, in many cases, been made landless and impoverished by, for instance, absentee landowners speculating on land (in the Zona Norte and in Guanacaste) or by the pulling-out of major employers like Chiquita (first in Limón Province and then in the Zona Sur near Golfito and on the Osa Peninsula). Many are left with simply no choice but to engage in the kind of activity – be it gold-panning, slash-and-burn agriculture or monobiotic fruit production – universally condemned by conservationists in the North.

Conservation in Costa Rica

Costa Rica has a long history of conservation-consciousness, although it has taken different forms and guises. As early as 1775, laws were passed to limit the destructive impact of *quemas*, or brush-burning, though the bulk of **preservation laws** were passed after 1845, concurrent with Costa Rica's period of greatest

THE CASE OF TORTUGUERO

National parks are now such an entrenched part of Costa Rica's landscape that they might be taken to have always been there. In fact, most have been established in the last forty years, and the process of creating them has not always been a smooth one.

Turtle Bogue (the old Miskito name for Tortuguero) has always been isolated. Even today, access is by boat or air only, and before the dredging of the main canal in the 1960s it was even more cut off from the rest of the country. Most of the local people were of Miskito or Afro-Caribbean extraction, hunting and fishing, and living almost completely without consumer goods. There was virtually no cash economy in the village, with local trade and barter being sufficient for most people's needs.

In the 1940s, **lumbering** began in earnest in the area. A sawmill was built in the village, and during the next two decades the area experienced a boom. The local lumber exhausted itself by the 1960s, but in the twenty-year interim it brought outsiders and a dependence on cash-obtainable consumer goods.

Simultaneously, the number of **green turtles** began to decline rapidly, due to overfishing and egg harvesting, and by the 1950s the once-numerous turtle was officially endangered. The alarm raised by biologists over their precipitous decline paved the way for the establishment, in 1970, of **Parque Nacional Tortuguero**, protecting 30 of the area's 35km of turtle-nesting beach and extending to more than two hundred square kilometres of surrounding forests, canals and waterways. The establishment of this protective area put former sources of income off-limits to local populations, and villagers who had benefited from the wood-and-turtle economy either reverted to the subsistence and agricultural life they had known before or left the area in search of a better one. Nowadays, however, many locals make a good living off the increasing amount of tourism the park brings, especially those with their own independent businesses.

The establishment of Parque Nacional Tortuguero effectively broke the **boom-and-bust cycle** so prevalent in the tropics, whereby local resources are used to extinction, leaving no viable alternatives after the storm has passed. In Tortuguero, the hardwoods have made a bit of a comeback, and the green turtle's numbers are up dramatically from its low point of the 1950s and 1960s. Considering the popularity of the national park, there's no doubt that conservation and protection of Tortuguero's wetlands can have lasting benefits for local folk, as well as local flora and fauna.

economic and cultural growth. That said, most of this legislation was directed at protecting resource extraction rather than the areas themselves – to guard fishing and hunting grounds and to conserve what were already seen as valuable timber supplies. In 1895, laws were passed protecting water supplies and establishing *guardabosques* (forest rangers) to fight the uncontrolled fires caused by the regular burning of deforested land and pasture by cattle-ranchers, while the forerunners of several institutions later to be important to the development of conservation in Costa Rica were founded by the end of the nineteenth century, including the Museo Nacional and the Instituto Físico Geográfico.

Much of the credit for helping establish Costa Rica's system of national parks in the second half of the twentieth century has to go to **Olof Wessberg** and **Karen Mogensen**, long-time foreign residents who in 1963, largely through their own efforts, founded the Reserva Natural Absoluta Cabo Blanco near their home on the southwest tip of the Nicoya Peninsula. The couple helped raise national consciousness through an extensive campaign in the mid-1960s, so that by the end of the decade there was broad support for the founding of a national parks service. In 1969, the Parque y Monumento Nacional Santa Rosa was declared, and in 1970 the **Servicio de Parques Nacionales (SPN)** was officially inaugurated. Spearheaded by a recently graduated forester, Mario Boza, the system developed slowly at first, as the law that established Santa Rosa really existed only on paper: neighbouring farmers and ranchers continued to encroach on the land for pasture and brush-burning as before.

Although it remains a mystery, the **murder of Olof Wessberg** in 1975 on the Osa Peninsula is an illustration of the powerful interests that are thwarted by conservation. Wessberg was conducting a preliminary survey in Osa to assess the possibility of a national park there (the site of modern-day Parque Nacional Corcovado). Although his assailant – the man who had offered to guide him – was caught, a motive was never discovered and the crime has not been satisfactorily solved.

MINAE, SINAC and Red

Nonetheless, despite the pressures of vested interests, the Costa Rican conservation programme moved forward in the early 1980s with the founding of **MINAE** (Ministerio del Ambiente y Energía), the government body entrusted with the overall control of the country's ecological resources. In 1988, the Arias government drafted a national conservation strategy, and, soon after his election victory in 1994, president José María Figueres started the drive to bring together all the various conservation efforts taking place throughout the country under direct government control. In 1995, the national parks, wildlife and forestry services were merged into **SINAC** (Sistema Nacional de Areas de Conservacion), a single agency within MINAE that had direct responsibility for the country's 29 national parks, 11 conservation areas and 167 other government-protected lands. For decades, much of the most important conservation work had been undertaken by privately (often foreign) funded initiatives, and so, in 1996, the **Red Costarricense de Reservas Naturales** was also founded, bringing the country's disparate patchwork of privately owned reserves and refuges under the control of a single administrative body subject to the same rules and regulations as state-owned parks. Privately funded conservation programmes are still vital, though, as they help to remove some of the financial burden from the beleaguered state coffers, which struggle to raise the revenue necessary to maintain the increasingly overstretched national parks. Indeed, private investment accounted for a large share of the funds the government raised to expand the size of its protected marine areas, in doing so boosting its total protected areas to 26 percent of the country.

Eco-paradise lost: pesticides, pollution and poaching

There are, however, flaws in this Garden of Eden, chief among them the importance of the **agro-export** economy. It can take half a century for land used to grow pineapples to recover sufficiently enough to support anything else, while the damage wreaked by the **pesticides** used in banana plantations – the country's major agro-export – is becoming an increasing threat. Foreign consumers attach an amazing level of importance to the appearance of supermarket bananas and pineapples, and about twenty percent of potentially dangerous pesticides used in the cultivation of bananas serve only to improve the look of the fruit and not, as it is often thought, to control pestilence. Travellers who pass through banana plantations on river trips in Costa Rica or who take river trips, especially along the Río Sarapiquí in the Zona Norte, can't fail to notice the ubiquitous blue plastic bags – the pristine appearance of Costa Rican bananas is due largely to the fact that they grow inside these pesticide-lined bags, which make their way into

GOING, GOING, GONE

At the end of 2013 scientists announced the discovery of an incredible 5000 new species in Costa Rica, including 277 new types of wasp alone. But the national parks and protected biological corridors have come too late for some. The favoured upper-canopy habitat of the **harpy eagle**, arguably the world's most powerful raptor, has been ravaged to such an extent that the bird is thought to have disappeared forever from Costa Rica's jungles. The number of sightings of the **giant anteater** in the last quarter of a century can be counted on the fingers of one hand. And the iconic **golden toad**, once abundant in Monteverde, has gone the way of the dodo, declared extinct in 2004, fifteen years after one was last spotted.

waterways where they are fatally consumed by fish, mammals (such as the manatee) or iguanas. In the Río Tempisque basin, on the Pacific coast, armadillos and crocodiles are thought to have been virtually exterminated by agricultural pesticides.

Not that agriculture is purely to blame for the country's **pollution** problems. In recent years, several high-profile hotels have been fined for damaging their local environment, and in 2008 the *Hotel de Occidental Allegro Papagayo* in Manzanillo was shut down after it was caught dumping sewage into a nearby estuary. Perhaps more alarmingly, the following year Parque Nacional Manuel Antonio – where conservation is always a balancing act thanks to the sheer number of visitors this tiny park receives – was found to be harming the very flora and fauna it was created to protect, and was almost closed after its leaking facilities polluted local rivers and coastline.

While Costa Rica became the first country in Central America to ban trophy hunting at the end of 2012, **poaching** in and around underprotected national parks and reserves is still a major issue. Turtle eggs are particularly vulnerable, being easily obtained and gathered in their hundreds, and while the beaches at Tortuguero are patrolled, those further south along the Caribbean coast at Moín are not. In the 2013 season, all but eight of the 1500 or so leatherback nests on Moín were ransacked by poachers. That year, conservation efforts in Moín had ceased in the face of armed threats from poachers, and in May 2013 the situation attracted global concern following the murder of 26-year-old conservationist Jairo Mora. In late 2016, four men were finally jailed for 35 years each for the crime, but the battle between conservationists and poachers on Moín beach continues.

Conservation initiatives

In recent years, Mario Boza, a prominent conservationist heavily involved in the founding of the national parks system, has advocated a **macro-conservation** strategy. By uniting concerns and "joining up" chunks of protected land, he argued, macro-areas provide a larger protected range for animals that need room to hunt, like jaguars and pumas, or require sizeable migratory areas, such as the endangered great green macaw (see box, p.234). Most of all, they allow countries to make more effective joint conservation policies: macro-conservation projects currently include the Corredor Biológico Mesoamericano (to create an unbroken stretch of jungle throughout all of Mesoamerica) and the Parque Internacional La Amistad (Costa Rica and Panama).

Another initiative, even more promising in terms of how it affects the lives of many rural-based Costa Ricans, is the creation of "**buffer zones**" around some national parks. In these zones, *campesinos* and other smallholders can do part-time farming, are allowed restricted hunting rights and receive education about the ecological and

---

CONSERVATION ORGANIZATIONS IN COSTA RICA

The following **conservation organizations** all work in Costa Rica. There are many more local operations working towards the same common goals.

Fundación Amigos de la Isla del Coco Aptdo 276-1005, Barrio Corazón de Jesús, San José (☎ 2257 9257, ⊚ cocosisland.org). Set up in 1994 to raise funds to preserve the unique flora and fauna of remote Parque Nacional Isla del Coco (see box, p.320), a UNESCO World Heritage Site.

Fundación Neotrópica Aptdo 236-1002, Paseo de los Estudiantes, San José (☎ 2253 2130, ⊚ neotropica.org). Well-established organization that works with several small-scale and (typically) local conservation initiatives in Costa Rica. Field offices in Turrialba, Puntarenas and on the Osa Peninsula; their main office in San José (opposite the Colegio Federado de Ingenieros y Arquitectos in Curridabat) sells posters, books and T-shirts in aid of funds.

Nature Conservancy 4245 North Fairfax Drive, Suite 100, Arlington VA, 22203-1606, USA (☎ 202 628 6860, ⊚ nature.org). US-based organization with a global remit – their work in Costa Rica focuses on the Cordillera Talamanca/Parque Internacional La Amistad and the Osa Peninsula. You can contact the local branch in Los Yoses in San José (☎ 2528 8800).

economic value of the forest. Locals may be trained as nature guides, and *campesinos* may be given incentives to enter into nontraditional forms of agriculture and ways of making a living that are less environmentally destructive.

In the past, Costa Rica's **waste-disposal problems** have given the country a garbage nightmare, culminating in a scandal in 1995 with the overflowing of the Río Azul site, San José's main dump. The government fully recognizes the irony of this – rubbish lining the streets of a country with such a high conservation profile – and in an admirable, typically Tico grassroots initiative, legions of schoolchildren are now sent on rubbish-collecting after-school projects and weekend brigades. Even more ingenious is the national movement that sends Costa Rican schoolchildren to national parks and other preserves as **volunteers** to work on conservation projects during school holidays, thus planting the seeds for a future generation of dedicated – or at least aware – conservationists.

Tourism

Over 2.6 million tourists a year come to Costa Rica – mostly from the US, Canada and Europe – an incredible number, considering that its population is just 4.8 million. Along with the charms of the country itself, Costa Rica's popularity is linked with the growing trend toward **ecotourism** – for the most part, tourists with a genuine concern for and interest in the country's flora, fauna and cultural life can choose from a variety

ECOTOURISM AND SUSTAINABLE TOURISM

"Ecotourism" and "sustainable tourism" are much touted, but difficult to define – and authentic ecotourism and/or sustainable tourism experiences are even harder to pin down. One of the best attempts to explain the meaning of the former has been put forward by ATEC, the Asociación Talamanqueña de Ecoturismo y Conservación (w ateccr.org), which seeks to promote, as it says, "socially responsible tourism", by integrating local Bribrí and Afro-Caribbean culture into tourists' experience of the area, as well as giving residents pride in their unique cultural heritage and natural environment.

"Ecotourism means more than bird books and binoculars. Ecotourism means more than native art hanging on hotel walls or ethnic dishes on the restaurant menu. Ecotourism is not mass tourism behind a green mask. Ecotourism means a constant struggle to defend the earth and to protect and sustain traditional communities. Ecotourism is a cooperative relationship between the non-wealthy local community and those sincere, open-minded tourists who want to enjoy themselves in a Third World setting and, at the same time, enrich their consciousness by means of significant educational and cultural experience."

ATEC

The Rainforest Alliance (w rainforest-alliance.org), meanwhile, has put forward a useful definition of sustainable tourism, which has much in common with ecotourism but is broader in scope, covering "all types of travel and destinations, from luxury to backpacking and bustling cities to remote rainforests".

"Sustainable tourism businesses support environmental conservation, social development, and local economies. Examples of sustainable business practices include conserving water and energy, supporting community conservation projects, recycling and treating wastes, hiring staff from the local community, paying them just wages and providing training, and sourcing locally-produced products for restaurants and gift shops. Sustainable tourism businesses take concrete actions to enhance the well-being of local communities and make positive contributions to the conservation of natural and cultural heritage. In doing so, they often cut down on their own costs and preserve the longevity of their businesses in addition to attracting responsible travelers. In order for sustainable tourism to thrive, it has to be profitable for business owners."

Rainforest Alliance

of places to spend their money constructively, including top-notch rainforest lodges that have worked hard to integrate themselves with their surroundings. If managed properly, low-impact ecotourism is one of the best ways in which forests, beaches, rivers, mangroves, volcanoes and other natural formations can pay their way – in *dólares* – while remaining pristine and intact.

Several pioneering **projects** in Costa Rica have set out to combine tourism with sustainable methods of farming, rainforest preservation or scientific research. The **Rainforest Aerial Tram**, which adjoins Parque Nacional Braulio Carrillo (and is now known as the Rainforest Adventures Costa Rica Atlantic), one of the most advanced of its kind in the Americas, if not the world, provides a fascinating glimpse of the tropical canopy – normally completely inaccessible to human eyes – but it also offers a rare safe and stable method for biologists to investigate this little-known habitat. Income from visitors is funnelled into maintaining and augmenting the surrounding reserve. The **Reserva Biológica Bosque Nuboso Monteverde**, meanwhile, preserves a large piece of complex tropical forest, giving scientists a valuable stomping ground for taxonomic study. Tourism is just one of the activities in the reserve, which has been a research ground for tropical biologists from all over the world, and provides revenue for maintenance and, more importantly, continued expansion.

More people, more problems

The success of the country's ecotourism initiatives have brought their own problems, however. The huge **growth of tourism** worries many Costa Ricans, even those who make their living from it, and many as yet unanswered questions remain. Is it just a fad, only to be replaced by another unprepared country-of-the-moment? What, if any, are the advantages of having an economy led by tourism instead of the traditional exports like bananas and coffee? Furthermore, how do you reconcile the need to attract enough visitors to make tourism economically viable with ensuring that this tourism remains low-impact?

MINAE vs the ICT

It is a problem made all the more difficult by ongoing arguments between two of the main organizations charged with managing the country's ecotourism industry: **MINAE**, the government body that, through SINAC, directly controls the country's network of national parks, and the **Costa Rican Tourist Board** (Instituto Costarricense de Turismo or **ICT**). Whereas MINAE is, despite severe underfunding, widely seen as having done a reasonably good job in ensuring that tourism doesn't overwhelm the parks' fragile ecosystems, the ICT is often regarded as putting commercial interests above environmental ones. In contrast to the somewhat impoverished state of MINAE, the ICT makes a lot of money out of tourism, much of it derived from the three percent tax collected on every occupied hotel room.

The ICT has, however, taken a step in the right direction with their development of the **Certificate for Sustainable Tourism** (@turismo-sostenible.co.cr). In an area that has traditionally been hard to quantify, the scheme helps shed light on the murky issue of just how eco an ecolodge or tour operator really is, by measuring how much they comply with the ICT's model of sustainable best practice and awarding them a rating of up to five "leaves"; as a company's rating increases, so do its benefits, which include publicity and promotion from the ICT, training and the like.

Foreign ownership, high prices and sex tourists

The question of who pays for Costa Rica's environmental wellbeing, though, is one that continues to provoke fierce debate. While the government actively welcomes contributions from **foreign sources**, many Costa Ricans are alarmed by what they see as the virtual purchase of their country by foreigners. Though many hotels and businesses are still Costa Rican-owned and -managed, North American and European ownership is on the rise, relegating many locals to low-paid jobs in the service sector. Gated **"gringo" communities** have sprung up along the Pacific coast, and across the country **rising property prices** are having a drastic effect on Costa Ricans, with many being priced out of their own communities.

At times, the government seems bent on turning the country into a **high-income tourist enclave**. North Americans and Europeans will still consider many things quite cheap, but Costa Rica is already the most expensive country to visit in the region, and the government has admitted that they have no qualms about discouraging "backpackers" (meaning budget tourists) from coming to Costa Rica. Better-heeled tourists, the thinking goes, not only make a more significant investment in the country dollar for dollar, but are more easily controlled, choosing in the main to travel in tour groups or to stay in big holiday resorts – ironically, the type of places that are often dogged by environmental scandal (see p.427).

Another flipside to Costa Rica's tourism success story is its ascendancy to one of the world's top **sex tourism** destinations. Prostitution is legal in Costa Rica, as long as the sex workers are over the age of 18, and it is estimated that approximately ten percent of foreign visitors are sex tourists. Disturbingly, paedophiles also come to Costa Rica, their underage victims stricken by violence, poverty and drug addiction. In 1999, Costa Rica's parliament passed a law against the sexual exploitation of minors, and while penalties are harsh and initiatives in place to educate taxi drivers, police officers, tour guides and hotel receptionists about the illegality of profiting from or promoting paedophilia, the problem is still prevalent.

Books

The most comprehensive volumes written on Costa Rica tend to be about natural history – many make better introductions to what you'll see in the country than the glossy literature pumped out by the tourist board. Frustratingly, many of the most informative works on both natural and cultural history are out of date or out of print (designated "o/p" in the list below). You'll find a number of the titles listed below in San José bookshops, but don't expect to see them elsewhere in the country.

Those interested in **Costa Rican fiction** (which is alive and well, although not extensively translated or known abroad) will have much richer and more varied reading with some knowledge of Spanish. Costa Rica has no single, internationally recognized, towering figure in its national literature, and in sharp contrast to other countries in the region the most sophisticated and best-known writers in the country are women. Carmen Naranjo is the most widely translated, with a number of novels, poems and short-story collections (plus some of the country's most prestigious literary awards) to her name. There are also a number of lesser-read writers, including the brilliant Yolanda Oreamuno, who together with an upsurge of younger women is tackling contemporary social issues like domestic violence and alcoholism in their fiction and poetry. The publication in 1940 of Carlos Luis Fallas's seminal novel *Mamita Yunai*, about labour conditions in the United Fruit Company banana plantations of Limón Province, sparked a wave of "proletarian" novels, which became the dominant form in Costa Rican fiction until well into the 1970s. Until recently, Costa Rican fiction also leant heavily on picturesque stories of rural life, with some writers – usually men – drawing on the country's wealth of fauna. There are also a number of *cuentos* (stories), fable-like in their simplicity and not a little ponderous in their symbolism, featuring turtles, fish and rabbits as characters.

TRAVEL NARRATIVE

Joe Bauer *Talking Tico: (Mis)adventures of a Gringo in and around Costa Rica.* An entertaining account of the author's travels around Costa Rica (and its neighbours), mixing historical vignettes with present-day encounters with xenophobic expats, giant moths and students at the University of Peace.

Robert Isenberg *The Green Season.* Written by a former *Tico Times* journalist, this book mixes essays and reportage on daily life in Costa Rica, taking in everything from football to traffic, venomous snakes to indigenous ceremonies.

Katherine Stanley Obando *Love in Translation: Letters to My Costa Rican Daughter.* Another book by a *Tico Times* journalist, *Love in Translation* blends an account of a US migrant's life in the country with a dictionary of Costarriqueñismos – Tico words, phrases and colloquialisms.

Paul Theroux *The Old Patagonian Express: By Train Through the Americas.* Rather out of date (Theroux went through almost 40 years ago), but still a great read. Laced with the author's usual tetchy black humour and general misanthropy, the descriptions of his two Costa Rican train journeys (neither of which still runs) to Limón and Puntarenas remain apt – as is the account of passing through San José, where he meets American men on sex-and-booze vacations.

CULTURE AND FOLK TRADITIONS

★**Paula Palmer** *"What Happen": A Folk-History of Costa Rica's Talamanca Coast.* The definitive folk history of the Afro-Caribbean community on Limón Province's Talamancan coast. Palmer first went to Cahuita in the early 1970s as a Peace Corps volunteer, later to return as a sociologist. The oral histories she collected from older members of the local communities – atmospheric testimonies of pirate treasure, ghosts and the like – are complemented by photos and accounts of local agriculture, foods and traditional remedies.

Paula Palmer, Juanita Sánchez and Gloria Mayorga *Taking Care of Sibö's Gifts: An Environmental Treatise from Costa Rica's KéköLdi Indigenous Reserve.* Manifesto for the future of Bribrí culture and ecological survival of the *talamanqueña* ecosystems, and a concise explication of differing views of the land and people's relationship to it held by the *ladinos* and Bribrí on the KéköLdi Indigenous Reserve.

CONSERVATION

★**Catherine Caulfield** *In the Rainforest: Report from a Strange, Beautiful, Imperiled World.* Published in 1986, but still one of the best introductions to the rainforest, dealing in an accessible fashion with many of the issues covered in the more specialized titles. Her chapter on Costa Rica is a wary elucidation of the destruction that cattle-ranching in particular wreaks, as well as an interesting profile of the farming methods used by the Monteverde community.

Gordon W. Frankie, Alfonso Mata and S. Bradleigh Vinson (eds) *Biodiversity Conservation in Costa Rica: Learning the Lessons in a Seasonal Dry Forest.* The first in-depth study of Guanacaste's endangered dry forest paints a detailed picture – biologically, environmentally, socially and politically – of this fragile ecosystem and its vital link to the country's other ecosystems.

Susanna Hecht and Alexander Cockburn *The Fate of the Forest: Developers, Destroyers and Defenders of the Amazon.* The best single book readily available on rainforest destruction, this exhaustive volume is written with a sound knowledge of Amazonian history. The beautiful prose dissects some of the more pervasive myths about rainforest destruction, and it's comprehensive enough to be applicable to any forested areas under threat in the New World tropics.

Luis Fournier Origgi *Desarrollo y Perspectivas del Movimiento Conservacionista Costarricense.* Seminal, if dry, survey of conservation policy from the dawn of the nation until the early 1990s, by one of Costa Rica's most eminent scientists and conservationists. In Spanish only.

HISTORY AND CURRENT AFFAIRS

Suzane Abel *Between Continents/Between Seas: Precolumbian Art of Costa Rica* (o/p). Produced as a catalogue to accompany the exhibition that toured the US in 1982, this is the best single volume on pre-Conquest history and craftsmanship, with illuminating accounts of the lives, beliefs and customs of Costa Rica's pre-Columbian peoples as interpreted through artefacts and excavations. The photographs, whether of jade pendants, Chorotega pottery or the more diabolical of the Diquís' gold pieces, are uniformly wonderful.

Elías Zamora Acosta *Etnografía Histórica de Costa Rica (1561–1615).* Hugely impressive archival research that reconstructs the economic, political and social life in Costa Rica in the years immediately following the Spanish invasion. A masterwork, distressingly difficult to get hold of. In Spanish only.

Richard Biesanz, Mavis Hiltunen Biesanz and Karen Zubris Biesanz *The Ticos: Culture and Social Change in Costa Rica.* An intriguing blend of quantitative and qualitative research, supported by personal interviews with many Costa Ricans, this book seeks to get under the skin of Costa Rican society, examining (among other things) government, class and ethnic relations, the family, health and sport, and managing to be rigorous and anecdotal at the same time.

Martha Honey *Hostile Acts: U.S. Policy in Costa Rica in the 1980s.* Those sceptical of elaborate conspiracy theories may have their minds changed by this exhaustively researched, weighty tome detailing the US's "dual diplomacy" against Costa Rica in the 1980s. In this heroic volume, and in contrast to her earlier findings in *La Penca: On Trial in Costa Rica,* Honey concludes that the 1984 La Penca bomber was a leftist Argentine terrorist with connections to Nicaragua's Sandinista government.

★**Steven Palmer and Iván Molina** (eds) *The Costa Rica Reader: History, Culture, Politics.* One of the best introductions to the country, this book features more than fifty texts by Costa Ricans, from essays and memoirs to histories and poems, interspersed with photographs, maps, cartoons and fliers.

Mitchell A. Seligson *Peasants of Costa Rica and the Development of Agrarian Capitalism* (o/p). The best single history available in English, although only a university or specialist library will have it. Much wider in scope than the title suggests, this is an excellent intermeshing of ethnic and racial issues, economics and sociology along with hard-core analysis of the rise and fall of the Costa Rican peasant.

WILDLIFE, NATURAL HISTORY AND FIELD GUIDES

Mario A. Boza *Costa Rica National Parks (Parques Nacionales).* Essentially a coffee-table book, this informed volume, written by one of the founders of the national park system, is a great taster for what you'll find in the national parks. The text is in Spanish and English, with stunning photographs throughout.

A.S. and P.P. Calvert *A Year of Costa Rican Natural History.* Although now very old – the year in question is 1910 – this is a brilliant, insightful and charmingly enthusiastic travelogue/natural history/autobiography by an American biologist and zoologist husband-and-wife team. It features much, much more than natural history, with sections such as "Blood Sucking Flies", "Fiestas in Santa Cruz" and "Earthquakes". The best single title ever written on Costa Rica, the only problem is finding it – try good libraries and specialist bookshops.

Joseph Franke *Costa Rica's National Parks and Preserves*. A comprehensive discussion of the system of national parks and wildlife refuges, with detailed information on hiking and trails, as well as a topographical and environmental profile of each one. Useful if you're intending to spend any time hiking in more than one or two parks.

★**Richard Garrigues and Robert Dean** *The Birds of Costa Rica*. This excellent, all-encompassing field guide to the country's myriad bird species is fast threatening Stiles and Skutch's tour de force (see below) as the birdwatchers' bible – succinct and portable, it makes the ideal handbook for everyday use in the field.

★**Adrian Hepworth** *Costa Rica: A Journey Through Nature*. Cherry-picking from the author's extensive portfolio, the second edition of this best-selling coffee-table tome features more of the lavish wildlife photography that made the original one of the most popular visual souvenirs of Costa Rica.

Daniel H. Janzen (ed) *Costa Rican Natural History*. The definitive reference source, with accessible, continuously fascinating species-by-species accounts, written by a highly influential figure – Janzen was involved on a policy level in the governing of the national parks system. The introduction is especially worth reading, dealing in a cursory but lively fashion with tectonics, meteorology, history and archeology. Illustrated with gripping photographs. Available in paperback but still doorstep-thick.

Sam Mitchell *Pura Vida: The Waterfalls and Hot Springs of Costa Rica*. Jolly, personably written but concise guide to the country's many little-known waterholes, cascades and waterfalls, complete with detailed directions and accounts of surrounding trails. Available in English in San José.

Donald Perry *Life Above the Jungle Floor: A Biologist Explores a Strange and Hidden Treetop World*. Nicely poised, lyrical account of Perry's trials and tribulations in conceiving and mounting his Rainforest Aerial Tram (see p.429). Most of the book deals with his time at Rara Avis, where he conceived and tested his tram prototype, the Automated Web for Canopy Exploration.

Fiona A. Reid, Twan Leenders, Jim Zook and Robert Dean *The Wildlife of Costa Rica*. This handy introduction to the main species you're likely to encounter, from mammals and birds to reptiles and amphibians, works well as a non-specialist field guide. The illustrations, particularly of the birds and mammals, are good and the species accounts detailed and informative – there's even a small section on insects, including butterflies, bullet ants and the extremely strange-looking tailless whip scorpion.

F. Gary Stiles and Alexander F. Skutch *A Guide to the Birds of Costa Rica*. Throughout Costa Rica, you'll see guides clutching well-thumbed copies of this seminal tome, illustrated with colour plates to aid identification. Hefty, even in paperback, and too pricey for the amateur, but you may be able to pick up good secondhand copies in Costa Rica.

Mark Wainwright *The Mammals of Costa Rica*. The most comprehensive guide to the country's mammal species, including the oft-overlooked bats, is an amalgamation of hundreds of field researchers' work and features detailed but accessible information on natural history, conservation and, interestingly, mythology. The animal tracks are useful, though there are better illustrations in other books of this ilk.

Allen M. Young *Sarapiquí Chronicle: A Naturalist in Costa Rica* (o/p). Lavishly produced book based on entomologist Allen M. Young's twenty years' work in the Sarapiquí area and featuring a well-written combination of autobiography, travelogue and natural science, centring on the insect life he encounters.

FICTION

Miguel Benavides *The Children of Mariplata: Stories from Costa Rica*. A slim collection of short stories, most of which are good examples of fable-like or allegorical Costa Rican tales. Many are written in the anthropomorphized voice of an animal; others, like *The Twilight Which Lost its Colour*, describe searing slices of poverty-stricken life.

Carlos Cortés *Cruz de Olvido*. Told in the macho, exhausted and regretful tone of a disillusioned revolutionary, this novel charts the return of a Costa Rican Sandinista supporter from Nicaragua to his home country, where "nothing has happened since the big bang". The narrative marries the storyteller's humorous disaffection with boring old Costa Rica and his investigation into the bizarre, excessively symbolic death of his son. In Spanish only.

Fabián Dobles *Ese Que Llaman Pueblo* (Spanish only); *Years Like Brief Days*. Born in 1918, Dobles is Costa Rica's elder statesman of letters. Set in the countryside among *campesinos*, *Ese Que Llaman Pueblo* is a typical "proletarian" novel. *Years Like Brief Days* is the first novel by Dobles to be translated into English, a story told in the form of a letter written by an old man to his mother, describing the village he grew up in and his eventful life.

★**Carlos Luis Fallas** *Mamita Yunai: El Infierno de las Bananeras*. Exuberant and full of local colour, culture and diction, this entertaining leftist novel depicting life in the hell of the banana plantations is a great read. It's set in La Estrella valley in Limón Province, where Fallas, a pioneering labour organizer in the 1930s and 40s, was instrumental in forcing the United Fruit Company to take workers' welfare into account. In Spanish only.

Joaquín Gutiérrez *Puerto Limón*. One of the best books of the "proletarian" genre, by one of the nation's foremost literary figures, who was also a prominent journalist. While very much focused on the gritty realism of labour conditions in mid-twentieth-century Costa Rica, the writing is lyrical and beautifully simple.

★**Enrique Jaramillo Levi** (ed) *When New Flowers Bloomed: Short Stories by Women Writers from Costa Rica and Panama*. Collection of the best-known Costa Rican women writers, including Rima de Vallbona, Carmen Naranjo, Carmen Lyra and Yolanda Oreamuno. Most of the stories are from the late 1980s, with shared themes of domestic violence – a persistent problem in Costa Rica – sexual and economic inequality and the tyrannies of female anatomy and desire. Look out especially for Emilia Macaya, a younger writer.

Tatiana Lobo *Assault on Paradise*. Costa Rica's first great historical novel tells the story of the arrival of the Spaniards and, as the title indicates, their destruction of the land and life of the indigenous peoples they encountered.

Carmen Naranjo *Los Perros no Ladraron; Responso por el Niño Juan Manuel; Diario de una Multitud; Ondina*; and *Sobrepunto*. In keeping with a tradition in Latin American letters but unusually for a woman, Naranjo occupied several public posts, including Secretary of Culture, director of the publishing house EDUCA and ambassador to Israel. She was widely considered to be an experimentalist, and her novels can be found throughout Costa Rica in Spanish only; her collection of stories *There Never Was Once Upon a Time*, however, is available in English.

★**Yolanda Oreamuno** *La Ruta de su Evasión*. Oreamuno had a short life, dying at the age of 40 in 1956, but by the time she was 24 she had distinguished herself as the most promising writer of her generation with her novel *Por Tierra Firme*. *La Ruta* – concerning a child sent to look for his father, who has disappeared, possibly on a drinking binge – displays her continually surprising, lyrical style. The search is both actual and spiritual, the novel a complex weave of themes. In Spanish only.

Barbara Ras (ed) *Costa Rica: A Traveler's Literary Companion*. This anthology is probably the most accessible starting point for readers interested in Costa Rican literature, with flowing and well-translated stories arranged by geographical zone. The best stories are also the most heartrending – read *The Girl Who Came from the Moon* and *The Carbonero* for a glimpse of life beyond the tourist-brochure images.

Yasmín Ross *La Flota Negra*. Originally a journalist from Mexico, Ross's *La Flota Negra* is one of the best-received novels set in Costa Rica in recent years. It takes as its starting point the story of the Black Star Line, the shipping company that brought so many of the Caribbean immigrants whose descendants now make up the population of Limón, along with the Pan-Africanist Marcus Garvey's visit to the province. In Spanish only.

Anacristina Rossi *La Loca de Gandoca/The Madwoman of Gandoca*. Rossi's popular novel is really "faction", documenting in businesslike prose and with tongue firmly in cheek the bizarre and byzantine wranglings over the Refugio de Vida Silvestre Gandoca-Manzanillo, including the surveying of the land of the indigenous Bribrí on the KéköLdi reserve.

Rima de Vallbona *Flowering Inferno: Tales of Sinking Hearts*. Slim volume of affecting short stories by one of Costa Rica's most respected (and widely translated) writers on social life, customs and – most poignantly, in the case of *Flowering Inferno* – the position of women.

Spanish

Although it is commonly said that everyone speaks English in Costa Rica, it is not really the case. Certainly, many who work in the tourist trade speak some English, and there are a number of foreign residents who speak anything from English to German to Dutch, but the people you'll meet day to day are likely to speak only Spanish. The one area where you will hear English widely spoken is on the Caribbean coast, where many of the Afro-Caribbean inhabitants are of Jamaican descent, and speak a distinctive regional creole.

If you want to get to know Costa Ricans, then it makes sense to acquire some **Spanish** before you arrive. Ticos are polite, patient and forgiving interlocutors, and will not only tolerate but appreciate any attempts you make to speak their language.

Pronunciation

The rules of **pronunciation** are pretty straightforward. Unless there's an accent, in which case stress the vowel with the accent (*tilde*), all words ending in "l", "r" and "z" are stressed on the last syllable, all others on the second to last. Unlike in the rest of Latin America, in Costa Rica the final "d" in many words sometimes gets dropped; thus, you'll hear "*usté*" for "*usted*" or "*¿verdá?*" for "*¿verdad?*" Other Costa Rican peculiarities are the "ll" and "r" sounds. All vowels are pure and short.

A somewhere between the A sound in "b**a**ck" and that in "f**a**ther"

E as in "g**e**t"

I as in "pol**i**ce"

O as in "h**o**t"

U as in "r**u**le"

C is soft before E and I, hard otherwise: *cerca* is pronounced "serka"

G works the same way: a guttural H sound (like the ch in "loch") before E or I, a hard G elsewhere: *gigante* becomes "higante"

H is always silent

J is the same sound as a guttural G: *jamón* is pronounced "hamon"

LL may be pronounced as a soft J (as in parts of Chile and Argentina) instead of Y: *ballena* (whale) becomes "bajzhena" instead of "bayena"

N is as in English, unless it has a tilde (accent) over it, when it becomes NY: *mañana* sounds like "manyana"

QU is pronounced like the English K

R is not rolled Scottish burr-like as much as in other Spanish-speaking countries: *carro* is said "cahro", with a soft rather than a rolled R

V sounds more like B: *vino* becomes "beano"

Z is the same as a soft C: *cerveza* is thus "servesa"

WORDS AND PHRASES

BASICS

Yes, No	Sí, No	**Open, Closed**	Abierto/a, Cerrado/a
Please	Por favor	**With, Without**	Con, Sin
Thank you	Gracias	**Good, Bad**	Buen(o)/a, Mal(o)/a
You're welcome	De nada	**Big, Small**	Gran(de), Pequeño/a
Where?	¿Dónde?	**More, Less**	Más, Menos
When?	¿Cuando?		
What?	¿Qué?	**GREETINGS AND RESPONSES**	
Why?	¿Por qué?	**Hello, Goodbye**	Hola, Adiós
Here, There	Aquí, Allí	**Good morning**	Buenos días
This, That	Este, Eso	**Good afternoon/night**	Buenas tardes/noches
Now, Later	Ahora, Más tarde	**See you later**	Hasta luego
		Sorry	Lo siento/Discúlpame

Excuse me	Con permiso/Perdón
How are you?	¿Cómo está (usted)?
I (don't) understand	(No) Entiendo
What did you say?	¿Cómo?
Do you speak English?	¿Habla (usted) inglés?
I don't speak Spanish	(No) Hablo español
My name is…	Me llamo…
What's your name?	¿Como se llama (usted)?
I am American/	Soy estadoudinense/
English/Australian/	inglés(a)/australiano(a)/
New Zealander/	nuevo(a) zelanda/
South African	africano del sur

DIRECTIONS

Do you know…?	¿Sabe…?
I don't know	No sé
How do I get to…?	¿Como llega a…?
Left, Right, Straight on	Izquierda, Derecha, Derecho
Where is…?	¿Dónde está…?
…the nearest bank	…el banco más cercano
…the post office	…el correo
…the toilet	…el baño/servicio
Is there (a hotel) near here?	¿Hay (un hotel) cerca de aquí?

ACCOMMODATION

Do you have a room…?	¿Tieneun cuarto/una habitacíon…?
…with two beds/	…con dos camas/
a double bed	una cama matrimonial
a single bed	una cama sencilla
It's for one person	Es para una persona
(two people)	(dos personas)
…for one night	…para una noche
(one week)	(una semana)
It's fine, how much is it?	¿Está bien, cuánto es?
Don't you have	¿No tiene algo más
anything cheaper?	barato?
Can one…?	¿Se puede…?
…camp (near) here?	¿…acampar (cerca de) aquí?
Hot water	Agua caliente
Cold water	Agua fría
Air-conditioned	Aire-acondicionado
Shared bath	Baño colectivo/ compartido
Ceiling fan	Abanico
Check-out time	Hora de salida
Taxes	Impuestos

TRANSPORT

Boat	Barco
Bus	Autobus
Train	Tren
Plane	Avion
Where is the bus station?	¿Dónde está el estación autobuses?
Where does the bus to…leave from?	¿De dónde sale el autobus para…?
I'd like a (return) ticket to…	Quisiera un tiquete (de ida y vuelta) para…
What time does it leave (arrive in…)?	¿A qué hora sale (llega en…)?
First	Primero/a
Last	Itimo/a
Next	Próximo/a

SHOPPING

I want to buy…	Quiero comprar...
I would like…	Quisiera...
Give me…	Deme…
one like that	uno así
What's that?	¿Qué es eso?
How much does it cost?	¿Cuanto cuesta?
It's too expensive	Es demasiado caro
What's this called in Spanish?	¿Como se llama éste en español?
ATM	Cajero de automatico
Credit card	Tarjeta de credito
Money	Dinero
Market	Mercado
Shop/store	Tienda

NUMBERS

1	un/uno/una
2	dos
3	tres
4	cuatro
5	cinco
6	seis
7	siete
8	ocho
9	nueve
10	diez
11	once
12	doce
13	trece
14	catorce
15	quince
16	diez y seis
20	veinte
21	veintiuno
30	treinta
31	treinta y uno
40	cuarenta
50	cincuenta
60	sesenta

70	setenta	**Today**	Hoy
80	ochenta	**Tomorrow**	Mañana
90	noventa	**Monday**	lunes
100	cien(to)	**Tuesday**	martes
101	ciento uno	**Wednesday**	miércoles
200	doscientos	**Thursday**	jueves
201	doscientos uno	**Friday**	viernes
500	quinientos	**Saturday**	sábado
1000	mil	**Sunday**	domingo
2000	dos mil	**January**	enero
1990	mil novocientos noventa	**February**	febrero
1991	mil novocientos noventa	**March**	marzo
	y uno	**April**	abril
First	Primero/a	**May**	mayo
Second	Segundo/a	**June**	junio
Third	Tercero/a	**July**	julio
		August	agosto

TIME, DAYS AND MONTHS

What time is it?	¿Qué hora es?	**September**	septiembre
It's (9) o'clock	son (las nueve)	**October**	octubre
It's half past (ten)	Es (las diez) y media	**November**	noviembre
Yesterday	Ayer	**December**	diciembre

A COSTA RICAN MENU READER

BASICS

Aceite	Oil	**Carambola**	Starfruit
Aceitunas	Olives	**Cas**	Pale-flesh fruit with sweet-sour taste
Ajo ("al ajillo")	Garlic ("in garlic sauce")	**Chinos**	Usually used for *refrescos*
Cebolla	Onion	**Fresas**	Strawberries
Cilantro	Coriander	**Guanábana**	Soursop; very large green mottled fruit with sweet, white flesh tasting like a cross between a mango and a pear. Mostly found on the Caribbean coast
Frijoles	Beans		
Huevos	Eggs		
Leche	Milk		
Queso	Cheese		
Salsa	Sauce		

MEAT (*CARNE*), FISH (*PESCADO*) AND SEAFOOD/SHELLFISH (*MARISCOS*)

		Guayaba	Guava; very sweet fruit, usually used for making spreads and jams
Atún	Tuna		
Bistec	Steak	**Limón**	Lemon
Cerdo	Pork	**Mamones chinos**	Spiny red or yellow fruits that look diabolical but reveal gently flavoured lychee-type fruit inside; somewhat like peeled green grapes, but sweeter and more fragrant. Usually sold in small bags of a dozen on street corners or buses
Corvina	Sea bass		
Jamón	Ham		
Langosta	Lobster		
Lomito	Cut of beef (filet mignon)		
Pargo	Red snapper		
Trucha	Trout		

FRUITS (*FRUTAS*)

Aguacate	Avocado		
Anona	Custard fruit; sweet, thick ripe taste. One of the best fruits in the country	**Maracuyá**	Passionfruit; small yellow fruits, sharp and sweet
Banano	Banana	**Moras**	Blackberries

Naranja	Orange
Papaya	Papaya/pawpaw; large, round or oblong fruit with bland orange flesh. Best eaten with fresh lime juice, and very good for stomach bugs
Pejibaye	A Costa Rican speciality, you'll find this small green-orange fruit (known as the peach palm fruit) almost nowhere else. Like its relative, the coconut, it grows in bunches on palm trees: the texture is unusual, as is the nutty flavour
Piña	Pineapple
Sandía	Watermelon
Tamarindo	Tamarind; a large pod of seeds, covered in a sticky, light-brown flesh. The unique taste – tart and sweet – is best first sampled in a *refresco*
Zapote	Large, sweet orange fruit, with a dark-brown outer casing

VEGETABLES (*VERDURAS*)

Chayote	Resembling a light-green avocado, this vegetable is tender and delicate when cooked, and excellent in stews and with meat and rice dishes
Fruta de pan	Breadfruit; eaten more as a starch substitute than a fruit
Hongos	Mushrooms
Palmito	Heart-of-palm; the inner core of palm trees, usually eaten in salads, with a somewhat bitter taste and fibrous texture
Plátanos	Plantains; eaten sweet
Zanahorias	Carrots

TYPICAL DISHES (*PLATOS*)

| Arreglados | Meat and mayonnaise sandwiches on greasy bread buns |

Arroz...	Rice...
...con pollo	...with chicken
...con carne	...with meat
...con pescado	...with fish
...con mariscos	...with seafood
...con camarones	...with shrimps/prawns
Bocas	Small snacks, usually eaten as an accompaniment to a beer
Casado	Plate of meat or fish, rice and salad, sometimes served with fried plantains
Ceviche	Raw fish, usually sea bass, "marinated" in lime juice, onions, chillies and coriander
Chicarrones	Fried pork rinds
Chilasquilas	Tortillas and beef with spices and battered eggs
Empanadas	Meat or vegetable patties
Frijoles molidos	Mashed black beans with onions, chilli peppers, coriander and thyme
Gallo pinto	"Painted rooster"; breakfast dish of rice and beans
Gallos	Small sandwiches
Pan de maíz	Corn bread; white rather than yellow
Picadillo	Potatoes cooked with beef and beans
Sopa negra	Black-bean soup with egg and vegetables
Tacos	Tortilla filled with beef or chicken, cabbage, tomatoes and mild chillies
Tamal	One of the best local specialities, usually consisting of maize flour, chicken or pork, olives, chillies and raisins, all wrapped in a plantain leaf
Tortilla	Thin, small and bland bread, served as an accompaniment to meals and, especially in Guanacaste, breakfast

DESSERTS (*POSTRES*)

Cajeta	Dessert made of milk, sugar, vanilla and sometimes coconut
Churros	Fingers of fried dough and sugar
Helado	Ice cream
Milanes	Delicate chocolate fingers
Queque	Cake
Queque seco	Pound cake
Tamal asado	Cake made of cornflour, cream, eggs, sugar and butter
Tres leches	Sponge cake soaked in milk and drenched with syrup

REGIONAL DISHES

CARIBBEAN

Pan bon	Sweet glazed bread with fruit and cheese
Patacones	Plantain chips, often served with *frijoles molidos* (see opposite)
Rice and beans	Rice and beans cooked in coconut milk
Rondón	Meat and vegetables stewed in coconut milk

GUANACASTE

Chorreados	Corn pancakes
Horchata	Hot drink made with corn or rice and flavoured with cinnamon
Natilla	Sour cream
Olla de carne	Rich, hearty meat stew
Pinolillo	Milky corn drink
Rosquillas	Corn doughnuts
Tanelas	Scone-like corn snack

Idioms and slang

Costa Rican Spanish is a living language full of flux and argot. Local slang and usage are often referred to as **tiquismos** (from *Costarriqueñismos*, or Costa Ricanisms) or, as Costa Ricans will say when enlightening the foreigner as to their meaning, "*palabras muy ticas*" (very Costa Rican words). Some of the expressions and terms discussed below may be heard in other countries in the region, especially in Nicaragua and El Salvador, but still they are highly regional. Others are purely endemic, including *barbarismos* (bastardizations) and *provincialismos* (words particular to specific regions of Costa Rica).

The noun "Tico", used as a short form for Costa Rican, comes less from a desire to shorten "Costarriquense" than from the traditional trend towards **diminution**, which is supposed to signal classlessness, eagerness to band together and desire not to cause offence. In Costa Rica, the common Spanish diminution of "ito" – applied as a suffix at the end of the word, as in "herman*ito*" ("little brother") – often becomes "itico" ("herman*itico*"). That said, you hear the -ito or -itico endings less and less nowadays.

Costa Rican Spanish often displays an astounding **formality** that borders on servility. Instead of "*de nada*" ("you're welcome"), many Costa Ricans will say "*Para servirle*", which means, literally, "I'm here to serve you". When they meet you, Costa Ricans will say "*Con mucho gusto*" ("It's a pleasure"), and you should do the same. Even when you leave people you do not know well, you will be told "*Que le vaya bien*" ("May all go well with you").

A COSTA RICAN DICTIONARY

An entertaining, illustrated dictionary of slang and *dichos* (sayings) for Spanish-speakers interested in understanding heavily argot-spiced spoken Costa Rican Spanish, **Nuevo diccionario de Costarriqueñismos**, by Miguel Ángel Quesada Pacheco, is a fascinating compendium, giving the regional location of word usage and sayings, what age group uses them and some etymology. It also reveals a wealth of localisms developed to describe local phenomena – witness, for example, the number of different words for "wasp". For English-speakers, *Love in Translation* (see p.431) is a good alternative.

Nicknames and a delight in the informal mix with a quite proper, formal tone used in spoken Costa Rican Spanish. Nicknames centre on your most obvious physical characteristic: popular ones include *flaca* (thin); *gorda* (fat); and *macha* (light-skinned). Terms of endearment are also very current in popular speech; along with the ubiquitous *mi amor*, you may also get called *joven* (young one).

Intimate address

It's difficult to get your head round forms of **second-person address** in Costa Rica. Children are often spoken to in the "*usted*" form, which is technically formal and reserved for showing respect (in other Spanish-speaking countries, children are generally addressed as "*tú*"). Even friends who have known each other for years in Costa Rica will address each other as "*usted*". But the single most confounding irregularity of Costa Rican speech for those who already speak Spanish is the use of "**vos**" as personal intimate address – generally between friends of the same age. Many people on a short trip to the country never quite get to grips with it.

Now archaic in European Spanish, "*vos*" is only used widely in the New World in Argentina and Costa Rica. It has an interesting rhythm and sound, with verbs ending on a kind of diphthong-ized stress: *vos sabés*, *vos quieres* (you know, you want), as opposed to *tu sabes/usted sabe* or *tu quieres/usted quiere*. If you are addressed in the "*vos*" form, it is a sign of friendship, and you should try to use it back if you can. It is an affront to use "*vos*" improperly, with someone you don't know well, when it can be seen as being patronizing. Again, Costa Ricans are good-hearted in this respect, however, and put errors down to the fact that you are a foreigner.

Everyday expressions

Here are some everyday **peculiarities** that most visitors to Costa Rica will become familiar with pretty quickly:

¡Achará!	Expression of regret: "What a pity!", like "¡Qué lástima!"
Adiós	"Hi", used primarily in the campo (country) when greeting someone on the road or street. Confusingly, as in the rest of Latin America, adiós is also "goodbye", but only if you are going away for a long time.
¿Diay?	Slightly melancholic interjection in the vein of "Ah, but what can you expect?"
Fatal	Reserved for the absolutely worst possible eventuality: "Esta carretera para Golfito es fatal" means "The road to Golfito is the very worst".
Feo	Literally "ugly", but can also mean rotten or lousy, as in "Todos los caminos en Costa Rica están muy feos" ("All the roads in Costa Rica are in really bad shape").
Maje	Literally "dummy", used between young men as an affirmation of their friendship/maleness: it's used like "buddy, pal" (US) or "mate" (UK). There is no equivalent for women, unfortunately.
¡Pura vida!	Perhaps the best-known tiquismo, meaning "Great!", "OK!" or "Cool!"
Qué mala/buena nota	Expression of disapproval/approval – "How uncool/great".

Luck and God

Both **luck** and **God** come into conversation often in Costa Rica. Thus, you get the pattern:

¿Cómo amaneció?	"How did you sleep?" (Literally, "How did you wake up?")
Muy bien, por dicha, ¿y usted?	"Very well, fortunately, and you?"
Muy bien, gracias a Dios.	"Very well, thank God."

Also, you will hear *dicha* and *Dios* used in situations that don't seem to have much to do with luck or divine intervention: "*¡Qué dicha que usted llegó!*" ("What luck that you arrived!"), along with such phrases as "*Vamos a la playa esta fin de semana, si Dios quiere*" ("We'll go to the beach this weekend, God willing"). Even a shrug of the shoulders elicits a "*¡Dios sabe!*" ("God only knows"). And the usual forms "*hasta luego*" or "*hasta la vista*" become in Costa Rica the much more God-fearing "*Que Dios le acompañe*" ("May God go with you").

"Where is your boyfriend?"

"*¿Dónde está su novio?/padres?*" ("Where is your boyfriend/family?") is a query women, especially those travelling alone, will hear often. **Family** is very important in explaining to many Costa Ricans who you are and where you come from, and people will place you by asking how many brothers and sisters you have, where your family lives, whether your grandmother is still alive... It's a good idea to get to grips with the following:

madre/padre	mother/father
abuelo/abuela	grandfather/grandmother
hijo/hija	son/daughter
hermano/hermana	brother/sister
tío/tía	uncle/aunt
primo/prima	cousin

Glossary

abastecedor a general store, usually in a rural area or *barrio* (neighbourhood), that keeps a stock of groceries and basic toiletries

agringarse (verb) to adopt the ways of the gringos

aguacero downpour

agua potable drinking water

ahorita "right now" (any time within the coming hour)

area de acampar camping area

area restringido restricted area

bárbaro fantastic, cool (literally "barbaric")

barrio neighbourhood (usually urban)

bomba petrol station

botica pharmacy

burro can refer to the animal (donkey), but is usually an adjective denoting "really big", as in "*Vea este bicho sí burro*" ("Come see this really big insect")

campesino peasant farmer, smallholder

campo literally countryside, but more often in Costa Rica "space", as in "seat" when travelling; thus, "*¿Hay un campo en este autobus?*" means "Is there a (free) seat on this bus?"

cantina bar, usually patronized by the working class or rural labouring class

capa rain gear, poncho

carro car (not *coche*, as in Spain)

cazadora literally, huntress; a beaten-up old schoolbus that serves as public transport in rural areas

chance widely used Anglicism to denote chance, or opportunity; like *oportunidad*

chiquillos kids; also *chiquititos*, *chiquiticos*

chivo cute

chorreador sack-and-metal coffee-filter contraption, still widely used

choteo quick-witted sarcasm, something Costa Ricans admire, provided it's not too sharp-tongued

colectivo an open-back truck used as a form of public transport in remote rural areas

conchos yokels, hicks from the sticks

cordillera mountain range

correo post office

dando cuerda colloquial expression meaning, roughly, to "make eyes at", in an approximation of sexual interest (men to women, hardly ever the other way around)

entrada entrance

evangélico usually refers to anyone who is of a religion other than Catholic, but particularly Protesta, even if they are not evangelical; such religions are also called *cultos*, belying a general wariness and disapproval for anything other than Catholicism

finca farm or plantation

finquero coffee grower

foco flashlight/torch

galletas biscuits

gambas buttresses, the giant above-ground roots that some rainforest trees put out

gaseosa fizzy drink

gasolina petrol

gringo not-at-all pejorative term for a North American (a European is usually *europeo*)

guaca pre-Columbian burial ground or tomb

güila child

güisqui whisky (usually bad unless imported, and astronomically expensive)

hacienda big farm, usually a ranch

hospedaje very basic *pensión*

humilde humble, simple; an appearance and quality that is widely respected

ICE Instituto Costarricense de Electricidad, the country's principal telecommunications provider

ICT Instituto Costarricense de Turismo, the national tourist board

indígena an indigenous person; preferred term among indigenous groups in Costa Rica, rather than the less polite *índio* (Indian)

invierno winter (May–Nov)

jornaleros day labourers, usually landless peasants who are paid by the day, for instance to pick coffee in season

josefino resident of San José

Limonenses Costa Ricans of Afro-Caribbean heritage

malecón seaside promenade

mal educado literally, badly educated; a gentle if effective insult, especially useful for women harassed by hissing, leering men

marimba type of large xylophone played mainly in Guanacaste; also refers to the style of music

mestizo mixed-race person, specifically indigenous/Spanish; not usually pejorative

metate pre-Columbian stone table used for grinding corn, especially by the Chorotega people of Guanacaste

MINAE Ministry of Environment and Energy

mirador lookout or viewing platform

morenos offensive term for Costa Ricans of African-Caribbean heritage (the best term to use is *Limonenses*)

muelle dock

Neotrópicos Neotropics: tropics of the New World

Nica Nicaraguan, from *Nicaragüense*

PAC Citizens' Action Party, the ruling political party

palenque a thatched-roofed longhouse inhabited by indigenous people; more or less equivalent to the Native American longhouse

pasear to be on vacation/holiday; literally, to be passing through

peón farm labourer, usually landless

personaje someone of importance, a VIP, although usually used pejoratively to indicate someone who is putting on airs

PLN National Liberation Party, the main opposition party

precarista squatter

puesto post (ranger post or ranger station)

pulpería general store or corner store

purrujas spectacularly annoying, tiny biting insects encountered in lowland areas

PUSC Social Christian Unity Party, historically one of Costa Rica's leading political parties

quebrada stream

rancho palm-thatched roof, also smallholding

redondel de toros bullring, not used for bullfighting but for local rodeos

refresco drink, usually made with fresh fruit or water; sometimes a fizzy drink, although this is most often called *gaseosa*

regalar (verb) usually to give, as in to give a present, but in Costa Rica the usual command or request of "*Deme uno de estos*" ("Give me one of those"), becomes "*Regáleme*"; thus "*¿Regáleme un cafecito, por favor?*" ("Could you give me a coffee?")

rejas security grille, popularly known in English as The Cage: the iron grille fencing you see around all but the most humble dwellings in an effort to discourage burglary

río river

sabanero Costa Rican cowboy

salida exit

sendero trail

SINAC National System of Conservation Areas

soda cafeteria or diner; in the rest of Central America, it's usually called a *comedor*

temporada season: *la temporada de lluvia* is the rainy season

temporales early-morning rains in the wet season

terreno land, small farm

Tico/a Costa Rican

UCR Universidad de Costa Rica (in San Pedro, San José)

UNA Universidad Nacional (in Heredia)

verano summer (Dec–April)

volcán volcano

Small print and index

A ROUGH GUIDE TO ROUGH GUIDES

Published in 1982, the first Rough Guide – to Greece – was a student scheme that became a publishing phenomenon. Mark Ellingham, a recent graduate in English from Bristol University, had been travelling in Greece the previous summer and couldn't find the right guidebook. With a small group of friends he wrote his own guide, combining a contemporary, journalistic style with a thoroughly practical approach to travellers' needs.

The immediate success of the book spawned a series that rapidly covered dozens of destinations. And, in addition to impecunious backpackers, Rough Guides soon acquired a much broader readership that relished the guides' wit and inquisitiveness as much as their enthusiastic, critical approach and value-for-money ethos. These days, Rough Guides include recommendations from budget to luxury and cover more than 120 destinations around the globe, from Amsterdam to Zanzibar, all regularly updated by our team of roaming writers.

Browse all our latest guides, read inspirational features and book your trip at **roughguides.com**.

Rough Guide credits

Editor: Rebecca Hallett
Layout: Anita Singh
Cartography: Rajesh Mishra, Lokamata Sahu
Picture editor: Yoshimi Kanazawa
Proofreader: Diane Margolis
Managing editor: Edward Aves
Assistant editor: Payal Sharotri

Production: Jimmy Lao
Cover photo research: Phoebe Lowndes
Editorial assistant: Aimee White
Senior DTP coordinator: Dan May
Programme manager: Gareth Lowe
Publishing director: Georgina Dee

Publishing information

This eighth edition published October 2017 by
Rough Guides Ltd,
80 Strand, London WC2R 0RL
11, Community Centre, Panchsheel Park,
New Delhi 110017, India
Distributed by Penguin Random House
Penguin Books Ltd, 80 Strand, London WC2R 0RL
Penguin Group (USA), 345 Hudson Street, NY 10014, USA
Penguin Group (Australia), 250 Camberwell Road,
Camberwell, Victoria 3124, Australia
Penguin Group (NZ), 67 Apollo Drive, Mairangi Bay,
Auckland 1310, New Zealand
Penguin Group (South Africa), Block D, Rosebank Office
Park, 181 Jan Smuts Avenue, Parktown North, Gauteng,
South Africa 2193
Rough Guides is represented in Canada by DK Canada, 320
Front Street West, Suite 1400, Toronto, Ontario M5V 3B6
Printed in Singapore
© Rough Guides, 2017
Maps © Rough Guides

456pp includes index
A catalogue record for this book is available from the
British Library
ISBN: 978-0-24128-065-2
The publishers and authors have done their best to ensure
the accuracy and currency of all the information in **The
Rough Guide to Costa Rica**, however, they can accept
no responsibility for any loss, injury, or inconvenience
sustained by any traveller as a result of information or
advice contained in the guide.
1 3 5 7 9 8 6 4 2

MIX
Paper from
responsible sources
FSC
www.fsc.org
FSC™ C018179

Help us update

We've gone to a lot of effort to ensure that the eighth
edition of **The Rough Guide to Costa Rica** is accurate
and up-to-date. However, things change – places get
"discovered", opening hours are notoriously fickle,
restaurants and rooms raise prices or lower standards. If
you feel we've got it wrong or left something out, we'd like
to know, and if you can remember the address, the price,
the hours, the phone number, so much the better.

Please send your comments with the subject line
"**Rough Guide Costa Rica Update**" to mail@uk
.roughguides.com. We'll credit all contributions and send a
copy of the next edition (or any other Rough Guide if you
prefer) for the very best emails.

Acknowledgements

Stephen Keeling: Thanks are due to Renzo and Grace
Sturmo in Monteverde; Chris in Puerto Jiménez; Ori and
her team at *Amor de Mar* in Montezuma; fellow trooper
Shafik Meghji; Rebecca Hallett in the UK for her judicious
editing; and lastly Tiffany Wu, the world's greatest travel
companion.
Shafik Meghji: Many thanks to all the locals, readers and
travellers who helped me out along the way. A special

muchas gracias must go to: Rebecca Hallett for her sterling
editing work; fellow author Stephen Keeling; Amos, Viviana
and all the staff at Reserva Rara Avis; Toine and Sara at
Montaña Linda Guesthouse in Orosí; Andy and all the staff
at *Orosí Lodge*; Huw and Kati at Travel Local; Wouter Zagt
and Noemi Clerkxs at Ecole; Fiona at Rickshaw Travel;
Alison Harvey; everyone at *Nayara Springs*; Jean, Nizar and
Nina Meghji; and Sioned Jones.

ABOUT THE AUTHORS

Stephen Keeling Stephen Keeling worked as a financial journalist and editor in Asia for seven years before writing his first travel book and has contributed to several titles for Rough Guides, including books on Central America, Mexico, Puerto Rico and Colombia. Stephen lives in New York.

Shafik Meghji An award-winning travel writer, journalist and broadcaster, Shafik Meghji has co-authored/updated over thirty Rough Guides, including to Australia, Argentina, Bolivia, Chile, India, Laos and Mexico. He writes regularly for print and digital publications, including *The Guardian* and the *Huffington Post*. Shafik is a member of the British Guild of Travel Writers, a fellow of the Royal Geographical Society, and a trustee of the Latin America Bureau. Twitter: @ShafikMeghji. Blog: unmappedroutes.com. Website: shafikmeghji.com.

Readers' updates

Thanks to all the readers who have taken the time to write in with comments and suggestions (and apologies if we've inadvertently omitted or misspelt anyone's name):

Ofer Holzer, Jana Leo, Martin Plackett, Peter Roth, Tine Snauwaert, Vicki Warthen.

Photo credits

All photos © Rough Guides, except the following:
(Key: t-top; c-centre; b-bottom; l-left; r-right)

1 Alamy Stock Photo: Michael Dwyer
2 AWL Images: Alex Robinson
4 Getty Images: John Coletti
5 4Corners: SIME/Pietro Canali
9 Alamy Stock Photo: Brian Atkinson (t); Yadid Levy (c). **Corbis**: Juan Carlos Ulate (b)
10 AWL Images: Michele Falzone
12 SuperStock: Danuta Hyniewska
13 Alamy Stock Photo: Neil McAllister (t). **Corbis**: Ingo Arndt (b)
14 Alamy Stock Photo: Nick Turner (b). **Corbis**: Robert Harding (t)
15 Getty Images: Wolfgang Kaehler (t). **SuperStock**: Juan Carlos Muñoz (b)
16 Alamy Stock Photo: FLPA (t). **Getty Images**: Nicola Paltani (b)
17 4Corners: SIME/Pietro Canali (t). **Alamy Stock Photo**: Siepmann (b)
18 Alamy Stock Photo: Al Argueta (t); Ian Woolcock (b)
19 Alamy Stock Photo: travelib (t). **Getty Images**: Johann Oswald (b)
20 Corbis: John Coletti (t). **SuperStock** (b)
21 Corbis: Keren Su (t). **Getty Images** (b)
22 Corbis: Rob Francis (t). **Getty Images**: DreamPictures (b)
23 Alamy Stock Photo: Hemis (t). **Corbis**: Bob Krist (b)
24 Getty Images: Myer Bornstein
27 Alamy Stock Photo: David Tipling (tl). **Corbis**: Lars-Olof Johansson (br); Roy Toft (tr). **Getty Images**: Gregory Basco (bl)
29 Alamy Stock Photo: Danita Delimont (bl). **Corbis**: Suzi Eszterhas (c & t). **Getty Images**: Kevin Schafer (br)
31 Alamy Stock Photo: Juniors Bildarchiv (b). **Corbis**: Mary Ann McDonald (cr); Paul Souders (cl). **Getty Images**: Gregory Basco (t)
33 Alamy Stock Photo: Adrian Hepworth (bl & cl). **Corbis**: Michael & Patricia Fogden (tr); Alex Mustard (br); Minden Pictures/Konrad Wothe (cr); Christian Ziegler (tl)
35 Corbis: Jeffrey Arguedas (tl); Ingo Arndt (b); Wil Meinderts (c); Bernard Radvaner (tr)

37 Corbis: Robert Francis (cl); George Grall (cr); Ivan Kuzmin (ca); Bence Mate (b); Paul Souders (t)
39 Corbis: John Cancalosi (cl); George Grall (bl); Joe McDonald (tl & tr); Paul Souders (cr); Konrad Wothe (br)
41 Corbis: Suzi Eszterhas (br); Tim Fitzharris (cra); Steve Gettle (tr); George Grall (cla); Christian Ziegler (bl). **Getty Images**: Glenn Bartley (tl); Christopher Jimenez (c)
43 Alamy Stock Photo: Oyvind Martinsen (bc). **Corbis**: Glenn Bartley (tr); Tim Fitzharris (tl); Steve Gettle (cr); Lars-Olof Johansson (bl & br); Thomas Marent (cl)
44 Getty Images: Alfonse Pagano
85 4Corners: Guido Cozzi
97 Corbis: Richard Cummins (t). **iStockphoto.com**: Dmitry Chulov (b)
116–117 Getty Images: Kryssia Campos
119 Robert Harding Picture Library: Marco Simoni
133 Alamy Stock Photo: Robert Fried
156–157 Alamy Stock Photo: Hemis
159 SuperStock: GIUGLIO Gil
185 Corbis: Suzi Eszterhas (b)
200–201 Corbis: JC
203 Getty Images: Nertog
238–239 Corbis: Ingo Arndt
241 Corbis: Rob Francis
269 Alamy Stock Photo: travelstock44 (t). **Corbis**: Kevin Schafer (b)
283 Alamy Stock Photo: Thornton Cohen (t). **Corbis**: Martin Siepmann (b)
299 Alamy Stock Photo: Andria Patino
319 Corbis: Franck Guiziou
339 Alamy Stock Photo: Jan Csernoch (b). **Robert Harding Picture Library**: Rob Francis (t)
356–357 Getty Images: Robert Harding World Imagery
359 Corbis: Konrad Wothe
381 Alamy Stock Photo: Claude Huot (t). **SuperStock**: Juan Carlos Muñoz (b)
406 Alamy Stock Photo: BLM Collection

Cover: *Río Celeste, Parque Nacional Volcan Tenorio* **AWL Images**: Michele Falzone

Index

Maps are marked in grey

Map symbols

The symbols below are used on maps throughout the book

✈	International airport	⚶	Viewpoint	— —	Ferry	
✈	Domestic airport/airstrip	▲	Mountain peak		Motorway	
♦	Place of interest	◭	Volcano	– – – –	Footpath	
♦	Museum	⚶	Springs		Unpaved road	
⊠	Post office	⌂	Cave		Pedestrian road	
ⓘ	Tourist information	⚶	Waterfall		Railway	
@	Internet	⚶	Surf beach		Wall	
☎	Telephone office	⚶	Windsurfing		Building	
⊞	Hospital	∴	Ruins/archeological site		Market	
⊞	Pharmacy/clinic	⚶	Ranger station/*guadaparque*		Stadium	
Ⓢ	Bank	⚶	Border crossing		Church	
★	Transport stop	⚶	Campsite		Cemetery	
⛽	Fuel station	⚶	Zoo		National Reserve/Park	
P	Parking	■	Tower		Beach	
⊥	Gardens	⚶	Forest activities		Swamp/mangrove	
⊠	Gate/entrance	⚶	Rock		Coral	
⌂	Refugio					

Listings key

- ■ Accommodation
- ● Eating
- ■ Drinking/Nightlife
- ● Shopping